Evaluating and Implementing
Hedge Fund Strategies

The experience of managers and investors

THIRD EDITION

Evaluating and Implementing Hedge Fund Strategies

The experience of managers and investors

THIRD EDITION

Edited by
Ronald A. Lake

Published by Euromoney Institutional Investor

Published by
Euromoney Books
Nestor House, Playhouse Yard
London EC4V 5EX
United Kingdom

Tel: +44 (0) 20 7779 8999 or USA +1 800 437 9997
Fax: +44 (0) 20 7779 8300
www.euromoneybooks.com
www.iibooks.com
Email: hotline@euromoneyplc.com
Email: ushotline@iinvestor.net

Printed by Cromwell Press

Contents

CONTENTS

Chapter 12: Asset-backed investing   149

Luke E. Imperatore

Chapter 13: Emerging markets   158

Bruce Richards and Louis Hanover,
Marathon Asset Management, LLC

Chapter 14: Convertible arbitrage: the manager's perspective   172

Michael A. Boyd, Jr and staff, Forest Investment Management

Acknowledgments

As H.G. Wells once wrote, 'No passion in the world is equal to the passion to alter someone else's draft'. I therefore owe the authors of the various chapters in this book an enormous measure of thanks for indulging my passion for wielding the red pen. More importantly, I thank them for their time, energy, insights and their indulgence. Several of the less polite contributors openly questioned what possessed me to undertake the effort of producing this book for a third time. In part the answer is that once three or four years have elapsed since the last edition, I finally forget what a pain in the neck it is. However, the other part of the answer is that I am determined to prove that George Bernard Shaw was wrong when he said, 'The road to ignorance is paved with good editions'.

Many other people contributed to this book (wittingly or unwittingly). These include the colleagues, clients, competitors and countless money managers we have met over the years. However, I would like to offer my very special thanks to: Mia Shapiro, for her invaluable discipline in corralling details; Stephanie Vallis, for being the 'big sister' who keeps everything on track; and Rick Lake, for his commitment, fraternity and determination. I smile because you're my brother. I laugh because you can do nothing about it!

Above all, thanks to Pam, Ben and Emily, for their patience and perseverance in reminding me that life is a book, every day is a new page and they are my co-authors; also to Cis Lake, the Mamaçita of all mamaçitas, whose love and memory is more than tongue can tell; and Herman Lake, the Father of our invention.

Ron Lake
Lake Partners, Inc., Greenwich, CT

Author biographies

Editor

Ronald A. Lake is president of Lake Partners, Inc., an investment consulting firm located in Greenwich, Connecticut. Lake Partners advises institutions and private investment groups on asset allocation, manager selection and programme supervision, with special expertise in hedge funds and alternative investments.

Contributing authors

Shuhei Abe is president, chief executive officer, and chief investment officer at SPARX Asset Management Co., Ltd., which is located in Tokyo. The firm manages various equity and hedged equity programmes in Japanese Equity.

Lee S. Ainslie III is managing partner of Maverick Capital based in New York and Dallas, Texas. The firm manages hedge equity funds.

James Berens, PhD, is a managing director and one of the original founders of Pacific Alternative Asset Management Co., LLC, an institutional fund-of-funds firm based in Irvine, California. He is involved in all stages of the investment process, focusing on asset allocation among various hedge fund strategies, and portfolio risk.

Antoine Bernheim, publisher of *The US Offshore Funds Directory* and Hedgefundnews.com, is president of Dome Capital Management, Inc., a New York-based firm he founded in 1984 to advise European investors. He is also chairman of Dome Securities Corp., a broker-dealer that specialises in raising capital for hedge funds.

Eric C. Bettleheim is a consultant at the law firm of Mishcon de Reya, Solicitors, based in London, England. He specialises in the regulation of financial institutions, derivatives, managed funds and commercial activities.

Jeff Bramel is vice president at DB Advisors, LLC, a subsidiary of the Deutsche Bank Group based in New York. DB Advisors manages the investment of Deutsche Bank's proprietary capital in hedge fund strategies.

Jonathan P. Bren is a principal at Hunt Financial Ventures, a private investment firm located in Dallas, Texas and New York, which allocates capital to, and incubates, hedge funds.

Michael A. Boyd, Jr is chairman and chief investment officer of Forest Investment Management located in Old Greenwich, Connecticut. The firm focuses on global convertible and other equity-linked securities arbitrage.

Ted Caldwell is founder and president of Lookout Mountain Capital, Inc., located outside Chatanooga, Tennessee. Lookout Mountain specialises in the evaluation, selection and monitoring of hedge funds.

Roddy Campbell founded Cross Asset Management in 1998. Located in London, the firm manages arbitrage and event-driven strategies in corporate equity and credit markets, specialising in Europe.

James S. Chanos is president of Kynikos Associates, Ltd. Based in New York, the firm focuses primarily on unhedged short selling of overvalued securities through the domestic Ursus Partners fund as well as Ursus International, Ltd., for international clients.

Alexandra Coffey is an analyst at Pacific Alternative Asset Management Co., LLC, an institutional fund-of-funds firm based in Irvine, California. She provides analytical support to the firm's investment management team.

Sarah Davidoff is an associate in the investment management department of the law firm of Skadden, Arps, Slate, Meagher & Flom, LLP, New York.

Peter Douglas is the principal of GFIA, Pte., Ltd., a Singapore-based research consultancy established in 1998. The firm researches and monitors Asian hedge funds on behalf of professional investors, and advises allocators and fiduciary investors on hedged strategies.

Barry Eichengreen is George C. Pardee and Helen N. Pardee Professor of Economics and Political Science at the University of California, Berkeley, California. He is also research associate of the National Bureau of Economic Research in Cambridge, Massachusetts, and research fellow of the Centre for Economic Policy Research in London.

Louis Hanover is the chief investment officer of Marathon Asset Management, LLC, New York. The firm specialises in the global credit markets and manages various hedge funds in emerging markets, convertible bond arbitrage, distressed debt and credit trading strategies.

Philip H. Harris is a partner in the investment companies and advisers group of the law firm of Skadden, Arps, Slate, Meagher & Flom, LLP, New York. He specialises in private investment funds, registered investment funds and related merger and acquisition transactions.

Lloyd Hascoe is managing director of Hascoe Associates, Inc., a family office located in Greenwich, Connecticut. He has overall responsibility for the firm and focuses on strategic investment policy and asset allocation.

James R. Hedges IV is the founder, president and chief investment officer of LJH Global Investments, LLC, a hedge fund advisory firm based in Naples, Florida.

Scott Higbee is an associate vice president in the New York office of Partners Group, an alternative investments firm based in Zug, Switzerland.

Nicholas S. Hodge is a partner in the Boston, Massachusetts office of the law firm of Kirkpatrick & Lockhart, LLP. He focuses on representing hedge funds, investment advisers, broker-dealers, real estate funds and other alternative investment vehicles.

Jason Huemer is the president of Synthesis Funds, a hedge fund incubator and seed investment firm located in New York. He also is the author of the monthly 'Hedge Row' column in the *Financial Times*.

Guy Hurley is the global head of manager selection at Financial Risk Management, Ltd., a London-based fund of hedge funds.

Luke E. Imperatore was most recently a managing director of Old Hill Partners, Darien, Connecticut, where he focused on business development and client services. The firm manages funds specialising in asset-backed securities.

IOSCO the International Organization of Securities Commissions, strives to cooperate to promote high standards of regulation to maintain just, efficient and sound markets.

Paul Isaac is chief investment officer at fund of funds firm Cadogan Management, LLC, New York. He has helped direct manager research and portfolio management at Cadogan since 1999.

Bruce I. Jacobs is a principal of Jacobs Levy Equity Management, Florham Park, New Jersey. Founded in 1986, Jacobs Levy has an institutional clientele and focuses exclusively on active management of US equity portfolios.

Lars Jaeger, PhD, is a founding partner of saisGroup, an investment firm specialising in alternative investment strategies based in Zug, Switzerland. SaisGroup merged with Partners Group at the end of 2001. He heads the risk management and quantitative analysis group.

Sohail Jaffer is managing director at Premium Select Lux, SA, an asset management company based in Luxembourg. He is a Council Member of AIMA and has edited and contributed to several international hedge fund publications.

Henry Kaufman is president of Henry Kaufman & Company, Inc., a financial and economic consulting firm based in New York.

Andrew S. Kenoe is a partner at the law firm of Skadden, Arps, Slate, Meagher & Flom, LLP, in Chicago, Illinois. He counsels clients on a wide range of domestic and cross-border transactional tax issues.

Michael A. Lawson is a partner at the law firm of Skadden, Arps, Slate, Meagher & Flom, LLP, in Los Angeles, California. He heads the firm's employee benefits group.

Stuart N. Leaf is chief executive officer of Cadogan Management, LLC, New York. He has been involved in the research, creation and management of Cadogan's multi-manager hedge fund portfolios since the inception of the firm in 1994.

Kenneth N. Levy is a principal of Jacobs Levy Equity Management, Florham Park, New Jersey. Founded in 1986, Jacobs Levy has an institutional clientele and focuses exclusively on active management of US equity portfolios.

Michael E. Lewitt is the president of Harch Capital Management, Inc., a money management firm based in Boca Raton, Florida, that specialises in non-investment-grade bonds and bank loans. Mr Lewitt is also author of *The HCM Market Letter*, a monthly review of the financial markets.

Roxanne M. Martino is the president and chief investment officer of Harris Alternatives, LLC. Harris Alternatives, which is based in Chicago, Illinois, offers alternative investment funds to individual and institutional investors.

Donald J. Mathieson is chief of the Emerging Markets Surveillance Division, International Capital Market Department, of the International Monetary Fund in Washington, DC.

Emma Mugridge is the director of AIMA (Alternative Investment Management Association) in London. Founded in 1990, AIMA is a not-for-profit trade association for the alternative investment community.

John Paulson is the president of Paulson & Co., Inc., in New York. The firm manages domestic and offshore funds focused on merger arbitrage.

Lois Peltz is the president and chief executive officer of Infovest21 in New York. In addition to providing an e-mail news service and *Strategy Focus*, a monthly publication, Infovest21 organises educational hedge fund events. She is the author of *The New Investment Superstars* published by John Wiley in 2002.

Christopher J. Pesce is managing director and global head of prime brokerage at Banc of America Securities, LLC, New York.

Michael A. Pintar is a former portfolio manager with Clinton Group based in New York.

Judith Posnikoff, PhD, is a managing director and a founder of Pacific Alternative Asset Management Co., LLC, an institutional fund-of-funds firm based in Irvine, California. She is responsible for interviewing, selecting and monitoring hedge fund managers, with a focus on the equity market-neutral and merger arbitrage strategies.

Bruce Richards is the president of Marathon Asset Management, LLC, New York. The firm specialises in the global credit markets and manages various hedge funds in emerging markets, convertible bond arbitrage, distressed debt and credit trading strategies.

Michael S. Rulle is the president and a principal of Graham Capital Management (GCM), LP, a Stamford, Connecticut-based commodities trading adviser.

Christopher Rupright is a partner at the law firm of Shartsis, Friese & Ginsburg, LLP, in San Francisco, California. He focuses on counseling investment advisory firms, and organising private investment pools, including hedge funds and offshore funds.

Thomas Schneeweis is director of the Center for International Securities and Derivatives Markets and Professor of Finance at the Isenberg School of Management, University of Massachusetts. He is also managing partner of Schneeweis Associates, a multi-manager investment consulting firm in Amherst, Massachusetts.

Paul Singer is general partner of Elliott Associates, LP, a New York-based investment firm. Mr Singer is also investment manager of Elliott International Limited, a Cayman Islands-based fund. The goals of both Elliot and Elliott International are to achieve a moderate return with low risk.

Eric Sippel is the chief operating officer and general counsel of Eastbourne Capital Management, LLC, a hedge fund manager in San Rafael, California. Prior to joining Eastbourne, he was a partner at the law firm of Shartsis, Friese & Ginsburg, LLP.

George Soros is the chairman of Soros Fund Management and is the founder of a global network of foundations dedicated to supporting open societies.

Richard Spurgin is assistant professor of finance at Clark University, Worcester, Massachusetts, and a partner in Schneeweis Partners, a multi-manager investment consulting firm in Amherst, Massachusetts.

Jeffrey Tarrant is the president and chief investment officer of Protégé Partners, a New York-based fund of hedge funds that invests with, and seeds, small and specialised hedge funds.

Mike Tremmel is a senior manager in the asset management practice in the Pacific Northwest region for Ernst & Young, LLP. He advises investment partnerships, offshore funds, registered investment advisers and other financial services entities.

Michael Waldron is director of research at the fund of funds firm Cadogan Management, LLC, New York. He has been involved in manager research and portfolio management at Cadogan since 1997.

Thomas Weber, PhD, is a founding partner and head of hedge fund investments at LGT Capital Partners AG, a fund of funds manager for alternative assets based in Switzerland, which invests in private equity and hedge funds on a global basis.

Part I

Introduction

Chapter 1

An overview of themes and issues

Ronald A. Lake
Lake Partners, Inc., Greenwich, Connecticut

The purpose of this book

'Meet Kate Reddy, hedge fund manager and mother of two. She can juggle nine different currencies in five different time zones and get herself and two children washed and dressed and out of the house in half an hour'. So reads the jacket cover on Allison Pearson's novel, *I Don't Know How She Does It,* which was published in 2002 and made it onto *The New York Times* book review best-seller list for a number of weeks. The book is characterised by 'humour, drama and bracing wisdom'. I know this only because the same jacket cover tells me so. I realise that the book is really not about hedge funds but rather 'the dilemma of working motherhood at the start of the twenty-first century' (again, the jacket covers tells me so). Yet the book bugs me a bit, for several reasons.

First, it irks me to think that Allison Pearson has probably already sold the film rights to her witty bauble of a book. I have not had any takers for the cinematic version of the vastly more informative tome that is now in your hands since its first edition in 1996.

Second, I suppose it is a mildly amusing sign of the times that after a three-year bear market, hedge funds have seeped into popular culture as something trendy. At least this is better than being reviled by the financial press and politicians as financial pirates who manipulate markets (remember how Malaysia's President Mahathir demonised George Soros after the collapse of the ringgit or how the Bank of England fingered him as the culprit who broke the pound?). However, there is something still unsettling about hedge funds becoming 'cool', especially when the pace of institutional interest is starting to pick up speed. The smart investor is always wary of the crowd, especially when the crowd is comprised of a herd of elephants.

Most annoying, though, is that even when the book is about hedge funds, it isn't about hedge funds. Rather than portraying hedge fund managers realistically as the hard working, insightful iconoclasts that they are, it falls back on some of the same old, tired stereotypes the industry has been tagged with for too long. Kate is a hedge fund manager at the fictional Edwin Morgan Forster, 'which ranks in the top 10 money managers in the United Kingdom and in the top 50 globally in terms of assets, and which, for five years running, has been voted money manager of the year'. Here is Kate addressing six new trainees:

> 'You will, I'm sure already be familiar with the term fund manager. Put at its simplest, a fund manager is a high-class gambler. My job is to study the form of companies around the world, assess the going rate in the markets for their products, check out the track record of jockeys, stick a big chunk of money on the best bet and then hope to hell that they don't fall at the first fence.'

Like Captain Renault at Rick's Café Americain in *Casablanca,* I am shocked, shocked to find that gambling is going on in here! How can such a refined and civilised pursuit as managing a hedge fund be sullied in such a way! I am sure that all hedge fund investors with any semblance of experience will recognise Kate Reddy's cartoonish characterisation for just what it is and respond with justifiably righteous indignation.

And like Captain Renault, we will all murmur a polite 'oh, thank you very much' when the croupier says 'your winnings, sir'. We are indignant perhaps because a small kernel of truth lurks within the humour of it all. Speculation is the 'bad rap' the industry must rise above but speculation is the vice that hedge fund investors and managers alike must always guard against precisely because the beauty (and danger) of hedge funds is that they can be so flexible in the way they invest.

Which brings us, surprisingly enough, to the purpose of this book. This third edition of *Evaluating and Implementing Hedge Fund Strategies* aims to foster an open and honest dialogue among managers and investors about what works and what does not work in hedge funds, what is attractive and what is unattractive, how to distinguish between the realities and the myths.

Since the second edition of this book in 1999, when there was only a modest shelf full of specialist volumes available, readers have benefited from a raft of new offerings on the industry. In particular, there are some excellent overviews. However, there still is no comprehensive survey, handbook or 'how to' manual. There never can be, because the field is too diverse, complex and dynamic. This book itself has been greatly expanded, revised and updated. Not only are the topics even broader than before, more than half of the authors are new. Yet it is neither primer nor procedural. Rather, it is a collection of essays written by and for professional investors as well as serious students seeking an insightful overview of the trends, developments and issues facing hedge funds. At one level, the chapters in this book are intended to delve into how hedge fund managers and investors 'tick'. At a broader level, though, the book is meant to have some enduring value as a set of reflections on the past, present and future of hedge funds. It is also meant to have some practical use. Hence the title for the book: *Evaluating and Implementing Hedge Fund Strategies.*

While the book has been written for a diverse audience comprising investors, institutions, intermediaries and money managers, each of the authors has taken a deeply personal approach to addressing the issues they believe are important. As editor, I asked the contributors to consider the following questions: How do you view your general area? What have been the trends? What is your particular approach and how has it evolved? From a conceptual point of view, what are the sources of risk and return in your area? What are their dynamics? How have they changed? What has not changed? As a hedge fund manager/investor, what has been your particular approach to exploiting these sources of risk and return? What strategies have worked over the years? What has not? Why? What is the outlook for your area? How do you expect things to develop going forward? What alternative scenarios are likely?

I am pleased to report that all of the contributors have succeeded in wrestling with these questions. I am also pleased to report that while many answers have been formulated, there are many that remain inchoate or elusive. This is only to be expected, again considering how diverse and dynamic the whole field of hedge funds is. Indeed, if there is any unifying conclusion to be drawn from this book, it is that hedge funds are so diverse and dynamic. When I set out to organise this book, I was concerned that we would end up with everyone saying the same thing. I should have known better. After all, put two hedge fund managers in a room and you will get three arguments. Even though the popular impression is that the hedge fund world is a monolithic one, surrounded by murk and mystery, pull aside the curtain and you will find some very serious (and ultimately very human) disagreements and divergences within the industry.

The structure of this book

The diversity, dynamics, disagreements and divergences that animate the hedge fund industry are reflected throughout the structure and content of this book. The topics addressed within the chapters have been divided into six broad sections:

Part I: Introduction
Part II: Evaluating opportunities – managers' strategies
Part III: Evaluating opportunities – investors' strategies
Part IV: Assessing risk and risk control
Part V: Hedge funds and public policy
Part VI: Legal and regulatory issues

'Part I: Introduction', includes this overview and five diverse chapters, which lay out the history and background of the industry, address the basic rationale for hedge funds and provide a basic set of definitions.

'Part II: Evaluating opportunities – managers' strategies', represents the 'supply side' of the industry. It is made up of presentations by 12 seasoned hedge fund managers who explore critically the challenges and opportunities they face within their particular discipline of investing, ranging from hedged equity investing to fixed-income arbitrage.

'Part III: Evaluating opportunities – investors' strategies', represents the 'demand side' of the industry. It comprises discussions by 10 hands-on investors of the uses and abuses, the pros and the cons of utilising hedge funds. Also included is the due diligence questionnaire developed by the Alternative Investment Management Association (AIMA), which is in Appendix 1.

'Part IV: Assessing risk and risk control', addresses what perhaps has become the most important topic within the field. It includes in-depth reviews by five practitioners who approach the issues from very different but related directions, as one is a manager, two are investors/intermediaries, one is an accountant/auditor and one is a prime broker.

'Part V: Hedge funds and public policy', explores how hedge funds relate to economic developments and how they affect the behaviour of securities markets. The four contributors not only share very thoughtful reflections on the issues but also offer some very useful guidance to policy makers.

'Part VI: Legal and regulatory issues', comprises five chapters that provide much needed clarity for those seeking guidance through the very complex tangle of undergrowth that surrounds hedge funds. Also included is an IOSCO report, which is in Appendix 2, on regulatory and investor protection issues.

Following are general reviews of the issues raised within each part of the book.

Understanding the beast – a review of Part I: Introduction

Asking someone to define what a hedge fund is reminds me of the old tale about the five blind men who try to define an elephant. The first blind man approaches the animal and gets hold of a leg. 'Ah, this animal is like a tree', he concludes. The next feels an ear. 'No, here's a wing.

It must be a sort of bird', and so on. So it is with hedge funds. Just when you think you have a firm grasp on any one part of the beast, you have to concede that someone else has identified something that may not be so apparent.

It is therefore impressive that Ted Caldwell in his chapter, 'Market gravity and hedge fund aerodynamics: the prudent approach to hedge fund classification', is able to draw such clear distinctions among the flora and fauna that make up the hedge fund landscape. The key is understanding the elementary nature of hedge funds, which Caldwell does by referring back to the original concept of a hedged fund as developed by A.W. Jones.[1] Lars Jaeger adds to the discussion by systematically analysing the sources of returns for hedge funds. The chapters of Antoine Bernheim and Lois Peltz provide further background by laying out the historical context within which hedge funds have developed. Antoine Bernheim gives a particularly telling explanation of what offshore funds are and how they have evolved into what they are today and more importantly how they continue to evolve in response to market developments and investor behaviour. Lois Peltz details the key events that are shaping the industry and what the implications may be going forward. Finally, Jon Bren offers a trenchant reality check, by relating broad principles to hard experience in 'Lessons learned from investing in hedge funds over the years'.

From an objective viewpoint, the common denominators among hedge funds would seem to consist of little more than the following: (i) they are commingled pools that are offered via private placements to a relatively limited number of institutions and sophisticated investors, and (ii) the manager receives an incentive fee. Beyond these characteristics, there is nothing monolithic or typical about the universe of hedge funds.

The reality is that there are hedge funds and there are hedge funds, and there are hedge funds. Some of the most well-known hedge fund managers attained celebrity-like fame (or in some cases infamy) in recent years, having achieved often spectacular performance with large, leveraged 'bets' on the direction of markets, currencies and interest rates. Other, perhaps less well-known managers have maintained a more traditional 'hedged' approach, while still others have focused on fairly narrow areas of specialisation, ranging from convertible arbitrage and short selling, to emerging markets, fixed-income arbitrage and quantitative 'market-neutral' strategies. Each has had periods when they were heroes and each has had periods when they were goats.

Even within these various 'types' of funds there are distinctions. Some are managed by seasoned professionals (cynics would say 'tired veterans'). Others are run by young start ups ('up starts'). Some are overseeing substantial assets ('too big and unwieldy'), while others are quite small ('untested and non-viable'). Certain managers adhere to well-defined investment disciplines ('inflexible'), while others are highly opportunistic in their approach ('unfocused').

Which (if any) of these types deserves to inherit the title of the True Hedge Fund? This question is touched on not just by Ted Caldwell, it is debated by virtually all of the contributors throughout the book. While categorising managers can be useful, more often than not the reality is that any given manager should be profiled as a bundle of characteristics, not a type. The issues are listed below.

The evolution of the hedge fund

The traditional definition

- US focus
- equity orientation; style specialisation

- hedged long-short
- low profile
- very small organisations

The contemporary definition
- global investment scope
- use of multiple asset classes; opportunistic
- derivatives used to hedge and/or augment positions
- high visibility
- large organisations

Proliferation of categories and approaches

Investment styles
- equities
- multi-strategy
- merger arbitrage; risk arbitrage
- convertible arbitrage
- fixed-income arbitrage
- strategic investing
- special situations
- closed-end fund arbitrage
- high-yield and distressed securities
- short selling
- pairs trading
- index arbitrage
- industry specialisation
- emerging markets
- etc

Portfolio manager techniques
- US versus global
- analytical versus quantitative
- hedged versus directional
- bottom-up versus top-down
- value versus growth
- fundamental versus technical
- concentrated versus diversified
- securities versus derivatives
- long-term investing versus short-term trading
- use of new issues, private placements, etc
- etc

The spectrum of return objectives
- high absolute returns
- relative returns

- stability of returns
- long-term versus short-term performance

The array of risk characteristics
- short-term volatility versus long-term performance
- volatility relative to a market index or benchmark
- consistency of returns
- risk of permanent loss
- portfolio diversification; concentration
- degree and type of hedging
- liquidity
- use of leverage
- exposure to interest rates, credit, volatility, other factors
- disclosure/trust/communication

Intelligence reports from the front lines – a review of Part II: Evaluating opportunities – managers' strategies

Since *all* investing is a matter of dealing with uncertainty and the passage of time, there will always be an eternal debate about who is more likely to succeed, the patient investor who maintains his conviction or the quick trader who is flexible and adaptable.[2] Likewise, there will never be agreement on whether it is more effective to be a top-down strategist who tries to anticipate macroeconomic trends and market developments, or a bottom-up analyst who concentrates on the characteristics of specific securities. To the former, who may regard himself as a visionary navigator, the latter resembles a highly trained but nonetheless near-sighted helmsman who may not have recognised his mistake of having signed on to the Titanic until it is too late. On the other hand, the latter, who styles himself after a fine crafts-man or connoisseur, may question the sanity of the former for having left terra firma in the first place. Trying to convince anyone that one approach is better than the other is often like discussing religion. No matter how tolerant you may be, when you know your way is right it is hard to understand how the other guy can be such an unenlightened heathen.

If there are any eternal truths, one of them is that there is no such thing as the 'world's best money manager'. There never has been. Another eternal truth is that the dispersion of results among hedge funds, even within a relatively narrow sub-sector of the industry, can be very wide. This is because managers have such tremendous latitude in what they can do. The fact is that there are great managers but no one outperforms all the time. Indeed, as history has shown, any manager eventually goes through a period(s) in which he underperforms, whether in absolute terms or relative to whatever benchmark is relevant. Furthermore, virtu-ally *all* investment styles go through periods of underperformance, whether due to changes in market conditions, overcrowding and too much money, or simple reversion to the mean. We have seen it happen in the past to growth stock managers, arbitrageurs, short sellers, market-neutral, macro players and the like.

The tide always turns, though. Furthermore, macro trends have transformed the investment process into a much more complex and global one. As Michael Lewitt points out in his chapter, 'Understanding credit cycles and hedge fund strategies', there are market forces that surround all money managers and all styles of investing. It may be perilous to assume one can outsmart the market but it is equally perilous to outsmart oneself by ignoring the market. Similarly, recognising market trends can inform the manager on where opportunities (and risk) will be.

These notions are at the very core of what it means to hedge market risk (or alternatively, to embrace market opportunity). Roddy Campbell, Shuhei Abe, Bruce Richards, Lou Hanover and Michael Rulle pursue very different strategies but for all of them the investment process entails identifying specific opportunities within trends. In 'European event and arbitrage investing', Roddy Campbell looks at bottom-up, event-driven investments within the context of the restructuring of Europe. In 'Long-short investment strategy in Japan', Shuhei Abe's broad, top-down view of the transformation of Japan's economy informs his approach to stock selection. Bruce Richards and Lou Hanover develop a framework for taking advantage of volatility arising from economic developments in 'Emerging markets'. For Michael Rulle's 'Trend following: performance, risk and correlation characteristics', the interplay between cyclical and secular trends is literally the name of the game.

There may be tides and winds that buffet all investors but perhaps one way to adapt is to dive beneath the waves where the forces are more muted. John Paulson in 'Adding alpha in merger arbitrage' and Jason Huemer in 'The hedge fund manager's edge: an overview of event investing' take up the banner of the 'micro' approach. Yes, there is always an ebb and flow of corporate activity, and John Paulson and Jason Huemer would be the first to tell you how this can put a spin on their areas of focus. However, these managers find opportunity in specific events, not the general trends. This is also the case for Luke Imperatore, who describes 'Asset-backed investing', where detailed analysis of specific pieces of paper can make or break an investment.

It would be overly simplistic to overemphasise this dichotomous portrayal of competing hedge fund strategies, macro versus micro. The fact is that there are many dimensions and shades of grey in this picture. Certainly the interplay of trends and specific events becomes most tumultuous in the day-in, day-out tension between the immovable object of the equity market and the irresistible force of stock valuation. While a number of the chapters in this part of the book explore some of the more exotic strategies, Lee Ainslie re-examines the basics. In 'Hedged equity investing', Lee Ainslie offers an insider's view of what it takes to run a classic hedged fund.

Another stream of activity in the hedge fund world is made up of a variety of disparate quantitative techniques. Again, even as such strategies are designed to mitigate the impact of market behaviour, trends and developments within the markets themselves have an inescapable influence on the efficacy of such strategies. For Bruce Jacobs and Kenneth Levy, the beauty of quantitative techniques is in designing portfolios to be unperturbed by the markets, as explained in 'Using a long-short portfolio to neutralise market risk and enhance active returns'. Fixed-income arbitrage is undoubtedly one of the more complex areas of the hedge fund world. Michael Pintar in 'Fixed-income arbitrage' elucidates many of the ins and outs of these complex strategies. Similarly, Michael Boyd reveals the dynamic nature of convertible arbitrage in 'Convertible arbitrage: the manager's perspective'. All three show how even the most advanced quantitative analysis must be tempered with a realistic understanding of how markets work. As one pundit once put it, 'The market is designed to fool as many people as possible at any one time'.

It is difficult to notice, but if there is agreement among the contributors on anything, it is that running a successful hedge fund is hard work that requires fortitude and perseverance. As Robert Wilson, a well-regarded hedge fund manager who is now retired, once said, 'In this business, 20 per cent of the time you feel omnipotent, 60 per cent of the time you feel frustrated, and 20 per cent of the time you feel merely despondent'. Few others would allow such an admission openly, but most would concur, at least in private.

Charting the seas – a review of Part III: Evaluating opportunities – investors' strategies

Why invest in hedge funds? In one of his movies, the ever-neurotic Woody Allen has a marvellous explanation for why he persists in behaving the way he does. He talks about a crazy uncle who thinks he is a chicken. Why doesn't he bring this relative to a psychiatrist? 'Because', Woody admits, 'I need the eggs'.

After a year like 1998, when hedge fund disaster stories were splashed on the business pages of every local newspaper, the story has some resonance to it. However, for every disaster, there were dozens and dozens of other funds that managed to navigate the rocks and storms without incident, or at least without fear of sinking, even if they did take on water. Perhaps another story is more appropriate. In late September 1998, I was hurrying through Grand Central train station in Manhattan, preoccupied with the questions of the day. This was at the height of investors' fears that global markets were in danger of being dragged down by the sinking juggernaut known as Long-Term Capital. Coincidentally, it was also a point in time when the tide of popularity for the film, *Titanic,* had finally reached an ebb. I suddenly noticed a T-shirt go by. It had a simple message: 'The ship sank. Get over it'. It may not have been an epiphany, but it did make me chuckle out loud.

Yes, a mighty ship, once thought invincible, sank under the weight of its own hubris. However, transportation did not cease. Many other ships sailed on. Indeed, hull design and navigational technology improved. In other words, before I abuse this analogy too much farther, investors allocate some portion of their money to a variety of hedge funds because they exhibit different patterns of returns, different sets of risk characteristics and thus different exposures to the market. Yes, for many private investors superior, absolute returns are the motivation for being in non-traditional investments. However, the other motivation is diversification. The validity of this rationale became increasingly apparent after March 2000, when the stock market bubble burst and hedge funds generally showed how being hedged could make a difference in the ensuing three-year bear market.

Tom Schneeweis and Richard Spurgin make it clear in their chapter, 'Quantitative analysis of return and risk characteristics of hedge funds, managed futures and mutual funds', that the performance of non-traditional investments *à la* hedge funds tends to be less dependent on the market or is even negatively correlated. Thus, as James Berens, Judith Posnikoff and Alexandra Coffey demonstrate in their chapter, 'Institutional investors: incorporating hedge funds into the asset allocation process', non-traditional investment vehicles such as hedge funds have grown significantly in popularity, partly due to their returns, partly due to their role in hedging or trading around market risk. Hedge funds are not going to replace conventional managers but the opportunity to enhance returns while reducing systematic risk can be a compelling motivation to invest in this area. A global perspective on these trends is provided by Sohail Jaffer in 'Analysing the evolution of the European hedge fund industry' and Peter Douglas in 'Hedge funds in Asia'.

The foundation for investing in hedge funds, or any investment for that matter, is understanding one's investment objectives and expectations. Perhaps it was said best by the great baseball player and inadvertent investment thinker, Yogi Berra, who once remarked, 'If you don't know where you are going, you might wind up somewhere else when you get there'. Determining a clear investment policy and understanding the investment environment is important in determining how and what kind of hedge funds an investor might utilise. Stuart Leaf provides his own thought-provoking version of a crystal ball for these questions in 'Understanding continuing trends in hedge funds'.

Developing an investment outlook is one thing. Understanding the behaviour of specific hedge funds is another. Roxanne Martino in 'The due diligence process', Thomas Weber in 'Quantitative analysis of hedge funds' and Jeff Tarrant in 'The life cycle of hedge fund managers' offer keen insights into assessing individual hedge fund managers. In particular, they share their experience in peering through the façade and digging behind the numbers to understand the realities of hedge funds. Rounding out the practical side of the process, Emma Mugridge makes available a valuable tool, the AIMA due diligence questionnaire, in Appendix 1.

All that is left is to integrate theory and analysis, and put together an actual investment programme. Lloyd Hascoe shares his personal experience in 'Utilising hedge funds: the experiences of a private investor', in which he provides a unique, decade-long case study. In marked contrast to Lloyd Hascoe's highly targeted approach, Jeff Bramel explores 'Hedge fund benchmarking and indexation', which has emerged as a tool for investors seeking to gain broad exposure to the asset class of hedge funds.

Before hiring a knife juggler, count his fingers – a review of Part IV: Assessing risk and risk control

Somerset Maugham, the author of the book *The Razor's Edge,* once wrote that there were three rules to writing a novel (unfortunately no one knew what they were). Similarly there are three rules to managing risk in a hedge fund. Fortunately, our contributors to this section do know what they are.

- *Rule 1.* As Paul Singer points out in 'Risk control and risk management', risk from a manager's point of view is a far more complex consideration than merely the simple but widespread notion of 'volatility'. It requires careful, thoughtful management and judgement of realistic expectations and potential surprise.
- *Rule 2.* Guy Hurley explains in 'Qualitative aspects of analysing risk and monitoring managers', that risk from an investor's point of view is ultimately a matter of judgement. This requires understanding a manager's character, culture and philosophy, and how these may change over time. In 'Hedge fund transparency', Jim Hedges delves into one particularly important aspect of the investor's process of gaining an understanding of, and trust in, a manager.
- *Rule 3.* Mike Tremmel makes it clear in 'Assessing risk and risk control: operational issues', that the best laid plans of managers and investors can come to naught if they are not implemented and administered with the proper controls. Chris Pesce elaborates on how critical 'The evolving role of the prime broker' can be. As more hedge funds engage in increasingly complex strategies, invest in more diverse global markets and utilise more exotic instruments, the need to control the trade and settlement functions as well as manage information and measure prices and performance will become commensurately more acute. None of these areas should be underestimated.

Stop me before I speculate again – a review of Part V: Hedge funds and public policy

On a flight to Hong Kong from Vancouver in November of 1997, I found myself sitting next to a fellow who turned out to be an engineer from Malaysia. Markets throughout the Pacific had been in a steep dive for a number of weeks and my seat-mate's eyebrows rose when I mentioned that I was in the investment business. 'Asian markets have been very difficult', he stated stiffly. Yes, I had heard something about that, I dead panned. 'You know why, don't you?' he asked pointedly. He then gave me a hard look as he spat out the answer. 'George Soros and all those other hedge funds'.

Such has been the power of the stereotype of hedge funds. For too many years, the financial press perpetuated the image of hedge funds as predatory speculators who move equity, fixed-income and foreign exchange markets by wielding enormous amounts of leverage and aggressively trading derivatives. Fortunately, members of the media have taken a more realistic, or at least less shrill, view as they came to realise the hedge fund industry represents only a thin sliver of the world's capital markets. After all, hedge funds are dwarfed by the insurance industry, mutual funds, pension funds, central banks and the proprietary trading desks of securities firms. Moreover, many hedge funds never trade any currencies or futures.

Are hedge funds to blame for bouts of market turmoil? Do they need to be regulated? According to the contributors in this section of the book the answer is: yes, no, maybe and then some. George Soros' 'Hedge funds and dynamic hedging' is excerpted from Congressional testimony delivered in 1994. It reads with surprising relevance and freshness in the wake of the events of 1998 and the post-2000 bear market. Henry Kaufman, in 'What bankers don't know', another prophetic piece, does know just where to lay the blame. In contrast, Barry Eichengreen and Donald Mathieson provide a scholarly approach to a difficult topic in 'Hedge funds and financial markets: implications for policy' which is excerpted from IMF Working Paper #166. More recently, the Securities and Exchange Commission has been much in the news regarding possible regulation of hedge funds. Jim Chanos' 'Short selling, hedge funds and public policy considerations' is adapted from his presentation at the Commission's roundtable on hedge funds which was held in May 2003. In addition to a clear and sensible explanation of the role of short selling in the markets, Jim Chanos also provides a very interesting practitioner's view of how a short seller analyses opportunities.

Taming the wild footnote – a review of Part VI: Legal and regulatory issues

Why bother to read the fine print in that turgid, impenetrable pile of paper known as the Prospectus? If you don't, you may some day wish you did. Hedge fund investing is not easy and it is not made any easier by the legal, regulatory and tax issues. The five chapters in this section will dispel any despair you may have about approaching this complex thicket of considerations. Phil Harris and his team provide a detailed road map for managers in 'Structuring hedge funds: an overview of business, legal and regulatory considerations for managers'. Eric Sippel and Christopher Rupright smooth the way for investors in 'Investing in hedge funds: an overview of business, legal and regulatory considerations for investors'. Eric Bettelheim's 'Marketing alternative investment funds: law and regulation in Europe' and Nicholas Hodge's 'Marketing alternative investments: law and regulation in the United States' simplify an otherwise bewildering array of details. Nicholas Hodge does double duty, analysing 'The evolution and outlook for regulation of hedge funds in the United States'. Finally, in Appendix 2 IOSCO shares their chapter on 'Regulatory and investor protection issues arising from the participation by retail investors in (funds of) hedge funds'. The latter two contributions are especially important as hedge funds are attracting a wider and wider audience of participants.

Lessons to be learned, re-learned and re-learned again

The holy grail of hedge fund investing can be summed up in one word: edge. Finding an edge is the theme that weaves its way through almost all of the chapters in this book. In some cases the word is used quite explicitly. In others, the word is too sacrosanct to utter or too steeped in mystery to be revealed to mere mortals. However, in the mundane world of slogging away at the chore of trying to add value, it is possible to develop a fairly straightforward checklist of what to look for, and what to avoid.

Potential sources of value added

- special set of skills, approach
- focused, responsive decision making
- cohesive organisation
- dedication and commitment
- balance of flexibility versus discipline
- niche opportunities; barriers to entry
- etc

Potential impediments to performance

- growth of assets under management
- adopting new techniques
- taking uncharacteristic risks
- refusal or inability to adapt
- refusal to admit mistakes
- loss of dedication and commitment, lifestyle changes
- change in objectives
- increasing organisational complexity
- organisational disruptions
- turnover of personnel
- lack of operational controls
- etc

Dynamics of the investment environment

- trending markets versus trading markets
- bullish environments versus bearish conditions
- strength of investment themes

- degree of market inefficiencies
- compression/dispersion of valuation discrepancies

Style cycles

- robustness of the style versus faddishness, susceptibility to corrections
- degree of inefficiency (opportunity) versus overcrowding
- number of seasoned professionals versus marginal entrants
- investor sentiment: oversupply of capital versus redemptions
- availability and terms of financing, margin

For investors, the solution to adding value must be guided by the careful determination of the blend of performance and risk control they seek, rather than in reacting to yesterday's style shifts. Success will follow for those who (i) practise the fine art and discipline of intelligently diversifying among different yet complementary managers and (ii) make sure their portfolio of managers is always structured to achieve their own carefully defined ends in an ever-changing world.

A fundamental issue is whether it is more effective to follow a core buy and hold approach to achieving and maintaining diversification by investment style and manager or whether more value can be added by engaging in some form of active, strategic asset allocation. In the first approach, the aim is to diversify among different strategies that have proven in the past to be effective over time, and to maintain a balanced allocation among them over the long term. This buy and hold approach requires patience and fortitude. If implemented with discipline, its chief advantage is that it can avoid the typical syndrome of dropping out of perfectly viable strategies when they are temporarily out of favour and chasing after hot areas when they are already peaking. Its chief disadvantage may be that it can be too conservative and backward-looking an approach (opportunities to add value by reallocating to new areas or changing trends will be missed).

The alternative is to take a strategic approach to asset allocation by trying to identify which areas or styles will outperform going forward. This timing approach requires a contrarian attitude and/or an ability to actively redeploy resources. If implemented with courage and good timing, its chief advantage is that it can add significant value over time. Its chief disadvantage can be that value is dissipated if too much reliance is placed on experimenting with promising but untested strategies that do not measure up, or if one's timing is simply wrong.

One underlying concern for those whose quest is to find an edge is how to understand and deal with underperformance. The real question is whether such underperformance is temporary or persists for a protracted period of time. If a manager is underperforming due to something that is peculiar to his particular approach, the analysis may be relatively simple. Is the manager still consistent in his approach or has he changed his stripes? Is he maintaining his investment disciplines or has he started taking uncharacteristic risks? Is the organisation and decision-making process intact or has it been affected by some disruptive change? Are the assets under management still appropriate to the manager's style? Has the manager lost his dedication or become distracted by some change in his personal circumstances? This is why monitoring managers is so critical. Or to quote Yogi Berra again, 'You can observe a lot just by watching'.

If one concludes that the source of the underperformance is transitory, this would be the worst possible time to throw in the towel. Rather, perseverance is warranted. Indeed, if one still has confidence in the manager, it may by an ideal time to top up one's allocation. After all, a good manager does not become stupid over night. On the other hand, if the conclusion is that the manager has truly lost his touch, the sooner one moves on, the better.

However, what if a manager is underperforming due to circumstances beyond his control? You may have found the best navigator in the business but if that navigator is on the Titanic it won't matter how good he is. Evaluating the outlook for investment styles, as opposed to investment managers, is far more difficult because it requires evaluating market trends.

The other underlying concern in the quest for an edge is unrecoverable loss (disaster). Often, the problem with a manager whose fund is in a state of collapse is stubbornness. As one pundit put it, 'Markets can remain irrational for longer than you can remain solvent'.[3] Getting out of the way is often smarter for a manager than proving he is right, or as Michael Simoff, a contributor to the second edition, often reminded me, 'If you are going to panic, panic early'. When a manager embraces risk, the investor must be fully cognisant and adjust accordingly. An investor once confronted a hedge fund manager famous for putting on enormous, concentrated positions in volatile futures markets. 'How do you sleep at night knowing your portfolio is so leveraged?' demanded the investor. 'How do you sleep at night knowing you've invested your money with me', was the cool reply.

Unfortunately, despite the clarity and simplicity of so many of these principles, it can be maddeningly difficult to get them to work. So many things can (and do) go wrong. It's as if hedge fund investors are just many coyotes, forever chasing Roadrunner with all those defective contraptions from ACME Supply Co, and never able to catch him.

Now that the industry has grown so much and so many investors have matured in so many ways, are there not some obvious guide posts to successfully selecting hedge funds? To answer this question, I would like to offer the following cautionary case study. To protect the innocent (and the guilty) I cannot name the manager involved but I can assure you the story is true.

If you have read Michael Lewis' book, *Moneyball: The Art of Winning an Unfair Game,* you know that it is not really about Billy Beane or baseball statistics but rather a delicious parable about the hedge fund investor's holy grail, namely finding an edge by identifying extraordinary talent. There is an interesting quote in Michael Lewis' book that is attributed to Cyril Connolly, author of *Enemies of Promise:* 'Whom the gods wish to destroy they first call promising'.

Promising was certainly the best word to describe Manager X when he announced plans to launch his hedge fund. Relatively few funds have been launched with such a full complement of attributes. The key man had served as understudy to an established manager in the business. He even had a record that he could point to, the results of a sub-portfolio for which he had been responsible. Maybe the performance figures weren't audited, maybe they were gross of fees, but you could easily pro forma the proposed fee schedule and see how impressive the numbers were. You could even arbitrarily divide by two and still get an impressive track record!

In addition to pedigree and record, Manager X was more than smart. Some even referred to him as a genius, so keen were his investment insights. Since he was smart, he travelled with all the other smart managers in the business. What a network of beautiful minds to draw upon.

In addition to pedigree, record, intelligence and network, our new candidate was backed by a solid team. The typical hedge fund start-up is a one or two-man band with a handful of junior analysts and maybe a few support persons, all housed in bare and cramped office space with basic, off-the-shelf turnkey systems provided by a prime broker. Not this time. Manager

X knew the importance of marshalling resources. On day one he would open his doors with a broad and deep team, complete with state-of-the-art portfolio systems, proprietary research, multiple lines of credit, the works. In fact, months before opening, the team would be running live with internal capital to make sure that all systems were working smoothly in advance of taking outside money. To top it off, many of the people involved already knew each other quite well or had worked together previously.

In addition to pedigree, record, intelligence, network and organisation, the new fund not only would launch with substantial capital, it would put a cap on contributions and immediately close to new investors to avoid any ongoing distractions from marketing. So excited were investors by Manager X's promise that the fund was oversubscribed long before launch date. The very large fund of funds groups were negotiating for capacity and the small fry were worrying about having their allocations cut back, prompting inflated requests for larger subscriptions in a vain attempt to game the situation.

Finally the fund was launched and investors settled back to watch expectantly for their due diligence on such a marvellous package of ideal hedge fund attributes to pay off. In the first few months, results were modest (impatient investors called it just plain flat). No matter. The manager was simply taking his time putting money to work. This was followed by a period of further modest (flat) results. One had to understand. The investment environment had become increasingly difficult. Then a steady erosion set in. The more that performance slipped, the greater the pressure to repair the damage. Finally 'erosion' gave way to outright draw down. Hot money investors were gnashing their teeth and whining loudly at conferences to anyone who would listen. The institutions were more professional and patient about it. They simply went about their business, quietly preparing their redemption notices.

What no one's due diligence had accounted for was the possibility that the manager might simply start off on the wrong foot. His investment calls were either too early or wrong, although the two are often indistinguishable. Once the redemptions started, the fund shrank dramatically, as did the organisation. Those investors that maintained confidence in the manager and stayed in found themselves wringing their hands as performance continued to erode, prompting further shrinkage in the organisation. Thus came the next wave of redemptions, exacerbating the downward spiral.

Of course, the postscript is that once the organisation shrank to a size that was more manageable for the manager and once he was finally able to clear his head after too long a stretch of uninterrupted frustration, the markets changed, his investment style swung back into favour, he made some smart moves and performance picked up briskly. Maybe the really smart money was the investor who added at that point, reasoning that Manager X had learned so many lessons by now, that he was better equipped than ever to run a hedge fund.

So we come back to the basic conundrum all investors must face, whether to persevere or move on. Even Kate Reddy knew this. Blast, I hate quoting Allison Pearson's book, but here is our friend, Kate, addressing those trainees again:

> If the horses I've backed do fall, I have to decide whether we shoot them right away or whether it's worth nursing that broken leg back to health. Remember, ladies and gentlemen, compassion can be expensive but it's not necessarily a waste of your money.

In closing, I offer two more quotes. The first is from Winston Churchill, who said, 'Never give in, never give in, never, never, never . . . .' The other is from W.C. Fields, who said, 'If at first you don't succeed, try, try again. Then quit. No use being a damn fool about it'. A veritable ying and yang of investment philosophy. Can they both be right? I will leave it to you to decide. In the meantime, I hope you find the material in this book to be valuable and useful and if you know any movie studio agents, please show them the book.

References

The following is a bibliography of books published in English on hedge funds and related topics. Please note that there are other works that are available in French, German, Italian and Japanese.

Anson, Mark Jonathan (2002), *The Handbook of Alternative Assets*, New York, John Wiley & Sons.

Baker, Richard H. (Ed.) (2000), *Operation of Hedge Funds and Their Role in the Financial System*, Congressional Hearing.

Barham, Sarah (2001), *Starting a Hedge Fund: A US Perspective*, Hong Kong, ISI Publications.

Barham, Sarah, and Ian Hallsworth (Eds.) (2002), *Starting a Hedge Fund: An Asian Perspective*, Hong Kong, ISI Publications.

Barham, Sarah, Ian Hallsworth and Gary Kitching (Eds.) (2002), *Starting a Hedge Fund: A European Perspective*, Hong Kong, ISI Publications.

Barnes, Claire (1995), *Asia's Investment Prophets*, London, Century.

Bekier, Matthias (1996), *Marketing of Hedge Funds: A Key Strategic Variable in Defining Possible Roles of an Emerging Investment Force*, New York, P. Lang.

Bernheim, Antoine (2002), *The US Offshore Funds Directory*, The US Offshore Funds Directory Inc.

Bernstein, Peter L. (1992), *Capital Ideas: The Improbable Origins Of Modern Wall Street*, New York, Touchstone Books.

Bernstein, Peter L. (1996), *Against the Gods: The Remarkable Story of Risk*, New York, John Wiley & Sons.

Bruce, Brian (Ed.) (2002), *Hedge Fund Strategies – A Global Outlook*, New York, Institutional Investor, Inc.

Caxton Corporation *et al* (2000), *Sound Practices for Hedge Fund Managers*.

Chance, Don M. (1994), *Managed Futures and Their Role in Investment Portfolios*, Charlottesville, VA, The Research Foundation of the Institute of Chartered Financial Analysts.

Chandler, Beverly (1998), *Investing with Hedge Fund Giants: Profit Whether Markets Rise or Fall*, London, Financial Times Prentice Hall.

Connors, Laurence A., and Blake E. Hayward (1995), *Investment Secrets of a Hedge Fund Manager: Exploiting the Herd Mentality of the Financial Markets*, Chicago, Probus Publishing.

Cottier, Philipp (1998), *Hedge Funds and Managed Futures,* New York, Peter Lang.

Crerend, William J., and Robert A. Jaeger (2000), *Fundamentals of Hedge Fund Investing: A Professional Investor's Guide,* New York, McGraw Hill.

Dunbar, Nicholas (1998), *Inventing Money: The Story of Long-Term Capital Management and the Legends Behind It,* New York, John Wiley & Sons.

Eichengreen, Barry (Ed.) (2002), *Hedge Funds and Financial Market Dynamics,* Washington, International Monetary Fund.

Goetzmann, William N., Jonathan Ingersoll and Stephen Ross (2001), *High-Water Marks and Hedge Fund Management Contracts,* Yale ICF Working Paper No. 00-34 (18 April).

Goldman, Sachs & Co. and Frank Russell Company (2001), *Alternative Investing by Tax-Exempt Organizations 2001 – A Survey of Organizations in North America, Europe, Australia and Japan.*

Golin/Harris Ludgate (2001), *The Future Role of Hedge Funds in European Institutional Asset Management,* survey.

Harvard Business School (1999), *Long-Term Capital Management, L.P. (A),* Boston.

HedgeWorld, *HedgeWorld Annual Compendium 2003,* Hong Kong, ISI Publications Ltd.

Hills, Richard (2002), *Hedge Funds: An Introduction to Skill Based Investment Strategies,* Bedfordshire, Rushmere Wynne.

Ineichen, Alexander M. (2003), *Absolute Returns: The Risk and Opportunities of Hedge Fund Investing,* New Jersey, John Wiley & Sons.

Jaeger, Lars (2003), *Managing Risk in Alternative Investment Strategies: Successful Investing in Hedge Funds and Managed Futures,* London, Prentice Hall.

Jaeger, Lars (Ed.) (2003), *The New Generation of Risk Management for Hedge Funds and Private Equity Investments,* London, Euromoney Books.

Jaeger, Robert A. (2002), *All About Hedge Funds,* New York, McGraw Hill.

Jaffer, Sohail (Ed.) (1998), *Alternative Investment Strategies,* London, Euromoney Books.

Jaffer, Sohail (Ed.) (2003), *Funds of Hedge Funds,* London, Euromoney Books.

Jobman, Darrell (Ed.) (2002), *The Handbook of Alternative Investments,* New York, John Wiley & Sons.

Jones, Gerald (Ed.) *et al* (1997), *Investment Policy: Anatomy of Alternative Investing,* Part One, Vol. 1, No. 2, Ithaca, International Center for Investment Policy.

Jones, Gerald (Ed.) *et al* (1998), *Investment Policy: Anatomy of Alternative Investing,* Part Two, Vol. 1, No. 3, Ithaca, International Center for Investment Policy.

Kaufman, Michael (2002), *Soros: The Life & Times of a Messianic Billionaire,* New York, Knopf.

Krieger, Andrew, and Edward Claflin (1992), *The Money Bazaar: Inside the Trillion-Dollar World of Currency Trading,* New York, Times Books.

Lake, Ronald A. (Ed.) (2003), *Evaluating & Implementing Hedge Fund Strategies: the Experience of Managers & Investors (Third Edition)*, London, Euromoney Books.

Lang, Peter (1995), *Marketing of Hedge Funds: A Key Strategic Variable in Defining Possible Roles Of An Emerging Investment Force*, Berne, St Gallen University.

Lavinio, Stefano (2002), *The Hedge Fund Handbook: A Definitive Guide for Analyzing & Evaluating Alternative Investments*, New York, McGraw Hill.

Lederman, Jess, and Robert Klein (1996), *Market Neutral*, New York, McGraw Hill.

Lederman, Jess, and Robert Klein (1995), *Hedge Funds: Investment & Portfolio Strategies for the Institutional Investor*, Burr Ridge, Irwin Professional Publication.

Lequeux, Pierre (2001), *Alternative Investments: Managed Currencies*, London, Euromoney Books.

Levy, Leon (2000), *The Mind of Wall Street*, New York, Public Affairs.

Lhabitant, Francois-Serge (2003), *Hedge Funds: Myths and Limits*, New York, John Wiley & Sons.

Lowenstein, Roger (2002), *When Genius Failed: The Rise and Fall of Long-Term Capital Management*, New York, Random House.

Maier, Nicholas W. (2002), *Trading With The Enemy*, New York, HarperBusiness.

Managed Funds Association (2003), *Sound Practices for Hedge Fund Managers*, Washington, DC, Managed Funds Association.

Masetti, Denis, and Simone Borla (2003), *Hedge Funds: A Resource for Investors*, New Jersey, John Wiley & Sons.

McCrary, Stuart (1999), *How to Create and Manage a Hedge Fund: A Professionals Guide*, New Jersey, John Wiley & Sons.

Moore, Keith, M. (1999), *Risk Arbitrage: An Investor's Guide*, New York, John Wiley & Sons.

Nicholas, Joseph G. (2000), *Market-Neutral Investing – Long/Short Hedge Fund Strategies*, Princeton, Bloomberg Press.

Nicholas, Joseph G. (2000), *Hedge Fund of Funds Investing: New Strategies for the Hedge Fund Marketplace*, Princeton, Bloomberg Press.

Nicholas, Joseph G. (2000), *Investing in Hedge Funds*, New Jersey, Bloomberg Press.

Nicholas, Joseph G. (2001), *Market Neutral Investing: The Essential Strategies*, New Jersey, Bloomberg Press.

Niederhoffer, Victor (1997), *The Education of a Speculator*, New York, John Wiley & Sons.

Owen, James P. (2001), *Prudent Investor's Guide to Hedge Funds: Profiting from Uncertainty & Volatility*, New York, John Wiley & Sons.

Parker, Virginia Reynolds (2000), *Managing Hedge Fund Risk*, London, Risk Books.

19

Peltz, Lois (2001), *The New Investment Superstars: 13 Great Investors and Their Strategies for Superior Returns,* New York, John Wiley & Sons.

Peters, Carl C., and Ben Warwick (1997), *The Handbook of Managed Futures & Hedge Funds: Performance, Evaluation, and Analysis,* Chicago, Irwin Professional Publication.

President's Working Group on Financial Markets (1999), *Hedge Funds, Leverage, and the Lessons of Long-Term Capital Management,* Washington DC.

PricewaterhouseCoopers (2003), *The Regulation and distribution of hedge funds in Europe.*

Schneeweis, Thomas, and Joseph Pescatore (1999), *The Handbook of Alternative Investment Strategies,* New York, Institutional Investor Books Inc.

Schneeweis, Thomas, and George Martin (2000), *The Benefits of Hedge Funds,* New York, Lehman Brothers Publications.

Schneeweis, Thomas, Hossein Kazemi and George Martin (2001), *Understanding Hedge Fund Performance: Research Results and Rules of Thumb for the Institutional Investor,* New York, Lehman Brothers Publications.

Schwager, Jack D. (1996), *Stock Market Wizards: Interviews with America's Top Stock Traders,* New York, Harper Business.

Schwartz, Martin, Dave Morine and Paul Flint (1994), *Pit Bull: Lessons from Wall Street's Champion Trader,* New York, Harper Business.

Slater, Robert (2001), *Soros: The Unauthorized Biography, the Life, Times, & Trading Secrets of the World's Greatest Investor,* Burr Ridge, Irwin Professional Publication.

Soros, George (2000), *Alchemy of Finance,* New York, John Wiley & Sons.

Soros, George (2001), *The Crisis of Global Capitalism,* New York, Public Affairs.

Soros, George, with Byron Wien and Krisztina Koenen (1995), *Soros on Soros – Staying Ahead of the Curve,* New York, John Wiley & Sons.

Staley, Kathryn F. (1997), *The Art of Short Selling,* New York, John Wiley & Sons.

Steinhardt, Michael (1999), *No Bull: My Life in and out of Markets,* New York, John Wiley & Sons.

Strachman, Daniel A. (2003), *Getting Started in Hedge Funds,* New York, John Wiley & Sons.

Swenson, David F. (2000), *Pioneering Portfolio Management – An Unconventional Approach to Institutional Investment,* New York, Free Press.

Temple, Peter (2003), *Hedge Funds: Courtesans of Capitalism,* New York, John Wiley & Sons.

Teweles, Richard J., and Frank J. Jones (Eds.) (1999), *The Futures Game: Who Wins, Who Loses, and Why,* New York, McGraw Hill.

Train, John (1980), *The Money Masters,* New York, Harper & Row.

Train, John (1989), *The New Money Masters,* New York, Harper & Row.

US Congress (1998), *House Committee on Banking & Financial Services, Bank Lending to and Other Transactions with Hedge Funds,* Washington DC, US Government Printing Office.

Warwick, Ben (Ed.) (1997), *The Handbook of Risk*, New Jersey, John Wiley & Sons.

Zlotnikov, Vadim (2003), *The Hedge Fund Industry: Products, Services or Capabilities?* New York, Sanford C. Bernstein & Co.

---

[1]   'Our market judgement has been very uneven, but if you're hedged, you can do it all on stock selection, which is where we're good.' A.W. Jones, quoted in *New Breed on Wall Street*, Martin Meyer, MacMillan, 1969.

[2]   Contrast the above quote with the following attributed to Michael Steinhardt, also taken from Meyer's *New Breed on Wall Street*: 'We emphasize leverage and stock selection, not hedges. You can delude yourself, but the hedging doesn't mean much'. Or the comment made by another manager: 'It's not a difficult intellectual problem for us. We're not wedded to any techniques. When the market changes, we just change along with it'.

[3]   The definition of an investment that is down 90 per cent is one that was down 80 per cent and then got cut in half.

Chapter 2

Market gravity and hedge fund aerodynamics: the prudent approach to hedge fund classification

Ted Caldwell
Lookout Mountain Capital, Inc., Lookout Mountain, Tennessee

Introduction

There is only one definitive attribute that yields a clear and concise definition for hedge funds, something you may never have encountered. This chapter presents the prudent approach to defining and classifying hedge funds, based on their original and unique triumph and the only characteristic that distinguishes hedge funds from other investment pools.

Most attempts to define hedge funds (and you have probably read hundreds) focus on descriptive traits common to many hedge funds, including the following. Hedge funds are lightly regulated, privately placed investments for the very rich or large institutions. They often borrow large sums to take big risks and they pay performance fees to managers that have most of their net worth invested in the fund.

Although these characteristics generally describe what most investors and the financial media consider a hedge fund to be, they are neither unique to, nor definitive for hedge funds. In fact, hedge funds are increasingly becoming available as registered, publicly offered products for multitudes of moderately wealthy individuals. They often borrow nothing, and take remarkably little risk. Sometimes they do not pay performance fees, and sometimes the managers do not have much of their net worth invested in the fund.

In short, none of the traits (individually or collectively) most commonly used to define hedge funds, tell us what a hedge fund really is. Hedge fund definitions using these characteristics are focused primarily on structural traits and continually mislead. So what really distinguishes hedge funds from all other managed investment pools?

The single, definitive characteristic that separates hedge funds from all other managed investment pools was central to the design of Alfred W. Jones' original hedge fund in 1949. Jones combined two conventional investing strategies normally associated with taking increased risk (short selling and leverage) into something counter-intuitive. He created a risk-averse investing system, designed to insulate investment skills from the gravity of the markets. Jones' system altered the relationship between risk and return from that normally required to invest in a given market.

Alfred Jones told his investors: 'The conservative nature of our operation [stems from] how differently we relate ourselves to the risks inherent in the stock market. [Our] unique hedging operation is merely the means for greater profit with equal risk, or equal profit with less risk than in conventional investment programmes.'[1] To fashion a clear and concise definition for hedge funds, all we must do is paraphrase what Alfred Jones told his investors (in the context of how he ran his fund):

> A hedge fund is a diversified, managed investment pool designed to extract returns from a given market, with less risk than is inherently required of traditional investors participating in that same market.

Market gravity: systemic risk and return

In the half-century following the establishment of Jones' original hedge fund, Modern Portfolio Theory[2] (MPT) evolved to provide the blueprint for institutional investing. Among other things, MPT maintains that the dominant risk and return that diversified investors acquire when investing in a market, are the systemic risk and return inherent for that market. To achieve higher returns than the market, you must accept higher risk. To secure lower risk, you must accept lower returns. In addition, MPT accurately quantifies the historical sensitivity for individual securities and whole portfolios to the gravity of the market.

Market risk in a conventional portfolio can be reduced (by going to cash), enhanced (by using leverage), or insured against (by using derivatives). Regardless, the dominant factor in the performance of assets invested in a market remains the systemic gravity of the market. Since the relationship between risk and return in traditional portfolios remains fundamentally anchored to the risk and return of the market, all traditional investing should be recognised as market-based strategies.

Consequently, a huge disconnect separates what Alfred Jones told his investors from MPT's fundamental assertion (that to achieve higher returns than the market, you must accept higher risk; and to secure lower risk, you must accept lower returns). Indeed, Jones articulated the antithesis of this, when he said his system provides the same returns with less risk, or greater returns with the same risk. Despite MPT, Jones' system did just that, and continues to do so!

The only way to reconcile the general truth asserted by MPT, and the reality of what Jones (and others that followed) actually accomplished, is by recognising superior investment skill. Yet, MPT is absolutely correct in declaring that superior investment skill is a rare commodity. A hedge fund manager may or may not possess superior investment skills. This is why the word 'designed' is such an important qualifier in my definition for hedge funds.

Hedge fund aerodynamics: a fundamental change in the risk–return profile

Alfred Jones always maintained significant assets in what he called the 'fully hedged' portion of his portfolio, where long positions were balanced by an equal value of short positions. This systematic approach allowed him to remain fully invested in the market, without being fully exposed to the systemic risk from the gravity of the market. It also shifted the attribution of returns in the fully hedged portion of the portfolio from the gravity of the markets to the investment skills of the manager.

The balance of Jones' portfolio remained exposed to the market, where returns were primarily attributable to the performance of the market. Jones always held a large number of positions in order to diversify, but he varied the net market exposure of his fund depending on his market judgement and that of his portfolio managers. Jones did not run a market-neutral fund, as many believe.

Jones was remarkably advanced in analysing his portfolio exposure and performance attribution, in the era before computers and the academic tools of MPT. He quantified the contributions from market-based returns, which he attributed to market judgement (market timing), and skill-based returns, which he attributed to superior stock-picking in the fully hedged portion of his portfolio. Jones even hired assistants to algebraically calculate the 'velocity' of stocks in relation to the market, to assist him in adjusting the effective valuation of stocks held long or short in the fully hedged portion of his portfolio (this is done today using beta).

Jones was not the first investor to utilise a basket of stocks sold short as a hedge against a general market decline. He was, however, the first to systematically employ this type of value-added hedging[3] at all times in a managed investment pool. He used the structure of a general partnership with performance-based compensation to establish his Fully Committed Fund in 1949 and then changed it to a limited partnership shortly thereafter. The limited partnership provided the original model from which the hedge fund industry has evolved.

So, what was the aerodynamic that allowed Jones to significantly overcome the gravity of markets? Jones fundamentally altered the relationship between risk and return in the fully hedged portion of his portfolio, simply by implementing an arbitrage. The related securities of his arbitrage were a basket of underpriced stocks (held long) and a basket of overpriced stocks (sold short).

Indeed, to extract returns from a given market with less risk than traditional investors have in the same markets, all hedge funds must employ some form of arbitrage for a significant portion of their assets. In addition, a system designed to extract returns from a given market with less risk than traditional investors is the only definitive characteristic that segregates hedge funds from conventional investment pools.

So, while the definition given above is sufficient and concise for general use, I expand on it a little for the classification system at the end of this chapter:

A hedge fund is a diversified, managed investment pool designed to extract returns from a given market, with less risk than is inherently required of traditional investors participating in that same market, by systematically employing an arbitrage strategy (or strategies) to considerably insulate investment skills from the gravity of markets.

The rationale for perpetual confusion: true versus nominal hedge funds

Clearly, my definition for hedge funds excludes a large number of funds that call themselves hedge funds, and that are regularly called hedge funds by the financial media. There is a reasonable explanation why this misleading custom came into common use, however, it does not suffice as a reasonable excuse for failing to prudently classify hedge funds.

So, how did it become common practice to define hedge funds using mostly structural characteristics (discussed at the beginning of this chapter), while neglecting the unique, fundamental shift in the risk–return profile achieved by true hedge funds?

Jones' system for fundamentally altering the relationship between risk and return for a portion of assets invested in a given market is conceptually simple, yet it is notoriously difficult for many to grasp. It is a concept that (until the millennium bubble burst) almost total-ly eluded the financial commentary on funds structured similarly to Jones', which have been called hedge funds since the late 1960s. The continuing failure of the media to recognise what really distinguishes true hedge funds perpetuates confusion among the investing public.

Had Alfred Jones been running a fully hedged portfolio in 1966, when *Fortune* magazine unveiled his 17-year-old operation, the financial media may have acquired and held a focus on the skill-based contribution of his hedged returns. However, in fact, Jones never ran a fully hedged portfolio. Although he always maintained a significant portion of assets within the hedged portion of his portfolio, the net market exposure of his fund varied considerably over the years, depending on the market judgement of his management team.

A single article in the spring of 1966, 'The Jones Nobody Keeps Up With'[4] by Carol Loomis, triggered the first great stampede into hedge funds. This article revealed the enormous success of Jones' fund, which had handily outperformed the best mutual funds over the prior five- and 10-year periods, after deducting an inconceivable 20 per cent profit reallocation to the fund manager.

Loomis's article also provided a virtual blueprint for how to set up and run a Jones-like fund. Although his concept of hedging was discussed, readers evidently focused more on the performance, the structure and the enormous incentive fees of Jones' operation. Aspiring hedge fund managers quickly calculated the impact of 20 per cent performance fees on their incomes, particularly when they could use leverage, and the rush to set up new funds was under way. The best information indicates several hundred hedge funds were established during the next three years, but Jones' notion of maintaining a conservative investing system within a sig-nificant portion of the portfolio was clearly lost on most of the imitation funds. Many funds appear to have been set up primarily to invest with leverage in a rising market, and to keep 20 per cent of the profits. Many failed after the market turned down in December 1968.

Funds structurally similar to Alfred Jones' have been called hedge funds ever since, with complete indifference to whether or not they significantly employ strategy to isolate invest-ing skills from the gravity of the markets. In addition, there is an uncomplicated rationale for the financial media's failure to grasp the unique and extraordinary value of true hedge funds in the years since.

The media converge on exceptions, rather than the norm, because that is what their audience wants. Funds that utilise leverage with little or no hedging have quite predictably provided the most spectacular returns, and also the most spectacular failures, so these are the funds that predictably garner the most attention. Meanwhile, the generally more attractive (but less sensational) long-term performance of true hedge funds continues to be largely ignored. Indeed, during the millennium bear market, some excellent hedge funds were actually panned in the media for preserving capital rather than producing spectacular gains.

Furthermore, many in the hedge fund industry are loath to have investors focus on what sets true hedge funds apart because the perpetuation of vague and confusing definitions serves the industry well. The value of hedge fund intermediaries is perceived to be greater when investors are less well informed. The 'friction' (ie, fees raked off at different levels) for hedge funds is enormous, making them a most attractive profit centre for multiple branches of major brokerage firms, and other intermediaries. The best information for investors rarely takes pri-ority over the best interests of the street.

Nominal hedge funds are not excited about being recognised as having market-based strategies because it might reasonably raise questions about outperforming appropriate benchmarks before performance fees are earned. Yet, even many true hedge funds are reluctant to have investors focus on the distinction between skill-based and market-based attribution because much of their performance (and performance fees) comes from the gravity of the markets, not skill. However, these are third-generation fee issues for another piece of writing. Enough heresy for now!

It is not my goal to reverse conventional use of the hedge fund moniker, but rather to provide investors with the appropriate template for distinguishing between true and nominal hedge funds. By recognising the distinction, investors will better understand the benefits and shortcomings of both true and nominal hedge funds, and their respective sub-classes.

True versus nominal: reduced risk for returns versus non-correlating returns

To construct a truly useful blueprint for classifying hedge funds, the 'Unified hedge fund classification system' (see the Appendix to this chapter) begins by drawing a proverbial line in the sand. On one side of the line, true hedge funds are divided into three logical peer groups. On the other side of the line, nominal hedge funds are divided into logical peer groups.

It should not be inferred that the distinction between true and nominal hedge funds imparts a value judgement that discounts the benefits of nominal hedge funds. The line is drawn to make the crucial distinction between two fundamentally different investing systems. Investors will find compelling investment opportunities on both sides of the line. Likewise, they will find unworthy opportunities on both sides of the line.

The two essential concepts for correctly distinguishing between true and nominal hedge funds are: skill-based investment strategies versus market-based investment strategies, and value-added hedging versus insurance hedging.

The distinguishing feature between skill-based and market-based investing systems is the source of expected returns, assuming the random selection of securities. Thus, the expected return for a market-based strategy is equal to the performance of the appropriate market benchmark for the portfolio.

While investment skill provides incremental performance for a market-based strategy, it provides essentially all of the performance for a skill-based strategy (that is, a fully hedged portfolio, or the hedged portion of a partially hedged portfolio). In addition, since random selection provides no skill factor, the expected return for a skill-based strategy (or the hedged portion of a partially hedged portfolio) is equal to zero. Any performance is a value-added performance, attributable to skill.

A major benefit of many nominal hedge funds is that they provide investors with low or non-correlating returns for their portfolio mix, but non-correlating returns from nominal hedge funds are still market-based returns. The skill-based returns of true hedge funds are also non-correlating. However, they fundamentally alter the risk–return profile for participation in a given market.

The advent of hedging with derivatives requires further clarification. There must be a distinction between insurance hedging (which is market-based) and value-added hedging (which is skill-based).

Buying insurance simply amounts to paying someone else to assume all or part of a risk that you do not want. To insure against a market decline that could decimate your stock portfolio, you can buy a put option on the stock index that most closely resembles your portfolio, or you can buy a customised put to replicate your portfolio. Different strategies utilising listed or unlisted derivatives (at a cost, and assuming the viability of counterparties) offer the holder of virtually any securities portfolio the opportunity to insure against a decline in the value of those securities, while keeping the benefits of an increase in their value. Buying portfolio insurance, like buying insurance on your home, is neither a skill-based nor a profitable venture. You are purchasing protection, and will collect only in the event of a loss, and only for the amount of the loss you insured against (the purchase of excess insurance for your home or your portfolio is not hedging; it is speculating).

Insurance hedging is the mitigation of market risk with expensive, market-based strategies, that only pay off in the event of a loss in the value of securities held. Value-added hedging is the mitigation of market risk with skill-based strategies that approximately neutralise the gravity of the market while pursuing profits within the hedge.

All value-added hedge strategies are forms of arbitrage that seek to profit from disparities in the value of related securities, usually baskets of related securities, regardless of the direction of the market. Value-added hedge strategies are true hedge strategies that approximately neutralise the directional force the market imposes on a given asset class. Again, with the market's gravity effectively neutralised, the dominant factor in the performance of value-added hedge strategies is skill. Thus, true hedge strategies are skill-based strategies.

Over the past half century, most funds that have utilised skill-based investing systems (including Jones' fund) have done so for only a portion of their assets. To draw the proverbial line in the sand, we must decide how large a portion of assets invested in skill-based strategies qualifies as a 'significant portion' to meet the definition of true hedge funds. Somewhat arbitrarily, but with considerable insight into the historical use of the system, this author chose 25 per cent of invested assets (not capital) as the minimum that must be invested in skill-based strategies, at all times, to qualify a fund as a true hedge fund. This is a very low requirement, but enough to alter the risk–return characteristics.

Recognising the definitive characteristic that set Alfred Jones' original hedge fund apart from traditional investment programmes is absolutely essential in understanding hedge funds. Prudence dictates that it is the basis for properly classifying hedge funds.

The 'Unified hedge fund classification system' (see the Appendix to this chapter) is an imperfect peer grouping scheme for an imperfect world. Initially published in 1996, it remains the only classification system to distinguish between true and nominal hedge funds. This classification system is a work in progress, and the update outlined in the following pages (version 1.6) will surely raise questions not yet sufficiently addressed. Your comments and criticism are welcomed, and may well spawn improvements to future versions.

Appendix

Unified hedge fund classification system, version 1.6[5]

Traditional investments

Traditional investing is characterised by the purchase, holding or sale – but not short sale – of primarily stocks, bonds and cash. The dominant variable in the performance of traditional investment management is the performance of the market. Except in rare cases, investment skills of the portfolio manager are relegated to the pursuit of incremental performance, relative to the appropriate market benchmark. Trust companies, insurance companies, mutual funds, pension funds and investment advisory accounts are the primary structures for holding traditional investment portfolios. The primary attribute for classifying traditional investments is asset class.

Non-traditional (alternative) investments

Alternative investments include all non-traditional forms of securities investing. Some major categories are: private equity and venture capital funds, real estate partnerships, oil and gas partnerships, commodities trading pools, true hedge funds and nominal hedge funds. The primary attributes for classifying non-traditional investments vary significantly.

True and nominal hedge funds share no definitive trait, and indeed they have fundamentally different risk–return characteristics. Though they often share structural and other characteristics customarily perceived (and frequently represented in the financial media) to be definitive for all hedge funds, these characteristics are only descriptive.

The primary attribute for classifying true hedge funds is strategy, whereas the primary attribute for classifying nominal hedge funds is structure.

True hedge funds

True hedge funds are diversified, managed investment pools designed to extract returns from given markets, with less risk than is inherently required of traditional investors participating in those same markets. They do this by systematically employing an arbitrage strategy (or strategies) with a significant portion of assets (at least 25 per cent of invested assets – not capital) to considerably insulate investment skills from the gravity of markets.

True hedge funds fundamentally alter the relationship between risk and return compared to traditional portfolios invested in the same markets. Like nominal hedge funds, true hedge funds are usually offered by private placement, they usually have performance-based fees for their managers, who usually have a significant personal stake in the fund – but none of these widespread characteristics are defining characteristics for true hedge funds.

There are only three major categories of true hedge funds: (a) Jones model funds, (b) relative value funds and (c) macro hedge funds.

(a) Jones model funds
Jones model funds are true hedge funds that invest almost exclusively in equity markets. They maintain no less than 25 per cent of invested assets within a value-added hedge structure at all times.

This original hedge fund model seeks to profit from the arbitrage between a basket of long equities and an equal value basket of short equities, maintained within the hedge at all times, but not necessarily with all assets. Any assets not within the hedge comprise 'net market exposure', which is expressed as a percent of capital.

Net market exposure (%) = (Longs − Shorts)/Capital

Throughout the 1990s, a growing number of managers set up 'equity hedge funds' that did little or no hedging. Thus, in 1995, I coined the name 'Jones model fund'[6] (with aggressive and conservative sub-classes) to distinguish equity funds that systematically and significantly hedge at all times from those that do not.

Conservative Jones model funds
Conservative Jones model funds mitigate market risk at all times by maintaining net market exposure from 0–100 per cent of capital inclusively, thus keeping any leverage within the hedge. This sub-class allows tremendous manager flexibility, and includes numerous sub-classes characterised by the use of different equity markets, sectors, regions, styles and exposure ranges.

- *Market neutral (or 'equal long-short') equity funds* constitute a subset of conservative Jones model funds that are 'fully hedged' (ie, they hold equal dollar long and short positions; some funds also balance by beta, sector and other variables). They normally have net market exposure of zero or stay within a narrow range around zero exposure.

Aggressive Jones model funds
Aggressive Jones model funds may occasionally or regularly amplify market risk by exceeding net market exposure of 100 per cent, thus using leverage outside of the hedged structure, or by going 'net short' with negative net market exposure. Nonetheless, they maintain a minimum of 25 per cent of invested assets within a value-added hedge structure at all times.

Alfred Jones' original hedge fund would have been classified in this peer group.

General equity sub-classes
Whereas some of the following groups are primary classes for traditional investment classification, they are secondary or lower classes under this system. These are useful sub-classes for Jones model funds, as well as for nominal equity hedge funds. The sub-classes listed here are neither comprehensive nor mutually exclusive, and order is a matter of preference.

- *Investment style sub-classes.* Growth, value, mixed, trading-oriented, etc.
- *Market capitalisation sub-classes.* Large cap, mid cap, small cap, and micro cap.
- *Geographic sub-classes.* Country-specific, global, international, regional or emerging markets sub-classes.
- *Industry sector sub-classes.* Healthcare, energy, telecommunications, technology, etc.

(b) Relative value funds
Relative value funds seek to profit from the arbitrage between closely related securities. Most articulate a goal of market neutrality or very low market correlation, but not all seek to fully hedge the portfolio. Strategies range from the arbitrage between highly diversified baskets of

related securities, to highly concentrated arbitrage bets on the spread between two related securities. Market risk is generally minimised, but other forms of risk (notably, model risk) can be substantial. The number of sub-classes utilising arbitrage strategies is virtually unlimited.

Capital structure arbitrage funds
- *Convertible arbitrage funds* go long convertible securities and short the underlying common stock.
- *Other capital structure arbitrage funds.*

Fixed-income arbitrage funds
Fixed-income arbitrage funds exploit price differentials between related fixed-income securities and/or derivatives.

- *Mortgage arbitrage funds* are primarily long mortgage-backed securities while hedging interest rate, volatility and prepayment risk.
- *Other fixed-income arbitrage (non-mortgage) funds.*

Merger arbitrage funds (risk arb)
Merger arbitrage funds specialise in the simultaneous purchase of stock in a company being acquired and the short sale of the acquiring company, thus making a directional bet that the deal will go through. They sometimes reverse this strategy.

Multiple strategy arbitrage funds
A substantial number of funds utilise multiple relative value strategies, which may include a combination of the above and/or a variety of index or other derivative arbitrage strategies.

(c) Macro hedge funds
Macro hedge funds seek to capitalise on changes in the relative values of securities, interest rates and/or currencies affected by regional or global economic change. They tend to be aggressive asset allocators, the use of leverage and derivatives tends to be substantial, and the method and degree of hedging may be highly concentrated or vary significantly.

Historically, macro hedge funds looked essentially like diversified funds of funds, with multiple sub-managers, and typically derived a significant portion of their returns from Jones model allocations within.

Due to the extreme concentration utilised in some forms of macro arbitrage (for instance, going short one currency against another), macro funds that do not clearly utilise a significant level of other value-added hedge strategies should arguably be classified as 'broad mandate nominal hedge funds'.

Nominal hedge funds

Nominal hedge funds fit the customary, structural description for hedge funds, but fail to employ a significant level of value-added hedging at all times. They are privately placed investments with performance-based fees for managers who often hold a significant personal stake in the fund.

Nominal hedge funds utilise market-based strategies, thus the dominant variable in their expected performance is the performance of the appropriate market benchmark. However, nominal hedge funds often make attractive allocations, by contributing returns with little or no correlation to the portfolio mix.

Short funds

Short funds seek to profit from the short sale of securities, primarily the stock of overvalued, fundamentally flawed or fraudulent companies.

- *Short-only funds* focus exclusively on the short sale of securities.
- *Short-biased funds* seek to profit primarily from the short sale of securities, but may buy securities as a hedge.

Special situations funds

- *Distressed securities funds* buy, and may occasionally short, the securities of companies under bankruptcy and/or reorganisation.
- *Opportunistic fixed-income funds* purchase debt securities that are undervalued due to mitigating circumstances.
- *Activist investing funds seek* to directly impact the value of securities held by influencing other securities holders, or by becoming activist shareholders.

Emerging markets funds

Emerging markets funds encompass a broad and growing classification with debt, equity and mixed sub-classes for investing, primarily long, in the securities of developing countries.

Nominal equity hedge funds

Nominal equity hedge funds are structured as traditional hedge funds, and they may use index options or some short selling, but they do not maintain a Jones model hedged structure.

- *Unleveraged equity funds*.
- *Leveraged equity funds*.

Broad mandate nominal hedge funds

Broad mandate funds are macro or mixed strategy funds that do not employ significant value-added hedging at all times.

Other alternative investments

- Private equity and venture capital funds.
- Real estate securities.
- Oil and gas partnerships, etc.
- Commodities trading pools.

---

[1] Taken from a report from Jones to the investors in his 'Fully Committed Fund,' 1961.

[2] Inclusive of the Capital Asset Pricing Model (CAPM).

[3] As opposed to insurance hedging, addressed in commentary that follows.

[4] Carol Loomis, 'The Jones Nobody Keeps Up With', *Fortune*, April 1966, 237–247.

[5] 'Unified Hedge Fund Classification', *Lookout Mountain Hedge Fund Review*, 3rd Quarter 1996, © Lookout Mountain Capital, Inc. Version 1.6 is the May 2003 revision. Subsequent updates to this classification may be obtained from www.Jonesmodel.info. Comments or suggestions should be sent to lkt_mtn@bellsouth.net or faxed to Lookout Mountain Capital, Inc. at (423) 821–9485.

[6] 'Jones Model Funds': LMC's Recommended Classification Name', *Lookout Mountain Hedge Fund Review*, 4th Quarter 1995, © Lookout Mountain Capital, Inc.

Chapter 3

Sources of systematic return in hedge funds

Lars Jaeger
Partners Group, Baar-Zug, Switzerland

Scott Higbee
Partners Group, New York, New York

Introduction

This chapter presents a discussion of the various sources of return in hedge funds. Hedge funds typically have two different return sources. The primary sources of return for hedge fund strategies are various risk premiums earned for exposing the investor to a variety of different systematic financial risks. The other primary return source is based on inefficiencies and price anomalies in public financial markets and the manager's skill to exploit them. However, the latter return source is not always easily distinguished from the former. Identifying risk premiums, exploiting market inefficiencies and understanding the underlying risk factors are critical components of building an optimal hedge fund investment portfolio.

Hedge funds have recently enjoyed a dramatic surge in attention. Investors now stretch beyond a select group of high net worth individuals that have traditionally made up a large majority of the asset class. Assets in hedge funds have increased by a factor of 10 in the last decade. The widespread view among asset managers is that hedge funds generate investment returns that are significantly more attractive than average equity and bond investments on a risk–return basis.[1]

Despite their recent momentum, hedge funds must address growing investor concerns about a persistent lack of transparency and diverse, partly unknown risks to continue the rapid pace of asset growth within the industry. Investors are becoming more familiar with and have started to ask more detailed questions about hedge fund return sources before making investment decisions. However, numerous investors remain sceptical of hedge funds and continue to view such investment vehicles as too mysterious and secretive. Related to this perception is the widely held belief that hedge funds generate returns solely through the identification of market inefficiencies not recognised by other market participants, which is incorrect. Another related misperception is that hedge funds constitute (similar to a betting or gambling strategy) a zero sum game (or even a negative sum game after accounting for fees and transaction costs).

In contrast, our view is that hedge funds primarily generate returns by assuming specific risks and earn risk premiums that can be readily analysed and understood by investors. In fact, risk premiums are equally the source of returns for most traditional investments (for example, the well-known equity risk premium). Conceptually hedge funds are nothing new, with the important difference being the underlying risk premiums are more diverse than those in traditional asset classes.[2]

Most hedge fund strategies operate in capital markets that exhibit a high degree of efficiency and liquidity such as global equities, foreign exchange, fixed-income and commodity markets. In line with theories in modern finance, most professionals do not believe that these markets consistently offer a free lunch (even to hedge fund managers). This creates some confusion and scepticism among investors. A significant part of this confusion arises from the inability of conventional risk measures and asset pricing theories to properly measure the diverse risk factors and return sources of hedge funds. A deeper understanding of hedge funds reveals that return sources are much more than pricing inefficiencies in public financial markets. The reality of hedge funds is that most strategies systematically earn risk premiums in exchange for assuming certain systematic risks. This chapter will illustrate some of these inherent return sources of hedge funds and will also discuss implications for the hedge fund portfolio (fund of funds) manager. Further, the discussion will remain qualitative rather than quantitative, but extensive references to the current academic literature on hedge fund return modelling are provided.[3] The chapter will also illustrate that the image of secrecy and mystique that still surrounds hedge funds is largely unjustified.

Hedge fund return sources
Risk premiums and manager skill

The discussion begins by distinguishing the following two principal sources of hedge fund returns (besides pure luck): economic risk premiums and manager skill. The consistently high, risk-adjusted returns of hedge funds suggest that financial markets are not completely efficient, and inefficiencies and price anomalies can be exploited through specific skills or competitive advantages of talented money managers. In asset pricing theory language, the corresponding return is referred to as alpha.[4] At the same time, hedge fund managers expose themselves to systematic risks and earn corresponding risk premiums,[5] which are the result of imperfect risk sharing in capital markets.[6] Asset pricing theory links these returns to beta.[7] Investors often lack an understanding of the fundamental difference between managers providing returns through an informational advantage or applying a certain investment skill to exploit market inefficiencies (alpha generation) and a manager generating returns by assuming systematic risks and earning corresponding risk premiums (beta generation). However, as described below, in practise the distinction is not always absolutely clear.

Beta risk premiums provide an inherent positive expected return over time, the source of which does not disappear if recognised by other investors (although beta risk premiums can fluctuate in size over time and can temporarily even become negative). As discussed in more detail below, the nature of risk premiums is directly related to the different economic functions of investors in financial markets. For hedge funds, these functions vary widely across their strategy universe.

Many investors believe that investing in hedge funds revolves around the search for alpha. However, the authors believe that the search for alpha must begin by understanding beta (ie, the assessment of systematic risk factors). Perceived price anomalies and apparent arbitrage opportunities are often related to risks and corresponding risk premiums.[8]

The two sources of hedge fund returns (risk premiums and market inefficiencies) are by no means mutually exclusive. However, despite certain overlaps and ambiguities in separating the two return sources, distinguishing what the authors refer to as risk premium strategies from pure skill strategies provides a proper framework for an analysis of how hedge funds generate returns.

The statement that risk premiums are a dominant source of hedge fund returns does not imply that manager skill is not essential or even meaningless. Manager skill and the direct exploitation of market inefficiencies are an important return source for hedge funds. The necessary competitive advantages (edges) of hedge fund managers can be categorised into informational edges and statistical edges. Informational edges are superior or faster access to or faster processing of price-relevant information, superior research capabilities, better knowledge about the behaviour patterns of investors, superior detection of mispriced securities or correctly timing the market. Statistical edges are based on recognising certain market conditions like price trends, seasonal price developments or conditional correlation features. It must be emphasised that statistical and informational edges often require a large amount of research and can disappear over time, for example, when other market participants copy and adopt a proven strategy. Further, even for strategies that rely mostly on risk premiums, manager skill is critical and expresses itself through premium identification, proper timing and execution and appropriate risk management by the hedge fund manager.

Modern asset pricing models and the battle surrounding alpha generation

Conventional finance theory states that consistent alpha generation is not possible in efficient markets. That theory is the well-known efficient market hypothesis (EMH).[9] In its strongest form, the EMH states that there is no price-relevant information available to any investor that is not yet reflected in market prices. However, most investment and academic professionals do not hold the EMH in its strong form to be true. The weak and semi-strong form variations of the EMH, however, have more numerous supporters (these two variations of the EMH exclude certain types of information from the information set that determine asset prices). The market efficiency debate between proponents of conventional finance theory and their counterparts (for example, advocates of behavioural finance theories) is waged over the interpretation of price and return anomalies.

To better analyse return sources of hedge funds and interpret them in the battle of alpha versus beta, it is important to be familiar with some of the basic assumptions of common asset pricing models, such as the Capital Asset Pricing Model (CAPM).[10]

1. *Normal return distribution.* Evaluation of risk and return can occur in a mean-variance framework.
2. *A single source of systematic risk.* There is only one priced risk for which investors are rewarded, which is the broad market risk.
3. *Frictionless trading.* There are no transaction costs, taxes, etc, and investors can sell short securities without any restrictions.
4. *Homogeneity of investor behaviour.* Investors act on identical and constant investment time horizons as well as on homogeneous expectations about returns, volatilities and correlations.

Normal return distribution

The assumption of normality becomes questionable when the probability distribution of investment outcomes is skewed (non-symmetric) or leptokurtic (possesses fat tails). Numerous hedge fund strategies have non-symmetric (negatively skewed) return distributions. It is furthermore commonly agreed that the return distribution of most financial instruments is leptokurtic. As an example, Exhibit 3.1 shows the first four moments[11] of different event-driven and relative value strategies.

It should be clear from Exhibit 3.1 that the conventional measure of risk, namely standard deviation, provides an insufficient basis for risk measurement for assets with significant higher moments. Investors usually have a preference for positively skewed outcomes and an aversion against negatively skewed and fat-tailed outcomes. This is not captured by a risk measure like the standard deviation that weighs each part of the distribution identically and does not sufficiently consider the probability of extreme events.

A good example of fat-tail risk combined with negative skews is the short option exposure of certain hedge fund strategies. Short option exposure refers to the risk–reward characteristics similar to those in selling naked options. The investor receives a fixed premium for being exposed to the possibility of large losses in unexpected stress events (the option ends up deep in the money). This profile helps to create impressive Sharpe ratios, and quantitative mean-variance based portfolio optimisations tend to recommend inappropriately large allocations to these strategies.[12] However, quoted risk-adjusted returns are clearly overestimated, as risk is only measured with historical standard deviations that do not consider the higher probability of extreme losses. Often the risk inherent in these strategies has usually not yet manifested itself during the manager's relatively brief performance history (a well-known example for a short option strategy was LTCM).

Standard mean-variance optimisation is not unambiguously appropriate when hedge funds are part of the investment portfolio.[13] One could go as far as arguing that the higher

Exhibit 3.1

Hedge fund returns and higher moments of their distributions

	Return (%)	Volatility (%)	Maximum drawdown (%)	Sharpe ratio	Skew (m)	Kurtosis (m)
Event Driven						
HFR	14.19	6.90	−10.78	1.33	−1.48	5.26
Tremont	10.48	6.43	−16.04	0.85	−3.54	24.33
Relative Value						
Convertible Arbitrage (HFR)	11.69	3.38	−4.84	1.96	−1.37	3.31
Convertible Arbitrage (Tremont)	10.23	4.88	−12.04	1.07	−1.22	4.39
Fixed Income Arbitrary (HFR)	8.58	4.64	−14.42	0.77	−1.82	9.68
Fixed Income Arbitrage (Tremont)	7.32	4.70	−12.47	0.49	−1.13	14.35

Note: The first four moments (mean return, standard deviation, skew, excess kurtosis) of the return distribution of event-driven, convertible arbitrage and fixed-income arbitrage strategy sector indices of Tremont and HFR. Additionally, the maximal drawdown and the Sharpe ratio (calculated with 5 per cent risk-free interest rate) are shown. Data is taken from January 1990 to December 2002 for the HFR data and January 1994 to December 2002 for the Tremont data.

Source: Authors' calculations.

risk-adjusted returns for hedge funds (when measured by mean and variance) are partly compensation (risk premium) for higher tail risk, that is, leptokurtosis, and the relatively higher probability of very low returns than very high returns, that is, negative skew.

A single source of systematic risk

This assumption is plainly false if applied to hedge funds, as hedge funds are subject to numerous other risks beyond broad market risk. There are various systematic risks beyond the broad equity market risk, such as low liquidity, credit risk and sector risk. In general, any non-diversifiable risk will carry a risk premium, that is, an expected return. Realising that single-factor models are insufficient to describe many financial instruments, researchers have developed numerous extensions of the one-factor CAPM model by including additional factors such as firm size or value factors (such as price-earnings ratio and price-book value) or macroeconomic factors (such as unexpected inflation or credit spreads) into their analysis. The Arbitrage Pricing Theory (APT) is the most frequently mentioned model of such and provides a more general (multi-factor) framework for explaining investment returns.[14]

Frictionless trading

This assumption is at best only partly true. Transaction costs are a factor of consideration for any investor. Furthermore, many investors are in reality constrained in selling short securities or investing in derivative instruments.

Homogeneity of investor behaviour

To add to the complication, hedge fund strategies are not buy and hold strategies. Managers change positions often, can make use of leverage and short selling and also invest in derivative instruments (all of which results in non-linear return profiles). This further invalidates the assumption of standard asset pricing models and their applicability to hedge fund returns.

The misperception that most hedge fund returns are solely the result of alpha generation can be linked to the inability of conventional finance theory to capture the diverse risks of hedge funds. Conventional finance theory, as described by the CAPM, teaches that expected investment returns are directly proportional to the amount of risk of the global market portfolio[15] (the proportionality factor is expressed by the beta of the investment). Any persistent excess return above and beyond the return for taking market risk is interpreted as being the result of particular manager skills, that is, as the manager's alpha. However, this interpretation of returns is severely flawed, as excess returns are often related to systematic risk factors, which are not considered in the model. Exposure to other systematic risk factors yields additional expected return unconditional to possessing superior information, short-lived market inefficiencies or the direction of equity markets.

Asset class factor models

Ideally, financial economists determine the set of risk factors for the factor models that can satisfactorily model hedge fund returns. For traditional investments, much work has been dedicated to examining the components of equity and bond returns, and numerous studies have successfully assessed the sources of return of traditional investments. In 1992 Sharpe introduced his seminal asset class factor model for the determination of return factors for mutual funds.[16]

The analogous detection of the specific performance drivers for hedge fund strategies with factor models has been the subject of debate in the academic and the financial communities in recent years. Based on Sharpe's work, Fung and Hsieh developed in 1997 one of the first asset class factor models for hedge funds to analogously determine systematic return factors.[17] In their work, Fung and Hsieh argue that hedge fund strategies are highly dynamic and create option-like (non-linear) return profiles, which cannot be modelled in simple asset class factor models (in their later research they explicitly incorporate option-type assets).[18] The recent literature offers an increasing number of studies around this question.[19]

Many of these studies indicate that particular sets of factors help to explain the performance patterns of the different strategy sectors with some explanatory power (which is, however, significantly lower than most traditional investments). However, the choice of the appropriate factors is not straightforward for most strategies. Most hedge fund professionals agree that beyond pure quantitative modelling, qualitative reasoning must supplement the analysis.[20]

Economic functions in capital markets

Further insight into risk premiums can be obtained by assessing the diverse economic functions of investor activity in financial markets. In fact, risk premiums and economic functions are strongly interlinked. The following provides a qualitative discussion of the relationship between hedge fund risk premiums and the various economic functions of hedge funds.[21] The most commonly known economic functions of hedge funds operating in the global capital markets are the following:

1. *Capital formation/efficient allocation of capital.* Providing companies access to capital.
2. *Risk transfer in financial markets.* Providing commercial hedgers with the possibility of transferring unwanted price risk for their business.
3. *Price transparency, liquidity and market efficiency.* Making markets more efficient and liquid; making a market for less liquid investments.
4. *Market completeness (granting option like exposures).* Creating a wide range of return profiles for investors (mostly through derivatives).

Capital formation/efficient allocation of capital

Equity risk premiums are compensation for the capital formation function that investors fulfil through buying company shares (and bonds), thereby providing the company access to additional working capital. Investors bear the risk of financial loss due to, for example, an economic downturn, less favourable earnings developments or bankruptcy. More generally, this function describes the efficient allocation of capital and includes the short selling of stocks of companies with deteriorating earnings outlooks. Two equity-related risk premiums are the 'small firm' premium which corresponds to the risks of investing in companies with lower market capitalisation (for example, key people management dependency, bankruptcy risk and lack of business diversification),[22] and the well-known premium on value stocks (low book to market ratios).

An often overlooked economic function of hedge funds is the introduction of new possibilities for companies to raise capital. Without hedge funds, many companies would face difficulties raising capital or would encounter significantly higher costs of capital. Two examples illustrate this.

- The emergence of convertible securities in recent years has given firms an additional option for raising capital and has thereby reduced the cost of capital for many firms. The support of hedge funds has been crucial to the expansion of the convertible securities market, and it is estimated that 70 per cent of new convertible issues are purchased by hedge funds.
- Hedge funds that specialise in distressed securities make a significant contribution towards reintegrating troubled companies back into the economic cycle and reducing the financial cost of failure.

Risk transfer in financial markets

Many futures strategies, especially trend-following strategies, fulfil an economic function that is very different from that of equity investors. Investors (speculators) in futures are willing to assume the natural price risks of commercial hedgers, thereby providing those hedgers with the possibility of transferring their undesired price risks and enjoying a higher degree of price stability. By fulfilling this function of risk transfer speculators in futures markets earn a corresponding premium, which could alternatively be called 'commodity hedging demand premium'.[23] A risk premium that is earned by some FX strategies is the positive interest rate carry between two currencies. The manager buys a currency with a high yield, and finances this with a low-yielding currency. This position carries the risk of unexpected currency movements.

Price transparency, liquidity and market efficiency

Investors who are willing to accept lower liquidity earn a liquidity premium. Such liquidity risk often goes together with credit risk, counterparty risk and mark-to-market risk (the latter is the risk of not receiving reliable prices to value the instruments). Credit and term structure risk premiums are connected to investing in fixed-income instruments with lower credit quality and longer maturity. In particular, fixed-income arbitrage strategies often expose themselves to a combination of liquidity, credit and duration risks, for example, through 'credit barbell' strategies (long short-term debt of lower credit quality and short long-term government bonds), TED spread trades (short Treasury bills versus long Eurodollar contracts), or off-the-run versus on-the-run (recently issued) Treasury bond positions.

Relative value strategies (often referred to as arbitrage strategies) provide capital markets with efficiency and price transparency. Their aim is to detect pricing inefficiencies through the application of proprietary valuation models to complex financial instruments (price anomalies have become extremely rare for instruments with simple structures). The manager provides the market with valuable price information based on his own (mostly highly sophisticated) modelling efforts. However, this is not a risk-free undertaking, as it is not guaranteed that the particular models are appropriate for the valuation and hedging process. It can be argued that part of the generated returns correspond to a complexity premium (or alternatively, an efficiency premium) related to the risk of mis-modelling the complexity of the underlying financial instrument and therefore trading the instrument at sub-optimal prices. Model risk can often lead to severe losses. As indicated above, for many relative value strategies the lower risk indicated by their standard deviation comes with significantly higher leptokurtosis and a negative skew – that is, the risk of extreme losses is higher than described by the normal distribution. As mentioned above, these strategies often earn what the authors call a 'higher moment risk premium'.

A general note on market efficiency and hedge funds: most 'hedge' funds base their decision-making process on fundamental analysis and superior information. This actually increases market efficiency. Hedge funds often act to counter price changes not based on fundamentals. Further, hedge fund managers are often the first to act when fundamentals change, and therefore support the fair valuation of securities. This trading reduces the likelihood of less informed investors purchasing securities at overvalued prices and selling them at undervalued prices.[24] Perhaps the accounting problems of numerous global firms in 2002–03 would have been discovered sooner if more market participants had focused not only on picking winners, but also on identifying losers (for example, Enron and WorldCom).

Market completeness: taking option-like exposures
Hedge fund returns have exposure to broad-based market indices and well-known risk factors such as equity markets, interest rate term structures and credit risk. However, as the trading styles are dynamic there is often an additional component to consider. A dynamic trading style will add an option-like element to returns. A distinction can be made with respect to the influence of market volatility on returns between strategies that are effectively short volatility, that is, they tend to show negative returns when general market volatility increases unexpectedly as in periods of global market crisis (for example, merger arbitrage, fixed-income arbitrage, FX carry or short options strategies), and strategies with long volatility exposure (for example, convertible arbitrage and managed futures). Long volatility strategies usually benefit from periods of market turmoil and unexpectedly and strongly increasing volatility in global financial markets (such as August 1998, September 2001 and June/July 2002).

Risk premiums for the individual strategies

Risk premiums as inherent sources of hedge fund returns are most apparent for several relative value strategies (fixed-income arbitrage, risk arbitrage, convertible arbitrage and equity market neutral). These arbitrage strategies[25] capitalise on pricing spreads between two or more related financial instruments. These spreads compensate investors for particular risks such as sector (or even firm) specific risk, credit risk, interest rate term structure risk, liquidity risk, FX risk, commodity price risk or deal risk (for example, for mergers). Further, relative value managers often provide the market with valuable price information based on their modelling. As argued above, the related systematic returns can be referred to as complexity premiums.

The returns of risk arbitrage strategies are based directly on capturing the spreads between the market prices of the target companies and the prices that acquiring companies offer. For this expected return, the risk arbitrage manager assumes the risk of the proposed M&A transaction not materialising, in which case the strategy is expected to incur heavy losses. One can say that risk arbitrage managers write put options on announced merger deals.

Managed futures are the main speculative market agent in futures markets, thus capturing what is above referred to as the 'commodity hedging demand premium'. Many global macro and managed futures managers capture the interest rate term premium (for example, by being long duration or convexity).

Exhibit 3.2

Hedge funds classified according to risk premiums they earn

	Long/ Short Equity	Equity Market Neutral (Stat Arb)	Equity Market Timing	Risk Arbitrage	Fixed Income Arbitrage	Convertible Arbitrage	Distressed Securities, Regulation D	(Trend-following) Futures strategies	Global Macro
Equity market risk premium	++		+	+			+		
(Corporate) event risk premium	++	++		++			++		
Small-firm premium	++	+		+			++		
Risk transfer premium								++	
Complexity premiums or 'efficiency' premiums		+			++	++	+		
Liquidity (mark-to-market risk) premium					+		++		
Term structure risk premium					+			++	++
Credit risk premiums					++	++	++		
FX risk premium								++	++
Extreme event risk premium		+		+	++	+			+

Source: Authors' own.

Long-short equity managers typically have simultaneous exposure to the broad equity market, to companies with small market capitalisation and to value stocks. The corresponding returns are the general equity risk premium, the small-firm premium and the low book-to-market premium.

Finally, the systematic return sources of the rather illiquid strategies like distressed debt or Regulation D bear great resemblance to the return sources of private equity investments.

Exhibit 3.2 summarises the diverse risk premiums in the hedge fund universe.

Strategies where manager skills matter most

Risk premiums as a source of return are less (if at all) obvious for opportunistic strategies like some global macro, short selling and long-short equity strategies. The returns of these strategies are to a larger degree derived from the individual manager's skill in forecasting price developments, detecting market inefficiencies and acting quickly upon certain market moves. The underlying opportunities are usually temporary and quickly disappear when acted on by other investors. The greatest potential for these 'pure skill-based' strategies is where information is not freely and broadly available, that is, in inefficient and less liquid markets (for example, small cap stocks). However, the distinction between manager skill and risk premium as a source of return is not always absolutely clear, and returns are often a combination of the two (for example, the above mentioned complexity risk premiums are often interpreted as an exploitation of market inefficiencies).

When a risk event has not yet occurred

One problem for the evaluation of risk premium-based strategies is that, while they earn returns due to the assumptions of certain risks, empirical measures of the underlying risks might be calculated for a time period that does not include a relevant risk event. This can lead to a severe underestimation of the real risk of a strategy.

The challenges for hedge fund investors

The tasks of a fund of hedge funds manager

A fund of funds approach, if properly structured and implemented, can add significant value to investors provided that the fund of funds manager adheres to some fundamental criteria in his investment approach regarding strategy allocation, manager due diligence, and risk management capabilities. The fund of funds manager has three key duties.

1. *Sector allocation (top-down analysis).* Deciding on the relative allocation of capital to various hedge fund styles. The goal is to invest in the right market sectors in the right market environment, and to achieve the appropriate level of diversification across different risk factors. In order to assess the real risk of a hedge fund strategy, the persistence of its returns, and its correlation to other strategies it is essential for a hedge fund allocator (fund of funds manager) to understand the various sources of returns within each type of hedge fund strategy.
2. *Manager evaluation (bottom-up analysis).* Evaluating the individual managers' strategies in a chosen style sector and performing a thorough manager due diligence process. The goal is to identify the best managers with the best skill set (highest alphas). In addition to the details of the strategy's characteristics and the edge or competitive advantage of the individual manager, the underlying hedge fund manager's firm structure should be thoroughly investigated and key personnel should be examined for integrity.
3. *Continuous monitoring/active risk management.* Monitoring open investments for inappropriate risk and style drift. Regular analysis and assessment of the managers' trading activities is an integral element of the overall investment process that feeds back into the top-down strategy sector evaluation and the manager due diligence process. Active risk management is the combination of regular analysis of the P&L, exposure, leverage and risk characteristics in the portfolio, and the ability to act in situations required to prevent unexpected and serious losses. The fund of funds manager needs to be able to quickly identify unexpected style drifts (a shift towards a different strategy than the one the manager formerly indicated) and undesired market bets, which do not match the risk profile. Leverage controls and risk limits need to be implemented and enforced efficiently (for

example, exposure and Value-at-Risk (VaR) limits, predefined maximal losses under various stress scenarios and leverage limits). The strategy's actual P&L performance and exposure profile should match the fund of funds manager's understanding of the strategy in different market situations.[26]

Strategy style risk and manager risk

Hedge fund investors must address two main categories of risks.

1. *Portfolio (style or strategy) risk.* The style risk of each strategy describes the a priori known risk of potential market behaviours affecting the entire strategy sector adversely, for example, equity market (directional) risk for long biased long-short equity, credit spread risk or equity market volatility risk for convertible arbitrage. Style risk can be market risk (changes in the market price of financial assets), credit risk (a counterparty does not meet or is not expected to meet its contractual obligations), liquidity risk (inability to execute transactions or unexpected decrease of funding opportunities), or a complex combination of all these risks.[27]
2. *Manager specific (structural or operational) risks.* These are the risks related to the possibility that the specific manager experiences a large unexpected loss due to, for instance, style drifts, operational problems, concentration in individual securities, fraud and business risks (for example, key people leaving).

An important difference exists between the two main risk categories. As discussed above, the systematic style risks of the individual strategy sector are essentially the return generators of most hedge fund strategies. Therefore, taking a certain amount of these risks is a prerequisite for obtaining expected investment results. Conversely, manager specific risk is unsystematic and does not correspond to an expected return.

Strategy or portfolio risk is best dealt with through appropriate diversification among various strategy sectors. Optimal diversification requires precise knowledge of the various strategy sectors including their return sources and their behaviour in favourable and unfavourable market environments. A comprehensive understanding of how past returns were generated is imperative to successful asset allocation. A diversified hedge fund portfolio contains strategies that demonstrate their respective strengths and weaknesses in different market environments.

Varying views exist on how to achieve sufficient protection against manager risk. One approach used by hedge fund allocators is to select 50–100 different managers, thus limiting the impact of a single manager blow-up in their portfolio. This results in diversification comparable to managing a corporate bond portfolio. However, this approach is sub-optimal and leads to efficiency losses as it results in an increased need for manager due diligence activities and less time spent per manager. In addition, it can quickly lead to over-diversification due to the inclusion of 'dead weight' managers, which often results in mediocre performance and an undesired correlation to equity markets. Active manager control and independent third party risk management can decrease manager risk significantly, and thus the number of managers needed in the hedge fund portfolio.[28] Consequently, one can also construct hedge fund portfolios with 15–20 managers, which are well diversified with respect to style risks.[29]

Implications for portfolio management of hedge funds

Sector allocation

Sector allocation has qualitative and quantitative components. A purely quantitative approach ignores the pitfalls of hedge fund portfolio optimisation, while a purely qualitative approach ignores the value of information about strategy features that can be obtained through a statistical analysis of risk, return and correlation features of hedge funds. As emphasised before, a significant part of the qualitative understanding is the assessment of the (economic) sources of return discussed above.

When looking at return and risk characteristics of hedge funds, a distinction is now commonly made between long biased strategies and other types of directional equity strategies (such as, for example, long-short equity, equity market timing, merger arbitrage) and non-directional strategies (such as relative value strategies, that is, equity market neutral, fixed-income and convertible arbitrage). Directional strategies are often considered as return enhancers in a hedge fund portfolio, while non-directional equity strategies serve as portfolio diversifiers. Directional strategies are generally more broadly exposed to market risk, that is, the risk of price changes in financial assets, while non-directional strategies take a higher degree of credit, liquidity, execution and complexity risks.

The allocation process is less a quantitative science than an art based on the allocator's experience. It should be stressed that no amount of statistical and econometric analysis can replace proper judgement. Empirical performance and correlation studies should serve as a general guideline for the hedge fund allocator, but he should equally consider qualitative elements such as an assessment of economic sources of return and risk, characterisation of premium-based or skill-based returns, and the determination of particularly hostile market environments (which might not yet have tested the strategy).

Manager due diligence

No amount of knowledge about positions and current risk levels can compensate for a lack of knowledge and confidence in the manager's strategy and his trading edge. The decision to allocate money to a particular manager is of ultimate importance for the investor. Each allocation to a manager involves the above discussed manager risks specific to his trading style and employed investment techniques (such as leverage, employed instruments and short selling). Two measures are essential in minimising these risks: proper due diligence and post-investment manager monitoring. Thorough due diligence should, without exception, be a requirement for an investment with a particular hedge fund manager, and should include obtaining a detailed understanding of each manager's individual trading strategy. Managers within the same strategy sector can differ with regards to strategy implementation, instrument diversification, hedging, use of derivatives, short selling and the degree of leverage.[30]

Unfortunately, many investors and fund of funds managers still rely too much on past performance when selecting managers, without pursuing thorough qualitative analysis. Qualitative aspects of the due diligence process involve understanding the manager's competitive advantages (edges), the investment style and attitude of the manager, details of the investment decision-making processes, the organisation and structure of the manager's operations, the trading facilities, and the character, quality and background of key people.

Active post-investment risk management

The different quantitative tools available to risk managers are: exposure analysis, correlation studies, Value-at-Risk (VaR) and its different variations, stress testing, scenario analysis, extreme value theory and credit risk models.[31] In contrast to risk measurement and analysis, risk management requires action and goes beyond simply measuring risk. Often, quantitative reports provide necessary data, but not sufficient information. While risk measurement aims to provide an objective assessment of how much risk is present in the portfolio, risk management consists of a variety of other (sometimes rather subjectively determined) factors, which also depend on the investor's risk profile. Active risk management ('risk management' should always be active) entails the dynamic and optimal allocation of risk among different assets and managers. Active risk management consists of defining and enforcing risk limits, performing dynamic portfolio allocation according to dynamic risk parameters, accepting certain risk factors and concurrently eliminating other risk factors that are deemed unacceptable.

Summary and conclusion

The very fact that hedge fund managers take risks is surely not undesirable. As discussed in this chapter, next to manager skills, risk premiums constitute a large part of hedge fund performance. However, risk that is unintended, misunderstood, mismanaged or mis-priced is not acceptable.

Following the argument that an essential part of hedge fund returns is taking risk premiums, some academics and professionals have asked themselves whether one can construct generic systematic trading programmes that pursue the same risk premiums (for example, a systematic strategy of writing options). If so, one could achieve similar returns to active hedge funds (and would obviously question the high fees of hedge fund managers).[32] This endeavour clearly contrasts with the view of the alpha protagonists in the hedge fund industry, to whom hedge fund returns depend unambiguously on the skill of the specific managers, which leads them to characterise hedge funds as absolute return or pure alpha generation strategies.

The truth is probably a combination of these two aforementioned views. However, it should be clear to the reader that hedge funds do not generate returns through mysterious and secretive means, but through a powerful combination of taking and managing particular risks (and earning the corresponding risk premiums) and relying upon the specific skills of highly talented managers.

A main reason for the persistent confusion about hedge fund return sources continues to be the inability of standard models in finance to adequately describe the diverse risks of hedge funds. There is an increasing amount of academic research related to the question of the return drivers of hedge funds. Most research to date has focused on expanding the Sharpe model of 1992 for systematic return drivers in traditional investment vehicles. The work by Fung and Hsieh, Agarwal and Naik, Schneeweis and Spurgin, and others has started to provide certain quantitative insights into what the systematic risk exposures of some hedge fund strategies could be, for example, for merger arbitrage, convertible arbitrage, equity market neutral and managed futures. These studies have shown that there is a systematic way of modelling hedge fund returns.[33] However, they also show that the proper choice of factors is not always clear. The authors hope for further analysis in this direction. A complete modelling of return drivers for all the different hedge fund strategies has yet to be developed. One conclusion of this chapter is that the hedge fund return puzzle remains far from being solved.

References

Agarwal, V., and N. Naik (2000), 'Multi-Period Performance Persistence Analysis of Hedge Funds', *Journal of Financial and Quantitative Analysis*, Vol. 35, No. 2.

Agarwal, V., and N. Naik (2000), *Performance Evaluation of Hedge Funds with option-based and Buy-and-Hold Strategies*, Working Paper (September).

Amin, G., and H. Kat (2001), *Hedge Fund Performance: 1990–2000: Do the Money Machines Really Add Value?*, ISMA Centre Working Paper 2001–5 (January), also available on www.ssrn.com.

Edwards, F., and M. Caglayan (2001), *Hedge Fund Performance and Manager Skill*, Working Paper (May).

Fama, E. (1991), 'Efficient Capital Markets: II', *Journal of Finance*, Vol. 46, No.5, p. 1575 (December).

Fama, E., and K. French (1992), 'The Cross Section of Expected Stock Returns', *Journal of Finance*, Vol. 47, No. 2, p. 427 (June).

Fama, E., and K. French (1996), 'Multifactor Explanations of Asset Pricing Anomalies', *Journal of Finance*, Vol. 51, p. 55.

Fung, W., and D. Hsieh (1997), 'Empirical Characteristics of Dynamic Trading Strategies: The Case of Hedge Funds', *The Review of Financial Studies*, Vol 2., No. 10.

Fung, W., and D. Hsieh (2000), 'Measuring the Market Impact of Hedge Funds', *Journal of Empirical Finance*, Vol. 7, p.1–36, also available on: http://faculty.fuqua.duke.edu/~dah7/vitae.htm.

Fung, W., and D. Hsieh (2001a), 'Benchmarks of Hedge Fund Performance: Information Content and Measurement Biases', *Financial Analyst Journal*, Vol. 58, p. 22.

Fung, W., and D. Hsieh (2001b), 'The Risk in Hedge Fund Strategies: Theory and Evidence from Trend-Followers', *The Review of Financial Studies*, Vol. 14, No. 2, p. 313 (Summer).

Fung, W., and D. Hsieh (2002), 'Asset Based Style Factors for Hedge Funds', *Financial Analyst Journal*, (September/October).

Fung, W., and D. Hsieh (2003), 'Alternative alphas and alternative betas', *The New Generation of Risk Management for Hedge Funds and Private Equity Investments*, Ed. Lars Jaeger, London, Euromoney Books, pp. 72–87.

Ineichen, A. (2000), *In Search of Alpha – Investing in Hedge Funds*, London, UBS Warburg (October).

Ineichen, A. (2001), *The Search for Alpha Continues – Do Fund of Hedge Fund Managers Add Value?*, London, UBS Warburg (September).

Jaeger, L. (2002a), *Managing Risk in Alternative Investment Strategies*, London, Financial Times/Prentice Hall (May).

Jaeger, L. (2002b), *Peering Into the Black Box*, IPE Publications (August).

Jaeger, L. (2002c), 'Risk Management and Transparency in the Construction and Monitoring of a Fund of Hedge Funds Portfolio', *Global Pension* (September).

Jaeger, L. (2002d), 'Sources of Return for Hedge Funds and Managed Futures', *The Capital Guide to Hedge Funds 2003*, ISI Publications (November).

Jaeger, L., M. Jacquemai and P. Cittadini (2002), 'Case Study: The sGFI Futures Index,' *The Journal of Alternative Investment* (Summer), Vol. 5, p.73.

Jaeger, L. (2003), *The Benefits of Alternative Investment Strategies In the Global Investment Portfolio*, Partners Group Research Publication, available on http://www.partnersgroup.net.

Jaeger, L., and W. Rutsch (2003), *The Significance of Liquidity and Transparency for Multi-Manager Portfolios of Alternative Investment Strategies*, London, Euromoney Publications.

Jaeger, L., and P. Säfvenblad (2003), 'Understanding return sources of hedge funds and private equity investments', *The New Generation of Risk Management for Hedge Funds and Private Equity Investments*, Ed. Lars Jaeger, London, Euromoney Books, pp. 37–56.

Lhabitant, F., and M. Learned (2002), *Hedge Fund Diversification: How Much is Enough?* Working Paper, HEC University Lausanne (July).

Mitchel, M., and T. Pulvino (2001), 'Characteristics of Risk in Risk Arbitrage', *Journal of Finance*, Vol. 56, No. 6, p. 2135.

Polyn, G. (2001), 'Hedge Funds Placed Under the Microscope', *Risk Magazine*, p. 12 (August).

Reilly, F., and K. Brown (1997), *Investment Analysis and Portfolio Management, Fifth Edition*, The Dryden Press.

Ross, S. (1976), 'The Arbitrage Theory of Capital Asset Pricing', *Journal of Economic Theory*, Vol. 13, No.2 , p. 341 (December).

Signer, A., and L. Favre (2002), 'The Difficulties of Measuring the Benefits of Hedge Funds', *The Journal of Alternative Investments* (Summer).

Schneeweis, T., and H. Kazemi (2001), *The Creation of Alternative Tracking Portfolios for Hedge Fund Strategies*, CISDM/SOM Working Paper, University of Massachusetts.

Schneeweis, T., H. Kazemi and G. Martin (2001), *Understanding Hedge Fund Performance: Research Results and Rules of Thumb for the Institutional Investor*, New York, Lehman Brothers Publications (December).

Schneeweis, T., and G. Martin (2000), *The Benefits of Hedge Funds*, Lehman Brothers Publications (August).

Schneeweis, T., and R. Spurgin (1998), 'Multifactor Analysis of Hedge Funds, Managed Futures, and Mutual Fund Returns and Risk Characteristics', *Journal of Alternative Investments* (Fall).

Sharpe, W. (1991), 'Asset Allocation: Management Style and Performance Measurement', *Journal of Portfolio Management*, Vol 2. No.18 (Winter).

Weismann, A., and J. Abernathy (2000), 'The Dangers of Historical Hedge Fund Data', in: *Risk Budgeting: A New Approach to Investing*, Ed. L. Rahl, London, Risk Books.

[1] See L. Jaeger (2003). However, hedge fund investors must exercise caution in the use of the standard deviation and linear correlation for risk and association measures in a portfolio as it is done in standard portfolio theory because this overly simplistic application in the case of hedge funds leads to some problems and often to flawed judgements.

[2] From this perspective it is actually doubtful whether hedge funds constitute a new 'asset class' as many protagonists of the industry proclaim.

[3] See the following article (and references therein) for a more quantitative discussion on hedge fund return sources: Jaeger, L., and P. Säfvenblad (2003), 'Understanding the sources of return for hedge funds and private equity investments', *A New Generation of Risk Management for Hedge Funds and Private Equity Investments*; Ed. L. Jaeger, London, Euromoney Books, pp. 37–56.

[4] Alpha can generally be generated by market timing and security selection.

[5] These are returns beyond the risk-free interest rate. The latter has nothing to do with a risk premium. In economic terms, the risk-free rate of return is the compensation to the investor for delaying consumption in exchange for (higher) future consumption.

[6] Systematic risks are risks that cannot be diversified away by investors. According to capital asset pricing theories systematic risks correspond to expected excess returns. In contrast, non-systematic risks, that can be diversified by the investors should therefore be avoided; see also the discussion below.

[7] The expression 'beta' is used here in a more general context referring to a variety of different risk premiums rather than a single risk premium, such as the equity premium in the Capital Asset Pricing Model (CAPM). See the discussion below.

[8] One example from the traditional world of equity investing is the fact that stocks with high book to price value (BV/PV) have outperformed other stocks significantly in past years. An argument raised by E. Fama and K. French is that investors pursuing a strategy of buying high BV/PV stocks provide 'recession insurance' to other investors; see Fama, E., French, K., (1992).

[9] The EMH in its three variations, the strong, semi-strong and weak forms, are discussed in detail by Fama, E. (1991).

[10] Most finance books cover the CAPM including its fundamental assumptions in great detail, for example, Reilly, F., and K. Brown (1997).

[11] The third and the fourth moment of a probability distribution describe the skew and kurtosis, respectively. The author notes for the purpose of mathematical correctness that the estimates provide no indication that these higher moments actually exist – that is, the corresponding integral converges.

[12] Further, the use of historical data for the purpose of hedge fund strategy and manager selection in combination with conventional portfolio optimisation techniques usually results in portfolios with inappropriately high non-considered risks and low liquidity (for example, large allocations to Regulation D and distressed debt securities).

[13] An interesting recent paper on the difficulties of measuring the effects of hedge funds in a portfolio and a consideration of higher moments in the optimisation is presented by A. Signer and L. Favre (2002).

[14] The APT was introduced by S. Ross in the early 1970s and first published in 1976 (see 'References').

[15] According to the CAPM and related asset pricing models as discussed in most finance textbooks, risk is two-fold. First, broad market risk is related to the volatility of the entire market. Secondly, (corporate) specific risk is the idiosyncratic risk of loss due to an adverse development, which affects the securities of a particular company. Note that, according to the CAPM, idiosyncratic (or unsystematic) risk does not earn the investor a higher expected return, because it can be diversified away.

[16] See the seminal paper by Sharpe, W. (1991).

[17] Fung, W., and D. Hsieh (1997).

[18] See their recent work: Fung, W., and D. Hsieh (2001).

[19] See the following articles for a further discussion: Schneeweis, T., and R. Spurgin (1998); Fung, W., and D. Hsieh (1997); Fung, W., and D. Hsieh (2001a); Fung, W., and D. Hsieh (2001b); Fung, W., and D. Hsieh (2002); Agarwal, V., N. Naik (2000b); Edwards, F., and M. Caglayan (2001); Mitchel, M., T. Pulvino (2001).

[20] T. Schneeweis *et al* (2001).

[21] The statement that hedge funds provide important economic value to financial markets and the economy as a whole is unfortunately in contrast to the often articulated view and widely held investor perception (especially outside the Anglo-Saxon world) that hedge funds offer no economic value. It has become quite popular among journalists to describe hedge funds as destructive market agents. This is mostly due to the persistent ignorance of many journalists with respect to hedge funds.

[22] See Reilly, F., and K. Brown (1997) (Chapter 7) and references therein for a further discussion on the small firm effect and related issues.

[23] See Jaeger, L., M. Jacquemai and P. Cittadini (2002) for more details and references.

[24] The increase of market efficiency provided by hedge funds may come at the price of higher short-term volatility, but with the benefit of lower long-term volatility and fairer prices. One must realise that market volatility, if it reflects true information, is good and desirable.

[25] Note that the word 'arbitrage' does not refer to the strictest meaning of the word here (which is 'generating a profit without risk'). In this context, 'arbitrage' means buying relatively undervalued securities, and selling overvalued securities. There is a risk involved here, specifically the risk that the undervalued securities become even cheaper and the overvalued ones more expensive.

[26] See also Jaeger, L. (2002c) for a more detailed discussion on risk and risk management issues for hedge fund portfolios.

[27] See Jaeger, L., and P. Säfvenblad (2003) for more details on systematic hedge fund risk factors.

[28] See Jaeger, L. (2002a) for a more detailed discussion on risk and risk management issues for hedge fund portfolios.

[29] Studies about how many managers are needed to reach sufficient 'manager diversification' in a hedge fund portfolio are presented in Schneeweis, T., and G. Martin (2000). Two studies about increasing correlations in portfolios with many different managers is presented by Armin, G., and H. Kat (2001); and Lhabitant, F., and M. Learned (2002).

[30] Note that leverage itself is not a risk type, but a way to increase and scale the risk and return distribution of a strategy. It can serve (in combination with others) as one indicator for a strategy's risk level.

[31] Issues of transparency and risk management are discussed in more detail in Jaeger, L. (2002c); see also Jaeger, L. (2002b); Jaeger, L. (2002a); Jaeger, L., and W. Rutsch (2003).

[32] See Polyn, G. (2001) and references therein (especially the study by the International Security Market Association). Academic research has also focused on the direct replication of the hedge funds with generic trading models; see, for example, the discussions by Schneeweis, T., and H. Kazemi (2001) as well as the paper by Fung, W., and D. Hsieh (2001b).

[33] A comprehensive summary of these efforts is provided by Fung, W., and D. Hsieh (2003).

Chapter 4

Historical overview of offshore hedge funds

Antoine Bernheim
Dome Capital Management, Inc., New York, New York

From humble beginnings

The world of offshore hedge funds began to develop in the late 1960s. Michael Steinhardt started his SP International, originally set up as a Panama company, in May 1968 and George Soros opened up the Double Eagle Fund NV, predecessor to the Quantum Fund NV, while working at Arnhold & Bleichroeder, in January 1969. Those were very modest beginnings. By the end of their first fiscal year, SP International SA had US$3.5 million in capital (31 January 1969) and Quantum Fund NV had US$6.2 million (31 December 1969). It was not immediately easy. In its first full fiscal year ended 31 January 1970, SP International lost 32.2 per cent (versus a loss of 14.4 per cent for the S&P 500) and it took approximately three years for the fund to recover its original net asset value (NAV) of US$100. By 1980, it still had less than US$20 million in capital. By then, however, Quantum had already put together a spectacular record multiplying its original NAV by a factor of 45 in 12 years and building its capital to US$380 million only to drop to under US$200 million the following year after a 22.6 per cent decline of its NAV.

The 1970s were difficult years in the financial markets and very few ventured in the area of offshore or onshore hedge funds for that matter. Cumberland Associates started in 1970 but did not have an offshore fund until 1984 (although they managed significant foreign accounts), Davidson Weil Associates opened Blackthorn Fund NV in October 1978 and Paul Singer who started Elliott Associates in 1977 did not have an offshore fund until 1994. It is only in the early and mid-1980s that things began to perk up as a result of several catalysts that changed the supply and demand for hedge funds.

First was the creation of the late Gilbert de Botton's Global Asset Management (GAM) in 1983. The firm started by the experienced Swiss banker who took a resolutely non-Swiss approach by organising its asset management business around individual offshore funds managed in large part by outside managers with clear performance information and a transparent fee structure. Gilbert de Botton was able to identify talented managers such as Niels Taub, Bernard Selz, John Angelo and Bruce Kovner and create funds around them in which GAM clients could easily invest.

The second catalyst in the development of offshore hedge funds in the 1980s was the emergence of a small number of exceptionally talented commodity traders who ventured out on their own and found a receptive audience among foreign investors, such as Bruce Kovner in 1983 and Paul Tudor Jones in 1985 to be followed by Monroe Trout and James Simon in 1988, and Louis Bacon in 1990. These traders were able to post spectacular returns as they made the important transition from trading commodities to trading financial futures at the time when trading in bonds, currencies and stock indices became dominant. Not only were their returns spectacular, in spite of a heavy fee structure, they were uncorrelated with the stock market and provided real diversification of risk.

The third catalyst of the early 1980s was the beginning of a bull market in the United States and the realisation by a few that corporate assets were undervalued and vulnerable to takeovers. A number of specialised hedge funds focusing on mergers and acquisitions started to offer high net worth individuals the opportunity to invest in an area that had been reserved to a few investment banking and brokerage firms. As risk arbitrage partnerships became more visible, a few foreign investors got their appetite whetted by the lure of high returns with the assumption of transaction, rather than market risk. Takeover players such as Carl Icahn, Asher Edelman and Irwin Jacobs became increasingly visible and paved the way for the build-up of several private investment partnerships. Coniston Partners established connections with a prominent Swiss investor and, in 1985, launched a companion offshore fund to their domestic partnership to take strategic blocks in companies and cause them to enhance shareholder value. By the end of 1989, it had become the fourth largest offshore hedge fund after Quantum, SP International and Bruce Kovner's offshore funds.

Still, by the end of 1989, the world of offshore hedge funds consisted of George Soros with a US$2 billion fund and all the other offshore hedge funds which totalled another US$3 billion in assets. At that time, Steinhardt's SP International had US$350 million and Julian Robertson's Jaguar Fund NV which had started in January 1986 had US$83 million in capital (versus US$500 million in Robertson's domestic partnerships). Foreign investors' interest consisted largely of the same original group of Quantum Fund investors which had been organised primarily in two funds of funds, Leveraged Capital Holdings set up in 1969 by Edmond de Rothschild's Banque Privée and Haussmann Holdings established initially in 1969 for the high net worth clients of the Paris-based Worms Group. These funds of funds placed a significant part of their portfolios in managed accounts as few hedge fund managers offered an offshore vehicle. Other important investors by 1989 included GAM, members of the Haussmann Holdings consortium such as Lugano-based Banca del Ceresio and Geneva-based Notz, Stucki et Cie, and Mirabaud et Cie, and a small number of other precursors such as Geneva-based Compagnie de Banque et d'Investissements (which later became Union Bancaire Privée) as well as a few private families.

Except for the hedge fund managers that had come out of a commodity trading background, hedge funds generally did not do well in the crash of 1987 and the risk arbitrageurs got decimated. However, the uncertainties within the brokerage and investment management community created by the crash and its aftermath got a number of people to think about going out on their own. Starting a hedge fund had become a tempting option.

When starting a hedge fund becomes an easy thing to do

Starting a hedge fund became much easier through a variety of factors which led the embryonic developments of the 1980s to the establishment of a significant hedge fund community in the 1990s. Some of those factors affected hedge funds in general and other offshore hedge funds more particularly. These included the development of:

- prime brokerage services;
- funds of funds; and
- directories and databases.

The development of prime brokerage services greatly facilitated the start-up of independent hedge funds by providing managers with turnkey back-office operations. Prime brokers enable money managers who trade at multiple securities firms to consolidate assets and record keeping in one place. They take over from the manager the responsibility for receiving and delivering funds and securities and recording the trades as they occur. They also provide financing and stock loans and many of them today offer significant execution capability in the global markets. The development of management and accounting reports by the prime brokers have enabled managers to have real-time access to their portfolio performance as well as accounting systems. Some prime brokers such as Furman Selz (now part of ABN Amro) and Bear Stearns began to supply turnkey offices with short-term leases, significantly lowering the working capital commitment required for new start-ups. In the late 1990s, prime brokers began also offering capital introduction services, matching hedge funds with investors. As business grew, more and more brokerage firms started to look at prime brokerage as a strategic activity: Morgan Stanley, Goldman Sachs and Montgomery (now part of Banc of America) and more recently Deutsche Bank and Lehman Brothers made a strong commitment to prime brokerage and have successfully developed these operations. Other banks and brokerage firms have attempted and failed or keep going with limited success.

The development of funds of funds has been another factor facilitating the development of new hedge funds. Until the passage of the Securities Markets Improvement Act of 1996, US hedge funds were limited to 100 investors and, as a result, hedge funds were forced to impose a relatively high minimum investment. This led to the development of funds of funds which facilitate access to a diversified portfolio of hedge funds with a significantly lower investment requirement. While not limited by the same regulations, the offshore market has seen a similar explosion of funds of funds offering investors diversification with a lesser investment commitment. These funds of funds are eager to place some capital with less seasoned managers as a way to demonstrate to investors that they are on the look-out for new talent. The asset gathering function provided by the funds of funds has helped the marketing efforts of newly established hedge funds and facilitated their growth.

The development of directories and databases was another factor in the growth of the business as it allowed performance information to be distributed more openly. Our own directory, *The US Offshore Funds Directory*, was the pioneer in the field in 1990 to be followed later on by others offering printed or electronically delivered performance information. In the late 1990s, the Internet further eased access to performance and other information. The result of the fast dissemination of information contributes to a more efficient allocation of capital and makes it increasingly difficult for a manager with a superior track record to remain undiscovered. When I first started in the business, one found out about managers through word of mouth, generally by speaking with other managers or brokers. Today, the capital introduction teams of the major prime brokers in addition to a variety of publications and databases put new managers on the radar screens of investors early on. On the other hand, the speed with which information circulates creates a potentially dangerous pattern where managers with little or no independent track record are able to gather assets more quickly than they can handle effectively. Certain managers who have an impressive resumé but not a proven track record in managing money independently have recently started up with US$500 million or more in capital. As some of these funds stumble, they may find themselves two or three years later with a lot less capital than they started with, as the speed with which information on new funds is disseminated creates capital flows in both directions and generally increases capital turnover.

Exhibit 4.1

Offshore hedge funds versus S&P 500: annual compound rate of return over calendar years (weighted by capital at the beginning of each year) (%)

	2002	*2000–2002* *(3 years)*	*1998–2002* *(5 years)*	*1993–2002* *(10 years)*
Hedge funds	3.2	5.4	8.4	13.5
S&P 500	–22.1	–14.6	–0.6	9.3

Source: Hedge Fund News.

Performance

Offshore hedge fund investors rode the wave of the explosion in financial assets in the 1990s. As was stated above, by the end of 1989, the total capital in offshore hedge funds was approximately US$5 billion of which George Soros' Quantum Fund accounted for US$2 billion. The real growth started in the mid-1990s and by mid-2003, according to *Hedge Fund News'* survey of offshore administrators, capital in offshore hedge funds exceeded US$490 billion. Extraordinary returns achieved in 1991, 1992 and 1993 paved the way for this growth which was briefly interrupted by a difficult 1994. In the second half of the 1990s, while assets were flowing into hedge funds, US equities roared ahead and hedge fund investors could not keep up with the indices. In fact, in the five years ended 31 December 1999, offshore hedge funds annual return stood at 18.3 per cent vs. 28.6 per cent for the S&P. Then the stock market bubble burst and interest rates collapsed leaving investors with bad bruises and no clear opportunity to make money. Hedge funds became the product *du jour* that banks around the world wanted to sell to their clients. In 2001, assets in offshore hedge funds grew by a whopping 28 per cent and again by 11 per cent in 2002. At the same time, performance declined markedly with hedge fund returns in the low single digit range, which nonetheless compared favourably to the negative returns of equities. The performance presented in Exhibit 4.1 is calculated to reflect the precise performance of offshore hedge funds by looking at each fund's capital at the beginning of a year, applying the net fund performance for the year to that capital and calculating a weighted average for each year. While the calculation does not take into account the intra year capital flows, it does capture capital flows on an annual basis and is an accurate picture of investors' performance.

Major trends

The major trends over the past few years in the offshore hedge funds' world are clearly visible from Exhibit 4.2.

The number of offshore hedge funds has been growing at a 20 per cent annual rate over the past 10 years, although growth in the number of funds has been slowing markedly since mid-2002. Capital in offshore hedge funds has been doubling every three years since 1991. Until, 2001, assets had grown primarily as a result of performance (65 per cent) and secondarily from capital inflows (35 per cent). In the last couple of years, asset growth has been primarily from capital inflows as performance has lagged. As the number of funds grew and

Exhibit 4.2

Selected statistics for offshore hedge funds, 1991–2002

	2002	2001	2000	1999	1998	1997	1996	1995	1994	1993	1992	1991
Single manager funds at beginning of year	737	647	609	494	448	375	308	248	197	123	104	88
Capital in US$ billion at beginning of year	150.4	117.6	113.0	76.7	70.6	49.4	34.80	30.2	34.90	17.4	11.9	7.8
Funds with capital >US$100 million at beginning of year	265	204	164	122	111	82	52	47	41	24	17	14
Five largest funds as % of total	15.3	16.6	20.5	24.4	29.4	35.4	42.9	38.9	45.9	50.6	51.5	54.7
Funds opened during year	124	171	140	200	114	106	80	70	68	77	35	33
Funds closed during year	86	58	58	49	40	27	27	29	33	12	14	12
Capital weighted rate of return (%)	3.2	5.9	7.1	25.8	1.7	25.0	20.3	20.3	−8.8	43.1	37.3	32.3

Source: Hedge Fund News.

the larger ones either closed to new investors, made distributions of capital or retired, the concentration among the largest funds has declined and the number of funds capable of attracting large investors' interest (those with capital over US$100 million) has increased at a disproportionate pace. There are more than 100 hedge fund groups with capital in excess of US$1 billion and more than 25 offshore hedge funds with capital in excess of US$1 billion.

Many of these trends were affected in the late 1990s by the surge in financial assets in the United States and, since then, by the growing interest in hedge funds on the part of institutions and distributors of financial products. As long as that continues, more and more managers are attracted to the independent and lucrative structure of the hedge fund and investors keep adding to their investments. The surge in hedge fund creation has been the result of a real exodus from:

- investment banks' proprietary trading and asset management divisions;
- institutional and mutual funds management companies; and
- people leaving larger hedge funds.

As these factors started to play out in Europe in the late 1990s, London became a major hedge fund centre. More recently, Asia has been seeing a surge of newly established hedge funds.

The development of offshore jurisdictions

Historically, a provision of US tax regulations made it unadvisable for foreign investors to invest directly in a US partnership trading securities since they would incur a tax in the United States on their realised capital gains. That provision, which was only removed with the Taxpayer Relief Act of 1997, was a critical factor in the development of an offshore hedge fund industry. When offshore hedge funds began to develop, the Netherlands Antilles was the jurisdiction of choice. It had a favourable tax treaty with the United States but the treaty only applied if the fund was set up in corporate form. Later on, as the treaty benefit disappeared, other jurisdictions started to compete with the Netherlands Antilles but the corporate form remained because of its familiarity to foreign investors. The British Virgin Islands, the Cayman Islands, Bermuda and the Bahamas offered alternatives to the Netherlands Antilles. All these jurisdictions share a low tax (in the case of the Netherlands Antilles) or no tax status. The legal environment has changed significantly in all jurisdictions in the 1990s with the adoption of new legislation affecting:

- the form or organisation available including limited liability (LLC) and limited duration (LDC) companies and partnerships (LP);
- mutual fund legislation; and
- anti-money laundering legislation.

It is beyond the scope of this chapter to review all the provisions that now govern the establishment of offshore hedge funds in each jurisdiction but it is appropriate to indicate the major elements which have made the offshore hedge fund market increasingly regulated.

The adoption of LLC legislation by most states in the United States in the 1990s (New York's LLC status came into effect in 1994) caused foreign jurisdictions to do the same in an increasingly competitive environment. The advantage of LLC and LP status is the pass-through treatment of income, expenses, gains and losses. The benefit of this pass-through is the ability to set up a master-feeder structure where a manager can run one single portfolio of securities (typically an offshore LLC, LDC or LP) into which will feed a US LP and a foreign corporation and possibly other special purpose feeders. The advantage of a master-feeder structure is obvious in terms of trading costs (no allocation of trades necessary and only one account reconciliation), financing costs (with a larger pool to serve as collateral), administration, accounting and audit costs and it also insures that the domestic and offshore funds have exactly similar results. With the adoption of enabling legislation in the main offshore jurisdictions in the early and mid-1990s, the master-feeder structure has gained wide acceptance by newly established funds with the result that an offshore hedge fund can be set up more quickly by a manager who otherwise may have waited longer to accumulate a critical mass of offshore interest.

Mutual fund legislation came into force beginning after 1993 to impose registration, disclosure requirements, record-keeping requirements as well as rights of action by shareholders. These developments came about to remedy the 'free-wheeling', unregulated image of offshore jurisdictions as part of a broader effort to curtail money laundering and other fraudulent acts in the wake of the Bank of Credit and Commerce International (BCCI) scandal of 1991. Bermuda had set supervisory regulations many years ago which required, among other things, disclosure of beneficial ownership or bank references for shareholders of Bermuda companies. Later on, it adopted additional statutes such as the Drug Trafficking Suppression Act and the 1993 Code of Conduct as well as a voluntary Code of Conduct for Bermuda funds in 1994 which give the Bermuda Monetary Authority significant compliance powers over funds, although neither registration nor licensing. The Cayman Islands Mutual Fund Law, first enacted in 1993, requires a fund to obtain a licence from the Cayman Islands government unless:

- the principal office of the fund is provided by the holder of a Cayman Islands mutual fund administrator licence; or

- the minimum investment in the fund is US$48,000; or
- the fund's equity interests are listed on a designated stock exchange.

The BVI Mutual Fund Act enacted in 1996 and amended in 1997 requires funds to register unless they have less than 50 investors or are made available only to professional investors. The Bahamas Mutual Fund Act of 1995 generally follows the approach of the Cayman Islands legislation and puts the Securities Board in charge of the supervision of mutual funds in the Bahamas. The common thread of these legislative changes is to create a supervisory infrastructure which can lead to additional regulations and enforcement.

While none of the jurisdictions want to kill the goose that lays the golden egg of the offshore business that is often their principal source of employment, the adoption of mutual fund legislation has gradually changed the pattern of competition. Historically, the British Virgin Islands (BVI) had maintained a leading market share (by number of funds) in the offshore hedge fund market. However, the uncertainties related to the BVI Mutual Fund Act of 1996 caused the BVI's market share for newly incorporated funds to decline significantly in 1997 and Cayman's approach to put the licensing burden on the fund's administrator rather than the fund itself has made it the jurisdiction of choice since then. In 2003, the Cayman Islands reached a 54 per cent market share among offshore hedge funds against the BVI's 25 per cent. Bermuda has maintained its position around 12 per cent.

The fight against money laundering has been a major issue in offshore jurisdictions since the BCCI scandal. Things moved quickly after the Financial Action Task Force of the OECD released a series of reports identifying countries as 'non-cooperative' jurisdictions in the fight against money laundering. By mid-2002, all the major jurisdictions where offshore hedge funds are domiciled had been removed from such lists and had implemented Know Your Customer regulations and agreed to cooperate in a global crackdown by the OECD on tax evasion. Governments in most of the Caribbean jurisdictions have also entered into bilateral tax information exchange agreements with the United States. At the same time, the US Patriot Act signed into law by President Bush in October 2001, imposes significant new anti-money laundering requirements on financial institutions, including banks and broker-dealers with which offshore hedge funds have accounts. Under regulations currently being considered, offshore hedge funds organised by US persons or selling ownership interests to US persons would be subject to US anti-money laundering rules. The anti-money laundering infrastructure built in the last few years in the offshore jurisdictions should make compliance with the upcoming regulations relatively easy, albeit with significant additional administrative costs.

The development of offshore administrators

US tax regulations adopted in 1968 which stayed in effect until 31 December 1997, required 10 administrative functions to be performed at an office outside the United States for a fund not to be subject to certain US taxes on its US source income. Known as the '10 Commandments', these functions included:

1. communicating with shareholders;
2. communicating with the general public;
3. soliciting sales of the company's stock;
4. accepting subscriptions of new shareholders;

5. maintaining the principal corporate records and books;
6. auditing the company's accounts;
7. disbursing payments of dividends, legal fees, accounting fees and directors' fees;
8. publishing or furnishing the offering and redemption price of the company's shares;
9. conducting shareholders' and directors' meetings; and
10. making redemptions of the company's stock.

These functions form the basis for the existence and activities of offshore administrators as they relate to offshore hedge funds. For many years, the business was divided among a handful of banks and trust companies located in the various Caribbean jurisdictions. The business was dominated by Curacao Trust International Company (Citco) which administered most of the big funds. As the number of offshore hedge funds increased and the complexity of legal structures and accounting issues grew, offshore administration attracted a number of new entrants in the late 1980s and early 1990s. As a result of such competition, the quality of service improved. Today, a dozen well-established firms compete for the business and offer services that extend beyond the traditional Caribbean locations. In particular, Dublin has become a major centre for offshore fund administration. Offshore administrators also offer their services out of the United States since the change of regulations effective 1 January 1998 relaxed the need to adhere to the 10 Commandments. However, because foreign investors place a great deal of value on confidentiality and an independent oversight of a fund's accounting practices, many of the functions previously required to be performed by offshore administrators continue to be handled by them. The business is going through a period of consolidation with the acquisition in 2002 of major offshore administrators by US-based financial groups such as Bisys, State Street Bank and Bank of New York.

Looking forward

The hedge fund market place has gone through an explosive growth phase since the mid-1990s and is becoming, as a result, more institutional in its investor base. With the recent declines in equities and interest rates, the bar has been lowered for hedge fund managers, and many institutional investors favour consistency over outstanding performance. They need to place large sums of money which only a limited number of hedge funds can handle. As a result, the market is likely to evolve into a two tier structure with large hedge fund groups operating more as risk managers and catering to the institutional market place, while smaller hedge funds serve a more entrepreneurial investor base and take greater risks to achieve the performance which hedge funds have traditionally been associated with. In addition, the free-wheeling environment which has led to the explosion in hedge fund creation over the past several years is likely to change. Barriers to entry will be raised as a result of US regulators looking to impose registration requirements and other obligations on hedge funds, the increasing role of institutions and the accelerating turnover of capital. The ability to stay in business long enough to thrive is likely to be tougher than what has been seen in the last few years. Offshore, the market place will resemble more and more that of the United States, as US institutional investors increasingly populate offshore hedge funds, large offshore funds of funds continue to beef up their US presence and US regulations increasingly apply across borders. However, hedge funds have now found a place among mainstream financial products and, unlike their humble beginnings, their future is no longer in doubt.

Chapter 5

Hedge fund trends: review and outlook

Lois Peltz
Infovest21, New York, New York

The early years of the new millennium have been critical ones for the hedge fund industry. The fact that hedge funds made money overall in spite of a negative stock market and limited opportunities reflected the value of the hedge fund concept, as shown in the simple comparison in Exhibit 5.1.

As a result, hedge funds became more mainstream. At one end of the spectrum, hedge funds are being offered to mass-affluent investors. At the other end of the spectrum, institutions are increasingly using hedge funds for active money management as replacements for long-only active managers. In a world where investors suffered three straight years of stock market losses, flat hedge fund gains tempted US pension plans and other institutions. As institutional interest has grown they have demanded more transparency. Growth is being fuelled by both developments.

Three years into the bear market, the hedge fund industry has more breadth and depth than it did previously, providing a strong base from which to grow further.

On the positive side there has been a steady flow of new managers as well as new products. Multi-strategy funds, registered funds and structured products continue to evolve. Institutional allocations and interest continues to grow on a global basis. Concerns for the industry include whether hedge funds will produce absolute returns or become more relative-return-oriented. Concern is growing over structured notes as interest rates remain low. Funds closing, funds blowing up and increased regulation all are issues. Going forward, investors and managers have lowered expectations for performance.

Outlook

Investors remain interested in hedge funds. While some may have delayed action due to

Exhibit 5.1

Comparison of benchmarks, 2000–02

	2000	*2001*	*2002*
S&P	−10.1	−13.0	−23.8
DJIA	−6.2	−7.1	−16.8
Nasdaq	−39.3	−21.1	−31.5
Hedge funds	5.0	4.6	−1.5

Source: Hedge Fund Research, Inc.

Exhibit 5.2

Distribution of hedge fund assets, 1990 and 1992 (%)

	1990	*2002*
Convertible arbitrage	0.5	5.3
Distressed securities	2.4	4.7
Emerging markets	0.4	2.2
Equity hedge	5.3	31.8
Equity market neutral	1.7	3.0
Equity non-hedge	0.6	4.0
Event-driven	3.8	12.2
Macro	71.1	9.4
Market timing	0.0	0.6
Merger arbitrage	0.6	2.0
Fixed income: total	**3.2**	**6.8**
Fixed income: arbitrage	3.2	2.1
Fixed income: convertible bonds	–	0.1
Fixed income: diversified	–	1.9
Fixed income: high yield	–	0.2
Fixed income: mortgage-backed	–	2.5
Regulation D	–	0.2
Relative value arbitrage	10.1	12.0
Sector	0.2	5.7
Short selling	0.1	0.4

Source: Hedge Fund Research, 'HFR Industry Analysis-2002 Year End Raw Data', 2003.

uncertainty about the economy and the markets, hedge funds remain one of the more attractive investments. Nevertheless, expectations for annual returns have been reduced to the 7 to 12 per cent range with annual standard deviation of 5 to 7 per cent and a maximum decline of 6 to 8 per cent per year.[1]

Size, asset flow and growth

Some estimate the size of the hedge fund industry at US$600 billion. While it is difficult to pinpoint the actual size of the industry due to fuzziness of definitions, some say US$600 billion may be too large due to double-counting. In actuality, there may be about 3,500–4,000 funds totalling perhaps US$350 billion. The difference may be due to inclusion of long-only funds, commodity trading advisers, funds of funds and managed accounts.

Many more strategies exist today and the percentage of assets those strategies represent have changed dramatically over the last decade. Today, the equity strategies dominate whereas in 1990, macro strategies dominated. Exhibit 5.2 reflects the changes in number and size.

Hedge fund assets are expected to quadruple over the next seven years, surpassing the US$2 trillion mark by 2010, according to a study by Putnam Lovell NBF and consulting firm NewRiver. The study predicts investors worldwide will sink roughly US$800 billion of new money into the asset class through the remainder of this decade – more than four times current estimates.[2]

According to this report, US and public pension plans will invest some US$527 billion in hedge funds by 2010, up from US$87 billion at year-end 2001. High net worth individuals will more than double their investments to more than US$1.2 trillion from almost US$400 billion in 2001. Of the US$1.5 trillion increase in global hedge fund assets by 2010, about US$800 billion will be new money and an estimated US$700 billion will come from market appreciation.

New managers and new funds

There has been a steady flow of new managers. The majority continue to come from larger, more established hedge funds. Investment banks, traditional managers and consultants are other sources. The lines between hedge funds and mutual funds continued to blur as more mutual fund managers defected to hedge funds or started their own hedge fund and as more mutual fund companies offered hedge funds.

Multi-strategy funds, registered funds, funds of funds, country-specific funds and structured products continue to proliferate.

Multi-strategy funds

Multi-strategy funds continue to grow in popularity as a means to alleviate capacity concerns. Investors get diversification more efficiently and cost-effectively as they have access to various strategies in a single vehicle. It also allows the investor to delegate tactical allocation to the manager.

On the negative side, however, due diligence and risk management are more complex. Detailed data is necessary for the investor to assess the overall portfolio's exposure to different types of instruments, sectors, geographical areas and leverage. Style drift can also be a concern.

Registered funds

Registered funds continued to emerge in record numbers. PaineWebber, Global Asset Management, Deutsche Bank, Oppenheimer, Bank of America and Man are among those offering registered funds of funds. There are about 20–40 funds of funds registered with the Securities and Exchange Commission.

Many of these funds are small, perhaps in the US$20–25 million range, having been seeded by the sponsor. Two main advantages for the sponsor are a wider audience and a lower minimum investment. Many of the minimums are at US$50,000. Some have been as low as US$25,000. This is not hedge funds for the masses but more the mass-affluent.[3]

Another plus from the investor's point of view is that independent boards of directors provide an extra layer of oversight. In addition, since registered funds are required to disclose the names of the managers in the fund of funds, greater transparency is provided.

Some say the costs are relatively high but may eventually come down. Management fees for a registered fund of funds may range from less than 1 per cent to 2.5 per cent. Performance fees can range from zero per cent to 10 per cent, or even 15 per cent with a hurdle. There may be an investor servicing fee which is an incentive/trail for the broker, which may range up to 1 per cent. The sales commission is upfront, a one-time fee. Also, registered funds have a tender offer rather than a redemption feature. Each time a tender offer is undertaken, legal costs are incurred.

The SEC seems to be taking a closer look at these products and moving at a slower approval rate than previously.

Structured products

Structured products continue to develop (structured leverage, principal protected notes, collateralised financial obligations and swaps). Structured products provide customised solutions for investors. Those who would typically not be hedge fund of funds investors, such as traditional debt buyers, do invest in collateralised fund obligations. These products attract investors with different goals, holding periods and other characteristics, increasing the diversity of a firm's investor base. Some institutions are more willing to make one major allocation to a fund of funds to replace an outsourced alternative asset allocation mandate.[4]

Structured deals allow managers to increase potential returns through the use of leverage. Structured products are a tool that funds of funds can use to achieve continued growth and more reliable cash flows. In 2002, two public hedge fund transactions (Man Glenwood Alternative Strategies and Investcorp's Diversified Strategies collateralised fund obligations) were rated. Standard & Poor's assigned ratings to US$374 million in floating and fixed-rate notes issued by Man Glenwood Alternative Strategies I. Man Glenwood Alternative Strategies I issued US$242 million of class A notes rated AAA, US$33 million class B1 and B2 notes rated AA, and US$41 million class C1 and C2 notes rated A. The rest of the issuance was class D, rated BBB. Man Glenwood Alternative Strategies invested the proceeds in 35 or more hedge funds.[5] Investcorp's collateralised hedge fund obligation, Diversified Strategies CFO, closed in June 2002 with proceeds of US$250 million. The transaction involved several classes of notes rated by Fitch, Moody's and Standard & Poor's as well as equity that was not rated. The proceeds were invested in Diversified Strategies Fund II, a fund of funds managed by Investcorp Management Services Limited, a Bahrain-based subsidiary of Investcorp Bank.[6]

Institutional developments

Foundations and endowments continue to increase their allocations while pension funds increase their knowledge of the area and also made allocations. Negative equity markets motivated endowments and pensions to turn toward alternative investments which are largely uncorrelated to stocks.

United States

Endowments and foundations

University and college endowments with more than US$1 billion in assets are allocating 9.6 per cent of their portfolios to hedge funds, according to preliminary results from the 2001 annual survey by the National Association of College and University Business Officers (NACUBO). The comparable figure for 2000 was 5.6 per cent. Smaller endowments, however, continue to invest little in alternatives.[7]

Endowments with less than US$100 million in total assets invested only 1.7 per cent in hedge funds. The average hedge fund allocation across endowments of all sizes was 2.9 per cent. The over US$1 billion group put an additional 3.5 per cent into event-driven and general absolute return strategies while all endowments put only 1 per cent into these strategies. The survey covered fiscal year 2001 (ending 30 June).

The largest endowments also invested much more heavily in other alternatives. They allocated 6.2 per cent to venture capital, 4.4 per cent to buy-out funds and 1.2 per cent to distressed securities. For all endowments, these percentages were at 1.5 per cent, 0.9 per cent and 0.3 per cent respectively. Adding together hedge funds, other absolute return strategies and various private equity investments, endowments over US$1 billion put 25 per cent into these alternatives compared with 6.6 per cent for all endowments.

NACUBO data also shows better performance for larger endowments similar to the pattern of comparative returns that emerged from the previous annual survey. However, endowments of all sizes were in the red for 2001 whereas they had enjoyed substantial gains in 2000. The average return was a 3.6 per cent loss in 2001 compared to a 13 per cent gain in the previous fiscal year.

The limited losses of larger endowments may be due to their greater asset diversification, particularly in alternative investments. Endowments with more than US$1 billion lost only 1.6 per cent while funds with less than US$100 million gave up 3.7 per cent. Those in between these sizes had losses in the intermediate range.

In past years, university endowments introduced hedge funds into their portfolios mainly to achieve diversification. However, today these investments are more likely driven by a growing need for returns to support school spending, as high spending rates and shortfall risk exists if returns are not met.

Among the endowments making their first foray into hedge funds in 2002 were Washington State University, which committed US$9 million to a fund of funds, and Mississippi State University, which allocated US$16 million to two funds of funds.[8]

Pension plans

Pension plans, driven by a need for higher returns in the slumping stock market, became more interested in hedge funds. They are driven by an urgent need for higher returns due to underfunding of retirement benefits.

With US$647 million in hedge strategies, the Teacher Retirement System of Texas is believed to be the largest pension investor in hedge funds as of 2001. A *Pensions & Investments* survey found that the next largest hedge assets belong to the defined benefit plans of Citigroup, World Bank and the Episcopal Church. Citigroup has US$560 million, World Bank US$516 million and the Episcopal Church US$346 million in hedge funds. Qwest has US$201 million pension assets in hedge funds, General Electric US$127 million and Philip Morris US$105 million.[9]

Among public pensions, the largest hedge asset holders after Texas Teachers were Pennsylvania Employees with US$340 million, Illinois Municipal Retirement with US$75 million, Louisiana State Employees with US$65 million and Cook County Employees with US$50 million as of 30 September 2002.

The combined hedge fund assets of the top 200 defined benefit plans add up to US$3.2 billion. However, this is a tiny sliver of the pensions' combined alternative investments, which weigh in at US$129.8 billion. The largest items in the alternatives category are private equity with US$77.5 billion and venture capital with US$25.3 billion.

Among those making their first commitments to hedge funds were the Nashville & Davidson County Metropolitan Benefit Board with a US$15 million mandate, the YMCA

Retirement Fund, which allocated US$100 million to two funds of funds, The Lathers Union Local 68 pension, which allocated US$2 million between two funds of funds and Seattle City Employees Retirement System which allocated to a fund of funds.[10]

A number of other pensions were said to be considering allocating to hedge funds, conducting allocation studies or educating themselves. These included The Florida State Board of Administration in Tallahassee, Teachers' Retirement System of Illinois, California State Teachers' Retirement System, and Blue Cross and Blue Shield Association.[11]

Europe

European institutions initially favoured private equity, and those that took the plunge are now experimenting with hedge funds. Time horizons tend to be one to three years. The pension allocation is currently very small. Switzerland and Holland lead in allocations to hedge funds with considerable interest growing in Sweden.

European hedge fund assets have quadrupled to more than US$60 billion over the past three years. Assets under management of the European hedge fund industry will grow to around €300 billion (US$294 billion) by the end of 2006 from an estimated 38 per cent annual growth, says a study by Oliver, Wyman and UBS Warburg.[12]

The allocation to hedge funds and private equity will be a small 2 per cent allocation of total assets, says pension fund consultant Watson Wyatt. The current allocation is 1 per cent. Depending on pension fund asset growth, investment in alternatives by the respondents could be between US$15–20 billion.[13]

Switzerland

Many of the major Swiss pension funds and insurance companies have an allocation in hedge funds. Examples include Nestlé, Swissair, City of Zurich, Swiss Life, Bloise Holding, Winterthur Leben and Swiss Post.

The big Swiss pension move into hedge funds was the result of an April 2000 amendment to Swiss pension fund law which recognised hedge funds as a separate asset class. The bear market of 2000 and 2001 and volatile stock markets have also been motivators.

Sweden

Swedish pension funds and other institutions have been changing internal regulations that will allow them to invest in hedge funds. The current estimate is that between 2 per cent to 5 per cent will be placed in mainly low volatility strategies. There are 2,300 private Swedish pension funds controlling SK120 billion (US$13 billion), according to the local pension fund association. The 30 largest pension funds have around SK77 billion (US$8 billion). Only a few funds, such as Volvo, are already invested in hedge funds.

Investor AB, the largest industrial holding company in Sweden, invested SK600 million (US$67 million) in a global long-short equity fund in 2002.[14]

Currently most institutions are outsourcing to funds of funds but some are investing directly in single-manager funds. Those with sizable monetary allocations, for example US$150 million and more, are likely to invest directly using their own specialist employees.

Swedish occupational pension arrangements, the Swedish ITP Plan and several Swedish National Pension Funds (AP1, AP2, AP3 and AP4) with US$20 billion are considering allocations.[15]

United Kingdom

Generally the £800 billion UK pension fund industry has been slower than their Dutch, Swiss and Nordic counterparts in allocating to hedge funds. It has been a hard sell to persuade UK hedge funds to even allocate between 2–3 per cent. UK pension fund law and regulations require the trustees of pension funds to obtain impartial advice. The main advisers, notably Watson Wyatt and Frank Russell, provide this service but it is a very small proportion of turnover in comparison to traditional fund advice.

Since many of the UK pensions were hurt by the negative stock market, as equities accounted for such a heavy part of the portfolios, they are now considering other routes including hedge funds.

UK pension funds are switching out of equities but prefer bonds to hedge funds and private equity, according to a Greenwich Associates survey of 390 of the largest private and municipal pension funds in the United Kingdom. Private equity only accounts for 0.9 per cent of total assets of the pension funds surveyed while the hedge fund proportion is only 0.1 per cent. Investment in hedge funds is likely to be slow in the next few years. Nevertheless, the trend toward asset diversification is accompanied by a dramatic increase in the use of specialty managers, including hedge fund managers.[16]

Chiswell, the specialist investment manager, released a study indicating that charitable funds in the United Kingdom are looking toward hedge funds and junk bonds to offset the fall in expected returns. Chiswell is forecasting a drop in long-term total returns of a typical charity portfolio to 7 per cent. The average return was 13.5 per cent between 1984 and 2000. Since charities cannot reinvest their income from dividends and interest, they are legally obligated to spend the money on their causes. There are about 190,000 registered charities in the United Kingdom, of which 10,000 are believed to invest in the stock market. Total assets are estimated at £50 billion.[17]

High-profile UK pension schemes that allocate money to hedge funds are drug company Astra Zeneca and food chain Sainsbury. Seven UK municipalities have been investing between 1–2 per cent of assets in hedge funds. Total portfolios in all assets range from US$400 million to US$3 billion. Their allocations range from 1–3 per cent.

Among those considering hedge funds are the main UK Railways Pension Scheme, South Yorkshire Pension Authority and Carnaud Metal Box (UK), which intends to allocate US$100 million to funds of funds.[18]

Japan

Life insurance companies

Japanese life insurance company interest in hedge funds has remained strong at a time when Japanese regional bank interest may be waning. Life insurance companies remain steadfast investors because of their longer-term view. The seven top Japanese life insurance companies, including Nippon Life and Sumitomo Life, are expected to have a combined total of ¥1.5 trillion (US$1.3 billion) invested in alternative products as of March 2003, up more than 20 per cent from the prior year.[19]

Four of the seven top insurers plan to increase their allocations. For example, Yasuda Mutual Life Insurance Company plans to double its investment to ¥350 billion (US$3 billion) now that it has acquired the expertise to evaluate hedge funds. Nippon Life says that it may increase its investment by up to ¥10 billion (US$89 million) though it does not plan to increase its investment at this time.

Trust banks

Japan's top trust banks report a rapid increase in the amount of client assets going into alternative investments. Mitsubishi Trust & Banking Corp reported ¥70 billion (US$626 million), more than triple the prior year's amount, going into alternative investments through the end of June. Sumitomo Trust & Banking Co. also saw investments triple to ¥58 billion (US$518 million) for the same time period. Both banks reported a sharp increase in hedge fund assets since they began offering such products.[20]

The banks have been increasing the amount of assets in their funds of funds. Many of these funds do not seek a high rate of return but rather strive to attain a set yield. The banks' clients include pension funds.

Regional banks

Regional banks in Japan have become less interested in hedge funds than they had been in prior years, largely due to performance. For example, if a fund of funds is generating 5 per cent returns now, once the investor takes out 3–5 per cent for hedging currency purposes, he is left with about 1.5 per cent, which is on a par with Japanese government bonds.[21]

However, when the investor began allocating to hedge funds makes a difference. Those investors that started in 1999 are generally satisfied. However, those that started later (in 2000 or 2001) have been hurt by performance. A number began investing after April 2001. At that time, legislation changed (bank accounts were no longer guaranteed by the government).

Some sources say regional banks are now becoming more interested in collateralised financial obligations and collateralised debt obligations. Many banks have been impeded by a need for liquidity in their portfolios, while others that are unfamiliar with hedge funds cannot meet regulatory requirements for managing risk.

Corporate pensions

If corporate pensions continue to experience negative return, many analysts expect a growing number of plans to be curtailed or disbanded.

Some pension funds have opted for passive investments linked to equity indices to avoid the risk of falling below their benchmark and to curb management fees. Others have invested in hedge funds in a bid for positive returns to help trim uncovered pension liabilities.

Retail market

Hedge fund investment trusts are growing in popularity in Japan. The number offered in 2002 was about 13 compared with four in 2001. Product size is estimated at ¥110 billion (US$984 million) compared with ¥10 billion (US$89 million) at the end of the previous year. These products traditionally targeted institutional investors due to their complicated nature but interest is growing in the retail sector due to individual investors' needs for steadier returns and the ability of the trusts to go short. Shinsei Bank, Daiwa Securities, Nomura Securities and Nikko Cordial launched unit trusts in 2002. The minimum investment is usually ¥5–10 million (US$40,000–80,000).[22]

Asia/Australia

Investments in hedge funds in Asia were estimated at US$35.6 billion by year-end 2002, reflecting an increase of 40 per cent from year-end 2001.

Hong Kong Jockey Club allocated US$100 million to a fund of funds; Australia's retirement system for Commonwealth employees, CSS/PSS, the second largest pension in the country, allocated A$100 million (US$51 million) to two funds of funds; and HostSuper, the Australian hospitality industry retirement system, allocated A$7 million (US$3.6 million).[23]

Those considering hedge funds include Master Superannuation Fund; The Government Superannuation Office of Victoria; Westscheme in Western Australia; and AV Super, Australia's retirement system for aviation employees.

Conclusion

On the positive side, the industry is broader and deeper than ever. Managers now come from all parts of the globe. Those managers that have survived the rocky early years of the millennium are more seasoned and experienced.

Hedge fund products are becoming more mainstream as investors realise their benefits. Retail products are now available as mutual funds and registered products. This growth however brings the threat of greater regulation.* Institutions worldwide are allocating to hedge funds. As both ends of the spectrum grow, the industry will need to respond to calls for more transparency and risk management.

* *Editor's note:* on 29 September 2003, shortly before this book went to press, the staff of the SEC issued its report entitled 'The Implications of the Growth of Hedge Funds', the culmination of its efforts following the Hedge Fund Roundtable held in May 2003. As of the date of this writing, the Commission itself had not taken any action in response to the report. One of the key recommendations of the staff was that the SEC consider 'requiring hedge fund advisers to register with the SEC as investment advisers, taking into account whether the benefits outweigh the burdens of registration'. In the staff's view, ' … registration of hedge fund advisers would serve as a deterrent to fraud, encourage compliance and the adoption of compliance procedures, provide the SEC with important information … and effectively raise the standards for investment in hedge funds from the "accredited investor" standard to that of "qualified client"'. See http://www.sec.gov/news/studies/hedgefunds0903.pdf for the full text of the report.

1   *Infovest21*, 'Cautiously optimistic outlook for 2003', 6 January 2003.

2   *Infovest21*, 'Study: hedge fund assets on the rise', 5 December 2002.

3   *Infovest21*, 'Closed-end funds still in their infancy', 20 March 2003.

4   *Infovest21*, 'S&P rates Glenwood structured note', 7 June 2002.

5   *Infovest21*, 'S&P rates Glenwood structured note', 7 June 2002.

6   *Infovest21*, 'Investcorp closes structured note deal with $250M', 27 June 2002.

7   *Infovest21*, 'Nacubo: Large endowments increase allocations by 10%', 12 February 2002.

8   *Infovest21*, 'Washington State University invests in Quellos', 17 July 2002; and *Infovest21*, 'Mississippi University enters hedge fund arena', 6 August 2002.

9   *Pensions & Investments*, 'Top 200 funds investing in hedge funds', 22 January 2002.

10 Infovest21, 'Nashville pension ventures into hedge funds', 1 April 2002; *Infovest21*, 'YMCA invests $100M in hedge funds', 24 June 2002; and *Infovest21*, 'Union pension diversified into hedge funds', 21 February 2002.

11 *Infovest21*, 'Florida State considers distressed fund', 18 September 2002; *Infovest21*, 'Illinois Teachers pension to discuss hedge funds', 24 July 2002; *Infovest21*, 'CalSTRS pondering hedge funds', 4 December 2002; and *Infovest21*, 'Blue Cross Blue Shield may seek convertible manager', 23 July 2002.

12 *Infovest21*, '38% annual growth estimated for European hedge fund industry', 10 September 2002.

13 *Infovest21*, 'Watson Wyatt: UK pensions to increase exposure to alternatives', 2 April 2002.

14 *Infovest21*, 'Swedish state pension funds considering hedge funds', 23 September 2002.

15 *Infovest21*, 'Swedish ITP considers hedge funds', 1 February 2002; and *Infovest21*, 'Swedish state pension funds considering hedge funds', 23 September 2002.

16 *Infovest21*, 'Greenwich Associates: UK pension shift into hedge funds is small', 7 November 2002.

[17] *Infovest21*, 'Chiswell: Charities in UK look at hedge funds', 25 March 2002.

[18] *Infovest21*, 'UK Railways Pension considering hedge funds', 27 September 2002; and *Infovest21*, 'Carnaud Pension Fund to allocate $100M to fund of funds', 21 October 2002.

[19] *Infovest21*, 'Top Japanese life insurers to increase hedge fund investment', 26 July 2002.

[20] *Infovest21*, 'Japanese Trust Companies: more customer assets go to alternative assets', 16 August 2002.

[21] *Infovest21*, 'Japanese regional bank interest waning in hedge funds', 11 July 2002.

[22] *Infovest21*, 'Investment trusts gain favor in Japan', 12 December 2002.

[23] *Infovest21*, 'Mesirow and Quellos selected by Hong Kong Jockey Club', 12 April 2002; *Infovest21*, 'Australia pension plan selects Harris and FRM', 4 January 2002; and *Infovest21*, 'Australian pension fund selects Barclays Fund', 13 March 2002.

Appendix A

Sampling of institutions using or considering hedge funds

United States/Canada

AIG
Allegheny County Retirement Board
Ameritech
Arapahoe County Employees
Arkansas Public Employees
Austin Police Retirement Board
Bass
Baxter International
Bell South
Bethlehem Retirement Fund
Blue Cross/Blue Shield
Boston City Retirement System
Boston Home
Boyce Thompson Institute for Plant Research
Bristol County Retirement System
Bristol General Retirement System
Brockton Contributory Retirement System
Caisse de Depot et Placement du Quebec
California Public Employee Retirement System
California Masonic Foundation
California State Teachers
Canada Life Financial Corp
Canadian Broadcasting Corp
Canadian National Railway
Caterpillar Inc
Central Laborers' Pension Fund
Chicago Art Institute
Chicago Firemen's Annuity Benefit Fund
Church Pension Fund (Episcopal)
Cigna Corp
Cincinatti Employees' Retirement System
Colorado Fire & Police Pension
ConAgra Foods
Conseco Corp
Constellation Energy Group
Cook County Employees' Annuity and Benefit
Corning Inc
Crown Cork & Seal
Dana Corp
Deere & Co

Delta Air Lines
Denver Public Schools Retirement System
Dominion Resources
Du Pont
Duluth Teachers Retirement Fund
Eastman Kodak
El Paso Firemen & Police
Eli Lilly
Fairfield Retirement Fund
Federated Department Stores
Florida State Board of Investments
Fort Worth Employees Retirement Fund
General Electric
General Motors
Gillette
Hartford, City of – Municpal Employees Pension
Haverhill Pension
Hearst Corp
Hercules
Hershey Foods
Hewlett Packard
Houston Firefighters' Relief & Retirement
Houston Municipal Employees
Howard Hughes Foundation
IAM National Pension Fund
IBM
Illinois Municipal Retirement Fund
Indiana Public Employees
International Paper
Isplat Inland
ITT Industries
Kern County Employees Retirement Association
Knoxville City Employees Pension Fund
Lathers Union Local 68 Pension
Lincoln Firemen & Policemen
Lockheed Martin Corp
Louisiana Firefighters
Louisiana State Employees Retirement System
Lucent Technologies
Manchester Retirement Allowance Funds
Masco
Marin County Employees Retirement Association
Massachusetts Bay Transportation Authority
Massachusetts Pension Reserve
Massachusetts Port Authority Employees
Massachusetts Public Employees Retirement Association

McKinsey Consulting
Memphis Light, Gas & Water
Merced County Employees Retirement Association
Merck
MetLife
Middlesex Retirement System
Mineworkers Pension Scheme
Minnkota Power Cooperative
Missouri Highway and Transportation
Montreal, City of
Nabisco
Nashville and Davidson County Metropolitan Benefit Board
New Hampshire Retirement System
New Orleans Firemen
New Orleans Retirement System
New York State Common
New York State Nurses Association
New York State Teachers Retirement System
New York Times
Nordson Corp
North Carolina Retirement
Norwalk City Employees
Nova Scotia Teachers
Ohio State Highway Patrol
Oklahoma Firefighters Retirement System
Oklahoma Law Enforcement
Oklahoma Police Pension and Retirement
Ontario Municipal Employees Retirement System
Ontario Teachers' Pension Plan
Pennsylvania State Employees Retirement System
Pentegra Group
Philadelphia Municipal Employees
Philip Morris
Pipe Trades Pension Trust
Plymouth County Retirement System
PNM Resources
Providence Employees
Public School Teachers Pension & Retirement Fund of Chicago
Quaker Chemical Corp
Qwest Communications
RJ Reynolds
San Antonio Police and Fire
San Diego County Employees Retirement Association
San Francisco City and County Retirement System
San Joaquin County Employees
SBC Communications

Seattle City Employees Retirement System
Sisters of Mercy Healthcare System
Skillman Foundation
Sterling Heights General Employees
Target Corp
Tennessee Valley Authority Retirement
Texas, Teacher Retirement System
TJX Co
Tulare County Employees
Tulsa Municipal Employees
UAL
UMWA Health & Retirement Funds
US West
Verizon Communications
Viacom
Virginia Retirement System
Walt Disney Co
Warhol Foundation
Wayne County Employees
Weyerhauser
Winterthur Insurance Company
World Bank
YMCA Retirement Fund

Europe

ABB Invest Foundation
Aegon
Algemeen Burgerlijk Pensionenfonds
AP Fonden 1, 2, 3, 4
APK Pensionstrasse
Astra Zeneca
BasellandSchaftliche Pensionskasse
Berne Teachers Pension Fund
Bloise Holding
BP Amoco
British Coal Staff Superannuation Scheme
Caisse de Depot et Placement du Quebec
Caparo Industries
Carnaud
Centrale Suiker Maatschappaj
Commerzbank
Costain Group
Helvetia Patria
ITP (Sweden)
KLM Pension Fund

Lansforsakringar
Manor
National Pensions Reserve Fund (Ireland)
Nestlé
Pensions Trust
PGGM
Prudential Plc
Sainsbury
Sampo Group
Seventh National Swedish Pension Fund
Shell Pensioenfonds Beheer
Shropshire County
Skandia Liv
South Yorkshire local municipalities
Swiss Air
Swiss Life Insurance Company
UK Railways Pension
Varma-Sampo
VEF
Volvo
Wellcome Trust
Winterthur Leben
Zurich City Workers
Zurich Insurance

Asia/Australia/Japan

Aisin Corp
Av Super
Commonwealth and Public Sector Superannuation (Australia)
Daido Life Insurance Company
East Japan Stationery Sales Pension Fund
Emerging Services Superannuation Scheme
Government Superannuation Office (Australia)
Hachijuni Bank
Health Employees Super Trust, Australia
Hitachi
Hong Kong Jockey Club
Host Plus (Australia)
Host Super (Australia)
Japan Travel Bureau
JGC Corp
KDDI
Master Superannuation Fund (Australia)
Nippon Life
Non-Government Schools' Superannuation Fund (Australia)

Retail Employees Superannuation Trust (Australia)
Retirement Benefits Board (Australia)
Sumitomo Life
Tokio Marine and Fire
Westscheme (Australia)

Appendix B

Important dates in hedge fund history

1949   The first hedge fund is set up by A.W. Jones, a journalist and academic.

1966   An article titled 'The Jones Nobody Keeps Up With' appears in *Fortune* magazine, describing the techniques and successes of A.W. Jones. The number of hedge funds grows in the next few years.

1967   Michael Steinhardt, along with two partners, Harold Berkowitz and Jerry Fine, starts his hedge fund with US$7.5 million.

1968   Assets in A.W. Jones' hedge fund peak at US$220 million.

1969   George Soros forms Quantum Fund with his partner at the time, James Rogers.

Leveraged Capital Holdings and Haussman Holdings, two funds of funds, are launched.

1973   US equity markets enter a two-year bear market.

Although the first hedge fund began in 1949, the first growth spurt did not occur until 1966–69 following Fortune *magazine's article on A.W. Jones. Steinhardt and Soros's original firms began in 1967 and 1969, respectively. However, between 1969 and 1974, the hedge fund industry contracted due to the bear market in stocks.*

1980   Julian Robertson starts Tiger Management with US$8.8 million.

1981   Odyssey Partners is launched by Jack Nash and Leon Levy with US$160 million.

1982   The bull market in US equities begins.

1986   *Institutional Investor's* cover article 'The Red Hot World of Julian Robertson'.

1987   The US stock market crashes in October.

Modern-day hedge fund history begins in the mid to late 1980s, when some of the large hedge fund managers such as Soros Fund Management and Tiger branch out and truly become global macro funds. Institutional Investor's *cover article on Julian Robertson attracted further interest to hedge funds. Hedge fund growth gained stronger momentum after the 1987 stock market crash.*

1989   A.W. Jones dies.

The Japanese market hits an all-time high, and then enters a period of extended decline.

1990   George Soros 'breaks' the Bank of England shorting the pound.

Equity markets tumble as Iraq invades Kuwait.

1992   Leon Cooperman leaves Goldman Sachs Asset Management to start Omega Fund.

'Macro' hedge funds score outstanding gains in emerging markets and European 'carry' trades.

1994   An unexpected rise in short-term rates lowers the value of certain hedge fund bond holdings, resulting in the 'Three David' incident with David Askin, David Weill and David Gerstenhaber, whose high-profile funds close down or suffer major losses.

John Meriwether launches Long Term Capital Management with several others from Salomon Brothers with US$1.25 billion in capital.

Michael Steinhardt of Steinhardt Management, with US$2.6 billion in assets, announces that he will retire at year-end, after 28 years in the business.

1995 Michael Vranos, former mortgage bond 'czar' at Kidder Peabody, starts a new hedge fund with Ziff Brothers Investments.

George Soros of Soros Fund Management sends letters to investors that the Quantum fund family is too large at US$10 billion. Currency, stock indices and bond futures can no longer be accommodated in all the firm's funds. Institutes change in how macro positions of funds are to be managed. Macro positions will first be taken by Quantum and Quantum Industrial Holdings. Allocations to be made only to Quasar and Quantum Emerging if market conditions permit.

Bruce Kovner of Caxton Corp returns significant amount of assets and focuses trading mostly on his own capital. He returned about two-thirds of US$1.8 billion managed.

1996 John Hancock Group, which owns John Hancock Funds, a major mutual fund company, decides to enter the hedge fund business in collaboration with Michael DiCarlo, the head of its equity department.

SEC issues no-action letter that allows hedge funds a way to make offerings to 401K investors without having to register as a mutual fund. The no-action letter addresses concerns raised by Panagora Asset Mgt. In 1995, the SEC had turned down a request from Panagora to market new investment pools to defined contribution plan investors without registering as a mutual fund.

creInvest, the first public investment vehicle structured like a fund of funds in Switzerland is set up as an offshore fund domiciled in the Cayman Islands and listed on the Zurich Exchange. It is launched with SF200 million (US$167 million). Bank Julius Baer is the lead underwriter. Castle Alternative is another Swiss-domiciled public investment vehicle to be set up that is structured like a fund of funds. LGT Non-Traditional Advisors raises SF180 million (US$150 million) for Castle Alternative Invest AG. Banque Syz comes out with Altin, the third publicly traded investment company in Switzerland.

Jeffrey Vinik resigns from Fidelity's Magellan Fund. He sets up Vinik Asset Management and launches two hedge funds, one US and the other offshore. Approximately US$800 million is raised in a short timeframe.

President Clinton signs the National Securities Market Improvement Act of 1996 into law, which becomes effective April 1997. This legislation introduces a new definition – a 'qualified purchaser', ie, a natural person with US$5 million or more of investments. 3(c)7 funds with qualified purchasers can now have more than 99 investors. US managers no longer have to be subject to a 12-month incentive fee if they are a registered investment adviser – all investors are qualified purchasers. Managers can now convert '99 investor funds' from 3(c)1 status to 3(c)7 status to have more than 99 investors.

The Taxpayer Relief Act of 1997 simplifies the application and principal office requirements known as the '10 Commandments'. According to the 10 Commandments, various administrative functions were required to be performed outside the United States to create a safe harbour for non-US investors. The principal office requirement is eliminated as of 31 December 1997.

The 'short-short' rule is repealed under the Taxpayer Relief Act of 1997, effective year-end, opening up the wider use of short selling by mutual funds.

1997 Odyssey Partners with US$3 billion in assets dissolves because it has become too large to easily invest.

SEC releases no-action letter for Internet product regarding hedge fund performance and related information over the Internet. Given to Lamp Technologies for its Hedge Scan Service.

Soros Fund Management reins in allocations it had made to outside managers in Quasar International Fund. Bulk of assets to be managed in-house. Largely managed as a fund of funds since its inception in May 1991.

Long Term Capital Management announces that it will return half of its US$6 billion in capital to investors. Distribution to be paid on 2 January 1998.

Dow falls 6.3 per cent and S&P is down 3.3 per cent for the month. About 75 per cent of the hedge funds in the MAR/Hedge database outperform S&P. About 45 per cent are positive.

1998 Bank Leu and Swiss Investment Co launch Leu Prima Global Fund, a fund of fund, the first hedge fund product registered in Switzerland, and which can be marketed directly to Swiss investors.

Grosvenor Capital Mgt, a US$3 billion fund of funds, sells a 70 per cent interest to Value Asset Management.

Asset Alliance acquires 50 per cent preferred equity and revenue sharing interest in Bricoleur Capital Mgt, as well as in JMG Capital Management and its affiliate Pacific Asset Management, and Metropolitan Capital Managers. Asset Alliance's stable of alternative investment managers now total US$1.3 billion with six managers.

The Russian government defaults and devaluation severely hurts hedge funds involved directly in that market, and indirectly affects funds trading in other emerging markets. Some funds temporarily suspend the calculation of net asset values and redemptions. III's High Risk Opportunity Fund and Dana McGinnis' Russian funds declare bankruptcy.

Long-Term Capital Management declines precipitously and is taken over by a group of 14 banks and brokerage firms. The immediate impact for the hedge fund community is widening of spreads in fixed-income positions, increased margin calls and a credit crunch. Following problems with the Shetland Fund in the mortgage markets earlier in the year, several mortgage arbitrage funds such as Ellington Capital and MKP Capital scramble to meet margin calls, reflecting difficulties in marking prices for illiquid securities.

BankAmerica Corp faces a federal lawsuit alleging the bank misled shareholders about its hedge fund exposure after announcing losses in a joint venture with DE Shaw.

2000 Michael Berger's Manhattan Capital Management is charged with among other things, fraud.

April 2000 amendment to Swiss pension fund law recognised hedge funds as a separate asset class.

California Public Employees Retirement System announces US$1 billion hedge fund programme.

2001   Pequot's Art Samberg and Daniel Benton split. Benton opens Andor in October.

Galleon co-founders – Raj Rajaratnam and Krishen Sud – split. Sud, along with others, set up Argus.

Incubators set up in significant numbers.

Structured notes become very popular.

Funds with lower minimums become more prevalent as major banks and brokerage firms develop product.

Michael Berger ordered to pay a US$20 million judgment against his bankrupt firm, Manhattan Capital Management.

Art Institute of Chicago files lawsuit against Integral Investment Mgt.

2002   Lipper & Co liquidates convertible securities portfolio and returns capital to investors. The funds are eventually deregistered. Other parts of the firm unravel due to redemptions.

Two public hedge fund transactions – Man Glenwood Alternative Strategies and Investcorp's Diversified Strategies collateralized fund obligations – were rated.

SEC begins formal fact-finding investigation to consider investor protection.

Acquisition trend is strong: Gartmore buys stake in Coda; Mellon acquires HBV Capital; BlackRock enters agreement to buy Cyllenius Capital; XL Capital takes stake in OneCapital Management; Brummer & Partners takes stake in Silver Kapital. Man Group acquires RMF, Pioneer acquires Momentum, Threadneedle takes stake in Attica, NIB takes stake in Harcourt Investment Consulting while Petercam Group increases stake in Concerto. Yankee Advisers sells a percentage to Refco while Mercantile Bankshares takes minority interest in Winston Partners. Robeco acquires Sage Capital while Gartmore acquires Riverview International and Neuberger Berman acquires LibertyView.

Beacon Hill informs investors that losses are double those reported. A number of lawsuits ensue.

Many European hedge funds close due to small assets, dismal asset raising environment, inexperience, and flat to negative performance.

Paris court finds George Soros guilty of profiting from insider trading in a 1988 takeover bid for Société Générale. Fined US$2.3 million.

2003   *January*

Eifuku, Tokyo-based long-short fund with assets of US$300 million, to shut down due to market volatility, prolonged Japanese bear market and poor performance.

Barton Biggs, chief global strategist at Morgan Stanley, announced that he will retire later in the year and take the helm at Traxis Partners – a new hedge fund.

SAC trader Michael Zimmerman and Lehman analyst Holly Becker have been formally notified by regulators that they may be facing enforcement action over possible insider trading. The two are husband and wife.

William von Mueffling leaving Lazard. He ran two very successful European hedge funds.

Kern County Employees Retirement Association announces a 3 per cent allocation to hedge funds.

February

AP Fonden 1, the Swedish National Pension Fund, announces its intent to invest 3 per cent (US$412 million) in alternatives.

A group representing one-fourth of investors who had invested about US$100 million in Michael Berger's Manhattan Fund accept a settlement of 10-15 cents on the dollar from the fund's auditor.

March

University of Texas Investment Management allocates US$175 million to Protégé Partners, their first investment in a fund of funds.

International Paper hires UBS O'Conner and Ramius Capital.

April

NASD censured and fined Altegris Investments of LaJolla for failure to disclose risks associated with hedge funds when marketing to investors. This was NASD's first enforcement action focusing on hedge funds.

Lancer files for Chapter 11 bankruptcy protection in a dispute over how the holdings are valued.

BlackRock agrees to acquire majority interest in HPB Management, a fund founded by Howard Berkowitz.

Man Group has record launch with US$725 million raised for Man Multi-Strategy Series 5. The prior record had been US$670 million for Man IP 220 Series 4 in October 2002.

The National Association of College and University Business Officers survey is released. Alfred University, Suny-Stony Brook, Yeshiva and University of Virginia have over 50 per cent of their portfolio in hedge funds. 266 endowments allocate to hedge funds in 2002. Average allocation is 5.1 per cent compared with 2.9 per cent in 2001.

May

The SEC holds a two-day Hedge Fund Roundtable. Topics discussed include marketing and distribution of hedge funds; disclosure, transparency and performance fees; valuation, allocation and use of commissions; strategies and market participants; enforcement/ fraud concerns; and assessment of current regulatory framework.

Morgan Stanley files petition to have Lauer removed as manager of the Lancer funds.

June

BNP Paribas and Zurich Financial Services sign a letter of intent regarding the transfer of certain structured products from Zurich Capital Management to BNP Paribas.

Philadelphia Public Employees Retirement System approves 5 per cent allocation for the US$3.8 billion plan to hedge funds.

Virginia Retirement System selects Ivy Asset Management as its adviser. Will allocate up to 3 per cent or US$1 billion of its US$35 billion plan.

July

The SEC alleges Lauer and Lancer with fraud.

Allegheny County Retirement allocates to JPMorgan Fleming fund of funds.

Nova Scotia Public Services Superannuation and Teachers Pension Fund allocates to long-short equity fund.

University of Montreal sues Lancer Group as they failed to return C$100 million of the plan's money.

Integrated Asset Management acquires Appleton International, a fund of funds, from PSG Investment Services for US$2.5 million.

August

Virginia Retirement System approves an additional hedge fund allocation of 3 per cent.

Bruce Cowen pleads guilty in US District Court in Miami to charges linked to the Lancer fund.

CSFB/Tremont investable hedge fund indices launched.

Fitch rates Man Glenwood Alternative Strategies II, a collateralised fund obligation.

Health Employees SuperTrust Australia make first allocation to fund of funds through Financial Risk Management and Quellos.

September

New York Attorney General Elliot Spitzer announces US$40 million settlement with Edward Stern's Canary Capital Partners regarding market timing and late trading of mutual funds.

Man Group assets exceed US$30 billion.

The staff at the SEC releases its report on the hedge fund industry. Recommendations include that managers register as investment advisers. Recommendations are to be considered by SEC commissioners.

UBS buys ABN Amro US prime brokerage business for US$250 million in cash.

CaLPERS selects Pacific Alternative Asset Mgt, UBS O'Connor and Financial Risk Management to replace Blackstone in managing the pension's US$1 billion in hedge fund assets.

Skandia Liv allocates US$250 million to hedge funds.

Massachusetts Pension Reserves Investment Mgt Board deciding who will manage US$1.4 billion in assets to be allocated to hedge funds.

Theodore Sihpol III, former registered representative at Banc of America Securities, charged with fraud for his alleged role in mutual fund trading.

Texas A&M endowment increases allocation to fund of funds managed by Quellos Capital Management.

Oklahoma Police Pension & Retirement System select Grosvenor to run US$70 million fund of funds.

University of Montreal pension plan writes off US$100 million investment in Lancer offshore fund.

October

A number of fund management firms receive subpoenas as the late trading and market timing probe of mutual funds widens.

Steve Markovitz, former portfolio manager at Millennium Partners, pleads guilty to securities fraud related to the late trading of mutual funds.

Chapter 6

Lessons learned from investing in hedge funds over the years

Jonathan P. Bren
Hunt Financial Ventures, New York, New York

Introduction

Mistakes? What mistakes? This is easy. Take a track record of a manager, stuff it into a proforma spread sheet, compare it to the record of other managers, make sure the correlation is low, then raise a bunch of money for this 'perfect' portfolio. Seems easy. A chimp could do it.

Well, it is not so easy and over the past 14 years I have made several mistakes and learned many lessons. Hopefully some of these lessons learned can help other allocators avoid the mistakes I made.

Past performance

The first criteria that most allocators use to evaluate a manager is track record. If the manager has performed well and the track record proves it, then most allocators will proceed with other parts of the due diligence process and then try to allocate to this manager. However, just because a manager has performed well does not mean that the manager will perform well going forward. I hate to admit it, but the lawyers are right when they include that standard disclaimer that 'past performance is not indicative of future performance'. I have seen too many allocators fall in love with a good performance track record and then overlook other due diligence issues to justify the positive conclusion that they have already arrived at in their minds.

The first thing I learned is to evaluate whether the manager was really adding value, or whether it was just a great time for his type of strategy. I always ask the manager, have you been swimming with the tide, or have you been swimming upstream? I saw too many fixed-income managers and arbitrage managers produce great numbers in the period from 1991–93. However, when the Federal Reserve increased interest rates and inverted the short end of the yield curve, many of these so called stars really suffered and in some cases went out of business. Looking back on the mistakes that were made, it seems so obvious how to avoid them. However, many of us get caught up in the glow of the good performance and cannot think of taking the chips off the table and moving on. It is always tempting for allocators to think that the positive performance will just continue. Adding to this bias to wait until the end, is the pressure to appease the end client invested in the fund of funds or the portfolio built for the end client.

The next thing to do is avoid feeling guilty about passing on a manager that performs well for all the wrong reasons. I felt pressure from clients for years because I decided to pass on investing with Long-Term Capital Management (LTCM) back in early 1995, thereby missing out on three years of extraordinary numbers. Since I missed the boat, several clients took some money away from me to invest with a fund of funds that would give them exposure to LTCM. Now it is easy to look back and say that I knew LTCM would fail, but that is not the case. I had no vision of a catastrophic failure that would shake the entire industry, but I knew the manager did not fit the fund I was managing. Having LTCM in my portfolio would have helped sell it, but letting client pressure force me to include a popular but inappropriate manager ultimately would have proved to be a very costly compromise.

The hard part of this lesson is that if you are early on your judgement and the manager continues to perform well, you begin to second guess your analysis and assessment. There's nothing worse than saying to a client or colleague, 'I am really concerned about the strategy and the manager's approach', then your client says, 'You have been saying that for a year and look at the track record'. This happened with several emerging market debt managers in 1997 up to August 1998 and also with several growth and momentum managers in late 1999 and early 2000. I remember asking a manager how he was selecting stocks and he told me that he let the market tell him which stock to buy by looking at the chart. If the chart was going up, it would continue going up until it stopped going up. Interesting logic, but not for me. So I passed on the manager in 1998 and watched him make a ton of money in 1999 and early 2000. A client friend of mine chastised me for missing the boat (again). The manager even told me that this was a new era for investing and that growth multiples were going to increase even from their historically high levels because the market and the economy were in a new 'paradigm'. I must have heard 'new paradigm' about 200 times. Well, that manager is now out of the hedge fund business and is acting as a consultant to franchise businesses on how to expand their base.

There are two important lessons about past performance. First, determine whether the manager really added value or was simply riding a wave. Second, do not be tempted to select a manager only on the basis of good performance in order to appease your clients or sense of greed.

This leads me to the next mistake I used to make. I never met a pro-forma I did not like. The problem with using pro-forma manager returns to structure a portfolio is that past market history is not going to repeat itself. Since markets do not run in uniform cycles, managers are not going to follow the same track as their pro-forma profile of past performance. Many of the managers that performed well for years in the late 1980s and the early 1990s have not performed as well since. Many from that period do not even exist any longer.

Adaptability

The best money managers are the ones that have shown that they can adapt to changing market conditions. Even when the current environment looks good for a specific strategy, the successful managers realise that this will not last forever and thus prepare for transition to a better strategy or approach. There is no reason that this concept cannot be utilised by the fund of funds allocator. To be a successful allocator, one will have to take a view on markets and strategies. There are good times and bad times for credit cycles, liquidity cycles and premium/multiple cycles. It was interesting to see how many fund of funds managers decided that it would be a good idea to start a technology-only fund of funds in early 2000. Of course the pro-forma looked great but the actual results were terrible. After 1998 no one wanted to invest in convertible arbitrage or any strategy that did not have perfect transparency or was not easy to understand. Of course, this was the perfect time to invest in these types of strategies.

The fund of funds managers and allocators who have performed well have had one thing in common. They have all been forward-looking and willing to adapt to changing market conditions. Now this sounds easy, but it requires the allocator to actually take a view, rather than following the easier and safer approach of just using a pro-forma of established managers. In June 1998, if one produced the perfect pro-forma with established managers that were not correlated, that pro-forma allocation would have suffered considerably in the second half of 1998 when the markets fell in the LTCM debacle. So allocators should take a view and be ready to reallocate to hedge fund sectors and strategies, knowing that they may be second guessed by investors.

Newer managers

If relying on past performance is so problematic, how does one review and evaluate newer managers with short track records? To complicate the picture, there is a big difference between managers who were involved in the portfolio process at a hedge fund or proprietary trading desk and managers who are new to the hedge fund management process.

Let's start with the easier of the two. Managers with no history of trading a hedge fund portfolio need time to prove themselves. Investors should wait to see how well the candidate can manage an absolute return portfolio. The newer managers that do have hedge fund portfolio management experience may be good at trading a portfolio, but terrible at managing a business. I have known some very successful proprietary traders who left their five feet of trading desk in lower Manhattan where everything was done for them, including their dry cleaning, and decided to start their own hedge fund in Greenwich, Connecticut, only to break down in tears when the Federal Express guy showed up and they did not know how to fill out the waybill. Managing an independent hedge fund takes so much more effort and skill than just running a portfolio at a bank or other established hedge fund. First, a good portfolio manager cannot manage the portfolio as well as before if he/she is also worrying about running the business. Operations, clearing, marketing and client service are all distractions for a portfolio manager and they cannot all be done successfully at the same time. Thus, building a management team that can provide the support in these non-portfolio management areas is paramount.

A further problem is that too many smart portfolio managers do not understand how the hedge fund business works. If a manager wants to raise assets and build a business, then he will have to play by the rules of the allocator community. Unless, the new manager is a well-known name coming from a well-known absolute return firm with a somewhat identifiable track record, then the manager will have to fit into the boxes created by the allocator community. The hardest thing for a new manager to accept is having to live in the world of monthly returns. Most new managers do not realise how sensitive most investors are to monthly returns with significant volatility. I have seen several managers who would not cut exposure, reduce risk and try to build a respectable monthly return profile and then be surprised that they could not raise any money. What concerns me more is when the newer manager raises assets during a good time for his strategy and then suffers redemptions after a period of bad performance. If the fast money leaves and other investors remain, the risk is that the manager tries to make the money back quickly to regain his 'high water mark' and get back to earning a performance fee. If market conditions dictate keeping a low-risk profile, the manager may get impatient and keep a higher-risk profile than is prudent. I have heard managers say to me that if they do not get back above their high water mark and earn

81

performance fees, then they may lose key support staff because they will not be able to pay them enough of a bonus to retain them.

Financing

Even when you think your manager has a solid trading approach and risk management process, one of the most important factors to evaluate is where the manager gets his financing from. If the manager does not employ any type of leverage or financing from his prime broker, then it is not much of a concern. However, for any type of fixed-income arbitrage or equity arbitrage strategy which requires the use of a balance sheet, the allocator better be sure how the various credit lines are set up.

When times are good, Wall Street will provide financing for almost everything. You want to finance your dog and then lease it back and derive a tax benefit at the same time? Wall Street will come up with some programme to achieve this. In 1994 and 1998, Wall Street was extending credit to almost anyone who wanted it. In 1994, when the Federal Reserve raised interest rates, many arbitrage trades inverted and suddenly had to be taken off. The managers lost a lot of money trying to liquidate but the lenders were in pretty good shape. However, in 1998, so much more leverage was extended than in 1994, as Wall Street competed fiercely to lend and trade with several hedge funds that looked more like bank proprietary trading desks leveraged 50 to one. The problem was that once the Russian default hit the markets in August 1998, liquidity evaporated and many of the financing sources themselves became extended. The equity underneath many of these hedge funds was wiped out or reduced to very little because the debt outstanding on many balance sheets was enormous. In 1998, many of the lenders panicked and scrambled to call in their lines first to beat the rush to the door. Lenders wanted to beat out the other lenders to try and recover whatever was left. Suddenly Wall Street was no longer the friend of the hedge fund and became the enemy in one quick turn. Lending sources were cut off and suddenly the highly leveraged funds were forced to sell to meet the new margin and lending limits.

Several hedge funds could have survived in the autumn of 1998 but their lenders pulled their credit lines and forced them to take even larger realised losses than necessary. It was like being a deep sea diver walking on the bottom of the ocean when suddenly there is a storm on the surface and the boat with all the air hoses attached decides to shut off your air and leave for safer harbours. The diver is stuck racing to the top before the air runs out, not taking into account the negative effects of racing to the surface too quickly. Several hedge fund managers did not make it to the top in time and the few who did suffered serious after-effects from selling precipitously. Since 1998, several of the large arbitrage firms have set up their own financing sources but most cannot and thus have to rely on the Street for their survival. All allocators should check with the manager to see what type of financing sources and credit lines are in place and determine how easily they can be taken away because when the sea gets rough, you know the lender will run for a safe harbour to ride out the storm and the lender does not care whether the manager is under water or needs his help more than ever.

Performance potential

Finally, the point in the lifecycle of a manager and the firm he has built, comes into play for future allocations. Past performance may be great but the question that remains is whether the manager can continue to perform as expected. Ego matters. Sometimes a manager can get very complacent when assets under management become large and seem secure, or he may decide to reduce risk in the portfolio in order to prevent redemptions in the near term. Some managers believe that since they have done well in the past, they will continue to do well even if market conditions change. I have seen too many managers who believe they are smarter than the market.

It is even worse when I hear allocators say, 'Look at the record. You can't argue with that. He must know what he is doing and who are we to question him?'. This drives me crazy. I saw this with short sellers in early 1991, fixed-income arbitrage managers in 1994, and the worst offenders were some long-short equity managers in 2001. All of them had great numbers and they went off a cliff when their discipline fell out of favour.

I look for managers who are hungry to succeed, not because they are arrogant but because they are highly motivated. This is a fine line to walk. Back in early 1995, I was invested with a global macro manager whose performance suffered in 1994, but he was worth a fortune personally. We decided to press our bet with this manager in early 1995 because we had the impression that his ego was big enough that he wanted to have a successful track record for the next several years and he did not want to slip out of the business with just US$1 billion in his pocket. Hunger to build a track record that investors remember you by is what I look for in a manager. This is more important than greed. Greed can make a manager do stupid things, especially when they are down and they see assets flowing out of the fund. The hardest part of the decision process is to allocate to or stick with a manager when the manager is experiencing a drawdown, or the strategy is out of favour and you do not know how the manager will react. Rare is the manager who can maintain a strong ego without becoming overconfident, but if you work hard to understand them, you will find them.

Part II

Evaluating opportunities – managers' strategies

Chapter 7

Adding alpha in merger arbitrage

John Paulson
Paulson & Co., Inc, New York, New York

Overview

Merger arbitrage is one of the oldest hedge fund strategies and has produced attractive returns for decades. The durability of the strategy is in its ability to generate positive returns over the long term irrespective of market direction. As shown in Exhibit 7.1 and Exhibit 7.2, over the past 10 years the Hennessee Merger Arbitrage Index has outperformed both the Standard & Poor's (S&P) 500 and the Hennessee Hedge Fund Index and delivered returns with low correlation and low volatility.

Merger arbitrage

In its most basic form, merger arbitrage captures the spreads in mergers involving public companies after terms have been announced. The spread is the discount between the offer price and the trading price. The target stock trades at a discount to the offer price to account for the risk of the transaction not closing, as well as for the time value of money. In its sim-

Exhibit 7.1

Merger arbitrage: 10-year performance, 1993–2003

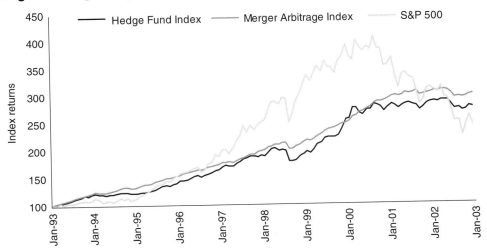

Source: Altvest using Hennessee Merger and Hedge Fund Indices.

Exhibit 7.2

10-year performance and correlations, 1 January 1993–31 December 2002

	Compound annual return (%)	*Standard deviation (%)*	R^2
Merger Arbitrage	11.6	3.8	0.26
Hedge Fund Index	10.7	7.2	0.45
S&P 500	9.3	15.5	1.00

Source: Altvest using Hennessee Merger and Hedge Fund Indices.

plest form, in a cash deal, one would merely purchase the stock of the target and tender it for the offer price at closing. In a fixed exchange ratio stock merger, one would go long the target stock and short the acquirer's stock according to the merger ratio in order to lock in the spread. The annualised return is the gross spread adjusted for the time it takes to close the transaction.

A unique aspect of the strategy is its ability to earn attractive returns that are not dependent on the market's direction. Shell's all-cash acquisition of Pennzoil announced in June 2001 illustrates this relationship.[1] Although the market declined as much as 30 per cent over the merger period (from 26 March 2002 to 2 October 2002), Pennzoil stock appreciated almost in a straight line, producing a steady return from deal announcement to closing, as illustrated in Exhibit 7.3.

Merger arbitrage becomes more complicated when the terms of the transaction become more complex. In addition to all-cash or all-stock deals, there are deals in which both cash and stock are offered; deals with stock collars in which the number of shares offered to target shareholders varies with the acquirer's stock price; stock deals subject to fixed or unknown pricing periods; stock deals with 'floors', 'caps' or 'walkaways'; as well as deals with other forms of consideration such as debt securities, new equity and contingent value rights. All of these features will have an effect on the spread, the profitability and the riskiness of investing in a merger transaction.

Once the mechanics of the deal are ascertained, the merger arbitrage manager must assess the risks and the probability of the deal closing. The success of a manager will depend on his ability to accurately analyse deal risk across hundreds of announced deals. To be successful requires very specialised skills unique to the arbitrageur. One must be an expert in evaluating the financing, legal, regulatory, accounting, market and business issues that may affect a deal's outcome. To properly evaluate these risks, the arbitrageur must have expertise in analysing merger agreements, financing agreements, strategic issues and financial statements, as well as federal, state and local regulatory issues. Failure to understand any of the many risks affecting a transaction could lead a manager to incorrectly estimate the probability of completion and to construct a sub-optimal portfolio.

Not a game for the inexperienced

While the strategy, when properly executed, can produce non-correlated, low-volatility returns, any individual deal may carry substantial risk. That is because the upside in a transaction is very small compared to the potential downside. While the annualised return may be

Exhibit 7.3

Shell/Pennzoil cash acquisition, 2002

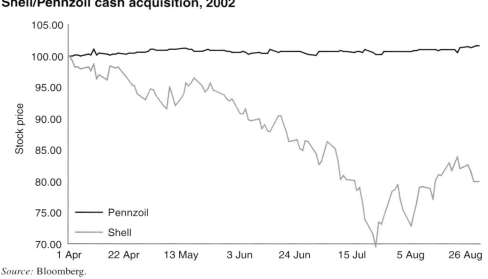

Source: Bloomberg.

high, the absolute return is small, and the downside can be 10 times, 20 times or even 30 times the amount of the potential gain. To avoid the risk of a deal breaking, most investors prefer to sell their stock after an offer has been announced to lock in the merger premium. While the investor may be better off selling on a deal announcement, the arbitrageur is uniquely qualified to assume the risk of deal completion in return for the remaining spread.

Adding alpha in merger arbitrage

While all merger arbitrageurs choose from the same universe of deals, each manager will structure his portfolio differently, choosing different deals in which to invest and allocating different weightings to each deal. As such, the performance of arbitrageurs will vary. In 2002, for example, using the Altvest database of 16 merger arbitrage managers who manage in excess of US$200 million, performance ranged from a negative 9.8 per cent to a positive 5.4 per cent. Over a three-year period, cumulative performance ranged from a positive 4.5 per cent to a positive 40 per cent, with one group of managers consistently occupying four of the top five positions and another group four of the five bottom positions. Clearly, while all managers are operating in the same space, not everyone is equal in the management of their portfolios.

A common approach to managing a merger arbitrage portfolio is to diversify a portfolio across a broad range of small positions. By minimising position sizes, the manager can protect himself from significant drawdowns in the event of an adverse deal outcome. This broadly diversified approach, however, should lead to no better than average returns. By diversifying across a wide base, such a portfolio will underweight higher return deals as well as include lower quality deals, causing overall returns to revert to the mean.

To do better than average, the arbitrageur must actively manage the portfolio and eliminate the higher risk, lower quality deals and assign larger weightings to deals with higher return profiles. To do so, however, an arbitrage manager must have broad-based skills to accurately analyse merger risks and estimate the probabilities of a deal's outcome. He can then construct a portfolio that minimises deal breakage while maximising exposure to higher return deals. If one is adept at evaluating the risk/return tradeoffs, this approach will lead to outperformance, both higher returns and lower risk. However, if a less capable manager attempts this more active strategy and incorrectly judges the risk/return tradeoffs, the result could be more volatility and below average performance.

While there are many good arbitrage managers, our particular strategy to manage the portfolio for outperformance is comprised of five basic principles:

- avoid deals that may break;
- optimise returns from the spread portfolio;
- weight the portfolio to possible competitive bid situations;
- focus on deals with unique structures that offer higher returns; and
- selectively short the weaker transactions.

Avoid riskier deals

Key to maximising performance is minimising exposure to deals that break. The downside relative to the upside is so great that one bad deal can consume the profits of numerous good ones. One must be able to anticipate which deals have a greater risk of non-completion and exclude those deals from the portfolio. The fewer broken deals one has in the portfolio, the greater the relative performance. The common characteristics of deals that break are poor earnings, an inability to consummate financing and/or regulatory obstacles. By eliminating deals that exhibit these characteristics, one can reduce the incidence of deal breakage.

Optimise spread portfolio

After excluding deals with higher risk, one must optimise the returns from the spread portfolio. Variables that can influence the performance in this category include the selection of deals, the relative weighting of positions, and the timing for entering and exiting the transaction. Portfolio construction in this area will be based on analysis of all the factors that affect a deal's outcome.

Overweight for topping bids

Key to adding alpha is overweighting the portfolio to those deals that have higher potential returns. The best example of higher return deals is an announced deal that receives a topping bid. Topping bids cause sharp spikes in the target prices and high annualised returns. Obviously, the bigger the weighting to such a deal, the greater the impact on overall performance. In the case of Quintiles, for example, Pharma Services bumped its offer by 28 per cent to US$14.50 from US$11.25, resulting in sharp gains in Quintiles' stock price after the deal was initially announced, as illustrated in Exhibit 7.4.[2]

The ability to consistently anticipate topping bids and overweight the portfolio to those deals will lead to consistent outperformance. Generally, the characteristics that lead to a higher bid include: a low relative valuation, an attractive target, an industry experiencing consolidation, no lock-ups and the company not having been shopped prior to deal announcement.

Exhibit 7.4

Effect of Pharma Services topping bid for Quintiles, 2003

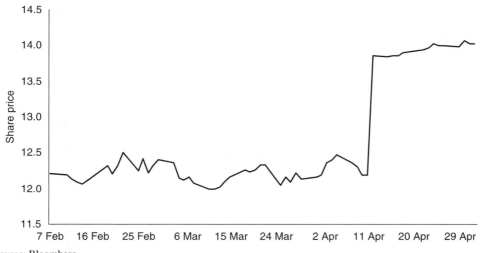

Source: Bloomberg.

Focus on deal structure

Other types of deals that offer high potential returns include cash/stock alternatives, stock collars and those deals with unusual structures. In a stock collar, the acquirer increases the number of shares offered to target shareholders if the acquirer's stock falls, in order to fix a dollar value to a deal. By setting up the spread at the upper end of the collar, one can earn above average returns if the acquirer's stock falls while still earning a positive return if the stock rises. In addition to offering higher potential returns, stock collars provide a hedge against a market downturn as the returns increase as the market falls.

Stock collars

There are numerous examples of collars, but one of the best ones we have seen was Nextlink's acquisition of Concentric.[3] In this transaction, Nextlink agreed to acquire Concentric for US$45 per share with the actual share ratio based on a collar from US$63–91. In the stock market craze of 2000, Nextlink ran from US$75 when the deal was announced in January 2000 to as high as US$123 in March 2000. We aggressively set up the spread when Nextlink traded above the collar, realising an attractive return from the positive spread. We also knew that we had tremendous additional upside if Nextlink ever fell below the upper end of the collar. In March 2000, the Nasdaq began to decline fiercely and Nextlink stock fell straight through the collar. As it fell, the returns from this transaction mushroomed, contributing over 80 basis points to our performance in April 2002, a month in which the market as a whole collapsed (see Exhibit 7.5).

Cash/stock

Cash/stock alternatives almost always offer the possibility of additional returns by maximising the allocation of the higher value alternative. The most attractive deals are those that offer

91

Exhibit 7.5

Stock collar profit matrix

Nextlink price (US$)	Merger ratio (US$)	Concentric value (US$)	Gain on Concentric (US$)	Gain/loss Nextlink (US$)	Profit (US$)	Annual return (%)
115.00	0.495	56.93	4.30	(2.97)	1.33	12.6
109.00	0.495	53.96	1.33	0.00	1.33	12.6
90.91	0.495	45.00	(7.63)	8.96	1.33	12.6
80.07	0.562	45.00	(7.63)	14.32	6.69	55.2
69.23	0.65	45.00	(7.63)	19.69	12.06	98.0
63.00	0.65	40.95	(11.68)	22.77	11.09	90.2

Note: As indicated by the table above, the profit per share increases from US$1.33 to as high as US$12.06 as Nextlink stock falls through the collar, producing annualised rates of return as high as 98 per cent.
Source: Paulson & Co., Inc.

cash or stock with no limitation on the amount of cash or stock elected. This structure provides the ability to create a free put or a call on the acquirer stock, which can lead to considerable returns depending on the volatility of the acquirer stock. HSBC's US$10 billion acquisition of Credit Commerciale de France (CCF) announced in April 2000 was such an all-cash or all-stock deal.[4] HSBC offered either € 150 in cash or 13 shares of HSBC for each share of CCF, which at the time of the deal's announcement were worth approximately € 150. If a manager just went long CCF at € 151, he would earn the full appreciation in HSBC stock if it went up, but would not lose if it went down as he could always elect the € 150 in cash. If on the other hand, the manager went long CCF and shorted 13 shares of HSBC per CCF share, he would make money if HSBC went down but would not lose if HSBC went up as he could elect stock to cover the short. Or, alternatively, the manager could short any percentage of the merger ratio to create varying levels of profit regardless of the direction HSBC moved. Exhibit 7.6 summarises the profit matrix.

Another way to augment returns is to focus on parts of the capital structure in a merger which may offer higher returns than the common stock. As part of HSBC's stock acquisition of Household International, announced in October 2002, HSBC also agreed to redeem Household's preferred stock at par plus accrued dividends.[5] Most arbitrageurs focused on the common stock and the preferred only traded up 10 points after the announcement, from US$50 to US$60, even though the redemption price was US$102. We bought the preferred at US$60 and continued buying all the way up to US$94, which equated to parity with the return from the common stock. At an average cost of US$75, we were able to earn 4.1× the return from the preferred stock relative to the common stock, even though the deal risk was the same (see Exhibit 7.7).

Selectively short weaker transactions

Another way to earn above average results is to short a transaction. By doing so, the arbitrageur makes money if a deal breaks and loses money if a deal closes. Generally, since spreads are tight and premiums are big, the loss is small if the deal closes relative to the gain

Exhibit 7.6

Annualised rate of return per CCF share (%)

Per cent short	0.0%	20.0%	40.0%	60.0%	80.0%	100.0%
Shares short	0.0	2.6	5.2	7.8	10.4	13.0
HSBC price (€)						
10.0	259.7	208.2	156.6	105.0	53.4	1.8
9.5	216.8	173.8	130.8	87.8	44.8	1.8
9.0	173.8	139.4	105.0	70.6	36.2	1.8
8.5	130.8	105.0	79.2	53.4	27.6	1.8
8.0	87.8	70.6	53.4	36.2	19.0	1.8
7.5	44.8	36.2	27.6	19.0	10.4	1.8
7.0	1.8	1.8	1.8	1.8	1.8	1.8
6.5	−6.7	1.9	10.5	19.1	27.7	36.3
6.0	−6.7	10.5	27.7	44.9	62.1	79.3
5.5	−6.7	19.1	44.9	70.7	96.4	122.2
5.0	−6.7	27.7	62.1	96.4	130.8	165.2
4.5	−6.7	36.3	79.3	122.2	165.2	208.2

Note: The table above computes the annualised returns from buying one share of CCF and shorting various amounts of HSBC ranging from 0 to 13 shares.

Source: Paulson & Co., Inc.

Exhibit 7.7

Household/HSBC merger: returns from arbitraging different parts of the capital structure

	Household preferred	Household common	Multiple
Acquisition value (US$)	102.00	30.90	−
Cost (US$)	75.00	28.40	−
Spread (US$)	27.00	2.50	−
Gross spread (%)	36.00	8.80	4.1×
Days to close	130	130	−
Annualised spread (%)	101.10	24.70	4.1×

Source: Paulson & Co., Inc.

if the transaction breaks. Since most deals close, picking the right deal to short is tricky and requires a fair amount of discipline. Generally, we look for poorly performing targets, weak acquirers, conditional merger agreements and financing contingencies.

We found all these attributes in Veritas' proposed acquisition of PGO Services announced in November 2001. While both companies were enthusiastic about synergies to be realised by merging their seismic operations, there were numerous problems with the merger. PGO had so much debt, US$2.6 billion, that it dwarfed the US$500 million market capitalisation of Veritas. Furthermore, PGO's earnings were declining and the merger was contingent on: 1) the sale of a highly speculative offshore oil prospect for US$250 million, 2) the maintenance of certain credit ratings, and 3) the ability to refinance certain debt. We shorted the deal soon after it was announced at an average spread of 15 cents. Ultimately, PGO's financial problems were so great that Veritas was forced to call off the merger, causing PGO's stock to plummet and Veritas' stock to rise. The spread blew out to US$6, causing a return approximately 40 times the money we had at risk. While the position was only 3.5 per cent of our portfolio, it accounted for approximately 25 per cent of our gains for 2002.

Just when you thought you understood arbitrage

While deals breaking can be an arbitrageur's greatest nightmare, some of our biggest gains have been in broken deals in which we were long. This happy set of circumstances can occur in a stock deal in which the stock of the acquirer, which the arbitrageur is short, implodes. In this situation, the acquirer typically runs into some type of problem that causes its stock to fall dramatically. If the acquirer's stock falls to a level which causes the target, whose stock is tied to that of the acquirer by the merger ratio, to fall to its pre-deal level, the target stock may disengage itself from that of the acquirer and stop falling. If the acquirer falls further, this will cause the spread to go negative, producing outsized gains for the arbitrageur.

One of the best examples of this situation is in Tyco's acquisition of CR Bard Inc (Bard), a highly profitable disposable medical products manufacturer, announced in May 2001.[6] Tyco originally agreed to acquire Bard for US$60 per share, a US$20 premium to its pre-announcement market price. However, in January 2002, as the deal drew near to closing, Tyco began to experience its well-publicised problems. This caused Tyco to drop from US$57.25 per share on 2 January 2002 to as low as US$23.10 per share on 5 February 2002. While Bard initially fell along with Tyco, once Bard reached US$50 it stopped falling. As Tyco fell further, the spread widened to US$20 causing outsized profits as shown in Exhibit 7.8.

Exhibit 7.8

Profiting from broken deals: Tyco's bid for Bard

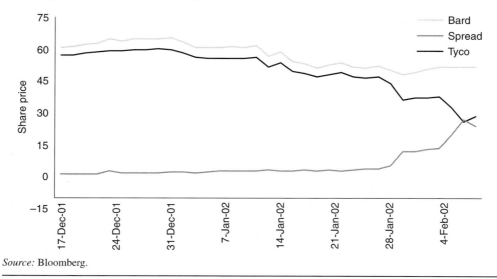

Source: Bloomberg.

Eventually, both companies called off the deal as Bard's shareholders would not approve the value implied by the merger ratio.

Globalisation

One of the major changes in arbitrage over the past decade has been the globalisation of the merger business. Companies compete globally and increasingly look at world market share rather than regional or national share. As an increasing percentage of deals transcend national borders today, merger arbitrageurs must be able to operate globally. Among numerous examples of cross-border activity are Procter & Gamble's acquisition of Wella AG of Germany to increase its share of the world hair care market, HSBC's acquisition of Household International to increase its exposure to US consumer finance, Nestlé's proposed acquisition of Dreyers to strengthen its ice cream market share and General Electric's proposed acquisition of Instrumentarium to increase its world share in medical monitoring equipment. Even deals between two domestic competitors will frequently involve cross-border issues. The best known example would be the proposed merger between General Electric and Honeywell, two US companies which received US anti-trust approval, only to be subsequently blocked by European regulators.[7]

While the globalisation of mergers has opened new opportunities for arbitrageurs, it has also provided new challenges. The successful manager must now be fully versed with corporate law across many countries and must become adept at trading in different markets and currencies. However, arbitrageurs are used to dealing with complicated issues. For example, understanding the legal framework for mergers in foreign countries is really no different than understanding the multitude of state laws in the United States. Corporations are organised in the United States under state law, not federal, and we must understand the different laws in numerous states, including Delaware, New York, Florida, Michigan, Ohio and others.

Merger bankruptcy

Another emerging area is in the acquisitions of bankrupt companies. As the level of bankruptcies reached historic highs in 2002–03, M&A activity in this context increased as well. Examples include US Steel's purchase of National Steel for US$1.1 billion completed in May 2003,[8] ST Telemedia's proposed US$240 million purchase of Global Crossing announced in May 2003,[9] and Berkshire Hathaway's US$570 million bid for Burlington Industries announced in February 2003.[10] Completion of these deals includes many of the same issues involved in stock mergers, such as regulatory approvals and financing.

There has been some controversy among investors whether participating in the reorganisation of bankrupt companies is appropriate for merger arbitrage managers. It is clear to us that the acquisition of a bankrupt company pursuant to an announced offer is an appropriate form of merger arbitrage. However, as distinct from distressed investing, the merger overlap will only occur *after an announced offer has been made*. In this case, the transactions can be set up as a spread, similar to a stock merger, in which the bonds purchased will be exchanged pursuant to defined terms for a package of cash, debt and/or equity securities. The spread is the difference between the value of the consideration received versus the price paid for the bonds. The similarities to a stock merger are many and include the defined consideration, the filing of an offer document, the need for a vote, the time period and the ultimate exchange.

The spreads in the merger bankruptcy area are typically wide. When National Steel bought all the assets of Birmingham Steel in December 2002, for example, the bondholders received a cash distribution of US$87. It was possible to buy the bonds at US$84 one month prior to distribution resulting in a gross spread of 3.6 per cent or 43 per cent annualised.

Recent trends

While merger arbitrage was traditionally practised by a small group of highly specialised managers, the boom in merger activity in the late 1990s attracted an abundance of capital from numerous sources. The rapid rise in merger activity was caused by the rising stock market which led to a plethora of multi-billion-dollar stock mergers. Merger activity reached US$2.7 trillion in 1999 and peaked at US$2.9 trillion in 2000,[11] dwarfing the traditional supply of capital from dedicated arbitrageurs and resulting in historically wide spreads. The wide spreads attracted capital not only from scores of new merger funds, but also from macro funds, multi-strategy funds and proprietary trading desks. Even with the increase in capital allocated to this strategy, the large volume of deals caused spreads to remain wide and returns to remain high. The Hennessee Merger Arbitrage indices achieved returns over 16 per cent net in both 1999 and 2000, with the better managers beating those returns.

However, the market changed dramatically in 2001. As the stock market declined, deal activity dropped and the economy slipped into recession. This caused spreads to tighten, deal risk to increase and merger arbitrage returns to fall. The capital allocated to the area was slow to retreat and overwhelmed the supply of deals. Pressure on spreads and increased deal risk caused average returns as provided by Hennessee to fall from 17.5 per cent in 2001 to 3.9 per cent in 2001 and to a negative 1.2 per cent in 2002.

The sub-par performance of merger arbitrage in 2001 and 2002 caused a perception in the hedge fund industry that one could not make money in the strategy and capital fled from the sector. The first to exit were the macro funds and the proprietary desks at investment banks that found it difficult to produce positive returns. Next were the multi-arbitrage funds who shifted funds to other arbitrage strategies. Lastly, merger arbitrage funds in general saw their capital fall as investors withdrew. In total, an estimated 80–90 per cent of the peak capital allocated to the strategy has exited.

Paradoxically, but not surprisingly, this reduction of capital committed to the merger arbitrage strategy has had a positive impact for those managers that remained. While deal activity has declined from peak levels, it stabilised at around the US$200 billion level by the end of 2002. The combination of reduced capital and stable deal activity has caused a supply/demand balance resulting in a widening of overall spreads and an improving market for merger arbitrage.

Conclusion

The merger arbitrage business will continue to prosper as a strategy. Merger activity will grow with the economy, as companies look to gain share, consolidate and expand through acquisitions. The level of deal activity will vary as a function of the health of the economy, the level of the stock market and the level of interest rates. While the strategy has its cycles based on the overall level of deal activity as well as the supply of capital, we expect returns will be commensurate with the hedge fund universe and will continue to be made with low correlation and low volatility.

Since merger arbitrage is a lot more than just capturing spreads, there is a wide variation among merger arbitrage managers. While the average return can be achieved by managing a highly diversified portfolio of small position sizes, to outperform the benchmark one must actively manage the portfolio. To do so successfully requires a high level of expertise and skill in the issues relating to mergers. Those managers who have this expertise can outperform the merger arbitrage indices on a consistent basis, producing above average returns with low correlation and low volatility in different market environments.

[1] 'Royal Dutch Shell to Become Lubes Leader with Pennzoil-Quaker', Press Release by Shell Oil Company, Inc issued 25 March 2002.

[2] 'Quintiles Transnational and Pharma Services Announce Agreement', Press Release by Quintiles Transnational Corp. issued 10 April 2003.

[3] 'Nextlink and Concentric Network Announce US$2.9 billion deal', Press Release by Nextlink Communications, Inc. issued 10 January 2000.

[4] 'Credit Commercial Recommended Offer By HSBC Holdings', Press Release by HSBC Holdings plc issued 3 April 2000.

[5] 'HSBC to Acquire Household International', Press Release by HSBC Holdings plc issued 14 November 2002.

[6] 'Tyco International to Acquire C.R. Bard', Press Release by Tyco International Ltd. issued 30 May 2001.

[7] 'EU Blocks General Electric's Planned Purchase of Honeywell', Press Release by European Commission issued 3 July 2001.

[8] 'National Steel Completes Sale of Assets to US Steel', Press Release by National Steel Corp issued 20 May 2003.

[9] 'ST Telemedia Increases Proposed Stake in Global Crossing', Press Release by Global Crossing issued 30 April 2003.

[10] 'Burlington Industries to be Acquired by Berkshire Hathaway', Press Release by Burlington Industries Inc issued 11 February 2003.

[11] *Source:* Bloomberg.

Chapter 8

The hedge fund manager's edge:
an overview of event investing

Jason Huemer
Synthesis Funds, New York, New York

Hedge funds and the efficient market hypothesis

In order to understand how hedge funds operate, it is first important to understand where they operate. Specifically, hedge funds operate within financial markets. How you regard the way hedge funds operate in these markets depends on your view of those markets, and in particular your view of their efficiency or lack thereof.

For decades, a debate has raged about the efficiency of financial markets generally and the stock markets in particular. To a large extent, this debate has been waged between the academic community (which has gone to great lengths to argue that the markets are fully efficient) and the financial services community, a group that has ultimately depended to a large extent on market inefficiencies for its livelihood.

In his seminal work on the subject, *A Random Walk Down Wall Street,* Burton Malkiel, captured the essence of the debate as follows:

> A random walk is one in which future steps or directions cannot be predicted on the basis of past actions. When the term is applied to the stock market, it means that short-run changes in stock prices cannot be predicted. Investment advisory services, earnings predictions, and complicated chart patterns are useless. On Wall Street, the term 'random walk' is an obscenity. It is an epithet coined by the academic world and hurled insultingly at the professional soothsayers.[1]

The academic theory breaks down into three discrete versions of the efficient market hypothesis (EMH): strong form, semi-strong form and weak form. Strong form, the most extreme case, posits that the market price reflects all information about a company, including public and private knowledge. Under this scenario, there is absolutely no edge to be gained through active management, and even inside information will not allow investors to achieve outperformance. Semi-strong efficiency consists of a market where stock prices reflect all public information, but not private information. In a semi-strong efficient environment, fundamental and technical analysis (the analysis of price action of a security) are still useless, but inside information conveys some form of advantage. Finally, there is weak form efficiency, where stock prices simply reflect historical trading patterns. In this least efficient of the three, technical analysis cannot work, but there is value to be gleaned from fundamental analysis.

Unfortunately, it is beyond the scope of this chapter to settle the EMH debate once and for all. While Burton Malkiel makes a convincing case for the academic camp, practical experience leads many market participants in the opposite direction. The essence of this tension is perhaps best captured by a wry observation from Fischer Black, the father of the Black-Scholes option pricing model and an academic who ultimately moved to private sector finance. The markets, Black is reported to have said, look a lot less efficient from the banks of the Hudson than from the banks of the Charles.[2]

Most practitioners, based on their first-hand experience, believe in extremely limited efficiency in the financial markets. Indeed, suffice it to say that the US$700 billion global hedge fund business owes its very existence to the fact that the markets seem to fall, at best, into the semi-strong efficiency category, and most likely are not even that efficient. In fact, the whole distinction between strong, semi-strong and weak seems somewhat arbitrary to those who have made their careers in trading and investment management. A more workable definition might be that while the markets are efficient in aggregate and over the long run, there are pockets of inefficiency, temporal or situation-specific, that hedge fund managers seek to exploit.

Today, the academic community may be moving toward this more practical view of the markets. After peaking in popularity in the 1970s, around the time of *Random Walk*'s first edition, the efficient markets hypothesis has gradually been chipped away by a series of anomalies that are impossible to reconcile with any rigid form of EMH, beginning in the 1980s with observations of excess volatility in equity markets. While many academics clung doggedly to the conventional wisdom of efficiency, over time the tide turned. As Yale University Robert Schiller notes: 'Wishful thinking can dominate much of the work of a profession for a decade, but not indefinitely' (Schiller, 2002).[3]

As old-fashioned theories of efficient markets have waned, in their place has come a school of economic and financial thought embracing behavioural finance and bounded rationality (indeed the 2002 Nobel Prize in economics was awarded to Daniel Kahneman for his work on irrational economic decision-making and bounded rationality). This framework replaces the prior overly simplistic view that economic actors behave perfectly rationally, and thus that markets are always efficient, with a view that economic actors behave like real people. That is, they may act rationally or not. This fairly common sense observation may seem obvious to any active Wall Street participant, but in academia it has been positively revolutionary.

Event-driven investing and temporary inefficiencies

Once one accepts the existence of some form of temporary inefficiency in the market place, it is fairly simple to understand the basic premise of event-driven investing. In essence, event-driven investing is about finding these temporary inefficiencies and capitalising on them. Specifically, event-driven investing looks for significant corporate events that create some sort of change in the status quo and set the stage for this type of inefficiency.

Broadly, event-driven investing looks at corporate events of all stripes. The events break down, however, into three major categories:

1. Mergers and acquisitions (including stock-for-stock transactions, cash tenders, hostile bids, bidding contests, minority squeeze-outs and companies for sale) are one of the largest

categories, and trading and investment strategies driven by these transactions would generally fall under the heading of risk arbitrage.

2. Companies subject to financial stress and distress, including companies in bankruptcy within the Chapter 11 process, offer a variety of investment opportunities, trading and buy-and-hold, that would typically be classified as distressed investing.

3. Finally, the 'other' category within event-driven investing is what is typically referred to as event equity or special situation investing. This broad strategy includes a number of corporate event types, with common themes including corporate spin-offs, split-ups, shareholder activism, leveraged recapitalisations and industry consolidation opportunities.

The common theme in all of these investment scenarios is a corporate event that creates disruption in the market place, usually resulting in some form of trading imbalance or information uncertainty. This dynamic frequently results in what a hedge fund manager would term a 'value gap', that is, a gap between the true value of a security and its market price. Since these inefficiencies are temporary, eventually these value gaps will close when the market properly revalues the security in question. It is here that event-driven hedge funds ply their trade, bringing their judgement, expertise and experience to bear in interpreting these situations in order to exploit these pockets of inefficiency and to capture these value gaps.

Hedge funds and their edge

In the lexicon of hedge fund managers, these inefficiencies would be exploited through the hedge fund manager's 'edge', that is, a competitive advantage relative to the market as a whole or relative to the manager's peer group. This notion of edge is one that recurs throughout the hedge fund industry and it is central to understanding how hedge fund managers operate and ideally thrive in the market place. While this edge takes many forms, its essence is what legendary hedge fund manager Michael Steinhardt would refer to as 'variant perception', taking a view of a situation that is at odds with the consensus. Often a manager's edge takes the form of an information advantage, and this is particularly true in event-driven strategies. In fact, in the view of many hedge fund managers, event-driven investing is the ultimate information game.

As the markets have evolved, gaining an edge, in information-based investing in particular, has become increasingly difficult (perhaps the best evidence that the markets are not strong-form efficient, is the fact that they have clearly become much more efficient over time). As an illustration, consider one of the investment industry's great apocryphal legends. As the story goes, a pivotal event in the history of the Rothschild clan was the historic trade made by the family upon Napoleon's defeat by Wellington at Waterloo in 1815. With advance notice of the outcome delivered by carrier pigeon to London, Nathan Rothschild was able to place a substantial bet on British government bonds well ahead of the market's move. As the market caught up, Rothschild's position soared in value, building on the foundation of wealth that would make the family the dominant financiers of their era.

In today's information age, where information has essentially become a commodity, an advantage of that order of magnitude is highly unlikely. Furthermore, with strict insider trading guidelines in place, an information advantage that significant could well be illegal. Nonetheless, information advantages do exist, even in today's more efficient markets, and it is the job of the hedge fund managers to seek them out. Often, the advantage can stem from superior efficiency in information processing. An event-driven manager of today may get their information early by being the first to wade through a complex legal document and to notice, and recognise the implications of, a particular clause in the fine print. In such cases, superior research and assiduous effort, like the Rothschild carrier pigeon, can put the manager ahead of the pack.

Perhaps more important, however, is the role of intuition and skill. One common mistake, and one that is lost in the coolly rational world of academic explication of the markets, is the assumption that an information advantage must be one of primary information. In fact, more often than not, it is second-order or meta-information, created when a manager assimilates information flow and synthesises entirely new information, drawing on the manager's judgement, expertise and experience. In other words, it is the conclusions that a manager draws from interpreting a stream of primary information that grant him the information advantage, the variant perception, that in turn conveys his or her edge.

Frequently, this edge relies on talent as much as or more than skill, drawing on abilities in pattern recognition, investor psychology, logic and rational decision-making, causal analysis, etc. Indeed, hedge fund management may be the ultimate IQ test, with manager returns providing a score. These processes are often unquantifiable, and indeed perhaps ineffable, often relying on a subconscious thought process masquerading as intuition or gut feeling. As a result, they tend to be lost or at least discounted in rigorous academic analysis of the markets. They are nonetheless real, however, and in fact are arguably the hallmark of all great hedge fund managers. In the final analysis, a manager's edge is the ultimate measure of talent and skill.

A note on risk premia and liquidity

Another important element of understanding the nature of hedge funds is in the source of opportunity for hedge fund managers. Specifically, how do these inefficiencies come about? How do hedge fund managers capture them? Broadly speaking, market anomalies tend to stem from two major disruptions: information-based inefficiencies and technical or trading imbalances. In each case, the approach and role of hedge fund managers is slightly different.

Information-based inefficiencies are fairly obvious. As previously noted, primary information flows with a high degree of efficiency, so few if any managers have the sort of 'carrier pigeon' advantage enjoyed by the Rothschilds 200 years ago. While there may be occasions where an investor enjoys a bona fide information advantage in primary information that was legally obtained (not inside information), such events are increasingly scarce in today's hyper-competitive investment environment where most low-hanging fruit gets picked immediately.

Far more common are those situations where the hedge fund manager is exploiting an advantage in second-order information. In this context, the question is not 'what is happening', but rather, 'what does it mean?' Here the hedge fund manager is bringing talent and expertise to bear in order to develop an information advantage in interpreting information flow. If the manager is correct, the market will come around to his or her view and revalue the securities in question accordingly. Frequently, the ability of the hedge fund manager to obtain this information advantage is prosaic: due perhaps to a more efficient, timely or assiduous information-gathering process. Sometimes it is a function of experience, where the manager is better able to fill in the blanks or make an intuitive leap in predicting outcomes.

In an abstract sense, what the manager is doing in this process is capturing a mis-pricing or value gap between these securities and their true or inherent value. This value gap also can be viewed as a risk premium, or the return in excess of the risk-free rate that investors require to hold a risk asset. So, in essence, hedge funds can be viewed as capturing risk premia that have been mis-priced. This is an important concept in understanding how hedge funds operate because it places risk squarely in the centre of the management process. Ultimately, for hedge fund managers, risk is not just about managing and protecting downside in the investment process (or generating true absolute returns) it is also the source of return itself.

The other major category of inefficiencies consists of technical or trading imbalances. Often these are the result of structural impediments to efficiency, such as limits on trading, uptick rules on short selling, limited windows where identical securities trade on different exchanges in different time zones and the like. As well, the driver for inefficiency may be a regulatory issue, including requirements that make certain market constituents forced sellers of securities, or tax rules that tilt the playing field in favour of certain tax-advantaged investors. Occasionally, the trading imbalance may be wholly irrational, such as when panicked investors flee a market en masse in informationless risk aversion.

In each of these cases, the adept hedge fund manager can and often does develop an edge. This edge can be as simple as nimble trading. For example, a trader may be able to move quickly before lumbering institutional investors get through investor committees and before perennially behind retail investors play catch-up the following day. It also may take the form of a trading advantage (many hedge funds get an early or first call from salespeople because they are large commission generators and as a result may be offered securities not shown to the rest of the market, including hard-to-borrow shorts). Often it is simply focus and discipline: the manager is simply more rational than the market at large, refusing to succumb to the timeless struggle between fear and greed that so often results in irrational behaviour among market participants. However, frequently the role of the hedge fund manager is simply to identify the order imbalance, recognise it as a non-fundamental phenomenon that will revert once balance is restored and step in opportunistically. In this regard, hedge fund managers can be viewed as the ultimate liquidity providers for the market.

Hedge funds' dual role as capturers of risk premia and liquidity providers to the market place is somewhat ironic given their position in the debate over market efficiency. In effect, because they step in to exploit these pockets of inefficiency and ultimately absorb the excess returns they offer, hedge funds are the ultimate police of market efficiency. As they arbitrage away pricing anomalies in the market place they are a critical element of the market's overall long-run efficiency. This also makes recent trends in the press and in regulatory circles especially counter-intuitive: given the invaluable service to free, fair, efficient and open markets that hedge funds play, it is particularly bizarre that so many observers have rushed to judgement and essentially made them the pariahs of the investment world. As with most witch hunts, there are vested interests at work behind the scenes. Hedge fund professionals can only hope that a better understanding of the industry and its inner workings will lead to a keener appreciation of the benefits of hedge fund investment programmes.

Corporate spin-offs: 3Com/Palm

Historically, one of the most intriguing, and profitable, sources of market inefficiency for event-driven investors has been corporate spin-offs. Among corporate spin-offs, few have reached the level of absurdity achieved by 3Com's spin-off of its PalmPilot division in 2000.

A mainstay of event-driven investing, the corporate spin-off presents several different investing opportunities: pre-spin-off an investment in the parent company often provides an opportunity to take advantage of dislocation and trading imbalances; between spin-off and distribution of remaining shares, investors may capitalise on a relative value gap by 'setting up the stub' (explained in greater detail below); and post-spin-off, value investors frequently benefit from long-term appreciation in shares of spun-off subsidiaries.

For the first two investment opportunities, an attractive spin-off opportunity will typically have several specific characteristics. First, the parent company is often in a prosaic or low-growth business and may be out of favour with Wall Street and the investing public. Second, the subsidiary to be spun-out is usually prized by the investing public, either because it is asset-rich or, more likely, it is a growth business in a sector the market values highly. Equally important, the division must be in some sense non-core within the context of the parent company's strategic direction.

As a result of the value differential, the true worth of the subsidiary in question may be obscured by the corporate ownership structure, creating an incentive to spin off the division in order to maximise shareholder value. The non-core status of the division makes such a spin-off more palatable to the parent company and to shareholders.

Within the context of the set-up presented above, 3Com/Palm was a textbook example of a spin-off investment opportunity, exhibiting all of these characteristics. Although it was a high technology company, 3Com was out of favour with the investing public despite the late 1990s technology boom. The company, which was founded in 1979 by entrepreneur Bob Metcalfe, derives its name from its three areas of focus: computers, communications and compatibility. A pioneer in computer networking, 3Com introduced the first network interface to connect IBM PCs through an ethernet LAN in 1983, and grew substantially as computer networking and the Internet expanded through the 1980s and 1990s. By the late 1990s, however, 3Com's business had slowed as it lost ground to larger rivals.

With its core business in networking infrastructure, 3Com seemed an odd parent company for PalmPilot, the leader in the market for hand-held connected organisers. In fact, although 3Com officials worked hard to rationalise the role of Palm in the company's stable of products, in reality the 3Com/Palm relationship was little more than a lucky accident, a by-product of the company's 1997 acquisition of modem-manufacturer US Robotics.

For its part, Palm was a dynamic, rapidly growing company with a product that was well known and loved by the broad investment public. The company was the brainchild of three entrepreneurs (Jeff Hawkins, Donna Dubinsky and Ed Colligan) who joined forces to found the company in 1992. Originally focused on development of graffiti software for hand-held devices, an approach that would become a trademark feature of future Palm devices, the company introduced its own line of hand-held computers shortly after it was acquired by US Robotics in 1995 in a US$44 million buy-out. From that launch, the company's business took off, and by the end of the decade PalmPilot had over 5 million users for its increasingly ubiquitous devices.

Even as Palm's fortunes were soaring, 3Com's core business was headed in the opposite direction. A distant second to Cisco in the networking equipment sector, the company had seen its revenues stagnate and its margins erode throughout the late 1990s. In fact, in its last full year as a 3Com division, Palm's growth vaulted ahead 116 per cent to US$570 million, accounting for fully 10 per cent of 3Com's total revenues. That level represented a five-fold increase, in nominal revenue and percentage of 3Com's top line, from just two years earlier.

An aggressive, and ultimately successful, event-driven trade would have been to go long 3Com shares in the summer of 1999 in anticipation of an announced spin off of the division. Although 3Com executives vigorously denied any intent to spin-off the unit, some industry observers had long speculated that a separation was in the offing. To informed observers, 3Com's claims of the division's core nature were viewed as somewhat artificial and strained. With Palm's business expanding rapidly, the potential windfall to 3Com of somehow monetising the asset was viewed as too enticing to pass up. Indeed, industry trade publication *Red Herring* in a June 1999 open letter to 3Com CEO Eric Benhamou, called for the company to divest Palm, for the benefit of both companies. As for timing, astute investors would surely have noted that the 1997 US Robotics acquisition, which was accounted for as a pooling of interests, required a two-year waiting period before the disposition of any material assets was allowed without significant tax consequences. By late 1999, the clock was running out on those two years.

Even if investors missed the opportunity to be early by purchasing 3Com prior to the announcement, however, there was still ample opportunity to jump into the trade. On Monday, 13 September 1999, the day 3Com announced its intention to spin off the unit, the company's shares traded up US$1.69 on heavy volume to US$28.94, for a one-day gain of over 6 per cent. However, that increase was nothing compared to where the stock was headed. As excitement over the pending Palm IPO mounted, so did interest in 3Com stock. After all, 3Com was due to receive a sizeable windfall from the IPO of Palm shares. For those investors interested in owning Palm shares, at least 80 per cent of the company's shares would be distributed to owners of 3Com stock in mid-year 2000. The resulting feeding frenzy pushed 3Com shares above US$100 by March of 2000, for a return of over 350 per cent in just a few short months.

The more traditional spin-off trade, however, occurred later, after the initial public offering of Palm shares in a classic 'setting up the stub' trade. The stub, in this case, refers to the stub equity created through a hedging transaction – here the parent company minus the spun-out division. The theory behind the opportunity is that the turmoil surrounding the parent and subsidiary company shares creates opportunities for fundamental mis-pricings, with value relationships moving out of alignment as a result of trade imbalances. This is particularly pronounced when the company being spun off is highly valued and the parent company is perceived as less valuable, creating a possibility for overvaluation of the subsidiary relative to the parent company.

The trade becomes possible because, in a typical corporate spin-off, the subsidiary is first listed via an IPO then the remaining shares are distributed to shareholders of the parent company. This creates two important preconditions for a stub trade: first, there is a period when the subsidiary can be stripped out of the parent company by shorting the number of subsidiary shares embedded in each parent company share; and second, the shares of the subsidiary will be received within a finite period of time, meaning the short position can be covered and the stub equity position becomes simple equity ownership in the parent company post-spin-off. Note that without this latter element (for example, in companies that own substantial stakes in other publicly traded entities with an open-ended holding period) any perceived theoretical mis-pricing may persist in perpetuity.

In a classic stub equity spin-off trade, the investor is most likely looking to capture a relative mis-pricing created by the activity around the spin-off. For instance, a spin-off may imply an earnings multiple of four times trailing 12-month earnings for the parent company versus a peer group trading range of 8–12 times for comparable companies. In such a case,

Exhibit 8.1

3Com/Palm value relationship, 2000

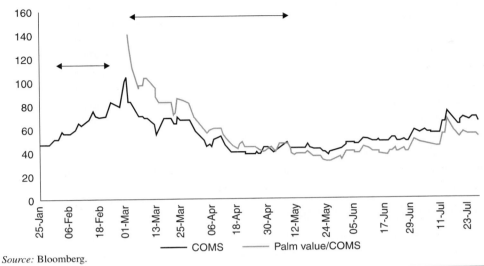

Source: Bloomberg.

the investor would likely set up the stub and hold it through distribution, awaiting a period of normality during which valuations could be expected to revert to peer group comparables. 3Com/Palm, however, represented an extreme case, as a result of the heightened level of excitement surrounding the PalmPilot offering. In fact, as can be seen from Exhibit 8.1, the value relationship in this case was so perverse that Palm's shares actually implied a negative value for 3Com, creating an opportunity for investors to purchase a share of 3Com and short the corresponding number of shares of Palm, ending up with their 3Com ex-Palm and cash, or a negative cost basis on their 3Com stub.

Of course, this raises a very simple question. While markets may not be perfectly efficient, they ought to be efficient enough that this type of anomaly cannot persist for long. So, why wasn't this spread quickly arbitraged away? In fact, the answer lies in one of the reasons the spread was there in the first place. There were profound technical inefficiencies in this trade in the sense that during this period Palm was not just hard to borrow for the purposes of selling short the shares, it was essentially impossible to borrow for the average investor. The reason was not just the popularity of the offering, but also the fact that while 3Com had initially planned to float roughly 20 per cent of Palm in the IPO, ultimately the issue was for only about 4 per cent of the company's shares. This combination of surging demand and thin supply proved to be not only a primary impetus of Palm's soaring stock price post-IPO (from US$38 issue price to over US$100 that day), but also a source of severe shortage for any investors looking to borrow the shares.

Some hedge funds (primarily larger funds with strong relationships on Wall Street) were able to find Palm stock in limited quantities and to set up the trade in a straightforward, fully hedged fashion. Others took advantage of their ability to trade actively in derivatives and options and set up the short end of the trade through swaps or through synthetic shorts, created through so-called put-call conversion trades, where an investor sells a call and buys a put at the same strike price. Unfortunately, these trades were not without friction and either were not highly scalable or saw much of the economics eaten away by premium. As a result, some intrepid managers simply took directional trades, figuring roughly that a US$50 billion market cap was somewhat excessive for a company with under US$600 million in total sales, no matter how hot its product. In fact, expressing this view through a simple short on 3Com at over US$70, which would have been easily executed throughout much of March, would have garnered an investor a handsome profit when the trade was covered below US$40 a share by early June.

As an aside, in an example of where sharp-eyed and sophisticated hedge managers can add value, there was actually a third trading opportunity at the tail end of the spin-off that a handful of managers exploited. In a truly risk-free arbitrage, a trade that is theoretically impossible in a fully efficient market, it was possible in late July 2000 to create the synthetic short position in Palm via a put-call conversion trade and then sell 3Com forward into the when-issued market for the stub equity, creating a profit of several dollars per share with no exposure whatsoever. While the trade was not highly scalable, it is a fascinating and rare example of a true arbitrage in modern markets.

Corporate split-ups: Canadian Pacific

If corporate spin-off transactions have historically been the most popular event equity trades for event-driven hedge funds, then corporate split-ups are a close second. Also known as 'sum-of-the-parts' plays and, in Europe, as 'holding company' trades these investments aim to take advantage of a major market inefficiency, usually referred to as a conglomerate discount. One of the best examples of such a trade in recent memory is the 2001 split-up of Canadian Pacific, at the time one of Canada's largest and oldest companies.

As the term implies, a conglomerate discount refers to the level at which a diversified corporation is valued versus the value of its various divisions when they are priced as free-standing entities. This discount, also known as a holding company discount or diversification discount, is found frequently throughout the markets and is the bane of corporate management teams of far-flung diversified corporations.

There have been numerous academic attempts to quantify and explain the prevalence of diversification discounts. Several theories have been put forth in an attempt to explain why such companies should be worth more split apart than joined together. One common argument is that the conglomerate approach obscures true value by interposing an opaque structure impeding the efficient flow of information. This information-based argument also frequently focuses on the difficulty of obtaining effective Wall Street research coverage for companies that defy industry classification.

The information inefficiency of conglomerates is intuitively compelling, but the issues behind the discount may be deeper and more fundamental. One indication that this could be the case is the history of such structures. Drawing on academic research which posited that conglomerates enjoyed substantial benefits of economies of scale and centralised resources, diversified holding companies were all the rage in the 1960s and 1970s. During that time, many conglomerates actually traded at a premium as a result of their diversified structure.

By the 1980s, however, investors had changed their views dramatically, punishing holding companies via conglomerate discounts. This reversal most likely reflects a more fundamental view of failings of the conglomerate structure, rather than simple misinformation or misunderstanding of the underlying businesses. In fact, among the more plausible academic theories is the argument that the market is accounting for inefficiencies bred by the diversified structure, in which strong operations in effect subsidise weaker, sometimes unprofitable, elements of the broader organisation.

Whatever the reason, conglomerate discounts are real and are difficult to dispel. In fact, for event-driven investors, the challenge is not to find conglomerate discounts – they actually are fairly commonplace. Rather, the challenge is to find a conglomerate discount that is imminently going to be closed. The key to successfully investing in such situations is finding management with a commitment to maximise shareholder value and the will and the means to make a meaningful change to restructure the business accordingly.

Although there are a number of tools to close a conglomerate discount (including paring back divisions and operating lines to a core strategic focus, issuing tracking stock for subsidiaries, and restructuring and decentralising management) perhaps the most effective tool is the corporate split-up, where the conglomerate is literally broken up into its constituent parts. The effect of such a reorganisation is potentially so profound, that event-driven investors are always on the prowl for corporate management teams willing to undergo such a radical transformation.

Such was the case with Canadian Pacific. One of Canada's largest companies, by the late 1990s Canadian Pacific was trading at a significant conglomerate discount estimated at anywhere from 11 per cent to over 30 per cent of fair value. Again, the conglomerate discount in itself was not news and was frequently commented upon, not least by the company itself. What was critical for investors to determine was whether management had the commitment and resolve to break up one of Canada's most prominent companies.

Tracing its roots back to the 1800s, Canadian Pacific's history was rooted in the history of Canada itself. The company began in 1881 when a consortium of Canadian businessmen extracted what in retrospect looked like a sweetheart deal from Canada's first prime minister to develop a rail line across the continent. In return for their commitment to construct the rail line, the Canadian Pacific founders received a substantial cash infusion, millions of acres of land, a guaranteed monopoly, and a commitment from the government to encourage traffic on the new route. With the rail line's success virtually assured, the company embarked upon an ambitious diversification plan just five years after its founding, an effort that ultimately would take Canadian Pacific into real estate, shipping, natural resources and agriculture, among other sectors. By the early 1980s, Canadian Pacific was the largest company in Canada by revenues, with over 160 subsidiaries.

By the mid-1980s, however, Canadian Pacific's bets on cyclical businesses were beginning to take their toll, and the company was struggling. Following a management change in 1985, the company began an aggressive programme of slashing cyclical and non-core divisions and focusing on profitable business lines. This programme continued until the mid-1990s, when the COO David O'Brien ascended to the CEO post. Following the sale of the company's Laidlaw division in 1997, Canadian Pacific consisted of five business divisions: PanCanadian Energy, CP Rail, CP Hotels and Resorts, CP Ships and Fording, the company's mining and minerals operation.

Despite a sweeping overhaul of the business from a decade earlier, however, Canadian Pacific still traded absolutely cheap. By August of 2000, with Canadian Pacific shares trading in the high US$20s to low US$30s, the company was trading at roughly an 11 per cent discount to management's estimation of fair value based on its own sum-of-the-parts analysis. While this was a meaningful improvement from the estimated 21 per cent discount the company found in September 1995, it still represented a substantial value gap. Furthermore, many outsiders found the company's analysis overly conservative and indeed the consensus estimates of fair value among sell-side research analysts at the time was almost US$6-a-share higher, placing the discount at over 30 per cent.

While there was no question that there was a substantial discount to fair value in Canadian Pacific's stock price, the question for investors was when, how and even if that value gap would be closed. Based on David O'Brien's positioning and rhetoric, it was clear that he intended to maximise shareholder value if possible. The question was: was it possible? How far could he go in the restructuring process? That is where fundamental event-driven research came into play.

For many event-driven hedge funds, despite an attractive conglomerate discount, Canadian Pacific didn't hit their radar screens until February 2000. It was then that David O'Brien clearly stated his intention to restructure the company and maximise shareholder value (and, most important, to do so within the next 12–18 months). That was followed up in September of that year with an announcement that the company's board of directors had retained RBC Dominion Securities to explore the feasibility of the five divisions operating as independent companies.

Things were starting to look interesting for event investors. Even so, it remained far from clear that the company would undertake a split-up. Many feasibility studies, such as the one undertaken by Canadian Pacific, end in a decision that falls far short of a full-scale reorganisation, and some result in no action at all. Finally, in January 2001, word began to circulate that Canadian Pacific management would be making a road show presentation to investors in the next few weeks. With no major corporate finance activity on the company's calendar, investors who had tracked the company closely saw this as a sign that an announcement was imminent.

At that point, a number of event investors began to establish positions in the company. With the stock having languished and settled into the high-US$20s, the analysis of the opportunity was fairly straightforward at that point. Canadian Pacific, with a collection of solid old economy stalwarts in its operating divisions and highly predictable cash flows, was trading absolutely cheap with little chance of a negative earnings surprise. In essence, the trade had little or no downside. At the same time, there was a high degree of upside option-ality to the trade, giving the overall risk–reward profile an attractive asymmetry. With the major residual risk being timing and opportunity cost, the trade was helped by the fact that the company enjoyed proactive management and was 12 months into an estimated 12–18 month process.

Ultimately, management announced its intention to split the company into five separate publicly traded companies on 13 February 2001. As Exhibit 8.2 shows, the response of the company's stock price in the short term was dramatic, with the announcement lifting Canadian Pacific shares from under US$30 to over US$40 within just a few months. Many event investors chose to exit at that point, and in fact by mid-May the conglomerate discount had largely been closed. The company officially split into its five parts on 3 October 2001, after which the combined shares of the five companies traded for slightly more than US$40 a share on balance, roughly where the company had been trading by the late spring and early summer pre-split-up. Whether they held for the short term or for the longer term, however, event investors' returns of over 30 per cent were quite attractive, particularly given the risk profile of the trade.

Exhibit 8.2

Canadian Pacific restructuring catalyst sends stock higher, 2001

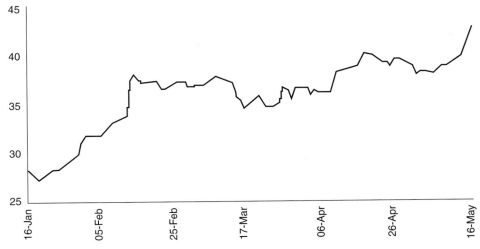

Source: Bloomberg.

Conclusion

The inefficiencies illustrated in the examples above, while extreme, are repeated in similar fashion in the equity markets every day. These inefficiencies may take the form of spreads on merger transactions that provide an arbitrageur with excess returns. Or, there may be a dramatic mis-pricing created as a result of the stigma and friction of a bankruptcy or reorganisation. Still other opportunities may parallel the Canadian Pacific split-up, the 3Com/Palm spin-off or a host of other such 'special situations' including shareholder agitation opportunities, recapitalisations, proxy fights, exchange offers and other major corporate initiatives.

In all of these cases, information gathering and information processing is the key to competitive advantage for managers. Even in the post-information age, as these examples illustrate, skilled managers can develop an edge in these information-intensive strategies through a combination of hard work and basic research coupled with judgement and skill in interpreting information flow to develop what legendary hedge fund manager Michael Steinhardt would have termed 'variant perception' versus the consensus view in evaluating these scenarios. Often this ability to see things differently is where true manager talent or native ability comes into play.

Much has been written and said about shrinking inefficiencies in the markets overall and about the ebb and flow of opportunities in event-driven investing. There is no question that the various elements of event-driven investing are subject to a high degree of cyclicality. This is particularly true of risk arbitrage, which tends to have a strong positive correlation to the business cycle, and of distressed investing, which tends to be negatively correlated to the business cycle. Even so, to the extent that event-driven investing relies on corporate events of any stripe, wherever they may arise, the future for event-driven investing opportunity flow seems secure. The business of business is business, as Milton Friedman noted, and that means change. Corporations will forever be buying, selling and restructuring their way into better businesses, creating fodder for event-driven investors for years to come.

[1] Malkiel, Burton Gordon (2000), *A Random Walk Down Wall Street, Seventh Edition*, New York, W.W. Norton & Company (June).

[2] Bernstein, Peter L. (1996), *Against the Gods: The Remarkable Story of Risk*, New York, John Wiley & Sons, p. 7 (September).

[3] Schiller, Robert J. (2002), 'From Market Efficiency to Behavioural Finance', *Cowles Foundation Discussion Paper No. 1385*, Yale University, p. 3 (October).

Chapter 9

Trend following: performance, risk and correlation characteristics

Michael S. Rulle
Graham Capital Management, LP, Stamford, Connecticut

Introduction

This chapter discusses how trend following achieves positive performance and why we believe it should continue to be a viable strategy. The chapter examines trend following in the context of a diversified portfolio of investments allocated across various hedge fund strategies. While trend following has a large investor base, the strategy may not be as broadly understood as many other hedge fund strategies. The analysis given here implies that institutional fund of funds managers and other allocators should give trend following a larger allocation than is traditionally assumed.

Systematic trend following is a macro strategy which trades futures and forward contracts in the currency, fixed-income, equity and commodity markets. Trend followers try to capture moves that persist between one and six months. Currently, there is over US$50 billion allocated to the managed futures industry, with a significant percentage being devoted to trend following. The futures and currency markets are the most liquid markets in the world and are accessed daily by hedgers, traders and investors. Trend following strategies benefit from these conditions, as it enables them to diversify across many different asset classes while being able to accommodate large capacity. While trends do not exist in all markets most of the time, they do exist in most markets some of the time. Trend followers create trading systems to profit from these trends. The basic trading strategy that all trend followers try to systematise is to 'cut losses' and 'let profits run'. The key issues from an investor's point of view are:

- sources of return;
- returns and volatility of returns; and
- correlation of returns and portfolio construction.

Trend following and sources of return

Returns have long option profile[1]

Trend followers create quantitative models to capture long-term trends while limiting the cost of doing so. These models create an expected return profile similar to being long options. A strategy has a long option profile when the strategy limits downside losses while potentially achieving very large upside returns. For example, trend followers use stop losses to achieve

Exhibit 9.1

Long call versus futures with a stop

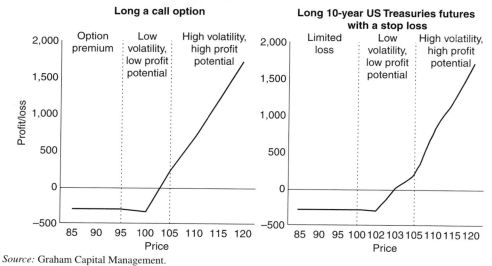

Source: Graham Capital Management.

limited downside exposures on their positions. Exhibit 9.1 presents the return profiles of a hypothetical long option position compared to an actual long futures trade with a 'stop loss'.

Trend followers are not literally trying to synthetically replicate individual options. Rather, a trend follower uses a combination of individual market strategies and portfolio design to create a synthetic portfolio of options. A trend follower achieves positive returns by correctly targeting market direction and minimising the cost of this portfolio. Thus, while trend following is sometimes referred to as being long volatility, trend followers technically do not trade volatility, although they often benefit from it.

William Fung and David Hsieh have performed an analysis demonstrating trend following's correlation and similarity to long straddle positions. At-the-money straddles are puts and calls with a strike price equal to the current market price of the underlying investment. Option models, such as Black-Scholes, would require a very small hedge for the holder of such a straddle. In other words, to replicate this straddle using the underlying market instrument requires the replicator to have almost no position in the underlying. However, as the market price of the underlying moves significantly higher(/lower), the straddle becomes increasingly long(/short) the market. A replicator of the straddle therefore would have to buy(/sell) the underlying in greater amounts as the market moved significantly in one direction. Since trend followers systematically stand ready to go long or short markets as trends emerge, their trading activity is very analogous to someone trying to replicate a long straddle position.

Trend followers will generally capture almost every ex-post long-term trend that appears in any market; however, there is a cost to capturing these trends. The cost occurs when trends seem to appear but end up reversing. The amount of that cost equals the distance between the entry price of buying/selling the particular futures contract, and the stop loss price of the particular model. This trading approach is similar to being long options because the stop loss creates a limited downside, and the continuation of the trend creates the large upside. Of course, if trends continually fail to materialise, these limited losses can accumulate to large

Exhibit 9.2

DAX futures contract (back-adjusted), February 2001–October 2001

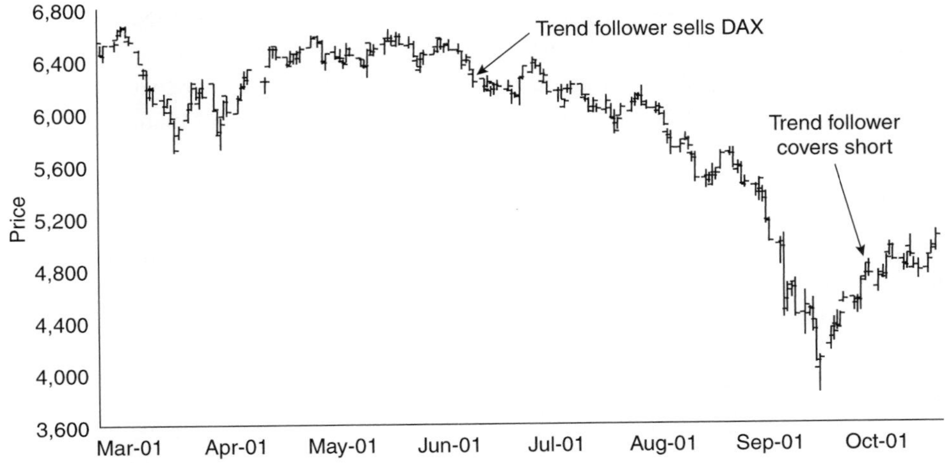

Source: Graham Capital Management.

losses. This is also true for any option purchase strategy. For trend followers, the option premium is paid for after an unsuccessful trade is closed when a stop loss has been reached. The premium can also be paid after markets have moved a great deal, profits have been made, and a reversal causes a trailing stop to be hit, and some of the profits reversed. Exhibit 9.2 provides an illustration of a trailing stop being hit after a major move in the DAX.

In general terms, it is easy to describe what a trend follower is trying to do, and the general way profits and losses are made. In effect, trend followers engage in a kind of long option replication strategy. Each trend follower has their own methods and models, and, as with any financial statistical activity, changing market structures will lead to evolutionary changes in models. The long option return profile, however, is common to all trend following programmes.

Trend following and quantitative models

Trend following uses proprietary financial models to achieve returns as do many hedge fund strategies and other financial markets activities. Some hedge fund styles which rely heavily, or exclusively, on quantitative models include: statistical arbitrage, convertible arbitrage, volatility arbitrage, mortgage arbitrage and fixed-income arbitrage. Other financial markets activities which also rely heavily on statistical modelling include: reinsurance, securitisation (including collateralised debt obligations, asset-backed securities and collateralised mortgage obligations), credit insurance, and asset allocation modelling and approaches.

All of these financial activities create strategies or financial instruments that can be invested in. Virtually all of them are traded or created by institutions or funds using proprietary trading models. Each of these proprietary financial models is a variation of known methodologies documented in financial literature. The same is true for trend following. There is an excellent range of academic literature documenting methodologies used by trend followers.[2]

A Bloomberg terminal can access 30 different statistical measures used by trend followers and other statistical traders. These appear for virtually every instrument quoted by Bloomberg that has a price series.

There are also certain trend following strategies that provide investors with complete model transparency. Some examples include passive strategies. Passive strategies (such as the MLM or sGFII indices) are usually either long or short in all traded markets at all times at fixed predetermined weights. They will use models which are simpler than active trend following, which is much more selective in getting long or short various markets. However, these passive strategies do provide investors with insight into trend following.

While trend followers use proprietary statistical modelling, investors still have access to its general principles. The methods used by trend followers are well documented in financial literature and can be intuitively understood. What distinguishes one manager from another, as with all investing, is how these methods are adapted and applied through time. Quantitative strategies need not be more opaque to investors than qualitative ones.

Speculators, hedgers and zero sum trading[3]

Since futures markets are literally derivative instruments, and are created by the act of buying and selling, it is easy to describe a market where all futures traders' profits add up to zero. If all futures traders were just speculators trading only with each other, and only had positions in futures markets, then, by definition, all profits and losses would sum to zero (plus the interest earned on margin cash).

To the extent the futures markets are dominated by speculators, the likelihood of total returns tending toward zero is increased. The opportunity for futures speculators as a whole to earn positive returns ultimately comes from the activity of hedgers who are an integral part of the futures market. Hedgers are usually thought of as operating businesses that hedge interest rate, currency and commodity risk. They may hedge interest rates in anticipation of selling debt or investing cash. For corporations, cross-border trade flows create an enormous amount of currency hedging outside the context of price speculative activity. Finally, commodity growers and producers are continually using commodity futures to hedge price risk.

The purpose of all commercial hedging activity is to shed unwanted price risk of some kind. As these risks are transferred to the futures markets it creates opportunities for speculators, trend followers and non-trend followers alike, to trade in a non-zero sum environment. Only an assumption that there are always offsetting hedgers simultaneously on the other side of all other hedging activity would make this untrue.

Additionally, many active investors, traders, market makers, and arbitrageurs trade futures and options in conjunction with underlying financial assets. Relative to futures speculators, these traders, although not engaged in commercial hedging activity, also function as hedgers. It is useful to discuss some examples because the financial community is a great source of hedging activity, which ultimately provides speculators, as a whole, with profit opportunity.

Convertible arbitrage traders buy convertible bonds and hedge interest rate and equity risk by shorting equities and interest rate instruments. The objective in convertible arbitrage is to realise the value of embedded equity options in the convertible bond while not taking any market risk. To hedge equity risk, the entire convertible arbitrage market is selling equity in a rising market and buying equity in a falling market. While natural equity holders will be on the other side, any imbalance in supply and demand will cause specialists and market-makers to take positions. This creates the potential for these intermediaries to hedge in the futures or options markets. When they do, they could be on the opposite side of the market as a trend follower entering a trade. A convertible arbitrage trader's interest rate hedging creates analogous opportunities for trend followers in bond futures markets.

An institutional investor may keep a balanced 60/40 mix in equities and bonds. Every time the portfolio manager rebalances he or she is buying bonds or equities as they fall (relative to each other) and selling bonds or equities as they rise. They may hedge this directly in cash markets or indirectly in the bond or equity futures markets. If the former, this 'programme' activity may still find its way to the futures markets as bond dealers and equity market-makers hedge their books.

Index arbitrage traders are continuously trading the basis between the cash markets and the futures markets. Every time they enter a trade, the arbitrageurs are buying or selling futures against the cash markets. They are indifferent to the direction of the market. From the perspective of the futures speculator, the index arbitrageur is a hedger. A US dollar-based global macro trader may be taking a long position in non-dollar fixed-income instruments. However, if the trader only wants interest rate exposure, he or she will sell the foreign currency and buy the dollar. If the dollar is trending down, the macro trader is providing a trading opportunity to the trend follower.

Nor does one have to make the case, as economists since Keynes have, that there is a 'natural risk premium'[4] provided to speculators for assuming this risk transfer. It does mean, however, that investors in futures-based strategies should have ample opportunity to earn a return greater than zero. The 'zero sum game' hypothesis of futures trading, while true in one sense, is largely irrelevant in practice when assessing trend followers, due to the ubiquitous presence of global hedging activity. The long track record of trend followers empirically supports this conclusion.

Returns and volatility of returns[5]

Annual volatility versus annualised volatility

Estimates are that the best of the hedge fund indices may overstate historical returns while the limited transparency of hedge fund portfolios means risk–return analysis can only be done by inference. However, investors can combine their knowledge of how certain strategies work with the available hedge fund index data to make reasonable judgements. We have chosen the CSFB/Tremont database for hedge fund strategies and the ZCM/MAR trend following index for trend following. The ZCM/MAR trend following index is used because it tracks the specific performance of systematic diversified trend followers. Both indices use a market weighted approach, maintain returns for defunct or non-reporting funds and only use forward data when a new fund is added. Since CSFB/Tremont only goes back to the beginning of 1994, any comparative data with ZCM/MAR trend following begins in 1994.

On a stand-alone basis, the risk-adjusted performance of trend following indices has been lower than some other hedge fund indices. However, in certain important ways, the differences between trend following and other strategies have been overstated and at times misinterpreted by the markets. To demonstrate this observation, Exhibit 9.3 compares the compound annual returns and annualised volatility, and the average rolling 12-month returns and annual volatility of each index.

Exhibit 9.3

Performance for period 1 January 1994–31 January 2003

Indices	Compound annual return	Annualised volatility of monthly returns	Average rolling 12-month return	Volatility of rolling 12-month returns
CSFB/Tremont Equity Market Neutral	10.99%	3.17%	12.11%	4.63%
CSFB/Tremont Multi-Strategy	9.25%	4.68%	10.00%	5.40%
CSFB/Tremont Fixed Income Arbitrage	6.76%	4.07%	7.70%	6.14%
CSFB/Tremont Event Driven	10.65%	6.24%	11.66%	9.19%
CSFB/Tremont Convertible Arbitrage	10.49%	4.88%	11.63%	9.57%
ZCM/MAR-Trend-Follower Advisors Index	10.03%	14.44%	9.87%	10.57%
CSFB/Tremont Long-Short Equity	11.48%	11.42%	14.51%	15.06%
CSFB/Tremont Dedicated Short Bias	0.49%	18.25%	0.06%	15.10%
CSFB/Tremont Global Macro	14.23%	12.59%	17.12%	16.12%
CSFB/Tremont Emerging Markets Index	4.83%	18.40%	7.29%	23.74%

Source: Graham Capital Management.

Exhibit 9.4

Statistics for period 1 January 1994–31 January 2003

Indices	Monthly volatility* upside	Monthly volatility* downside	Upside/ downside	Skew	Excess kurtosis
CSFB/Tremont Equity Market Neutral	0.73	0.38	1.93	0.14	0.06
CSFB/Tremont Dedicated Short Bias	3.96	2.60	1.52	0.85	2.00
ZCM/MAR-Trend-Follower Advisors Index	2.80	2.05	1.36	0.32	0.02
CSFB/Tremont Long-Short Equity	2.51	2.08	1.20	0.25	2.95
CSFB/Tremont Global Macro	2.56	2.41	1.07	−0.03	1.62
CSFB/Tremont Emerging Markets Index	3.27	3.81	0.86	−0.48	3.25
CSFB/Tremont Multi-Strategy	0.80	1.36	0.59	−1.29	3.13
CSFB/Tremont Convertible Arbitrage	0.73	1.42	0.51	−1.59	4.02
CSFB/Tremont Event Driven	0.92	2.35	0.39	−3.32	21.22
CSFB/Tremont Fixed Income Arbitrage	0.44	1.57	0.28	−3.21	15.82

*Volatility relative to zero return.

Source: Graham Capital Management.

Exhibit 9.4 compares monthly upside volatility, monthly downside volatility, skew and kurtosis for each of the hedge fund indices. Skew measures the statistical likelihood of a return in the tail of a distribution being higher (positive skew) or lower (negative skew) than that predicted by a normal distribution. Kurtosis (fat tails) measures the statistical likelihood of there being more returns (high kurtosis) or less returns (low kurtosis) in the tails of distributions than that predicted by normal distributions. Exhibit 9.5 shows the autocorrelation of each strategy's returns, based on one-month lag, two-month lag and three-month lag.

Exhibit 9.5

Autocorrelation for period 1 January 1994–31 January 2003

Indices	One-month lag	Two-month lag	Three-month lag
SFB/Tremont Convertible Arbitrage	0.569	0.434	0.159
CSFB/Tremont Fixed Income Arbitrage	0.409	0.102	0.027
CSFB/Tremont Event Driven	0.344	0.149	0.031
CSFB/Tremont Emerging Markets Index	0.299	0.010	−0.020
CSFB/Tremont Equity Market Neutral	0.300	0.193	0.092
CSFB/Tremont Long-Short Equity	0.159	0.060	−0.046
CSFB/Tremont Dedicated Short Bias	0.067	−0.073	−0.035
CSFB/Tremont Global Macro	0.055	0.046	0.085
CSFB/Tremont Multi-Strategy	−0.034	0.075	0.184
ZCM/MAR Trend-Follower Advisors Index	0.066	−0.111	−0.075
S&P 500 Total Return Index	−0.021	−0.040	0.097

Source: Graham Capital Management.

Autocorrelation is simply the correlation of a given month's returns relative to a previous month's returns.

As shown in Exhibits 9.4 and 9.5, the four strategies with the largest skew, highest kurtosis and lowest upside/downside volatility (that is, fixed-income, event-driven, convertible arbitrage and emerging markets) also had the highest autocorrelation. While there is no necessary statistical link between autocorrelation and these other measures (for example, equity market neutral has high autocorrelation, but no skew or kurtosis and a high upside/downside volatility ratio) they appear to go together with certain trading strategies. As discussed below, high positive autocorrelation seems to be linked to strategies which have a short option profile. This short option profile, in certain strategies, will also create negative skew and high kurtosis. The trend following index had a small negative autocorrelation with a two-month and three-month lag. Although not shown in this table, when serial correlation is done for trend following using three or six-month time windows, the negative serial correlation rises to approximately (−0.25). From 1983 to mid-2002, the negative serial correlation of returns for three-month and six-month time windows, respectively, was (−0.24) and (−0.26) for the ZCM/MAR trend following index.

Exhibit 9.6 compares modified Sharpe ratios for the various strategies. What stands out here in particular is that for some of the strategies there is a significant difference in the Sharpe ratios, when calculated using monthly annualised versus rolling 12-month data. The change in the Sharpe ratio of trend following compared to, for example, convertible arbitrage is significant. Sharpe ratios are usually calculated using annualised monthly volatility numbers.[6] This may lead to misleading inferences for strategies with returns that have high autocorrelation. This annualisation process is most appropriate when predicting annual volatility for strategies whose monthly returns are uncorrelated to each other. Sharpe ratios calculated this way can understate or overstate actual annual risk when the underlying monthly returns of the strategy have positive or negative autocorrelation.

Strategies with high autocorrelation, negative skew, positive kurtosis and higher downside volatility will tend to have more losses (kurtosis) of greater magnitude (skew) than predicted

Exhibit 9.6

Sharpe ratio comparison

Indices	Modified Sharpe ratio* (monthly)	Modified Sharpe ratio** (rolling)	% difference
ZCM/MAR-Trend-Follower Advisors Index	0.69	0.93	34.8%
CSFB/Tremont Emerging Markets	0.26	0.31	19.2%
CSFB/Tremont Multi-Strategy	1.98	1.99	0.5%
CSFB/Tremont Long-Short Equity	1.01	0.96	−5.0%
CSFB/Tremont Global Macro	1.13	1.06	−6.2%
CSFB/Tremont Event Driven	1.71	1.27	−25.7%
CSFB/Tremont Equity Market Neutral	3.47	2.61	−24.8%
CSFB/Tremont Fixed Income Arbitrage	1.66	1.25	−24.7%
CSFB/Tremont Convertible Arbitrage	2.15	1.22	−43.3%
CSFB/Tremont Dedicated Short Bias	0.03	0.00	N/A

* Annualised return ÷ annualised volatility.

** Rolling 12-month return ÷ volatility of rolling 12-month return.

Source: Graham Capital Management.

by the annualisation method used to calculate most Sharpe ratios. Therefore, these strategies may have overstated risk-adjusted performance when this method is used. Conversely, it appears that strategies with higher upside volatility, positive skew, positive kurtosis and negative autocorrelation will tend to have more gains (kurtosis) of greater magnitude (skew), than predicted by the annualisation methodology. When the Sharpe ratio calculation is done on an annual basis using rolling 12-month data, no other statistical calculation is performed. Rolling 12-month returns and volatilities will tend to smooth the impact of the non-symmetrical and autocorrelated monthly returns of different hedge fund strategies. Later, it will be demonstrated that the use of rolling data may help create more optimal portfolios.

Long option profile strategies and short option profile strategies

Trend following has a higher Sharpe ratio and convertible arbitrage, for example, has a lower Sharpe ratio when annual rolling numbers are used. This is due primarily to the autocorrelation of their monthly returns. Trend following's long option profile seems linked to its negative autocorrelation (particularly for three and six-month time windows), positive skew and high upside/downside volatility ratio. Convertible arbitrage, on the other hand, has a 'short option' profile that appears linked to its positive autocorrelation, negative skew, high kurtosis and low upside/downside volatility ratio. Exhibit 9.7 graphically depicts the monthly return distributions of both the trend following and the convertible arbitrage indices.

Previously we explained why trend following has a long option profile. Many other hedge fund strategies clearly exhibit a short option profile. Credit oriented and convergence strategies and certain market-neutral strategies often fit this description. Fixed-income and mortgage arbitrage, emerging markets debt, risk arbitrage, distressed debt, convertible arbitrage (particularly strategies that assume significant credit risk) and mean reverting

Exhibit 9.7

Return distribution (%)

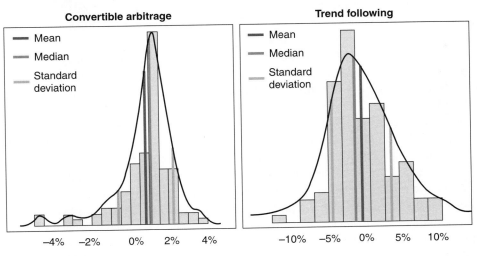

Source: Graham Capital Management.

market-neutral statistical arbitrage strategies are examples of strategies which can also exhibit optionality.[7] To get a better understanding of what it means for a strategy to have a short option profile we will analyse credit-oriented convertible arbitrage and risk arbitrage. Convertible arbitrage strategies which hedge all credit risk through credit derivatives are not prone to having this short option profile.

A strategy exhibits a short option profile if it has a high percentage of limited upside trades or months and a low percentage of larger downside trades or months. Corporate bonds fit this description perfectly. They have a limited upside return because they earn a defined fixed coupon and are usually callable if interest rates decrease very much. In exchange for receiving a fixed cash flow, the corporate bondholder assumes a larger downside risk due to potential credit deterioration, or bankruptcy. Convertible bonds are hybrid securities whose value is typically 85 per cent corporate bond and 15 per cent equity option. For an arbitrageur, a convertible bond has both a short option profile (corporate bond) and a long volatility (embedded equity option) profile. However, if credit quality severely deteriorates, the bond value dominates. That is, the arbitrageur will lose more money on the bond than made on volatility. Additionally, convertible bonds, particularly lower credits, are not as actively traded as underlying equity markets. Monthly prices, and therefore returns, can appear more stable and consistent than they really are.[8] Of course, as the annual numbers show, convertible arbitrage still has had good risk-adjusted returns. However, annualised volatility numbers understate the risk of convertible arbitrage.

The same point can be made about risk arbitrage. Risk arbitrageurs buy equity of an acquisition target once a deal has been announced and hope to earn the remaining deal spread, while risking the much larger loss from the deal not closing. Since a very high percentage of deals close, risk arbitrage will have a high percentage of limited upside winning trades and a low percentage of large downside losing trades. Risk arbitrage has also had good risk-adjusted returns. However, its annualised volatility numbers understate the strategy's risk.

Empirically, autocorrelation, both positive and negative, appears to be consistently linked to the strategies with known optionality. To repeat, the statistical existence of auto-correlation in monthly returns results in an understatement or overstatement of actual annual volatility when annualising monthly volatility. However, as demonstrated by the equity market-neutral index, autocorrelations and optionality do not need to appear together. However, the strategies of convertible arbitrage, fixed-income arbitrage, event-driven (both risk arbitrage and distressed debt), and emerging markets all have attributes in common which help explain why these strategies have both optionality and autocorrelation. They are either less liquid strategies (distressed debt, emerging markets, mortgage markets and con-vertible bond markets) and/or strategies which have a 'fixed carry' component (each of the aforementioned plus risk arbitrage).

Less liquid securities are usually formally valued monthly when fund managers get esti-mates from their prime brokers and other dealers. Since trading activity is comparatively low, values can appear more stable month to month than is really the case. This phenomenon contributes to serial correlation. Secondly, many of these strategies have a fixed carry com-ponent. This is usually reflected in positive interest carry or, as in the case of risk arbitrage, value accretion as the estimated deal closing date approaches. This also contributes further to serial correlation. These strategy attributes, as discussed earlier, are designed to have frequent but limited upside months and less frequent but larger downside months. This creates their short option return profile.

Trend following, particularly for three and six month time windows, has negative serial correlation. Thus, its annual volatility can be overstated by annualising monthly volatili-ty. Trend followers are subject to major reversals in markets (as can be visually seen in the DAX contract example in Exhibit 9.2). Usually, trend followers achieve their largest downside periods through the give back of previously unrealised gains. For a profitable position, the net effect over the entire period is positive, although achieved in this volatile fashion. It is this return tendency of trend following which creates its negative serial correlation and it is the investment philosophy of 'cutting losses and letting profits run' (the implicit long straddle position cited earlier in Fung and Hsieh) which creates the long option return profile of trend following.

Correlation of returns and portfolio construction

Trend following and correlation

Exhibit 9.8 shows the correlation of trend following with the CSFB/Tremont indices, the S&P 500 and the Lehman Brothers Bond Index based on both monthly and the 12-month rolling data. Both approaches produce similar results.

Exhibit 9.9 shows the correlation of all strategies to the S&P 500 during positive and negative performing months for the S&P.

Exhibit 9.10 looks at the best and worst performing months of the S&P 500 since 1987 and compares the returns of the ZCM/MAR trend following index with the S&P 500 as well as their correlation.

The correlation characteristics of trend following with the equity market and other hedge fund strategies is compelling for investors seeking portfolio diversification. Trend following has had positive correlation during strong periods for the S&P 500 and negative correlations during very weak periods for the S&P 500. This is what one should expect from a long option

Exhibit 9.8

Correlation analysis, 1 January 1994–31 January 2003

ZCM/MAR Trend-Follower Advisors Index versus:	*Monthly*	*Annual*
CSFB/Tremont Convertible Arbitrage	−0.12	−0.19
CSFB/Tremont Dedicated Short Bias	0.30	0.44
CSFB/Tremont Emerging Markets Index	−0.19	−0.15
CSFB/Tremont Equity Market Neutral	0.17	−0.01
CSFB/Tremont Event Driven	−0.22	−0.14
CSFB/Tremont Fixed Income Arbitrage	−0.01	0.09
CSFB/Tremont Global Macro	0.33	0.36
CSFB/Tremont Long-Short Equity	−0.10	−0.41
CSFB/Tremont Multi-Strategy	−0.05	−0.14
Lehman Brothers Treasury Bond Index	0.39	0.47
S&P 500 Total Return Index	−0.27	−0.09

Source: Graham Capital Management.

Exhibit 9.9

Correlation analysis, 1 January 1994–31 January 2003

S&P 500 Total Return Index versus:	*Down months*	*Up months*	*Difference*
ZCM/MAR-Trend-Follower Advisors Index	−0.55	−0.16	0.39
CSFB/Tremont Equity Market Neutral	0.23	0.33	0.10
CSFB/Tremont Dedicated Short Bias	−0.56	−0.48	0.08
CSFB/Tremont Multi-Strategy	−0.01	−0.11	−0.10
CSFB/Tremont Global Macro	0.09	−0.05	−0.14
CSFB/Tremont Long-Short Equity	0.39	0.24	−0.15
CSFB/Tremont Convertible Arbitrage	0.30	0.06	−0.24
CSFB/Tremont Emerging Markets Index	0.49	0.12	−0.37
CSFB/Tremont Event Driven	0.58	0.13	−0.45
CSFB/Tremont Fixed Income Arbitrage	0.26	−0.25	−0.51

Source: Graham Capital Management.

strategy. Trend following also has had a negative correlation to equities in bear markets while other hedge fund strategies have generally exhibited positive correlation to the S&P 500 during these same periods.

Trend following and portfolio construction

As discussed earlier, the annualisation method for calculating Sharpe ratios produces misleading results for hedge funds with autocorrelation. The 12-month rolling analysis performed earlier implies that the annualisation of monthly data results in overstated Sharpe ratios for hedge fund strategies with positive autocorrelation. If portfolio construction relies on annualised returns and volatilities, it will tend to over allocate to high positive serial cor-

Exhibit 9.10

Trend following and S&P 500 returns (%)

Worst	S&P Total Return Index (monthly)	ZCM/MAR Trend-Follower Advisors (monthly)	Best	S&P Total Return Index (monthly)	ZCM/MAR Trend-Follower Advisors (monthly)
Oct-87	−21.59	1.84	Jan-87	13.51	10.01
Aug-98	−14.46	11.49	Dec-91	11.44	22.03
Sep-02	−10.87	4.81	Mar-00	9.78	−2.73
Feb-01	−9.12	1.03	May-90	9.75	−7.06
Aug-90	−9.04	8.81	Jul-89	9.03	1.20
Nov-87	−8.32	11.33	Oct-02	8.80	−4.80
Sep-01	−8.08	6.03	Oct-98	8.13	−0.19
Nov-00	−7.88	6.79	Jul-97	7.96	8.64
Jul-02	−7.80	6.79	Dec-87	7.78	8.18
Jun-02	−7.12	10.75	Apr-01	7.77	−7.42
Jan-90	−6.71	3.13	Nov-01	7.67	−10.02
Mar-01	−6.34	8.17	Nov-96	7.56	7.02
Aug-01	−6.26	3.04	Jan-89	7.33	7.03
Apr-02	−6.06	−2.16	Feb-98	7.21	−0.55
Dec-02	−5.88	5.65	Feb-91	7.15	−0.68
Aug-97	−5.60	−4.77	Nov-90	6.46	0.32
Sep-00	−5.28	−3.79	Sep-98	6.41	6.21
Jan-00	−5.02	1.60	Oct-99	6.33	−6.35
Average:	−8.41	4.47	Average:	8.34	1.71
Correlation coefficient:		−0.206	Correlation coefficient:		0.386

Source: Graham Capital Management.

relation strategies (for example, fixed-income or convertible arbitrage) and under allocate to negative serial correlation strategies (for example, trend following) as a whole, when constructing high Sharpe ratio portfolios.

This can be demonstrated by performing two different pairs of optimisations (four in total). The first two optimisations compare the absolute highest Sharpe ratio portfolios using two different methods. One portfolio is optimised to create the highest annualised monthly Sharpe ratio and the other portfolio is optimised to create the highest rolling annual Sharpe ratio. These portfolios produce very different results which are then compared across a variety of monthly statistics. The second pair of optimisations sets a target rate of return of 10 per cent for the same 10 indices and again performs the same comparative analysis to find the highest Sharpe ratio portfolios using the two different methods of calculating these ratios.

The data used for the optimisations were for the period beginning January 1994 and ending January 2003. The only constraint put on the optimisations was that no strategy could be allocated less than 5 per cent or more than 30 per cent. Each portfolio was rebalanced monthly to achieve the initial weightings on an ongoing basis. 'Portfolio One' is always the designation for the optimised portfolios creating the highest annualised monthly Sharpe ratio.

Exhibit 9.11

Return and volatility analysis

	Portfolio One monthly optimisation	*Portfolio Two rolling 12-month optimisation*
Returns (%)		
Annualised monthly	9.44	9.61
Rolling annual	10.24	9.85
Volatility (%)		
Annualised monthly	2.77	3.33
Rolling annual	5.18	4.52
Modified Sharpe		
Annualised monthly	3.41	2.89
Rolling annual	1.97	2.18

Source: Graham Capital Management.

Exhibit 9.12

Comparative portfolio weightings (%)

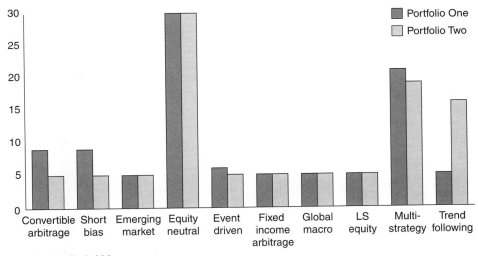

Source: Graham Capital Management.

'Portfolio Two' is always the designation for the optimised portfolios creating the highest rolling annual Sharpe ratio.

The first analysis below seeks to find the highest absolute Sharpe ratio by optimising among the 10 total indices. Portfolio One was optimised using the traditional method which optimised based on monthly returns, volatility and correlations. Portfolio Two was optimised based on rolling annual returns, volatility and correlations.

Exhibit 9.11 compares returns and Sharpe ratios for the two portfolios.

By definition, Portfolio One had a higher Sharpe ratio when calculated using annualised monthly returns and monthly volatilities. Conversely, also by definition, Portfolio

Two had a higher Sharpe ratio when calculated using rolling annual returns and rolling annual volatility.

The two methods for calculating the Sharpe ratio result in very different answers. For example, Portfolio One's Sharpe ratio declines from 3.41 to 1.97 simply by changing the method of calculation to using rolling annual returns and rolling annual volatility. When the annualised monthly Sharpe ratios are compared, Portfolio One appears better: 3.41 vs. 2.89. However, when the rolling annual Sharpe ratios are compared Portfolio Two appears better: 2.18 vs. 1.97. As stated in the previous section, we believe the rolling 12-month numbers gives a more accurate picture of actual historical Sharpe ratios.

As seen in Exhibit 9.12 Portfolio Two has a 16.3 per cent allocation to trend following, while it has a 5 per cent allocation in Portfolio One. Is there another way to compare the two portfolios, besides the two methods of calculating Sharpe ratios, to get a sense of which one has the better risk–reward performance?

To determine this, the two portfolios were evaluated by comparing their monthly performance since 1994 using a variety of different measures. Exhibit 9.13 gives the results.

As can be seen in Exhibit 9.13, Portfolio Two does appear to have better statistical performance. Portfolio Two had a higher upside volatility, lower downside volatility, higher average winning month, positive skew, lower kurtosis, higher Sortino ratio and a lower maximum drawdown. Portfolio One was superior in that it had 10 winning months per year vs. 9.4 winning months per year for Portfolio Two. For any investor with a time horizon longer than a few months, Portfolio Two appears superior. Yet, as seen in Exhibit 9.12, the traditional

Exhibit 9.13

Risk–reward analysis

	Portfolio One monthly optimisation	*Portfolio Two rolling 12-month optimisation*
Monthly returns		
Mean (%)	0.76	0.77
Median (%)	0.77	0.66
Volatility		
Upside (%)	0.63	0.79
Downside (%)	0.50	0.42
Ratio	1.26	1.88
Sortino ratio*	5.54	6.67
MAX drawdown	3.50	1.34
Calmar ratio**	2.71	7.19
Skew	−0.18	0.28
Kurtosis	0.78	−0.13
Average win (%)	0.98	1.10
Average loss (%)	−0.38	−0.41
Winning months/year	10.00	9.40

*Annualised return/annualised downside volatility.

** Annualised returns ÷ maximum drawdown.

Source: Graham Capital Management.

method of calculating Sharpe ratios makes it appear as if Portfolio One had the best risk–reward performance. Optimising using rolling annual data created a superior portfolio because it better captured the impact of autocorrelation, skew, kurtosis and upside/downside volatility. It created a portfolio with superior performance characteristics than the traditional method which is biased toward short option profile strategies.

The second pair of optimisations was performed on the same hedge fund indices, except in this instance the annual returns were set equal at 0.80 per cent per month (about 10 per cent per year). The same constraints of a minimum 5 per cent and a maximum 30 per cent were

Exhibit 9.14

Return and volatility analysis

	Portfolio One monthly optimisation	*Portfolio Two rolling 12-month optimisation*
Returns (%)		
Annualised monthly	10.03	10.03
Rolling annual	11.41	10.46
Volatility (%)		
Annualised monthly	3.12	4.05
Rolling annual	6.56	4.89
Modified Sharpe		
Annualised monthly	3.21	2.47
Rolling annual	1.74	2.14

Source: Graham Capital Management.

Exhibit 9.15

Comparative portfolio weightings (%)

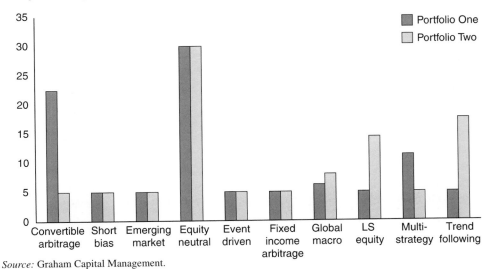

Source: Graham Capital Management.

125

Exhibit 9.16

Risk–reward analysis

	Portfolio One *monthly optimisation*	*Portfolio Two* *rolling 12-month optimisation*
Monthly returns (%)		
Mean	0.80	0.80
Median	0.79	0.60
Volatility		
Upside (%)	0.68	0.95
Downside (%)	0.64	0.47
Ratio	1.06	2.02
Sortino ratio*	4.51	6.21
MAX drawdown (%)	3.98	1.76
Calmar ratio**	2.51	5.68
Skew	−0.33	0.46
Kurtosis	1.23	0.20
Average win (%)	1.07	1.30
Average loss (%)	−0.55	−0.52
Winning months/year	10.00	8.70

*Annualised return/annualised downside volatility.

**Annualised returns ÷ maximum drawdown.

Source: Graham Capital Management.

used. The results are presented in Exhibits 9.14, 9.15 and 9.16. As can be seen from the data, the same pattern exists as in the first optimisation. Once again, as seen in Exhibit 9.14, the two methods for calculating Sharpe ratios for Portfolio One result in significantly different outcomes. The annualised monthly method produces a 3.21 Sharpe ratio versus 1.74 for the rolling annual method. For Portfolio Two, the Sharpe ratios are similar using either method. The annualised monthly method makes Portfolio One appear better, while the rolling annual method makes Portfolio Two appear better.

Exhibit 9.15 shows that Portfolio One has a large allocation to convertible arbitrage and a low allocation to trend following while Portfolio Two allocates a large amount to trend following. The difference between the two portfolios comes largely from a reduction in convertible arbitrage and multi-strategy, and an increase in trend following and long-short equity.

As can be seen in Exhibit 9.16, Portfolio Two has an improved risk–reward profile. Portfolio One has more winning months per year but Portfolio Two has better upside volatility, lower downside volatility, lower max drawdown, higher average winning month, lower average losing month, positive skew and lower kurtosis. It appears that Portfolio Two, which has the higher allocation to trend following, is the better risk-adjusted portfolio.

Each of the optimisations that solved for the highest rolling annual Sharpe ratio resulted in a portfolio with better risk–reward performance for investors with a time horizon longer than a few months. This supports the proposition that the rolling annual method is more accurate than the annualisation method for calculating Sharpe ratios for hedge fund strategies. These portfolios all had higher allocations to trend following, lower maximum drawdowns and higher Sortino and Calmar ratios. Increased allocations to trend following appears to create a more risk-averse portfolio. A portfolio with a higher probability of a lower drawdown should be considered preferable to the investor, everything else being equal. Conversely, if one wanted, through leverage, to set the maximum drawdown of the two Portfolio Twos, equal to that of the two Portfolio Ones, the investor would have achieved a higher return at the same drawdown level.

The above analysis is obviously not meant to suggest these optimised weights are what is actually recommended for a particular portfolio. This ultimately depends on a variety of factors including individual manager selection, relative risk weightings in each strategy, forward forecasts of market conditions for each strategy, and targeted absolute return and risk levels. However, this analysis demonstrates that the positive portfolio characteristics of trend following, as presented in this chapter, will result in hedge fund investors having improved performance by allocating to trend following.

Conclusion

As long as trends appear in global markets, trend followers should be able to earn positive returns. Additionally, as long as hedgers exist, there will be ample opportunity and capacity for futures traders as a whole to be profitable.

While trend following, on a stand-alone basis, has had a higher volatility profile than many other hedge fund strategies, this difference may have been overstated. When calculating Sharpe ratios by annualising monthly volatility numbers, one does not capture the autocorrelation of returns inherent in many hedge fund strategies. The practical effect of this has been to overvalue short option profile strategies and undervalue long option profile strategies when evaluating risk–reward performance. By using a rolling 12-month methodology, which tends to smooth data, one can effectively capture the impact of optionality and autocorrelation in measuring the risk–reward profile of a strategy.

Trend following's second unique quality, which is related to its long option return profile, is its correlation characteristics. It is one of the only strategies which is negatively correlated to stocks during negative equity markets and which also exhibits an increase in correlation when equity markets are very positive. However, its largest benefit to a diversified portfolio of hedge funds arises from its high negative correlation when the equity market declines.

Proper hedge fund portfolio construction requires forecasting returns, correlation, volatility, as well as individual hedge fund and overall portfolio optionality. This chapter has provided evidence, through a rolling 12-month methodology, that portfolios which are constructed with a meaningful allocation to trend following can create more risk-averse investments. If portfolio construction relies only on monthly returns, volatility and correlations, they may ignore the effects of autocorrelation, skew, kurtosis and upside/downside volatility, thus creating sub-optimal portfolios for time horizons longer than a few months. Asset allocators should explicitly factor in these statistical elements when determining their optimal portfolios. If they do, it will more likely result in a higher allocation to trend following than previously considered.

References

Agarwal, Vikas, and Narayan Y. Naik (2002), 'Performance Evaluation of Hedge Funds with Option-based and Buy-and-Hold Strategies,' *Working Paper* (August).

Amin, Gaurav S., and Harry M. Kat (2002a), 'Hedge Fund Performance 1990–2000: Do the 'Money Machines' Really add Value?' *ISMA Centre for Education & Research in Securities Markets, Working Paper Series.*

Amin, Gaurav S., and Harry M. Kat (2002b), 'Who Should buy Hedge Funds? The Effects of Including Hedge Funds in Portfolios of Stocks and Bonds' *ISMA Centre for Education & Research in Securities Markets, Working Paper Series.*

Brooks, Chris, and Harry M. Kat (2002) , 'The Statistical Properties of Hedge Fund Index Returns and Their Implications for Investors,' *Journal of Alternative Investment*, Vol. 5, pp. 26–44.

Brown, Stephen J., and William N. Goetzmann, 'Hedge Fund with Style,' Working Paper, No. W8I73.

Edwards, Franklin R., and Mustafa Onur Caglayan (2001), 'Hedge Fund and Commodity Fund Investment Styles in Bull and Bear Markets,' *Journal of Portfolio Management*, Vol. 27, pp. 97–108.

Favre, Laurent, and Jose-Antonio Galeano (2002), 'Portfolio Allocation with Hedge Funds: Case Study of a Swiss Institutional Investor,' Working Paper.

Fung, William, and David A. Hsieh (2001a), 'Asset-Based Hedge-Fund Styles and Portfolio Diversification,' *Financial Analyst Journal*, Vol. 58, pp.16–27 (September).

Fung, William, and David A. Hsieh (2001b), 'The Risk in Hedge Fund Strategies: Theory and Evidence from Trend Followers,' *Review of Financial Services*, Vol. 14, pp. 313–341.

Fung, William, and David A. Hsieh (2002a) , 'Hedge-Fund Benchmarks: Information Content and Biases,' *Financial Analyst Journal*, Vol. 58, pp. 22–34.

Fung, William, and David A. Hsieh (2002b), 'The Risk in Hedge Fund Strategies: Theory and Evidence from Fixed Income Funds,' *Journal of Fixed Income*, p.14.

Harris, Lawrence (1993), *The Winners and Losers of the Zero-Sum Game: The Origins of Trading Profits, Price Efficiency and Market Liquidity*, University of Southern California.

Jaeger, Lars (2002), *Managing Risk in Alternative Investment Strategies*, London, Financial Times Prentice Hall.

Karas, Robert, *Looking Behind the Non-Correlation Argument*, Website: www.aima.or aima-site/researchll toct99.htm.

Kat, Harry M. (2002), 'Managed Futures and Hedge Funds: A Match Made in Heaven,' Working Paper (November).

Kaufman, Perry (1998), *Trading Systems and Methods*, New York, John Wiley and Sons.

Krokhmal, Pavlo, Stanislav Uryasev, and Grigory Zrazhevsky (2002) 'Comparative Analysis of Linear Portfolio Rebalancing Strategies: An Application to Hedge Funds,' *The Journal of Alternative Investments*, Vol. 5, pp. 10–30.

Lhabitant, Francois-Serge (2001), 'Assessing Market Risk for Hedge Funds and Hedge Funds Portfolios,' Social Science Research Network Electronic Library (August).

Martin, George (2002), 'Making Sense of Hedge Fund Returns: What Matters and What Doesn't,' *Derivatives Strategies*, Vol. 4, No. 11.

Radalj, Kim, *Risk Premiums and the Forward Rate Anomaly: A Survey*, Department of Economics, University of Western Australia.

Schneeweis, Thomas, and Georgi Georgiev (2002), *The Benefits of Managed Futures*, CISDM and School of Management at University of Massachusetts.

Schneeweis, Thomas, and Richard Spurgin (2002), 'Quantitative Analysis of Hedge Fund and Managed Futures Return and Risk Characteristics', *Evaluating and Implementing Hedge Fund Strategies*, Second Edition, R. Lake (Ed.), London, Euromoney Books, pp. 262–275.

Spurgin, Richard, 'Some Thoughts on the Sources of Return to Managed Futures', CISDM and School of Management, University of Massachusetts. www.graniteonline.com/Articles_papers,_etc/Source_of_CTA_Returns.pdf.

---

[1] 'The Risk in Hedge Fund Strategies: Theory and Evidence from Trend Followers', William Fung and David A. Hsieh (2001b). The authors demonstrate that trend following returns are highly correlated with buying straddles (call and puts) on markets, in particular, 'look back' straddles.

[2] *Trading Systems and Methods*, Perry J. Kaufman (1998). Kaufman provides an excellent overview of trend following and other systematic programs in this 700 page text and provides an 11 page bibliography.

[3] 'Some Thoughts on Sources of Return to Managed Futures' Richard Spurgin. 'Quantitative Analysis of Hedge Fund and Managed Futures Return and Risk Characteristics' Thomas Schneeweis and Richard Spurgin (2002). Both articles discuss sources of returns for managed futures relating to the existence of hedgers.

[4] 'Risk Premiums and the Forward Rate Anomaly: A Survey', Kim Radalj, Department of Economics, University of Western Australia. Radalj examines the unbiased forward rate hypothesis (UFRM) as well as Keynes' insurance theory of speculation first proposed in Keynes', *A Treatise on Money, Volume II*.

[5] Both Brooks and Kat (2002), and Amin and Kat (2002) stress the importance of factoring skew, kurtosis and autocorrelation into risk–reward analysis for hedge funds. Traditional mean-variance analysis will tend to understate risk for high autocorrelation, negatively skewed and high kurtosis strategies.

[6] The annualisation of a monthly volatility number is calculated by multiplying the monthly volatility number by an annualisation factor. This factor is sometimes called the 'square root of time' (in this instance that would mean $\sqrt{12}$, or 3.46).

[7] William Fung and David A. Hsieh (2002b) make the point that many fixed-income and credit oriented strategies can be modelled as a short position in look back straddles in interest rate spreads.

[8] Brooks and Kat, ibid. The authors also discuss autocorrelation being linked to lower liquidity strategies.

Chapter 10

Using a long-short portfolio to neutralise market risk and enhance active returns

Bruce I. Jacobs and Kenneth N. Levy
Jacobs Levy Equity Management, Florham Park, New Jersey

Introduction

Investors traditionally focus on identifying securities they expect to perform well and adding those winning securities to their portfolios. Few investors take advantage of losing securities, unless it is to avoid them or to sell those that happen to be included in their portfolios. However, selling losing securities short has the potential to add at least as much value as purchasing winning securities long. Furthermore, combining winners and losers in a single portfolio offers advantages in terms of pursuit of return and control of risk that are not available in long-only portfolios.[1] We examine below a long-short portfolio designed to eliminate exposure to equity market risk and return while providing returns from stock selection. A market-neutral long-short portfolio is constructed so that the dollar amount of securities held long equals the dollar amount of securities sold short and the short positions' price sensitivity to market movements equals and offsets the long positions' sensitivity. Since the portfolio's value does not rise or fall just because the broad market average rises or falls, the portfolio is said to have a beta of zero. This does not mean that the portfolio is riskless. It will retain the risks associated with the selection of the individual stocks held long and sold short. However, with insightful security selection, the portfolio will reap commensurate rewards.

Setting up a market-neutral long-short portfolio

Exhibit 10.1 illustrates the operations needed to establish a market-neutral long-short strategy, assuming a US$10 million initial investment. Keep in mind that these operations are undertaken virtually simultaneously, although they will be discussed in steps.

In the United States, the Federal Reserve Board requires that short positions be housed in a margin account at a brokerage firm. The first step in setting up a long-short portfolio, then, is to find a trustworthy 'prime broker' to administer the account. This prime broker clears all trades and arranges to borrow the shares to be sold short.

Of the initial US$10 million investment, US$9 million is used to purchase the desired long positions. (The application of the remaining US$1 million is discussed below.) These are held at the prime broker, where they serve as the collateral necessary, under Federal Reserve

Exhibit 10.1

Setting up a market-neutral long-short portfolio

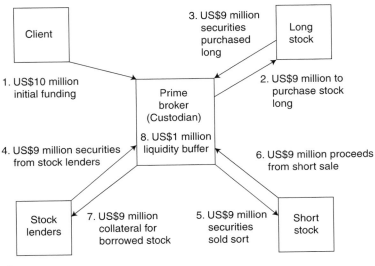

Source: Authors' own.

Board margin requirements, to establish the desired short positions. The prime broker arranges to borrow the securities to be sold short. Their sale results in cash proceeds, which are delivered to the stock lenders as collateral for the borrowed shares.

Federal Reserve Board Regulation T requires that an equity margined account be at least 50 per cent collateralised to initiate short sales.[2] This means that the investor could buy US$10 million of securities and sell short another US$10 million, resulting in US$20 million in equity positions, long and short. As Exhibit 10.1 shows, however, the investor has bought only US$9 million of securities, and sold short an equal amount. The account retains US$1 million of the initial investment in cash.

This 'liquidity buffer' serves as a pool to meet cash demands on the account. For instance, the account's short positions are marked to market daily. If the prices of the shorted stocks increase, the account must post additional capital with the stock lenders to maintain full collateralisation; conversely, if the shorted positions fall in price, the (now over-collateralised) lenders release funds to the long-short account. The liquidity buffer may also be used to reimburse the stock lenders for dividends owed on the shares sold short, although dividends received on stocks held long may be able to meet this cash need. Normally, a liquidity buffer equal to 10 per cent of the initial investment will be sufficient.

The liquidity buffer will earn interest for the long-short account. We assume the interest earned approximates the Treasury bill rate. The US$9 million in cash proceeds from the short sales, which have been posted as collateral with the stocks' lenders, also earn interest. The interest earned on these proceeds is typically allocated among the lenders, the prime broker and the long-short account; the lenders retain a small portion as a lending fee, the prime broker retains a portion to cover expenses and provide some profit, and the investor receives the rest. The exact distribution is a matter for negotiation, but we assume the amount rebated to the investor (the 'short rebate') approximates the Treasury bill rate.

The overall return to the market-neutral long-short portfolio thus has two components: an interest component and an equity component. The performances of the stocks held long and sold short will determine the equity component. As we will see below, this component will be independent of the performance of the equity market from which the stocks have been selected.

Performance in bull and bear markets

Exhibit 10.2 illustrates the hypothetical performance of a market-neutral long-short portfolio under two scenarios. The top half of the exhibit (the bull market case) assumes the market rises by 30 per cent, while the long positions rise by 33 per cent and the short positions by 27 per cent. The 33 per cent return increases the value of the US$9 million in long positions to US$11.97 million, for a US$2.97 million gain. The 27 per cent return on the shares sold short increases their value from US$9 million to US$11.43 million; because these shares are sold short, this translates into a US$2.43 million loss for the portfolio.

The net gain from equity positions equals US$540,000, or US$2.97 million minus US$2.43 million. This represents a 6 per cent return on the initial equity investment of US$9 million, equal to the spread between the returns on the long and short positions (33 per cent

Exhibit 10.2

Hypothetical performance of market-neutral long-short portfolio in bull and bear markets (US$ million)

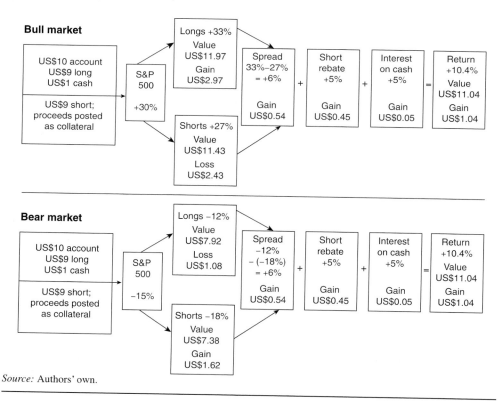

Source: Authors' own.

minus 27 per cent). As the initial equity investment represented only 90 per cent of the invested capital, however, the equity component's performance translates into a 5.4 per cent return on the initial investment (90 per cent of 6 per cent).

We assume the short rebate (the interest received on the cash proceeds from the short sales, which fluctuates with market rates) equals 5 per cent. This amounts to US$450,000 (5 per cent of US$9 million). The interest earned on the liquidity buffer adds another US$50,000 (5 per cent of US$1 million). Thus, at the end of the period, the US$10 million initial investment has grown to US$11.04 million. The long-short portfolio return of 10.4 per cent comprises a 5 per cent return from interest earnings and a 5.4 per cent return from the equity positions, long and short. (On the other hand, if the shorts had risen more than the longs, the spread would be negative, providing a lower, perhaps even negative, return. Also, if interest rates had declined, the interest earnings would be lower.)

The bottom half of Exhibit 10.2 illustrates the portfolio's performance assuming the market declines by 15 per cent. The long and short positions exhibit the same market-relative performances as above, with the longs falling by 12 per cent and the shorts falling by 18 per cent. In this case, the decline in the prices of the securities held long results in an ending value of US$7.92 million, for a loss of US$1.08 million. The shares sold short, however, decline in value to US$7.38 million, so the portfolio gains US$1.62 million from the short positions. The equity positions thus post a gain of US$540,000 (exactly the same as the net equity result experienced when the market rose). The interest earnings from the short rebate and the liquidity buffer are the same as in the bull market case, so the overall portfolio again grows from US$10 million to US$11.04 million, for a return of 10.4 per cent. (Obviously, if the shorts had fallen less than the longs, or interest rates had declined, the return would be lower.)

A market-neutral long-short portfolio is designed to return the same amount whether the equity market rises or falls. A properly constructed market-neutral portfolio, if it performs as expected, will incur virtually no systematic or market risk; its return will equal its interest earnings plus the net return on (the spread between) the long and short positions. The equity return spread is purely active, reflecting the investor's stock selection skills, neither diluted nor augmented by the underlying market's return. This active equity return should reflect the enhanced flexibility that long-short portfolio construction affords the investor in actively pursuing returns and controlling portfolio risk.

Benefits of long-short

Exhibit 10.2 assumes equal profitability of the long and short positions (3 per cent on either side of the market). However, short positions may actually be able to offer greater profitability than long positions. There are both theoretical and practical reasons for believing so.

Investors' expectations about the future performance of a security differ. Some investors are optimistic, others pessimistic. Without complete freedom to sell short, however, the views of pessimistic investors may not be fully reflected in the security's price. Some stocks will thus be overpriced. Those stocks about which there is the greatest divergence of opinion will be the most overpriced.

Overpricing may be supported by fads and bubbles. Overpricing may also be supported by corporate publicity and by brokerage house recommendations and research reports. Corporations tend to publicise good news in a timely manner, whereas bad news is subject to delay, 'window dressing' and outright fraud. Brokers and analysts favour buy over sell rec-ommendations. Brokers have more to gain from buy recommendations, as anyone may buy, generating commissions for the broker, whereas only those who already own the stock (and a small number of short sellers) will sell. Furthermore, analysts, swayed by their firms' investment banking relationships, have been reluctant to issue negative reports that could offend current and potential corporate clients.

In a market in which prices tend to reflect over-optimism on the part of investors and in which short selling is restricted, inefficiencies may be concentrated in overpriced stocks. In such a market, there are likely to be more profitable opportunities for selling short overpriced stocks than there are profitable opportunities for purchasing underpriced stocks.[3]

Nevertheless, the real benefits of long-short are not dependent upon the existence of greater inefficiencies in overpriced than underpriced stocks. Rather, they flow from the increased flexibility allowed by the long-short construction process.[4]

This increased flexibility reflects, most obviously, freedom from the short selling con-straint imposed on long-only portfolios. Consider, for example, a long-only investor who has a strong negative view about a company. The strongest position this investor can take is to exclude the company's stock from his or her portfolio. As the typical US stock constitutes only 0.01 per cent of the capitalisation of the US equity universe, not holding the stock trans-lates into a portfolio underweight of 0.01 per cent relative to the underlying market. Such a minute underweight can hardly be expected to contribute a great deal to the portfolio's per-formance! By contrast, the long-short investor's ability to underweight the stock is limited only by the investor's tolerance for risk.

However, long-only investors face limitations on their portfolio positions more subtle than, although perhaps just as costly as, the absolute constraint on short selling. Consider a long-only investor whose selection universe consists of the stocks in a given market index and who measures performance against that index. In order to achieve a return over and above that of the underlying index benchmark, the investor must be able to overweight securities expected to earn above-average returns and underweight securities expected to earn below-average returns.

Consider, for example, a stock that constitutes 5 per cent of the underlying benchmark. If the stock is expected to offer an above-benchmark return, the investor will want to over-weight the stock in his or her portfolio. Establishing an overweight, however, requires investing more than 5 per cent of the portfolio's capital; a 1 per cent overweight, for exam-ple, requires a 6 per cent portfolio position. The long-only portfolio's ability to take active positions is limited by the need to allocate capital to what are essentially passive, bench-mark positions.

The long-only portfolio's scope of 'activity' may be further reduced by the need to contain portfolio weights in order to control portfolio risk. Departures from benchmark weights, needed to produce above-benchmark (or excess) returns, introduce residual risk relative to the bench-mark. The more the portfolio departs from securities' weights in the underlying benchmark, the greater is the probability that its return will diverge from (perhaps falling short of) the return on the benchmark. Thus, for a long-only investor, controlling a portfolio's residual risk means controlling the portfolio's weighting of each security.

This may require limiting underweights as well as overweights. Consider again a stock that constitutes 5 per cent of the underlying benchmark index. This time, however, the investor expects the stock to do poorly, and wishes to underweight it. Excluding the stock from the portfolio would constitute a 5 per cent portfolio underweighting; this is a significant position in terms of the portfolio's residual risk. If the stock, against the investor's expectations, performs well, the portfolio's performance relative to its underlying benchmark could suffer. To limit portfolio risk, the investor is likely to hold some position, albeit an underweighted one, in the stock, even though the investor expects a sub-par return from that particular security.

A properly constructed long-short portfolio does not face such restrictions on its ability to take active positions. As noted, because stocks can be sold short, its ability to underweight stocks is not limited to their weights in an underlying index. In fact, in market-neutral long-short, there is no underlying benchmark index restricting positions, long or short. The offsetting long and short positions eliminate systematic risk and, with it, the benchmark. Long-short portfolios do not have to converge to securities' benchmark weights to control portfolio residual risk; nor do they need to allocate capital to essentially passive positions in order to achieve desired over or under-weightings. In long-short, virtually all equity positions are active. Portfolio risk is controlled by the proper combination of securities held long and sold short.

In this regard, we cannot overemphasise the importance to long-short management of an integrated approach to portfolio construction. An integrated approach is one that considers the risks and returns of all the securities, long and short, simultaneously. While it is possible to combine a separately constructed short portfolio with a separately constructed long portfolio, the result offers but negligible benefits and does not represent a true long-short portfolio. Only an integrated approach, resulting in a single long-short portfolio, offers the investor true benefits in terms of enhanced flexibility in pursuing return and controlling risk.[5]

Adding back market return

A market-neutral long-short portfolio offers an active return from the specific securities selected to be held long or sold short, plus a return representing an interest rate. The neutral strategy does not reflect either the return or the risk of the underlying equity market. As Exhibit 10.2 illustrated, the value added from stock selection skill, represented by the long-short spread, is independent of the performance of the equity asset class from which the securities were selected.

That value added can be transported to other asset classes via the use of derivatives overlays. An investor can, for example, add back the risk and return of the equity market by purchasing stock index futures equal in amount to the investment in the long-short strategy. The resulting 'equitised' long-short portfolio captures the performance of the underlying market while allowing the investor to benefit from the enhanced flexibility in stock selection afforded by long-short management. Other derivatives overlays may be used to establish exposures to, for instance, fixed income and foreign equity. In effect, long-short construction allows the investor to separate the security selection decision from the asset allocation decision.

The 'transportability' of the long-short spread implies that the identity of a long-short portfolio is flexible. A market-neutral long-short portfolio offers a return (and risk) from security selection on top of a cash return. An equitised long-short portfolio offers the security selection return on top of the equity asset class return. Long-short portfolios do not constitute a separate asset class; but the existing asset class to which they belong will depend upon the choice of derivatives overlay.[6]

Some concerns addressed

Long-short construction maximises the benefit obtained from potentially valuable investment insights by eliminating long-only's constraint on short selling and the need to converge to securities' benchmark weights in order to control portfolio risk. However, while long-short offers advantages over long-only, it also involves complications not encountered in long-only management.

Many of the complications are related to the use of short selling. For example, shares the investor desires to sell short may not be available for borrowing, or shares that have been sold short may be called back by their lenders. Short selling is also subject to various exchange rules that can delay or prevent short sales. Uptick rules, for example, forbid short sale of a stock if the stock's last price change was a decline. Such rules can give rise to opportunity costs.

We have estimated that the cost associated with securing and administering lendable stocks typically averages 25–30 basis points (although it may be higher for harder-to-borrow shares). This cost is incurred as a 'haircut' on the short rebate the investor receives from the interest earned on the short sale proceeds.

A more serious impediment to long-short strategies may be the discomfort many investors feel with the idea of shorting. Perhaps this reflects an association of shorting with speculation. However, shorting is no more inherently speculative than active long investment. Although losses on short positions are theoretically unbounded (as a stock's price may rise without limit), the potential for such losses can be curtailed by diversifying short positions across a large number of stocks and by scaling back positions as prices increase.

Other perceived impediments to long-short investing are just as illusory. Take, for example, the issue of trading costs. A long-short portfolio that takes full advantage of the allowed leverage will engage in about twice as much trading activity as a comparable unlevered long-only strategy. The additional trading costs, however, must be weighed against the expanded potential for return. Most investors will be willing to pay the additional trading costs in exchange for the expected incremental return. Nevertheless, leverage is not an inherent part of long-short. Given capital of US$10 million, for example, an investor could choose to invest US$5 million long and sell US$5 million short; trading activity for the resulting long-short portfolio would be roughly equivalent to that for a US$10 million long-only portfolio.

The differential between management fees for a long-short versus a long-only portfolio is also largely a reflection of the leverage involved. If one considers the management fee per dollar of securities positions, rather than per dollar of invested capital, there should not be much difference between long-short and long-only. In addition, if one considers the amount of active management provided per fee dollar, long-short may be revealed as substantially less costly than long-only! As we have noted, long-only portfolios contain a sizeable 'hidden passive' element; only overweights and underweights relative to the benchmark are truly active. By contrast, virtually the entire long-short portfolio is active.

Since it does not have to converge to securities' benchmark weights in order to control risk, a long-short strategy can take larger positions in securities with higher (and lower) expected returns compared with a long-only portfolio whose ability to take active positions is limited by benchmark weights. It does not necessarily follow, however, that a long-short portfolio is riskier than a long-only portfolio. The long-short portfolio will incur more risk only to the extent that it takes more active positions and/or engages in more leverage. Both the portfolio's 'activeness' and its degree of leverage are within the explicit control of the investor. Furthermore, proper portfolio construction should ensure that any incremental risks and costs are compensated by incremental returns.

The importance of investment insights

Long-short portfolio construction, with the flexibility it affords in pursuing returns and controlling risk, enhances the investor's ability to implement investment insights. Whether or not it will enhance portfolio returns will depend ultimately on the efficacy of those insights. Besides analysing the operational considerations involved in long-short management, investors need to evaluate carefully the value-adding potential of the security selection approach underpinning it.

We believe that the best insights into security behaviour come out of a quantitative approach that enjoys both breadth and depth. The equity market is complex; it is subject to a myriad of influences. Mispricing arises from investors' cognitive errors, such as herding or over-reaction, and from companies' differing abilities to adapt to changing economic fundamentals. Furthermore, the nature of mispricings changes over time. The complexity of the market demands continual research and an investment process that combines human insight, plus finance and behavioural theory with state-of-the-art quantitative and statistical methods. Intensive statistical computer modelling of a wide range of stocks and a variety of proprietary factors allows breadth of inquiry combined with depth of analysis. Breadth of inquiry maximises the number of insightful profit opportunities that can be incorporated into a portfolio and provides for greater consistency of return. Depth of analysis, achieved by taking into account the intricacies of stock price behaviour, maximises the 'goodness' of such insights, or the potential of each one to add value. Breadth and depth together help to ensure consistent value added, whether in long-short or long-only portfolio management.[7]

---

[1]   Assuming some element of active turnover. Otherwise, any individual short can only produce a maximum gain of 100 per cent, while an individual long, theoretically at least, can appreciate endlessly.

[2]   For more on initial and maintenance margins required by law, by exchanges and by brokers, see Bruce I. Jacobs and Kenneth N. Levy, 'The Long and Short on Long-Short', *Journal of Investing*, Spring 1997.

[3]   For more on this, see Bruce I. Jacobs and Kenneth N. Levy, 'Long/Short Equity Investing', *Journal of Portfolio Management*, Fall 1993 and (in translation) *The Security Analysts Journal of Japan*, March 1994.

[4]   See, for example, Bruce I. Jacobs and Kenneth N. Levy, '20 Myths About Long-Short', *Financial Analysts Journal*, September/October 1996.

[5]   For more on this, see Bruce I. Jacobs, 'Controlled Risk Strategies', in *ICFA Continuing Education: Alternative Assets* (Charlottesville, VA: Association for Investment Management and Research, 1998). For a technical discussion, see Bruce I. Jacobs, Kenneth N. Levy, and David Starer, 'Long-Short Portfolio Management: An Integrated Approach', *Journal of Portfolio Management*, Winter 1999.

[6]   For more on alpha transport, see Bruce I. Jacobs and Kenneth N. Levy, 'Alpha Transport With Derivatives', *Journal of Portfolio Management*, May 1999.

[7]   See, for example, Bruce I. Jacobs and Kenneth N. Levy, *Equity Management: Quantitative Analysis for Stock Selection* (New York: McGraw-Hill, 2000); Bruce I. Jacobs and Kenneth N. Levy, 'Engineering Portfolios: A Unified Approach', *Journal of Investing*, Winter 1995; and James A. White, 'How Jacobs and Levy Crunch Stock for Buying and Selling,' *Wall Street Journal*, 20 March 1991, C1.

Chapter 11

Fixed-income arbitrage

Michael A. Pintar, CFA
Clinton Group, New York, New York

Introduction

The fixed-income arbitrage strategy provides an attractive risk-adjusted return while exhibiting low correlation with returns on equity or fixed-income markets. The strategy has evolved over the past several years from one that has often performed like a short option position into a much more stable strategy with often positively convex characteristics. This chapter will attempt to explain the fixed-income arbitrage strategies, some of the risks pertaining to these strategies and how to mitigate them. This chapter will also explore different approaches that can be taken to minimise some risks inherent in fixed-income arbitrage portfolios.

Fixed-income arbitrage strategies and their risks

The fixed-income arbitrage strategy involves the purchase or sale of one fixed-income security versus an opposing trade in that of another in order to profit from relative movements or accrue positive carry over time. The securities involved generally include: investment-grade government and government agency bonds, exchange-traded futures, interest rate swaps and options.

   The fundamental premise underlying this strategy is that fixed-income markets display inefficiencies. The inefficiencies can be structural, as in the case where tax, accounting or regulatory issues drive certain market participants to use products for uneconomical reasons. Structural inefficiencies can also relate to market segmentation where certain market participants are restricted from trading in particular products or markets. The inefficiencies in fixed-income markets can also be due to liquidity preference. Liquidity driven inefficiencies are caused by certain market participants' need or desire for specific securities, usually for hedging-related purposes. These flows usually last for only a short period of time. Due to the often very large size of the flow, this can create dislocations in the normal relationship between two products. In taking advantage of both types of inefficiencies, structural and liquidity-driven, the fixed-income arbitrage strategy often involves taking an opposing position to the specific flow causing the anomaly. In providing this countervail, the fixed-income arbitrage participant will seek to minimise exposure to systematic factors unrelated to the flow causing the anomaly. Therefore, the fixed-income arbitrage strategy involves structuring trades that minimise the exposure to systematic risk factors while maximising the profit from anomalies caused by structural or liquidity-driven flows. The three broadly defined strategy types employed to take advantage of these anomalies are: yield curve, spread and options trades.

Yield curve trades

Yield curve trades often refer to very basic structures such as steepeners or flatteners, which involve taking opposing positions in two maturities on the yield curve. These trades seek to profit from changes in the slope of the yield curve. Given that the slope of the yield curve is largely a function of the expectation of future short-term interest rates, the risks in these positions are directly related to anticipated central bank action. This obviously makes these trades very 'macro' or subject to the direction of yields. Given the intention of the fixed-income arbitrage strategy to avoid speculation on macroeconomic factors and to have as little correlation with the fixed-income markets as possible, the use of multiple curve maturities is much more appropriate.

These so-called butterfly positions involve taking positions in three or more maturities on the yield curve. Butterfly trades seek to take advantage of anomalies on the yield curve without taking a view on the slope of the yield curve itself. The structuring of yield curve trades in this manner reduces the exposure to macroeconomic factors such as movements in short-term interest rates.

Movements in the short-term interest rate are usually the single largest determinant of the change in the slope or steepness of the yield curve. As the short-term interest rate decreases, the yield curve tends to become steeper. This is due to the expectation that future short-term interest rates will have to increase to offset the reduction in the current short-term interest rate. The converse is also true. This negative correlation between the short-term interest rate and the steepness of the yield curve reduces the volatility of the forward rates.

The incorporation of multiple yield curve maturities does not necessarily eliminate exposure to systematic risk. This is because each of the maturities along the yield curve exhibits different volatility. The reason for this goes back to stability of the forward rates. In order to dampen the volatility of forward rates, longer maturities need to move less than shorter maturities under normal circumstances. There are times when this is not the case, such as when short-term interest rates approach zero and monetary policy is neutral or ineffective. When this happens, intermediate and long-term maturities will often exhibit more volatility, as these maturities will attempt to predict future short-term interest rate movements. Also, supply and demand for the fixed-income products in intermediate to long-term maturities will determine the direction of yields, as short-term rates will exhibit very little volatility. This is currently the case in Japan where overnight rates are effectively zero and the Bank of Japan provides stimulus through outright purchases of Japanese government bonds along the yield curve. Therefore, almost invariably the yield curve flattens in rallies and becomes steeper in sell-offs.

In addition, different maturities across the yield curve will also exhibit different correlations with absolute movements in the short-term interest rate. The reason for this is somewhat related to volatility but also due to the actions of market participants as short-term rates change. Some market participants need to hedge their assets or liabilities dynamically. These market participants, who are usually not value-conscious, will tend to hedge using the same maturity as their liabilities. If enough of these market participants have the same maturity hedging needs given a particular movement in yields, the maturity on the yield curve will exhibit correlation with short-term interest rates.

For example, if the average duration of mortgage portfolios in the US market is five years, the five-year maturity will tend to exhibit more volatility and will have higher correlation with short-term rates than would be the case otherwise. This can create opportunities for fixed-income arbitrage participants because the five-year maturity will tend to exhibit richness or cheapness as yields change. For instance, if hedging-related fixed-rate swap paying from a mortgage hedger caused a cheapening of the five-year maturity on the interest rate swap curve relative to the two-year and the 10-year maturities, a strategy involving a receive-fixed position in a five-year interest rate swap versus pay-fixed positions in both two-year and 10-year interest rate swaps could take advantage of this. However, a simple equal risk allocation to the two maturities opposite the five year could expose the position to directional risks. This equal risk weighting does not properly take account of the systematic risk factors of volatility and macroeconomic correlation. In addition, simple equal risk weighting such as that in the example may expose the butterfly position to other risks such as convexity.

Convexity is the change in duration given a change in yields. This second order effect, if not accounted for will lead to a residual long or short interest rate risk position. All else being equal, convexity increases as duration and cash flow dispersion increases. For this reason, butterfly positions that are short the wings, or the yield curve maturities opposite the middle maturity, will be short convexity. The converse is also true. For butterfly positions involving short to intermediate maturities there is usually negligible risk. However, for butterfly positions involving long-dated maturities the risk can be substantial. To hedge this risk, the arbitrage participant will need to either purchase or sell short-dated options depending on the butterfly position. The butterfly position can also be adjusted at inception to minimise the convexity risk or the position can be adjusted as yields change in order to keep the position dollar value of a basis point (DV01) neutral.

Butterfly positions often use market-neutral weightings in order to mitigate systematic risks. This involves weighting the yield curve maturities according to either their historical or implied volatilities or employing statistical techniques such as simple regression to determine the market-neutral weighting. More sophisticated tools such as principal component analysis or factor models can also be used to attain a market neutral weighting across the yield curve maturities. The construction of these models varies, but most involve weighting each of the yield curve maturities involved in the butterfly to their respective exposures to pre-defined risk factors such as parallel yield curve shifts, change in slope or change in curvature.

Spread trades

Spread trades are the broadest strategy type in fixed-income arbitrage. The most common spread trades involve:

- government versus government or government versus agency bonds;
- basis trades, which involve the purchase or sale of government bonds versus opposing positions in exchange-traded futures contracts; and
- asset swap trades, which involve the purchase or sale of fixed-rate government or agency bonds versus opposing positions in interest rate swaps.

The governments versus governments or governments versus agency bonds spread trades are very straightforward and are typically taken to exploit a valuation difference between the securities. The valuation difference could involve an excessive or inadequate yield spread driven by temporary supply and demand. It could also be due to liquidity reasons such as in the case of on-the-run versus off-the-run bonds. The valuation is often due to a difference between the respective financing and borrowing rates of the two bonds. In these cases, the forward or carry-adjusted yield spread will determine the proper valuation.

Aside from the assumed risks related to liquidity premium such as flight-to-quality or benchmark premium risks, which are usually assumed by the fixed-income arbitrage participant in these strategies, there can be other systematic risks. These risks vary from implicit credit risks, such as in the case of government versus agency bond spreads, or monetary policy risks such as in the case of cross-currency government versus government spread trades. Often it is impossible or impractical to properly hedge these risks in a cost-effective manner. Therefore, it becomes important to analyse whether the performance of the trade will be disproportionately affected by the systematic risks such as credit or monetary policy rather than the liquidity-driven risks related to supply and demand for these bonds.

A basis trade involves the purchase or sale of futures contracts versus opposing trades in bonds deliverable into that futures contract. A standard bond future contractually obligates the short position to deliver to the long position a bond meeting the specifications of the contract. This delivery will take place on a future date also specified by the contract. As this delivery takes place at a future date, not a spot date, the futures contract price will imply a rate of financing on the deliverable bond to that future date. This financing rate will be determined not only by the supply and demand for the futures contract relative to the bonds deliverable into that futures contract but also by the short-term interest rate. In order to hedge this short-term interest rate, the basis trade strategy will also involve the use of an over-the-counter instrument called a repurchase agreement (repo) or reverse repurchase agreement (reverse repo). These instruments also hedge the short-term interest rate risk of the futures contract as the term of the repo or reverse repo can be tailored to match the delivery date of the futures contract. The rate attainable on the repo or reverse repo will often determine the attractiveness of the basis trade as it is directly comparable to the implied financing rate on the futures contract.

Another risk in a basis trade not relating to supply and demand comes from the embedded delivery option in the futures contract. This embedded option exists because a bond futures contract usually specifies not just one bond but instead a basket of bonds acceptable for delivery into that futures contract. This basket of bonds may contain issues with very different maturities and thus very different DV01s. The short position owns an option because the short position can choose the bond they wish to deliver to the long position. Conversely, the long futures position is short this option. The value of this option will be influenced by the volatility not only in the level of rates but also in the slope of the curve. Thus, in order to avoid being exposed to systematic risks associated with long or short options positions, the basis trade must be hedged with offsetting options positions. Multiple options are used because the cheapest-to-deliver bond will change not only as the level of rates change but also as the yield curve slope changes. Through the use of delivery option models, the embedded option can be valued. From the option valuation, the volatility is implied and compared to those of other fixed-income products. It can then be determined whether it is cost-effective to hedge the option.

Asset swap trades are another of the spread trades common in fixed-income arbitrage. Asset swap trades include:

- asset swaps which involve the purchase of fixed-rate bonds versus pay-fixed positions in interest rate swaps;

- reverse asset swaps which involve the sale of fixed-rate bonds versus receive-fixed positions in interest rate swaps; and
- box trades that involve one of each position.

The outright asset swap or reverse asset swap trades involve taking exposure to systematic risk while the box trades seek to hedge some of this risk. There are many different asset swap structures but all involve the following components:

- fixed rate on the bond;
- fixed rate on the swap;
- financing or borrowing rate on the bond; and
- floating rate on the swap, which is usually term Libor.

Asset swap spread widening or tightening is largely driven by macroeconomic factors such as movements in the short-term interest rate and its associated effect on the shape of the yield curve. There is also a credit component to asset swap spreads. As has been explained, as short-term interest rates decline, usually the yield curve will tend to become steeper. This steepening of the yield curve will entice market participants, such as corporations, to transform their fixed-rate liabilities into floating-rate liabilities. The reason for this is to save on interest costs, as the short-term floating rate is much lower than the longer-term fixed rate. This transformation of liability exposure involves the market participant receiving fixed versus paying floating on an interest rate swap. The interest rate swap term will generally match the maturity of the liability exposure. This could be either an existing liability or a new fixed-rate debt issue. The effect of this receiving of fixed rates by market participants will cause asset swap spreads to contract. Conversely, when short-term interest rates increase, the incentive is eliminated and market participants will wish to lock-in the interest rate of their liability. They will do so by paying fixed on an interest rate swap. This will tend to cause asset swap spreads to widen.

Asset swap spreads are also influenced by other systematic risks such as general credit spread movements. The underlying rate on an interest rate swap is Libor, which is calculated based on a sample of bank funding rates. Therefore, the level of Libor will be determined partly by the current as well as the expected future credit of the banks comprising the Libor panel. This gives asset swap spreads an inherent exposure to general bank credit risk. This will tend to widen asset swap spreads when credit risks increase and tend to tighten them when credit risks decline.

The systematic risk factors, such as short-term interest rate and credit, associated with asset swap or reverse asset swap positions, can be mitigated through an asset swap box trade. A box trade involves initiating an asset swap position on one part of the yield curve and a reverse asset swap position on another part of the yield curve. The attractiveness of this position is that it isolates the richness or cheapness of one bond and that of another versus the Libor curve. For instance, if an off-the-run 30-year US Treasury bond was yielding 20 basis points less than a pay-fixed position in an interest rate swap to the maturity of that same bond, while an off-the-run 10-year US Treasury note was yielding 40 basis points less than a receive-fixed position in an interest rate swap, a box trade may be attractive if the difference in rates between where one can lend and borrow the respective Treasuries is not exorbitant. To construct the box trade, the fixed-income arbitrage participant would purchase the off-the-run 30-year Treasury versus pay-fixed on an interest rate swap matching the maturity and the DV01 risk of the bond and also sell the off-the-run 10-year Treasury versus receive fixed on an interest rate swap matching the maturity and the DV01 risk of the note. In addition, the fixed-income arbitrage participant will lend the 30-year Treasury and borrow the 10-year Treasury generally for the same term in the repo market.

The weighting of the respective positions in the box trade will usually be according to their respective DV01 risks. This will hedge the position against general spread widening or tightening associated with any changes in real or perceived credit risks. The weighting could also be adjusted to be slightly long or short asset swap spreads. This would be done if there were a correlation between the shape of the asset swap spread curve and the level of asset swap spreads. The carry in a box position will be determined by the relative asset swap spreads of the two opposing positions, the funding and borrowing rates on the two bonds and the bonds' respective DV01s.

Options trades

Options trades can involve either short-term or long-term expirations on a fixed-rate bond, a futures contract or an interest rate swap. As short-term option prices are influenced most by absolute movements in an underlying security, positions in them are often referred to as gamma trades. As long-term option prices are influenced most by changes in the implied volatility of the option they are referred to as vega trades. Options trades are implemented to take advantage of a discrepancy between the implied volatility on an option and the historically observed or anticipated volatility of the underlying security. The strategies could involve outright long or short options positions, or could involve opposing options positions in different expiries, on different products or on different maturities along a yield curve.

Outright long or short options trades involve the purchase or sale of an option with a particular expiry on a particular product. The rationale behind these trades could be that the amount of theta or time decay of the option will differ from the profitability or loss of the delta hedging. The rationale could also be that the implied volatility on the option position will move favourably to the position. Although the ultimate loss of any outright long option position is known at inception, this strategy involves a payment of an often large premium. This can make the trade costly if that premium is not adequately recovered through delta hedging. The position could also be subject to large mark-to-market risks if the implied volatility moves in an unfavourable direction to the position.

Conversely to a long outright option position, the ultimate loss in a short option position is unknown. The losses in outright short options positions can often be quite substantial. The reason being that there is a chance of large market moves or gaps that make dynamic or any frequent hedging of the short option position impossible. Any outright options positions inherently lend themselves to systematic risks because the profitability or loss will be determined by the magnitude and frequency of market movements. To minimise exposure to these risks, opposing long and short options positions can be taken. These positions can minimise or eliminate the largely systematic gamma or vega risks of the option while taking advantage of relative mispricings between options. Depending upon which type of risk, gamma or vega, one wishes to hedge, different weightings are used.

Vega trades are generally hedged to be neutral to movements in implied volatility. This is called a vega-neutral weighting. These weightings attempt to neutralise the predominant risk factor in these options positions. The profit or loss in vega trades will be determined primarily by the relative changes in the implied volatility of the expirations or maturities. These relative changes take place due partly to the realised volatility of the underlying but more due to the supply of and demand for the option.

An example of this is in Europe, where European life insurance demand for zero coupon callable bonds leads to consistent selling of long-dated options on European interest rate swaps called swaptions. The selling of these swaptions leads to depressed levels of long-dated implied volatility. The reason for the selling of the swaptions is in order for the issuer of the zero coupon callable bond to monetise the option, or sell it for a premium, they become long through their issuance of the callable. Conversely, this is the same option the insurance company is short but they, unlike the issuer, maintain their short option position. Therefore, the net effect of this issuance is more supply in long-dated swaptions leading to persistently low long-dated implied volatility. A fixed-income arbitrage strategy to take advantage of this would be to purchase these cheap swaptions while selling either shorter or longer-dated swaptions. The weighting in this position would usually be vega neutral in order to hedge the predominant risk factor in the position. Weighting the trade vega neutral will often result in the position being long or short residual amounts of gamma. This will affect the carry of the position but the net risk is usually negligible. Also, attention should be paid to how the structure will perform over time if nothing changes. This is called analysing the roll down. This analysis will help determine the attractiveness of the position as vega trades often take a considerable amount of time in order to work due to the structural nature of the underlying supply and demand imbalances.

Gamma trades are generally hedged to movements in the underlying security. This is called a delta-neutral weighting. Although the absolute movement between the two underlying securities will largely determine the profitability of gamma trades, relative changes in implied volatility will have mark-to-market implications. Gamma trades can involve very simple short-dated options positions where one wishes to speculate on absolute movements in the underlying security. They can also involve more complex rationales. An interesting type of gamma trade involves taking positions in options with the same expiration but with different maturities across a yield curve. These positions are referred to as conditional yield curve trades because the position will have exposure to the underlying yield curve if yields move in a particular direction. These trades are implemented when a discrepancy exists between the actual or anticipated volatility of the underlying yield curve and that implied by the options market. Conditional curve trades can be structured using straddles, strangles or only puts or calls. The fixed-income arbitrage participant would use just puts or calls if they wished to have exposure to a particular yield curve position only if yields moved in a particular direction.

For example, if a yield curve butterfly position looked attractive due to the cheapness of a particular point on the yield curve but the butterfly position was highly correlated with the direction of yields and the options market was not properly accounting for the directionality of the underlying curve position, a conditional curve trade could be implemented. This structure would give the fixed-income arbitrage participant exposure to the underlying yield curve position only when it is usually most favourable to the underlying curve position. The structure would leave no exposure if the market moved in a direction usually associated with an unfavourable movement in the underlying yield curve position. Therefore, a positively convex position in an underlying yield curve trade is obtained.

Another structure involves taking positions in options with the same expiration but on different products. These positions are called conditional spread trades. The rationale for these positions is generally the same as the conditional curve trades. They are taken when an underlying spread position, such as an asset swap, is desired but the participant wishes to hedge out the directionality of the underlying spread position. As it has been established, asset swap spread positions have correlations with the direction of the market and are thus subject to systematic risk. Structuring asset swap spread trades conditionally not only eliminates this systematic risk but also creates positive convexity. Again, this is due to the increased exposure to the underlying position when the market moves in a direction usually associated with favourable moves in the underlying asset swap spread and reduced exposure in moves usually associated with unfavourable moves in the asset swap spread.

The ability to create these positively convex positions for zero cost is due to market segmentation. Options on different products and maturities often have very different end-users and thus often have very different supply and demand characteristics which can lead to pricing anomalies.

Portfolio risks

Aside from the market risks specific to fixed-income arbitrage strategy types, there are also those inherent in entire fixed-income arbitrage portfolios of which managers must be aware. Although there are several, two in particular are especially pertinent for this strategy: positioning and leverage.

Positioning

Due to the attractiveness of the fixed-income arbitrage strategy from a standpoint of risk-adjusted return, large amounts of capital have been deployed to exploit these opportunities. At the same time, the amount and timing of information relating to arbitrage opportunities has increased. This is due to the banking and brokerage community's investing of significant resources in the trading and sales relating to this strategy. As a result, there are a substantial number of participants focused on the same opportunities within the same fixed-income markets. Although the effects of this are more efficient and smoothly functioning fixed-income markets, inevitably, one risk into which this does translate is that of positioning.

The positioning of large numbers of fixed-income arbitrage participants within the same fixed-income arbitrage trades can lead to unattractive characteristics. Although somewhat unintuitive, the volatility of fixed-income arbitrage strategies can often be much higher than would be the case without the arbitrage interest, especially following large moves. This is due to very different risk limits across different types of accounts. Those having very tight stop loss limits will be forced to exit a position after very little mark-to-market loss. This will cause those still holding the position to experience a more adverse move than would be the case otherwise. This increased volatility makes it difficult to properly size trades initially.

For instance, if a measure such as Value-at-Risk (VaR) is used in order to weight risks evenly across different strategies, an unreasonable amount of risk may be assigned to a position. This is because VaR analysis has no way of measuring not only the potential for increased volatility but also the potential for increased correlations due to positioning. This could lead to very faulty assumptions being made about the true amount of risk in a fixed-income arbitrage portfolio.

In addition to the increased downside volatility and possible faulty VaR assumption to which positioning risk can lead, incorrect assumptions about the validity of the trade may also be made. This is due to the often inconspicuous nature of the flow. This makes it very difficult to discern whether there has been a real shift in supply and demand, and thus possibly a change in the validity of the arbitrage trade, or whether the flows are technical in nature as in those related to the unwinding of positions.

There are ways to mitigate positioning risk in a fixed-income arbitrage portfolio. The easiest is to avoid crowded trades through the use of market intelligence. At times, this is difficult, if not impossible. Even if it were possible, it may not be the best solution. The reason that a strategy is often crowded is due to the attractiveness of the position. Thus, one could be foregoing an attractive opportunity due to positioning risk. Therefore, minimising risk to the entire portfolio is more suitable. In order to accomplish this, extensive diversification across markets and strategies should be used. In addition, VaR is useful but should be combined with stress testing to improve its effectiveness.

VaR is defined as the predicted largest loss of an instrument, position or portfolio over a period of time that one could expect given a specific level of confidence under a normal distribution. There are two distinct methods of calculating VaR: parametric and simulation. Parametric, as the name implies, sets parameters for estimating the VaR of the portfolio. These parameters are based on:

- the risk of the positions in the portfolio;
- the volatility of the positions in the portfolio; and
- the correlation between the positions in the portfolio.

There are two drawbacks to the parametric approach. First, the parametric approach does not account for the non-linearity of positions populating fixed-income arbitrage portfolios. Second, the risk parameters, particularly the volatility and the correlation, can deviate much more frequently and much more severely than those predicted under a normal distribution due to incalculable variables such as positioning of other fixed-income arbitrage portfolios. To overcome these drawbacks, VaR can be calculated based on simulations.

Simulated VaR involves generating scenarios and re-pricing the portfolio to measure changes in the value. The simulations can be based on historical periods or based on random paths such as in Monte Carlo simulation. Since the simulation methods involve re-pricing the entire portfolio under these different scenarios, non-linear positions such as options will be properly calculated. Unfortunately, historical and Monte Carlo simulations do not fully address the second drawback of VaR. This is because the simulations are based on either historical events that may be due to circumstances that are no longer valid or based on simulated paths that may not be able to account for certain variables. To overcome this, VaR can be supplemented with stress tests based on subjective scenarios to produce a more realistic sense of risk given non-quantitative variables and during extraordinary market environments. For instance, if there are significant speculative positions in particular yield curve maturities, instruments in a spread or options expirations that the participant has identified, tests can be run that shock these particular positions at the same time to see how negatively this impacts the portfolio. This exercise is important in determining the real worst-loss case as it assumes no relief from historical correlations of positions and it incorporates what the manager believes is the largest conceivable shock based on their market intelligence. Therefore, the risk of potential positioning problems in fixed-income arbitrage portfolios can be identified, examined and hopefully mitigated.

Leverage

Leverage is obviously an important component in any arbitrage strategy. Since the fixed-income arbitrage strategy seeks to profit from relatively small movements between instruments, the use of significant leverage is vital in attaining a sufficient return on capital. This is because the strategies employed are market-neutral and thus usually exhibit less volatility than an outright long or short position. Therefore, the leverage used in the fixed-income arbitrage strategy can be viewed as an enhancement to the return on these low-risk positions. However, with this use of leverage come some risks that should be minimised through some common sense measures.

Leverage in this strategy can be implicit, as in the case of derivatives contracts or explicit in the case of asset financing but both involve the need for a line of credit from a financial institution or counterparty. The ability to maintain this credit will depend on the volatility of the securities in the portfolio. The borrower's perceived credit will also be taken into account. In addition, the ability and willingness of the counterparty to extend this credit is also a vital factor. In the past, there have been several cases where the ability or willingness of one or several financial institutions to extend credit became impaired. This impairment was, at times, related to problems specific to a particular financial institution but, at others, related to more systemic types of financial risk.

To avoid the situations where the ability or willingness of a financial institution to extend credit becomes impaired, it is important for fixed-income arbitrage managers to have credit lines with a number of potential counterparties. This reduces the risk of an inability to maintain leverage as well as reduces potential counterparty credit risk. In addition, when at all possible and economical, explicit financing of assets should be locked up for a specified term. This reduces the exposure to roll over risk associated with financing or borrowing assets. This is especially important during times of systemic financial risk.

It is also important for a fixed-income arbitrage portfolio to maintain an adequate reserve of cash or cash equivalents. Although this may seem intuitive for any leveraged portfolio, it is even more important in this strategy. This is due to the absolute amount of leverage, which tends to be greater due to the lower implied volatility of the strategy. If the volatility of the securities within the portfolio increase and the correlations between strategies increase, such as in the fall of 1998, without a sufficient amount of excess cash it can be very difficult to maintain positions.

In addition, by holding sufficient amounts of excess cash, fixed-income arbitrage accounts can take advantage of the downside volatility caused by the unwinding of attractive positions due to forced liquidations or stop losses. Although this excess capital on hand will reduce the return on capital on the portfolio, over time the reduced volatility should increase the risk-adjusted return or Sharpe ratio on the portfolio.

Also, although it may be possible for a fixed-income arbitrage portfolio to attain a large amount of leverage, it may not always be prudent to do so. This is due to the liquidity risk inherent in this strategy. Liquidity risks can involve serious risks to the stability of the portfolio such as in the case of a downward spiral. This is where the unwinding of leveraged positions has a greater negative effect upon the value of the remaining positions than the amount of cash released. Liquidity measurement and control can reduce this risk.

Liquidity measurement and control techniques involve estimating the tradable amount or float of any given position and then setting a maximum percentage of that float that is prudent for the portfolio to hold. Although there is a substantial amount of guesswork involved with the estimation of the liquidity, it is a useful exercise. The analysis will help avoid the initiation of large positions in illiquid securities despite the attractiveness of the opportunity. In the estimation process the manager should also be aware that the liquidity in the position would change as market dynamics change. In volatile periods, such as those that involve financial system stress, the liquidity in positions will evaporate quickly. Also, there is no one correct percentage for every fixed-income arbitrage portfolio to use as a limit. The limit will vary depending on the other characteristics of the portfolio such as diversification, VaR and the amount of free capital that is available.

Conclusion

The fixed-income arbitrage strategy has gone through a transformation due partly to the events of the autumn of 1998 but also due to the increased sophistication of fixed-income end-users. This increased sophistication means that there remain very few, if any, riskless opportunities of which to take advantage. Although this has made the fixed-income arbitrage strategy more difficult to apply, and with often times lower expected returns, there have been some favourable by-products. The fixed-income arbitrage strategy now has an increased focus on constructing portfolios that minimise exposure to systematic risks while still giving scope to profit from opportunities created by market segmentation and temporary supply and demand imbalances. It has also led to increased trading in more liquid positions by the fixed-income arbitrage players as well as an increased focus on structuring positions that have positive exposure to event risk. This transformation from a short volatility strategy to a long volatility strategy has made the fixed-income arbitrage strategy a more stable, and hopefully, more appealing strategy for institutional investors.

Chapter 12

Asset-backed investing

Luke E. Imperatore
Greenwich, Connecticut

Introduction

The goal of this chapter is to provide an overview of the asset-backed security (ABS), structured finance and securitisation markets, including their evolution and their attractiveness from an investment perspective.

ABSs constitute an ever-growing segment of the US, European and global capital markets. In the past two decades, the ABS market has enabled companies and banks to finance a wide range of assets in the public debt market and has attracted a variety of fixed-income investors. Asset securitisation techniques, while complex, have won a secure place in corporate financing and investment portfolios because they offer issuers a cheaper source of funding and investors a superior return than would otherwise be possible.

The ABS market had its genesis in the mortgage-backed security market, which was created by Louis Ranieri at Salomon Brothers Inc in the 1980s. It has grown in recent years to be the largest fixed-income market in the world, dwarfing even the US Treasury market. In its most generic sense, ABSs are issued by special purpose vehicles (SPVs) whose sole assets are underlying pools of loans, receivables or other property rights.

The ABS market has grown dramatically over the past two decades because it serves a variety of useful purposes, including:

- packaging cash flows from asset pools that have previously been too difficult for a large class of institutional buyers to invest in due to:
    - a large number of small assets (ie, loans) that require specialised administration and tracking;
    - relative illiquidity of the underlying collateral when viewed on an individual loan basis;
    - specialised servicing needs; and
    - the critical mass required for efficiently entering many markets;
- transferring risk from the underlying asset pools to various classes of security holders, especially institutional buyers, according to their risk appetite;
- dramatically increasing the liquidity and velocity of the underlying collateral classes through the increased liquidity in the ABS side of the market; and
- increasing the financing flexibility and liquidity for originators and issuers.

Some market participants peg the beginning of the non-mortgage-backed ABS market as March 1985 when Sperry Corporation issued a security backed by a computer lease. During that same year, the first auto loan-backed ABS was issued by Valley National Bank and Marine Midland in the amount of US$60 million. Two years later, the Republic Bank of

Exhibit 12.1

ABS issuance, 1990–2002

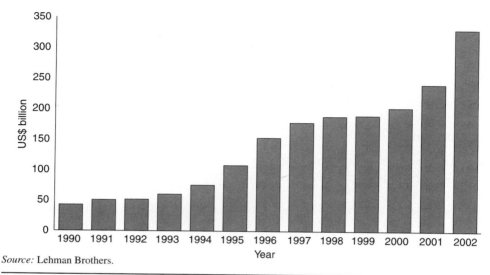

Source: Lehman Brothers.

Delaware issued the first credit card-backed ABS. By 2002, the ABS market had grown to US$329.3 billion (see Exhibit 12.1).

ABS growth arose from the development of three sectors: automobile loans, credit card receivables and home equity loans. Further growth of the ABS market has occurred across a range of less developed sectors, including manufactured housing loans, equipment leases, business loans and utility bills (see Exhibits 12.2 and 12.3).

As the structuring and documentation of ABSs have become more routine and streamlined, the securitisation market has truly soared in North America and has taken off in Europe as well. Securitisation markets, which in the past were largely limited to conforming residential mortgages, now include everything from commercial mortgages to David Bowie's future royalty streams.[1]

The primary driver behind the growth of the ABS market is due to the fact that securitisation structures offer both issuers and investors distinct advantages over more traditional investment vehicles for many asset classes.

Advantages for ABS issuers

The advantages to ABS issuers are numerous but include the following:

- assets/collateral that otherwise would be too small or cumbersome to be purchased directly can be pooled;
- cash flows are directed to the security holders with the residual interest being retained by the equity holder (who is typically the issuer); and
- structural leverage is often created for the issuer, who can leverage his equity and free up capital for increased origination, or other uses (ie, the velocity of the issuer's capital is increased).

Exhibit 12.2
Breakdown of ABS issuance, 1990

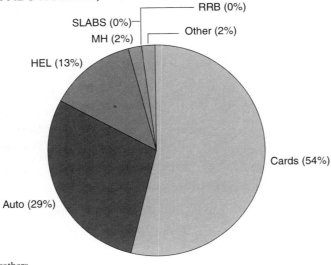

RRB (0%)
SLABS (0%)
Other (2%)
MH (2%)
HEL (13%)
Cards (54%)
Auto (29%)

Source: Lehman Brothers.

Exhibit 12.3
Breakdown of ABS issuance, 2002

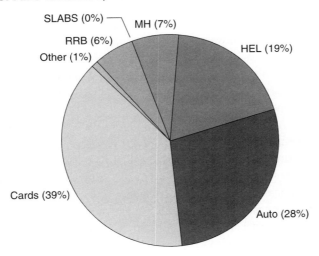

SLABS (0%)
MH (7%)
RRB (6%)
HEL (19%)
Other (1%)
Cards (39%)
Auto (28%)

Source: Lehman Brothers.

Advantages for ABS buyers

The advantages to ABS investors over traditional methods relate to the following.

- Greatly improved liquidity versus holding collateral directly (eg, the greater liquidity of a mortgage-backed bond versus a whole loan security).

151

- Lower transaction costs for holding ABS versus holding and servicing the underlying collateral.
- Enhanced ability to diversify between asset classes. Investors (particularly smaller ones) can invest in a variety of ABS bonds across collateral pools that heretofore may have been beyond their reach.
- Enhanced diversity of collateral pools. Today's ABS pools are often highly diversified geographically as well as by borrowers to meet strict underwriting and rating agency criteria. Prior to the emergence of the ABS market, only the largest of institutional investors could obtain the diversification of collateral that is available today.
- Foreign investors today have access to deep, and growing, collateral pools that they would have been all but shut out of previously. The impact of foreign purchases of US ABS paper cannot be underestimated, as it is an important part of funding the US current account deficit.

Technical aspects of the asset-backed market

The assets underlying an ABS are usually illiquid and private in nature. Securitisation makes these assets available for investment to a much broader range of investors. The 'pooling' of assets makes the securitisation large enough to be economical and to diversify the qualities of the underlying assets. The pool is held by a SPV that is set up as a stand-alone, bankruptcy-remote entity that takes title to the assets. It is the cash flows from these assets that are 'passed through' to the investors in the form of an ABS. A significant portion of the securitisation (ie, the senior tranche) usually qualifies for an investment-grade rating, which enables the issuing company or bank to raise funds at an attractive rate, while freeing up capital and retaining customer relationships and servicing revenues.

The cash flow from the underlying assets, or collateral, provides the debt service to the securities issues by the SPV (typically a trust). The trust is administered by a trustee for the benefit of the trust security holders and is governed by a trust indenture. The trustee, in turn, employs a servicer who administers the underlying collateral and liquidates collateral when it is in default. Today's servicers have become highly specialised and efficient in administering the underlying collateral pools.

The cash flow of the trust is split between the various security classes according to the trust indenture and is paid out according to it in a fashion that is generally referred to as the 'waterfall'. Generally the securities of the trust are fashioned into a senior/subordinate structure that creates structural leverage for the lower-rated (or unrated equity) tranches. It is these generic senior/subordinate structures (and their many permutations) that enable the senior tranches to garner investment-grade ratings. It is this flexibility in structuring a trust's cash flows that has fuelled the ABS market's spectacular growth. In turn, the complexity that often comes with structuring these cash flows has also led to abuses in the market in some instances.

Economics of the ABS market

The economics of the securitisation process are driven by interest rates and the ratings arbitrage associated with dividing the cash flows from the overall securitisation pool into various tranches with different characteristics.

The simplest form of ABS is pure pass-through, mortgage-backed securities (MBSs) of conforming mortgage pools backed by a US government guarantee. In MBS, hundreds, thousands or even tens of thousands of individual mortgages are pooled together and deposited in a trust. The trust then issues securities that are collateralised by, and amortised by, the cash flows of the real estate underlying those mortgages. By buying US$1 million of securities issued by a US$1 billion trust, an investor gains significant diversification benefits in terms of prepayment and loss predictability.

Investors in ABSs create much-needed liquidity for originators and servicers. Mortgage brokers originate individual loans and then sell them to banks or other servicing operations, which then fund them by issuing MBSs, which are purchased by insurance companies. Each entity has carved out their specific niche within the process, and has transferred the other aspects of the mortgage business to those more willing or able to take on those risks. Over time, these pass-through securities evolved into the ABS market that we know today. Early deals were done primarily by one of two types of issuers: banks and troubled credits. Banks, facing the impending changes in regulatory capital requirements that were being implemented in the mid-1980s, issued ABS not as a source of funding, but as a means of freeing up capital by removing assets from their balance sheets. Troubled credits, such as Chrysler, whose non-investment-grade rating had effectively shut them out of the corporate markets, used the ABS market as a source of 'tiering' their borrowing. By transferring high-quality assets such as pools of auto loans into a bankruptcy-remote subsidiary, they were able to sidestep questions about the company's long-term viability. Investors needed to focus only on the performance of the collateral (for which Chrysler could provide extensive historical data) and Chrysler's ability to service the collateral in order to become comfortable with the transaction.

Once investors became comfortable with the notion that large pools of assets (other than mortgages) exhibited predictable loss and payment characteristics, every consumer asset was fair game for securitisation. Boat loans, recreational vehicle loans and credit card balances soon followed, with credit cards soon becoming one of the largest sectors in the ABS market. Home equity loans (a MBS/ABS hybrid) are currently the largest sector within the ABS market, accounting for around 40 per cent of domestic issuance.[2]

More esoteric deals are now commonplace, with catastrophe bonds, tobacco settlements and rock star royalty streams all packaged into securities.

ABS legal structures also allow for considerable creativity in carving up the cash flows from the issuing entity. For example, if a pool of US$1 billion auto loans is dropped into a trust, the trust can issue five bonds, or tranches, of US$200 million each, with the shortest receiving the first US$200 million in cash flows from the US$1 billion pool and the second receiving US$200 million in cash once the first tranche is paid off, etc. In addition, carving up the cash flows allows for the reallocation of credit risk within the trust. For instance, one of those five tranches could receive payments only if there were collections on the underlying collateral in excess of what was needed to pay the other four tranches. Again, the objective is to redistribute characteristics of the collateral so that the overall trust can be funded in the most efficient manner. A money market fund may be an aggressive buyer of AAA-rated one-year paper, but restricted from purchasing securities that have a final maturity of greater that 24 months. On the other hand, an insurance company with long liabilities may want a longer average life, or may be more willing to take additional credit risk.

There are numerous enhancements incorporated into ABS structures designed to protect investors against a number of risks to varying degrees. First, the collateral itself is transferred into a bankruptcy-remote special purpose entity to eliminate the risk that it will be considered an asset of the originator, and therefore subject to claims from creditors. This is critical, as

153

the principal purpose of ABSs is to tier the funding of assets of a higher credit quality than the parent. In the event of a bankruptcy of the parent, the underlying collateral should continue to perform as before. If Ford closed its doors tomorrow, your monthly loan payments on your Ford Explorer would continue as before. If that loan (and therefore those monthly payments) were part of a securitisation, those payments would be collected by the trustee and remitted to bondholders just as before.[3]

In addition to any senior/subordinate structures that may exist in an ABS security, there are typically numerous forms of over-collateralisation, reserve accounts and excess spread that form the first line of defence against losses, and make the servicer and originator of the collateral sensitive to the performance of their loans. If a pool of auto loans with an average APR of 10 per cent are transferred into a trust, which then issues 5 per cent coupon bonds, the excess spread of 5 per cent is returned to the owner of the collateral net of any losses that may have occurred. So, if historical losses for an originator have been 2 per cent, the transaction has a cushion for additional losses of 3 per cent before the bondholders lose money. That first 3 per cent of credit exposure are borne by the issuer (in the form of foregone income), incentivising them to service the pool to the best of their ability to control losses. Oftentimes, excess spread will be deposited into a reserve account and released to the issuer either at maturity, or when the account reaches some predetermined size. Usually, there are loss and delinquency triggers that are monitored by the trustee that can trap additional cash.

The trustee is responsible for administering the trust, distributions on the bonds and, in the event of a servicer termination, either hiring a replacement servicer or stepping into that role themselves. In transactions where the servicer is considered weak, a backup servicer will be identified (and paid) from the outset. A 'hot backup' will usually be paid a monthly fee to compensate them for loading all of the current loan information onto their platform in order to reduce the time needed to take over servicing if that becomes necessary.

Opportunities for hedge fund investors in ABS markets

The tremendous growth of the ABS market throughout the 1990s has created a plethora of opportunities for investors. In addition, individual ABS issues, while relatively homogenous in their structure, are quite unique regarding their underlying collateral.

Another interesting characteristic of the ABS market is that the bonds are typically amortising and pay principal and interest on a monthly basis. Moreover, credit quality and duration of off-the-run issues will become dynamic as issues amortise. All of these factors contribute to a market that is fragmented and often less transparent than meets the eye.

Niche opportunities in ABS

As the ABS market has matured, the new issue side of the business has become highly efficient. Institutional buyers routinely purchase US$25 million blocks of deals (or larger) with minimum effort, as the underwriter and ratings agency typically have all of the relevant information tied up in a readily recognisable form. The initial offering is almost certainly the only time that the market operates in a state of pure price transparency.

The secondary market is perhaps the exact opposite. Information is not readily available. Historical performance of the underlying collateral pools must be gathered and analysed. Pricing is opaque. Moreover, many securities become 'orphaned' as their size and remaining life shrink due to amortisation, making them unattractive to most institutional buyers. In essence, by focusing on investment opportunities that are both too small for typical institutional investors and yet too sophisticated for individual investors, a hedge fund can construct a portfolio of fixed-income investments, which generates high monthly income with low price volatility.

Managers willing to do the credit work on these orphaned bonds can be rewarded with attractively priced portfolios where much of the risk has already been wrung out of the underlying collateral pools.

Distressed/high-yield opportunities in ABS

An interesting subset and evolving niche strategy in the ABS market is the distressed market. The ABS market really only came into its own in the second half of the 1990s. As a result, problem credits did not begin to surface until the last few years. Unlike the corporate bond market where there is a large, established community of distressed investors, the ABS market does not have an equivalent. Therefore price volatility can be quite high in troubled names, presenting attractive investment opportunities. Examples include manufactured housing, franchise, collateralised debt obligations (CDOs) and others.

Distressed/high-yield CDOs: a classic example of many sellers and few buyers

CDOs are ABS structures backed by high-yield bonds, highly leveraged loans, asset-backed bonds and other asset classes. These structures are designed to arbitrage interest rate spreads between the underlying collateral and the weighted cost of debt capital issued by the APV, typically a trust. A typical CDO structure is illustrated in Exhibit 12.4.

You will note that the weighted cost of capital ranges from Libor + 85 to 110. The average coupon on the underlying collateral pool of bonds or loans ranges from 200 to 350 (highly leveraged loans) or a fixed rate of 10 per cent more, typically, for high-yield bonds. This results in an excess interest spread (Yield – Cost of debt capital) of 115 to 240 basis points. It is this arbitrage that enabled dealers to attract significant equity capital to CDOs resulting in issuance of over $80 billion of high-yield CDOs, also known as collateralised bond obligations (CBOs) from 1996 to 2000. Equity holders were expected to earn a return in excess of 15 per cent on their investment after applying historical default and recovery rates to the high-yield collateral pool. Debt investors were driven by the attractive spreads of the respective rated classes of bonds relative to other securities with similar ratings. For example, AAA-rated corporate paper of the same duration trades at a spread of Libor flat to 10 basis points; therefore, these CBO securities offered a spread 'pickup' of 35 to 50 basis points. The AAA rating also implied a highly remote risk of principal loss, using historical default and recovery performance assumptions for the high-yield collateral.

The opportunity to purchase distressed CBO debt securities in the secondary market at substantial discounts to intrinsic value is the result of the underperformance of the underlying high-yield loan and bond collateral since 2000. The dramatic increase in high-yield default rates coupled with a substantial drop in recovery rates has resulted in a significant deterioration in the performance of substantially all CBO debt securities created since 1996. Historical average annual high-yield default rates have been less than 3.5 per cent since inception of the market in 1986. Historical recovery rates over the same period have been in

Exhibit 12.4

A typical CDO structure

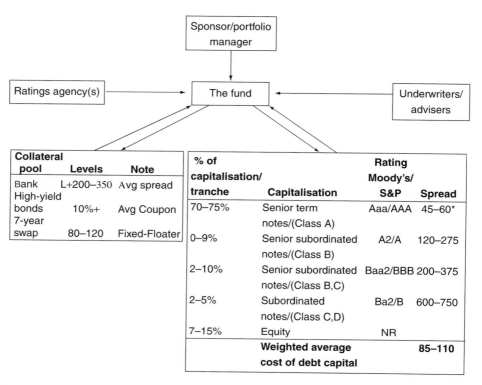

Collateral pool	Levels	Note
Bank High-yield	L+200–350	Avg spread
bonds 7-year	10%+	Avg Coupon
swap	80–120	Fixed-Floater

% of capitalisation/ tranche	Capitalisation	Rating Moody's/ S&P	Spread
70–75%	Senior term notes/(Class A)	Aaa/AAA	45–60*
0–9%	Senior subordinated notes/(Class B)	A2/A	120–275
2–10%	Senior subordinated notes/(Class B,C)	Baa2/BBB	200–375
2–5%	Subordinated notes/(Class C,D)	Ba2/B	600–750
7–15%	Equity	NR	
Weighted average cost of debt capital			**85–110**

* Represents floating tranche only; fixed tranche range 160–180 bps.

Sources: CSFB, Bloomberg.

excess of 40 per cent. In the last three years annual high-yield default rates have averaged over 8.3 per cent which is nearly double the average annual default rate of the previous 13 years. Recovery rates, currently averaging 34 per cent, have dropped over 12 per cent during the same period.

The deterioration of CBO collateral is evidenced by the dramatic increase in downgrades of CBO securities over the last two years. Of the outstanding CBO securities issued from 1996 through 2000, over 70 per cent have been downgraded, leaving the original CBO investor with a distressed security that no longer meets their investment criteria.[4]

Specifically, many bank asset-backed commercial paper programmes or 'bank conduits' were original investors in AAA-rated CBO securities. These CBO securities were purchased based on their rating and the attractive spread relative to comparably rated securities and the banks' cost of funding. As these CBO debt securities migrate down the rating spectrum, the appetite of the bank conduit diminishes as additional reserves are required to be held by the bank, diluting the return on investment.

There is limited liquidity available to purchase distressed CBO debt securities in the secondary market. This has created a compelling opportunity for investors capable of analysing the CBO structure and the performance of the underlying high-yield assets.

Several hedge funds have recently entered the secondary market for CBOs to fill this liquidity void and take advantage of the opportunity to generate substantial risk-adjusted returns for their investors.

Conclusion

The enormous growth and success of the ABS market lies in its unique ability to efficiently aggregate smaller, illiquid assets into bundled securities which are widely accepted and traded in global capital markets. The resulting securities markets have become enormous funding sources for a wide variety of consumer, as well as commercial, activities.

In fact, ABS funding activity has grown so much that many view it as creating various 'bubbles' in the economy whether it be in consumer credit, housing or some yet undiscovered market. Nevertheless, as a hedge fund manager in structured credit, we are largely agnostic to whether ABS structures are enabling consumers to be more free-wheeling than they otherwise would have been. Instead we explore 'bubbles' for what they might offer after they have burst – with a careful eye towards avoiding collateral damage during the 'bursting' phase.

Being a total-return buyer versus a ratings-driven one, we can buy credits for their intrinsic value when others may be prohibited from buying. Our preference is to be always looking in less-trafficked areas of the capital markets and the ABS securities, because of their complex asset classes and tranching structures, oftentimes offer just that. However, less-trafficked areas are not limited to distressed securities only and can often include the senior securities of an issue which, for various reasons, have been shunned or overlooked by the institutional community, providing a very rich purchase for the hedge fund buyer.

Whether across various credit tranches or in our asset classes, the opportunities in the ABS market remain abundant. Buying right and being diversified is the best long-term strategy for 'hedging' our portfolio risk and providing superior risk-adjusted returns to investors.

---

[1] The bonds of which incidentally have come under ratings pressure as his record sales have stalled in recent years.

[2] *Source:* Lehman Brothers.

[3] Using Ford Motor as an example, an investor in a Ford securitisation is theoretically indifferent as to Ford Motor's viability as an ongoing entity. However, in reality, if Ford left the auto business the resale value of Ford cars (ie, the ultimate collateral backing the ABS issue) would plummet, significantly altering the expected net losses in the pool of loans. Moreover, since the originator of the loans also acts as the servicer in most ABS transactions, a new servicer would need to be hired to fill that role. Although that servicer may end up being perfectly competent over time, there would be disruptions in the short term as they converted loan information and loaded it onto their servicing and collection platform. For this reason, the market is quite sensitive to changes in servicers.

[4] *Source: Default and Recovery Rates of Corporate Bond Issuers*, Moody's Investors Service, 2000.

Chapter 13

Emerging markets

Bruce Richards and Louis Hanover
Marathon Asset Management, LLC, New York, New York[1]

Introduction

The development of emerging market debt as an active, viable and widely traded investment class ironically owes its beginnings to a dark period in Latin American financial history. Mexico's default on its commercial bank obligations in 1982 marked the beginning of a wave of sovereign defaults to spread across Latin America, which subsequently cut off valuable capital and rendered the region 'lost' for the remainder of the decade.

It was not until the late 1980s, after the completion of Mexico's Brady exchange, that the international capital markets began to finally reopen its doors to Latin America. The Brady plan, named after US Treasury Secretary Nicholas Brady, engineered a solution that effectively securitised billions of non-performing bank debt into attractively structured bonds. The Brady concept, initially designed to facilitate the re-entry of the United Mexican States back to the global capital markets, would ultimately be applied to other countries in default, (including countries in eastern Europe, Asia and Africa), enabling these sovereign borrowers to regain access to international credit.

The first few Brady exchanges in effect planted the seeds for a burgeoning secondary market place of securitised emerging market paper. A total of seventeen countries (see Exhibit 13.1) ultimately participated in issuing Brady bonds, totalling approximately US$170 billion. The majority of Brady debt was issued by Latin American credits in the first half of the 1990s, with Argentina, Brazil, Mexico and Venezuela representing 78 per cent of total issuance. With each exchange, the increasing breadth of tradable countries and different types of fixed-income products attracted an ever-increasing number of participants, including institutional investors, mutual funds, insurance companies and pension funds. From the ashes of the 'lost decade', a new asset class was born.

Mexico: a true success story

The tale of Mexico provides a microcosmic perspective of the opportunities and pitfalls the emerging market bond universe has to offer. After issuing the first Brady bonds in 1990, the Salinas administration ostensibly put the country on the right track with a sensible mix of policies. By the end of 1993, Mexico had amassed US$25 billion in international reserves, a four-fold increase in four years.[2] Mexico's entry into the North American Free Trade Agreement (NAFTA) in 1994 was the country's crowning achievement and Mexico's Brady bonds rallied to reflect this development. External bond spreads that were quoted at 600 basis points prior to the announcement, tightened to about 260 basis points (Mexico's five-year debt spreads currently trade +150 basis points over US Treasuries).

Exhibit 13.1

Original Brady/exchange issue amount (US$ billions)

Country	Pars	Discounts	Other Brady debt	Total Brady debt issued	Per cent of all Bradys
Latin America					
Argentina	12.67	4.32	8.47	25.45	15.0
Brazil	10.49	7.29	32.88	50.66	29.9
Costa Rica	na	na	0.59	0.59	0.4
Dominican Republic	na	0.33	0.19	0.52	0.3
Ecuador	1.91	1.44	2.78	6.13	3.6
Mexico	22.40	11.77	2.73	36.90	21.7
Panama	0.26	0.045	2.92	3.22	1.9
Peru	0.18	0.57	4.12	4.87	2.9
Uruguay	0.53	na	0.54	1.07	0.6
Venezuela	7.33	1.27	9.95	18.55	10.9
Non-Latin					
Bulgaria	na	1.85	3.28	5.13	3.0
Ivory Coast	na	0.07	1.26	1.33	0.8
Jordan	0.49	0.16	0.09	0.74	0.4
Nigeria	2.05	na	na	2.05	1.2
Philippines	1.89	na	2.32	4.21	2.5
Poland	0.90	2.99	4.02	7.90	4.7
Vietnam	0.23	0.02	0.29	0.55	0.3
Total	**61.34**	**32.11**	**76.43**	**169.88**	**100**
Per cent	36.10	18.90	45.00	100.00	

Source: Merrill Lynch.

In December 1994, just as the country's prospects had turned up, a devaluation of the Mexican peso (dubiously dubbed the 'Tequila Crisis'), less than five years after carrying out the initial Brady exchange, threatened to push Mexico back to the brink of 'welfare' status. The well-documented peso devaluation, principally a result of a gross imbalance in the country's current account, stunned the emerging market debt world and marked the first significant emerging market crisis of the new decade. For many investors who had embraced emerging market investments after being introduced to the first Brady bonds, the Mexican peso devaluation was a rude awakening, as it introduced investors to the high level of volatility associated with this asset class (see Exhibit 13.2).

The tumultuous spring that ensued quickly dispelled any notion of investing in emerging markets for income. By early March 1995, the Emerging Market Bond Index (EMBI) fell over 20 per cent from the previous December.[3] The Mexican peso traded down to MXP7.45/US$, a loss of over 50 per cent from pre-devaluation levels. Although, Mexican debt bore the brunt of selling, with sovereign credit spreads reaching +2,200 basis points from a level of +500 basis points months earlier, other prominent Latin credits like Argentina were also hard hit as a wave of contagion spread throughout the region (the Argentina floating-rate bond (FRB) due in March 2005 lost half of its market value during this short period) (see Exhibit 13.3).

Mexico and its asset class eventually recovered as the US Treasury led a bailout package that provided critical capital to Mexico, which helped restore confidence to the emerging markets. Remarkably, by mid-1996, the investment community found itself in the midst of another torrid love affair with the emerging markets. Investors seemed to have reversed course as emerging market countries, including Mexico, were once again successful in attracting investment capital. Mexico's current account deficit had been adequately addressed and the country was growing again. As a result, Mexico was able to successfully place a US$1.75 billion 30-year global Eurobond, becoming the first emerging market country to issue a pure 30-year bond. By late 1997, the EMBI touched a historic tight of +330 basis points vs. US Treasuries, 1,600 basis points tighter from its peak of +1,900 basis points in March 1995. Emerging markets as a class appeared to have the wind at its back.

However, as any experienced student of emerging markets can attest, this asset class is subject to frequent 'feast or famine' periods. Almost on cue, in the summer of 1998, global markets came under intense pressure after Russian authorities declared it would devalue its currency and default on its local currency debt. The markets were caught off guard as investors and hedge funds had amassed huge commitments in local market Russian debt (called GKOs) with exposure to the currency. In the weeks that followed, a massive de-leveraging process began to unfold in the global capital markets, leading to a liquidity crisis that caused the collapse of Long Term Capital Management and endangered the viability of the entire global financial system. This event prompted the Federal Reserve to hold emergency sessions and adopt measures to restore confidence in the financial markets. In short, an emerging market crisis ignited a systemic capital markets catastrophe. The indiscriminate and vicious sell-off entangled all 'risky' financial products. Even Mexico, which was on a path to investment-grade status, was not spared, as evidenced by the fact that the United Mexican States bonds due 2026 fell 36 points (as Mexican external debt spreads widened 900 basis points).

Exhibit 13.2

Mexican Brady bond spreads, 1993–95

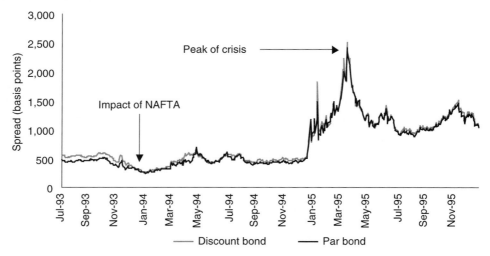

Source: Marathon Asset Management, LLC.

To avert a complete meltdown in the world's financial markets, the Federal Reserve injected large amounts of liquidity into the system, most notably with three consecutive interest rate cuts. When the clouds began to clear in October 1998, emerging market assets regained its footing, but the asset class was badly damaged and the losses were staggering.

Investor interest steadily returned and, amazingly, neither the Brazilian real devaluation in January 1999, nor the crash in global equity values in 2000, nor the protracted default in Argentina during 2001 had any sustained impact on global emerging market debt between 1999 and 2003. Investors were again drawn to the emerging markets.

With little fanfare, in the spring of 2003, eight years after devaluing its currency and a year after obtaining the long coveted status of investment grade, the Mexican authorities voluntarily retired the last of its Brady bonds (named the 'Par series') at par, 16 years ahead of schedule. This action was symbolic in that Mexico became the first country to enter and actually complete a Brady programme. The grave state of affairs during the spring of 1995 is now but a distant memory.

The Mexican story of the 1990s is impressive because the country managed to not only survive but actually prosper amidst its own growing pains and the uncertainty of global capital flows. On many fronts, Mexico today is vastly different from its days when it first entered NAFTA and devalued its currency in 1994, as its economy is far larger, more diverse and dynamic with international reserves in excess of US$50 billion and its public finances on solid ground.

While it is clear that the Mexican economy benefited from free trade with the United States, the Mexican authorities were also responsible for bringing about their country's success through the implementation of appropriate policy measures and delivering a sound economic programme since its devaluation. After the Tequila Crisis, Mexican policy-makers properly concluded that managing market expectations ultimately shapes market sentiment, which in turn influences capital investments. Through all of its trials and tribulations, the Mexican story has been a huge success as it serves as a model for other emerging market countries.

Exhibit 13.3

Argentine FRB spreads, 1994–95

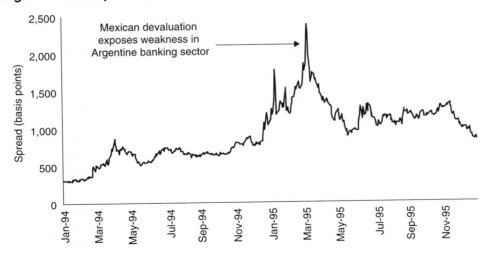

Source: Marathon Asset Management, LLC.

Clearly, Mexico has not been the only tale of 'boom and bust' in the last 15 years. In fact, Russia's return from its 1998 financial debacle is in many ways even more extraordinary than Mexico's story. Russia's spectacular meltdown created global 'contagion' as the developed markets were rendered volatile, illiquid and completely dysfunctional. Renowned money managers were brought to their knees as the depth of the collapse in valuations in the world's capital markets proved overwhelming. The Russia 12.75 per cent bonds due in 2028 were priced near par in June 1998 but fell to 18 cents on the dollar within four months of issuance, an implicit yield in excess of 60 per cent. Less than five years later, these exact bonds trade above 160, equating to a yield of less than 7.5 per cent! The transformation of the Russian economy from a selective default credit to one that is on the path to investment-grade status (rated a BB rating by Standard & Poor's and its debt trading 300 basis points over US Treasuries) is the greatest turnaround story the sovereign debt market has witnessed in recent memory.

As the market evolves

As is evident by now, the common theme that reverberates through the emerging markets world is one of recurring volatility. This inherent volatility reflects not only the nascent nature of these economies but also the vagaries of capital flows and the disaggregate way information is disseminated to the market. These 'boom and bust' cycles evidenced in regular waves can be a cruel and painful lesson for those who simply employ 'buy-and-hold' investment strategies. Still, recent return data suggests, while individual emerging market stories can be marked by dramatic events and volatility, the asset class has proven to be remarkably successful. The EMBI[4] has been the top performing debt class every year for the past four years, gaining an average of 14 per cent per annum. Given the various credit concerns of the debtor nations that comprise this asset class, diversification is obviously a critical ingredient for success.

Many emerging markets managers have structured their funds to take full advantage of the various degrees of volatility in the emerging markets. In order to effectively trade emerging market debt, investment managers must understand that volatility is often highly extreme. While volatility is not necessarily a good thing, if it is harnessed properly it can be incredibly advantageous from a trader's perspective. Emerging market debt continually presents opportunities due to the 'dislocations' and inefficiencies that develop regularly. In effect, smaller positions (less leverage) can produce comparable or better risk-adjusted returns for a hedge fund manager. In light of this, a disciplined investment programme with diversified strategies that aim to capture both the routine market swings from a directional standpoint and also arbitrage the anomalies that persist in the external debt market represent a viable strategy for many emerging market hedge funds. Views expressed through the local interest rate and foreign exchange markets, as well as the utilisation of derivatives including options and credit default swaps (CDS) can help to optimally monetise inefficiencies in the emerging markets. In addition, select hedge fund managers will strategically attempt to identify and analyse distressed companies or 'special' situations domiciled in the emerging markets.

In contrast, the government bond market of the G-10 countries represents a highly liquid commodity that is much more efficient and much less volatile. As a result, investors in G-10 debt must assume a higher degree of leverage and risk to capture relatively small inefficiencies when they arbitrage or trade bonds in G-10 markets.

A world of opportunities

The universe of the most viable and tradable external debt is included in JP Morgan's Emerging Market Bond Index Plus (EMBI+), a variant of the original EMBI that was introduced in January 1991 (the original EMBI only included bonds issued from a Brady facility). The EMBI+ is a total return index that tracks the performance of external bonds including Bradys, Eurobonds and loans. The EMBI+ is comprised of 90 US dollar-denominated sovereign debt issues with an average outstanding balance of US$2.7 billion per issue, representing 19 countries: Argentina, Brazil, Bulgaria, Colombia, Ecuador, Egypt, Malaysia, Mexico, Morocco, Nigeria, Panama, Peru, the Philippines, Poland, Russia, South Africa, Turkey, Ukraine and Venezuela.

While the external debt market is characterised by the 'Brady' label, in recent years, the availability of emerging market fixed-income products has expanded beyond the original 'Bradys' or Eurobonds, reflecting a growing base of investors and pointing to a maturation of the market. The universe of emerging market debt-related products is quite broad and includes options on most liquid instruments, credit default swaps (CDS) and foreign exchange-based rate structures. Today, the global Eurobond market has developed alongside the Brady bond market as countries have utilised the capital markets to finance budget deficits and roll over existing debt at lower rates. Global Eurobonds, which are simply straight or plain vanilla debt issued by a sovereign or corporation entity, have in greater frequency replaced existing Brady bonds in the secondary market.

In addition, the accessibility of many local markets continues to increase. The JP Morgan ELMI+ (Emerging Local Markets Index Plus) provides a glimpse of the vast number of local markets that offer tradable products. Included in this index are: Argentina, Brazil, Chile, China, Colombia, the Czech Republic, Egypt, Hong Kong, Hungary, India, Indonesia, Israel, Mexico, the Philippines, Poland, Russia, Singapore, the Slovak Republic, South Africa, South Korea, Taiwan, Thailand, Turkey and Venezuela (see Exhibit 13.4).

Exhibit 13.4

EMBI+ spread, 1998–2003

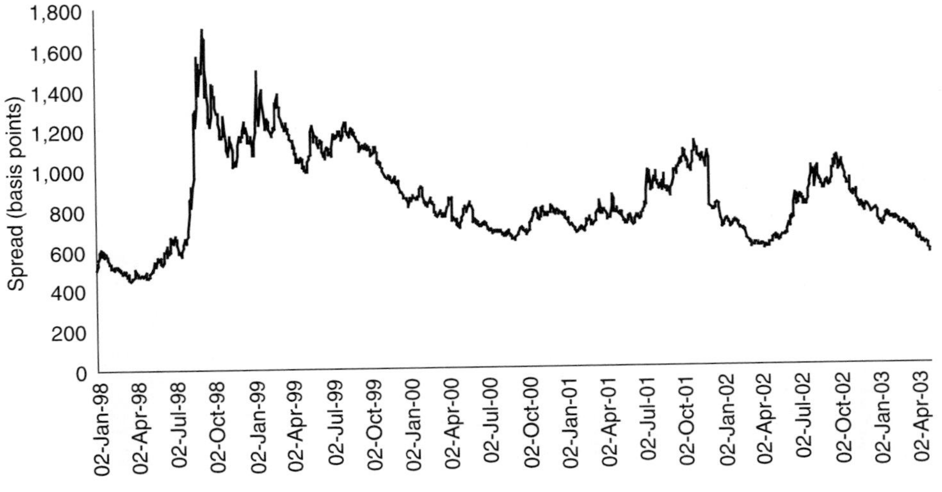

Source: JP Morgan Chase.

Emerging markets versus other debt classes

Volatility and returns

Conventional bond wisdom suggests that fixed-income investors generally desire a stable and predictable market place. This is principally due to the fact that fixed-income pays investors interest income regardless of the pricing considerations of the underlying asset. To put it in more technical terms, as prices remain steady in a spread-based market, the cost of carrying a short position outweighs the cost of capital to fund a long position, thereby making volatility generally undesirable. Solvency, rather than appreciation, is the most important component for investors. However, in the emerging market debt world, this is not always the case. Volatility almost invariably creeps into every emerging market story, as endogenous and exogenous developments have proven to disturb emerging market asset prices.

Historically, emerging markets have traded with an annual standard deviation in excess of 20 per cent, which is more in line with volatility experienced in the equities market than the typical 5–8 per cent levels of volatility evidenced in most fixed-income asset classes. In fact, volatility in the emerging markets exceed by three-fold the annual volatility of every other major debt classes, including US government bonds, mortgage-backed securities (MBS) and corporate bonds. Indeed, risk metrics confirm that emerging markets are the most volatile asset class in the fixed-income space. The Brazil C bond, considered to be the benchmark (and most liquid) instrument in the emerging market debt world is a good proxy of general volatility for this asset class. Since issuance, the Brazil C bond's average annualised volatility has been over 20 per cent during the past decade with five discrete periods where volatility exceeded 70 per cent (see Exhibit 13.5). Given this high absolute level of volatility, a simple buy-and-hold strategy leads to greater exposure than many long-only, index-based investors would like to assume.

Volatility can certainly be viewed as a negative but it can also be considered a characteristic that regularly supplies meaningful opportunities. Despite the high level of volatility,

Exhibit 13.5

Brazil C bond volatility, 1994–2002

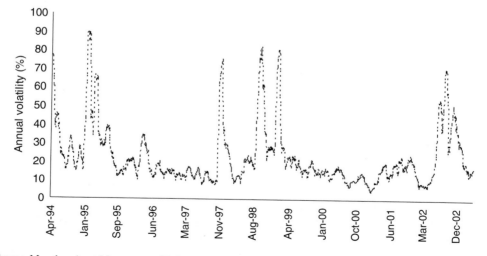

Source: Marathon Asset Management, LLC.

Exhibit 13.6

Risk versus reward characteristics of various assets, October 2001–March 2003

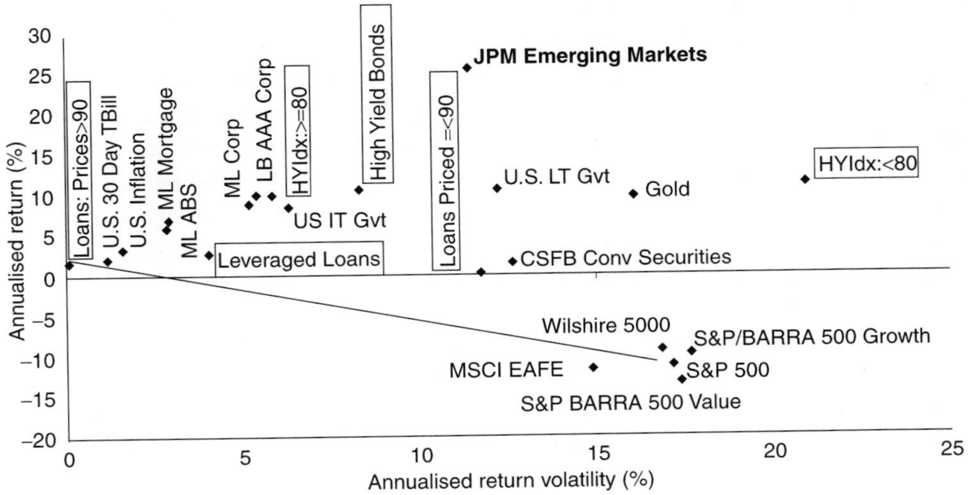

Source: Credit Suisse First Boston.

emerging market debt has delivered superior returns relative to its peers in the fixed-income sector. As Exhibit 13.6 illustrates, emerging market sovereign debt continues to be one of the top performing asset classes on both an absolute and risk-adjusted basis. In other words, investors have been more than adequately compensated for assuming the higher level of risk. In the period between October 2001 and March 2003, we see that emerging market debt not only delivered one of the highest returns among all asset classes but it did so with even less volatility than the US Treasury 10-year note! The S&P 500 Index, during the same period, dropped an average 8 per cent annually with almost twice the amount of risk.

We should note that while the superior performance of emerging market debt in recent years is indeed a reflection of vast improvements in various local markets, the asset class has also benefited from an investment environment increasingly interested in adding yield and diversification to supplement more traditional portfolio allocations. Given the severe market correction in global equity prices in recent years, investors have gravitated towards the emerging market debt space as an alternative source of long-term returns. Moreover, slow global growth has compressed government rates to historic lows in the G-10 markets, thereby increasing the allure of high-yielding assets.

Liquidity

The EMBI has consistently been the cheapest and perhaps the most inefficient asset class in the capital markets. In the face of this, critics of emerging markets have often charged that the asset class lacks sufficient liquidity to make it worth investing. In truth, the common perceptions about the 'lack of liquidity' in emerging market debt are proved to be completely erroneous when measured against actual statistics from the secondary market place.

Admittedly, local currency denominated debt issues can be illiquid but US dollar-denominated issues, which account for upwards of 90 per cent of all portfolio holdings, are both relatively liquid and transparent. Dollar-denominated issues in the EMBI have an average value of nearly US$2 billion, with the largest 10 issues having a face value of US$5 billion on average.[5] The top 10 issues in the EMBI+ have a face amount of US$8.7 billion per issue, considerably larger than agency and corporate bond issues in the United States. In contrast, the average size of a US high yield-bond issue is only about US$300 million.

Moreover, daily trading activity is quite robust with at least 15 major money centre banks and investment banks acting as market-makers and providing liquidity with active two-way markets. While the benchmark emerging market issues are not on equal footing with on-the-run US government bonds, emerging market issues are substantially more liquid than is typically assumed. The bid–offer spread on an average sovereign debt issue is approximately 0.5 points, which is comparable to the bid–offer spread for many BBB-rated US corporate bonds and less costly than most high-yield bonds.

In addition, emerging markets is one of the few fixed-income asset classes that provides 'live' broker prices so that market-makers can transact with transparency in price. The higher degree of transparency has in effect reduced the average bid–offer spread over the years, similar to what transpired in the US Treasury market and MBS market. A repurchase market (repo) is also available, enabling investors to actively establish short positions by borrowing bonds in the repo market. This is important for money managers who rely on hedging to manage risk or shorting as a means to profit.

Strategies

There are many strategies deployed by emerging market debt managers. Most of the strategies can be grouped into one of the following three buckets: a) arbitrage b) directional trading and c) special situations in sovereign and corporate debt. Arbitrage includes pairs trading arbitrage, where the purpose is to actively exploit pricing disparities that occur between similar securities issued by the same sovereign or corporate entity; yield curve arbitrage, where the objective is to profit from the changing shape of the yield curve; and relative value arbitrage, where the goal is to capture the price discrepancies that exist between related credits. In directional trading, a trader looks to take outright long or short positions to capitalise on strong technical swings or positive/negative fundamental developments. Hedge funds also enjoy the opportunity to selectively participate in special situations (sovereign restructurings and corporate workouts) as deeply discounted debt presents tremendous opportunities if the ultimate outcome is a successful restructuring. All of these strategies can be employed in both the local and external markets.

Directional external and local market trades

Emerging market debt is comprised of government and corporate debt issues in countries that are generally assigned non-investment grade ratings (typically because of impaired debt service in the past). This universe of debt has an outstanding balance of US$1.5 trillion[6] and is comprised of external and local (or domestic) debt. The external debt markets, which are primarily US dollar-denominated, include Brady bonds, sovereign global debt, corporate debt, commercial paper, money markets, loans and receivables. Local currency markets are denominated in local currency terms, which include sovereign debt, corporate debt and the currency markets.

Arbitrage trading

Due to the segmentation and permutations between Brady bonds, Eurobonds and local currency bonds along a sovereign yield curve, an investment manager is able to arbitrage one bond against another by taking a long position in the sovereign debt of one country and simultaneously shorting a related security within the capital structure of the same country.

Distressed situations

Exceptional opportunities to purchase sovereign and corporate emerging market debt materialise during stressful macroeconomic periods. Selectively purchasing sovereign, corporate and bank debt at deeply discounted levels is challenging, as the political, economic, accounting and legal frameworks are less developed, less transparent and differ from country to country. Money managers who wisely position themselves to take advantage of an improving macroeconomic picture, however (eg, during the Asian and Russian distressed debt crisis) can be rewarded handsomely. In 2003, we see a similar opportunity in select Latin American distressed corporate and sovereign credits.

Below are two examples of actual trades that have been established in the market place by hedge fund practitioners.

Arbitrage: Brazil euro-denominated versus Brazil dollar-denominated bonds

In May 2002, Brazilian global bonds denominated in euros experienced a severe sell-off that coincided with broader emerging market weakness. As the market began to price in the possibility of a Brazilian sovereign default during the summer of 2002, higher US dollar priced sovereign assets declined and Brazil's sovereign yield curve sharply inverted. Euro-denominated Brazilian global bonds were especially hard hit as European retail holders sold en masse. The same bonds, rich to its dollar counterparts just months earlier (due to an unusual demand for euro-denominated paper), began to trade at steep discounts.

For example, compare the Brazil 9.5 per cent euro-denominated bond due 5 October 2007 against the Brazil C bond, which is the most liquid dollar-denominated, intermediate sovereign bond (see Exhibit 13.7). At the height of the selling, despite a lower dollar price, comparable coupon and a shorter maturity, the euro-based bond traded eight points below the 8 per cent Brazil C bonds of 15 April 2014 after trading 10 points above at the start of the year. From a credit perspective, this made little sense as all these issues were *pari passu*, thus creating an arbitrage opportunity. If Brazil defaulted, the arbitrage would have been profitable as the arbitrageur had taken 'dollars out' of the country given the price of the Brazil Eurobonds were trading at a discount to the dollar bonds (for example, the C bond). If the situation in Brazil improved, the curve would normalise and the spread between the two bonds would invariably contract. The two greater risks associated with this trade were: a) a mismatch in currencies and b) marked-to-market risk in the event that the spread continued to invert.

The currency risk could be easily hedged in the currency or futures markets and so the bigger risk was the latter.

The Brazilian yield curve did normalise once selling abated and investors again began to search for yield. The intermediate euro-denominated global bonds, the hardest hit during the crisis, recovered dramatically, converging to their dollar counterparts.

Exhibit 13.7

Brazil C bond versus Brazil 2007 (€)

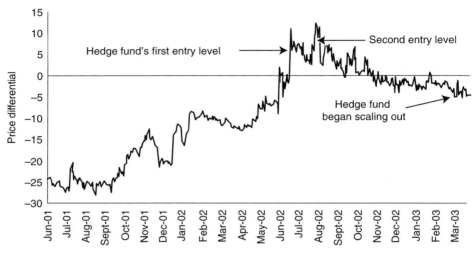

Source: Marathon Asset Management, LLC.

Cross credit arbitrage: PDVSA 7.5 per cent 2028 versus Venezuela 9.25 per cent 2027

A strike at PDVSA, the state run oil company of Venezuela, which began in December 2002, brought oil production in Venezuela to a virtual halt and left the currency vulnerable by early 2003. The bolivar depreciated approximately 28 per cent in January 2003 and ultimately forced the Venezuelan monetary authorities to declare capital controls and set the foreign exchange rate at 1,600. At one point, with oil production at 20 per cent of normal rates, floating-rate Venezuela DCB bonds that were due on 18 December 2007 touched a four-year low as the Venezuela sub-index of debt fell by more than 10 per cent.

PDVSA's bonds weakened as the ratings agencies lowered Venezuela's sovereign rating, citing its reduced cash flows from oil revenues. This decline in PDVSA's bonds represented a cross-credit arbitrage opportunity versus the sovereign bond of Venezuela. Due to PDVSA's relationship with CITGO and the fact that future oil receipts were escrowed offshore in a US dollar account (some interest was in effect already funded), the company's capacity to remain current on its debt obligations was highly likely, despite the strike. Conversely, the sovereign ability to pay its debt was questionable as Venezuela's fiscal account continued to deteriorate. A possible arbitrage existed to take a long position in PDVSA's bonds 7.5 per cent 2028 against an offsetting short position in the Venezuela 2027 bonds.[7]

This trade could be initiated at almost an equal dollar price in January 2003 when heavy selling led to undue supply in PDVSA paper. In short, this trade enabled the arbitrageur to express a bearish view on the country and also capture the cheapness of PDVSA. In better times, PDVSA's bonds due in 2028 had traded as high as 20 points above the Venezuela 2027s. Furthermore, a hedge ratio could be determined based on the prevailing relationship and historical trading pattern between PDVSA's 2028 and Venezuela's 2027 bonds, as highlighted in Exhibit 13.8.

Exhibit 13.8

PDVSA 7.5% 2028 versus Venezuela 9.25% 2027

Source: Marathon Asset Management, LLC.

By March 2003, Venezuelan bonds moved sharply higher, as weakened political opposition and renewed vigour by Chavez, combined with the resumption of oil production, enabled PDVSA to increase oil production to nearly 40 per cent of its capacity. Even as Venezuelan bonds recovered more than half their losses, PDVSA's facility based bonds outperformed their sovereign counterpart.

The current market

According to the World Bank, there are currently 156 developing countries (referred to as developing nations, low income nations, or Third World countries with a per capita income of less than US$9,205) in the world. These countries encompass 84 per cent of the world's population and 75 per cent of sovereign states. Factors that positively influence the performance of emerging market debt are: strong global and domestic growth rates, higher commodity prices for commodity exporting countries, controlled inflation combined with disciplined monetary policy, stable and adjustable currency rates and steady capital flows.

According to the International Monetary Fund, 'the relatively strong risk-adjusted performance of emerging market bonds, mounting disenchantment with equities and low yields on safer government bonds have kindled institutional investor interest in emerging market bonds. Emerging market bond mandates were initiated by institutional investors in the fourth quarter of 2002 and most emerging market bond managers expect continued inflows. A further technical factor seen supporting the market this year is the high amount of coupon and amortisation payments coming due in 2003. Some US$20 billion in sovereign payments are due from EMBI+ countries, and some US$30 billion from EMBIG (diversified), against a backdrop of falling gross insurance. Brazil, Colombia, Mexico, Venezuela, Russia, Turkey and The Philippines all have bonded payments substantially exceeding US$1 billion (over US$4 billion in the case of Brazil, Turkey, Russia and

Mexico). The baseline outlook of positive but slow global economic growth; limited inflationary pressure; low yields on major domestic government bonds; and continued progress in strengthening the balance sheets of the household, corporate and financial sectors in the economies, could create a favourable environment for emerging market bonds.'[8]

The outlook

The outlook for emerging market credits is always murky, which in essence is what defines the emerging markets. However, the asset class offers significant yield to fixed-income investors and the investment environment is in the midst of a phase where the search for the holy grail is yield. What has further bolstered the asset class as of late is the fact that emerging market sovereign debt is devoid of the corruption that has scandalised many US companies. Corporate scandals have taken its toll on the US high-yield market place in recent years, and as a result, investors have increasingly allocated funds to emerging markets, contributing to strong capital flows into sovereign emerging market bonds and creating a virtuous cycle.

As the industrialised world (United States, Europe and Japan) recovers, the impact on growth in emerging markets should prove positive. The extent to which each local economy can benefit from greater external stimulus is a function of locally driven variables such as fiscal and monetary policies, the strength of international trade and commitment to reform. Absent a major crisis unfolding (for example, Brazil), the emerging market sovereign debt sector should once again outperform its fixed-income counterparts.

Conclusion

The emerging market sector is well known for its high volatility. For those who are able to capture the price swings and dislocations that occur in the emerging markets, returns can be quite favourable. However, volatility can be a double-edged sword. Since emerging market debt trades at higher yields, most traditional emerging market debt managers attempt to generate returns by earning the generous spread over Treasuries. During the past decade, the annualised mean return for the EMBI has been in excess of 12 per cent, which reinforces the notion that investors can reap attractive returns if they can withstand the volatility and violent downswings.

Most hedge funds have little in common with traditional fixed-income managers. As briefly seen in the examples of trades discussed above, a hedge fund is able to post returns through capital appreciation generated by capturing price disparities rather than through interest income. A hedge fund can build a core portfolio that is balanced with:

- offsetting positions that are part of the same capital structure;
- long and short positions with comparable duration (the combined position will not be significantly affected by small changes in interest rate levels); and
- relative value strategies that involve offsetting positions in closely related countries (for example, Brazil versus Argentina).

The four years from 1999 to 2003 have been very kind to emerging market hedge funds. However, the ultimate test was 1998 when Russia defaulted and the debacle of Long Term

Capital wreaked havoc on the market. At that time, the universe of emerging market hedge funds lost in excess of 35 per cent, according to industry sources, a drop that not surprisingly resulted in the closure of several emerging market hedge funds. In 1998, the Hedge Fund Research (HFR) Emerging Markets Index was down 33 per cent. One year later, the same index reported positive returns, up nearly 56 per cent. Not surprisingly, Value-at-Risk (VaR) analysis has proven to be of little use as a risk management tool for emerging market investors as historical pricing has given little indication as to the magnitude and timing of future volatility and ultimate price points.

The objective of any hedge fund is to consistently generate high absolute returns irrespective of the direction of the market. Healthy fundamental and technical conditions are key for the emerging markets. However, regardless of the direction of the market, a hedge fund manager with an active and opportunistic perspective can profit, given an intelligent approach to making investments and managing risk. Given this, it is important to build a balanced and diversified portfolio consisting of long positions, hedged with offsetting short positions and with risk spread across different countries and sectors. Managers with a more active trading approach employ a predetermined exit strategy and stop loss at both the trade and portfolio levels. If managed prudently, a hedge fund manager can generate an attractive and consistent return in a bear, bull or consolidating market. In this vein, emerging markets, as an asset class, are not only viable but can also be rewarding.

References

Brauer, J. (1999), *Brady Bonds: A Decade of Volatility*, Emerging Markets Research, Merrill Lynch & Co (December).

Kim, G., J. Byun and A. Ying (2003), *Emerging Markets Bond Index Monitor.* Emerging Markets Research, JP Morgan (April).

International Monetary Fund (2003), *World Economic and Financial Survey,* Washington DC (March).

Global Fund Analysis (2002), *Global Fund Analysis Research Report: Fixed Income Arbitrage Issue* (May).

---

[1] Marathon Asset Management, LLC, located in New York, is a Registered Investment Advisor (RIA) with the Securities Exchange Commission (SEC) in the United States, registered with the Financial Services Authority (FSA) in the United Kingdom (MCap Global Finance Ltd.), and a Commodity Pool Operator (CPO) and a Commodity Trading Advisor (CTA) with the CTFC and NFA. Marathon Asset Management, LLC, New York has no affiliation with any entity similarly named.

[2] *Source:* JP Morgan Chase.

[3] *Source:* JP Morgan Chase.

[4] *Source:* JP Morgan Chase.

[5] Global Fund Analysis, *Fixed Income Arbitrage Issue*, May 2002.

[6] *Source:* JP Morgan Chase.

[7] At a price differential of six points, the PDVSA 2028 trade about 380 basis points tighter in yield. The duration difference was about two duration years; 8.5 on the PDVSA 2028 and 6.5 on the Venezuela 2027 (9.25 per cent due 15 September 2027).

[8] International Monetary Fund, *World Economic and Financial Survey,* March 2003, Chapter III, p. 62.

Chapter 14

Convertible arbitrage:
the manager's perspective

Michael A. Boyd, Jr and staff[1]
Forest Investment Management,[2] Old Greenwich, Connecticut

Introduction

Wall Street is known for continuous creativity and innovation in the financial markets. Seemingly limitless combinations and permutations of securities and risk spreading characterise this creativity. In this chapter, there is an overview of the evolution of the modern convertible securities market. There will be an attempt to demonstrate that convertible arbitrage, a time tested alternative investment technique, can be used as a complementary strategy to augment both fixed-income and equity portfolios.

The issuer's side of the convertible securities market

Convertible bonds (CBs) have been used as a financing tool by issuers for over 100 years, but in this chapter, the convertible securities market is defined as having commenced in the 1950s and having continued through to the present. In the period 1950–70, the issuer universe was small, with a correspondingly small number of investors. Convertible securities were the financing vehicle of choice for emerging technology and service companies, as well as conglomerates. The securities issued were primarily subordinated convertible bonds with long-dated maturities or junior convertible preferred stocks. These instruments served either as acquisition currency or to bolster the issuer's balance sheet at a lower rate of interest than bank loans or straight debt. Furthermore, because they were issued at a premium to the conversion price, they had less dilution of the equity base than a common equity issue. In comparison with the protection afforded bondholders today, the indentures of those issues were weak.

The period from 1980 through to the present has been characterised by a dramatic change in the nature of convertible issuance from this earlier period. Average maturities have declined from 25 years to seven years. At the same time, issue size has increased. Currently, US$1 billion issues are not uncommon. Total worldwide outstanding issuance has surpassed US$550 billion,[3] and as a consequence, some investors now consider convertible securities a separate asset class in the portfolio allocation model. Credit quality has also increased during this period. Today, approximately 59 per cent of all issues outstanding are investment grade, with 19 per cent rated BB, and 22 per cent rated B or below.[4] These percentages assume an assignment of an equivalent rating to the US$122 billion of convertibles that are not rated by any agency.

The type of issuance has also changed dramatically from the structures of a simple bond or preferred equity to a wide array of sophisticated instruments. These include bonds, preferred, or equity equivalents, with short or long maturities, varying conversion ratios, contingent convertibility, contingent call provisions, staggered puts, exchangeable credit, and various settlement procedures upon call, put or redemption. This wide flexibility in structure has attracted a number of issuers who would historically not consider a convertible issue. Issuers can tailor an issue to achieve balance sheet, cash flow or tax planning efficiencies.

The investor's side of the convertible securities market

In the period 1950–80, the universe of investors interested in the convertible securities market was limited. It was comprised mostly of individuals, dedicated institutional convertible funds, high-yield funds, Wall Street trading desks and hedge boutiques. In 1973 a seminal event occurred. The Chicago Board of Options Exchange (CBOE) opened its doors for membership. Standardised listed options with readily ascertainable prices were introduced. This was followed later in the decade with the Chicago Board of Trade's introduction of the Treasury futures, and in 1983, the CBOE introduction of equity index options. The 1990s witnessed further growth in hedging instruments, such as credit default swaps, asset swaps, variance swaps and interest rate swaps. With an expanded, more visible and liquid hedging mechanism, financial market participants were better equipped to effectively hedge specific risks out of their portfolios.

As hedging of risk became more accepted in concept by financial managers, interpretations of laws were changing. The 'Department of Labor' sanctioned short selling by ERISA accounts, and the IRS changed the interpretation of unrelated business taxable income (UBTI) to permit short selling without incurring tax liability within tax-exempt accounts. These changes laid the underpinnings for a widespread acceptance of hedging as a risk control mechanism. This led to the convergence of a variety of market participants. These included hedge funds, trading houses, bond investors, equity managers, banks and insurance companies. Thus, hedging financial instruments in the markets as an institutional strategy was born.

Over the same period on Wall Street, a change took place in the mindset toward trading and risk taking. Hedging became an accepted means by which to manage many forms of financial market risk, just as it had been for decades in physical commodities. The increased use of short selling by convertible and option hedgers necessitated a growth in the stock loan capabilities of Wall Street. Financing of overnight loans, rebates and margining of positions became a large source of revenue for brokers. Prime brokers offering these capabilities created the conditions for talented traders to be lured away from trading desks and into money management, offering alternative strategies to large pools of assets. This backdrop set in motion the growth of hedge funds and the wide array of alternative strategies, which are discussed in this book. Convertible arbitrage is a core strategy in the alternative asset class and as a result has grown dramatically since 1990. By 2003, convertible hedge funds, as an investor class, began to suffer from a supply–demand imbalance; there were more available funds for investment than there was new issuance to absorb these funds without disturbing pricing balance in the market place. Hence, from an issuer's perspective, the terms available for borrowing in the convertible market became more attractive than any other financing source.

What is a convertible security?

Convertible securities today are structured with a multitude of features. They range in their claim on the issuer's capital structure, from senior secured debt to preferred equity. Convertibles have many features that non-convertible corporate debt instruments contain. They include calls, puts, sinking funds, floating coupons, step-up coupons, zero coupons and protective clauses upon the occurrence of certain events. All convertibles allow for convertibility, or in a recent innovation, contingent convertibility into the underlying shares of the issuer, the dollar value of those shares, or, in some instances, into the value of some other asset. The contingent feature is a development that sets a bar above the 'normal conversion price' for which the underlying asset must trade in order for the holder to have the right to convert. This has allowed for a lower share count assumption by the issuer for earnings per share calculations, and as a result, has enticed more issuers to the convertible asset class. There are many varieties of convertibles. For simplicity, the focus of discussion will be on a fixed strike convertible bond.

A convertible bond is a corporate security, issued with a reduced bond yield, in exchange for a conversion feature. This allows the holder to convert the security into a fixed number of shares of the company's underlying common stock at any time prior to maturity or redemption of the instrument. The intrinsic value of the convertible is the maximum of the straight debt value or the conversion value. The investor is willing to accept a lower coupon for the possibility of benefiting from stock price appreciation. Typically, the convertible security is call protected for a number of years, after which the issuer may induce conversion or call the security for cash (see Exhibit 14.1).

Since the holder of a convertible security may convert it into a predetermined number of shares of the issuer's common stock, there is a varying degree of correlation between the convertible security's value and that of the related equity security. As the common stock price appreciates or depreciates, the convertible security's valuation follows. However, the degree to which a change in value of the underlying security is reflected in the value of the con-

Exhibit 14.1

Typical convertible bond profile

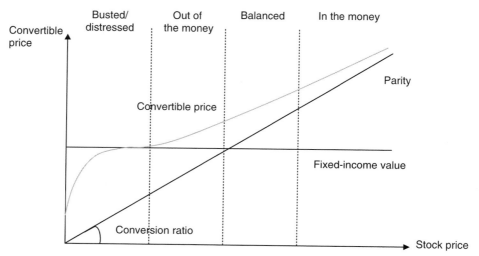

Source: Forest Investment Management.

vertible security depends upon the convertible security's premium over conversion value, or premium over investment value.

The premium over conversion value, or equity premium, is defined as the amount paid for a convertible security in excess of the value receivable upon conversion into the underlying security. For example, if a bond trading at par (US$1,000) converted into 10 shares of an US$80.00 stock, the conversion value (also known as parity value) would be US$800. The premium level, therefore, would be the difference between the US$1,000 par value and the US$800 conversion value, a total of US$200 in premium. Since premium is typically expressed in percentage terms over conversion value, this security would have a 25 per cent premium (US$200 ÷ US$800).

The premium over investment value is defined as the amount paid for a convertible security in excess of the value that the convertible would trade at if it were a non-convertible, fixed-income instrument.

There are various factors that affect the level of a convertible security's premium over conversion value. In the model discussed below, the value of a convertible bond is heavily dependent on:

- the underlying equity volatility;
- equity dividend yield;
- call protection remaining;
- level of interest rates; and
- years to maturity.

Other factors that have varying degrees of impact include:

- equity float;
- short borrow-ability; and
- size of issue.

In the case where the underlying equity is low, the convertible security acts more like a fixed-income instrument, causing a higher equity premium to develop as it trades closer to investment value. Thus, investors pay more for the convertible security's yield component rather than its equity component, or option value. Conversely, as the common stock appreciates, valuing the convertible security higher than par value, the equity premium falls since there is increasing likelihood the issuer will force conversion. The narrowing degree of equity premium at these levels is often a function of the amount of call protection left in the security and the volatility of the underlying equity. While this premium relationship generally holds true over time and across a broad range of prices between investment value and potential call point, there is rarely in practice a linear correspondence between the price of a given convertible security and that of its underlying security. A convertible security, because of its hybrid nature, responds differently to various market forces than a pure equity instrument such as common stock.

A synopsis of convertible hedging theory

In theory, hedging positions in convertible securities employs the short sale of the underlying equity security or related instruments that creates an offset to the long position. The principal risk in the purchase price paid for the convertible security is offset by the proceeds realised from the short sale of the underlying security. Therefore, due to the inverse correlation, the price fluctuation in either position is theoretically offset by a contra price fluctuation in the related position. The gain, which would be realised from an increase in the resale of a long convertible security position, would be offset against the loss, which would be realised from an increase in the repurchase of the short underlying security position. The theoretical net result of all the movements should be either a neutral or profitable dollar outcome.

Additional profit potential could be derived from a premium expansion, which could be caused by the convertible position moving from an undervalued relationship to one that is overvalued. Conversely, losses may occur when premiums contract, causing an undervalued relationship between the convertible security and its underlying common stock. Actual hedging activities are more sophisticated than the preceding theoretical discussion would imply.

Cash and carry trades

One of the original convertible arbitrage strategies was referred to as 'cash and carry'. The concept here is to buy a convertible bond and sell an appropriate amount of shares (see Exhibit 14.2), as determined by the hedge ratio. The hedge ratio, or delta, is the theoretical number of shares short which protects the investor from moves either up or down in the underlying stock price. Assumptions are made in a scenario analysis of the price that the convertible will trade in a stock move up, down and unchanged. Convertible arbitrage trades are identified by the amount of return one can attain if the scenario assumptions are correct. Profits are generated by the coupon income, short stock interest income, and net profits of the bond and short stock positions. Returns in this strategy are often enhanced by leverage (not shown in this example).

Exhibit 14.2

Simplified 'cash and carry' template

Simplified 'cash and carry' template

Hypothetical Bond ABC 1/1/10	Short proceeds rate = 3%
Coupon = 5%	Stock dividends = 0
Current stock price = 80	Conversion ratio = 10
Current bond price = 1000	Hedge ratio (shares) = 8

	Scenario of one-year holding period		
	Down	*Unchanged*	*Up*
Stock price	60	80	100
Bond price	850	1000	1170
Net P/L bond and stock	10.00	0.00	10.00
Short rebate	24.00	24.00	24.00
Coupon income	50.00	50.00	50.00
Capital required (onset)	1000.00	1000.00	1000.00
Simple ROR (%)	8.4	7.4	8.4

Source: Forest Investment Management.

The analysis above is limited in its approach because it does not identify the profit opportunities of re-hedging, or delta hedging, the position optimally. Delta hedges are made to keep the up and down scenarios at equal rates of return. The frequency and rate of change in the delta is muted by the analysis and therefore underprices the volatility component. It also does not accurately account for other sensitivities inherent in the valuation of the convertible. This was the primary strategy before the broad acceptance and use of volatility-oriented convertible pricing models.

The impact of stochastic models on the convertible market

The advent of quantitative convertible pricing models allowed arbitrageurs to move to an option-based model approach. The first models assumed static credit spreads that would not change over different enterprise values of the issuer. The models would also assume a single volatility estimate for the life of the security (no volatility surface). These models, given inputs of a single credit spread and volatility, would give the investor theoretical values for their long convertible, short stock investment, and sensitivities commonly referred to as 'the greeks':

- delta;
- gamma;
- rho;
- sigma;
- theta; and
- vega.

These sensitivities include the position's exposure to parallel shifts in stock prices, risk-free interest rates, credit spreads, short stock dividends or volatility.

The limitations of these models came back to haunt model-based investors in times of crisis. During market stress periods, credit spreads, risk-free interest rates, and stock prices moved violently and independently. Without an effective credit hedge, a realisation was imposed on the investor: one needs to account for the correlation of market factors that contribute to the fair pricing of the convertible or find a way to hedge the credit spread component. (A simplified example of how an investor could estimate one of these correlations is discussed in the section 'A simplified approach to valuing stock price–credit spread correlation' below.)

The coming of age of the credit derivatives market has allowed volatility-oriented convertible managers to isolate credit risk. In effect, it allows these investors to implement their strengths in volatility pricing and hedging techniques. They are able to use many of the tools developed by equity derivative specialists in their investment process. Although these hedges are rarely perfect, this has led to a more competitively priced market place for the subset of convertible issues where a liquid market of credit derivatives exists for that credit, such as asset swaps and credit default swaps. The other side of these trades has enabled credit investors to gain exposure to convertible securities' credits, without exposure to volatility pricing and hedging costs.

A crowded market for convertible arbitrage

Convertible arbitrage has grown significantly in sophistication over the last decade. The progress in valuation techniques of option pricing, and, more recently, credit pricing, has led to greater transparency of fair value of these instruments. The initial quantitative arbitrage entrants were experts at volatility pricing, taking advantage of the convertible asset class as a source of mispriced, often underpriced, equity options. Recently, with the advent of liquid credit derivative markets, volatility players are able to isolate their option from their credit exposure. The outperformance of the convertible arbitrage asset class versus other market-neutral strategies, and the relative ease of credit hedging, has lured many volatility arbitrage players to the convertible market. Their investments are limited to the hedgeable credit universe, which is characterised by better quality and seniority. The size of capital being deployed by these players and the leveraged nature of their trades, versus the size of the convertible market has led to lower expected returns for the pure convertible volatility arbitrage player. Outright investors have also grown in sophistication with their ability to access third party quantitative models. Although most of these models are limited in scope, they have brought the outright investor to acquiesce in the concept of theoretical fair value and subsequently increased their acceptance of convertibles as a viable investment alternative to equities and corporate debt. This has led to the convertible market being monitored by a more diverse group of investors. Although a more crowded market than the past, relative value opportunities abound for the experienced manager who can look through the limits of pure volatility arbitrage and single-factor models, characterised by fixed credit spreads with no allowance for correlation to other pricing sensitivities.

Credit analysis of convertible bonds

There are numerous methods of credit analysis. The approach that Forest Investment Management follows in performing convertible credit analysis is a two-pronged process. It combines aspects of both traditional credit analysis as well as an option-based default model to approximate the behaviour of credit securities, using dynamic stock price and volatility scenarios. The research process begins with a comprehensive review of the capital structure of a company to assess its overall credit strength using traditional credit metrics such as leverage ratios and debt service capability, as well as the company's ability to access capital. The resulting analysis, coupled with a qualitative assessment of the company's credit drivers, provides the input for the quantitative credit model.

This approach is highly dependent on our 'forward look' of the capital structure. Effectively analysing and pricing the credit risk of a convertible bond requires a thorough understanding of the capital structure of the company. The convertible bond value is contingent on the terms and conditions written into the security's indenture. These terms and conditions define the rights due to the convertible bondholder relative to other debt holders in the event of certain fundamental and structural changes to the credit.

The quantitative modelling of the credit component of a convertible bond is based on a modified 'Merton' model approach that allows for dynamic and forward-looking measures of a company's capital structure, asset volatility and leverage in order to estimate the probability of default. The basic thesis is that equity can be considered a call option on the market value of a firm's total assets with a strike price equal to the book value of the firm's debt. By the application of derivative asset pricing theory (a generalisation of the options pricing theory of Black, Scholes and Merton), empirically observed equity risk can be decomposed into its constituent asset risk and leverage components. In this respect, default estimation is used for valuation of the credit component of the convertible bond, in conjunction with the observed market price of credit in order to establish the economic price of the credit for the individual issuer.

The anticipation of default by Merton-type models is expressed as a probability distribution. Theoretically, a corporate bond price should be equal to the present value of its cash flows discounted at rates that are the sum of the riskless discount rates plus the expected loss rate and a risk premium. The riskless rates can be estimated from the pricing of Libor by means of a term structure model. The expected loss used is equal to the probability of default multiplied by the loss given default. The risk premium should be proportional to each bond's systematic risk, which in turn is determined by the default probability. This means that the options adjusted spread (OAS) of the bond should be a function of the default probability. The default probability can be calibrated to an OAS from the observed price of credit in the cash bond market and credit derivatives markets to approximate the convexity[5] of the convertible bond.

According to the model, default occurs when the borrower's assets are depleted to such an extent that minimum payment of liabilities cannot be met. The 'probability of default' derives from the dynamic success or failure of the borrower. There are three basic types of information needed to derive the default probability of a firm: financial statements, market prices of the firm's equity, and subjective assessment of the firm's future prospects and risk. Financial statements, by their nature, are inherently backward looking. Market prices, by their nature, are inherently forward looking because investors form debt and equity prices as they discount the firm's future. The most effective default measurement tools, therefore, use both market prices and financial statement analysis.

There is an increasing number of credit modelling vendors that employ some extension of the 'Merton' model including Moody's KMV® and CreditGrades™. Moody's KMV Creditedge for example, uses an extension of the Black-Scholes-Merton framework to produce a model of default probability that assumes the firm's equity is a perpetual option with the default point acting as the absorbing barrier for the firm's asset value. When the asset value hits the default point, the firm is assumed to default. A default database is used to derive an empirical distribution relating the distance-to-default to a default probability. This model uses this option nature of equity to derive the underlying asset value and asset volatility implied by the market value, volatility of equity and the book value of liabilities.

The dynamic modelling of credit risk results in increased granularity compared to using traditional rating agency grades. The benefit of using this approach is that it eliminates much of the qualitative distortion inherent in traditional credit analysis.

A simplified approach to valuing stock price – credit spread correlation

As described earlier, a convertible bond is an instrument that has the characteristics of both corporate debt and equity. Therefore, both the interest rate and the stock price drive the price of the convertible bond. In addition, the convertible bond's value is subject to the issuer's default risk. During 2002, the credit market exhibited historically high volatility and high correlation with the equity market and risk-free interest rates. In this section, we attempt to explore a credit model that specifies a deterministic relation between credit spread and stock price.[6] The non-stochastic nature of this model provides us with a simple and efficient valuation process, as well as an observation of 'constant delta' and 'negative gamma'[7] for credit-sensitive convertible bond issues. Later in this section, we will examine the statistical method adopted to estimate the parameters for the credit spread/stock price relationship.

Consider buying one convertible bond at price P_{CB} and shorting H shares of stock at price P_S. The investor's dollars at risk (DAR) is:

$$DAR = P_{CB} - H*P_S*C \qquad \text{(Equation 1)}$$

where
C = the conversion ratio
H = hedge ratio
DAR = the portion that we need to discount using a risky rate

The remainder of the bond price ($P_{CB}-DAR$) can be discounted using the risk-free rate. Traditionally, convertibles were valued using a single static credit spread across the stock price spectrum. Thus, when the stock price approaches zero, H is reduced to near zero, DAR is close to P_{CB}, and the convertible bond resembles a high-yield straight debt. When the stock price rises, and parity is much higher than par value, at this point H is increased to near 100 per cent, and DAR is close to points premium[8] due to the equity hedge. The convertible bond resembles the profile of a risk-free bond plus an equity option. In the credit model, however, the convertible bond valuation differs significantly from the traditional picture. We employ the following credit model:[9]

$$CS(P_S) = \beta_0 + \beta_1 \exp(-\beta_2 \cdot P_S) \qquad \text{(Equation 2)}$$

where
$CS(P_S)$ = credit spread at stock price P_S
β_0 = the tightest credit spread possible for the issuer
$\beta_0 + \beta_1$ = the widest credit spread
β_2 = a decay coefficient indicating how fast the credit pricing deteriorates as the stock price declines

This model specifies an exponential functional form between credit spread and the stock price. By using a functional form, we made the assumption that credit spread is perfectly correlated with stock price. Although this model has significantly simplified the complex relationship between the two quantities, it does provide us with a credit/stock perspective consistent with historical observations and allows a more intuitive discussion. An alternative approach is to assign a separate random process for the credit spread, with some pre-specified or varying correlation with the random process for the stock price.

To use the above credit model, we need to estimate the βs. One approach is to use the historical credit spread and stock price movement to infer β_1 and β_2. Another approach is to derive the βs from an issuer's financial statements through fundamental analysis, as discussed in the previous section, 'Credit analysis of convertible bonds'. Here, we will only examine the first approach. Rearranging Equation 2, and taking the natural logarithm on both sides, we have:

$$\ln(CS(P_S) - \beta_0) = \ln(\beta_1) - \beta_2 \cdot P_S. \qquad \text{(Equation 3)}$$

With a pre-specified β_0, we can apply linear interpolation between $\ln(CS(P_S)-\beta_0)$ and P_S. As a result, the slope is $-\beta_2$, and the interception is $\ln(\beta_1)$.

The application of the credit model has the following implications on convertible bond valuation. First, for credit-sensitive CBs (low β_2), delta is little changed over a wide range of stock prices ('constant delta' or 'cash and carry'), as a result, gamma diminishes. Second, in the low-stock-price area, gamma becomes negative because credit deteriorates causing the convertible to fall in price at a rate faster than the stock does. Third, the theoretical convertible bond value is often much lower than it would be using a static credit spread. This is the result of the model taking into account the falling bond floor. The irony is that this model displays a hedging profile used for years by managers before the acceptance of quantitative models. The more things change, the more they remain the same.

For a further discussion of model adaptations, see the 'Addendum' at the end of this chapter on the trinomial tree method and the implicit finite difference method.

Risk management

The risk to a portfolio constructed on the basis of theoretical value is any change in the value of the original inputs, or the improper hedging of the original output sensitivities. In the simplified model above, the inputs used were the risky rate, the risk-free rate, credit spread, decay coefficient and equity volatility. There are three broad categories of risk in these inputs:

- interest rate risk (rho);
- credit spread risk (sigma); and
- equity volatility risk (vega).

After a position has been included within a portfolio, any change in the absolute value of an input can cause a drop in the theoretical value of a security.

There are several hedging techniques available to offset these different model risks. Shorting fixed-income instruments, such as Treasuries, or using interest rate swaps and interest rate options can offset long interest rate risk. Long credit spread risk can be offset by shorting corporate fixed-income instruments or using credit derivatives such as credit default swaps, credit index products such as Morgan Stanley TRACERS[SM] and JPMorgan HYDI[SM].[10] Long volatility risk can be mitigated by selling equity options, equity index options, or entering into variance swaps.

Model input risks are just some of the risks in a convertible arbitrage portfolio. What are these other risks and what are some of the ways these risks can be measured and managed? The primary exposure to capital inherent in an arbitrage position is the difference between the long and short market values, plus or minus the notional value of derivatives. This is known as the 'unhedged exposure'. Capital is rarely at risk for this total exposure, but is more frequently at risk for a lesser amount that is sometimes hard to quantify. A portfolio can be analysed to calculate the theoretical negative impact caused by changes in model inputs: interest rates, credit spreads and equity volatility. This effect is expressed as a percentage of the net asset value (NAV). At times, these risks can offset each other. For example, a corresponding widening in credit spreads will be offset by the benefit from an increase in volatility.

A portfolio can also be stress tested to determine the economic impact of changing market conditions. Value-at-Risk, (VaR) analysis is one such measurement. Some managers find VaR a useful risk tool, while others find it difficult to apply to convertible portfolio risk analysis due to the complexities of the convertible arbitrage strategy. However, stressing a convertible arbitrage portfolio by changing the model inputs to predetermined levels and combinations could result in a meaningful scenario analysis, and resultant NAV impact. This type of output is readily understandable and adjustable for changing economic environments.

Other risks that impact the performance of a portfolio fall into the categories of 'structural' and 'operational'. The investor should consider what guidelines a manager uses to structure the portfolio. Sector, industry and individual position exposure limits should be clear. Credit quality concentration, minimum hedge percentage, maximum naked position, position loss limits, security type, notional derivative exposure, liquidity, and geographic limits and levels should also be ascertained.

Another set of facts that should be ascertained before an investor selects a manager falls into the operational area. Who are the prime brokers? How do you measure counter-party risk exposure? Are sources of financing secure for a leveraged portfolio? Is there a lock-up, and if not, what are the withdrawal procedures? Does the manager provide transparency? Does the fund obtain third party verification of pricing? Is there a deep bench of talent or are investors relying on a superstar? As you can see, there are a number of subjective and not so apparent risks in the decision process leading to an investment in a convertible arbitrage manager.

Investment portfolio applications

Due to the hybrid nature of convertibles and the inherently skewed relationship between upside potential and downside risk, convertible securities can be used as part of alternative equity and/or alternative fixed-income strategies. Convertible arbitrage strategies, if managed properly, are designed to generate streams of returns with low volatility that are non-correlated with traditional asset classes and investment strategies. They can be utilised more effectively as 'complements' rather than as 'alternatives' to manage risk and achieve return targets in the total portfolio.

Presented in Exhibit 14.3 are comparative total rates of return for various asset classes vis-à-vis the returns for convertible arbitrage. The returns of our market-neutral Forest Fulcrum Strategy are included for illustrative purposes as representative of the class of convertible arbitrage.[11] We have not included a comparison to a convertible arbitrage index as a benchmark because we believe to do so would be of limited value in that it is composed of returns from varied and disparate convertible arbitrage strategies. Among the participants in the convertible arbitrage benchmarks, there are marked differences in their size, longevity, risk profile, leverage employed, hedging, global asset allocation and portfolio configuration.

There are a number of strategies that a portfolio manager may employ within the context of a convertible arbitrage trade. A portfolio manager may prefer a portfolio of volatility-oriented positions, whereas another may prefer a credit sensitive, high-yield portfolio that employs leverage and credit insurance. Allocations of capital may vary widely between domestic US and offshore issues. Some managers may deviate from a market-neutral position to one that is slanted to a bull or bear bias. Some managers may employ all the forms of insurance available to control risk, while others may utilise only a select few within their portfolio.

The Fulcrum Strategy, as a discrete, clearly identifiable and time-honoured strategy, is designed and implemented as a classical 'market-neutral' convertible arbitrage technique to

Exhibit 14.3

Comparative total returns (%)

	Forest Fulcrum (net)	S&P 500 Total Return	Merrill All-Convert Index	Citigroup Broad Inv. Grade (BIG)	Citigroup BB-rated	Citigroup High Yield Index	Citigroup 10-year Treasury	Citigroup 1-month T-bill
Latest month, April 2003	1.17	8.23	4.71	0.88	4.53	6.21	0.00	0.09
Latest three months	3.35	7.64	6.61	2.22	7.46	11.26	1.93	0.28
Year-to-date	6.75	4.82	8.57	2.30	10.25	15.39	1.03	0.38
Latest 12 months	12.27	−13.36	4.29	10.45	2.83	9.64	14.89	1.47
Latest two years (ann.)	8.71	−13.00	0.18	9.14	6.06	7.09	10.29	2.03
Latest three years (ann.)	11.80	−12.99	−3.97	10.21	8.22	4.95	10.35	3.18
Latest four years (ann.)	12.06	−7.72	3.88	7.88	5.77	2.63	6.99	3.58
Latest five years (ann.)	10.11	−2.45	4.82	7.56	5.94	2.63	6.96	3.73
Since March 1993 (ann.)	12.57	9.43	9.39	7.25	8.49	7.03	6.64	4.11
Calendar years								
2002	6.05	−22.13	−3.71	10.09	−2.75	−1.52	14.66	1.65
2001	14.31	−11.91	−3.95	8.52	13.48	5.44	4.01	3.69
2000	21.90	−9.15	−11.70	11.59	2.96	−5.68	14.45	5.65
1999	6.85	21.03	44.32	−0.83	2.24	1.73	−8.41	4.44
1998	0.32	28.57	8.21	8.71	8.05	3.60	12.88	4.55
1997	17.34	33.34	18.99	9.64	12.76	13.19	11.27	4.88
1996	20.16	22.99	14.30	3.62	8.99	11.28	0.07	4.95
1995	29.80	37.53	24.75	18.53	22.62	19.54	20.84	5.37
1994	−6.89	1.27	−7.08	−2.85	−1.34	−1.10	−5.64	3.84
1993 (March to December)	15.67	7.66	14.13	5.94	11.30	12.46	6.18	2.42

Sources: Forest Investment Management and Bloomberg Professional.

achieve a balanced risk–return profile on either side of the standstill rate of return. In the parlance of options terminology, a portfolio constructed and managed under the Fulcrum Strategy is analogous to an income bearing straddle consisting of a put option and call option purchased at the same strike price plus the standstill rate of return.

The Forest Fulcrum Fund and the more popular convertible hedge fund indices, such as the HFRI Convertible Arbitrage Index or the Goldman Sachs Convertible Arbitrage Index, as representative of convertible arbitrage, have been consistently profitable during the bear market that began in 2000. Based on empirical observation, convertible arbitrage perfor-

Exhibit 14.4

Comparable volatilities (annualised standard deviation) (%), as at April 2003

	Forest Fulcrum (net)	S&P 500 Total Return	Merrill All-Convert Index	Citigroup Broad Inv. Grade (BIG)	Citigroup BB-rated	Citigroup High Yield Index	Citigroup 10-year Treasury	Citigroup 1-month T-bill
Latest 12 months	5.38	21.01	11.48	2.69	13.72	15.30	7.65	0.08
Latest two years (ann.)	5.80	18.19	10.39	3.56	11.06	13.00	7.77	0.24
Latest three years (ann.)	5.27	18.15	15.45	3.30	9.69	12.00	6.99	0.51
Latest four years (ann.)	5.45	17.88	17.07	3.29	8.57	10.60	6.73	0.49
Latest five years (Ann.)	6.10	18.76	16.96	3.30	8.26	10.31	6.97	0.45
Since March 1993 (ann.)	5.49	15.55	13.12	3.66	6.47	7.78	6.72	0.38
Calendar years								
2002	5.16	19.73	11.14	3.58	12.92	13.74	8.63	0.04
2001	6.69	19.05	14.90	3.64	8.24	11.94	6.78	0.32
2000	4.10	16.43	21.97	2.71	4.42	6.48	5.05	0.12
1999	4.21	12.62	16.03	2.62	2.72	4.00	4.71	0.05
1998	7.42	20.59	15.26	2.52	6.77	8.95	6.28	0.17
1997	0.76	15.27	8.47	3.44	3.31	3.05	6.04	0.10
1996	1.22	10.35	7.81	4.08	3.31	2.57	6.77	0.06
1995	2.19	4.92	6.09	3.46	3.08	2.99	5.54	0.11
1994	7.33	10.20	6.65	4.13	4.84	4.88	6.86	0.17
1993 (March to December)	2.10	6.34	5.47	2.57	2.25	2.01	5.03	0.06

Sources: Forest Investment Management and Bloomberg Professional.

mance ebbs and flows over a rolling three- to five-year cycle as observed in Exhibit 14.3. Over that cycle, convertible arbitrage strategies have performed well versus traditional asset classes, with lower volatility as shown in Exhibit 14.4.

On a risk-adjusted basis, using the Sharpe ratio as a proxy for risk-adjusted measurement, convertible arbitrage has outperformed traditional asset classes and investment strategies by a wide margin (see Exhibits 14.5 and 14.6).

The returns also have a low correlation to those of traditional asset classes and investment strategies, as shown in Exhibit 14.7.

Correlation may vary on a one-year horizon, but as the horizon is lengthened, the correlation coefficients tend to decline. While non-correlation over discrete horizons is important, investors become more concerned when they perceive that the equity market, as reflected by the Standard & Poor's index, is at an inflection point in the investment cycle, as shown in Exhibit 14.8.

Additionally, there has been a low correlation to interest rate sensitive investments as measured by the 10-year United States Treasury as shown in Exhibit 14.9.

Exhibit 14.5

Risk/return profiles of selected benchmarks, March 1993–April 2003

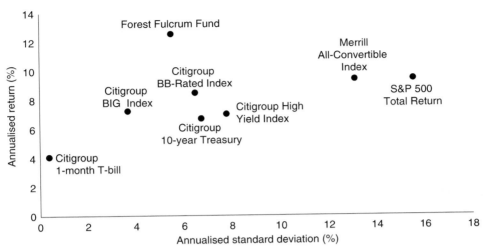

Sources: Forest Investment Management and Bloomberg Professional.

Exhibit 14.6

Comparative annualised Sharpe ratios, as at April 2003

	Forest Fulcrum (net)	S&P 500 Total Return	Merrill All-Convert Index	Citigroup Broad Inv. Grade (BIG)	Citigroup BB-rated	Citigroup High Yield Index	Citigroup 10-year Treasury
Latest 12 months	1.92	(0.64)	0.30	3.18	0.17	0.59	1.67
Latest two years	1.13	(0.78)	(0.12)	1.92	0.41	0.44	1.05
Latest three years	1.56	(0.84)	(0.39)	2.03	0.54	0.20	1.00
Latest four years	1.48	(0.56)	0.10	1.26	0.29	(0.03)	0.52
Latest five years	1.01	(0.23)	0.15	1.12	0.30	(0.05)	0.48
Since March 1993	1.46	0.40	0.45	0.83	0.67	0.40	0.39
Calendar years							
2002	0.85	(1.24)	(0.43)	2.26	(0.28)	(0.16)	1.45
2001	1.50	(0.76)	(0.44)	1.28	1.14	0.20	0.08
2000	3.55	(0.84)	(0.70)	2.05	(0.56)	(1.72)	1.62
1999	0.57	1.24	2.13	(1.97)	(0.77)	(0.64)	(2.76)
1998	(0.52)	1.13	0.31	1.57	0.52	(0.06)	1.26
1997	14.82	1.67	1.54	1.31	2.22	2.53	1.02
1996	11.25	1.60	1.14	(0.29)	1.16	2.30	(0.67)
1995	9.67	5.52	2.83	3.45	5.00	4.28	2.52
1994	(1.45)	(0.19)	(1.63)	(1.59)	(1.03)	(0.97)	(1.36)
1993 (March to December)	7.26	1.06	2.51	1.78	4.68	5.87	0.98

Sources: Forest Investment Management and Bloomberg Professional.

Exhibit 14.7

Comparative correlation coefficients (versus monthly returns for the Forest Fulcrum strategy), as at April 2003

	S&P 500 Total Return	Merrill All-Convert Index	Citigroup Broad Inv. Grade (BIG)	Citigroup BB-rated	Citigroup High Yield Index	Citigroup 10-year Treasury	Citigroup 1-month T-bill
Latest 12 months	0.10	0.52	0.11	0.49	0.47	0.20	0.46
Latest two years (ann.)	0.15	0.13	0.20	0.17	0.16	0.16	0.14
Latest three years (ann.)	0.06	0.15	0.15	0.22	0.19	0.06	0.13
Latest four years (ann.)	0.07	0.00	0.19	0.17	0.14	0.13	0.17
Latest five years (ann.)	0.08	0.06	0.06	0.17	0.20	0.04	0.11
Since March 1993 (ann.)	0.01	0.13	0.17	0.23	0.24	0.06	0.19
Calendar years							
2002	0.00	0.42	0.24	0.37	0.37	0.12	0.40
2001	0.19	0.00	0.29	0.00	0.04	0.23	0.41
2000	0.28	0.11	0.43	0.32	0.02	0.20	0.37
1999	0.14	0.24	0.02	0.15	0.21	0.15	0.47
1998	0.03	0.29	0.16	0.27	0.49	0.33	0.33
1997	0.25	0.04	0.34	0.33	0.22	0.31	0.01
1996	0.46	0.11	0.52	0.53	0.40	0.57	0.58
1995	0.15	0.05	0.09	0.05	0.14	0.17	0.75
1994	0.06	0.33	0.06	0.18	0.11	0.12	0.09
1993 (March to December)	0.07	0.12	0.49	0.50	0.15	0.40	0.06

Sources: Forest Investment Management and Bloomberg Professional.

Over the periods measured above, we conclude from the correlation analysis that the returns from convertible arbitrage have low correlation with the primary equity and bond markets in all market environments. On a five and 10-year basis, convertible arbitrage correlation coefficients have been consistently low in relation to the other asset classes measured.

Over time, investors may realise higher total returns due to lower volatility. We tend to view this process as '. . . winning by not losing, over time, rather than timing . . .'.

Alpha and convertible arbitrage performance

The large rise in equity markets during the 1990–2000 period, and the subsequent decline from 2000–03, encompassing periods of high and low volatility, affords an excellent time-frame to measure the excess return potential of the convertible arbitrage strategy. In order to measure the alpha of a manager, one must have an appropriate benchmark, and as stated above, we at Forest Investment Management feel that there is no readily comparable benchmark. An index of active convertible arbitrage managers suffers from non-comparability because of differing styles, leverage employed, risk profiles and geographical allocation. The measurement of alpha, using the returns of a passive index simply approximate excess absolute returns due to a near zero beta.

Exhibit 14.8

Comparative equity market correlation coefficients, March 1993–April 2003 (versus Standard & Poor's 500 Stock Index, total rate of return)

	Forest Fulcrum (net)	S&P 500 Total Return	Merrill All-Convert Index	Citigroup Broad Inv. Grade (BIG)	Citigroup BB-rated	Citigroup High Yield Index	Citigroup 10-year Treasury	Citigroup 1-month T-bill
Up equity markets								
Latest three years	0.32	1.00	0.48	0.40	0.13	0.01	0.52	0.14
Latest five years	0.09	1.00	0.09	0.26	0.14	0.23	0.19	0.04
Since March 1993	0.04	1.00	0.38	0.01	0.12	0.02	0.03	0.03
Down equity markets								
Latest three years	0.11	1.00	0.46	0.27	0.36	0.37	0.52	0.02
Latest five years	0.06	1.00	0.56	0.34	0.46	0.50	0.53	0.07
Since March 1993	0.11	1.00	0.56	0.25	0.48	0.53	0.41	0.03
All equity markets								
Latest three years	0.06	1.00	0.79	0.40	0.57	0.57	0.63	0.05
Latest five years	0.08	1.00	0.72	0.27	0.51	0.51	0.39	0.01
Since March 1993	0.01	1.00	0.73	0.06	0.54	0.53	0.09	0.12

Sources: Forest Investment Management and Bloomberg Professional.

Exhibit 14.9

Comparative bond market correlation coefficients (versus Citigroup Benchmark 10-year US Treasury Note Index, total rate of return), as at April 2003

	Forest Fulcrum (net)	S&P 500 Total Return	Merrill All-Convert Index	Citigroup Broad Inv. Grade (BIG)	Citigroup BB-rated	Citigroup High Yield Index	Citigroup 10-year Treasury	Citigroup 1-month T-bill
Up bond markets								
Latest three years	0.13	0.40	0.07	0.72	0.21	0.13	1.00	0.33
Latest five years	0.30	0.25	0.20	0.77	0.19	0.21	1.00	0.21
Since March 1993	0.17	0.11	0.12	0.60	0.07	0.12	1.00	0.10
Down bond markets								
Latest three years	0.12	0.75	0.68	0.94	0.29	0.11	1.00	0.34
Latest five years	0.19	0.21	0.03	0.89	0.14	0.04	1.00	0.35
Since March 1993	0.10	0.05	0.10	0.82	0.13	0.13	1.00	0.27
All bond markets								
Latest three years	0.06	0.63	0.38	0.91	0.31	0.28	1.00	0.06
Latest five years	0.04	0.39	0.31	0.92	0.22	0.25	1.00	0.02
Since March 1993	0.06	0.09	0.12	0.86	0.08	0.02	1.00	0.08

Sources: Forest Investment Management and Bloomberg Professional.

In Exhibit 14.3, the average annualised excess return of this strategy experienced during a period encompassing both an explosive bull market and a vicious bear market affords a high degree of comfort to a potential investor in this strategy.

Going forward, we believe that convertible arbitrage managers can continue to produce a high Sharpe ratio if they possess skills in credit and volatility pricing, along with an ability to recognise the self-hedging aspect of a convertible's embedded warrant against its credit exposure. Another source of value will be the manager's ability to recognise when to shift exposure between volatility and credit. Finally, the ability of a manager to quantify the correlation of market factors and the related impact on convertible pricing and hedging techniques, will uncover relative value trades that will be overlooked by his competitors.

In closing, we have attempted to illustrate how convertible hedging as an investment strategy pursued with discipline can enhance portfolio returns, while reducing downside volatility. We believe, that for those investors who are seeking to balance risk and return within a diversified investment portfolio, and who have more than short-term investment objectives, convertible arbitrage is a viable, disciplined approach that has endured many market cycles.

Addendum

The Black-Scholes partial differential equation (PDE) for derivative pricing is shown below:

$$\frac{\partial C}{\partial t} + (r_I - d_I)S \; \frac{\partial C}{\partial S} + \frac{1}{2} S^2 \sigma^2(S,t) \; \frac{\partial^2 C}{\partial S^2} = r_I \, C$$

where:
C = derivative price
S = underlying asset price
r_t = deterministic riskless interest rate with time dependence
d_t = constant dividend yield and/or borrow cost
$\sigma(S, t)$ = deterministic local volatility surface

The above equation includes two extensions to the Black-Scholes theoretical framework, specifically, term structure of interest rates (first introduced by Merton) and the local volatility surface (dependent on asset price and time). It is an inhomogeneous PDE where the second and third terms on the right are the convective and diffusion components respectively. The convertible bond pricing involves the solution of this derivative equation, while also considering the structured bond component (that is, present value of the face value at bond maturity, coupons, embedded call or put provisions etc).

The solution of the Black-Scholes equation must be obtained numerically. The equation must be discretised and the derivatives in the equation approximated by their difference counterparts, for example, $\partial C/\partial t \sim (C_{t1} - C_{t2})/(t_1 - t_2)$. Once the equation has been discretised in both dimensions (time and asset price), the present value of the derivative is obtained by solving the equation backwards in finite time increments from maturity.

There are three main methods of solving the equation backwards in time. These are the explicit, implicit and Crank-Nicholson methods.[12] Exhibit 14.10 shows how the different methods calculate the node values backwards in time ($t_1 < t_2$).

Exhibit 14.10

The different methods of calculating node values back in time from t_2 to t_1 with $t_1 < t_2$

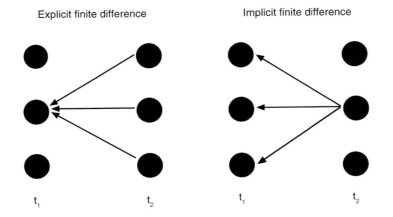

Source: Forest Investment Management.

Explicit finite difference methods calculate one node at t_1 from the three nodes at t_2 while implicit finite difference methods calculate three nodes at t_1 from one node at t_2. The Crank-Nicholson method is an averaging technique of the explicit and implicit methods.

The trinomial tree method of solving the PDE falls under the explicit finite difference category and is a very popular technique. In essence, it models the path of the underlying asset price process forward in time until maturity. It then determines the present value of the risk-neutral probability-weighted payoffs at maturity, backwards in time. Risk neutral probabilities are calculated at each step going forward in time, to satisfy the no arbitrage condition. The expectation of the three nodes must equal the riskless interest rate and the variance must equal the variance of the stochastic process. The popularity of this method stems from its ease of implementation and its intuitive link to the theoretical framework. However, it suffers from one significant shortcoming, which presents a formidable challenge as the Black-Scholes theoretical framework is extended. This shortcoming is the fact that the explicit finite difference method is only convergent when the condition below is satisfied:

$$\frac{\Delta t}{(\Delta \ln S)^2} \leq \frac{1}{\sigma(S,t)^2}$$

This means that as the nodes (in time and S) in the trinomial tree are being built forward in time, all nodes have to satisfy the convergence condition above, the no arbitrage condition (to ensure that the risk-neutral probabilities are non-negative) and internal nodes within the tree have to allow transition to them from two nodes immediately prior for computational efficiency. Since Δt, S and $\sigma(S, t)$ are now allowed to vary and the asset space nodes are themselves a function of $\sigma(S, t)$, the forward in time growth of the trinomial tree is non-trivial.

Unlike the trinomial tree approach, the implicit finite differences method does not attempt to model the underlying asset price movements. Instead it takes the PDE as given and simply solves it discretely. Therefore, it loses its intuitive appeal. However, the key advan-

189

tage here is that it can be theoretically shown that this method is unconditionally stable allowing Δt, S and $\sigma(S, t)$ to vary independently. The computation is carried out by first log - transforming the equation, setting up the nodes independently in log asset price space and time. Calculate backwards in time from maturity by specifying von Neumann boundary conditions at the edges of the log asset price space. Therefore, additional routines are not required to ensure algorithm convergence, and arbitrage principles and reduction of computational efficiency are not required.

The trinomial tree approach requires that the total number of nodes to be calculated are fixed at $(n + 1)^2$, where n is the number of time steps. However, in the implicit finite difference approach the number of nodes is given by $n*m$ where again n is the number of time steps and m is the number of asset price steps. Since asset price steps (m) is set independently, a substantial gain in computational efficiency is achieved for a large number of time nodes (n). Finally, the greeks of the derivative security obtained from the implicit finite difference method are significantly more stable than those obtained from the trinomial tree method.

---

[1]   Thanks to Jay Madia, Robert Min, John McDonald, Jingyan Wang and Scott Watson.

[2]   Notice of disclaimer: the inclusion of the returns from the Forest Fulcrum Strategy is for illustrative purposes only, and not for the purpose of promoting the strategy or the firm. Past performance is not necessarily indicative of future results.

[3]   Goldman Sachs Convertible Research, 2003.

[4]   Forest Investment Management assignment of equivalent credit ratings.

[5]   Convexity is a measure of the curvature in the relationship between bond prices and bond yields.

[6]   Avantis, Angelo (2001), *Credit Risk in Convertible Bonds*, London, Risk Books, Chapter 7, p. 261.

[7]   In the traditional convertible bond model, the delta varies with respect to stock price. The lower the stock price, the lower the delta. Gamma, defined as the change in delta per unit of stock price change, is always positive. This is true because in a static credit spread convertible bond model, on a given day, the bond floor is constant regardless of the stock price movement, and the option portion (CB value less bond floor) is the only component that is sensitive to the stock price. In the deterministic credit spread model, however, the bond floor no longer holds still. As the stock price declines, the bond floor also declines due to the widening effect of the credit spread. To hedge the decline of the bond floor, additional shares are needed besides those used in hedging the option portion. Therefore, delta does not necessarily decline as the stock price declines ('constant delta'). In low-grade convertible bonds, the credit is so sensitive to the stock price that as the stock declines, delta actually increases, this will lead to the 'negative gamma' observation.

[8]   Points premium is defined as bond market minus conversion value.

[9]   Avantis, Angelo (2001), *Credit Risk in Convertible Bonds*, London, Risk Books, Chapter 7, p. 261.

[10] The JPMorgan High Yield Debt Index (HYDI) is a liquid, tradable and diversified credit index consisting of a basket of credit default swaps. Each credit default swap in the index expresses the tradable credit spread to Libor of its reference security, and so the index represents a basket of diversified credits. Similarly, the Morgan Stanley TRACERS index product aggregates 49 individual credits into a tradable basket, allowing users to express views on the underlying credit spread, backed by the five-year structure and liquidity of the underlying market for credit default swaps.

[11] The inclusion of the returns from the Forest Fulcrum Strategy is for illustrative purposes only, and not for the purpose of promoting the strategy or the firm. Past performance is not necessarily indicative of future results.

[12] Brockhaus, Oliver, Michael Farkas, Andrew Ferraris, Douglas Long and Marcus Overhaus (2000), *Equity Derivatives and Market Risk Models*, Risk Books, Chapter 8.

Chapter 15

Hedged equity investing[1]

Lee S. Ainslie III
Maverick Capital, New York, New York

Introduction

'Heads – I win. Tails – you lose.' At some point in life, most people eventually realise that this is not such a hot deal. Yet, in the past decade a reincarnation of this proposition has wildly proliferated in the financial world – hedge funds. 'Let's invest your money. If we win, I keep 20 per cent (or sometimes more!) of the winnings. If we lose, you lose.'

Since A.W. Jones first uttered the phrase 'hedged fund' about 50 years ago, the term mysteriously lost a critical 'd' to become 'hedge fund'. This omission is rather appropriate as many of these funds are anything but hedged. Indeed, for many funds the word 'hedge' seems wildly out of place. The only common denominator among hedge funds today that I can find is that we all have found a way to charge the aforementioned performance fee.

Some fund managers would take offence at my description of the performance fee structure as essentially a riskless proposition, especially given that 'high water marks' are now rather standard. High water marks ensure that a manager will not charge a performance fee until any previous losses have been made up, so that the manager theoretically pays back a portion of the losses by working for free until the investor is whole. However this pay back only has value if the manager produces positive, sometimes very positive, returns (keep in mind that if a manager is down 50 per cent then up 50 per cent, he is still down 25 per cent cumulatively) and no discount is given for the time value of this capital. Of course if the manager closes shop, then high water marks have the same value as they do on a pier.

Despite this reality, the incentive fee structure is the most effective motivator in the investment world, and directly relates the interests of the manager to those of his investors. Not only does this fee structure attract many of the best and brightest investors, but the hedge fund structure also allows a manager to pursue strategies designed to optimise risk–return. This mode of investing is a marked contrast to a US mutual fund manager who must follow constraints imposed by Congress over 50 years ago. A mountain of empirical evidence shows that after all fees and expenses hedge funds have over time delivered superior risk–return profiles.

However, this common denominator, this riskless proposition for the hedge fund manager, raises a host of important questions for those analysing such funds. How does a fund generate returns, and how sustainable is this process? Is the manager able to justify such a fee structure? How does the manager add value, and can this be clearly demonstrated? Does the investor clearly understand the risks that the manager is taking, and are these risks justified by the net returns? The analysis of and answers to these questions vary greatly from strategy to strategy and fund to fund. At Maverick Capital, the principals of the firm are the largest investors, and hence we continually ask these very questions of ourselves.

The term 'hedge fund' was not always such a misnomer. The original concept was the result of a very intelligent, and somewhat daring, insight by A.W. Jones in 1949. He combined two concepts, leverage and shorting, both of which were considered to be quite risky in that day, to develop a rather conservative investment strategy. By investing borrowed capital in short securities (which profit through price declines), Jones lowered his exposure to the market while increasing his invested capital. By maintaining this balance of long and short investments, the market was largely 'hedged' out, and returns were driven by security selection.

This simple strategy is employed in many different ways by hundreds of equity hedge funds today, including Maverick Capital. Our goal is to preserve and grow capital, and we believe that over time this hedged equity approach will prove to be the best way to achieve this objective. However, we have recognised and addressed many of the risks inherent to this strategy. I hope the following discussion will shed light on how we have approached and analysed our own hedged equity strategy.

Net exposure and long-short ratio

The concept of net exposure is a critical one in understanding vehicles employing this strategy. If for every US$100 of equity a fund invested US$150 in long securities and US$100 in short securities (which profit through price declines), only US$50 is net long the market, creating a net exposure of 50 per cent [(US$150–US$100)/US$100]. In this example, the fund has US$250 invested in the equity markets, even though only US$50 is exposed to the vagaries of the stock market.

While net exposure is the most prevalent measure of hedging in the investment community, I believe that another measure, which I refer to as the 'long-short ratio', provides much more insight into the degree of hedging. Net exposure indicates what percentage of net assets are net long the market, but the long-short ratio describes the balance of longs and shorts. Consequently, this ratio is a more significant determinant than net exposure of a portfolio's ability to perform in different environments and to produce returns that are not correlated to the market. To demonstrate the importance of the long-short ratio, let us look at two different portfolios:

	Portfolio A	Portfolio B
Long exposure (%)	150	75
Short exposure (%)	(100)	(25)
Net exposure (%)	50	50
Long-short ratio	1.5x	3.0x

Obviously, both of these portfolios have a net exposure of 50 per cent, but these exposures were achieved in different ways. If one assumes average stock-picking, that is, both long and short investments perform equivalent to the market, and no value is added on either side, then net exposure is quite predictive. In a down 15 per cent market, both of these portfolios would be down 7.5 per cent, or 50 per cent of –15 per cent. Algebraically, long exposure times long performance plus short exposure times short performance equals total performance:

Portfolio A $\quad (150\% \times -15\%) + (-100\% \times -15\%) = -7.5\%$

Portfolio B $\quad (75\% \times -15\%) + (-25\% \times -15\%) = -7.5\%$

In my experience, however, most investors hope their managers will perform better than average and will add value by selecting long securities that outperform the market and short securities that underperform the market (or produce 'alpha' in investment lingo). To see the importance of long-short ratios, assume that in this down 15 per cent market the managers of Portfolios A and B are able to select longs that outperform by being down only 10 per cent and shorts that underperform by being down 20 per cent. With equivalent long and short performance assumptions, the results of Portfolios A and B are quite different:

Portfolio A $\qquad$ $(150\% \times -10\%) + (-100\% \times -20\%) = +5.0\%$

Portfolio B $\qquad$ $(75\% \times -10\%) + (-25\% \times -20\%) = -2.5\%$

The lower long-short ratio allows Portfolio A to produce positive returns, assuming some alpha during a significant market drop. Although 5 per cent outperformance on an un-levered basis may be considered unusual in a traditional investment environment, at Maverick our long equity investments have outperformed the S&P 500 and the Morgan Stanley World indices by substantially more than 5 per cent per year. Our short equity investments have underperformed these indices by an even greater margin. As you can infer, over time we have developed a spread in returns between our longs and shorts that is much larger than the 10 per cent spread used in the above example.

Another question worth pondering: how much alpha is required to break even in a down market? Again, while net exposure is of no value in regard to this question, the long-short ratio makes the answer rather clear. For Portfolio A, with a long-short ratio of 1.5 times, the shorts must decline 50 per cent more than the longs for the entire portfolio to break even. For Portfolio B, with a long-short ratio of 3.0 times, the shorts must decline three times as much as the longs to break even. In other words, if the longs of both portfolios are down 10 per cent, then in order to break even the shorts of Portfolio A need to decline in price by 15 per cent, compared to a 30 per cent decline in shorts required for Portfolio B, as shown below:

Portfolio A $\qquad$ $(150\% \times -10\%) + (-100\% \times -15\%) = 0.0\%$

Portfolio B $\qquad$ $(75\% \times -10\%) + (-25\% \times -30\%) = 0.0\%$

Of course, a lower long-short ratio is not necessarily better. In some scenarios the higher long-short ratio would produce a better return, but it is an important measure of the degree of hedging. Net exposure gives insight into expected performance if security selection is just average. The long-short ratio helps analyse performance assuming superior security selection, or positive alpha. Net exposure reflects the degree to which performance is dependent on the market, whereas the long-short ratio reflects the degree to which performance is dependent on security selection.

Leverage

One of the implications of analysing long-short ratios is the notion that higher leverage can be beneficial, which is contrary to common wisdom, by allowing lower long-short ratios and therefore a greater degree of hedging. In a pure hedged equity investment strategy, leverage can be represented by gross exposure, the sum of the absolute value of long and short investments divided by net assets. As we can see by comparing Portfolios A and B above, if two portfolios have equivalent net exposure the portfolio with the higher gross exposure, and consequently a lower long-short ratio, is more hedged.

However, common wisdom is not completely incorrect. As leverage increases, the risk–return profile of any portfolio degrades. For example, if you lever a portfolio two to one, risk will increase two-fold, but returns will only improve two-fold minus the cost of leverage. Therefore, risk increases more than returns increase, resulting in a poorer risk–return profile.

The critical question in evaluating a manager's use of leverage is how far the risk–return profile can be degraded and still be attractive. Many arbitrage strategies rely on this evaluation. By arbitraging two sets of securities that are theoretically equivalent, returns can be achieved with virtually no risk. Such investments have an incredible risk–return profile, but typically provide rather small returns. Consequently, most arbitrage managers use leverage (sometimes astronomical levels of leverage). Of course, such leverage leaves little room for error. Although many of these managers may not consciously arrive at these decisions in this fashion, their implicit belief is that the risk–return of their underlying arbitrage positions is so attractive that it can withstand the negative impact of leverage and still be worthwhile.

This analysis is also useful for hedged equity strategies. Has enough risk been hedged out to justify the leverage employed? The answer to this question varies widely from fund to fund. The simple strategy of having long and short investments can lead to very significant or very little risk and volatility depending on how it is implemented. To judge whether or not different managers implement a hedged equity strategy with appropriate levels of leverage, several statistical measures, such as Sharpe or Sorrentino ratios, can be quite helpful in judging past returns.

Unless an investor is looking to increase market exposure, higher leverage should go hand in hand with a higher degree of hedging. The degree to which a fund is hedged can be inferred by the replies to questions such as: How correlated are the fund's returns to the market's return? How consistent are the returns? How does the fund perform in down markets? Analysing daily returns, although frequently unavailable, can prove to be much more insightful than monthly returns.

Finally, in evaluating the use of leverage one should be assured that the manager is not employing hidden leverage. In reporting leverage some managers include only the investment value or collateral requirements of derivative instruments rather than the full notional value of such investments. During periods of unusual volatility even delta-adjusted notional values can be quite misleading. In a pure hedged equity fund, such as Maverick, leverage is typically obtained through the margining of long and short equity investments. However, many funds secure leverage through other instruments such as repos, futures, swaps and other derivatives. Such sources of leverage can be rather expensive, leave the borrower with the credit risk of the lender, can be subject to changing collateral requirements and are often difficult to quantify.

Market timing in a hedged strategy

Today many funds exist that on average maintain low net exposures and long-short ratios, but perhaps should not be considered hedged. Investors should understand how different managers attempt to add value in order to analyse the impact of different market conditions on returns and to judge the sustainability of returns. Low net exposures and long-short ratios should just be the first step of such analyses for hedged equity funds.

In discussing exposures and ratios most managers will offer either snapshots on specific dates or figures that are averaged over a period of time. Either of these presentations can hide the variability of these figures. A manager who constantly maintains his long-short ratio between 1.4 and 1.6 attempts to add value in a different manner than the manager whose average long-short ratio is 1.5 but who has had ratios as low as −2.0 and as high as +4.0. The second manager is attempting to create performance through his ability to time the market (to decide when to bet against the market and when to be very unhedged and actually be levered long the market). This manager wants market risk because he believes he can add value through these timing decisions and is willing to maintain outsized market exposures.

Of course there is no right or wrong approach. Different individuals have different skill sets and experience and consequently attempt to generate performance in different ways. However, potential investors should understand how the investment philosophy attempts to create value and whether or not this attempt is successful. Once one understands the drivers of performance, the sustainability of these drivers can be evaluated.

Risks within the hedge

Maintaining consistently low long-short ratios and net exposure levels does not in itself ensure that the overall portfolio is hedged. If a fund is long Hong Kong and short Germany, is that a hedge? How about a fund that is long financial stocks and short technology stocks? Long small capitalisation stocks, but short large cap stocks? Long low beta value stocks, but short high beta growth stocks? Long individual stocks, but short index-related futures or options? Since there is some small positive correlation to global equity markets, each of these scenarios provide some small degree of hedging, but are the correlations strong enough to be an effective hedge?

Maverick's solution has been to maintain consistent low net exposures and long-short ratios on a beta-adjusted basis within each region and each industry in which we invest. As a result we have a balance of longs and shorts in Japan and in the United States, as well as within retail, healthcare and other sectors. Since we place a premium on liquidity, both our long and short investments have always been focused on larger capitalisation names. By maintaining long and short sub-portfolios with similar characteristics and correlations, performance is driven by the ability to add value through stock-picking (not market timing or attempting to successfully rotate sectors).

At first blush, the concept of being hedged within each region and industry may sound quite similar to pairs trading. This phrase describes an investment style in which two very similar stocks, for example, Ford and General Motors or Sainsbury and Tesco are paired off against one another by owning one security and shorting its peer. Such trades are usually driven either by an apparent valuation discrepancy in two companies that are perceived to be very similar or by the need for an offsetting trade to hedge out certain risks in an investment.

In my experience, more often than not, one side of such trades works well while the other side does very little or even suffers negative returns. Moreover, maintaining both investments ties up significant capital. I believe that such trades often result from an unwillingness or inability to make difficult investment decisions. When two similar companies trade at very dissimilar valuations, rarely are both valuations wrong (either the companies are not as similar as they first appear, or one valuation proves to be justified and does not change). Likewise, the desire to offset certain risks may be a substitute for the effort to evaluate those risks.

The advantage of a pairs trading strategy is that the correlations of a number of different macroeconomic risks are taken into account. In our judgement, by maintaining low net exposures and long-short ratios in each region and industry, most of these risks are greatly reduced, and yet the flexibility exists to achieve a superior return on capital. Just as importantly, each and every investment is just that, an investment that is expected to produce a profit, not just to serve as a hedge.

Hedging instruments

One of the most common potential hedging problems arises from the use of index-related futures and options to create short exposure. Many hedge fund managers apparently have little confidence in their ability to select securities that will underperform the market. The use of such instruments may be appealing as they appear to be easy and efficient tools, but such instruments preclude any possibility of creating alpha, or adding value, on the short side. On the contrary, the costs of such instruments ensure negative alpha.

While the use of these instruments can be effective in some market environments, often such hedges prove to be poorly correlated to the movements of individual stocks. Several times in history the market has placed a premium on large, liquid, stable stocks such as those that comprise the S&P 500 Index. During such periods the S&P 500 can substantially outperform individual securities, as seen by the relatively paltry performance of broader-based indices, such as the Russell 3000, or unweighted indices, such as Value Line.

Not only does a fund using index-related puts and other market-related instruments incur additional costs, but such a fund gives up income in the form of short rebates. So why are some managers so quick to forgo the opportunity to profit beyond just a drop in the market through shorting individual securities? This is because shorting stocks can be quite difficult, as is discussed below.

Hedge fund investors are theoretically sophisticated investors. If a sophisticated investor wishes to simply lower his exposure to the equity market, he can sell futures or buy puts himself. Going back to one of the questions I posed in the beginning: does a manager deserve to charge a performance fee for conducting transactions that the investor could conduct himself?

Challenges of shorting

After professing our ardent belief in the value of hedging, we are often asked, 'If hedging is so fantastic, why not maintain zero per cent net exposure and a long-short ratio of 1:1?'. Good question. I believe that there are several fundamental disadvantages to short selling, and as a result we want to maintain a positive equity bias. However, it is critical in our minds that our net exposure and long-short ratio be low enough that our performance can have virtually no correlation to the market and that we have a realistic chance of producing positive returns in down markets.

In our experience, shorting stocks is often an uphill battle for several different reasons, some of which are obvious, some of which are not. The first and most apparent disadvantage of short selling is the fact that over time you are fighting the natural upward trend of the market. This trend has been more pronounced in the past several years, and investors can lose sight of the fact that the market has gone through long periods when returns were minimal. During the 14-year period from the middle of 1968 to the middle of 1982, the S&P 500 appreciated by less than 1 per cent a year! However, even if my crystal ball told me that we were about to enter a similar period, we would still maintain a positive bias given the other challenges of the short side.

The old saying 'unlimited downside, limited upside' is quite true in short selling and has some unfortunate consequences. It is impossible to make more than 100 per cent on a short sale, and even that event is exceedingly rare. However, it is quite possible, and not altogether uncommon, to lose a multiple of the original investment in a short. In long investments we often are able to own stocks for years that may double or quadruple in price (we had one stock that appreciated 20-fold in less than four years). Unfortunately, for a short investment even a 50 per cent return is quite strong, so the maintenance of strong returns on the short side requires more constant replenishment of good ideas and the significant effort required to produce those ideas.

With short investments, poor selections are naturally pressed. When a short investment is not working, and a stock appreciates, the size of the position also increases. As a short works, and declines in price, the size of the position becomes smaller. As a result, poor short investments are increased, and the strong investments are decreased. Of course this trend works in the opposite way on the long side.

On the short side, an investor constantly faces a host of issues that do not exist on the long side. To short a stock, an investor must be able to borrow the security. On the NYSE you must have an uptick to short a stock, and long sellers must take priority over short sellers for market orders. On Nasdaq an up-bid is required to sell short. As onerous as these regulations may be, short selling can be much more difficult outside the United States. For example, in Japan virtually all shares are called in twice a year for dividend payments, which forces all short sellers to cover their positions. In any locale once a stock has been successfully borrowed and shorted, the investor must then live with the continual threat of buy-ins and squeezes.

Quite importantly, when an investor shorts a stock, he is betting against a management team that possesses much greater knowledge of the company than the investor and is typically working very hard to create value and prove the short investors wrong. Working with a management team as a shareholder is a much easier task. As a short seller your communication may be strained at best, and you have no ability to impact your investment positively. On the long side, an investor often has the opportunity to work with management to improve shareholder value or offer useful industry insight. Importantly, management can undertake a number of actions, such as selling the company or buying back stock, which can instantly ruin a short.

Finally, many investors do not recognise how the above drawbacks impact the security selection, trading and back office requirements of short investments. Compared to the ever-growing, gigantic talent pool experienced with long investments, there are relatively few traders, analysts, stock borrowers and portfolio managers with meaningful experience on the short side. Shorting stocks is far more challenging than buying stocks in every aspect and level of the organisation, forcing many organisations to shy away from these investments.

As these disadvantages to shorting are considered, I believe that in the longer term a portfolio should have a positive bias. This subjective decision is supported by the long-term returns of short-only funds as well. However, in my judgement, to be considered truly hedged, this positive bias should be low enough that the portfolio is not significantly correlated to any benchmark and has the ability to generate profits even in bear markets. Many funds today have a difficult time demonstrating their ability to achieve this balance.

Security selection risk

The strategy of maintaining a balance of longs and shorts within each region and each industry sector reduces a variety of different macroeconomic risks, including market, currency, political, interest rate and industry sector risks. This is not to say that a truly hedged equity strategy is a lower-risk strategy. These macroeconomic risks have been transferred to security selection risk, which I believe is a far preferable risk. As a result, in a truly hedged equity strategy, performance is driven by stock-picking, not by the ability to time markets or rotate sectors within the market.

I consider security selection risk preferable to macroeconomic risks, as market timing decisions are much more difficult to predict correctly on a regular basis. Compared to individual stocks, macro investments are far more likely to be impacted by outside factors over which neither any investor nor any management team has any control. Many macro investments are essentially zero sum games in which investors are as likely to win as to lose over the long term. The sustainability of returns of a portfolio is driven by the predictability of the underlying individual investments. As a result many macro funds tend to display greater volatility. Having said all this, the type of investment risk that a manager takes should be driven first and foremost by the individual strengths and experience of that manager.

Recognising that a truly hedged equity strategy purposely produces outsized security selection risks, steps should be taken to mitigate these risks. Perhaps the most important mechanism to reduce security selection risk is diversification, which can help ensure that no one position and no one mistake can be too costly. The desire to spread stock picking risks over a number of different securities must be balanced against the negative impacts of spreading research resources so thin that an intimate understanding of a company or industry is lost. In such cases, diversification can become 'di-worse-ification'.

Setting maximum and minimum position sizes helps enforce several disciplines, including diversification. Minimum position size limits guard against 'di-worse-ification'. Many investors dislike minimum position size limits for the exact reason I favour such limits (they force decisions). As an investment declines in price, position sizes can shrink to an insignificant size. Position size limits drive an investor to decide whether such a position should be liquidated or whether such a position is worth increasing. As discussed below, I believe forcing such decisions keeps the portfolio focused on the best ideas. On the short side, maximum size limits can serve as an important ceiling to reduce losses from large short investments that are going the wrong way.

Many theories exist on how loss-limit rules should be implemented and executed, and for different investment styles appropriate rules can vary widely. In my judgement, the critical function of loss-limit rules is to help the manager recognise errors and reduce security selection risk.

A factor often overlooked in reducing stock-picking risk is liquidity. Despite some portfolio managers' belief to the contrary, all investors are human, and, therefore, will make mistakes. The ability to recognise these errors and recover from such mistakes is a critical factor in performance. The liquidity of each underlying position drives the ability to quickly reverse course and mitigate the cost of errors.

Non-equity risk

Many hedged equity funds employ strategies other than simply investing in long and short equities. Taking investments such as bonds, commodities and currencies into account when attempting to analyse how truly hedged a fund is or how consistently the fund has added value can be quite difficult. Perhaps a more important question is: should one bother?

Over the past couple of decades investors have taken an increasingly dim view of public companies that grow for the sake of growth by acquiring a disparate set of businesses. 'Conglomerate' became a bad word. The argument against conglomerates holds that an investor should have the flexibility to select businesses in which he would like to invest, rather than have different businesses forced on him by the management of a company. Likewise, someone who invests in hedge funds should have the ability to invest in the currency or commodity funds he believes are the best in their business rather than have a currency trading operation forced on him by one of his managers whose expertise lies elsewhere.

In some firms the same individual or individuals handle both equity and macro investments. Unless these individuals happen to be exactly equally skilled in both arenas, their investors would perhaps be better served if the manager focused his time and energy on the strategy in which he excels. The appropriate question for investments outside the core competency is not whether these investments can be profitable, but rather whether these investments can deliver a risk–return profile as strong as that of the primary strategy. An investor should not have to suffer any dilution of the firm's critical skill set. Finally, I believe that the historical returns of most mixed funds prove that the risk–return of such entities is not optimal. Only a handful of investors, such as my former boss, Julian Robertson, have ever demonstrated the ability to excel in several different investment arenas on a consistent basis.

Global investing

Why invest outside the United States when your expertise and relationships are primarily American? How do you compete against firms that are based in local markets and staffed by local professionals? When these questions are posed (which is almost a daily occurrence), I am usually able to resist the urge to give irritating replies such as 'easy money'. I believe that maintaining an international portfolio is not only profitable, but also an element essential to the production of superior returns in a hedged strategy.

Global competitiveness increases every day. To understand the competitive environment of a film manufacturer in New York or a software vendor in California, one should have a strong understanding of their primary competitors who happen to be based in Japan and Germany, respectively. Perhaps the US investor is best equipped to analyse a Swiss pharmaceutical firm that generates two-thirds of its revenues and profits in the United States. Of course this benefit is bi-directional. An understanding of US companies is critical to analysing multinational companies based outside the United States.

International experience also provides a sense of balance and perspective to valuations and investment trends. Dealing in a variety of markets gives an investor experience in a wide variety of different macro and competitive environments that can then be applied to different situations.

While US investors face some disadvantages in competing against local investors, applying the knowledge and expertise of global investing can more than compensate for these drawbacks. The US equity market is by far the most competitive and over-analysed market in the world. Sell-side research outside the United States is typically not of the same quality, thereby giving buy-side investors greater opportunity to add value. Western investment techniques can often be quite helpful in exploiting the relative inefficiency of many international markets.

Perhaps the biggest advantage that an international fund enjoys over a competitor who is focused on just one country or region is the fact that the international investor only invests in a particular market when he sees opportunity. Funds focused on one area are forced to invest in that country or region, whether they foresee significant opportunity or not. The ability to shift capital to the regions with the most promising opportunities allows an investor to maximise returns.

If one believes in the logic that a US investor should just invest in the United States, then it would naturally follow that an investor based in Texas should just invest in Texas. Before long I will only be investing in the lemonade stand started by my children. I do not believe that an investor should unnecessarily limit himself to a narrow range of opportunities.

For the hedged investor, international markets can be particularly fruitful and useful. The inefficiency and less competitive nature of these markets can create significant returns. Unlike traditional managers, a hedge fund can virtually eliminate the macroeconomic risks of such markets by maintaining a hedged discipline. How does a truly hedged equity fund invest in markets where short selling is impossible, such as Russia? It does not. A truly hedged fund only invests in markets where macro risks can be hedged.

Finally, international investing creates not only the potential to improve returns, but also the potential to lower the volatility of the portfolio through diversification. If properly executed, an international portfolio can both enhance returns and lower risk (a true win-win).

Large cap versus small cap

Another common argument with which I disagree is the concept that small stocks offer better long and short opportunities. Note that I am avoiding the age-old discussion of whether small or large stocks perform better over time. For a truly hedged equity manager, this argument bears little relevance. The important question is whether or not it is easier to add value in small stocks on both the long and short side, and if so, is this advantage significant enough to offset the disadvantages of investing in smaller cap stocks.

The small stock argument often starts with the assumption that the chances of outperforming are greater as an investor is more likely to gain an informational edge or a 'knowledge advantage' (a very similar argument is implied in the theory that one should only invest locally). However, in today's world, public information on small and large companies is distributed with amazing efficiency and is available through a myriad of sources. Smaller companies often have much higher business risk than larger companies, as smaller businesses are typically more focused on fewer, or even single, products or lines of business. This increased business volatility can be difficult to predict and analyse for both long and short investors.

By investing in stocks with smaller capitalisations an investor may be foregoing one of the most significant advantages of investing in public markets – liquidity. One of the primary reasons that Maverick has always focused on larger capitalisation stocks, on both the long and the short side, is that we make a lot of mistakes. Even when we have not erred, the world has a funny way of transforming once terrific ideas into embarrassing investments. When this happens, we simply pick up the phone and sell (or cover). By focusing on larger-cap, more liquid securities we minimise the cost of these mistakes by quickly putting them behind us. The costs associated with trying to exit illiquid investments can be quite significant.

Portfolio issues

While the above discussions give some insight into the hedged equity framework within which we live at Maverick, our approach to stock-picking has not been mentioned. Of course, this strategy only produces significant performance if one can manage a long portfolio that outperforms the market and a short portfolio that underperforms the market. This process is comprised of both security selection and portfolio management.

I believe that the ability to consistently outperform and underperform requires a willingness and ability to apply many different security selection methodologies and techniques. An investor must be armed with scores of paradigms and approaches to stock-picking at all times and have the wisdom to recognise which method should be applied in each situation. At Maverick our analyses typically focus on the fundamentals of the business, the quality of management and the reasonableness of valuation. Since security selection is too important and too broad of a topic to address in any detail in this chapter, I will focus instead on the management of a portfolio of such selections.

While our portfolio decisions are driven by fundamental analyses, we certainly do not ignore technical and quantitative analyses, which have come into vogue once again. Unfortunately, as the onslaught of technology, capital and knowledge is applied to such analyses the ability to create a sustainable advantage through these means becomes less and less likely. Today a manager can put a state-of-the-art charting tool on his desktop for a small monthly fee. Indeed, a manager without such technology is at a disadvantage as such analysis is so prevalent that technical buy and sell recommendations quickly become self-fulfilling prophecies in the short term. Just as I would not run a marathon without running shoes, I would not run a portfolio without technical tools – but in neither case am I gaining an advantage as my competitors have the same equipment.

Assuming perfect liquidity and ignoring tax consequences, every day a security is not sold, it is essentially bought, since at the end of the day that security is owned and the opportunity to invest that capital elsewhere has been forsaken. The term 'hold' is useless, in my way of thinking. If one does not believe that the expected risk–return profile of a stock is attractive enough to purchase the stock, then why hold that stock? That capital should be deployed in a stock that is a buy. The recognition of this logic forces an investor to evaluate constantly every security in the portfolio and ensure that the risk–return at the current price is still attractive enough to merit further or increased investment. If not, the security should be liquidated, and that capital should be redeployed in investments that are attractive enough to warrant investment. In my judgement, this buy or sell discipline and the ongoing re-evaluation of each security is critical to developing superior returns.

Furthermore, a portfolio should be continually rebalanced. In the utopian world, the size of each position would be commensurate with the manager's estimation of the risk and return of that position from that price that day. To approach this ideal, the relative size of each position should be constantly reviewed and actively determined, that is, increased or reduced. This philosophy again shows the value of liquidity. With less liquid securities the cost of adjusting position sizes, in terms of the impact on execution prices, may preclude an investor from efficiently rebalancing the portfolio.

I am often surprised by how many managers forget the notion of 'sunk costs'. The price at which a stock was originally purchased or shorted should be irrelevant to any current decision (other than tax considerations) regarding the fate of that holding. Too often managers focus on trying to lock in a certain profit or return on each security (looking backwards to the cost of a position rather than forward to the risk–return of a position from the current price). Likewise, I find target prices of little value. In a world where competitive environments and market conditions change constantly, a prospective estimation of fair value, and hence potential return, must be continually re-evaluated and updated.

Some argue that the degree of leverage should change as the manager finds more or less opportunity. However, the implicit assumption of varying levels of investment is that the manager has the ability to predict the performance of his own fund. If a fund is truly hedged then such a prediction should be quite difficult to make. I would also argue that any manager that believes that his fund is about to enter into a period of poor performance should make significant changes in the underlying investments, rather than just reduce leverage to these investments.

Maintaining a consistent level of investment enforces an important discipline through periods of poor performance. When equity decreases, leverage increases, typically at exactly the wrong time. This unplanned leverage increase can lead to a dangerous spiral where the detrimental impact of poor investments has a greater and greater impact on returns as equity declines and leverage continues to climb. By maintaining consistent investment levels the manager is forced to review and reduce positions during such periods (exactly when such action is necessary).

Evaluating trading

Maintaining an efficient portfolio that is constantly adjusted to reflect proper weightings and risk controls, as discussed above, can increase both execution costs and tax costs for US investors compared to less active styles (the issue of taxes is discussed in the next section). I believe that trading should be viewed as a potential profit centre, one that can be evaluated in several ways.

Before judging the effectiveness of trading execution, a manager should assess the effectiveness of trading decisions. This requires an arbitrary distinction between investment decisions and trading decisions, which we at Maverick look at on a monthly basis. We measure the difference between actual month-to-date performance and what our performance would have been had we not executed any trades that month, in other words, if we still owned the exact same portfolio we owned at the beginning of the month. Importantly, our systems allow us to look at this analysis on a security-by-security basis so that we can study our past trading mistakes and successes and learn from both.

To evaluate execution, we judge every single trade execution versus both the closing price and the volume-weighted average price (VWAP) of the security the day of execution. In my judgement, a trader can add significant value through his or her understanding of the short-term supply/demand picture for a security. Therefore, the traders at Maverick are expected to buy stocks below both the closing price and the VWAP, and sell stocks above these levels. The measurement of execution versus the close relates the profit or loss on that trade that day, while studying execution versus VWAP shows the opportunity cost of actively trading. A trader attempts to use his or her skill and knowledge to achieve an execution superior to these yardsticks. If a trader is not able to demonstrate consistently the ability to beat these measures, then perhaps the manager should instead employ a trader who carefully participates in all trading activity throughout the day and does not attempt to add value.

Buy-side traders share the blame or credit for poor or strong executions with their counterparts on the sell side. Hence, these measures are also very useful tools for evaluating brokers.

Clearly circumstances can arise that make these measurements of executions versus close and VWAP for any single trade of little use. However, over a period of time the cumulative totals of these measures can give great insight into which firms are more concerned for their clients and which firms are more concerned for their own proverbial yachts. At Maverick we share the relative results of these analyses with our trading partners and have found that this knowledge has helped engender a very healthy competitive environment.

While effective trading can improve results, creating performance solely through trading has proved to be a very difficult way to create value on a sustainable basis. Therefore understanding whether a manager is focusing on selecting stocks or selecting bids and offers is critical. Contrary to the common vision of the portfolio manager who stares at a quote screen all day, I would argue that the greater the separation between the manager and the traders, the greater the odds for success in both functions.

Taxes

One school of thought is that investment managers should ignore tax consequences and focus on investing. Indeed, several times in this discussion I assume no tax consequences to simplify the discussion. In reality, every trading decision has tax consequences for US investors. In my judgement, balancing these consequences with other considerations is a critical part of the decision-making process. The logic that a portfolio manager should be able to juggle concerns such as market conditions, accounting issues, integrity of management, valuation methodologies, technical analysis, and the like, but that tax concerns, which are clearly defined and very quantifiable, are too difficult for this same manager, befuddles me. I view the analysis of the tax impact of portfolio activity to be one of the easiest decisions I am faced with every day.

I am often surprised that so many hedge fund investors pay so little attention to the impact of taxes on returns. For US investors, the 'taxability' of returns is just as important as the rate of expected return. To demonstrate how dramatically the tax profile of different strategies can impact bottom line returns, let us look at two different portfolios that both return 20 per cent per year over a 20-year period. Portfolio A (as in Arbitrage) realises all of its gains every year, while Portfolio B (as in Buffet) only realises gains at the end of the 20-year period. US$1,000 invested in Portfolio A would be worth US$11,253 at the end of 20 years, while US$1,000 in Portfolio B would accrete to US$32,587. These figures assume that you are a citizen of the United States (home of the brave and of capital gains taxes), you are honest (you pay your taxes), your tax adviser is overpaid (you have no losses to offset these gains), and you live in a wonderful state without state or local income taxes (for example, Texas).

The 'A as in Arbitrage' comment was made to highlight the inefficiency from a tax standpoint of many arbitrage strategies. As we have seen, hedged equity investing shares many traits with arbitrage strategies, so many investors understandably assume that a hedged equity strategy shares a similar tax profile. Fortunately for me, and unfortunately for the IRS, this is not necessarily a valid assumption.

Most arbitrage funds realise almost every gain and loss every year. In other words, all profits are short term. In contrast, a hedged equity strategy can generate all types of taxable income (unrealised gains, income, short-term and long-term realised gains). One disadvantage of a hedged equity strategy is that all realised gains from short selling are short term by definition whether the holding period is two days or 20 years. However, the manager has tremendous flexibility as to when these gains have to be recognised. By carefully selecting the most tax-efficient stock lot for every sale and cover, by closely watching the dates that different lots become long term, by actively avoiding wash sales, and, most importantly, by being a longer-term investor, the tax efficiency of a hedged equity strategy can be very attractive.

One common perception which is incorrect is the notion that high turnover automatically leads to high taxes. Again, the tax impact of an investment style does not depend on how often a stock is traded nearly as much as how intelligently the stock is traded. Intelligent turnover can actually be quite helpful in reducing taxes through proactively realising losses. As one can infer, from the comments regarding the importance of constantly re-evaluating every position and of forcing buy or sell decisions, I believe that high turnover is a healthy sign of an active manager who is seeking always to maximise the return of his portfolio.

If one is attempting to judge to what degree a manager tends to add value through trading versus investing, the average holding period (the length of time between the initiation and final liquidation of a position) is a telling statistic. If, instead, an investor is trying to focus on tax efficiency, then looking at a breakdown between unrealised gains, long-term and short-term gains and income is much more effective than drawing conclusions from turnover. Analysing K-1s from different investors over a variety of time periods is perhaps the most useful tool in understanding the tax efficiency of different funds.

Analysing returns

As construed above, true hedged equity investing is a rather straightforward and logical investment strategy. So why is this approach not more common? Returns in such a strategy are almost purely driven by the manager's ability to add value through security selection. The challenge of hedging out the very factors that drive most managers' performance, market and industry sector moves, and of relying almost solely on the ability to pick stocks is one that many choose to avoid.

Unfortunately, many money managers strive unsuccessfully not to lose value. Some studies have shown that over time only 25 per cent of mutual funds outperform the market. For managers competing in this arena, producing market-equivalent returns is a significant achievement, even though such performance results from adding no value. To move to a strategy where performance is primarily driven by the ability to add value can be a daunting proposition for traditional managers.

To understand a manager's ability to add value, I believe one should focus on alpha, or the amount of performance not attributable to the market. In a hedged equity strategy, alpha can be measured in two ways. First, by comparing total performance to the performance of a relative index adjusted for the net exposure of the fund. For example, if a hedge fund that focuses on large capitalisation US equities and maintains average net exposure of 50 per cent is up 17 per cent during a period of time that the S&P rose by 10 per cent, the alpha would be 12 per cent [17% – (10% × 50%) = 12%]. Looking at alpha in this manner shows how much of a manager's return was 'given' to him by the market, and how much of the return is attributable to the value added by the manager.

This analysis has two drawbacks. Finding a relative index can be quite difficult. For example, the S&P 500 is commonly used to represent US equities even though the index is comprised of larger capitalisation stocks. The S&P 500 has gone through long periods in which it was dominated by a handful of securities, and the average price move of the stocks in the index was quite different from the price move of the index itself. Another concern is that different levels of gross exposure can influence this measure of alpha, as shown in the description of a long-short ratio.

To eliminate this gross exposure bias, analysing the returns of both long and short investments on an unlevered basis versus the returns of a similar index can be quite useful. Obviously, one would hope that a manager would be able to demonstrate the ability to select longs that outperform the market and shorts that underperform the market on a consistent basis. Managers who tend to use market-related instruments to create short exposure, rather than shorting individual securities, are quickly exposed by this analysis. However, looking at separate alphas for long and short investments eliminates any consideration of the value the manager may add through his selection of the balance of long and short investments (or market timing).

To review the success of market timing one can study the difference between actual performance and derived performance assuming constant long and short exposures. For example, if for a period of time a fund maintained an average of 150 per cent of equity invested in long securities and 100 per cent of equity in short securities and if on an unlevered basis the long portfolio was up 10 per cent and the short portfolio was down (creating a profit) 5 per cent, the derived performance would be +20 per cent [$(150\% \times 10\%) + (-100\% \times -5\%) = 20\%$]. If the fund's actual performance during this time was 25 per cent, then the manager added 5 per cent of value through shifting his long and short exposure. Although the fund averaged 150 per cent in longs and 100 per cent in shorts, this balance must have been shifted towards the long side during one or more strong market periods and shifted lower during weaker periods for the market.

Unfortunately, this analysis ignores several costs and risks to shifting net exposure that may be difficult to quantify. Allowing net exposure to reach greater extremes can create a significant increase in the volatility of returns. This analysis also does not take into account the execution costs and tax impacts of the higher turnover that results from the shifting of net exposure. Perhaps most importantly, one cannot evaluate the cost of the investment in time and resources to attempt to time the market. Would the performance from security selection have been better if the time devoted to market timing had been invested instead in picking stocks? In light of these more subtle costs, I believe that one must be able to demonstrate significant and consistent improvements in performance through market timing to justify regular shifts in net exposure.

Looking at such derived performance can provide insight into the manager's ability to time other shifts in the portfolio as well. As discussed above, a manager who invests in different regions around the world has a significant potential advantage in his ability to deploy capital into regions where opportunities are available and reduce or eliminate exposure to a region where less opportunity is perceived to exist. To judge how effectively a manager has shifted assets in recognition of such opportunity, one can compare actual overall performance to the performance derived from looking at the weighted average of regional performance, or the total of each region's performance multiplied by the average asset allocation of that region. If the manager is skilful enough, or lucky enough, to move assets into regions before they enjoy strong performance and out of regions before they suffer poor performance on a regular basis, overall performance could be higher than the performance of any one region.

A similar analysis can be done on different asset breakdowns, such as industry groups or market caps.

Of course one can easily end up with reams of numbers that may look impressive but provide little insight. In my judgement, the goal of such analyses should be to understand in what ways are a strategy and a manager creating value and in what ways is value being destroyed. Once the means of value creation have been identified, one can attempt to judge the consistency and sustainability of this value creation.

Often the most difficult step in conducting such analyses is obtaining necessary data. Some funds do not track such data, and some choose not to share such information. If such figures are available, the greater the frequency (daily is better than monthly) and the longer the time period, the more useful and meaningful the results of such studies will be. Of course, the greater the manager's transparency, the greater the investor's ability to understand and analyse the strategy.

I believe that the manager of any business should constantly analyse and re-analyse his business and performance in order to recognise and then address mistakes and weaknesses. The money management business is a bit unique in that performance can be quantified in so many different ways. The quantification of decisions and processes that comprise different components of performance allows both the manager and the investor to find flaws, improve results, compare to others and judge sustainability.

Selecting a hedged equity manager

I have one final, and probably most important, thought on the evaluation of different investment strategies. Know the manager. No matter how intensive the due diligence process is or how frequently one communicates with a manager, an outside investor is never going to be in a position to understand every trade, risk or mistake. At the end of the day, an outside investor is investing in an individual or a team more than in a strategy. This need to have a strong belief and trust in the manager is especially critical in hedge funds, given the amount of latitude and flexibility that these entities enjoy. The development of such a relationship can start with references that include current investors, brokers, former employees and former employers. I have even had potential investors hire private investigators who spoke to family and friends. I believe that a manager should have an investment in his fund that is significant in terms of his net worth, as a percentage of the fund's total assets, and in absolute dollars. All too often the flaws of a fund are only evident when it is too late, and the confidence that an investor has in the manager may ultimately be the most important consideration.

This chapter reflects my approach and thinking. I am quick to recognise, however, that there are many ways to create value and make money. Furthermore, the types and amount of risk that I believe are worthwhile will be considered too conservative by some and too aggressive by others. I am in no way trying to suggest that Maverick's strategy is the only or the best approach to money management. Maverick's investment philosophy is simply the most logical to me. By sharing how we have considered different issues, and the logic behind our conclusions, I hope to have improved the understanding of a hedged equity strategy.

---

[1] © Lee S. Ainslie III.

Chapter 16

Understanding credit cycles and hedge fund strategies

Michael E. Lewitt
Harch Capital Management, Inc., Boca Raton, Florida

'For historians each event is unique. Economics, however,
maintains that forces in society and nature behave in repetitive ways.
History is particular; economics is general.'

Charles Kindleberger
Manias, Panics and Crashes: A History of Financial Crises (1978)

'[A]ll facts and personages of great importance in world history occur,
as it were, twice...the first time as tragedy, the second as farce.'

Karl Marx
The Eighteenth Brumaire of Louis Napoleon (1852)

Introduction

The analysis of credit cycles involves an understanding of monetary policy, financial and industry innovation, and regulatory change. However, the ability to identify in advance those moments when credit cycles veer into crisis also requires imagination, an appreciation of human folly and a willingness to imagine worst case scenarios. In order to identify times of maximum risk, understanding human psychology is at least as important as understanding economics. Credit cycles involve a combination of historical, sociological, political, economic and psychological factors that are both unique to each specific cycle and common to all cycles. Hard and soft data must be examined. The unhappy truth is that markets don't learn their lessons very well. Financial history tends to repeat itself. The only questions are when and to what degree.

Hedge fund managers charged with preserving capital and producing positive returns in both good and bad markets must pay particular attention to the etiology of credit cycles and particularly those extreme turning points that lead to financial crises that can consume years of returns in the blink of an eye. Hedge fund investors seeking positive uncorrelated returns in all types of markets must determine which strategies and managers are best suited for particular points in the credit cycle. By reviewing in detail the characteristics of the most recent credit cycle as it affected the US corporate bond market, it may be possible to gain a greater

Exhibit 16.1

Historical speculative-grade default rate extrema

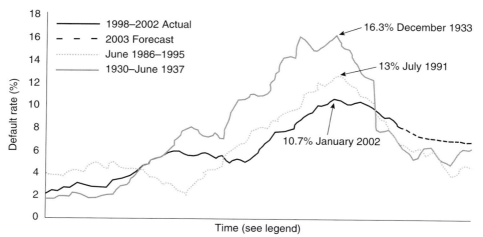

Source: Moody's Investors Service, February 2003, *Default & Recovery Rates of Corporate Bond Issuers, A Statistical Review of Moody's Ratings Performance*, 1920–2002, p.1.

appreciation of the warning signs that investors should heed in managing their own money (or their clients' money) or giving it to others to manage.

A century of accelerating credit cycles

The financial markets have experienced three horrendous credit cycles since 1920 (illustrated in Exhibit 16.1):

- the Great Depression (1930–37);
- the high-yield bond and real estate market collapse (1990–91); and
- the aftermath of the internet bubble (2000–02).

Over the last two decades, extreme credit cycles have occurred with greater frequency than before, rendering consistent hedge fund returns more difficult to achieve. Two of the three worst credit market cycles in the last 80 years occurred during the last 15 years (see Exhibit 16.2). If one includes the relatively short-lived but severe collapse of the credit markets in 1998 in the wake of Russia's default and the collapse of Long-Term Capital Management, three of the most extreme credit cycles of the last 80 years have occurred in the last decade.

The condensation of credit cycles and the increasing incidence of credit dislocations is a consequence of the globalisation of the world economy, technological advancements in the electronic transmission of information (accelerating the velocity of market data travelling around the globe), and financial innovations such as derivatives and securitisation that blur the distinctions among markets and asset classes. The confluence of these developments has perversely made the markets more informed but less informative. Information and capital rocket around the world at unprecedented velocities and volumes, leaving investors with less time to process market data before reacting. Today, a pin dropping in Argentina can cause

Exhibit 16.2

Spread to worst in the domestic high-yield market, 1984–2002 (bp)

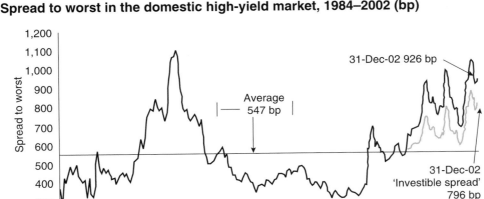

Source: JP Morgan, January 2003, *2002 High Yield Review*, p. 103.

simultaneous ripples (or waves, or in rare cases tsunamis) as far away as Japan. By the time the pin drops, it may already be too late for investors to protect their capital. In a financial world dominated by innovation and new products that blur the traditional distinctions between debt and equity, disruptions in the credit markets are certain to affect all hedge fund strategies in all asset classes.

Credit cycle acceleration and contagion

The increasing frequency and severity of extreme credit events points to the heightened risk of contagion among markets and asset classes. Contagion risk, which damaged so many hedge funds in 1998, is heightened in three areas today. First, large hedge funds, mutual funds and other institutional investors tend to have overlapping securities holdings, facilitating the spread of market dislocations from one sector or asset class (such as emerging market debt) to another (such as mortgages or corporate debt). Moreover, in a sector like convertible arbitrage, which is dominated by a handful of very large firms, different hedge funds tend to have many overlapping holdings. A problem in one hedge fund (for example, a flood of unanticipated redemptions) could trigger forced liquidations that may adversely affect the holdings of other large funds.

Second, a limited group of institutions act as prime brokers and lending counterparties to the universe of hedge funds. As a result, these financial institutions may discover in market crises much higher credit exposures than they anticipated to vulnerable companies and industries. It is very difficult for large hierarchical institutions to understand and monitor these risks, whose understanding requires expertise across a variety of disciplines.

Third, the proliferation of 'funds of funds' has effectively created a pyramid effect in which investors at the bottom of the pyramid are in a position to trigger liquidations all the way up the chain due to factors that may be entirely unrelated to individual hedge fund performance. While heightened contagion risk has been mitigated by a more careful utilisation

Exhibit 16.3

The 10 largest bankruptcies

Company	Date	Assets (US$ billion)
WorldCom, Inc	21 July 2002	103.9
Enron Corp	2 December 2001	63.4
Conseco, Inc	18 December 2002	61.4
Texaco, Inc	12 April 1987	35.9
Financial Corp. of America	9 September 1988	33.9
Global Crossing Ltd	28 January 2002	30.2
USL Corp	9 December 2002	25.2
Adelphia Communications	25 June 2002	21.5
Pacific Gas and Electric Co	6 April 2001	21.5
Mcorp	31 March 1989	20.2

Source: www.BankruptcyData.com.

of leverage after the lessons learned in 1998, it still remains a significant threat to financial market stability and hedge fund returns. In order to evaluate contagion risk, hedge fund investors must be provided with transparency (on a confidential basis) in order to have access to the type of data on the underlying holdings of the funds in which they are invested.

This chapter will review the macroeconomic factors that contributed to the recent boom-and-bust cycle in an attempt to provide investors with a road map to which they can refer in handicapping future cycles and structuring their portfolios accordingly.

The etiology of the 1997–2002 credit cycle

The 2001–02 credit collapse has the dubious distinction of being the longest in duration of the last 80 years. From peak to trough, this down-cycle was the most sustained on record. While the two previous extreme cycles saw the default rate fall by 50 per cent in the 12 months following their peaks, the current cycle peaked in January 2002 but only declined by 30 per cent in the subsequent 15 months. The year 2002 marked the nadir of a credit cycle that saw historic increases in the total number and dollar volume of defaults. The default rate has only been higher during the Great Depression, and the world has never before seen the sheer magnitude of the defaults that occurred in 2001 and 2002. This cycle culminated with the largest default in history, the well-publicised US$103.9 billion bankruptcy of WorldCom, Inc, which had been rated investment grade only shortly before its demise. Moreover, seven of the largest bankruptcies in history had the dubious distinction of occurring during 2001–02 (see Exhibit 16.3).

Rather than hoping that history will not repeat itself, hedge fund investors can only hope that history will not repeat itself for them. In order to do so, they need to acquire an understanding of the factors that create the conditions conducive to extreme credit events.

Macroeconomic factors

Monetary policy

Monetary policy is either an art or a very inexact science. Whatever it is called, however, the

Federal Reserve is far more likely to get it wrong than get it right. As Charles Kindleberger argues: 'even when the supply of money was neatly adjusted to the demands of an economy, and mistakes were avoided, the monetary mechanism did not stay right very long. When government produces one quantity of a public good, money, the public will proceed to make more...'.[1] It is hardly coincidental that frequent credit market dislocations have occurred in a period (the last 15 years) in which the world's central banks (particularly in the United States and Japan) have run extremely lax monetary policy (see Exhibit 16.4). When the government mints money, the money has to find a home somewhere. All too often that home is one of excess.

The simultaneous and interconnected stock market, credit market and capital spending bubbles that occurred at the end of the 1990s actually originated much earlier in the decade as the Federal Reserve bailed out the US banking system from the weight of bad corporate and real estate loans. By sharply reducing interest rates, the Federal Reserve enabled banks to rebuild their balance sheets by borrowing at low rates and investing and earning an artificially positive spread on lower risk assets (primarily Treasury bills). As the Clinton administration aggressively reduced federal deficits, the Federal Reserve did little to tighten liquidity. Brief episodes in 1994 and 1997 did little to reverse the inexorable tidal wave of liquidity unleashed on the markets during the decade despite the short-term pain incurred by fixed-income investors when interest rates rose.

Accommodative Federal Reserve policy made possible an explosion of US corporate borrowing in the latter half of the 1990s. 'Annual borrowing by non-financial corporations as a percentage of non-financial corporate GDP darted from 3.4 per cent in 1994 and 3.7 per cent as late as 1996 to a previously unparalleled 9.9 per cent in the first half of 2000, this during a period when non-financial corporate (nominal) GDP was itself increasing at an average annual rate of 5.7 per cent. As a result, by the first half of 2000, non-financial corporate borrowing on an annual basis had more than quadrupled with respect to 1994 and

Exhibit 16.4

Growth of money zero maturity (MZM) money stock, 1987–2002 (%)

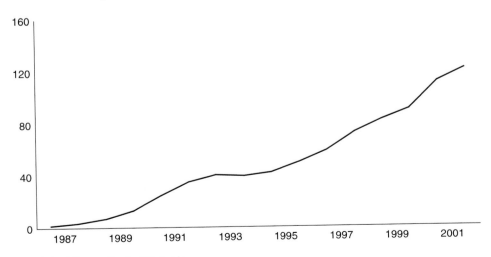

Source: Federal Reserve Bank of St. Louis.

non-financial corporate debt as a proportion of non-financial corporate GDP had reached 85 per cent, the highest level ever, up from 72.2 per cent in 1994'.[2] This borrowing financed huge corporate equity buy-backs at prices that now look stupidly high and an explosion of unnecessary capital expenditures that has left in its wake a legacy of overcapacity that will take years to work off.

Private borrowing supplanted government borrowing as the Clinton administration made deficit elimination a policy priority (a priority the Bush II administration has jettisoned with a vengeance, with significant implications for future credit cycles). As a result, private expenditure far exceeded private disposable income. The financial balance-of-payments of the private sector moved from its historical norm of between –3 and –4 per cent of GDP to an unprecedented negative –5.5 per cent of GDP in the third quarter of 2000. When private spending came more into line with income in the latter half of 2000, the boom was over. This huge negative –5.5 per cent gap was plugged by a huge increase in private borrowing, most of which was incurred by consumers since corporations had stopped spending in the face of stock market and credit rating agency scrutiny. While this imbalance was corrected, lower interest rates slowed the pace of change by providing incentives for more borrowing and spending so that in the fourth quarter of 2002 the gap was still a negative –1.1 per cent. Despite the popping of the stock market bubble, the private sector (primarily consumers) was still spending more than it was earning.

One of the aspects of this credit cycle that differentiated it from earlier ones was the surprising strength of consumer spending in the wake of massive corporate layoffs and general economic malaise. Consumer spending held up far longer than most experts believed it would, and far longer than in previous cycles. The biggest risk in the downside of any credit cycle is debt deflation, a collapse in the value of the assets collateralising debt. This occurred in the United States in the 1930s and in Japan in the 1990s. It also occurred in the US real estate industry in 1990–91 and the US and global telecommunications industries at the end of the 1990s. Nonetheless, as of the beginning of 2003, the collapse of equity values that began in March 2000 had not yet led to meaningful debt deflation (beyond the telecommunications industry) in areas such as residential and commercial real estate. There are several reasons for this. First, only 4 per cent of household debt consisted of margin debt on stocks. Second, the lowest interest rates in a generation led consumers to borrow against their homes to maintain spending levels; 70 per cent of household debt is mortgage debt, and low interest rates have fuelled demand for housing and helped maintain housing prices. Third, the psychology of consumers proved to be extremely resilient despite massive layoffs and stock market losses. While consumer spending began a fairly steady downturn in mid-2002, the fact that consumer spending had dropped sharply in earlier periods of economic malaise rendered the consumer's obduracy one of the most surprising features of this cycle.

Declining corporate profitability

Perversely, the latest corporate credit cycle coincided with a steady decline in corporate profitability (which actually peaked in 1997) and pricing power and increasingly legitimate fears of deflation. This went unnoticed at the time because contemporaneous government statistics overstated profitability and productivity improvements. Only during the summer of 2002 were these earlier government figures restated, revealing a true picture of declining corporate profitability. However, careful observers of corporate credit throughout this period were aware that corporations were finding it increasingly difficult to increase revenues.

The 'reverse Plaza Accord' of 1995 was a turning point for US corporate profitability. This agreement was designed to weaken the US dollar against the Japanese yen, relieving the suffering Japanese manufacturing economy from the early 1990s pressures of a rising yen. The result of this agreement was a rising US dollar that put severe pressure on the US manufacturing sector and attracted record inflows into US dollar-denominated assets (contributing to the coincident equity and credit market bubbles).

Corporate profits peaked in the third quarter of 1997 and continued to decline through early 2003, particularly outside the financial sector. This is a direct result of increasingly global competition in the manufacturing sector and flew in the face of demonstrable (although probably over-hyped) improvements in productivity. According to the Bureau of Economic Analysis (BEA), corporate profits declined from US$556 billion in 1997 to US$518 billion in 1999 to US$462 billion in 2000. Lower corporate profits coincided with an increasing lack of pricing power on the part of corporations. The annual increase in product pricing actually fell sharply beginning in 1995 to its lowest point in the 1990s in the 1998–2000 period.[3] Average annual profits (net of interest) for the years 1998, 1999 and 2000 fell by 7.5 per cent in the non-financial corporate sector and almost 18 per cent in the corporate manufacturing sector compared to 1997.[4] Between 1995 and 2000, world manufacturing prices actually fell at a steep average annual rate of 4 per cent. During this same period, new investments continued to be made despite the deteriorating prospects for earning an adequate return on investment. To place this in the context of the late 1990s stock market bubble, corporate profits were dropping just as stock prices were being inflated to unprecedented (and unjustifiable) valuations and borrowing in the private sector was skyrocketing.

Regulatory changes

Several regulatory changes contributed to the 2000–02 credit downturn. The first occurred in the securities industry. In the category of 'be careful what you wish for,' issuers were provided with the long-sought-after ability to speed up the bond issuance process with the introduction of Rule 144A in April 1990. With Rule 144A, the Securities and Exchange Commission amended the private placement rules to permit issuers to sell bonds to institutional investors more easily. Rule 144A offerings are not reviewed by the SEC prior to issuance. As a result, these underwritings can be completed on an accelerated timetable, limiting the time available for underwriters to perform thorough due diligence and for attorneys, accountants and other professionals to properly police issuers and underwriters. Most of the new issues sold since 1995 have been Rule 144A deals (see Exhibit 16.5 in relation to high-yield issues). This explosion of Rule 144A issuance rendered due diligence a lost art and laid the groundwork for an increasing incidence of accounting problems and faulty corporate disclosures in the corporate bond market.

A second regulatory change in the securities industry was passage of the Private Securities Litigation Reform Act of 1995 (PSLRA), which made it far more difficult for underwriters, accounting firms and law firms to be sued for fraud. This legislation effectively codified the US Supreme Court's 1994 decision in *Central Bank of Denver v. First Interstate Bank of Denver*, which held that accounting firms, investment banks and law firms could not be sued for 'secondary liability'. In order to recover from these parties, a plaintiff would have

Exhibit 16.5

High-yield new issues, 1991–September 2000

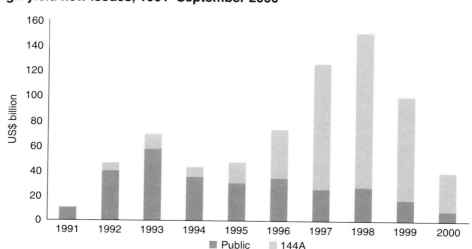

Source: Credit Suisse First Boston, *2002 Annual Review*, CSFB Global Leveraged Finance, Vol. 1.

to show that they were primarily liable for fraud, a much higher standard than secondary liability. Being at the scene of the crime and looking the other way was no longer enough to hold professionals to a high standard; from this point onward, they would have to be actively involved in the fraud. While limiting frivolous securities lawsuits was the ostensible (and sensible) aim of the PSLRA, this legislation came at a time when financial markets were becoming increasingly complex and the opportunities to commit fraud were increasing. Coupled with Rule 144A, the PSLRA left investors with little recourse as the incidence of corporate accounting fraud increased sharply in the late 1990s. Only with the Sarbanes-Oxley Act of 2002, passed in the wake of the Enron and WorldCom scandals, would an attempt be made to put some teeth back into the securities laws.

Deregulation of two other industries, telecommunications and energy (particularly unregulated utilities), resulted in a flood of bond financings in the latter half of the 1990s and a tidal wave of defaults in 2000–02.

The Telecommunications Reform Act of 1996 was intended to stimulate competition among local and long-distance providers of telecommunications services, between new local service providers and incumbent Bell monopolies, and between cable and telecommunications companies. This legislation unleashed a frenzy of speculation as investors (with a hearty slap on the back from Wall Street) convinced themselves that 'convergence' among different parts of the telecommunications sector would dramatically increase demand for telecommunications services. The result was an unprecedented volume of bond issuance in the telecommunications space (see Exhibit 16.6).

If the high-yield market meltdown of 1990–91 was tragic, the 2000–02 collapse was surely farce. Convergence turned out to be both a delusion and another type of contagion. The technology, media and telecommunications (TMT) firms at the heart of the much-ballyhooed 'New Economy' attracted so much capital that 39 million miles of fibre were laid (enough to circle the earth 1566 times). Today less than 5 per cent of this cable is being

Exhibit 16.6

Media/Telecom as a percentage of total new issues (proceeds), 1993–2001

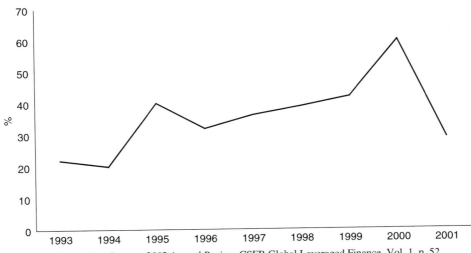

Source: Credit Suisse First Boston, *2002 Annual Review*, CSFB Global Leveraged Finance, Vol. 1, p. 52.

utilised. The torrent of global liquidity made available the capital to fund the massive over-building of telecommunications capacity. Much of this additional investment ended up in the hands of companies such as Global Crossing and 360Networks that ended up in bankruptcy court where their lenders recovered only a small fraction of their investment. This was a global phenomenon. Virtually all of the state-owned European telecommunications companies borrowed tens of billions of dollars to participate in auctions of 3G technology before realising that demand for this technology was years (or decades) away, threatening their credit ratings and burdening their balance sheets with debt that will take decades to repay.

The symbiosis of the equity and credit bubbles is demonstrated by the disproportionate impact of defaults in the telecommunications sector. In 2001, telecommunications defaulters constituted 25.8 per cent of issuers by dollar volume and 16.1 per cent as a percentage of issuers. In 2002, an almost unthinkable 56.4 per cent of defaults by dollar volume and 31.2 per cent of defaulting issuers were in the telecommunications sector. Combined with defaults by other TMT issuers, so-called New Economy companies accounted for 75 per cent of defaults by dollar volume and 47 per cent by number of issuers in 2002 (a record year for defaults).[5] It is no accident that the industry sector that led the equity bubble bore the brunt of the credit bubble collapse.

A similar phenomenon occurred in the energy industry, which in the case of Enron's broadband unit actually attempted a convergence between the energy and telecommunications industries. Energy deregulation unleashed a flood of investment by non-regulated utilities. Much of this capital ended up being raised for energy trading businesses, which were initially perceived to be immature but promising enterprises. Unfortunately, a combination of undeveloped markets and greed led to a complete collapse of energy trading. Rating agencies belatedly came to understand the circular (and therefore flawed) nature of the logic that rendered these companies wholly dependent on investment-grade ratings to be able to be considered viable trading counterparties in the first place. As a result of this deregulation debacle (which also inflicted permanent harm on the California economy), defaults by companies in the energy and utility sector constituted 7.6 per cent in dollar volume and 11.4 per cent in number of issuers of total 2002 defaults.[6]

Financial innovation

One of the important roles that Wall Street performs is to create products to absorb systemic liquidity. Perhaps the most significant financial innovation of the last 20 years has been the explosion in the securitisation of financial assets. Securitisation took off in the 1970s with the development of the mortgage-backed securities market. Today, virtually any kind of financial asset can be bundled and resold to a different set of buyers. Even hedge funds have been securitised. In 2002, Man Group plc, the world's largest hedge fund manager, and Investcorp, the Bahrain-based investment company, raised US$750 million of new capital through the issuance of collateralised fund obligations (CFOs) that used hedge fund interests as the underlying collateral.

Henry Kaufman has argued convincingly that the securitisation of financial assets has contributed to the increasing volatility of financial markets. By transforming illiquid or non-marketable assets (for example, individual residential mortgages or automobile loans) into liquid and marketable securities, securitisation belies the fact that the assets underlying these securities are illiquid and difficult to accurately value in volatile markets. Securitisation may also impair the credit process by shifting investors' attention away from the underlying assets to the more liquid assets being securitised.[7]

The corporate bond and bank loan markets have been major beneficiaries of securitisation. The credit collapses in 1990–91 and 2001–02 were both facilitated by financial innovation that created demand for high-yield bonds. In the 1980s, financial firms such as Columbia Savings & Loan, First Executive and others became primary outlets for high-yield bonds. In

Exhibit 16.7

US CBO issuance as a percentage of US high-yield bond issuance, 1995–2001

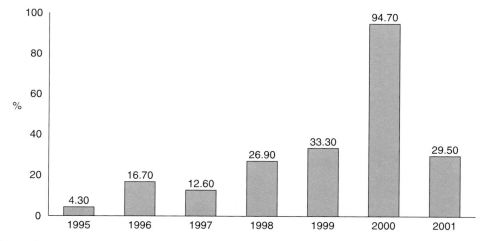

Source: Credit Suisse First Boston, *2002 Overview of CBOs/CLOs*, p. 8.

the 1990s, the mantle was assumed by securitisation vehicles known as collateralised debt obligations (CDOs).

In the late 1990s, an explosion in the issuance of CDOs created demand for high-yield bonds and bank loans. CDOs are highly leveraged structures that issue investment-grade rated debt in various tranches. The capital raised is then invested in a diversified pool of high-yield bonds, bank loans and other instruments. CDOs can take several forms, the two broadest categories being collateralised bond obligations (CBOs) with the underlying assets consisting of high-yield bonds) and collateralised loan obligations (CLOs), with the underlying assets generally consisting of 70 per cent bank loans and 30 per cent bonds). In order for a CDO to maintain the investment-grade ratings on its debt, it must adhere to a number of strict covenants, including stringent diversification requirements. These requirements have effectively created demand for new issues in marginal companies and industries, weakening the overall credit quality of new issuance (as well as of CDO collateral pools). These structures have evolved over the course of the 1990s to increase the types of assets they can hold. By the end of the new issue boom, CBOs became the buyer of last resort for many B-rated bond issues, particularly those in industries that had poor default histories. Bank loans were structured into quasi-bonds (with long-dated bullet maturities and/or soft asset collateral) to meet the structural demands of CLOs.

The role played by these pools of capital in the new issue market is clearly seen in Exhibit 16.7 and Exhibit 16.8, which show how CBO issuance in the United States and Europe was not only increasingly large in absolute dollar terms but also in comparison to the volume of new issues being brought to market. According to Credit Suisse First Boston, the CBO market grew from US$3.5 billion in 1990 to US$21 billion in 1996 to US$178.5 billion by the end of 2001, equivalent to 24.2 per cent of total high-yield bonds outstanding as of that time.

The unhappy truth is that the flood of CBO issuance facilitated a flood of mispriced high-yield bond issuance that failed to compensate bondholders for the equity risk involved in

Exhibit 16.8

European CDOs as a percentage of Western European high-yield new issuance, 1995–2001

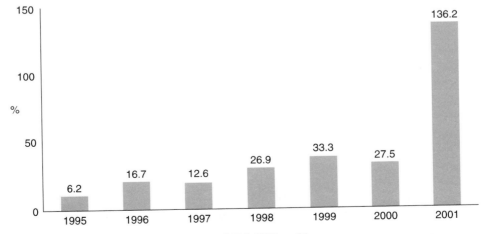

Source: Credit Suisse First Boston, *2002 Overview of CBOs/CLOs*, p. 24.

owning a high-yield bond. It was inevitable that the market would trade down to levels that would properly reflect this equity risk.

The growth of the nascent European new issue high-yield bond market was enormously facilitated by the creation of European CBOs. By accounting for more than 100 per cent of the volume of new issuance in 2001, these structures could not sate themselves on the new issue market and had to hunt in the secondary market for assets.

Tracking the dark side of the credit cycle, CDOs came under severe ratings pressure as the credit cycle turned downward. As of 4 October 2002, Moody's Investors Service (Moody's) had taken negative action on 238 CDOs with more than US$129 billion in assets, representing 40.5 per cent of initial CDO assets rated by Moody's. Standard & Poor's (S&P) had taken negative ratings action on 108 CDOs representing over US$60 billion in assets, representing 37.6 per cent of initial CDO assets rated by S&P. Fitch had taken negative ratings action on 108 CDOs with over US$60 billion of assets, representing 38.7 per cent of initial total CDO assets rated by Fitch. As of October 2002, 312 CDOs managed by 136 different firms had been downgraded by one or more of the three credit agencies that rate these structures. Looking behind this data, the damage to CBOs was much worse than the damage to CLOs. Moody's has found that a significantly greater percentage of CBOs have been subject to negative credit ratings (either downgrades or placed on credit watch with negative implications) than CLOs.[8] This is attributable to the huge disparity between the low recovery rates on defaulted bonds, which comprise 100 per cent of CBO collateral, and the much higher recovery rate on syndicated bank loans, which comprise 70 per cent or more of a typical CLO's collateral. Needless to say, by the end of 2002 the issuance of new CBOs had ground to a halt while CLOs remained a viable product.

The manifestations of the 1997–2002 credit cycle

The macroeconomic factors that led to a flood of low quality new bond issuance in 1997 and 1998 led to an all-too-predictable credit collapse three to five years later. This was an uncanny repeat of the earlier high-yield bond boom-and-bust cycle. Similar to the late 1990s, the late 1980s saw a significant increase in high-yield bond new issuance, much of which was tied to financially driven leveraged buy-outs that resulted in a slew of large bankruptcies of well-known companies such as Federated Department Stores (owner of Bloomingdales), Macy's Department Stores, Southland Stores (owner of 7–11s), and E-II Holdings (owner of Samsonite, Culligan and other name brands). For anyone paying attention, the writing was on the wall in the late 1990s.

Lower quality new bond issuance

One of the key indicia of credit cycles is the quality of new bond issuance. As Exhibit 16.9 shows, the issuance of lower rated credits was extremely high in the years preceding the 1990–91 and 2001–02 spike in default rates.

The percentage of issuers rated below Ba1–Ba3 grew modestly from 62 per cent of the speculative-grade universe in 1996 to 65 per cent in 2002, both very high rates in historical terms. The average first-time speculative-grade rating deteriorated from B1 to B2 during 2002. Moody's points out that the expected default rate doubles from B1 to B2. Speculative-grade issuers rated in the Caa1–C rating range increased from 14 per cent in 2001 to 18 per

Exhibit 16.9

Percentage of new issues rated B or less, 1980–2002

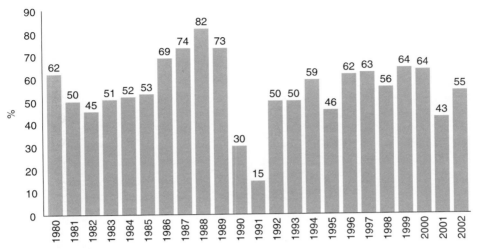

Source: JP Morgan, January 2003, *2002 High Yield Annual Review*, p. 60.

cent in 2002, again high rates in historical terms (particularly in view of the fact that approximately 50 per cent of C-rated bonds ultimately default).

Deterioration in credit quality

Moody's studies demonstrate that credit ratings are useful forward-looking indicia of credit deterioration. Historical analysis illustrates that credit ratings decline as an issuer moves closer to its default date, and such declines tend to accelerate as the default date looms closer. However, there is no reason why an investor has to wait until default to be alerted to the increasing risk of default and what it means for individual investments and a broader portfolio, asset allocation or investment strategy. There is more than sufficient historical data from the last 20 years of corporate bond issuance and performance to identify troubling trends in advance.

Credit rating actions illustrate the extent of the damage that has occurred since 2000 (for which the credit rating agencies deserve their share of the blame for over-rating issuers during the bubble). In 2001 and 2002, respectively, 27 per cent and 25 per cent of speculative-grade issuers were downgraded. Investment-grade companies also showed serious ratings erosion. Investment-grade ratings have actually been eroding since 1997, which coincided with the peak of corporate profitability. The downgrade rate of investment-grade issuers increased from 15 per cent in 2001 to 22 per cent in 2002. Previously solid A2-rated companies saw 20.6 per cent of their ranks downgraded during the year. A huge volume of fallen angels (investment-grade companies that are downgraded to speculative grade) flooded the corporate bond market in 2002 and significantly changed the landscape of fixed-income investing by swelling the high-yield bond market and creating the most attractive risk–reward opportunities for investors in a decade, as demonstrated by the subsequent rally in corporate bonds that occurred between October 2002 and June 2003. In 2002, 171 issuers lost their investment-grade ratings and accounted for 11 per cent of the speculative-grade universe (see Exhibit 16.10).

Exhibit 16.10

Annual fallen angel totals, 1983–2002

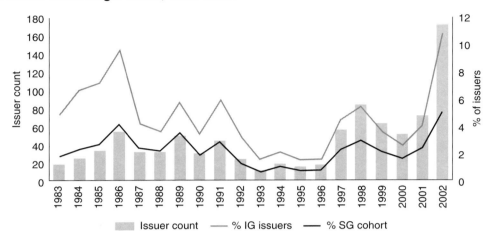

Source: Moody's Investors Service (2003), *Default & Recovery Rates of Corporate Bond Issuers: A Statistical Review of Moody's Ratings Performance, 1920–2002* (February) p. 12.

Exhibit 16.11

Annual US downgrade rate and annual change in industrial production, 1983–2002

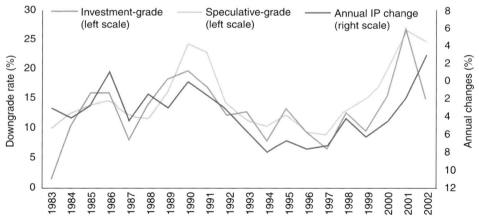

Source: Moody's Investors Service (2003), *Default & Recovery Rates of Corporate Bond Issuers: A Statistical Review of Moody's Ratings Performance, 1920–2002,* (February), p. 11.

Moody's bond studies show a close correlation between deterioration in credit quality (as measured by credit rating changes) and broad economic activity. The annual percentage change in total US industrial production, as shown in Exhibit 16.11, highlights a –0.51 contemporaneous correlation with investment-grade ratings downgrades and a –0.79 correlation with speculative-grade downgrades.

Record default rates

Defaults were the most public face of the credit meltdown. According to Moody's, the total dollar volume of defaulted debt increased by a troubling 34 per cent annualised rate between 1996 and 2002, with the largest increases coming in 2001–02. Worldwide in 2001, 212 issuers defaulted on US$135.1 billion of debt, a record that was quickly swamped in 2002 when fewer issuers, 141, defaulted on an even greater US$163.4 billion of debt.

The average size of default increased for speculative-grade issuers from US$436.2 million in 1996 to US$1,294.0 million in 2002 and for investment-grade issuers from US$591.5 million in 1998 to US$8,201.8 million in 2001 and US$5,159.4 million in 2002. Some 19 issuers representing more than US$55 billion (34 per cent of total defaults), including such well-known names as WorldCom, Inc, Marconi Corporation, Plc and Kmart Corporation, defaulted in 2002 within one year of holding investment-grade ratings. The collapse of a number of household investment-grade names greatly shook the confidence of the credit markets, particularly the investment-grade corporate bond market that was unaccustomed (and arguably ill-equipped, leaving an opening for more nimble hedge funds) to dealing with defaults.

In 2002, defaults were a global phenomenon in an increasingly globalised world. According to Moody's, the share of US issuers that defaulted was the lowest since World War II, with US issuers making up 64 per cent of defaults by dollar volume and 62 per cent as a percentage of issuers. To place this in historical perspective, between 1920 and 2002, US-based corporate bond issuers have represented on average 91 per cent of defaults as a percentage of issuers and 90 per cent of defaults as a percentage of dollar volume. The increase in European defaults accompanied the opening of the European high-yield bond market. This market was effectively non-existent prior to the early 1990s. The chickens began to come home to roost in 2001, when European defaults constituted 4.2 per cent of defaults by volume and 7 per cent in number. In 2002, the chickens overran the chicken coop, with European defaults constituting 23 per cent by volume and 19 per cent by number of total global defaults. The European high-yield market was particularly decimated because a disproportionate percentage of its high-yield issuance came in the telecommunications area and came out of the United Kingdom, the European capital market most closely linked with the United States. Some of the largest global defaults were European telecom companies such as NTL Communications Corp (US$8.5 billion), Telewest Communications PLC (US$5.2 billion) and United Pan-Europe Communications NV (US$5.1 billion).

Low recovery rates

Investors also experienced record low recovery rates (the ultimate measurement of the damage done) on defaulted corporate bonds and bank loans in 2001 and 2002. Recovery rates are influenced by a number of factors, including the macroeconomic environment, the credit cycle, lender behaviour, industry factors, and the specific reasons for the default event and the severity of the underlying problems that caused it. Declining recovery rates in the current cycle have coincided with economic weakness and lender skittishness resulting from the systemic stress that such a default rate produces on suppliers of credit.

In 2001, recovery rates for lower tiers of issuers' capital structures fell to nearly half their historical averages. This is illustrative of the fact that corporate enterprise value (defined as the sum of net debt plus equity) became highly extended during the bubble as a combination of cheap debt and high equity prices raised total corporate valuations into the

Exhibit 16.12

Average defaulted bond recovery rates by security and priority (US$)

Priority in capital structure	Average recovery			
	1982–2002	1982–2000	2001	2002
Secured bank loans	61.6	67.3	64.0	51.0
Equipment trust	40.2	65.9	NA	38.2
Senior secured	53.1	52.1	57.5	48.7
Senior unsecured	37.4	43.8	35.3	34.0
Senior subordinated	32.0	34.6	20.5	26.6
Subordinated	30.4	31.9	15.8	24.4
Junior subordinated	23.6	22.5	NA	NA
All bonds	37.2	39.1	34.7	34.3

Source: Moody's Investors Service (2003), *Default & Recovery Rates of Corporate Bond Issuers: A Statistical Review of Moody's Rating Performance, 1920–2002*, (February), p. 20.

stratosphere. This was particularly true in the TMT companies that dominated defaults during this period. Once reason returned, enterprise values moved closer in the direction of historical norms (although they remain high by historical standards at the beginning of 2003), drastically shrinking the total value available to creditors. As a result, the recoverable value of the underlying businesses accrued to the senior-most capital and there was little left for unsecured debt and equity holders. See Exhibit 16.12, which lends further context to the poor relative performance of CBOs versus CLOs discussed earlier. The 2001–02 period represents a nadir in recovery values for corporate lenders. The average recovery rate for unsecured debt was less than 35 cents on the dollar compared to a historical average of 41.6 cents on the dollar for the 1982–2002 period. Once telecommunications debt is excluded, however, the average recovery rate rises to 41.8 cents on the dollar, slightly higher than the average rate over the last 20 years.

By every measure, the downside of the 1997–2002 credit cycle has been extremely painful for investors.

Conclusion

Are investors doomed to fall victim to persistent credit cycles, or can preventative measures be taken to avoid them and the losses they cause? The 1997–2002 credit cycle was more severe than earlier episodes of credit malaise, but it was driven by many of the same factors that caused earlier downturns. A combination of lax monetary policy, regulatory changes and financial innovation created a classic boom-and-bust cycle. There were ample warning signs that things were getting out of hand in the late 1990s, but the pressure to produce short-term performance held even the most sophisticated managers hostage to the madness of crowds.

As the corporate bond market experienced its best performance in two decades between October 2002 and June 2003, warning signs of another credit downturn were emerging. These signs (a flood of new issuance by weaker credits, the ability of issuers to borrow at uneconomically stingy yields and spreads) were similar to those that preceded the credit collapses in 1990–91 and 2000–02. Moreover, these warning signs were accompanied by troubling macroeconomic problems, including a weak dollar, a growing US current account deficit, a simultaneous economic slowdown in the United States, Europe and Japan, an abrupt shift from US federal budget surpluses to huge deficits and a threat of deflation sufficiently palpable to lead the Federal Reserve to publicly express its concern.

Hedge fund investors and managers are well-served by an understanding of the circumstances that lead to credit bubbles and the ability to identify the symptoms of bubbles before they pop. The most easily identifiable symptoms are statistical measures of credit quality that far exceed historical norms. If they can identify these warning signs, hedge fund practitioners should structure their portfolios with sufficient liquidity and flexibility to maintain decent returns while retaining the ability to liquidate positions and limit their downside when the inevitable credit crunch arrives. The most obvious measures would include reducing leverage (including derivatives exposure) and migrating individual security holdings into more liquid names. In effect, hedge funds will need to act as anti-momentum investors and increase their margins of safety as the warning signs flash more brightly. Knowing how to identify the warning signs, and then taking protective steps, can significantly improve long-term hedge fund returns and mitigate the booms and busts that tend to occur repetitively. If such steps are taken, tragedy need not lapse into farce.

References

Mikuni, Akio, and R. Taggart Murphy (2002), *Japan's Policy Trap: Dollars, Deflation and the Crisis of Japanese Finance,* Washington DC, Brookings Institution Press.

Minsky, Hyman (1986), *Stabilising an Unstable Economy,* New Haven, Yale University Press.

---

[1] Kindleberger, Charles (1989), *Manias, Panics and Crashes: A History of Financial Crises*, New York, Basic Books, Inc.

[2] Brenner, Robert (2002), *The Boom and the Bubble: The United States in the World Economy*, New York, Verso.

[3] Ibid.

[4] Ibid.

[5] Moody's Investors Service (2003), *Default & Recovery Rates of Corporate Bond Issuers: A Statistical Review of Moody's Rating Performance, 1920–2002* (February).

[6] Ibid.

[7] Kaufman, Henry (2000), *On Money and Markets*, New York, McGraw Hill.

[8] Moody's Investors Service (2003), *Moody's Deal Score Report, CDO Deal Summary Performance, February 2003* (11 April).

Chapter 17

European event and arbitrage investing

Roddy Campbell
Cross Asset Management, London

Introduction

When I was asked to contribute to the third edition of *Evaluating and Implementing Hedge Fund Strategies* I rather looked forward to pontificating on event-driven and arbitrage techniques. After all, I have been writing on the subject in investor letters for many years, after practising it for 22 years I should know something about it, I quite like showing off, and it was about time I appeared in a serious and intelligent book.

Then I looked at some of the other contributors for this edition, and read some of the chapters in previous editions, and panic gently set in. They were clearly so much more knowledgeable, dedicated, experienced, successful and lucid than I am, and more to the point, had written about event and arbitrage investing at least as well as I could.

Consequently, I went back and reread my brief from the editor, and reread the topic he had given me, and saw the light. It had Europe in the title, and clearly he wanted me to write about this great new market that had suddenly appeared, right at the end of the 20th century. I would not be shown up because I would be able to focus my comments on event-driven investing, which includes capital structure arbitrage, merger arbitrage, distressed securities, corporate restructurings, bankruptcies and so on.

I do not include strategies at the macro end of event-driven, which might include major sector bets. Nor do I include trading methods that rely over heavily on value as a first filter, even value-with-a-catalyst. For my purposes, event-driven must include an announced, inevitable, or highly likely corporate event; and therefore by implication a timetable within which each trade should be completed.

European event and arbitrage investing

I have always maintained that Continental Europe throughout the 1980s and most of the 1990s was a place from which the professional event-driven investor and arbitrageur was lucky to return with his trousers still on. I know I nearly lost mine on many occasions.

Those of you who have been to school and studied geography will know what and where Europe is, but it is worth stating it clearly.

Europe is a large land mass just off the coast of Britain

The history of Britain is simple. We have gone around the world conquering countries and colonising them, and generally making those areas safe for capital markets arbitrage.

It is worth noting, semi-humorously, that all countries where arbitrage has been successfully practised on a consistent basis over a sustained period of time were once British colonies (the United States, Canada, Australia, New Zealand, Hong Kong, Ireland, South Africa and even India). This does not mean that having been a British colony is an automatic invitation to arbitrageurs to roll up (experience in Zimbabwe and Pakistan has been mixed). It is however a pretty good place to start in my experience and is summed up in Campbell's first law below.

Campbell's first law: arbitrage has never worked in countries that have never been ruled by Britain

Sadly for Europe, none of it has really ever been a British colony. The consequence is that it has never been a place safe for arbitrage. Latin America, Russia and China have never been British colonies and they too are areas where event-driven and arbitrage investing could not be described as consistently attractive investment strategies. Arbitrage and event investing depends upon your host country not being able to confiscate your money if they do not like what you are doing. This has not been the case in Europe, although they have often disguised confiscation as a 'change of rules'.

Those of you who take the narrow geographical point of view, that Britain is part of Europe, please suspend that belief for the duration of this chapter. If it makes it easier, think of Britain as the 51st state.

On a more serious note, there are various conditions required in some mixture or other to successfully, predictably and profitably practise event-driven investing. These include:

- a stock market with rules;
- a regulator with rules; or
- a court system with teeth and precedent;
- a bankruptcy and/or administration system;
- a takeover or merger code;
- shareholders who care;
- anti-trust and other industry regulatory bodies who know what they are doing;
- governments that intervene predictably, if at all;
- shareholders who generally act to maximise their profits; and
- non-executive or other constraints on management.

Less long-windedly, I could sum these up in three requirements:

- a level and visible playing field;
- a decent body of precedent of corporate law decisions; and
- an ability to predict the behaviour of participants and comprehend their motives.

It is less than controversial to state that these conditions did not pertain in Europe before the introduction of the euro (the 'Trojan horse' of Europe, of which more later). I could list examples but these would be selectively chosen to make my case, so let me just ask a few test questions about Europe in the years 1980–98.

- Can you name a public French company that has gone bankrupt or undertaken a formal restructuring?

- Can you name a hostile takeover in Germany?
- Can you name a competent and independent national anti-trust body in Europe?
- Can you name a successful example of shareholder activism?

Some of you will be able to answer 'yes' to one or more of the above questions, but not many of you. With the exception of the generally positive German anti-trust record, I struggle to think of a meaningful 'yes' answer to any of those questions for the period in question.

So why propose a fund, in 1998, intended to specialise in UK and European event-driven investing and arbitrage, when my own first law states that arbitrage does not work in Europe? To answer this question we need to look a little at the history of post World War II Europe and see what might have changed in the last decade.

The post war history of Europe changed in 1979 and 1980 with the elections of Margaret Thatcher and Ronald Reagan. To simplify their electoral platforms, they believed that governments did not create wealth or employment, the private sector did. They further believed that government involvement, based on the view that governments know better, generally destroyed wealth and employment.

Margaret Thatcher and Ronald Reagan set in place the conditions under which the United Kingdom and United States could recycle employment out of old industries into new. Consequently, unemployment levels in the two countries are low in comparison to most of Europe.

Campbell's second law: government involvement spells danger for arbitrageurs

European governments have had a strong belief in government intervention in the economy, in companies and in markets. Remember that Francois Mitterand nationalised the banking sector in France shortly after his election as French President in 1981. Note in general that the European Union began as a Coal and Steel Community and then became an agricultural support system through the Common Agricultural Policy. Observe labour laws in most countries in Europe.

Now, I am no economist and so will supply no statistics of any reliability but Europe is characterised by steadily increasing unemployment, an ageing population and low levels of job creation. The contrast with the United States needs no highlighting but the contrast with the United Kingdom is startling (we also have a more racially diverse population due to colonial immigration policies and so have a better base to manage future population change).

At some point in the 1990s, and it varied from country to country, people realised that governments, indeed, do not create jobs. Even governments realised that they cannot create jobs. Most importantly, workers realised it because they could see the relentless pressure on costs in all businesses, as white-collar jobs were shed in banking and insurance and blue-collar jobs in industry. So governments throughout Europe realised that in the modern world their power to improve the lives of their citizens was significantly less than they had believed or hoped and that the best thing they could do was admit they could do nothing. Rather, what they could do was to create conditions in which the market would take over.

As you might imagine, although it might be difficult for an American audience to fully realise this, these are not sentiments or theories that can even be uttered in Europe, let alone offered to electorates as a platform. So what happened was two-fold:

- politics ceased to exist, in the sense that different political parties offered more or less the same menu as each other;
- politicians and governments agreed to cede more and more power to Brussels, so that they could say to their electorates 'We are powerless, it is against European Union law'.

This is the first mention of Brussels in this chapter, but Brussels and the euro hold the key to the whole subject of Europe as an event-driven environment, and in fact give rise to my next law. By Brussels I mean the central (unelected) machinery of the European Union, essentially the European Commission and its civil service.

Campbell's millennium law: national governments in Europe have now lost all power to interfere in capital markets

The millennium law is, I admit, still rather forward looking and will never be quite true, but it is truer by a factor of a hundred times than the status quo ante, which went something like the following.

European national governments cannot resist interfering in capital markets. They range from the dirigiste to the socialist, and tweaking the allocation of capital is, they believe, a right and good thing to do, and defending national jobs and businesses is, they believe, a healthy and vote winning thing to do.

Now, I would not claim that European governments have lost for all time their desire to interfere, but it is now true, legally, that they have lost a great deal of their ability to do so. European law has removed their ability to subsidise, protect and rig their national interests to a very large degree.

- The European Commission wrote repeatedly to Portugal in 2000 forbidding it to prevent the takeover of the Champalimaud Group by Banco Santander of Spain, which was eventually allowed to proceed in the teeth of Portuguese government opposition to the continuing creeping ownership of the Portuguese financial sector by large Spanish banks.
- The Commission forbade France to use its 'golden share' in protecting TotalFinaElf from possible foreign takeover at the time of the agreed merger between TotalFina and Elf in 2000.
- The Commission has to permit national subsidy, for example Britain's emergency package to the private company British Energy (essentially Britain's entire nuclear power industry) in 2002–03, still under investigation and attack by the EU.
- The Commission has completely neutered the ability of national anti-trust authorities to permit national or regional champion mergers, for example, blocking the Swedish merger of truck companies Volvo and Scania in 2000 against the strongly expressed desire of Sweden to permit it.

It is difficult to do justice to the scale of power handed over by national governments to Brussels in its various forms and also to other supranational bodies. This happened through the 1980s and 1990s but only really had a major impact on the markets in which I operate when the capital markets were (more or less) unified by the introduction of the euro.

Campbell's next law: the euro *est arrivé*

One could argue for ever about the design of Europe by its (French, mainly) architects and whether it has turned out as they wished. What is true is that they envisioned a bloc that could, in financial and political terms, present a counter-weight to the absolute dominance of the United States and at the time, the Soviet Union. This required a single market place and centralised political institutions that could transcend the weight of national ones.

The introduction of a common currency ran alongside these desires. It would undoubtedly be more efficient, it would prevent the markets attacking government policies through the currency and bond markets and, in the mind of the dirigiste designers, it would create a currency that would rival the US dollar in a way that would enhance Europe's power and prestige.

What this has done in my world is validate and solidify a trend that had been going on for decades, namely the transfer of powers from national regulators, courts and law makers to Brussels. The psychological impact on voters, companies, shareholders and politicians has been stupendous.

I described the euro earlier as the 'Trojan horse' of Europe. I do not believe that the designers of the project and its political supporters in Germany and France really understood the extent to which it would permanently neuter the financial ability of countries to be different, the extent to which at the macro level it would remove their ability to print money and run budget deficits and the extent to which at the micro level power is transferred to companies and capitalists away from politicians. It seemed to me that the wave of corporate activity that followed the euro introduction was a direct effect and showed the real extent to which companies now had power.

Another law: shareholders own the companies they own shares in

Let's look at shareholders. Before the euro, a French savings institution would collect all its savings in French francs, whether in the form of insurance, retirement accounts, mutual funds, whatever, and would be compelled, for currency risk reasons, to keep the vast majority in franc assets, typically French shares, bonds, money markets and property. The euro means three things:

- there is now no currency risk in diversifying into assets in the Benelux, Germany, Italy, Spain, Portugal, Finland and so on, and the irreversible introduction of the euro has removed the last shred of political or country risk;
- the French government cannot access those savings as easily as before; and
- the institution has to compete with other pan-European asset managers on investment performance.

Look again at the third point. What it means is that institutional shareholders have started to care about their performance and not just the chairman's knighthood (or local equivalent).

In France this has spelled the end of the *Noyau Dur*, literally hard core. This referred to a group of key shareholders who would do what the government told them. In France this was easy to police because of the Enarques. The Enarques are the ruling class of France and have all been to school together. Imagine a whole country run by Harvard Business School graduates and you get the picture.

In France the core shareholders were instructed to hold and retain shares in key companies (banks, insurance, defence, media, oil and so on) and ensure that those companies were run in the interest of France. This made the companies takeover proof. It also meant that if a French company was in danger of being taken over, the Enarques got on the phone and rustled up some core shareholders to acquire stock and see off the invader.

Now when there is a controversial takeover, not only are governments less willing and less able to become involved but their ability to use tame shareholders to achieve the end they want regardless of the impact on the financial performance of those shareholders is extremely limited.

A global background

Relax, nothing too geo-political. The changes in laws which transferred powers from national governments to Brussels (generally in connection with the creation of a genuine single market and the introduction of the euro) have created the conditions for free capital markets in Europe. However, none of this would have happened if not for the trends and conditions that made these changes and policy adoptions almost compulsory.

The United States has helped create a global economy; we have lower barriers to trade than ever before; we have the closest ever to a market economy worldwide; the Soviet Union is gone. This makes the world faster moving, especially given the changes in technology that have occurred. Europe has adapted rationally, by making it easier to compete and recycle its workforce. It has problems ahead, especially in micro labour market legislation and practice, and in its demographics, but the first wave of change has been to give the market a chance.

Back to arbitrage

I set up Cross Asset Management in 1998 to exploit these structural and behavioural developments. I took this action precisely because Europe (ex-United Kingdom), which had long been a barren area for arbitrage and event-driven investing, was finally changing. Furthermore, I took this action despite my own experiences in the past, as the following war story from the Netherlands illustrates.

In the late 1980s, when I was working for the hedge fund IFM, we bought sufficient shares in a company called Audet to prevent the agreed merger with VNU going ahead. An agreed public company merger in Holland had never failed before. We were paying above the value of the all-stock offer to acquire shares in the belief that the company was worth much more and that VNU or another acquirer would pay more later. We were acting in the knowledge that a major Dutch shareholder was of the same mind and intended to refuse the offer and between us we owned sufficient shares to prevent the merger.

Holland had a takeover code, which stated that the acquiring company was unable to raise its bid after a certain point but would need to lapse the bid and make a new one after waiting some statutory period. We were buying shares after the bid-raising deadline had passed, in the sure knowledge that the company could not raise its bid under Dutch securities law.

The day after the bid closed, and should therefore have lapsed, we were informed that the bid had been raised by 10 per cent, the other key shareholder had accepted, and all our trades on the stock exchange for the previous few days were being cancelled since we must have been in possession of inside information that the bid was going to be raised. Since the bid could not be raised and we were actually bracing ourselves for a fall in the stock price (albeit temporarily, we hoped), this came as an unpleasant surprise but there was nothing we could do without exposing ourselves in public to accusations of insider trading levelled at us by a national stock exchange.

Now, every story is different and unique. In this one the Dutch sorted out their Dutch affairs to their satisfaction and the (partial) loser was the Anglo-Saxon raider. That is not a unique story and we emerged with a profit on that occasion, but the surprise of the wholly unexpected regulatory intervention was a chastening experience. In many other cases we retreated wounded.

It was apparent by 1997–98 even to a blinkered one-eyed Euro-sceptic Thatcher-voter that there were changes occurring in capital markets in Europe. Most obviously securities firms in Paris, Frankfurt and so on were closing down and moving their pan-European operations to London, which had a very significant effect on type and homogeneity of behaviour.

I divide this effect into two parts. Firstly, shareholders exhibit group behaviour. Put them all in London and they will, chameleon-like, adopt similar London-style behaviour and gradually shed their French-ness or German-ness. Secondly, there is what I loosely term the Goldman Sachs effect, which is the Americanisation of advice offered to corporates by the (generally global and American) investment banking community. For example, Pechiney of France, which as I write is the subject of an unsolicited takeover offer, has appointed Goldman and JP Morgan to strengthen its French advisory base of BNP and Rothschild.

Let's look again at the list of conditions necessary to successfully, predictably and profitably practice event-driven investing:

- a stock market with rules;
- a regulator with rules; or
- a court system with teeth and precedent;
- a bankruptcy and/or administration system;
- a takeover or merger code;
- shareholders who care;
- anti-trust and other industry regulatory bodies who know what they are doing;
- governments that intervene predictably, if at all;
- shareholders who generally act to maximise their profits; and
- non-executive or other constraints on management.

I summed these up earlier as follows:

- a level and visible playing field;
- a decent body of precedent of corporate law decisions; and
- an ability to predict the behaviour of participants and comprehend their motives.

I recall presenting the thesis that 'European event-driven is the next profit opportunity' to US investors in 1998 and 1999 and those who knew the area were rightly sceptical about whether the backdrop provided any justification for the investment opportunity I was proposing. They felt there was absence of clarity of corporate law and asked questions about how many lawyers I had on retainer in Frankfurt, Paris, Milan and Stockholm. With considerable knowledge of anti-trust they asked penetrating questions about Karel van Miert, the Competition Commissioner and the competition landscape. They knew, and if they didn't I told them, that European shareholders and management did not operate in a clear relationship as profit maximising owners and managers.

All I could do was say, 'Wait and see'. I felt very strongly that Europe was on the brink of substantial change that would result in corporate events in the hundreds and thousands in an environment where the market would, generally, be king.

Back to the future

I could list tens, hundreds, of examples showing how right I was and how clever I am, which of course is true but that is not the point of this chapter. Francis Fukuyama wrote in 1990, followed up by his book *The End of History*, about the triumph of liberal democracy over other forms of human organisation. I felt then that capitalism had also triumphed over all other forms of human commercial structures, both in its ability to bring material wealth increases but equally powerfully in its greater ability to deliver human satisfaction to individuals in the form of freedom, endeavour and self-expression.

It sounds foolish and almost certainly is, to say that the changes in European capital markets in the last few years can in any way be placed alongside the fall of the Soviet Union or the Berlin Wall, but they are all effects of the great lead the United States has over the rest of the world. In the early 1980s there was a list of the world's top 10 industries and the United States was world leader in only one, aerospace. The Japanese controlled sectors such as computers, chips, steel and cars. Within 10 years the United States was back on top in nearly all important growth areas.

Europe wants some of what the United States has (at the moment economic growth and job creation) and has rationally reacted by opening up to two ways in which it seems the United States has obtained this lead:

- no politics (there is minimal choice in Europe now of political system); and
- market capitalism.

The introduction of true and free market capitalism into a continent with an established and strong rule of law and concept of property is a pretty powerful cocktail. European event-driven investing seems safe for years to come as a strategy. However, don't tell anyone, or we'll be deluged with capital!

Chapter 18

Long-short investment strategy in Japan: capitalising on the dynamic structural change occurring in Japan

Shuhei Abe
SPARX Asset Management Co., Ltd., Tokyo

Introduction

The past six years have been a period of dramatic growth for the Japanese hedge fund industry, with the number of Japanese long-short equity managers increasing significantly over the past 18 months. From a handful of managers in 1997 when SPARX introduced SPARX Long-Short Fund Ltd, we estimate that there are more than 100 dedicated Japan long-short managers today, with aggregate assets under management in excess of US$12 billion. This chapter aims to unravel the dynamics behind this recent rapid growth by covering the following two areas.

- Dynamic structural change in Japan, which is creating opportunities for long-short equity investors by highlighting the differences between winners and losers among Japanese corporations.
- Our experience, which describes how SPARX as an investment manager capitalised on this investment opportunity.

Dynamic structural changes in Japan

Our principal premise launching the SPARX Long-Short Fund in the late 1990s was our belief that Japan is undergoing dynamic structural change. In order to capitalise on this change, we believed that a long-short equity investment approach based on fundamental stock selection was the ideal investment strategy. As shown in Exhibit 18.1, Japan is shifting from a bureaucrat-led system to a market-driven system. The pyramid on the left shows Japan's post-war, socio-economic model, which was often referred to as 'Japan Inc'. Simply, bureaucrats and banks were in control, directing economic activity and capital flows. This system experienced enormous success through export-driven growth supported by controlled competition in the domestic economy.

The ultimate objective of the 'Japan Inc' system was to distribute wealth from productive sectors to less efficient sectors. The strategy started with support for Japanese strategic growth industries, such as textiles, steel, colour TVs, semiconductors and automobiles, which then became the nation's cash cows. The Ministry of Finance (MOF) effectively collected

Exhibit 18.1

Japan: transfer of power

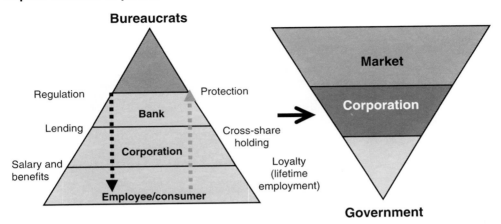

Note: This new environment is challenging Japanese managers to put the market ahead of long-standing relationships.

Source: SPARX.

profits from these export-oriented companies via taxation and redistributed these profits to small-scale farmers, regional governments and other structurally vulnerable domestic sectors through grants and other supportive measures. More importantly, the system sheltered both strong and weak companies by limiting competition in the domestic economy.

The beginning of the end of the 'Japan Inc' era was signalled by the Plaza Accord in 1985, which brought massive appreciation of the yen and put severe pressure on the profitability of exporters in Japan. The strengths of the centrally organised system became weaknesses; in particular, the stability fostered by cosy ties among bureaucrats, banks and corporations limited the flexibility needed for the Japanese economy to overcome the challenges faced since the bursting of the bubble. However, while genuine changes at the macro level have been few and far between, significant developments at the micro level hint at a new era in which consumers, voters and shareholders will have more control over their destiny. For example, corporations have substantially reduced cross-shareholdings, thus facilitating greater competition and an improved awareness of the importance of corporate governance and return on equity. Some companies will adapt to the changes in the environment and thrive, while others clearly will not undertake the necessary measures to remain competitive. This differentiation between winners and losers is an ideal starting point for a long-short investor.

The emergence of Japan's post-war industrial system

Looking back, one should not forget that Japan experienced miraculous economic growth during the post-war period. Japan's GDP grew from ¥8.5 trillion in 1955 to ¥490 trillion in 2000, or more than 57.6 times.

This amazing economic growth was accomplished by creating a structured export-driven system for selected industries. Japan has relied on this export orientation to fuel its growth

233

Exhibit 18.2

Post-war socio-economic model of Japan

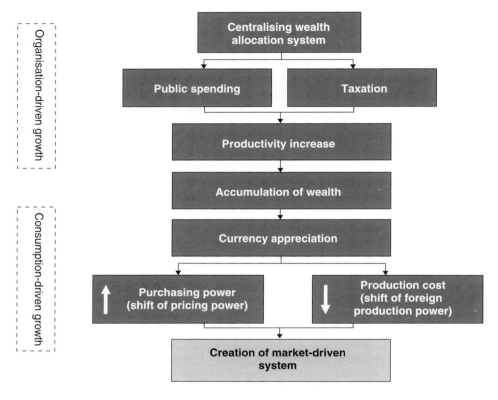

Source: SPARX.

over the past six decades. The country's original post-war industrial system was structured by selecting a few strategic industries (for example, automobiles and electronics) that the government believed would play key roles in the future economic development of Japan. Each strategic industry received special governmental support and companies within these industries found success and security through their respective *keiretsu*, or business groupings. Each *keiretsu* was centred around a main bank, which was responsible for the allocation of capital among group companies. The ties among the companies of a *keiretsu* went beyond simple cooperation: group companies held shares in other *keiretsu* members in a system of cross-shareholdings called *mochiai*, with the main bank generally holding the most shares due to its central position within the group. This *keiretsu* system experienced phenomenal success and facilitated rapid expansion. At the peak in 1986, *mochiai* accounted for more than 66 per cent of total outstanding shares on the Tokyo Stock Exchange.

At the same time, the government offered many programmes to support and protect the strategic industries. Among the support programmes implemented were high import tariffs, numerous regulations to prevent outsiders from entering markets and incentives to encourage repeat demand from the country's captive consumers. The close cooperation between the government and the favoured strategic industries created an environment in which a few powerful companies dominated each major domestic market and were able to control pricing fully with the approval, tacit or otherwise, of the authorities. This pricing control allowed companies to generate consistent profits from domestic operations, which then could be used to enhance the competitiveness of their export activities.

Starting in the 1970s, these companies began aggressively exporting into foreign markets. At first, cheap prices were the only advantage Japanese corporations could offer. However, with stable domestic profit bases to rely on, companies were able to amass the necessary resources to improve product quality and many products eventually achieved recognition as the best in the world. Using this export-oriented formula, by the early 1980s, many of these companies had become the dominant players in their respective global markets.

In this environment, the system sheltered both strong and weak companies. Government policies favoured the large *keiretsu*, and also ensured that strong companies did not crush the weak. As a result, the stock market through the bubble period had little incentive to differentiate between winners and losers, which meant, of course, that long-short equity was not a viable investment strategy during that time.

Dismantling Japan's post-war industrial system

Japan's industrial success did not go unnoticed. By exploiting domestic consumers to drive the country's export strategy, the Japanese government created a structural trade surplus. Japan's trade partners generally accepted the surplus while Japan was still a developing country working its way out of the devastation of World War II. By the 1980s Japan had clearly become a wealthy country through its spectacularly successful export policies and the trade surplus became a lightning rod for criticism. As repeatedly seen in history, any system with overwhelming success or excessive growth will eventually reach a point at which this growth rate becomes unsustainable. The rapid and massive accumulation of wealth by 'Japan Inc' finally reached a limit in 1985, when the Group of Five leading industrialised economies engineered a dramatic appreciation of the yen under the Plaza Accord. By drastically limiting the profitability of Japanese exporters, the Plaza Accord effectively brought an end to 'Japan Inc'. The introduction of market forces into Japan's socio-economic model severely diminished the ability of bureaucrats and the banks to control the economy and started the shift from the left triangle in Exhibit 18.1 to the one on the right.

The magnitude of this transfer of power in Japan cannot be underestimated. The paradigm shift is occurring in spite of strong resistance from politicians and bureaucrats. The historical power structure is being dismantled by market forces, which are gradually moving Japan toward structural reform and, ultimately, true economic recovery. The market is beginning to assume the role previously played by bureaucrats and the banks, and the emerging system is finally starting to clean up the excesses of the past.

Today, Japan is exhibiting clear signs of the breakdown of the old system. For example, the MOF simply ran out of ways to protect the Long-Term Credit Bank of Japan and Nippon Credit Bank, two key players in 'Japan Inc' from nationalisation in 1998. Another indication of change is the reduction in the share of *mochiai* on the TSE from the historic high of 66 per cent to less than 30 per cent today. Likewise, the system of lifetime employment and seniority-based promotions has given way to layoffs and other forms of involuntary separation, as well as performance-based personnel evaluation systems. The ties that bound Japanese companies to the old ways of doing business have fallen away and many enterprising businesses with dynamic management in Japan have already implemented significant changes to increase profitability and improve shareholder returns.

At the micro level, those companies that successfully adapt to the new system will be rewarded. Conversely, we have already seen the market punish companies unable to change and adjust to the post-bubble environment and we expect this trend to increase in scope in the future.

To better understand the overall context, we believe that Nissan Motor illustrates one of the most successful cases of 'old Japan' transforming itself into 'new Japan'. Prior to the 1930s, the largest automobile manufacturer in Japan was Ford Motor Company of the United States. In 1936, the Automobile Manufacturing Business Act was passed, restricting the production of automobiles to 'Japanese' companies with more than 50 per cent ownership by 'Japanese' shareholders. This provided an opening for Nissan, which was founded in 1933, and its rival, Toyota, as Ford was eventually forced to shut down its operations in Japan in 1940.

Nissan became part of the then powerful Fuyo *keiretsu*, which was anchored by the former Industrial Bank of Japan (IBJ, now part of Mizuho). Nissan closely aligned itself with the bank by accepting IBJ executives as president, and at the peak, borrowing more than ¥2 trillion and paying ¥100 billion of interest on an annual basis. Nissan represented a typical *keiretsu* participant, holding *mochiai* shares of more than 1,390 *keiretsu* companies at one point. In accordance with usual practice, potential shareholders' profit was redistributed from stronger companies of the *keiretsu* to weaker ones through business arrangements that were not structured to maximise the returns to shareholders of individual group companies.

This system succeeded during the growth era, but as the domestic economy stalled and the yen strengthened, it began to extract a heavy toll on the company. By the time Carlos Ghosn of Renault took the helm of Nissan in July 1999, the company was losing market share and money, and was suffering from an oppressive debt load. In truth, the future of the company was in jeopardy.

Mr Ghosn's mandate was clear: generate profits and increase returns to shareholders, including Renault, which currently holds 44 per cent of the outstanding shares of Nissan. In the restructuring that has taken place, the company liquidated its cross-shareholdings and sold non-core businesses. Management also slashed procurement costs, which consumed approximately 60 per cent of revenues, while reducing net automotive debt to zero and improving return on equity to levels above 10 per cent. During this period, Nissan's market value increased by 32 per cent, while the overall market fell 47 per cent. Nissan, once on the verge of bankruptcy, is now one of the most profitable corporations in Japan.

At SPARX, we strongly believe that dynamic structural changes in Japan will continue to create clear differentiation between winners and losers among Japanese companies and thus provide a fertile source of investment opportunities for equity long-short investment strategies.

The SPARX experience of long-short investing in Japan

Since our firm's beginning, the phrase 'macro is the aggregate of micro' has been the core foundation of our investment philosophy. Simply stated, we aim to know the companies or the businesses in which we invest. Alternatively, we believe a company's intrinsic value cannot be accurately evaluated without a thorough understanding of the underlying business.

Our investment approach focuses on business, people and price. When we visit a company, we assess the growth potential of the market in which it operates, the corporate strategy laid out by the management and the quality of earnings generated by that business. Based on a series of both qualitative and quantitative analyses, a three-year projection of earnings is built to derive the intrinsic value of the company. The difference between the company's intrinsic value and market price is called the 'value gap' and we aim to participate in the narrowing of this undervaluation. Of equal importance in our process is the identification of the catalyst that will narrow this gap. In the past, we have observed that the market may never recognise the undervaluation, and many Japanese companies remain firmly entrenched at these low valuations. In other words, a cheap stock can always stay cheap without a catalyst to unlock the underlying value of the company.

The second, and equally important, facet of our investment objective is to achieve our return target with minimal volatility. We believe that investing based on a company's intrinsic value provides a margin of safety or built-in stabilising effect. We buy when the company is trading below its intrinsic value and sell as the stock price nears the intrinsic value. On the other hand, if the market price is well above its intrinsic value, we would look for a catalyst that would trigger a deterioration of its high premium and may sell short the company. Once the market price corrects to or under its intrinsic value, we will buy back this position. Without intrinsic value, which is used as a yardstick, we would be vulnerable to the volatility of the market.

However, the calculation of a company's intrinsic value is not a static, one-time event. In Japan, market volatility, the idiosyncrasies of the market and general business conditions are dynamic. For example, in 2002, market valuations for Japanese electronic components manufacturers were based on monthly orders. In 2003, the market focused on future earnings although current monthly orders remained sluggish. In this case, the risk premium declined, causing a multiple expansion. Earnings visibility for the electronic components sector has awarded higher price/earnings multiples to companies within the sector. Therefore, it is also essential to understand the signals transmitted by the market because the market may indicate that previous assumptions are no longer valid.

Kenwood illustrates this process. Founded in 1946, Kenwood, formerly known as Torio or Kasuga Radio, started as a high-end wireless device manufacturer. A series of successful products contributed to the cachet of the 'Kenwood' brand, which eventually led to the expansion of the company's business portfolio to include home electronics, car audio and electronics, and wireless devices. However, the company focused on expanding sales rather than improving profits.

During the heyday, the different products in the company's portfolio supported one another. However, the impact of the less profitable home audio division was felt as the domestic economy stalled and a number of products reached saturation points. Moreover, Kenwood decided to expand its reach into the ultra-competitive mobile handset market. These mis-steps, coupled with losses resulting from inventory write-offs and equity write-downs, resulted in a negative shareholder equity position. The future of the company was in the hands of Kenwood's main bank, Asahi Bank (now known as Resona Bank).

At this point, Kenwood's falling stock price reflected market participants signalling scepticism over the company's future. However, we took a closer look and saw a much brighter future. For SPARX, this represented an opportunity in which the market price was well below the intrinsic value of the company. From our perspective, the prescription, or catalyst, for Kenwood's revival was clear: stick to core competence, restructure non-core balance sheet items and deliver profit to shareholders. Nevertheless the obvious question, 'who can execute that plan?' remained the biggest issue. Fortunately, the main bank brought in new management that not only recognised the problem but tackled it with utmost conviction. Asahi Bank executed a debt-for-equity swap to strengthen the company's balance sheet and provided additional commitment lines to secure working capital. Within three months, the new management, under the strong leadership of president and CEO, Haruo Kawahara, forcibly attacked the company's main illnesses. The home audio division was significantly restructured and nursed back to profitability through significant headcount reduction and closure of production facilities. Furthermore, Kenwood exited the loss generating mobile handset business and increased wholesale prices among 'Kenwood' brand products. These decisive actions quickly returned the company to profitability. Over this period, Kenwood's market value dipped below ¥8 billion at the peak of the crisis but steadily recovered to the point at which it was valued close to ¥60 billion in mid-2003, or 7.5 times from the lowest point. Though Kenwood is an extreme case with a huge value gap, we believe that a comprehensive knowledge of each investment is the best way to mitigate risk.

Up to now, we have focused mostly on the long side of the portfolio. However, many of the outlined concepts are applicable to identifying short candidates. The major difference lies in the greater emphasis of monitoring market momentum, which will be explained in greater detail.

Unlike the long portfolio's investment universe which consists of all of the 3,500 listed companies in Japan, the short portfolio's investment universe is dramatically smaller. In general, short candidates are usually trading above a market capitalisation of ¥50 billion or approximately US$400 million. Using this figure as the demarcation line, there are approximately 650 companies. This number shrinks further to about 400 companies when considering stock lending availability. Based on this much smaller universe of companies, we then first identify stocks showing strong momentum and then decipher the drivers of this strength to create a shortlist of candidates.

In most cases, short candidates meet one of the following four criteria:

1. exhibit a negative value gap based on our intrinsic value analysis;
2. at a key turning point based on our analysis of market momentum;
3. subject to major catalysts that may induce a decline in stock price; and
4. serve as a hedge against a risk in the long portfolio.

While the starting point of analysis for long candidates is calculating their intrinsic value, potential short candidates are identified by carefully monitoring stock price movements. Within the short universe, we utilise a series of proprietary screening techniques based on quantitative measures and then conduct further fundamental research to derive an intrinsic value.

As previously mentioned, a stock's market momentum is a critical consideration in the process of selecting short candidates. In most up markets, stock prices tend to benefit from positive momentum which is self-reinforcing. In these situations, we try to identify turning points suggested by technical analysis or other key triggers such as earnings announcements or significant corporate events. Based on this analysis, we closely watch the price movement to determine the entry point for our short positions. Although a catalyst is important, we have observed many cases where a stock price declined because it advanced too much or the catalyst itself became apparent only after the decline. Therefore, market momentum is key to the decision-making process. If a stock price is advancing strongly and the overvaluation continues to widen, the potential profit in a short position is quite significant once momentum reverses. The boom and bust of a bubble is the best example of this scenario.

However, the inflection point is the most difficult to pinpoint in a rising market. For example, prices may continue to appreciate and shrug off the appearance of a slight deterioration in fundamentals. Alternatively, the market may have already moved before a catalyst is identified. In any case, stock prices tend to react before a change in fundamentals. For this reason, it is critical to best understand the underlying forces that fuel a stock's momentum and then simulate multiple scenarios. In the end, after all the analysis is complete, the decision concerning the timing of the entry point comes down to a qualitative one.

Lastly, we also consider entering into short positions to hedge against long portfolio risk. These positions are not pair trades, but ones entered to protect select long positions in the fund. BARRA and other risk analysis tools are used to better understand the portfolio risk that is inherent in the long portfolio. Once identified, individual hedge positions are created to somewhat offset such risks. However, it is important to note that this trading tactic is secondary to our objective of earning a return on any short positions. In the end, we aim to construct the fund's long and short portfolios on a stock-by-stock basis with the goal of generating performance within each.

Innovative product delivery capability

For any investment manager looking to raise money, identifying and stimulating investors' demand is always a challenging task. This is where creative innovation in product delivery comes into play. In this section, we discuss our experience of delivering a long-short equity fund to Japanese investors, as regulations governing domestic distribution of investment funds in Japan are often a mystery to foreign observers.

SPARX's challenge in delivering a long-short fund to Japanese retail investors started in the late 1990s, when various steps toward deregulation in the financial sector began to occur in Japan. The timing coincided with the rise of strong demand for absolute-return products among financial intermediaries in Japan.

In 1996, the Hashimoto Cabinet announced a series of financial deregulation packages known as the financial Big Bang. One of the most dramatic changes affecting the asset management industry was the amendment of the Investment Trust Law, which governed the Japanese onshore funds, or investment trusts. This abolished many barriers to entry for managers of investment trusts and many newcomers with innovative product ideas entered the market. Also under the new Securities and Exchange Law, various restrictions imposed on distribution of offshore funds in Japan were relaxed. This deregulation eventually enabled SPARX to deliver a long-short fund to Japanese retail investors but many obstacles remained before the ultimate goal could be reached.

One such non-regulatory obstacle was the underdeveloped market to facilitate short sale transactions in Japan. For example, the only method for Japanese onshore funds to create short positions was through the costly, inconvenient and heavily regulated margin transaction facilitated by the stock exchanges. Short sales through over-the-counter margin transactions, which would provide less costly and more convenient means to create short positions on more available names, were not yet available for onshore funds.

With such obstacles to overcome, the alternative solution was to launch an offshore fund to be distributed in Japan. Until 1998, only Organisation for Economic Cooperation and Development (OECD) domiciled funds, such as Luxembourg or Dublin funds, could be distributed in Japan, and the local restrictions in these domiciles rendered short positions impossible. However, as part of the Big Bang deregulation, offshore funds distributed in Japan expanded to include funds domiciled in non-OECD countries. This deregulation enabled Bermuda or Cayman-based funds meeting certain standards to be distributed in Japan. SPARX took advantage of this deregulation to structure the first equity long-short offshore fund to be distributed in Japan. Nevertheless, this was not an easy path to pursue.

Despite relaxation of the rules, the fund service providers and regulatory authorities were quite slow and cautious in adapting to this new change. Therefore, a considerable amount of energy and time was spent in explaining and gaining consensus. This cautious stance stemmed from the substantial difference in regulatory practices and approaches of regulators in Japan, Luxembourg or Dublin versus those of Cayman or Bermuda, which operate under a completely different regulatory framework. As a result of countless discussions among various parties, including the regulators, consensus and understanding formed slowly. This agreement enabled SPARX to launch the first yen-denominated, Cayman-based long-short equity fund in June 1999.

This breakthrough had a tremendous impact on the industry, not only because SPARX was able to deliver an innovative product to Japanese investors but also because it showed that a small independent investment company like SPARX, without the strong lobbying power of larger financial groups, could bring about a major difference in advancing the asset management industry.

As demand for long-short equity products was stimulated and spread to Japanese pension funds and financial institutions, regulators allowed over-the-counter stock lending, along with further deregulation in other areas. In response, SPARX launched the first onshore fund utilising over-the-counter short transactions in April 2000. At present, the number of onshore equity long-short funds utilising over-the-counter margin transactions totals more than 35, with the short balance totalling approximately ¥180 billion at the end of April 2003.

Conclusion

With the severe decline in the Japanese equity market over the last decade, we have observed a significant shift in the shareholder base of companies. The key implication for investors is that Japanese companies can no longer ignore their shareholders. In fact, the shareholder's voice will only grow louder over time. As a result, companies must begin to think about the efficient use of assets and generating a sufficient rate of return.

Furthermore, in this environment it is becoming easier to differentiate between the winners and losers. The tough business environment as well as waning influence of the banks are primary reasons for this. Going forward, dynamic structural change in Japan should continue to create opportunities for the long-short equity investor. In the end, we will see that Japan's bureaucratic-led system was unable to withstand global market forces.

Part III

Evaluating opportunities – investors' strategies

Chapter 19

Analysing the evolution of the European hedge fund industry

Sohail Jaffer[1]
Premium Select Lux, SA, Luxembourg
AIMA Council Member (Benelux) (Alternative Investment Management Association)

Introduction

AIMA, the Alternative Investment Management Association, is an international, not-for-profit trade association whose objectives are to work with and for its members (comprising fund managers, banks, brokers and service providers), to encourage sound practices and to educate investors and other interested parties on the topic of alternative investment strategies and related subjects, such as transparency, due diligence and risk management.

While it does not actively promote individual funds or products, AIMA is an increasingly pivotal element of the hedge fund industry with member companies based in 42 countries (at the time of going to press). This positioning enables the Association to work closely with experienced and professional hedge fund practitioners and collate educational information for the use of interested parties. To that end, AIMA is regularly contacted by institutional investors seeking general advice and specific assistance on accessing further information (though not products). Examples of recent AIMA projects for the community include the expansion of the series of generic due diligence questionnaires,[2] the commissioning and publication of the *Guide to Fund of Hedge Funds Management and Investment* and the co-foundation of the Chartered Alternative Investment Analyst (CAIA)[3] qualification in conjunction with the CISDM of the University of Massachusetts.

The purpose of this chapter is to analyse the various developments and issues relating to the increase in institutional activity in the European industry; both on the supply and buy sides. In this chapter we shall look at:

- an overview of the European industry;
- the regulatory environment;
- current investor and media perceptions;
- the institutions' requirements for investments;
- the range of companies and institutions currently allocating to hedge funds;
- advantages and disadvantages;
- the institutions' allocation process;
- the due diligence process;
- fee structures;
- future developments; and
- the conclusion, including projected growth.

An industry overview

Estimated assets within the global hedge fund industry at the end of 2002 were approximately US$600 billion (according to HFR, Inc[4]), although this figure varies according to different sources. As Exhibit 19.1 attests, the industry has seen a steady growth in the last 12 years.

Likewise, the number of funds within the industry is commonly estimated at about 6,000. The growth in fund numbers increased rapidly, particularly after 1998, although this growth slowed in 2001–02.

'Hedge funds' is a term which covers a broad range of skill-based investment strategies that attempt to generate positive returns regardless of market direction. For this reason, it is, perhaps, more appropriate to refer to them as alternative investment strategies. They are not traditional (long only) as they have the ability to go short. However, they can be long or short-biased and, thus, may not be fully hedged. It is best to consider these funds as an important source of diversification for any traditional portfolio.

Ideally, hedge funds should focus on generating returns primarily from disciplined investment management processes based on investment skills, and not from asset class exposure. They should use rigorous risk controls and generate returns that exhibit low correlations with traditional asset classes. Due also to their low correlations with equity returns, these funds tend to perform well relative to equity returns in adverse market environments, as shown in Exhibit 19.2.

According to *EuroHedge*[5] in January 2003, European hedge fund managers were managing 181 funds comprising total assets of US$8,813 million (see Exhibit 19.3).

In the past, the 'traditional' hedge fund investor was the private investor/family office. This has been changing considerably in recent years. Institutional investors have become aware of the benefits of hedge funds as they seek diversification within their portfolios. This became a pressing necessity as the bear market unfolded in 2000–02. Assets and returns of traditional fund managers and pension funds, for example, fell to dangerously low levels. The institution's fiduciary responsibilities require it to consider all investment possibilities in

Exhibit 19.1

Growth in global hedge fund assets, 1990–2002 (US$ billion)

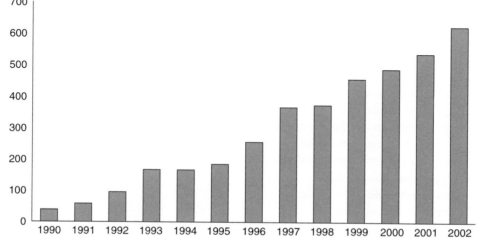

Source: HFR, Inc.

Exhibit 19.2

Traditional and hedge fund index performance, 2000–02 (%)

Benchmarks	2002	2001	2000	Three-year bear market
MSCI World $	−19.5	−16.5	−12.9	−49.0
S&P 500	−22.1	−11.9	−9.1	−43.1
CSFB Tremont Index	3.0	4.4	5.2	12.6
*European manager data:**				
European long-short $	2.3	3.0	18.7	9.8
European long-short £	5.8	14.4	5.9	20.8
European long-short €	2.5	2.8	16.1	9.5
Macro $	4.9	5.7	8.7	20.7
Fixed-income $	8.9	7.5	17.1	35.1
Global equity $	0.1	0.2	15.7	0.8
Managed futures	14.0	8.0	12.5	39.7
Combined arbitrage, of which:	3.4	9.6	20.3	32.8
Event-driven $	1.9	5.9	19.1	24.6
Mixed arbitrage	2.6	13.0	21.4	36.3
Stat & quant arb	2.1	6.4	23.8	29.0
Convertibles	6.1	13.5	19.1	40.3

* *EuroHedge*, January 2003 (data used for three-year bear market covers the period March 2000 to March 2003).

Note: all figures rounded to closest tenths.

Sources: EuroHedge; CSFB/Tremont (www.hedgeindex.com).

Exhibit 19.3

An overview of European hedge fund managers' funds and assets, January 2003

Type of fund	Number of funds		Total assets (US$ million)	
European long-short		47		2,367
Global equity*		22		977
Arbitrage, of which:		55		2,344
Event-driven	10		647	
Convertibles	12		558	
Mixed arbitrage	14		617	
Stat & quant	19		522	
Macro		20		696
Fixed-income		16		1,814
Emerging markets/Asia		17		508
Other, of which:		4		107
Distressed securities	2		55	
Global multi-strategy	2		52	
Total		**181**		**8,813**

* Including four US long-short equity funds.

Source: EuroHedge.

order that it meets its performance objectives. If one considers the performances of the traditional indices shown in Exhibit 19.2 as a guide to the traditional portfolio's fall, it is easy to understand the move to more active and less correlated performance.

The extensive range of strategies available within this sector fulfils different objectives for different investors. For example, conservative investors may find the 'market-neutral' fund attractive, as it aims to add value and returns through active management while reducing risk through being both long and short securities in certain industry sectors or geographical areas. Of course, nothing is guaranteed though this can seem more attractive as an introduction to hedge funds compared with the short seller who employs a technique that anticipates price decline on borrowed securities (a strategy that has proven its worth in the bear market but may not fare too well when we return to a bull market). The main strategies and their characteristics are described later.

Institutional investors include insurance companies, reinsurance companies, banks, corporate pension funds, private pension funds, public pension funds, endowments and foundations. Increasingly, such groups have reached a degree of understanding, developed over a lengthy period of time, in which they have attained a level of comfort in the sector. The US market has been at the forefront of investment and an increasing number of European institutions have issued mandates in the last couple of years, such as AP7 (one of the Swedish state-owned pension funds), which has allocated to one fund of funds in Europe and one in the United States. Recent private comment to AIMA by pension funds investing a percentage (minimum 5 per cent) in alternative investment strategies states that their overall portfolio returns are still negative but by single digits as opposed to many of their peers who are still showing negative figures in high double digits. In the market environment of 2003, with the political pressures in many countries forcing urgent consideration of reforms for pension funds particularly, there is a fundamentally sound case for the revision of investment parameters to move from passive to active, from long-only to long-short and other alternative investment strategies.

In Europe, we have seen some institutions make investments in hedge funds in multiple ways. For example, there are two European pension funds that allocate directly to hedge funds. One, if not both, run hedge fund strategies internally and they also have a joint venture which offers fund management services to other parties and, finally, they each offer stock lending capabilities to other parties. Hedge funds have the ability to go long and short and pay a fee for this service.

The income streams comprise returns from internally managed portfolios, returns generated from investments in external hedge funds/funds of hedge funds and fees from stock loan. While these entities are at the cutting edge, there are other institutions around the world that have employed these types of income generation for some time.

On the supply side, institutions such as AXA have developed their asset management services in this arena. Investment banks such as Deutsche Bank, HSBC, Merrill Lynch and Citigroup have highly developed asset management groups structuring and distributing hedge fund and fund of funds products to retail and institutional investors not only in Europe but globally.

Regulatory environment

Fund management companies and/or funds are regulated in certain jurisdictions throughout Europe. The following is a simple overview and should not be relied upon as legal advice.

In France, at present it is not permitted to market offshore funds without authorisation from the Commission des Opérations de Bourse (COB) and/or the Ministry of Finance; a fund domiciled in an OECD jurisdiction requires approval from the COB and a non-OECD domiciled fund requires Ministry approval. To date, no offshore fund has obtained authorisation. European Union funds do not require the Ministry's approval. The COB has recently issued new regulations permitting the marketing of foreign funds in France and introducing a new 'fund of alternative funds', an OPCVM de fonds alternatifs, which may invest up to 100 per cent of its assets in hedge funds. There is a recommended minimum investment subscription of €10,000 in such a fund of alternative funds. Existing or new fund managers will be required to submit a business plan specifying investment in hedge funds to the COB for approval or licensing, respectively; full disclosure will be required. An OPCVM will need to include specific risk warnings in its prospectus. Examples of an appropriate business plan and amendment to a prospectus are shown on the COB website. There are restrictions as to the underlying funds within an OPCVM and those of a fund of alternative funds must be listed on a regulated market (although a standard of simplified OPCVM may invest up to 10 per cent or 50 per cent, respectively, in unlisted funds).

The COB has clarified that, where the prospectus or investment management agreement specifically provides that investment in a hedge fund may be undertaken, an OPCVM or manager will not be regarded as marketing the fund to its investors. However, if a French investment manager were to receive a commission from an underlying fund or its promoter, marketing will be implied (and that would also breach rules as to conflict of interest). A fund of alternative funds must have its marketing plan approved by the COB; its intended distribution channels, advertising and sales training must be detailed. Its target investors should be relatively knowledgeable.

At present, it is not possible to register or run a hedge fund in Germany and promotion of hedge fund products in Germany is not permitted. 'Repackaging' of products (by registering funds in an offshore jurisdiction and operating 'advisory' vehicles from Germany) is possible but the imposition of high taxes means it is not practical. Index-linked certificates are the most favoured structure for retail funds of funds. The government's finance minister announced an effort to create onshore regulation in March 2003 and these are expected to be drafted and approved by early 2004. It is anticipated that some types of alternative investment funds (both domestic and foreign) and retail funds of funds will be permitted in Germany from 2004 with the implementation of European guidelines on investment funds.

In Luxembourg, the Commission de Surveillance du Secteur Financier (CSSF) issued Circular No. 02/80 in December 2002, setting out a new legal and regulatory framework applicable to Luxembourg-domiciled hedge funds and funds of hedge funds, and clarifying rules which apply to Luxembourg domiciled collective investment schemes using alternative investment strategies.

In Ireland, non-UCITS foreign funds may not generally be advertised or marketed in Ireland without approval of the Central Bank of Ireland (CBI). Since December 2002, retail funds of unregulated funds have been permitted by CBI Notice NU 25. Irish Stock Exchange (ISE) listed hedge funds are able to 'passport' into Europe.

Recent tax 'amnesties' granted to Italian investors have led to the growth of hedge fund investment in Italy. However, there are significant tax disincentives for investing in foreign, non-UCITS funds as the increase in NAV of an offshore fund is taxed as income.

In Sweden, a fund manager must be regulated in Sweden. Retail sales may be made, subject to requirements as to transparency and diversification, custody and administration by a Swedish bank.

In the United Kingdom, the Financial Services Authority (FSA) regulates investment management companies, including hedge fund managers. A hedge fund cannot be domiciled in the United Kingdom. All UK hedge fund managers must be authorised and regulated. The United Kingdom adopted the UCITS directive on collective investment schemes in 1985 but unregulated collective investment schemes (as hedge funds generally are termed) may not be advertised in the United Kingdom by an authorised UK-based manager, nor may people in the United Kingdom be invited to participate in such a scheme. The FSA is working with the UK industry, through AIMA, to clarify the existing promotion regime and has issued Consultation Paper 176 on Bundled Brokerage and Soft Commission.

Perceptions

Hedge funds have been perceived in the same light as derivatives: high octane investments and very risky. However, in response to the ever-tightening risk controls demanded by the institutional investor and, more relevantly, the greater knowledge acquired by investors that these strategies can reduce the volatility of the overall portfolio, the professional hedge fund industry has proven its commitment to risk control.

A key element of the misperception of the industry comes down to regulation or the perceived lack of it. In fact, it is important to note that many hedge fund managers are fully regulated. As previously noted, the Financial Services Authority (FSA) in the United Kingdom regulates these managers as any other investment manager. The FSA does not, however, regulate the funds (all of which are offshore, there being no onshore regulation). The fact is that a form of strong regulation exists to ensure that there is a sound business structure. The same applies in most jurisdictions except the United States, where hedge fund managers with 99 or fewer clients may make unregistered, private offerings.

The unrealistic views are slowly being changed, with a growing number of professional financial publications assigning journalists to the hedge fund business. This leads to greater understanding among those who have, in the past, made assumptions based on exaggerated and overly-magnified misperceptions. Yet, there is no denying that hedge funds, like all other investment areas, have experienced their own problems.

There have been notable hedge fund failures in the United States and Japan. In one instance in the United States, there were allegations that performance figures had not been accurately calculated and/or reported and accusations of fraud have been levied. To date, the European industry has experienced few problems of this nature.

Having perceived these investments as 'risky', institutional managers may hesitate to mention hedge funds because it involves perceived career risk. They believe that their careers could be impaired if a) the investor is doing something that other investors are not, and b) more importantly, the investment choice does not work. Such concerns are diminishing as the number of institutional investors in hedge funds increases.

Institutions are gaining knowledge and experience, thereby transforming their previous perceptions. The media, as ever, tend still to focus on the bad stories rather than the good, although this is changing for the better. AIMA and its membership is actively working on re-educating all parties: media, institutional investors and private investors/family offices.

Investor requirements

Simply, these can be defined as:

- *Returns.* Institutions are increasingly expected to achieve superior total returns compared to their benchmarks, especially as they need to make up for the losses they have experienced in 2000–02. They are looking for specialist managers who can add value by increasing their overall portfolio returns.
- *Liquidity.* When the underlying investments are easily traded, the expectation is that the fund should be more liquid, not less.
- *Diversification.* Low correlation with current investments, if handled correctly, can result in improved portfolio stability and increased returns.
- *Risk management.* Through diversification and non-correlation, overall portfolio risk should be reduced.
- *Transparency.* Many, though not all, hedge funds are able to offer daily portfolio or exposure reports through their administrator or prime broker. In particular, this allows fund of funds managers to create tailor-made risk and return reports for their investors while not revealing positions, thereby keeping both parties satisfied.

Certain types of investors are more likely to invest in hedge funds. For instance, the trustees of endowments, foundations and private pension plans are more likely to have business or investment backgrounds, so they are more likely to understand the investment concept and, perhaps, may have had personal experience with these types of funds. In the case of a public or corporate pension plan, however, the trustees may also comprise individuals without financial backgrounds. No serious fiduciary will permit investment in a complex and/or new investment area if they do not understand it.

Every week, there are more and more reports about institutions investigating or investing in hedge funds. In April 2003,[6] it was reported that the Ontario Teachers Pension Plan, Canada's second largest public pension fund, had increased its exposure to hedge funds (including managed futures and funds of funds) by C$613 million (US$416.8 million) in 2002. While having experienced an overall investment loss of 2 per cent on its C$66.2 billion portfolio, it noted that the loss was significantly reduced due to its exposure to alternative investments.

Other non-European institutions that have announced they are beginning to look at hedge funds include Boeing,[7] Purdue University,[8] Nordson[9] and Sompo Japan Insurance.[10] In Europe, however, the trend has been slower, particularly in the United Kingdom. JP Morgan Fleming Asset Management surveyed 171 large UK pension funds, managing £364 billion (US$575 million) and only 8 per cent have invested in hedge funds. None of the largest 10 currently invests, though 7 per cent say they would definitely invest in the future while 36 per cent have not ruled out the possibility (more than two-thirds of which would use a fund of funds rather than invest directly into underlying hedge funds).[11] Continental European institutions are less conservative, however, with institutions such as ABP, PGGM, Swiss Life, Nestlé and AXA having been involved in the industry for some years.

Education is key for these investors. They are becoming increasingly interested in attending hedge fund industry events (even speaking at them) although the majority still prefer private educational sessions. Within Europe, AIMA has held investor forums and meetings in France, Italy, Switzerland, Spain, Germany, The Netherlands and Sweden in recent

Exhibit 19.4

Descriptive statistics of portfolio performance, 1990–2001

	Average annual return %	Standard deviation	Monthly min. %	Monthly max. %	Sharpe ratio
Portfolio A	10.7	8.1	−6.3	7.4	0.65
Portfolio B	11.4	6.9	−5.9	6.7	0.86

(Portfolio A: 50 per cent US equity, 50 per cent Salomon Bond).

(Portfolio B: 40 per cent US equity, 40 per cent Salomon Bond, 20 per cent EACM).

Source: EACM, Evaluation Associates Index (www.eacm.com).

Exhibit 19.5

Performance in hostile markets (%)

	Sep 2002	Jul 1999 – Sep 1999	Jul 1998 – Aug 1998	Aug 1997	Feb 1994 – Mar 1994
S&P 500	−44.73	−6.24	−15.37	−5.60	−6.96
Specialist credit	7.45	3.93	−5.48	0.86	−0.68
Relative value	14.54	3.23	−1.87	0.91	−0.30
Equity no bias	18.72	4.86	−0.43	1.99	1.00
Equity short bias	78.36	6.56	22.35	1.05	9.34
Equity long bias	−12.87	2.67	−12.44	1.21	−3.21
Directional trading	21.06	1.53	1.94	−1.56	−0.89

Source: Financial Risk Management (2002), utilising FRM indices.

years and provides the investors with complimentary access to its research and other educational and information tools.

Recent research on *Alternative Investments in the Institutional Portfolio*[12] shows that institutions can maximise return potential by allocating between 10 per cent and 20 per cent to alternative investments, including hedge funds. For instance, Exhibit 19.4 shows how the introduction of alternative investments to a portfolio can generate greater returns while reducing risk (standard deviation).

The true measure of hedge funds can be seen in Exhibit 19.5, which shows their performance in relation to long-only portfolios in adverse markets. In nearly every instance, the returns of hedge funds have been marginally negative or notably positive in periods when the S&P 500 declined.

The alternative investment industry, including hedge funds, is careful to mention that past performance is not necessarily indicative of future results. However, the low correlation of hedge funds to long-only funds in recent bear market environments is attractive.

Range of investors

While it is possible to analyse hedge fund demand broadly by type of investor, it is impossible to provide accurate figures on who is investing where. This is due to investors being reluctant to reveal investments in anything other than 'traditional' areas and the hedge funds not wanting to reveal the source of their capital. When the first edition of this book was published in 1996, approximately 70 per cent of hedge fund assets came from high net worth individuals and 30 per cent from institutional investors. Anecdotal evidence indicates that the ratio is now closer to 60/40.

Private banks now consider hedge funds to be an integral part of the asset allocation process for their clients and are, in essence, taking on the role of a fund of funds manager. This is because they will undertake the responsibility of conducting due diligence on all potential managers and have developed the expertise to understand the strategy and monitor all risk elements. While this service was created for internal clients originally, a number of private banks are now offering products externally.

Banks are placing proprietary capital into hedge funds as well as creating their own funds. Today, most large investment banks offer funds of funds and single manager funds, which they sell on to their internal clients as well as to institutional investors and, in some cases, through the independent financial advisor community. With traders leaving proprietary desks, some institutions recognise the value in placing capital with the manager as he starts his new venture. A number of larger hedge fund managers in Europe have been seeded by their previous employers in this way.

Those institutions with long-term investment horizons, such as pension funds, reinsurance companies and endowments, are finding a suitable vehicle in hedge funds which, as stated earlier, have been showing relatively strong returns over recent years. It should be noted that, as with other alternative investments such as managed futures, quality returns can be achieved and it is strongly recommended that an allocation is not withdrawn just because returns have been negative for a couple of months. With many institutions having experience in private equity/venture capital (where lock-ups can be lengthy and the market is illiquid) the concept of hedge fund investment with a long-term view is viable.

Institutional corporate treasurers from companies such as major automobile manufacturers are making allocations. Exact amounts are unknown, due to the secrecy surrounding their investment strategies.

For retail investors outside of Europe, the main investment accumulation centres are the United States, Canada, Japan and the Middle East.

In Europe, we are seeing retail investors in the United Kingdom, France and Germany allocating to hedge funds, although this trend has not taken hold with any great note. This is primarily due to the adverse publicity, regulatory restrictions and lack of understanding surrounding these investments. This limits the appeal of the products to the European retail investor, although, through their other investments (such as pension funds), they may already have limited exposure to hedge funds, albeit unknowingly. In the United Kingdom, institutions such as Deutsche Bank and HSBC have created retail funds of funds structures such as Individual Savings Accounts (ISA). In France, the supermarket, Carrefour, has offered a fund of funds at its outlets, while in Germany, Deutsche Bank launched its retail fund of funds in 2001 and raised in excess of US$1.4 billion.

Venture capital specialists are taking equity stakes in hedge funds. Such relationships are symbiotic as, in some cases, the hedge fund manager may invest in venture capital. A recent development has been the creation of specialist companies whose business model is to take an equity stake in the manager, offer marketing/distribution services and take a percentage of fee income.

Exhibit 19.6

The advantages and disadvantages of hedge funds

Advantages	*Disadvantages*
Diversification across asset classes	High minimum investment levels
Low correlation to world financial markets	Restricted transparency (to current investors only)
Enhance return of total portfolio	Perceived career risk
Reduce risk of total portfolio	
Access to experienced, specialist investment strategies and fund managers	

Source: Author's own.

The final category is the fund of funds. Most existing and potential investors have neither the skill nor infrastructure to make direct investments in hedge funds. The first step is often to allocate to fund of funds managers who have the necessary experience. The manager will allocate to a number of specialist hedge fund managers with varying strategies, thereby diversifying the investment. Diversification assists risk control of the overall portfolio and also deals with the 'career' risk identified earlier.

The advantages and disadvantages of hedge funds

Risk is of great concern to the investor. The perception has been that hedge fund strategies are highly leveraged and volatile and will ultimately negate any positive returns achieved by other investment areas of the portfolio. This perception is changing. Nowadays, investors ask the right questions and do not invest if they are uncomfortable with the strategy or any element of the fund structure, including leverage. In turn, managers have realised that they must demonstrate stringent risk controls in all areas of fund management. The topic of risk management is discussed as much now by the industry as it was by the investor community. Through a careful, extensive due diligence process, the investor can acquire an understanding of a hedge fund's strategy, the company and its employees, and, only then, make an allocation. Specialist risk consultants (for hedge funds specifically) are now in existence (see Exhibit 19.6).

Allocation process

The markets have fallen drastically in recent years, returns and assets have dropped, terrorist activity has led to increased claims, which has led to increased insurance premiums, pension funds are underfunded and some parts of the world are on the edge of recession. Investors have not experienced such pressure for some time. Index-tracking alone generated solid returns in the past to enable portfolios to meet and even exceed their benchmarks. It is imperative that these same institutions take meaningful steps to turn around their faltering portfolios and employ more active management.

There are three parts to the educational process: individual, departmental and institutional. A typical pattern is:

1. Investment officer/department will undertake to investigate product range, either in-house but, more probably, through specialist external consultants. It is more likely that investigation will occur outside the institution, due to the fact that, generally, there is a lack of internal expertise.

2. A good knowledge base has been attained and now a 'champion' emerges at the board level. They may need to be educated or, in such case as the individual who already has personal or business experience with these strategies, he will be in an ideal position to influence strategy decisions.

3. For some of the pension fund community, an integral element of the allocation process is to appoint an actuary or other consultant to develop this knowledge base to a level where an appropriate presentation can be made to the investment board.

4. The investment board then allocates an agreed amount with a set limit, often subject to conditions, such as a maximum percentage allocation, overall level of risk and expected annual returns.

5. Once this is agreed, the investor considers various strategies to decide which will best fit with their objectives.

6. Various managers will be approached. Initial contact with managers is made in many ways: via investment consultants, conferences, media attention, prime brokers, third party marketers and referrals.

7. The due diligence process will then begin.

With specific return objectives set, the investor will have chosen the strategy(ies) that best fit the portfolio. Once an allocation has been made to a fund, most investors will have reasonable access to reporting on positions and returns of each fund (through the administrator or prime broker). Some institutional investors now demand full transparency before investing. If the manager is prepared to provide this information, the norm is for each party then to agree to a format for the provision of aggregate return and risk data that meets the needs of the investor's portfolio. In the past, there were some funds that denied the investor reasonable information, stating only that their track record speaks for itself. These days are past. The vast majority of funds have realised that transparency can attract capital, while opacity may retard the growth of assets under management.

As mentioned earlier, one way in which the institutions invest in hedge funds is through the multi-manager fund or fund of funds. The benefits of this method is that the investor need only undertake due diligence on one manager, leaving the responsibility to the manager to choose the strategies (to meet the investor's requirements) and select the underlying funds. The institution need only put up one minimum investment, instead of one to each manager. This method is highly attractive to institutions and is a logical first step. This method continues to attract institutions as they enter into the alternative investment arena. Once greater knowledge and understanding is acquired, then the institution will consider investing directly into single-manager hedge funds.

In a survey of 376 entities with hedge fund assets totalling more than US$350 billion, conducted by Deutsche Bank,[13] a range of investors (banks, pension funds, endowments/foundations, family offices, funds of funds, insurance companies and others) were asked about their concerns. While allocations into funds of funds are larger than those directly into hedge funds, investors still express concern about fund of funds investing although, as Exhibit 19.7 shows, the trends are positive overall.

Exhibit 19.7

Concerns about investing in funds of funds

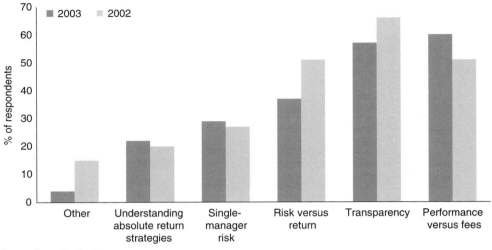

Source: Deutsche Bank.

The argument for funds of funds is diversification of risk and return. The responsibility for due diligence and monitoring is passed from the investor to the manager. It should be noted that there is an increasing number of sector/strategy-specific funds of funds being offered, such as a fund of long-short equity hedge funds. Diversification narrows but can be of more interest to some investors who are only looking for exposure in a particular area.

The fund of funds industry offers structured products. For example (and as referred to earlier), investment banks in Germany and the United Kingdom have created funds of funds within a retail wrapper, such as the Individual Savings Account (ISA) in the United Kingdom.

Others offer capital guaranteed products (closed end) in which a percentage of the assets raised remain in safe securities while the balance is invested in underlying hedge funds. The investor is guaranteed 100 per cent of his investment on redemption. Products have been structured with the focus on principal protection, leverage, tax issues, risk management and other purposes. Thirty one per cent of those surveyed by Deutsche Bank that do not currently invest in structured products plan to do so in the future.

Due diligence

Due diligence is the most important part of the entire allocation process. It can be, indeed should be, an intense operation. Questions that should be posed include asking how much leverage is used, are derivatives used, is the fund spread among different market sectors, has a single transaction accounted for much of the return, and how much of his own money does the manager have in the fund? The key points to thorough manager due diligence for any investor are:

- *Structure.* Including registered activities, regulatory registration and full background on the principals.

- *Performance.* Thorough investigation of past performance, markets traded and maximum capacity.
- *Strategy.* Its principles, trading philosophy, evolution of strategy through increased money under management or other influences.
- *Risk.* How the fund is hedged, the amount of leverage employed and how risk is calculated.
- *Research.* Is there any annual budget and how is research undertaken (through external specialists)?
- *Administration.* Which company is used externally and their controls, management and incentive fees applied, prime broker used and leverage extended on fund, lock-up periods.

A series of seven generic due diligence questionnaires is available on application, and at no charge to institutional investors, from AIMA. The series comprises questionnaires for those selecting the services of: hedge fund managers, futures fund managers, prime brokers and administrators.

The amount of time that due diligence takes varies, though the majority of decisions are taken between one and nine months.

All fund managers will have a disclosure document in which they will outline much of the above. There is no substitute for qualitative due diligence, however. Investors should go to the manager's office, meet the entire manager team, including support staff, to get a feel for the solidity of the company. Many investors underestimate the importance of the fund's counterparties. Enquiries should be made about the fund administrator and prime broker.

Risk management is high on the investor's checklist. It should be acknowledged that it is both the investor's and the manager's responsibility to ensure that they are each aware of the others' investment objectives. The investor is advised to ensure a thorough check if performance drops and no exact explanation can be given (through the administrator or prime broker generated reports on performance, volatility and positions). Risk controls should be undertaken by both parties. The norm is for investors to expect monthly reporting and over 50 per cent of investors review their hedge fund holdings on a monthly basis.[14] The trend is that fund of funds managers require greater transparency than other types of investors. Their clients, mainly institutions, demand agreed upon aggregate portfolio data, specifically: risk monitoring, strategy drift monitoring, sector concentration, leverage and cross-ownership.

There is a demand among hedge fund service providers (particularly fund administrators) to offer a variety of other services. It is common practice in Europe that all fund managers with offshore funds will employ third party administrators, specifically separate entities. The administrator, who is responsible to the client (not the fund), thus prepares the net asset value (NAV) of the fund using details of all transactions within a defined period. With access to the fund portfolio, investors are beginning to ask for further services from the administrator, such as risk reporting, aggregate risk calculations (VaR) and risk monitoring (interpreting risk reports).

Fee structure

The final part of the negotiation is the fee structure. Each of the following institutions takes a fee and, in the case of a fund of funds, an incremental layer is added.

- Hedge fund manager.

- Administrator (registers fund; issues shares; does legal and tax work; calculates fees, reports to manager and investor).
- Custodian (assumes receipt and payment obligations for subscriptions and redemptions; monitors brokers).
- Prime broker (settles and clears trades; reports to manager and, if required, investor; stock lending and risk management).

The standard method of manager recompense is through a management fee and incentive or performance fee. There is no exact formula for this as it is entirely at the discretion of the manager and agreement of the investor. However, an average for a hedge fund manager would be a 1–2 per cent annual management fee plus a 15–20 per cent performance fee on all positive returns, calculated annually, quarterly, or monthly by agreement. Fees are based on the NAV of the fund or on the NAV per share. The fund of funds manager may add an average 1 per cent management and 10 per cent performance fee.

There is some discontent amongst investors with regard to the performance fee as it allows the manager to benefit with investor returns, but lose nothing with investor losses. Investors now look for manager investment in the fund and high water marks.

Also, it can be unfair for the investor who joins the fund mid-term following a successful period only for profit to be lost before the next calculation date: the investor is paying a fee for negative performance on the overall fund. The perfect equalisation policy would achieve the following:

- the investor pays a performance fee directly related to the performance of his investment;
- he would bear the same capital risk per share as all other investors;
- the NAV per share would be the same for all shares;
- the NAV would accurately reflect the fund's performance; and
- the arrangements would be easily understood by the investor.

Experienced investors are setting their own fees, although for some of Europe's larger, experienced and successful hedge fund managers, this does not happen. For those at the top of the performance tables (for a sustained period of time) moves have already been made to increase fees for new and existing investors. The purpose is to ensure committed investors support the company's infrastructure in difficult markets.

In the first quarter of 2003, we are beginning to see the effects of this fee structure. Hedge fund managers, particularly, have established their businesses and costs on the premise that they will perform above the benchmark set with their investors. While many have performed well in the bear market, some have not met their benchmark and thus are funding the company and fund on the management fee only, and not the performance fee as well. Several hedge fund manager and fund closures have begun. Smaller specialists are closing, also. Positive performance but low assets means a much smaller steady income for the manager. Anecdotal comment puts the expected attrition figure for Europe during 2003 at up to 15 per cent of all managers.

The future

A recent hedge fund financial risk management survey by KPMG[15] found that industry practitioners believe transparency to remain one of the most significant challenges in regard to risk management, although it can be dependent on strategy. KPMG surveyed European hedge fund and fund of hedge fund managers with combined assets of €39 billion and Luxembourg hedge fund administrators with combined related assets under administration of €23.7 billion. Related to this is the regularity, depth and accuracy of NAVs provided. For example, the ability to take daily and weekly statements by many underlying funds (particularly those trading exchange-listed products) means that hedge fund managers appear to have more comprehensive risk management tools relative to their fund of funds colleagues. Together with risk management issues such as liquidity, underperformance, style drift and credit risk, transparency is a key issue for the industry.

Assets will continue to climb, although there has been a marked slowdown at the beginning of 2003. If hedge funds perform negatively, they may not be seen as fulfilling their portfolio diversification role, thus assets are redeemed. Ironically though understandably, even if they perform well they may see redemptions due to investor losses sustained in their traditional portfolios. Investors, particularly institutions, are underfunded. While seeking to minimise losses through alternative investments, their needs are immediate thus they redeem and go to cash.

In Europe, we will see a number of manager closures due to lack of assets and poor performance, though the great majority of funds are expected to prove their worth, survive the market and increase assets due to the attrition of others and their positive returns. There will be consolidation as well as some managers returning to an institutional environment, remaining focused on trading and not on running a business.

Regulations will continue to be clarified and refined. AIMA works both formally and informally with key regulators across the continent to enhance existing regulation. Opportunities for establishing product and distribution are expected to increase in France and Germany in 2004.

A greater focus on asset pricing practices and NAV calculation will be seen by both investors and the industry. In-depth research and *A Guide to Sound Practices for Hedge Fund Administrators* are due out in late 2003.

Education will and must increase. There are still investors and their advisers who remain unclear on the specifics of the hedge fund industry. Key topics will continue to be addressed both through research and more practical developments.

---

[1] The author would like to offer special thanks to Emma Mugridge, AIMA Director, for her invaluable contribution to this chapter.

[2] AIMA's *Series of Seven Due Diligence Questionnaires* is available to its member companies and institutional investors only, on application.

[3] Chartered Alternative Investment Analyst (CAIA): www.caia.org.

[4] Hedge Fund Research, Inc: www.hfr.com.

[5] *EuroHedge*, January 2003 (www.hedgefundintelligence.com).

[6] 'Hedge fund exposure grows at Ontario Teachers; deficit seen', 2 April 2003, *Infovest21* (www.infovest21.com).

[7] 'Boeing pension group explores hedge funds; lowers expectations', 1 April 2003, *Infovest21*.

[8] 'Purdue University considering boosting hedge fund exposure', 21 March 2003, *Infovest21*.

[9] 'Nordon considering possible hedge fund allocations', 17 March 2003, *Infovest21*.

[10] 'Sompo Japan Insurance to consider alternatives', 14 March 2003, *Infovest21*.

[11] 'UK pension funds continue to be cautious about hedge funds', 1 April 2003, *Infovest21*.

[12] *Alternative Investments in the Institutional Portfolio* commissioned by AIMA, T. Schneeweis/V. Karavas/ G. Georgiev, CISDM, University of Massachusetts (2002).

[13] 'Alternative Investment Survey Results: Part 2 – Inside the Mind of the Hedge Fund Investor'. March 2003. (capital.introduction@db.com).

[14] 2003 Deutsche Bank Alternative Investment Survey.

[15] 'Hedge Fund Financial Risk Management Survey', KPMG (2003).

Chapter 20

Hedge funds in Asia

Peter Douglas[1]
GFIA Pte Ltd, Singapore
AIMA Council Member (Singapore) (Alternative Investment Management
Association)

Introduction

Asia's core attraction to global allocators is that there are some world class managers who typically still have capacity. Cyclicality, renewed investment interest in Asia and resulting liquidity flows are rapidly increasing demand and, to a certain extent, supply.

Allocating to a hedge fund manager is the result of a search for talent allied with capacity, and this is no different in Asia. However, global allocators looking to managers in Asia will find some different characteristics, some driven by the youth of the industry, some by the nature of the underlying capital markets and some cultural.

Intention of this chapter

This chapter provides an overview of the industry in Asia, primarily for the benefit of potential allocators. While I have tried to include hard data, reporting schedules and a very rapidly developing industry mean that the numbers will inevitably be out of date by the time you read this; qualitative comment is of far more commercial value. I have therefore tried to provide as much qualitative colour to the picture as possible, and have emphasised the commercially useful over the statistically perfect wherever possible.

Information is attributed wherever appropriate. Otherwise, opinions and observations are my own and not necessarily those of the Alternative Investment Management Association (AIMA) or of GFIA Pte Ltd.

Overview

Global allocators are beginning to review the universe of hedge fund managers in Asia more seriously, and are beginning to allocate capital to take advantage of quality managers, even as some of the more directional capital leaves the region.

The fastest growing source of new members for the Alternative Investment Management Association (AIMA is the industry body for the hedge fund industry) is Asia, with 21 per cent of global membership in the region as of 2003.

A survey at the beginning of 2003 suggested that global allocators had the order of 2.5 per cent of their assets in Asian strategies, and their intention in aggregate was to increase this over a six-month period by 44 per cent.[2] Even if the actual rate of growth does not match that

Exhibit 20.1

Average assets under management by manager location

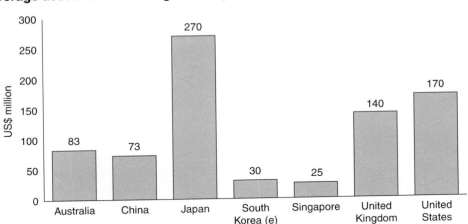

Note: (i) Australia is heavily skewed by two managers – median size is probably comparable with Singapore; (ii) China includes Hong Kong; (iii) total excludes offshore-domiciled managers.
Source: AsiaHedge, April 2003, except South Korea estimate, GFIA April 2003.

intention (and in the first half of 2003, *AsiaHedge,* the journal for the Asian hedge fund industry, reports that aggregate assets only increased by 6 per cent), there is no doubt that Asia is rapidly becoming an inescapable part of the hedge fund world.

According to Eurekahedge, a Singapore-based specialist hedge fund broker, there are 330 Asian hedge funds, including Japan and Australia, in 2003, which is an increase of 14 per cent in six months.

If we slice this to include only funds with US$50 million or more under management and at least a 12-month history, we arrive at a universe of 53 funds. Looking at the numbers slightly differently, *AsiaHedge* estimates that 35 per cent of management groups had less than US$50 million of assets under management (see Exhibit 20.1).

Research conducted by GFIA, an independent researcher of Asian hedge funds, suggests that there are some smaller and newer funds that, qualitatively, deserve serious attention (sometimes because they are spawned by an already stable organisation), and that the universe of funds that might pass an initial screen by a fiduciary investor would approach 100.

Applying a rough and ready 80:20 rule to these numbers, we could assume that about 20 would at any one time be appropriate for serious consideration. While this is a small absolute number, it is probably about the same ratio of total funds to quality candidates as the hedge fund universe in either the United States or Europe, and it is certainly a large enough universe to keep an analyst busy full-time. However, the geographic dispersion (see Exhibit 20.2) of the managers' locations means that, although first-level screening can arguably be done anywhere in the world, qualitative due diligence, including building trust and confidence with a manager, can be tough for allocators without a physical presence in the region.

When I first started researching Asian hedge funds in 1998, a common complaint was that, with no more than one or two exceptions, they were mostly aggressive mutual funds with a performance fee. While I do not think that was ever a totally fair criticism, it is

Exhibit 20.2

Location of decision maker

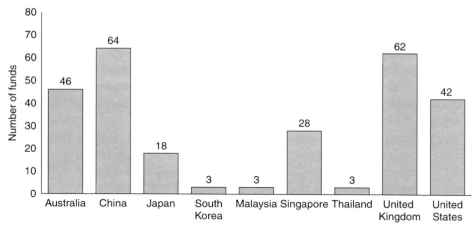

Note: (i) Many Japanese managers are domiciled offshore and the total for Japan therefore understates the number of Japan-based strategies; (ii) China includes Hong Kong; (iii) total excludes offshore-domiciled managers. *Source:* Eurekahedge, September 2003.

true that the universe was initially dominated by fundamentally driven, long-biased, directional long-short equity managers (see Exhibit 20.3). Some of the early Asian hedge funds were unashamedly chasing the highest returns possible from equity implementation of macro-type thematic bets.

There is still a predominance of equity long-short managers, and the majority of those are still broadly Jones-model managers who may do best in sideways or rising markets. However, within the catch-all category of equity long-short, there are single-country, sector-specific, model-driven, trading and other niche strategies as well as, of course, a huge divergence of manager styles. Recently – and understandably in a liquidity-driven bull market – many equity managers have become significantly directional and increased market exposure.

Intuitively, managers based in the region should have better access to information and therefore better performance, but there is no hard research to suggest this is the case. There are some powerful Asian strategies run from London, New York, and other locations ex-Asia. The manager breakdown by location broadly is as follows.

Japan has some large managers, aided by the (relative) liquidity of the stock market and availability of stock borrow. Given that the restructuring of Japan is being emphasised at the micro level (even if by default due to the lack of restructuring at the macro level), it is not surprising that equity long-short is the dominant strategy. Most Japan managers have a dual office structure, with an onshore and an offshore base, driven by tax considerations. Many in fact have no, or a token presence, onshore, with London, Singapore and Sydney being popular locations. Interestingly, the indigenous managers are now gaining some visibility, with two of the largest locally run funds being around US$1 billion of assets. An increasing number of Japanese financial institutions have set up internal hedge fund management operations. GFIA expects to see more local Japanese managers gain visibility over the next 12 months. There is also some fund of funds presence in Tokyo.

Exhibit 20.3

Strategies of Asian managers

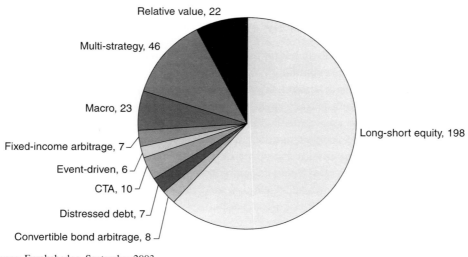

Source: Eurekahedge, September 2003.

Hong Kong has a substantial industry, aided by the relative depth of the conventional money management industry there. The majority of Hong Kong funds are therefore equity long-short, with a smaller number of successful fixed-income and relative value players. There are a couple of global funds of funds with local presence, and at least four indigenous fund of fund groups. As the world slowly comes to terms with the awesome reality (no longer do we talk of 'potential') of the Chinese economy, demand for strategies that understand China is increasing, and that expertise is, typically, concentrated in Hong Kong.

Singapore has a newer and relatively small industry (although numbers of managers are on a par with Hong Kong), but is demonstrating a couple of niches in Japan strategies, and relative value and other non-equity strategies (driven by the number of banks that have proprietary trading centred in Singapore, as a key source of management talent). A small number of global funds of funds have some representation in the Republic. Singapore's core strength is that for senior professionals it offers a more comfortable quality of life than any other investment centre in the time zone outside Australia; furthermore the regulatory environment is extremely friendly to boutique operations.

Australia has a vibrant hedge fund industry, stimulated significantly by the growing tendency of local institutions to make allocations to alternatives – more than 30 retirement funds now have explicit allocations to hedged products, and both the number and volume of assets committed is growing rapidly. Many managers are however very small, but the top half a dozen are receiving meaningful allocations from global managers and there are at least two billion-dollar managers in Australia. Strategies represented are an eclectic mix, including domestic, regional and Japanese strategies.

The Asian capital markets still limit opportunities for event-driven managers, statistical arbitrage traders, and pure market-neutral players, though there are examples of all these types within the industry. However, in the search for talent and capacity, there is enough here to keep the global allocator interested.

Appetite for capital

In 2002, 66 new hedge funds started in Asia, raising an aggregate US$1.7 billion.[3] That is an increase of over 30 per cent in the number of funds, with an average of US$25 million per launch (though the median would be significantly lower than this). The picture for 2003, at the time of writing, is accelerating, with 80 new funds launched so far, including 21 with more than US$10 million. Subjectively it feels as if the typical quality of start-up is improving, partly as the footprints of those who have gone before help newcomers avoid mistakes, and partly as financial institutions are now shedding real muscle into the market place, with star professionals looking for second careers. Furthermore, as more and more seasoned allocators trawl Asia for talent, managers are exposed to global competition and a global standard of organisational competence.

As shown in Exhibit 20.4, the typical Asian hedge fund is still a small business. Sixty-three per cent of Asian hedge funds have less than US$50 million under management (although the same may be substantially true for the US industry). *AsiaHedge* calculate that the five largest funds in the region control 26 per cent of the assets, though that concentration has been weakening over the last year as the industry deepens.

Doing some 'quick and dirty' math, the majority of Asian managers probably generate less than US$1 million per year in revenues, for a business that needs at minimum two or three highly experienced financial professionals, and usually must service an international client base. One-third of funds have less than US$10 million under management and of these 46 per cent have been in business for over a year, and still have less than US$10 million of assets. That is a great deal of personal commitment for the managers running those strategies.

Even in the United States and Europe, many start-ups struggle to achieve critical mass. However, in Asia even managers who bring significant credibility to a new operation can find it difficult to achieve scale quickly. There are several reasons for this.

Exhibit 20.4

Assets under management by fund

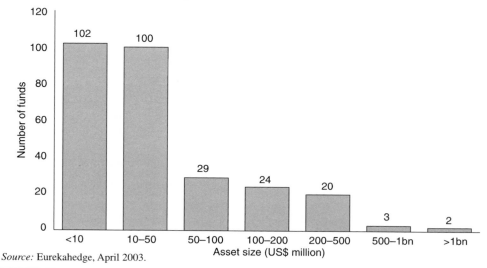

Source: Eurekahedge, April 2003.

First, the industry is young. Only a few more than 100 funds have been running for more than three years (and only 50 or so for more than five years) and therefore the supply of graduates carrying with them a track record and reputation from existing firms, is limited. Ultimately, the industry will of course outgrow this constraint, but for now, constraint it is. Asia is not a conventional lifestyle destination for professionals leaving careers in the United States and Europe to resettle, so apart from a few hedonists in Singapore and Sydney, few experienced professionals choose to relocate to Asia from elsewhere. Consequently, in Asia talent typically is new to the hedge fund industry, usually from long-only asset management houses, or proprietary trading, with the learning curves widely associated with those career paths, and resulting hesitation on the part of allocators to invest at the inception of a new strategy. One of the implications for an allocator is that the organisation needs to show a good learning feedback loop (often an excellent manager new to the industry will produce the best returns after 12–18 months running a hedge fund, when he or she has learned the hardest lessons). Allocators need to be sensitive to where in the learning cycle the manager is.

Secondly, many allocators are unfamiliar with the capital markets in Asia, and therefore are less comfortable with strategies in this area. The nature of the markets here has some implications for the industry, too.

Regulatory environment

This is unsurprisingly a short section. Most hedge funds, including those in Asia, are structured as offshore funds in lightly regulated jurisdictions, although the manager may often be located in a recognised financial centre with a good level of financial regulation. Furthermore, to date, most Asian allocators and investors have preferred to invest in such structures. A long discussion of regulations would be fruitless, with the exception of some comment about the appearance of regulated retail-oriented products, which are feasible, though arguably not that important yet, in several jurisdictions.

The industry in Asia typically offers Cayman structures, US limited partnerships and separate accounts. Global allocators face few regulatory hurdles. In most cases, allocators need only confirm as part of their organisational due diligence process that the onshore management company is appropriately regulated and licensed (their counterparty risk will be with a type of structure with which they are very familiar).

Some managers in some jurisdictions (Australia and Japan) offer domestic funds for local investors who find offshore structures difficult to utilise for tax or other reasons.

Australia, Hong Kong, Japan and Singapore all allow retail offerings of hedged products. The requirements in each jurisdiction differ, and as always the commercial realities of distribution and demand will dictate whether a manager wishes to offer product to local retail markets and whether therefore the cost of a domestic structure is warranted. To date, only Japan has seen significant retail demand, with Australia making some headway. In Hong Kong and Singapore, retail demand for onshore products has been slow to appear.

Characteristics specific to Asian strategies

Asia is not a single market. Depending on their strategy, managers may focus on one single market, a small handful of the friendliest, or 14 different markets (the number of markets included in the widely used MSCI indices). Geographically, remember that after your 13-hour flight from London (or your epic multi-hop trek from Chicago, losing a day of your life in the process) to Singapore, the geographic centre of the region, you still have a seven-hour flight to Tokyo or Seoul, a four-hour flight to Hong Kong, a five-hour flight to Shanghai and a seven-hour flight to Sydney. Although almost all financial professionals speak English, you will have to negotiate taxi drivers speaking in a host of languages you do not understand and a different currency in each country. Best not to forget whether you should be thinking of Christian, Buddhist, Hindu, Muslim, or a host of other country-specific holidays (such as respect for the Aged Day, International Women's Working Day and Picnic Day) when you're planning your itinerary.

All the Asian markets have different characteristics, in terms of the sectors represented, trading patterns, liquidity, and importantly, availability, cost and convenience of stock borrow. This of course creates arbitrage and diversification opportunities, but the dictum that 'in a bear market the only thing that goes up is correlation' is as true of public equity in the region as any other asset class globally.

Compared with developed markets, there is less corporate activity in public markets (and therefore few event-driven strategies), but there is a resilient and sustainable supply of distressed paper; typically thin fixed-income markets but, from high-quality issuers, a fairly high-quality supply of convertible bonds; and some large, but very inefficient, derivatives markets. The opportunity set is coloured differently in Asia.

Liquidity is a rapidly moving target, meaning that accurate hedging is often either difficult or expensive, or both (market neutral is at best a target, not a measurable result, in Asia). Gap risk can be high, and the clever arbitrage strategies have a habit of exhibiting nasty 'tails' from time to time. Allocators must demand higher returns to compensate for these risks.

To ensure a supply of consistently profitable trades, a large proportion of managers are multi-strategy in fact if not in name. This can be difficult for allocators who both prefer a clear definition, or use quantitative optimisation models that work best with clean strategies. Moreover, allocators need to differentiate between style drift and perfectly legitimate changes in capital allocation within a fund. This is partly because Asia is (is always?) in transition, and that is also true of its capital markets. What might be a red light elsewhere in the world may be pragmatic in Asia. One of the better Japan long-short equity managers, for example, says 'I would much prefer to do my research, find my Microsoft, and run it for several market cycles, and when it's right to do that, I will, but over the last few years market conditions have dictated that I trade', and he does, sometimes moving net long to net short and back within a month (and by doing so has annualised over 10 per cent a year since inception three years ago). Will I still back him when he finds his Microsoft, despite the dramatic strategy shift this will entail? In principle, yes, as his strategy will very much follow his deep understanding of the market structure, which is what he is paid for.

Asian hedge fund shops are, broadly, split into those run by western, or western-minded managers, and indigenous local managers. Cultural differences can be overstated (at the end of the day, capitalism is capitalism). However, I would make a couple of comments (necessarily general, remember, Asia is not homogenous). First, in most Asian countries, going independent is considered a one-way street, with no way back into conventional employment. That is an extra disincentive (and, conversely, an extra badge of courage) for Asian managers to set up. A number of really good managers in the region do not have the polished marketing presence of the established hedge funds in Mayfair or Manhattan. Although a good allocator will see through the polish or lack of it, it is a hindrance to rapid growth. Finally, many

Asian business people have a culture of control, both of people and of cash. Many indigenous firms are characterised by a hierarchy that feels odd to an allocator used to looking at a more collegiate organisation, and many are frankly under-resourced in terms of numbers and calibre of support (and sometimes investment) staff, in the interests of cash conservation. I spend a great deal more of my time than my peers elsewhere in the world understanding organisational risk (it is a key defining success factor in allocating to Asian hedge funds).

An advantage, however, is the very real manager diversification between indigenous and foreign managers. One of the very good Japan long-short managers I track, owned and managed by local professionals, typically has negative or very low correlations with its foreigner-operated peer group that cover a similar universe of stocks in superficially very similar strategies. The demonstrable quantitative difference is explained definitively by very cultural, qualitative differences in the mindset of the professionals in the business.

Allocators do need to spend more time on their Asian managers, and this, with the double whammy of distance (awkward time zones, long flights and infrequent face-to-face contact) slows the rate of investment.

The silver lining, and this is a big one, is that most Asian managers have capacity. Although we're beginning to see some strains amongst the better known Japanese specialists, there remain several world class pure Japan managers with capacity. In the Asia ex-Japan space, although good managers are beginning to reach capacity, only a few are closed to new capital. This window is closing rapidly, however, and every week I receive another note from a manager who is closing to new investors. The capacity window in Asia is still open, but it is imminently shutting as it has elsewhere in the world.

Managers do go out of business, and about 30 funds have left the universe during 2003 to date (about 10 per cent of the universe, comparable to or even slightly lower than other regions). Although the rationale for closing is not always publicised, the list mostly comprises funds that were consistently too small to be profitable. I can only spot two 'accidents' among them, and neither were widely held.

A typical equity long-short manager in Japan would have capacity of perhaps US$500 million, and in Asia ex-Japan, maybe US$200 million. Liquidity has been increasing, but underlying capacity is rising more slowly due to constraints on short availability, the need to apply leverage and an increased number of market participants. There are more than 70 Japan long-short funds that have assets of less than US$500 million (of which, from experience, at least 30 would warrant some interest from a fiduciary investor); in Asia ex-Japan, 42 funds have less than US$200 million, and the same empirical screen yields another 30 or so of interest to the professional investor.[4]

Adding all this up, GFIA estimates that currently the good managers in the region still have an aggregate capacity somewhere between US$5 billion and US$9 billion. Given that in the first half of 2003 market liquidity has been imploding and we may be at a cyclical low in market capacity, this capacity is likely to increase. In terms of sourcing good capacity, allocators focusing exclusively on the United States and Europe are missing a large part of the potential universe.

Allocators that are prepared to do the work have a window of opportunity to find high quality talent, in strategies that may well have little correlation to their existing holdings (and actually find that the manager is happy to take their money).

A final implication of the lack of capital in Asia is that, generally, information flows are good, as managers realise they must be flexible to woo investors. However, I am beginning to see a little more reticence at the margin – again, Asian managers are importing the standards of managers in more developed jurisdictions. For example, a specialist Asian fund of funds I worked with obtained ongoing full position disclosure from all but one of the equity managers in its portfolio. I switched capital from a US-based fund to a very similar strategy based in Hong Kong (with similar quant characteristics but about half the capital) purely because the information flow from the Midtown-mafia manager was always late, thin and inflexible, while the Asian manager was happy to provide virtually any information I needed, immediately. This is an extreme example but not untypical.

Asian appetite for hedged products

Across the region, the major private banks have been active for many years selling hedged products (largely funds of funds) to wealthy families and individuals. Since 2000, this product push has reached down to the priority banking level, so the middle class professional with a few hundred thousand dollars in the bank has typically already been exposed to hedged, and in particular, fund of fund products. As always with the private banking industry, hard numbers are not available but sales are reported to be substantial. This may partially explain why the response to retail funds of funds has been weak (much of the demand has been satisfied already).

Some funds of funds groups (such as MAN group, Charles Schmitt in Hong Kong and Quadriga) have packaged their products successfully to appeal to a wider spectrum of distribution such as independent financial advisers (IFAs) and stockbrokers.

While demand from private banking clients across the region appears broadly homogenous at the institutional and fiduciary investor level, the region exhibits diverse characteristics.

Japan accounts for approximately 10 per cent of global demand for funds of hedge funds,[5] and much of this has been from long-term investing institutions such as life assurance companies (this group alone is estimated to have invested US$9 billion)[6] and banks (US$4.5 billion).[7] Many of Japan's institutional investors have been exposed to the industry since the early to mid-1990s and are now among the world's more sophisticated allocators.

Hong Kong has a number of sophisticated family offices who are very familiar with hedged assets. Generally, however, Asian family offices are relatively unsophisticated in allocating to alternatives, and have smaller amounts of liquid assets than their US or European counterparts as typically they are managing excess liquidity of a family business and not the proceeds of the sale of a business. At least two major fiduciary investing institutions have made allocations to hedge funds, advised by traditional asset consultants as part of a formalised portfolio construction process; in this respect, Hong Kong resembles other institutional markets in Europe and elsewhere. Although the total assets are not large, there is a depth of understanding of hedge fund allocation skills in the territory.

Demand from Singaporean institutions has been muted, though this has been changing and two major public sector institutions have taken the asset class seriously. Reported forthcoming changes in the legislation controlling trustee investments may accelerate allocations from other fiduciary investors here. Family offices here have not yet made concerted strategic allocations.

Australian superannuation funds have been quietly making allocations for two to three years now, and it is estimated that by end-2002 about 25 Australian superannuation funds had allocated, in aggregate, significantly in excess of US$400 million to hedged assets,[8] either through a portfolio of single manager funds or funds of hedge funds. For most of these funds, their current allocation is seen as a test, and the aggregate amount invested could grow quite sharply in the near term. There appears to be at best moderate interest from family offices.

Other Asian markets such as Taiwan and South Korea are making inroads. South Korea in particular looks interesting as at least two major institutional investors have made allocations (in a largely homogenous environment, visible trendsetters can prove a powerful catalyst).

Current environment

One of the themes evident in the Asian hedge fund industry is how the 'alpha from beta' seekers are being replaced by more mainstream allocators. The international money in Asian hedge funds has often been attracted by the Asian growth story. Some managers (in particular some of those located outside the region) have built good businesses riding the waves, but hedge funds are not the best way to ride a liquidity driven bull market. During 2002, and continuing into 2003, there was a gradual erosion of holdings by 'Asiaphile' investors, replaced with allocations from large global allocators who were less impressed with the Asia story than with the simple fact of managers doing the right job, with available capacity. While the number of these allocators is currently small (around 15–20 houses appear to have credible research awareness of the region), both the number of managers on the radar screen, and the number of allocators interested, appear to be growing.

One interesting phenomenon of the last few months, as Asian markets have raced ahead, is that dedicated hedge fund allocators have been including absolute return long-only equity managers in their searches.

Despite the second half of 2002 being treacherous as markets were buffeted by global events and, especially in Japan, domestic distortions, managers generated positive returns for their investors. The ABN Amro Eurekahedge index returned a creditable 4.4 per cent in 2002, and annualised at about 8.8 per cent since its inception in January 2000. Asian equity remains very cheap though arguably some weaker issues have been swept up in the rush and are no longer good value, and credit is strong. More managers are beginning to use their balance sheets aggressively and, in aggregate, manager volatility will increase, and the risk of accidents with it. Some of the arbitrage strategies are finding life difficult as hedging remains expensive. The increasing supply of stock borrow is matched by increased demand, and, while liquidity is currently good, it is never a given in Asia and gap risk always remains. The consistent performers currently include distressed debt strategies (where continued supply suggests returns may be sustainable), and fixed income, where a dearth of players ensure consistent opportunities. The more aggressive long-short managers have of course been performing strongly in 2003. The better traders continue to do well, though some of the more fundamentally driven managers have been proven right in recent months. In Japan, the micro restructuring argument supporting allocations to long-short strategies remains as strong as ever; foreigners are buying and liquidity is picking up.

A number of managers have reshaped their strategies in reaction to recent market conditions. Some have widened their universe (Japan managers beginning to add Korea, for example). Some are emphasising trading, as I've discussed. Many new start-ups have focused on non-equity sectors of the capital markets.

Future developments

I can see no reason why the number of managers in the region should not continue to grow at a net 25 per cent per year or more. As the capital market industry continues to change, increasing numbers of competent managers will seek to build independent businesses.

Aggregate capacity is currently sufficient to meet demand, though we are beginning to see the better managers move to soft closing (where they are selective about what capital they accept, to preserve capacity for preferred investors), with several hard closing and declining any new capital. Once this point is reached, however, Asia will experience similar capacity constraints as elsewhere in the world.

Increasingly, global allocators will have to include Asia in their universe (not to do so would mean excluding an increasingly meaningful slice of the global opportunity set).

In summary, the inefficiencies in Asian capital and information markets can create good returns and, in the near term, these returns are being amplified by good market liquidity. Investors should expect both returns and volatilities to be higher, strategy by strategy, in Asia than in a developed market. However, the universe of Asian managers is less and less directional, and increasingly able to capture returns from a wider range of opportunity sets.

[1] The author would like to thank Paul Storey, editor of *AsiaHedge*, for his comments, suggestions and contribution to the scope of this chapter, and Eurekahedge for access to their database. Low Jeng-Tek, research assistant, and Enio Shinuhara, MBA participant, both of INSEAD, contributed significantly to the revision of this chapter.

[2] *Source:* Deutsche Bank, *Alternative Investment Survey,* 2003.

[3] *Source:* Bank of Bermuda.

[4] All these figures are sourced from Eurekahedge's database.

[5] *Source:* Barra Consulting 2001. The author believes that although Barra's absolute numbers will have changed significantly in the intervening two years, the ratio cited is probably relatively stable.

[6] *Source:* AIP Tokyo estimate, September 2002.

[7] *Ibid.*

[8] *Source:* Basis Point Consulting (a Sydney-based market research firm).

Chapter 21

The life cycle of hedge fund managers

Jeffrey Tarrant
Protégé Partners, New York, New York

Introduction

The life cycle of hedge fund organisations is one of the most important, and least analysed, dimensions of investing in hedge funds. With over a decade of institutional history, the industry now has been established long enough to learn that hedge funds, like many other businesses, experience forces of growth and decay that create a finite life cycle far more defined than in traditional money management. Yet hedge fund investors, especially recent entrants into the business, largely ignore the existence of a life cycle. Newer, mostly institutional, investors have elected to tilt their hedge fund portfolios in favour of established brand name hedge funds, not realising that many of those organisations may already have experienced their best and brightest days. I believe that catching a hedge fund firm in the sweet spot of its life cycle is one of the most important dimensions an investor needs to achieve outstanding results.

My thesis is that people and organisations change, especially when exposed to an increase in personal fortune. For an available reference to support this thesis, look no further than the text in your hands. This is the third edition of this book. The last edition, printed in 1999, contained chapters from approximately 49 contributing authors roughly evenly divided between hedge fund managers, investors and service providers. Approximately half of those authors have had one or another significant changes, some positive but most negative, in their businesses, including:

- key management turnover;
- retirement;
- business spinouts;
- the sale or merger of the firm;
- internal management disputes (legal and otherwise);
- large losses; and
- business closing and/or business exit.

While all of the authors are outstanding individuals, many have experienced great changes in their organisations that might or might not be in the best interests of their investors.[1] I believe this underscores the need for understanding the dynamics of the hedge fund organisation life cycle.

Interestingly, the focus of many due diligence efforts has recently shifted to protect against fraud. Frauds are difficult to avoid. If a person wants to defraud you or the fund, they will invent ways that even the savviest investor will not be able to prevent. Investors now frequently perform background checks on the principals of hedge fund firms. While a noble pursuit, its premise (that people and behaviour do not change) is indeed faulty. Few recognise that the most important analysis in hedge funds is not to avoid the fraud but to analyse the changes in successful organisations. While frauds make headlines, much more money was lost in brand name hedge funds such as Julian Robertson's Tiger Fund or Long-Term Capital Management than was lost in frauds such as Michael Berger's Manhattan Fund.

Wealth management begets wealth creation (for the manager)

Before we examine the life cycle of the hedge fund manager, we should examine the ultimate, and often unspoken, goal of most managers. The money management business is a great source of wealth creation for money managers (and sometimes for clients as well). Further, the largest wealth created by legends in the business has come from selling their businesses, rather than from growing their portfolio. For evidence, try to calculate how much more money the likes of Claude Rosenberg, Michael Price and Sir John Templeton made by selling their investment management companies at a multiple with how much they made in their personal accounts as investors before the sale of the firm.

If we assume that most legendary money managers are intelligent folk, we conclude that they know where to make their real fortune. The only question that remains is: can business valuation multiples be applied to the hedge fund business? To answer this question, one needs to know the primary differences between hedge fund management and traditional money management.

1. Hedge fund styles are generally capacity constrained. This is the first and most important rule that is often overlooked.

The standard formulas to value a traditional money management business are always related to assets under management (the so-called scalability of the asset management fees). The value of an asset management firm is a function of assets under management (AUM) and performance (which probably but not necessarily is a condition to greater AUM) (see Exhibit 21.1).

We all want our managers to be successful, but not at the expense of performance. Unfortunately, another rule of successful hedge fund investing, that size is the enemy of performance, conflicts with the ability of an asset management firm to achieve a high business valuation.

Since most hedge fund styles are capacity constrained, the value of the hedge fund firm is constrained as well (see Exhibit 21.2).

It is very important to know if a sale of the business is an objective lurking deep in the mind of your manager. An obsession with building a scalable hedge fund business might add more uncertainty about future performance, given that most hedge fund strategies are not scalable. The unfortunate consequence of the asset gathering mentality is the creation of a capital bloated hedge fund, lacking the focus and edge that created the historically attractive risk/return.

Exhibit 21.1
Value of traditional asset management firm

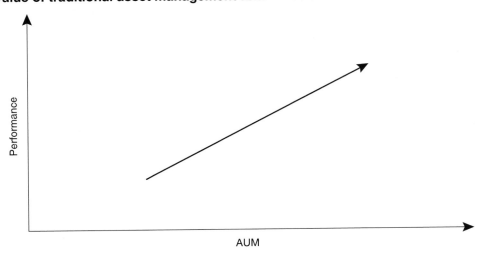

Source: Author's own.

Exhibit 21.2
Value of hedge fund asset management firm

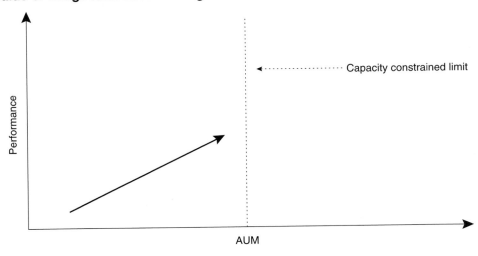

Source: Author's own.

2. Hedge fund fees, which are performance related, are higher than traditional money management fees. A hedge fund manager can make an excellent living without selling his management firm.

Even if the objective of a money manager is not to sell the firm, the inherent high fee structure of hedge funds can create an unstable environment for the hedge fund manager. A well-known observer of the asset management business, Byron Wien of Morgan Stanley Asset Management, observed the following:

> Unlike some others, I do not think we are in a hedge fund bubble that is going to end in disaster. I expect a number of new and old funds to close down, but the concept will endure. What is becoming apparent to me, however, is that the basic structure of an individual hedge fund may be unstable and that is something important for investors to think about. The case for instability starts with the fact that the two largest and best-known funds have changed structure dramatically. Tiger Management effectively closed down and returned investors' money, while Soros Management changed its focus from aggressive macro management to an endowment orientation and most of the outside investors took back their money. Both of these funds had outstanding records over a longer time but ran into a difficult two-year period. Size was blamed for some of the trouble; both had reached around US$20 billion.[2]

As is underscored by Byron Wien, hedge funds can destabilise as they succeed and grow. Before exploring the reason why, the maths of the hedge fund business must be discussed.

The maths of the hedge fund business

Hedge funds have historically charged '1-and-20' fees (that is, a 1 per cent asset management fee and a 20 per cent performance fee). In the early days of the business, hedge funds managed US$50–200 million and were regarded as niche boutiques, earning sufficient fees to cover the costs of the business and provide a good living to the money managers.

As can be seen in Exhibit 21.3, if a hedge fund manages US$100–200 million, the firm revenues in a year can range from US$4–14 million depending on performance. This was once considered to be a successful business model. I still consider it to be one of the great wealth creation businesses but the growth of the industry and ambitions of hedge fund managers have redefined the meaning of success and pushed asset growth to new heights. However, if assets under management grow to the range of US$500 million to US$8 billion, business revenues move to eight digits (10s of millions) from seven digits (millions). This is an important shift.

Exhibit 21.3

Annual revenues of a hypothetical hedge fund business

Performance (gross rate of return) (%)	AUM (US$ million)					
	100	200	500	1,000	5,000	8,000
15	4	8	20	40	200	320
20	5	10	25	50	250	400
25	6	12	30	60	300	480
30	7	14	35	70	350	560

Source: Author's own.

Tarrant's rule of eight digits

Having invested money on behalf of Forbes 400 families, institutions and foundations, and having been involved in the creation and direction of several business enterprises, I have come to the conclusion that things change whenever more than US$10 million in perceived gains or losses are generated in an organisation. I guess in a certain respect, eight digits are considered to be real money and thus create real concern.

When eight-digit losses occur, someone will lose a job. Management assigns responsibility to an unsuspecting person since obviously no one will take credit for losses. While this may be obvious, the more interesting analysis occurs when an eight-digit figure is positive and attributed to a success.

While failures and losses are orphaned, successes and profits have many fathers. Unfortunately, in business there is no DNA testing that can determine the true father of the success, so it is left to the interpretation of contracts (employment and otherwise) and the creativity of the claimant and/or their lawyers to determine the rights to the fruits of success.

Why does this relate to the hedge fund business? It does so because the success and profits we are talking about are significant to the balance sheet of an individual. An eight-digit sum is large enough to affect the personal wealth of most individuals. An eight-digit sum, if not shared with the talent in the firm that created that sum, will drive out entrepreneurial talent.

Therefore, I believe it is important to understand how the hedge fund business evolves in relation to the wealth of its principals. It is my premise that people and organisations change when the wealth of those involved changes. It is, therefore, useful to develop a new dimensional analysis for hedge fund managers, given the profitability of the business and the relevant cause and effect of wealth on the individual and the organisation.

The five phases in the life cycle of the hedge fund management firm

Phase 1: entrepreneurial

The first phase is the initial 18 months after the start of a hedge fund business. The hedge fund manager has probably left another hedge fund organisation, a mutual fund, a Wall Street trading desk or a securities firm as a sell-side analyst. In a successful firm in this phase, the principals have invested significant capital relative to their net worth and probably have raised money from early investors. The money manager/entrepreneur is highly motivated for financial and personal achievement reasons. The critical issue an investor in the hedge fund must understand, after being convinced that the team is potentially a good money manager, is whether the entrepreneurial firm has sufficient and stable capital to survive the following few years regardless of the market environment. It is important to know the source of the capital and its stability during this period.

Start-up risks, such as operational and back office issues, were much more of a concern to me in the early days of hedge funds than they are today. With outsourced resources available at their fingertips, a hedge fund can acquire seed capital, outsourced administrative services, compliance, trading, marketing and risk analysis. Few of these outsourced resources were available a few years ago. Today the manager can spend his time focused on value creation skills, that of money management.

Phase 2: wealth creation

Fortunately, during the wealth creation phase the objectives of the investor and the manager are usually aligned. The hedge fund manager is focused on the primary investment process from which he derives a competitive advantage. Through this focus the manager has the chance to generate returns and create wealth for the investors and the principals of the firm. Many consider the period between the first year and fifth year to be the best years to invest with hedge fund managers.

According to a study prepared by Cross Border Capital:[3]

- young funds outperform seasoned funds after adjustments for the risk of failure;
- the youngest decile beats the oldest by 970 basis points per annum; and
- investors should buy funds in their first three years of existence.

In addition, Byron Wien observes:

> Our hedge fund group at Morgan Stanley Asset Management determined that large funds lag medium-sized funds across the board. Young funds tend to do better than mature ones.[4]

I agree with these observations and have built a business investing with focused hedge managers that are disciplined enough to restrict their asset size, especially during the wealth creation phase. Most good money managers are disciplined; however, one of the most important disciplines is not to be lured by the siren song of the asset gathering business.

Phase 3: wealth enjoyment

After four to five years of managing a successful hedge fund (or perhaps sooner with a very successful fund), the hedge fund manager accumulates enough wealth that his lifestyle can change dramatically. Outstanding managers may earn tens or hundreds of millions of dollars cumulatively in five years. For an investor to think that this wealth effect will not have a dramatic effect on the manager, his lifestyle, family and organisation is naive. One of the first lessons I learned when I studied economics is that money is not static. It moves and wants to move into things like houses, cars, airplanes, art, golf courses, private islands, hunting estates and more. Taken to the extreme, the time enjoying the fruits of success can cause a drag on the manager's focus.

On the other hand, some managers are more ascetic and philanthropic. For those people, money moves to noble causes in the form of private foundations and charitable activities. What can be a great benefit to society, however, can still be a distraction away from money management.

While we applaud the manager for his success and his contribution to society as a producer, consumer and philanthropist, I believe the manager should honestly assess his continued devotion to investment management as his life changes. Hedge fund investment management is more than a full-time job, and the manager and its investors should be aware of the distractions of wealth. If a manager does feel strongly about philanthropic endeavours, it might make more sense for the manager to continue to focus on his business and reduce and/or contribute his fees to the charity. An increasing number of managers (including our firm) have chosen this path and have generated millions of dollars of benefits to non-profit organisations. In that way, the manager can focus on the value-added skills that created past performance, and the philanthropic cause can directly benefit from fee reduction or sharing. If there is a considerable time commitment for the philanthropic endeavours, the manager may want to consider shifting his focus, retiring as a money manager and devoting his time to charitable activities. Increasingly, we see hedge fund managers that recognise the need to manage this time commitment by funding professional non-profit management teams to execute the manager's philanthropic vision, while allowing the manager to continue to focus the majority of his time on investment management.

Phase 4: wealth preservation

Now the manager has amassed a personal fortune. His 'get rich' mentality has been replaced by a 'stay rich' mentality, which in turn can overtake his investment style. Hedge fund managers are paid well to take smart risks. Once a manager has amassed a fortune by any measurement, he has an inclination to reduce risk significantly. When this occurs, the expected return characteristics can drop significantly based on the manager's reduced risk profile. This might or might not fit the client's objectives.

Due to his compressed time schedule, the manager might hire young protégés and attempt to transfer years of knowledge, expertise and judgement to the individuals who are pre-Phase I in their wealth development. The hedge fund instability that Byron Wien identified begins when the manager has difficulty in retaining younger, talented protégés, who might have higher return needs and/or entrepreneurial aspirations.

Phase 5: wealth succession and/or distribution

Once the manager has successfully preserved wealth, he must think about larger concerns than his own needs. After a few younger analysts leave the firm, the hedge fund manager recognises a need to create a succession plan. Though he created the firm on the basis of his investment judgement, the manager attempts to codify the investment process so that the informational 'DNA' of his edge can be passed on to the next generation within the firm. Unfortunately, few hedge fund firms have been able to capture the founding hedge fund manager's judgement into an institutionalised process. As a result, the prospective results are unlikely to resemble the past.

Sustaining an edge in the hedge fund business is gruelling. If the manager is not willing to continue the pace of work that was required in the earlier phases, then he must pass the baton to a new generation of associates and partners. At this moment, the potential for a serious degradation in the firm occurs. If the best talent within the firm is not part of the founder's wealth succession and/or distribution plan, then the firm's instability increases. Some sure signs of instability include:

1. discussion of the potential sale of the firm to any entity other than employees;
2. farming out money to managers to absorb excess capital and to generate portfolio ideas;
3. new product proliferation and discussions of extending the firm's brand to unrelated investment areas;

4. sponsoring new external hedge funds or spinouts from within the firm, creating an incentive problem when trying to keep the talent internally: top talent will want to spinout, while the remaining talent left behind in the firm might be second rate; and

5. transferring ownership of the firm to family members who have not proven their investment prowess.

Once the hedge fund manager 'farms out' money or 'spins out' internal groups, he enters a different business. The firm begins to look more like a fund of funds or a hedge fund incubator. The manager may have discovered a way to protect his revenue stream but an investor cannot know if he has the right skills to manage other people's money (let alone his own) in this fashion.

Conclusion

Hedge fund investors should recognise the life cycle of the hedge manager and incorporate that dimension into the allocation of their hedge fund assets. Just as institutions learned over the last years to first shift assets from bonds to stocks and then to separate small cap and large cap stocks within that allocation, so, too, may institutional investors begin to allocate capital to both the large brand name hedge funds and to smaller, emerging hedge fund managers in an effort to diversify the portfolio across the phases of the life cycle.

Sophisticated hedge fund investors will not favourably receive those hedge fund managers that are 'asset gatherers'. I only ask these managers to read two books written by Al Reis: *The 22 Immutable Laws of Branding* and *Focus: The Future of Your Company Depends on It*. These books were given to me by one of the most focused and longest standing members of the hedge fund community. He believes, and I agree, that all investors should read these books. For the brand name hedge fund managers that want to extend their brand into new forms of investment management, I would refer you to Al Ries' '10th Law of Branding: The Law of Extensions', which states 'the easiest way to destroy a brand is to put its name on everything'.[5] In *Focus: The Future of Your Company Depends on It*, Al Ries underscores that most successful firms focus on their competitive advantage and do not dilute their focus into new areas outside their circle of competence.[6]

Some of the greatest investment masters have retired with full knowledge about the issues outlined in this chapter. If you analyse what some of the great, retired hedge fund managers have done with their own personal fortunes, you will discover that the early investors in emerging hedge fund managers were many of the legendary names of the investment business. If investing with emerging managers is good enough for these seasoned veterans, institutions should not be far behind with a similar strategy. Most of these sophisticated investors know (perhaps first hand) the inside secret of the hedge fund business, that there has never been a successful hedge fund that has managed more than US$8 billion over a sustained period.

As a result, due diligence should incorporate the stage of the life cycle of the hedge fund management firm and an investment portfolio should be constructed with this added perspective in mind.

---

[1] This, of course, is no reflection on the editor of the book, who has invited me to contribute not only to the previous edition but also to this one!

[2] Byron Wien, *The Inherent Instability of Hedge Funds,* Morgan Stanley Equity Research, 29 April 2002, p. 1.

[3] Cross Border Capital, *Absolute Return Fund Research,* April 2001.

[4] Wien, p. 2.

[5] Al Ries and Laura Ries, *The 22 Immutable Laws of Branding,* 'The Law of Extensions', New York, HarperCollins Publishers, 2002. p. 49.

[6] Al Ries, *Focus: The Future of Your Company Depends on It,* New York, HarperCollins Publishers, 1996.

Chapter 22

Utilising hedge funds: the experiences of a private investor

Lloyd Hascoe[1]
Hascoe Associates, Inc, Greenwich, Connecticut

Hedge funds and private investors

Private investors are no longer the primary source of capital for hedge funds. Over the past few years, institutional investors have been entering the arena in a big way. However, unlike institutional investors, private investors, as owners of the investable assets, are clearly identifiable people with human concerns and unique personalities. The intensely personal nature of private finance drives family investing activities. To better understand the perspective on hedge funds and their appropriateness for private investors, I offer the experience of my family, the Hascoe family.

First, it is important to outline the evolution of the Hascoe family investment office, Hascoe Associates, and identify the factors that have led to the extensive use of hedge funds to achieve our investment objectives. In order to understand our investment strategy I will provide some history of Hascoe Associates that I hope will help in the understanding of our family's risk profile, which provides the framework for our investment philosophy and strategy. Finally, I will provide my views on where the hedge fund industry is headed and where I would like to see it go from a private investor's viewpoint.

Evolution of a family investment office

Hascoe Associates was created in the early 1980s as a result of the sale of the family's operating businesses. The sudden liquid wealth created by the sale of these businesses caused considerable apprehension, as we were unaccustomed to managing substantial financial assets. The skills necessary to invest capital prudently are quite different than those that were required to build our operating businesses. Therefore, we were hesitant to rush into an investment programme without careful preparation. Since we knew the painstaking effort that it took for us to build wealth over many years, we adopted a 'go slow' attitude, common to private capital, which resulted in us following a very methodical investment process.

The sale of an entrepreneurial, closely held business, to a large multinational US corporation for stock and cash, presented us with many complex and difficult investment management issues. Perhaps the foremost issue faced was how to best invest and preserve capital over the long term. Is it better to trust your assets completely to outsiders such as one of the well-established trust banks or is it preferable to actively manage the assets in-house? Answers to questions like this are never clear, and they are often subject to change. Given our entrepreneurial 'do it yourself' background, we set out to manage our asset allocation decisions in-house while delegating the actual day-to-day investment management process to external professionals.

Our situation was complicated by the fact that we realised our liquid wealth almost overnight. The family went from being overwhelmingly invested in operating companies, to holding large amounts of liquid assets including a concentrated equity position in a large US multinational. At the time, Hascoe Associates did not exist and our collective investment experience was quite limited. The Hascoes, like so many other families in our situation, did not have a history of holding and investing financial assets. This lack of investment experience provided short-term risks as well as long-term opportunities. In the long term it provided us with extensive possibilities, as the investment landscape was unlimited. In the short term, we became overwhelmingly invested in municipal bonds and continued to hold our concentrated equity position. Fortunately, being undiversified was a profitable strategy for us during this period. The early 1980s turned out to be an ideal time to be buying bonds and our concentrated stock position proceeded to quadruple in price before it was gradually sold.

Although the 1980s and 1990s produced high returns on financial assets, we were concerned about the inherent long-term volatility of the stock market. Therefore we would never commit the high level of assets to traditional equity investing which would be required to maintain and build long-term wealth. Yet, we clearly recognised that over the long term we would need to realise the high, real returns on capital which equities offered. The possible loss of value due to inflation, income and estate taxes, and the growth in the number of family members necessitated returns which have historically only been available through equity type investments. Balancing our risk and return requirements, we sought after-tax returns of municipal bonds plus 400 basis points at risk levels one-third of the stock market.

While in the short term we were able to avoid major disasters (and in fact did exceptionally well) we realised that we needed to develop a long-term professionally managed investment programme. This led to the creation of Hascoe Associates. The office was created shortly after the sale of our operating assets. The staff consisted of my father, Norman Hascoe; Herb Ornstein, his CFO; a secretary; and myself. We quickly grew and began building a fully functioning family investment office to perform the investment, accounting and personal support functions required for the Hascoe family.

Today, Hascoe Associates employs eight professionals with a full complement of support staff. We have a dedicated investment team that formulates and implements our many investment programmes, which includes a multi-strategy hedge fund portfolio, a private equity portfolio and a traditional fixed income programme. We have developed or acquired the skills necessary to evaluate investment strategies, conduct full manager due diligence, perform extensive research and risk analysis, and implement portfolio development. We also have a real estate portfolio, which is managed by a successful real estate investment and development company, Bryant Development Corp, owned and operated by my brother, Andrew Hascoe.

Private investors and risk

As we set out to develop our investment programme we faced a critical question. How does a wealthy family maintain hard-earned assets in real terms while minimising or avoiding market volatility? On the one hand, equities are the asset class of choice for those seeking long-term growth, as the late 1980s and 1990s showed. On the other hand, the historical volatility of equities is an anathema for investors concerned with capital preservation as the last few years have shown. Hascoe Associates is a good example of utilising a diversified hedge fund programme to meet the challenge of achieving high investment returns while enjoying lower volatility. The Hascoe family's aversion to risk is not unique and derives from how the family wealth was originated. Our discussions with other family investment offices show us that their appetite for risk is remarkably similar.

It is not surprising that risk tolerance is similar among wealthy families as the factors that led to the creation of their wealth share many common characteristics. In many cases, a family's assets are created by an older generation that may not have been prepared to manage the wealth that resulted from their own success. Typically, the wealth creating generation's objective is wealth preservation while the subsequent generations seek capital growth. The generation managing wealth faces the very real competing pressures of wealth preservation versus long-term growth in the capital base. Like other families, the Hascoe family has to continually manage these conflicting pressures to meet the objectives of current and future generations. These issues will become particularly acute as each generation matures and assumes a greater role in the family's finances. My point in highlighting these issues is to help the reader understand just how important and complex an issue like risk management is to the private investor.

With these risk constraints in mind, we began our programme by formulating a long-term investment strategy. We realised that we needed to diversify the family's assets from its overwhelming allocation to municipal bonds, which was increasing over time as we continued to liquidate what was a highly concentrated stock position. Our reasons for diversification were two-fold and are the typical, classic, portfolio considerations. First, we desired to lower our risk by spreading our investments among a variety of asset classes and managers. Secondly, through careful selection of strategies and vehicles with high or stable returns and low correlation characteristics, we desired to increase our return while simultaneously lowering risk. As previously mentioned, we considered our after-tax hurdle rate to be the yield on our intermediate municipal bond portfolios plus 400 basis points.

Once you understand how most private investors view risk, it is possible to see how Hascoe Associates eventually embraced a multi-strategy hedge fund concept as an equity surrogate. While private investors desire high absolute returns, they also want to prevent large losses. The conundrum of realising high growth with low volatility presented us with a very difficult investment task. We have met this challenge over time through a well-constructed portfolio of hedge fund strategies. We believe that, with careful manager and strategy selection, hedge funds will continue to allow us to realise higher risk-adjusted returns than would otherwise be possible utilising traditional investment vehicles.

Discovering hedge funds

In constructing our new investment programme, we were constrained by the aversion to buy-and-hold equity strategies due to their relatively high historic volatility. Mindful of our risk profile, we found the long-run return of the stock market attractive but we were very unsettled by the possible high volatility it can display. We were also uncomfortable with the possibility of the stock market performing poorly over extended periods of time, which has indeed happened in the past few years. Although equities had performed splendidly during the better part of the 1980s and 1990s, history and common sense indicated that the markets could not possibly go up forever at above normal rates of return, and that the equities would endure sustained periods of uninspiring performance and significant volatility which indeed has turned out to be the case.

The time horizon for private investors is unique in the investment world in that individuals and family generations have finite lives, whereas most institutions theoretically have infinite time horizons. That is, while an overall family strategy can have an almost infinite time horizon; individuals view their risk reward balance differently during the various stages of their lives. The multi-generational aspects of families further complicate this situation. Each generation has a different investment time horizon at distinct points in time. Each generation may have a different tolerance for the volatility and/or poor performance that the stock market can exhibit for extended periods of time. In addition, private investors typically do not have the ongoing capital inflows to their portfolios that many pension funds enjoy. Private investors do not have the same ability to average their cost basis down while waiting for the market to turn and therefore are not bailed out over time. This is the primary reason that private capital tends to seek absolute investment returns and this is what began our investigation of hedge funds.

We began to focus our energies on learning more of the intricacies of Wall Street in the hope that we could better understand how professional money managers managed their own wealth. If anybody had discovered the investment world's Holy Grail, that is, higher returns with lower risk, he would probably be one of Wall Street's pros.

During our investment apprenticeship we held innumerable discussions with the leaders in the Wall Street community on how to best invest. Invariably the discussion would lead to a concept called 'proprietary trading' which was very foreign to us. Slowly we began to understand that proprietary trading was how the Street's own capital was invested to earn superior risk-adjusted returns. As one Wall Street executive put it, 'We do not buy stocks . . . we sell them . . . '. That statement still sticks in my mind as testimony that the Street invests its own capital quite differently than their customers. The implication was that, compared to outsiders, Wall Street firms had an edge when investing their own capital. In addition, our sense was that proprietary trading techniques might offer us the ability to invest opportunistically rather than using the traditional methods used by most small investors. This was the right strategy for us as it allowed us to utilise our entrepreneurial style and apply it to our investment and decision-making process.

Achieving higher returns and lower risk

Through our analysis of risk versus return, we realised that the vast majority of efficient frontier studies were based on institutional models where their investment returns are not taxed. These models are woefully lacking for private, taxable investors as they fail to incorporate the impact of taxes. This means that on an after-tax basis it is extremely difficult for private investors to keep up with the traditional efficient frontier. Hedge funds, through their freedom to use leverage and greater investment flexibility, allow private investors to partially compensate for taxes while also reducing risk. The higher Sharpe ratios potentially achievable through the use of hedge funds should allow private investors to recapture some of the returns lost to taxes. Once again it is plain to see that private investors have very different demands than those of institutional investors. This may help explain why private investors have been so attracted to the hedge fund industry.

In our discussions with Wall Street professionals we found that by using proprietary trading techniques we could invest capital in high-return, low-risk strategies. Fortunately for Hascoe Associates, we discovered that proprietary trading techniques were accessible through a previously unknown (to us at least) investment vehicle, the hedge fund. The hedge fund seemed to offer us the investment alternative that we were seeking. We recognised that although some of these strategies individually were higher risk than the S&P 500, a diversified group of hedge funds could be put together to gain the advantages of a portfolio effect. This can be accomplished because within different hedge funds there are such a variety of underlying strategies, exposures and leverage.

As our interest in hedge funds peaked we were immediately attracted to the multi-strategy concept and its diversification benefits. A solid multi-strategy programme can allow the private investor to invest with world-class managers, while diversifying individual strategy and manager risk. These attributes are particularly important given the high information hurdles inherent in the hedge fund industry. At the inception of Hascoe's multi-manager strategy, information on managers was far more difficult and time-consuming to gather than it is today. Many of the consultants and databases that now exist were not available until relatively recently. Our initial thinking was that we should find a good fund of funds manager; however, we concluded that we could develop the expertise in-house to construct our own multi-manager programme. Due to our entrepreneurial background we were confident that we could not only learn the business but implement and create our own tailor-made programme.

We began our programme by investing in a core of funds with lower risk strategies where we had the added benefit (and in retrospect danger) of having a personal relationship with the managers. The advantage of investing with someone with whom you also have a personal relationship is that there is a higher level of trust and communication than is otherwise possible. However, you run the danger of being less objective when dealing with friends who also manage your money.

Our experience with our multi-manager, multi-strategy fund is similar to that of many other private investors that I know. We built our programme in a methodical fashion around a core of lower-risk strategies. We focused on hedged arbitrage strategies that performed consistently well, giving us confidence that we were on the right track. Our experience with these core managers remains favourable and we still maintain some of these investments today.

Over time, we have added capital to our hedge fund programme. This has enabled us to add new managers and strategies with a variety of different return, volatility and correlation characteristics. We only choose our managers and strategies after careful analysis, utilising numerous risk exposure models, which allows us to analyse a variety of risk and opportunity factors (refer to the Appendix to this chapter for an example). These models help us to adjust the portfolio according to the opportunities and risks in the world financial markets. Our current programme employs approximately 10 different managers utilising a large number of investment strategies. The number of underlying investment strategies is dictated only by the number of opportunities that present themselves. We feel that it is prudent for investors to diversify among managers as well as by investment strategy due to the quite chilling prospect of an individual investment totally 'blowing up'. It would be an understatement to say that our confidence in our multi-manager programme would have been shaken if we had invested with a manager who blew up. However, over time, we have in fact reduced the number of managers in our programme. When we first started our programme our view was to diversify among single-strategy managers and we quickly grew to over 20 managers. Since then we have been able to reduce the number of managers by adding a number of multi-strategy managers.

With the growth of the hedge fund industry, much of the money going into hedge funds has tended to gravitate to the most experienced and successful managers, swelling assets under management to well over US$5 billion for a number of managers. Concerns began to grow about their ability to attain the proper risk–reward profile. At the same time, managers not only started to close their doors to new capital inflows, but also began to significantly limit investors' ability to exit by changing withdrawal terms. As a consequence, we found ourselves less able to move between managers and strategies. Since our liquidity was being reduced at the manager level, our ability to be in the right place at the right time was also reduced, potentially hurting our returns and increasing our risk. Therefore, we shifted our strategy toward adding the best and the brightest multi-strategy managers to our portfolio. These managers have the ability to shift allocations between strategies as the investment environment presents opportunities. Although we would rather have the ability to make more of those strategy allocation decisions ourselves, we think that the risk of being somewhat limited from making strategy selection decisions ourselves is more than offset by the manager's ability to tactically allocate at will between ever increasing types of investment strategies. The evolution of our programme is illustrated in Exhibits 22.1 to 22.6.

Returning to Hascoe Associates' original premise for investing in hedge funds, namely realising high risk-adjusted returns, we are very pleased with the results that we have experienced. During the past 12 years we have been able to realise a Sharpe ratio of roughly two-and-half times that of the S&P 500 while earning a very similar return (see Exhibit 22.7).

As our programme continues to evolve, we anticipate continuing to push up our returns without substantially increasing risk. The intention is to build gains over time by continuing to place capital opportunistically. We have always maintained that private investors who seek

Exhibit 22.1

Hascoe investment programme allocations, 1991

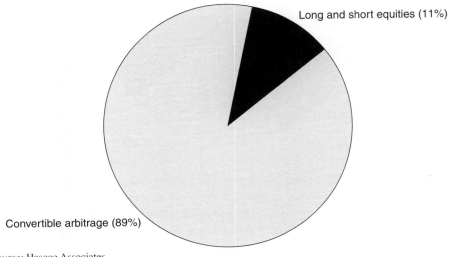

Source: Hascoe Associates.

Exhibit 22.2

Hascoe investment programme allocations, 1993

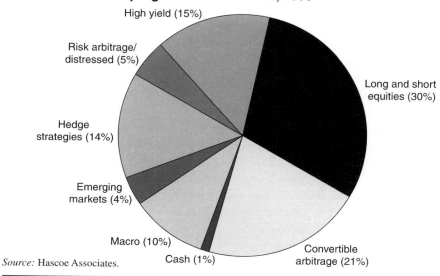

Source: Hascoe Associates.

Exhibit 22.3

Hascoe investment programme allocations, 1995

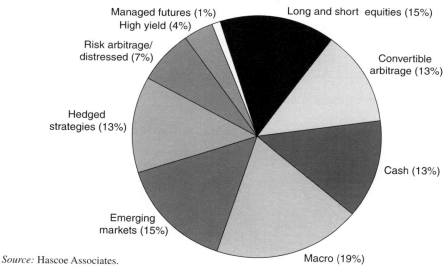

Source: Hascoe Associates.

stock market exposure should instead utilise long-short equity hedge funds. The volatility in equity valuations over the past couple of years has proved that thesis. However, you must find the managers who really hedge their positions and utilise shorting to generate returns. More recently we have also become interested in distressed managers. The current economic environment has caused difficulty for many companies but created new opportunities for smart hedge fund managers. We are always investigating new hedge fund strategies and will

Exhibit 22.4

Hascoe investment programme allocations, 1997

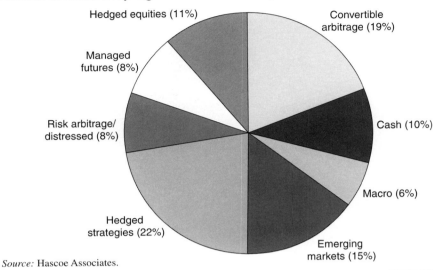

Source: Hascoe Associates.

Exhibit 22.5

Hascoe investment programme allocations, August 1998

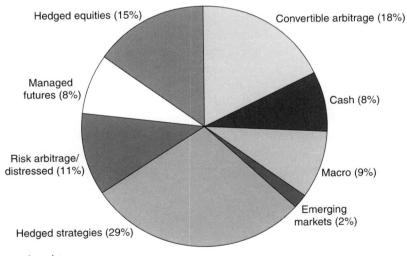

Source: Hascoe Associates.

reallocate capital to them, if appropriate, as a means to increase our returns while enhancing our diversification.

The future of hedge fund investing

Clearly, we believe that the time and effort that we have devoted to our hedge fund strategy

285

Exhibit 22.6

Hascoe investment programme allocations, December 2002

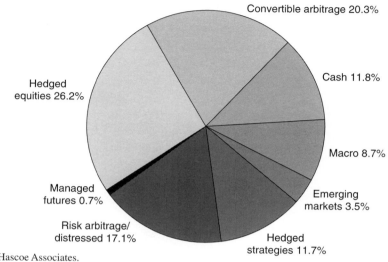

Source: Hascoe Associates.

has paid off. Our programme has met our risk-adjusted return expectations quite well. Looking to the future, we share the view of many other private investors that the hedge fund industry will allow us to continue to achieve the risk–return profile that we seek. However, the landscape has become more complex and risky. There are now thousands of hedge funds, many of which have only started operations in the last few years. Lucrative fee structures, the ability to call their own shots and freedom from complex organisational structures, have lured many traditional investment managers, often the best talent from Wall Street and the mutual fund industry, into creating their own hedge funds. Nowhere else can Wall Street professionals generate a level of success from the fruits of their own talent and discipline. As these 'hedgies' break out on their own, investors will be presented with more opportunities but also additional risks. Many of these managers mistakenly believe that they have the ability to manage a hedge fund because of their success in managing traditional investments. Nearly two decades of favourable financial market performance has helped many hedge fund start-ups post good returns. A good investment return during this period does not necessarily correlate with good investment management, and many of these managers have got caught in this difficult environment. As the financial markets revert to their long-term mean, it has been painful for many. Time will tell which managers will make it.

As I have mentioned, when we began investing in hedge funds, information was scarce and good managers were mostly found through referrals. We had to gather all of our intelligence independently and virtually in a vacuum. Our office was forced to develop a large database of managers, along with their documents and performance statistics. Fortunately, while the industry has become more complex, it has also evolved to the point where the information/due diligence void has been filled by databases, websites, newsletters, independent marketers and specialised consultants. Our office derives a great deal of benefit from the fact that we can devote less time and effort to data collection which thereby allows us to focus more time and energy on the actual portfolio analysis and decision-making process.

Exhibit 22.7

Annualised risk versus annualised return, January 1994–December 2002 Hascoe programme versus indices (%)

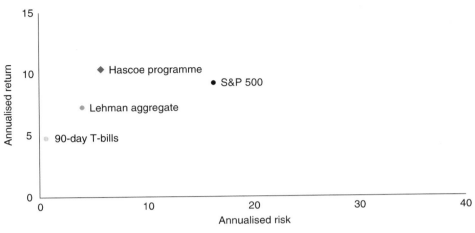

Source: Hascoe Associates.

Another significant trend occurring in the hedge fund industry is the increasing diversity of managers and strategies. The benefit to investors is clear. The menu of investment strategies has mushroomed to include a wide array of strategies ranging from global macro to convertible bond arbitrage. Far more specialised strategies are also available. For example, if you are interested in convertible arbitrage, it is now possible to find not only a US convertible arbitrage manager but also one who focuses internationally, or on privately negotiated convertible transactions.

What is most interesting is that investors can now add strategies to their programme which have return and correlation characteristics that are specifically attractive to them, but that have been previously unavailable to private investors due to a lack of convenient investment vehicles. Furthermore, within an individual strategy, investors often can choose the specific risk profile that they prefer. If an investor wants an aggressive convertible arbitrage allocation, he can choose a manager that uses a lot of leverage. If an investor wants to be conservative, he can allocate to a manager that uses little leverage, avoids credit 'bets', or is oriented towards hedging volatility.

Leverage is a key determinant of risk, and it has become easier for investors to manage their overall portfolio exposure in ways that were largely unavailable in the past. For example, we can now choose managers who utilise less leverage during periods when we believe that the interest rate environment is not favourable. Conversely, we can increase returns by reallocating to more leveraged managers when the interest rate outlook is favourable. However, leverage also has a dark side. The same leverage that allows a manger to amplify returns can also amplify losses. In the past 20 years there have been numerous examples of hedge fund managers making the mistake of putting all of their eggs in one basket, leveraging those eggs and then getting it wrong, wiping out most or all of the investors' money.

The general increase in the choices of investment strategies today allows investors to better focus their asset allocation in areas that they feel are attractive. However, this greater

287

selectivity forces investors to accept much greater responsibility for their investment decisions than they may have had to in the past. Some investors view this greater responsibility as a burden rather than a benefit. They may be better off utilising a consultant, a fund of funds or investing with more diversified or discretionary managers who will make these allocation decisions for them. For Hascoe Associates, the responsibility is welcomed because we seek to manage our risk profile closely and have greater control of our portfolio's characteristics.

I believe that hedge fund investing will continue its evolutionary process of greater manager and strategy selection as well as more efficient information dissemination. However, today there is an enormous amount of capital entering the industry. On the one hand, this has allowed better managers to increase fees and decrease liquidity. On the other hand, the increase in competition for capital has allowed investors to seek out better terms from up and coming managers.

The enormous growth of the hedge fund industry has coincided with even larger growth in the mutual fund industry. Private investors are increasingly comparing many of their hedge fund managers with the lower-cost alternatives of traditional mutual funds. While there are many distinct differences between these two investment vehicles, in many cases the comparison is justified. Recently, there has been a relaxation of the laws governing mutual funds. We are beginning to see hedge fund strategies become available in the mutual fund format. Specifically, at the time of this writing, there are a number of market-neutral and hedged managers offering their strategy through equity mutual funds. At the same time there is increased scrutiny of hedge funds by the regulators as the big investment banks are attempting to 'retailise' the hedge funds business with offerings ranging from registered funds of funds to principal guaranteed products with US$25,000 minimums.

As the opportunities increase for traditional managers to earn performance-based compensation, and a chance to call their own shots, we think that the industry will remain dynamic and continue to grow. There have been some notable setbacks as many hedge fund managers got knocked around by the market's increased volatility. While the total amount of capital devoted to hedge funds has increased dramatically, so have the number of managers and strategies. Although this may dilute returns, we also expect an increase in opportunities as the best and brightest uncover new ideas and strategies.

This chapter began with the reasons why the Hascoe family as a private investor was originally attracted to hedge fund investing. The main rationale for a private investor to embrace hedge funds continues to be the desire for better risk-adjusted returns. In Hascoe Associates' experience, our multi-strategy programme has been able to meet our goal of achieving long-term equity market returns with significantly reduced risk. The return and risk characteristics that we have experienced would have been impossible to achieve had our investment menu been limited to traditional investment vehicles. We believe that we will continue to realise attractive risk-adjusted returns as world financial markets and the hedge fund industry continue to evolve.

---

[1] The author would like to offer special thanks to Tom Kuntz and Luke Imperatore for their assistance.

Appendix

The Factor Sensitivity model: a hypothetical example

Manager	A	B	C	D	E	F	G	H	I	J	K	L	M	Portfolio
Allocation (%)	4.9	8.7	6.6	8.4	7.1	9.4	9.1	8.7	8.6	7.6	8.0	4.7	8.2	100
Characterisation of returns:														
Income and st. capital gains attribution (%)	25	100	15	40	100	95	70	90	15	95	35	70	100	
LT capital gains attribution (%)	75	0	85	60	0	5	30	10	85	5	65	30	0	
Tax efficiency (%)	26	42	23	29	42	41	35	40	23	41	28	35	42	35
Factor sensitivity:														
Asia	0	1	1	1	1	2	2	0	0	2	2	2	0	1.08
Latin America	0	0	0	5	0	0	0	0	0	0	0	1	0	0.47
Russia and eastern Europe	0	0	0	6	0	0	0	0	0	0	0	0	0	0.50
Western Europe	0	1	8	2	0	0	4	0	2	0	4	4	0	1.51
Spreads and premiums	6	7	0	0	7	8	2	1	0	7	4	0	2	3.44
US real estate	3	0	0	0	0	0	0	0	0	0	0	0	0	0.15
US dollar	0	1	1	4	1	1	3	0	2	1	1	4	0	1.44
US equity	0	3	1	1	2	3	2	5	7	3	2	2	0	2.54
US interest rates	2	3	2	3	2	3	3	2	2	3	5	5	5	3.06
Key-man	10	10	10	10	10	7	10	3	10	10	5	10	10	8.71
Leverage	1	7	3	2	2	7	5	1	0	7	0	5	0	3.13
Illiquidity of underlying securities	6	3	3	8	3	5	2	6	3	5	7	2	1	4.19
Risk–return expectations:														
Before-tax return	15	16	24	30	20	14	22	28	16	18	24	28	8	20.04
After-tax return	11.18	9.28	18.41	21.36	11.60	8.27	14.21	16.86	12.27	10.64	17.35	18.09	4.64	13.21
Downside risk	20	10	20	50	12	10	12	25	15	12	22	30	4	18.31
Risk–reward ratio	0.56	0.93	0.92	0.43	0.97	0.83	1.18	0.67	0.82	0.89	0.79	0.60	1.16	0.84
Liquidity of investment*	A	A	Q	A	A	A	A	A	Q	A	A	M	D	

* A = Annual; Q = Quarterly; M = Monthly; D = Daily.

Note: This exhibit is a scaled-down version of our Factor Sensitivity model using actual managers in a hypothetical blend. This model attempts to analyse the aggregate sensitivity of a multi-manager portfolio to a variety of political, economic, psychological and market factors. Each manager's direct performance sensitivity to events in the listed factors is ranked on a scale from 0 to 10 (from low to high). These sensitivities are then asset-weighted and aggregated for the portfolio as a whole. In a snapshot, the model simultaneously can offer both a risk and an opportunity analysis of the portfolio's current or proposed composition.

Chapter 23

Quantitative analysis of hedge funds: a simple comprehensive framework

Thomas Weber
LGT Capital Partners, Pfäffikon, Switzerland

Introduction

Every investor looks at historical performance data

Hedge fund data is becoming a commodity. Investors and interested parties can view hedge fund indices and individual funds' track records via the Internet or purchase hedge fund databases for a few thousand dollars. Analysing historical performance characteristics remains the easiest and also one of the most important criteria for selecting hedge funds. The ratios and computations used for hedge fund analyses differ from traditional measures, as hedge funds typically have absolute return objectives rather than beating index-related benchmarks. The ratios also tend to become more and more sophisticated because hedge funds can do so many things; that is, invest in almost any security or asset class.

A simple and structured framework for quantitative analysis

Every hedge fund investor has his own set of ratios and analyses that he abides by and is familiar with. Readily available analytical packages provide ample computation power with ever more exotic and sophisticated ratios with new and interesting names. This chapter gives a description of a simple framework for quantitative analysis of hedge funds. It will show a sample one-page summary of statistics that displays the most important quantitative information for a single manager in a structured and intuitive way. The framework is applied to a particular fixed-income arbitrage manager. The chapter summarises the benefits of quantitative analysis, and concludes with the points that qualitative due diligence is paramount and quantitative analysis is necessary but not sufficient.

Some caveats

Short history and limited observations

Let us start with some caveats regarding the use of hedge fund data. Some apply only to index or peer group comparisons whereas others pertain to individual funds. The first problem with hedge fund data is its short history. Although the first hedge fund was launched in 1949, the real growth of the industry did not commence before the late 1980s, and the greatest explosion of hedge funds only started in the mid-1990s. This means the data cover limited economic, stock market, interest rate, or other cycles and developments.

Hedge funds normally report their performance on a monthly basis. Sometimes weekly or daily estimates are available. This limits the types of analysis in contrast to listed securities, for which tick data is available. Another pitfall is that newer hedge fund managers may only provide track records that are unaudited composites of historical accounts and strategies and might not correspond to the current investment philosophy, process or team.

Survivorship and selection bias

Hedge fund databases tend to have a higher degree of survivorship bias as they cannot control the providers of the performance data, which are normally the hedge fund managers themselves (or their administrators). Funds that have closed or shown bad performance might stop delivering their data to the database. Although some databases keep dropouts in the database, this computation is an extra effort not many undertake.

Furthermore, quite a few hedge funds with long records do not provide the databases with their data. Often these funds are closed and do not want to attract potential new investors; or they are just secretive about their strategy and performance. Others might be newer funds that do not want to report performance data until they can show satisfactory results. Thus, databases may not represent the hedge fund industry or the respective hedge fund styles fully.

Inconsistent style classifications with heterogeneous funds

Another issue that complicates the use of databases involves the classification of hedge funds. Different database providers use different style categories or may classify managers differently, even if they use the same categories. The problem stems from the heterogeneity and complexity of many hedge funds. Often certain funds pursue multiple strategies and could therefore be classified in different categories, or might belong in different categories at different points in time. A correct classification requires detailed knowledge of the hedge fund manager's investment strategies and a detailed set of style categories.

A specific problem exists with using hedge fund composite or hedge fund style indices. Due to the heterogeneity of the individual funds the constructed index shows a too diversified, that is, small risk, and cannot be used as a proxy for an individual fund of that style. As an example, one convertible hedge fund manager might pursue a US strategy whereas another could be active in Japan. They might end up in the same 'convertible bond arbitrage index' but have different risk–return characteristics. Even within such a relatively narrow category, the dispersion of performance among managers can be very wide and uncorrelated. The problem with data analysis is that the constructed indices do not accurately describe the risk–return parameters for a typical fund (if there is such a thing as a 'typical' fund) of that style but only for the diversified universe of funds. Therefore, one would be better off using the average return and the average risk of all funds in a specific style category (and not the index) to analyse the impact of adding this type of fund to the portfolio. This is shown in Exhibit 23.1, which compares the downside deviation of an index of hedge funds with the downside deviation of the average fund within the same style category. The average long short hedged manager for example showed a downside deviation of more than 10 per cent versus 4 per cent for the index of long short hedged managers.

Exhibit 23.1

Hedge fund style indices versus averages – indices underestimate risk

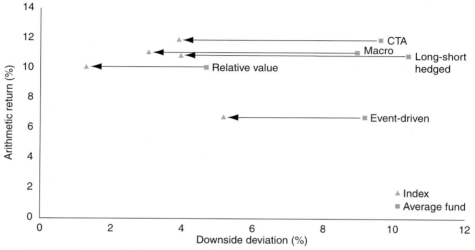

Sources: Hedgefund.net and author's own computations (data from November 1997–February 2003).

Normal distribution versus 'fat tails'

Underlying many computations, ratios and optimisations is an assumption that returns are normally distributed. Similarly, risk management models and guidelines often are based on two or three standard deviation events. Some hedge funds, though, can have very negative or positive surprises. Their performance data can be sharply skewed rather than exhibiting a normal distribution, which makes the usage of optimisers and other sophisticated analytical tools questionable. Improving the sophistication of your analysis by adding more complex distributions that account for skewness and kurtosis does not address the fact that distributions of hedge fund returns frequently change with varying time windows.

Conclusion

There are two conclusions to draw from these caveats. First, good data should be used – that is, a long audited track record of a specific entity from reliable sources. On the other hand, the quality of data will be inferior to that of traditional securities and even mutual funds. Therefore, one should not become too sophisticated in developing ever-more complicated quantitative models but use one's creativity in identifying good data and qualitative measures.

A simple framework for quantitative analysis of hedge funds

Overview

A useful framework for quantitative hedge fund analysis can be developed without inventing new ratios and computations. Rather, widely used analyses can be structured into five categories, which give a comprehensive overview of the characteristics and qualities of the fund:

- performance;
- risk;
- efficiency;
- consistency; and
- correlation.

Within each category it is possible to combine established mathematical and statistical ratios with easy-to-understand analyses that appeal to one's common sense.

Such a structured quantitative analysis can be tailored to the individual investor's objectives and requirements. Different investors might perceive and evaluate the categories and ratios differently; for example, one investor might be extremely interested in low risk or volatility whereas another is more concerned with correlation to an index or his current portfolio. A comprehensive analysis, however, looks at all categories and ranks them accordingly.

As illustration, all the ratios discussed in the following sections are applied to a specific fund and a summary analysis is displayed in Exhibit 23.2.

Return

Return is the most looked at figure pertaining to any investment. In the long run it is the only measure that matters, assuming the investor was able to live with the observed volatility or other risk factors that were associated with the performance. The higher the better, unless one was designing structured options on an asset that require the asset to finish within a specific performance band.

Geometric return and the power of compounding

The accepted methodology of calculating 'average' returns is to use the geometric mean because it implies compounding of the returns. This is the best assumption unless gains are withdrawn on a regular basis. The problem with arithmetic returns becomes obvious when looking at an extreme case, as in Exhibit 23.3.

The arithmetic return shows an annual return of 25 per cent although the portfolio has an ending value of 1,000 which was also its initial value. The geometric mean assumes reinvestment, which means the return of year two was lost in year three and therefore the total return is zero.

The power of compounding is an important concept in finance that is often underestimated. An investment returning 15.75 per cent p.a. doubles within five years. After an additional six years with the same annual performance the initial investment has quintupled. However, the compounding works both ways. If in the example the return in only one annual period had been a loss of 30 per cent and the returns for the other 10 years remained at 15.75 per cent p.a., the initial investment would only have tripled. The conclusion is simple: a stable performance tends to be better than a volatile one.

Rolling returns

In addition to looking at a fund's cumulative, annual and monthly returns, the computation of rolling returns gives an interesting insight into the characteristics and qualities of the returns. Rolling periods with a length that matches the investor's time horizon can show how consistent a fund might have been in meeting the investor's expectations. Looking at average,

Exhibit 23.2

Performance of sample fund (data from January 1991 to February 1994)

1. Return	Fund	Index[*]
Total return (%)	73.55	41.50
Geometric mean p.a. (%)	19.02	11.59
Rolling 12-month returns (mean) (%)	24.70	9.64
Rolling 12-month returns (max) (%)	36.19	26.32
Rolling 12-month returns (min) (%)	15.94	4.48

2. Risk	Fund	Index
Standard deviation (%)	6.23	10.68
Downside dev. p.a. (T-bill 4.5%)	2.19	5.73
Maximum drawdown (%)	−3.50	−5.10
Maximum drawdown (length in months)	3	3
Maximum drawdown (recovery in months)	5	1
Average of 5 maximum drawdowns (%)	−1.69	−3.73

3. Consistency	Fund	Index
Number of months	38	38
Number of positive months	32	26
Percentage of positive months (%)	84	68
Average monthly return (up months) (%)	1.92	2.48
Number of negative months	6	12
Percentage of negative months (%)	16	32
Average monthly return (down months) (%)	−0.89	−2.31

4. Efficiency	Fund	Index
Sharpe ratio p.a.	2.33	0.66
Sortino ratio p.a. (T-bill)	5.99	1.15
Gain/loss ratio	11.49	2.32
Annual return/5 max. drawdowns	14.64	2.59

5. Correlation	Fund	Index
Correlation	0.38	1
24-mon. correlation (mean)	0.46	1
24-mon. correlation (max)	0.75	1
24-mon. correlation (min)	0.07	1
# months fund +, index + / %	21	55
# months fund −, index + / %	5	13
# months fund +, index − / %	11	29
# months fund −, index − / %	1	3

6. Monthly returns fund (%)	1991	1992	1993	1994
Jan	1.50	1.61	1.90	1.47
Feb	0.80	1.80	1.94	−1.29
Mar	−0.13	1.72	2.41	
April	−2.90	1.61	1.56	
May	−0.49	1.34	1.62	
June	0.39	1.68	1.93	
July	−0.27	2.09	2.79	
Aug	0.62	2.43	2.98	
Sep	0.36	1.78	1.89	
Oct	2.84	1.55	1.43	
Nov	3.20	1.27	0.40	
Dec	9.44	1.11	−0.27	
Year	15.94	21.92	22.58	0.16
Max	9.44	2.43	2.98	1.47
Min	−2.90	1.11	−0.27	−1.29

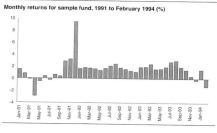

Cumulative performance, 1991 to February 1994

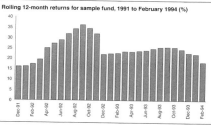

Monthly returns for sample fund, 1991 to February 1994 (%)

Rolling 12-month returns for sample fund, 1991 to February 1994 (%)

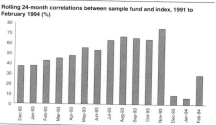

Risk and return, 1991 to February 1994

Rolling 24-month correlations between sample fund and index, 1991 to February 1994 (%)

[*] The index used is the Standard & Poor's 500.

Source: Author's own.

Exhibit 23.3

Arithmetic and geometric return

	Year 1	Year 2	Year 3	Arithmetic return p.a.	Geometric return p.a.
Value of portfolio	1,000	2,000	1,000		
Annual return (%)		100	−50	25	0

Source: Author's own.

minimum and maximum rolling returns can give greater insights into the cyclicality of returns, which may be relevant for an investor seeking to time an investment. In the example given in Exhibit 23.4 the worst annual return would have been under 6 per cent and the best would have been over 36 per cent.

Risk

Risk puts the return figure into perspective. The phrase 'high risk–high return' captures the basic concept. Risk analysis in general, but in particular in the framework of hedge funds, has to show whether the achieved return is a result of higher risk or manager skill. However, the concept of risk in the financial world is extremely broad and deep. There are many dimensions to what constitutes risk for investors and how it should be quantified and analysed. Several measures are illustrated in the section 'Risk' in Exhibit 23.2 and are discussed further below.

Standard deviation and downside deviation

This chapter focuses on the traditional definition of risk as variability of returns as measured by standard deviation. The lower the standard deviation, the lower the variability of returns and hence the risk of the investment. One of the benefits of standard deviation is its simple computation and its wide usage. On the other hand, there are some pitfalls associated with this statistic. For example, it is based on the assumption of normally distributed returns, an assumption that hedge funds do not always fulfil. Another drawback is the fact that standard deviation is a symmetric measure that penalises high positive as well as high negative returns.

Therefore, for hedge funds, which typically aim at avoiding negative returns, a more appropriate measure should be used. The downside or semi-deviation computes the volatility of returns below a specified benchmark, and therefore does not penalise high upside volatility. The benchmark can be any value but normally refers to the mean return, the risk-free rate (T-bills) or a hurdle rate of zero per cent.

Although standard and downside deviation generate similar types of results, the contrast between the two allows a detailed analysis of an investment's volatility by distinguishing good (upside) volatility from bad (downside) volatility.

Drawdown

Standard and downside deviation are widely used but they are not very intuitive. Explaining standard deviation by saying that two-thirds of the returns lie within a range around the mean that is plus/minus one standard deviation is not obvious to many people.

A much more concrete measure is the drawdown analysis, which looks at the largest consecutive loss for an investment. The drawdown shows:

- the maximum losing streak in per cent of an investment;
- how long the period of losses lasted; and
- how long it took to recover the loss.

In addition to looking at the largest drawdown, it makes sense to look at the average of all drawdowns. This gives an indication of whether the largest drawdown was an exceptional event or may be likely to occur again soon.

Efficiency

The analysis of the efficiency of an investment combines the preceding two concepts of return and risk into one. Efficiency tells you how many units of return were generated for incurring one unit of risk. Thus, the higher the efficiency, the higher the return that was generated given a certain level of risk. (See the section 'Efficiency' in Exhibit 23.2.)

Sharpe and Sortino ratios

The most widely used ratios are the Sharpe ratio and the Sortino ratio. The Sharpe ratio is computed by dividing the excess return (return over the risk-free rate) by the standard deviation. The Sortino ratio on the other hand divides the excess return by the downside deviation. If you computed your downside deviation not below the risk-free rate but below zero or any other number, you should compute the excess return accordingly. It is important to specify the hurdle rate and the way it is being computed in order to be able to compare figures, in particular if you compare data from different sources.

Other measures of efficiency

Other measures of efficiency include the gain/loss ratio, which relates positive and negative returns to the magnitude of the monthly returns. It is computed by dividing the number of positive months by the negative ones and multiplying this by the ratio of up-month performance divided by down-month performance. The higher the number, the greater the efficiency.

The annual return divided by the average or maximum drawdown figure is another way to show the relationship between the upside and the downside. A ratio below one means that an average annual return could be destroyed by the maximum/average drawdown. There are limitations in interpreting this figure. For example, a particular fund might have large drawdowns followed by substantial gains, which might lead to an above average annual performance.

Consistency

The consistency of returns is reflected in the dispersion of the rolling 12-month returns as displayed in Exhibit 23.4. Another check is to look at the number of positive and negative monthly returns as well as their magnitude, as shown in the section 'Consistency' in Exhibit 23.2. It is important to note that the return patterns of different styles vary significantly. Relative value strategies tend to have the highest percentage of positive monthly returns, whereas trend

Exhibit 23.4

Rolling 12-month returns for sample fund, 1991 to February 1994 (%)

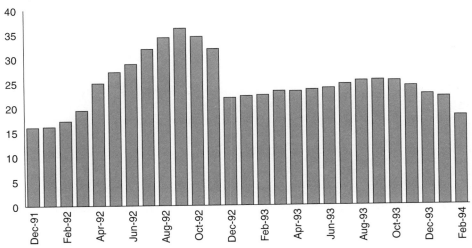

Source: Author's own.

followers/Commodity Trading Advisers (CTAs) are at the other end of the spectrum. They often just have a couple of months per year with strong trends and high positive performances. In months without clear trends they try to minimise the downside. Relative value funds typically have 80–100 per cent positive monthly returns versus 50–80 per cent for CTAs. On the other hand, the CTA's average positive monthly return is much higher than that of the average relative value fund. The point is, a consistency analysis is most relevant when comparing funds of the same style or strategy.

Measuring consistency is important because it tries to capture the basic objective of hedge funds, that is, to generate positive returns no matter what an index does. Therefore, looking at the average performance of the fund when the relevant index is up or down gives an interesting indication of how consistent the fund's performance on average was. In the example shown in Exhibit 23.2 the average monthly performance in months when the S&P was up came to 1.5 per cent, whereas it amounted to 1.4 per cent in S&P down months. This is an extremely consistent pattern and confirms the low correlation as discussed later.

Snail trail

One interesting and comprehensive consistency analysis is the so called 'snail trail'. This analysis integrates three factors:

- the over or underperformance of one manager versus another manager, an index or his peer group;
- the manager's relative volatility versus another manager, an index or his peer group; and
- how relative performance has changed over time.

In Exhibit 23.5 each point on the graph represents a 24-month period. The first point denotes what out/underperformance the manager achieved versus his peer group and whether his risk

297

Exhibit 23.5

Sample fund versus HFR event-driven index 24-month rolling returns

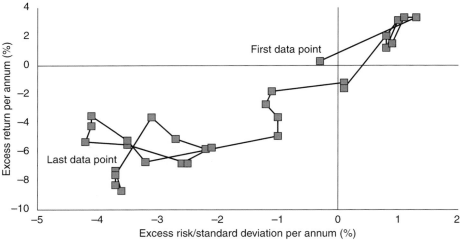

Source: Author's own.

was above or below that of his peer group. Each following point looks at the next succeeding 24-month time period. The analysis shows whether a manager was able to achieve his outperformance because of an above average risk and how his strategy's risk–return characteristics have changed over time. This analysis can also help to detect changes in a manager's aggressiveness or defensiveness as compared to his peers.

Traditional correlation analysis

An important benefit of non-traditional assets and hedge funds is their low correlation to traditional investments like equities, bonds and cash. Therefore, hedge funds have a diversification benefit: adding them to a traditional portfolio improves the return–risk relationship of the portfolio. A correlation analysis examines the relationship between a hedge fund's returns and those of a benchmark index, as in the section 'Correlation' in Exhibit 23.2 and in Exhibit 23.6. The range of indices for comparison can be broad. Often traditional securities indices are used, for example, the S&P 500 (for US equities), the MSCI World (for global equities) or the Salomon Brothers World Government Bond Index (for bonds). On the hedge fund side, style and composite hedge fund indices from different data providers can be used. However, indices can also be tailor-made, for example to replicate the current portfolio to which the analysed fund should be added. Finally, the comparison of the fund's performance to another fund can be of interest.

Hedge funds, perhaps with the exception of short-only funds, cannot be a pure hedge to traditional market downturns and also generate returns when the traditional markets are up. A correlation analysis, however, shows how strongly the benchmark's and the fund's returns are related. A correlation of one means that fund and index move in the same direction and the same magnitude. A correlation of minus one, the other possible extreme, means that the fund and index are perfectly negatively correlated. A correlation

Exhibit 23.6

Risk and return, 1991 to February 1994

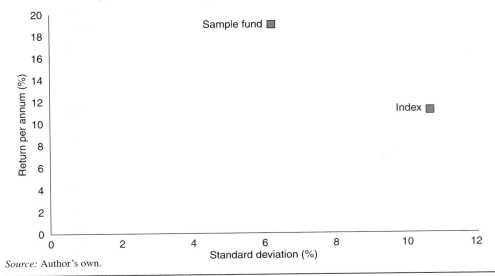

Source: Author's own.

Exhibit 23.7

Rolling 24-month correlations between sample fund and index, 1991 to February 1994 (%)

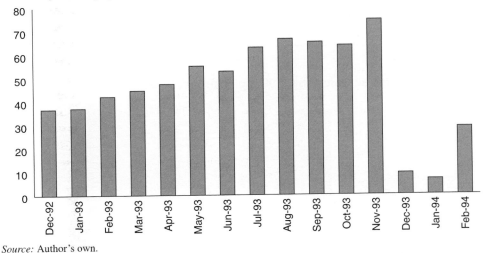

Source: Author's own.

around zero means that the returns of the fund and index do not seem to be dependent on each other.

In order to have statistically significant results a correlation analysis should examine at least 24–36 data points. In addition to looking at the correlation over the whole period it is interesting to look at rolling correlations over 24–36 month periods in order to analyse the stability of correlations over different market cycles (see Exhibit 23.7).

Fund performance versus index performance

A more intuitive way of looking at correlation is the analysis of the monthly returns of the fund versus the comparison benchmark. There are four different possibilities of looking at the monthly returns:

1. fund up–index up;
2. fund down–index up;
3. fund up–index down; and
4. fund down–index down.

Cases 2 and 3 represent months with negative correlation. However, the investor is particularly interested in case 2, which pertains to instances when the fund has positive performance in a negative index month.

The section 'Correlation' in Exhibit 23.2 shows five months in which the fund went down when the index was up, but 11 months when the fund went up and the index went down. Or expressed differently, of the 12 down months for the index, the fund went down in just one. This observation of low correlation and consistent performance irrespective of the benchmark index is also supported by the analysis of the fund's performance in index up and index down months (see the section 'Consistency').

Monthly returns

Finally, it is interesting to look at individual monthly returns and analyse their distribution, that is, the minimum, maximum and average returns as well as the clustering of good or negative performance streaks (see Exhibit 23.8).

Exhibit 23.8

Monthly returns for sample fund, 1991 to February 1994 (%)

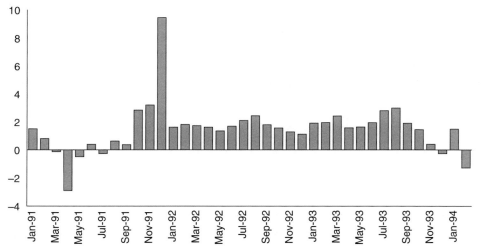

Source: Author's own.

Case study

Investment strategy

The data in Exhibit 23.2 are for a fund that pursues a relative value fixed-income arbitrage strategy and aims at achieving a stable return (annualised at 15 per cent) irrespective of developments in the fixed-income markets. The fund invests in collateralised mortgage obligations, other mortgage-backed securities of high credit quality and a variety of derivative instruments. Most of the securities are guaranteed by federal or state agencies and carry a rating of Aaa or Aa. The fund can use leverage of up to three times equity. Detailed guidelines exist regarding risk management, for example, regarding diversification and liquidity of investments. The company manages US$600 million in equity and employs five investment professionals and a number of other staff.

Interpretation of summary analysis

The analysis of performance shows good results. It shows a typical pattern for relative value funds with stable monthly returns. Except in the start-up period, none of the rolling 12-month returns are below the fund's stated objective of 15 per cent and the track record is longer than three years, which should be about average for the hedge fund universe at that time.

The data show a very low standard deviation of 6.2 per cent and downside deviation of 2.1 per cent. The maximum drawdown occurred early in the history of the fund and amounted to 3.5 per cent, which was recovered over five months. Other than that, only two more negative monthly returns of −0.27 per cent and −1.29 per cent were observed, but very recently.

The good performance and risk numbers result in excellent efficiency with a Sharpe ratio of over two and a Sortino ratio of nearly six.

Consistency is also high. Only six out of 39 months showed negative performances and the average performance in up months is 1.9 per cent and in down months is −0.9 per cent. It is particularly interesting to note that the fund's performance in index up and index down months is 1.5 per cent and 1.4 per cent respectively. At this point the question of the index for comparison should be discussed. It could be argued that a fixed-income benchmark might be better suited, or even a style index of mortgage-backed securities or relative value hedge funds. The benefit of using the S&P 500 is its widespread use and the stated return objective of the fund, which is 15 per cent per annum.

The correlation to the S&P 500 could be a little lower than 0.39. However, in 11 months when the index was down, the fund showed a positive performance, whereas in only five months did the index go up but the fund went down (see Exhibit 23.9).

All in all, the fund displays a good to excellent quantitative result with a small consolidation in the last couple of months. However, the fund in our example is the now well-known Granite Fund managed by David Askin! Despite its stellar statistical record, it went to zero in the month following our data series for a variety of reasons.

Complex investment strategy and instruments

Mortgage-backed securities (MBS) arbitrage is one of the most complex and difficult hedge fund strategies. In addition to all the concepts and problems associated with fixed-income arbitrage (such as interest rates, yield curve, volatility, convexity and credit risk) one has the

Exhibit 23.9

Cumulative performance, 1991 to February 1994

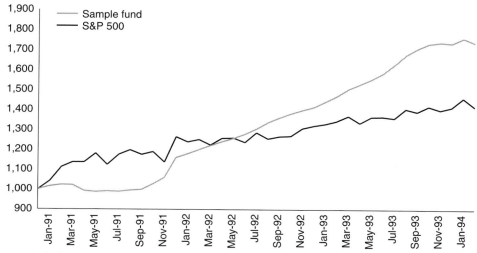

Source: Author's own.

problem of prepayment risk and extremely complex, illiquid and difficult to value derivative instruments. Whereas a reduction in interest rates normally increases the value of an interest-paying instrument, with MBS this is not always the case. An example would be when interest rates fall sufficiently that mortgages are prepaid and refinanced. The modelling of all the risks, and in particular the prepayment risk of MBS, can be extremely complex and research intensive. One hedge fund manager in this area used one of the first privately owned Cray supercomputers for this purpose, a task that is now done by a computer network.

The other aspect of risk lies in the complexity of derivative instruments. In addition to straight puts and calls there are interest only (I/O) strips, principal only (P/O) strips and inverse floaters and ever new and exotic types of derivatives. Not only is it difficult to value these instruments but also liquidity is often low.

Unexpected interest rate increase in 1994

The year 1994 was a difficult one for hedge funds and traditional money managers. An unexpected interest rate increase in February 1994 reduced the liquidity of the MBS market, a problem often associated with very complex strategies. The manager who had a variety of I/Os and P/Os to create a market-neutral portfolio saw the value of his P/O strips decline more than his I/O strips appreciated because there was only limited demand for this type of paper. The manager did not realise the losses and allegedly published net asset values based on estimated prices rather than dealer bids. When prices continued to fall he had to sell off the most liquid positions after margin calls from his brokers. When further calls occurred he had to sell positions with large discounts to their value.

Some of the brokers accelerated the fall of the fund as they knew the manager had to liquidate his positions at all cost. Some brokers allegedly sold positions the same day to other counterparties with profits of 50–100 per cent. The whole process is still being investigated and it is expected that the investors might recover 10 per cent or more of the NAV from the brokers.

Conclusion

A complex investment strategy does not necessarily have to lead into a catastrophe. In the first quarter of 1994, 12 managers who pursued similar leveraged strategies as the fund discussed showed no worse returns than negative 2 per cent. However, no matter how attractive a fund may look based on quantitative analysis, statistics are no substitute for a clear understanding of the risks underlying a given investment strategy.

Summary

There is a reason for all prospectuses stating 'past performance is no guarantee for future performance'. Quantitative analysis is not sufficient to identify successful hedge funds. It must be accompanied by a thorough qualitative due diligence and ongoing risk monitoring after an investment has taken place. Qualitative due diligence must look at the four 'P's: the people, the process, the performance and risk characteristics, and the partnership details of the fund. Risk monitoring must focus on qualitative and quantitative aspects. When developments show up in the numbers it might already be too late to react. Ongoing communication with the hedge fund manager and other people in his firm and the industry might help to detect early warning signs.

Yet quantitative analysis has a lot of reasonable uses. The framework discussed earlier provides a comprehensive overview of a fund's performance and risk characteristics. In this respect it can be used as a starting point for more detailed analyses. It can also be used as a framework to rank different funds. Such a peer group ranking system can be tailor-made, as the weights of the different categories or ratios can be individually determined.

Quantitative analysis is an important tool for hedge fund evaluation. With so many more hedge funds offering their services every day, one of the most important applications of quantitative analysis can be to weed out uninteresting managers and zero in on the most promising candidates that then warrant thorough qualitative due diligence.

Chapter 24

Institutional investors: incorporating hedge funds into the asset allocation process

James Berens, Judith Posnikoff and Alexandra Coffey
Pacific Alternative Asset Management Company, LLC, Irvine, California

Introduction

As institutional investors review their cumulative portfolio losses since 2000 (estimated in the trillions of dollars), hedge funds stand out as having continued to deliver good returns, certainly on a relative basis but even in absolute terms. Largely as a result of their strong absolute performance in a troubled equity market environment, flows into hedge funds are estimated to have been US$16.3 billion in 2002 alone.[1] Notable billion-dollar plus hedge fund investors include CalPERS, the Ontario Teachers Pension Plan, the ABP, General Motors pension funds and the top five US university endowments.

In addition to the absolute returns provided by hedge funds, these institutional investors recognise that hedge funds tend to have a very attractive risk profile that, when included within a traditional portfolio allocation, can improve overall portfolio characteristics. While these attractive risk characteristics were in fact widely known starting in the mid to late 1990s, the reality of dismal returns from most public asset classes has led to a keener appreciation of the diversifying properties hedge funds bring to an overall portfolio.

However, even as these properties have become more fully appreciated, hedge fund blowups, meltdowns and frauds continue to be a high-profile deterrent to full acceptance by the institutional investment community. As demonstrated by the headline cases of hedge fund disasters, treading carefully through hedge fund waters is a skill and time commitment that few investors possess. Thus, as US pension plans and other institutions increasingly turn their attention to the portfolio benefits of hedge funds, they are relying more and more on experienced and institutionally focused funds of funds managers and consultants to help them achieve their hedge fund investment objectives.

This chapter will provide a review of how hedge funds differ from traditional long-only investments, how those differences can be incorporated to benefit an institutional portfolio and the practical matter of how institutions are currently using hedge funds.

What defines a hedge fund?

Hedge funds, because of their strong absolute performance in the troubled equity market environment of the last few years, have recently become the investment choice 'du jour'. The term hedge fund is so broad and widely used that it is difficult to define precisely. For some, a hedge fund is any investment pool where a performance-based fee is charged. It is unfair, however, to lump all such funds together as they can be extraordinarily diverse in terms of their investment styles and performance characteristics. Thus, where hedge funds fit and what role they play within the portfolio of an institutional investor can also be extremely diverse.

Even today, the actual definition of a hedge fund is still hazy but the common definition is a loosely regulated investment pool that has the primary portfolio characteristic of being hedged. In other words, the manager of a hedge fund will invest both long and short (or engage in other offsetting securities transactions) in order to dampen or eliminate the impact on return of various systematic factors, primarily that of the overall equity market or of interest rates. Returns are thus driven primarily by security selection, not by any systematic market exposure (with the exception being pure macro strategies). With lack of regulatory oversight and an investor base initially comprised primarily of high net worth individuals, hedge funds have tended to operate without previously set investment constraints, in that they have the ability to sell short, use a broad array of investment instruments or securities and be opportunistic. Interestingly, hedge funds by design operate without many of the constraints identified by Roger Clarke and his colleagues[2] that institutions typically place on their investment managers (such as no shorting and limits on portfolio turnover). Furthermore, Clarke et al. find that such constraints negatively impact returns.

Much of the return generated by hedge funds can thus be traced to their ability to trade freely or opportunistically in response to various market conditions, leading to their promise of good absolute performance rather than good relative performance. The focus on absolute performance rather than relative performance and the entrepreneurial aspects of the managers results in hedge funds traditionally charging a performance fee, or 'carry', where the performance earned is shared between the portfolio manager and the investor. A fixed management fee is also typically charged. In any event, today's institutional investor is increasingly focused on what the underlying investment exposures are as opposed to the fund structure or even how the fund defines itself.

Where do hedge funds fit in an institutional portfolio?

The role hedge funds can play within an institutional portfolio can be as varied as the hedge fund strategies themselves. However, hedge funds most commonly appear in institutional portfolios in one or more of the following three asset allocation approaches.

Traditional allocations

Some institutions are using hedge funds as an absolute return diversifier (see Exhibit 24.1 for the low historical correlations between hedge funds and traditional asset classes) as hedge funds can fit quite easily as part of the traditional equity or fixed-income allocation of the portfolio. In addition, as Exhibit 24.2 demonstrates, the addition of hedge funds can do much to increase the risk-adjusted performance of a traditional allocation. For example, when using hedge funds as an equity replacement, instead of going through the policy changes necessary to allocate a specific dollar amount to hedge funds (as a separate allocation), some institutions will instead construct a portfolio of long-short equity hedge funds and add them to their equity allocation in order to lower the overall beta on their portfolio. Most long-short hedge funds are invested primarily in domestic US equities, so the returns generated by managers in this particular strategy are generally fairly highly correlated to the US equity market. Thus, an allocation to long-short equity hedge funds can legitimately play a role as a portion of the domestic equity allocation. As a general rule, however, because of the effect of short selling, the equity market risk (as measured by beta) of a group of hedge funds will likely be less than that of the overall market. Thus, the impact of their addition on the effective equity market exposure of the overall equity allocation should be recognised and accounted for by investors.

Dedicated short selling hedge funds that focus primarily on domestic equities (although in a decidedly different manner) can also fit as part of the standard equity allocation, providing an insurance-like hedge. However, investors must be cognisant of the fact that the typically negative correlation of the short sellers with the US equity market can significantly alter the overall portfolio's effective equity market exposure.

Alternatively, an allocation to traditional fixed-income securities may be replaced with an allocation to hedge funds, specifically those with a fixed-income focus. This can be in the form of managers who trade different fixed-income securities (for example, the bonds of distressed or bankrupt companies) or those who go short as well as long the bonds (for example, sovereign debt hedge funds). This strategy of replacing traditional fixed-income exposure with that gained through hedge funds is becoming especially popular now in the current low interest rate environment. Hedge funds may be shorting bonds or have an active strategy in place for managing interest rate risk. As interest rates go up, bond prices go down, and hedge funds with their shorting capability are in a position to potentially benefit from either move. This fixed-income replacement or enhancement strategy allows institutional investors to lower their exposure to interest rate risks, obtain higher returns and at the same time capitalise on fixed-income volatility. For example, distressed debt hedge funds, because they invest primarily in debt-related instruments, can be and often are included as part of a fixed-income allocation. Due to the relatively low duration of the distressed securities, the addition of distressed debt hedge funds provides a return premium but little additional volatility risk to a traditional fixed-income allocation.

Exhibit 24.1

Hedge fund correlation matrix, January 1998–December 2002

	CBH	DD	CH	SDMH	LSE	SS	EMN	MA	S&P 500
Convertible bond hedging (CBH)	1								
Distressed debt (DD)	0.83	1							
Credit hedging (CH)	0.83	0.88	1						
Sovereign debt and mortgage hedging (CDMH)	0.55	0.53	0.55	1					
Long-short equity (LSE)	0.74	0.76	0.63	0.31	1				
Short selling (SS)	−0.63	−0.70	−0.58	−0.15	−0.77	1			
Equity market neutral (EMN)	0.57	0.55	0.53	0.17	0.73	−0.47	1		
Merger arbitrage (MA)	0.73	0.74	0.73	0.28	0.74	−0.63	0.76	1	
S&P 500	0.50	0.50	0.46	0.06	0.62	−0.83	0.38	0.57	1
T-bills	0.17	−0.01	0.01	−0.03	0.27	0.04	0.49	0.38	0.10
Lehman aggregate	−0.24	−0.15	−0.22	0.01	−0.19	0.22	−0.01	−0.22	−0.30

Source: Pacific Alternative Asset Management Company Manager database.

Exhibit 24.2

Impact of hedge fund on traditional portfolios, 1994–2002

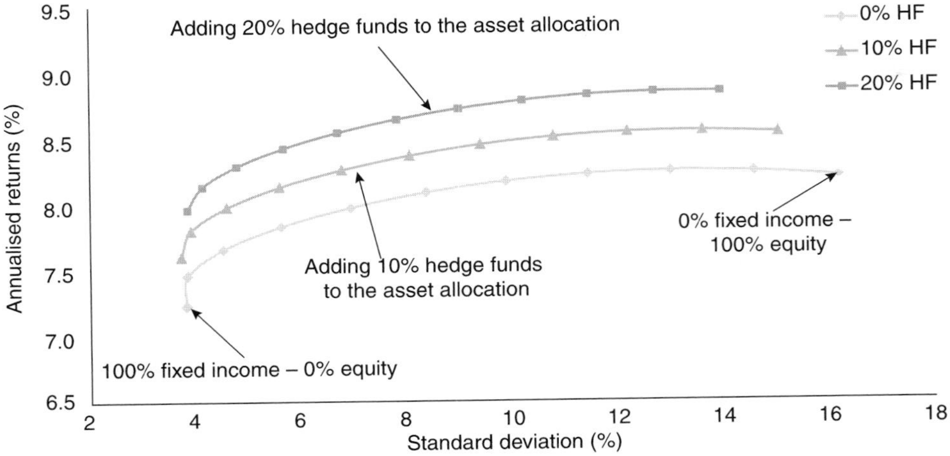

Sources: Fixed income: Lehman Brothers US aggregate; Equity: Russell 3000; Hedge funds: Credit Suisse First Boston Hedge Fund Index (CSFB).

Various market-neutral[3] hedge fund strategies also have debt-like return characteristics (relatively low volatility and correlation to other asset classes) so they can also fit as part of a fixed-income allocation. The inclusion of both distressed debt and market-neutral hedge funds would act to increase the overall expected return of the fixed-income allocation and add little if any portfolio volatility. Increasingly, a combination of the two hedge fund sub-asset categories is being recognised as an extremely attractive fixed-income alternative.

'Alternatives' allocation

Hedge funds can also fit quite well as part of an institutional portfolio's 'alternatives' allocation, usually by providing fairly consistent returns and relatively low volatility as compared to other alternatives such as private equity, venture capital and timber and agricultural land. The Yale University endowment, for instance, had 25 per cent of its assets allocated to hedge funds in 2002.[4] This approach is perhaps the most prevalent strategy that institutional investors use for their hedge fund allocations although it involves a total policy allocation to alternative assets with hedge funds treated as a separate strategy within the overall alternatives allocation. This strategy for hedge fund investing by institutional investors is usually put into place and guided by the institution's investment consultants. The hedge fund allocation, in combination with other alternative assets such as real estate, private equity and venture capital, allows for enhanced liquidity within the overall allocation while maintaining the high, but often risky returns, of the other generally illiquid alternative assets. This approach has become particularly popular in the last few years as many of the less liquid alternative assets mature and institutional investors are shifting these assets into hedge funds as a source of liquidity.

One interesting approach within an alternatives allocation is to combine absolute return hedge funds and private equity. As most allocations to private equity require a five-year or longer 'lock-up' with little if any realisable return generated over that period, the addition of absolute return hedge funds can provide a flow of stable absolute returns with low volatility and better liquidity terms. It should be recognised, however, that each of the hedge fund categories generally lessens volatility, increases liquidity and lowers expected returns for an overall allocation to alternatives. Due to the lower liquidity requirements within this allocation, distressed debt and public-private, long-short hybrid funds are often used in this context.

Portable alphas

Another role for hedge funds within an institutional portfolio that has seen remarkable success is the use of hedge funds in conjunction with financial futures to provide index-plus returns. Institutions typically implement this approach through the use of derivatives to transport alpha from one asset class to another. The strength of the equity markets in the late 1990s and the shift to index-based investing (given the realisation of the difficulties in consistently adding alpha with a long-only investment programme) propelled institutional interest in the portable alpha concept. In basic terms, in an index-plus programme, index futures or a swap are used to generate the returns of the desired index (less Libor which is the implied cost of funding) and a portion of the dollars allocated are invested in a pool of hedge funds in order to generate alpha (in excess of Libor). The combination of the two components should result in the return of the index plus the returns of the hedge fund portfolio less Libor. As long as the hedge funds can generate a return in excess of Libor plus a small amount to cover transaction costs, the return on this portable alpha package will exceed that of the index (hence the name 'index-plus'). The alpha or value-added from the hedge fund portfolio is ported to the return of the equity index. Market-neutral and absolute return focused strategies, because of their consistent ability to generate a positive alpha with relatively low volatility, are particularly appropriate categories for this application.

Stand-alone/dedicated allocation

More recently, the most common means of incorporating hedge funds into an institutional asset allocation has been to create a new investment allocation and call it the 'hedge fund' or 'absolute return' category. The impact on the portfolio's return will be substantially the same as the previous three methods, but will ultimately depend on which of the institution's other asset classes gets reduced as a result of the hedge fund allocation. For example, for an institution with indexed equities, if the hedge fund allocation received 5 per cent while the cash allocation was decreased by 5 per cent, and all other allocations were left unchanged, the effect on the portfolio return of this approach and the portable alpha approach would be identical in the aggregate.

Given that this method is essentially incorporated within the previous three, one might wonder why it has become the dominant means for institutions investing in hedge funds. Our belief is that the reason is inherent in the institutional investment process itself: a stand-alone allocation means that the hedge funds are appropriately categorised, separately tracked and benchmarked. In this context, the whole process for an institution is familiar. Either the institution or a selected consultant can conduct a search for hedge funds, perhaps involving a request for proposal (RFP). Those funds deemed most attractive can be researched thoroughly and invited to a finals presentation, and the chosen fund(s) can then be monitored and benchmarked (facilitated by the proliferation of reasonable peer groups and indices). The whole process works just as it might for a traditional large-cap US equity manager. Due to these characteristics, the most common allocation in this context has been to well-diversified multi-strategy funds of funds.

Issues for institutions investing in hedge funds

Regardless of where institutional investors slot hedge funds into their asset allocations, it is critical for them to realise that investing in hedge funds is different from investing with traditional managers. Hedge funds have traditionally been seen as operating opaquely, often not disclosing to investors the underlying investment process or investment strategies and almost never revealing actual trades or portfolio positions. Hedge funds have little or no required regulatory oversight (although currently there are indications that this may change, particularly in the United States as the Securities and Exchange Commission is in the midst of an extensive review of hedge fund activities),* thus pre-hire due diligence and ongoing monitoring are critical. Issues related to the use (if any) of leverage, liquidity, portfolio valuation and reporting all need to be addressed. Additionally, hedge fund investments are made through funds that typically have fairly restrictive liquidity and reporting terms and which pay the manager a performance or incentive fee. This stands in complete contrast to the typical long-only traditional investment made via a separate account with complete transparency, daily liquidity and investor control via their custodian.

Institutional investors have reacted to the differences inherent in hedge fund investing by attempting to overlay the traditional separate account methodology. This has considerable drawbacks when applied to hedge funds. Specifically, many of the top performing managers (and even some start-ups!) are reluctant to manage separate accounts away from their funds. Separate accounts with these managers tend to underperform their funds, which may be due to lack of oversight but is more likely the result of managing without regular incoming flows. Many strategies and/or securities cannot or should not be managed within a separate account format. For example, separate accounts lack the limited liability features of investing in a fund and thus the investor may face margin calls directly if leverage is used. Position size or concentration may become an issue if the manager is trading securities that cannot be easily allocated across various accounts or investors.

Perhaps the greatest negative impact that an institutional investor may create by attempting to treat investing in hedge funds the same as investing with traditional managers is that they impose constraints on the manager. This may take the form of restricting the investment universe, disallowing certain strategies, or requiring the manager to remain fully invested. Additionally, some institutions by their charter (particularly some public pension plans) do not allow for the use of short selling or leverage, constraints on either of which may prevent the use of some traditional hedge fund strategies altogether. All of this constrains the opportunity set for the manager and limits expected return without necessarily reducing risk. Hedge funds by their very nature have different risks than do traditional managers and limiting their investment options may in fact increase overall risk. Specifically, it may be best for a manager to limit exposures in some instances and increase them in others in order to minimise volatility or avoid investing in a poor environment. Placing constraints on the manager may limit his or her ability to adjust to market conditions and thus negatively impact performance.

Recurrent threat of hedge fund regulation

Finally, the hedge fund industry itself is changing for the better to meet the demands of institutional investors. The first US Securities and Exchange Commission (SEC) inquiries into hedge funds began in 1968 when the SEC set out on an extensive fact finding mission and discussed the possibility of taking steps to regulate the hedge fund industry. In 1970, responding to the regulation threats by the SEC and the market events of 1968–69, Carol Loomis, in an article for *Fortune*,[5] wrote that hedge funds may face 'disastrous happenings' from the SEC. Loomis detailed in her article how hedge funds had reached 'crisis numbers' and how the impact of hedge funds on the market had been approached by the regulators with an attitude that is best described as bitter.

Some 30 years later, in response to the implosion of Long-Term Capital Management, the President's Working Group and the SEC set out again to determine what steps were needed to regulate the hedge fund industry and protect investors. Again, in May 2003, the SEC approached hedge funds as 'high-risk' investment vehicles that need to be regulated in order to protect the general public.

The underlying theme of the SEC inquiries and the threats of regulation have centred on increased disclosure requirements and forced registration with the US SEC. However, due to investor pressures, not regulation, more US-based hedge fund managers are already registering with the US SEC. Additionally, more hedge funds are now being offered by traditional investment managers and by boutique firms run by managers already with experience and comfortable with managing within an institutional framework. The information made available to investors is improving as managers recognise investors' concerns, particularly those of institutional investors. In many ways, the simple presence of large-scale institutional money (both direct and indirect) is accelerating the transformation of hedge funds into a component of the mainstream investment management industry.

Advantages of using a fund of funds

The critical components of hedge fund investing for institutions include portfolio diversification and manager selection. Studies conducted on hedge funds have shown that the distribution of hedge fund returns resembles most closely the distribution of individual stock returns rather than the return distribution of well-diversified security portfolios such as mutual funds. This means that to achieve their risk and return targets over their investment horizons, institutional investors should invest in portfolios of hedge funds, not single hedge funds. Hedge fund portfolios should be diversified by sub-strategy, investment style and manager in order to mitigate the risk associated with either a single investment style or single manager.

Internal research done at Pacific Alternative Asset Management has shown that manager selection is more important than strategy selection in building hedge fund portfolios.[6] Due to their idiosyncratic nature, hedge fund strategies have a higher level of manager-specific risk than do public market strategies such as long-only equity or fixed-income investing. There is also a lower level of familiarity and comfort on behalf of both investors and hedge fund managers in dealing with one another. This means that investors must prudently both select and monitor the managers in which they invest by utilising a fundamental investment process that parallels those used by responsible equity managers.

Unfortunately, these tasks are difficult to accomplish for hedge fund investing because accurate, up-to-date quality hedge fund data are not easily obtained or deciphered, including the identification of superior managers. Therefore, investors must devote considerable resources to these tasks in order to gain the desired results. For this reason, sophisticated institutional investors are increasingly relying on the services of professional fund of funds managers of proven quality. In addition to statistical analysis, experienced fund of funds managers can provide the necessary qualitative components of successful hedge fund investing rather than simply relying on quantitative analysis of historical performance data as provided by the various proprietary databases.

The hedge fund due diligence process as conducted by an experienced fund of funds manager will include a thorough review of the investment strategy and process of a candidate manager. This will specifically focus on identifying the underlying risks of the investment process and strategy, including the remaining residual risks such as 'tail' risk (this cannot be done based solely on historical return data but should also include analysis of actual portfolio holdings). The due diligence process will also include a thorough review of the suitability, liquidity and pricing of the underlying securities included in a manager's portfolio (including whether or not the pricing or valuation is conducted independently of the fund manager). Additionally, an in-depth check of the fund manager and senior staff's personal backgrounds should also be conducted with an emphasis on the manager's reputation for honesty and truthfulness. This is best done by relying on one's network of contacts throughout the investment industry (both hedge fund and traditional) in order to go beyond the list of provided references.

In addition to the extensive pre-hire due diligence necessary for successful hedge fund investing, ongoing due diligence and monitoring of the individual hedge funds must be done in order to protect against manager style drift, the assumption of excessive risks, illiquidity in the underlying investments and valuation issues. This is a significant part of the benefits to be gained through the use of an experienced fund of funds manager that has the resources and the infrastructure necessary to deal with these tasks. Also, much as is done for portfolios of individual stocks, portfolios of hedge funds need to be continually assessed in terms of diversification, performance attribution, achievement of the expected risk and return objectives, and removal and replacement of individual managers. Again, these functions are best left to those with experience and success in managing portfolios of hedge funds across various hedge fund cycles and investment environments.

Clearly, a fund of funds greatly simplifies the due diligence requirements for an institutional investor, a major advantage given the limited or reduced staffing levels at most pension plans or other institutions. The most significant advantage, however, of a fund of funds approach is to substantially reduce the primary risk that worries institutional investors (that of a hedge fund blow-up). Recent anecdotal evidence indicates that this risk is so well handled by the fund of funds community that the primary risk for an institution investing in a fund of funds is not blow-up risk but rather simply mediocre absolute returns.

Conclusion

Although the hedge fund industry is growing to meet its predicted US$1 trillion demand over the next few years, the components needed to develop an institutionally attractive product are still in their infancy. Some of these components include such necessities as client education, institutional marketing, transparency around processes and valuations, and sophisticated client service meant especially for the institutional clientele. The rate of growth for the hedge fund industry, especially in the institutional sector, is dependent on the mechanisms put in place to educate clients and the ability to manage hedge fund assets on the scale required by institutions. Funds of funds have grown in the industry as institutions realise that qualified and experienced funds of funds have the capacity and due diligence resources to handle large allocations of money, funding skilled managers, and the ability to offer the level of client service that institutional investors require. Regardless of the mechanism used to obtain the exposure, hedge funds have matured as an industry and delivered the kind of results that legitimately merit the consideration of institutional investors.

* Editor's note: on 29 September 2003, shortly before this book went to press, the staff of the SEC issued its report entitled 'The Implications of the Growth of Hedge Funds', the culmination of its efforts following the Hedge Fund Roundtable held in May 2003. As of the date of this writing, the Commission itself had not taken any action in response to the report. One of the key recommendations of the staff was that the SEC consider 'requiring hedge fund advisers to register with the SEC as investment advisers, taking into account whether the benefits outweigh the burdens of registration'. In the staff's view, ' ... registration of hedge fund advisers would serve as a deterrent to fraud, encourage compliance and the adoption of compliance procedures, provide the SEC with important information ... and effectively raise the standards for investment in hedge funds from the "accredited investor" standard to that of "qualified client"'. See http://www.sec.gov/news/studies/hedgefunds0903.pdf for the full text of the report.

[1] *The Wall St. Journal Online,* 3 March 2003, 'Choose Your Fund: Hedge or Mutual'.

[2] Clarke, Roger, Harindra de Silva, and Steven Thorley (2002), 'Portfolio Constraints and the Fundamental Law of Active Management', *Financial Analysts Journal,* Vol. 58, No. 5 (September/October), pp. 48–66.

[3] Market neutral is the phrase generally used to describe a collection of investment strategies that capture small mispricings between closely related securities and thus aim to deliver returns uncorrelated with the overall market. Market-neutral strategies are intended to have zero market risk as measured by beta (hence market 'neutral').

[4] 2002 Yale University Endowment Letter.

[5] Loomis, Carol (1970), 'Hard Times Come to the Hedge Funds', *Fortune.*

[6] Berens, James L., and Judith F. Posnikoff (2001), 'Market neutral investing through funds of funds', *The Capital Guide to Alternative Investments,* 2001 edition, pp. 123–128.

Chapter 25

Quantitative analysis of return and risk characteristics of hedge funds, managed futures and mutual funds

Thomas Schneeweis
University of Massachusetts, Amherst, Massachusetts

Richard Spurgin
Clark University, Worcester, Massachusetts

Introduction

The past decade has witnessed a dramatic rise and fall in the use of stock and bond mutual funds as stand-alone investments or as part of an investor's diversified portfolio. Moreover, previous research (Sharpe, 1992; Elton et al., 1995) has shown that for stock and bond mutual fund investors, multi-factor models often provide improved explanatory power regarding the return structure of these investment vehicles. Within the past decade, several studies (Fung and Hsieh, 1997a, 1997b; Liang, 2001; Agarwal and Naik, 2000b; Schneeweis et al., 2002, 2003) have explored sources of return for actively managed assets such as mutual funds, hedge funds and managed futures (for example, commodity trading advisers). In this research, hedge funds and commodity trading advisers have been shown to have different trading styles (for example, long and short positions and leverage) and trading opportunities (for example, commodity and currency markets) than traditional stock and bond mutual fund managers. As a result, for hedge funds and managed futures, factors which incorporate the possibility of trending prices (up or down), as well as short positions, may capture their relative return movement.

In this chapter a common set of factors are used to describe return movement across each of the asset classes studied (commodity trading advisers, hedge funds and mutual funds). Results indicate the set of factors which explain returns to mutual funds, hedge funds and managed futures are somewhat asset class and strategy dependent. In short, for certain equity sensitive mutual funds and hedge funds, the factors explaining asset return are similar and the relative hedge fund investments can be regarded more as return enhancers than risk diversifiers. In contrast, for other hedge fund and managed futures strategies, the factors explaining asset return may differ from those explaining mutual fund returns such that the hedge funds and managed futures strategies may be regarded as risk diversifiers.

In the next section, there is a brief review of previous research on the sources of return to hedge funds and managed futures. As discussed above, these research results show that the sources of the expected return for various equity or credit sensitive hedge fund strategies (for example, hedge equity or distressed debt) may be similar to those in traditional asset classes such as stocks and bonds, while the returns to certain hedge fund strategies (for example, market-neutral, convertible hedge) often depend on different factors than traditional stocks and bonds (Fung and Hsieh, 2002; Schneeweis and Spurgin, 1998). In fact, it is due to the different return opportunities and return drivers for certain hedge funds that the benefits of risk diversification (relative to traditional stock and bond investments) exist. In the consequent section, the data and methodology used for this analysis is described. The approach used in this study is similar to that conducted in an earlier version of this study (Schneeweis and Spurgin, 1999). The results are subsequently presented. The results are also consistent with our earlier analysis; that is, the same basic market return and risk factors may be used to better understand the fundamental return characteristics of mutual funds, hedge funds and managed futures. As important, once these market factor relationships are understood, they may be used as a basis for asset allocation across various traditional and alternative investments.

Sources of return to hedge fund and managed derivative investments

Previous research on hedge funds and managed futures (Schneeweis and Spurgin, 1999; Spurgin and Schneeweis, 2003; Fung and Hsieh, 2000c; Agarwal and Naik, 2000a) has compared historical hedge fund and commodity trading adviser (CTA) returns with certain economic variables with the goal of identifying those factors that explain historical return performance. As early as the mid-1990s, Mitev (1996) conducted a factor analysis which suggested a five factor model for CTAs. Mitev concluded that the CTAs in his sample fell primarily into 1) trend following strategies, 2) surprise or stop loss control models, 3) agricultural markets, 4) spread strategies (primarily interest rate) and 5) fundamental economic factors or global markets. While this research sheds light on how CTAs perform relative to one another, it did not address the underlying source of CTA return relative to general economic variables or trading approaches. Recent CTA analysis has extended this analysis into reviewing how CTA returns are consistent with returns to a look back option (Fung and Hsieh, 2001) or respond to various trend following indices (Spurgin and Schneeweis, 2003) which are designed to track CTA-based trading strategies.

In contrast to hedge funds, CTAs derive much of their return from trading derivatives. However, the derivatives market is, by definition, a zero sum game. Theoretical studies of derivative market structure have identified many potential sources of this risk premium in trading derivative-based products. In short, empirical and theoretical research has indicated that CTAs may offer the opportunity for risk-adjusted returns even within a zero sum game market.

Futures and options investors may simply hold positions that mimic the return of the underlying cash asset, which would yield a positive expected return if, as with stock index futures, the underlying asset had an expected return greater than the cost of financing.

Speculative traders offer liquidity to hedgers. An imbalance between hedging demand from long hedgers and short hedgers may create opportunities to earn returns by purchasing (providing) the excess supply (demand) from the hedging community.

Transaction costs in futures and options markets are generally lower than for comparable cash instruments. Low transaction costs may allow derivatives traders to exploit information about an asset's value that is too small for investors in cash instruments to utilise profitably.

Academic studies have shown that momentum-based trading strategies are profitable over time. While most of these studies were conducted on equity markets, such that the momentum profits may not be large enough to cover the cost of transacting the trades, derivative markets have been shown to earn these returns because of their low transaction costs and high leverage.

Options traders may be able to create positions that offer a risk premium in exchange for accepting exposure to certain portions of the return distribution of the underlying security.

Options traders also have the ability to create positions that may profit from changes in expected volatility of the underlying asset. Investors in cash instruments can only profit from changes in the value of the underlying asset. Within the past decade, academic research on the sources of hedge fund returns has also developed. Fung and Hsieh (1997a) use factor-analytic approaches to determine the common factors that help explain hedge fund return patterns. Fung and Hsieh identify five general investment approaches (distressed, global/macro, systems, systems/opportunistic and value) that are shown to explain most hedge fund return variation. Of these five groups, global/macro, systems and systems/opportunistic were shown to have factors not easily explained by the factors common to stock funds, bond funds, distressed funds or value funds.[1] Thus, for the hedge funds and managed futures funds, theoretical and empirical models of return estimation may necessarily be based on the anticipated trading style of the hedge fund manager. For instance, hedge funds focusing on pure zero risk arbitrage positions will have the risk-free rate as a benchmark. If the hedge fund focuses on long international equity then international equity benchmarks similar to those used for traditional international mutual funds may be regarded as standard (Fung and Hsieh, 1997). Many factors have been proposed to explain the higher risk-adjusted returns earned by hedge funds in recent years as compared to mutual funds that trade similar assets (Fung and Hsieh 1997a; Ackermann, 1999; Liang, 2001; Schneeweis et al., 2003). In brief, results show that most hedge fund strategies have exposure to the same market factors that affect traditional stock and bond funds including equity market exposure, interest rate exposure, credit risk exposure and option-based return characteristics.

Thus, to the degree that different factors explain the returns to managed futures, hedge funds, and stock and bond mutual fund returns, each may provide investors exposure to unique sources of return and provide an important source of return to a diversified investment portfolio. It is important to point out, however, that for certain hedge fund strategies that trade similar securities as traditional mutual funds, the factors which explain returns may be similar. In those hedge fund strategies, the investment may be regarded primarily as a return enhancer rather than a risk diversifier.

Data and methodology

The methodology used in this chapter is similar to that used in an earlier version (Schneeweis and Spurgin, 1999). Returns for all data series are expressed as monthly holding period returns and cover seven years from January 1996 to December 2002. Hedge fund indices are provided by Hedge Fund Research (HFR) and Evaluation Associates Capital Management (EACM). CTA indices are provided by CISDM (formerly MAR), Barclay Trading (Barclay) and EACM. Lipper stock and bond mutual fund indices are used to represent mutual fund returns. The comparison asset class benchmarks include the Standard & Poor's 500 stock index (S&P 500), Russell 2000, the Lehman US Aggregate Bond Index, Lehman High Yield, Goldman Sachs Commodity Index (GSCI) and the Lehman Global Aggregate Index. The Managed Futures Securities Based (MFSB) Index is used as a proxy for trend following CTA-based trading return.[2] Other indices employed in the study include the MSCI World Equity Index and the return on US 30-day Treasury bills. The source for the non hedge fund data is Bloomberg.

Statistical tests include descriptive risk and return characteristics, correlation analysis and multiple regressions. The correlation analysis exhibits correlations with nominal and absolute values of the cited factor indices. Multiple regression analysis is conducted using CTA, hedge fund, and stock and bond mutual fund indices as the dependent variables and the nominal (S&P 500, Russell 2000, Lehman US Aggregate, Lehman High Yield and MFSB) and absolute (Russell 2000, Lehman Aggregate and Lehman High Yield) indices as explanatory variables. Absolute values are used to capture elements of market volatility in each represented asset class. The following factors are based on common sources of return to mutual fund, hedge fund and managed futures trading strategies.

- *A natural return to owning financial and real assets.* This is modelled by including the nominal value of stocks (Russell 2000) and bonds (Lehman US Aggregate and High Yield).
- *Flexibility to use both long and short positions to benefit from market timing skill.* This is captured with the absolute value of the monthly returns of the underlying asset markets.
- *Market inefficiencies that result in temporary trends in prices.* A proxy for this is the Managed Futures Securities Based Index which captures the return to a moving average strategy using four futures market segments: physical commodities, currencies, interest rates and stock indices.

Results

Managed futures, hedge funds, mutual funds, stock and bond indices: descriptive statistics

Exhibit 25.1 gives descriptive statistics of the data used in this study. Included are the average annual return, standard deviation, maximum and minimum monthly return, the information ratio and Sharpe ratio for each of the CTA, hedge fund, and stock and bond mutual fund indices. Exhibit 25.2 shows a subset of the indices plotted in return/standard deviation space.

Results in Exhibit 25.1 and Exhibit 25.2 are consistent with the hypothesis that stock and bond funds, hedge funds and managed futures investments have different risk and return structures. Exhibit 25.2 shows that during the period studied (1996–2002), most of the hedge fund categories offered higher risk-adjusted returns than would have been available by allocating assets to the S&P 500 and cash. These results, however, could be the result primarily of the unique market conditions existing over that time period (for example, declining interest rates and credit spreads). While results in Exhibit 25.1 provide evidence that these assets have different historical risk–return trade-offs, it does not explain what the determinants of those returns are. The following sections describe the results of correlation and multivariate analysis of the returns. Results indicate that certain asset management strategies (for example, mutual funds) derive their return primarily from the nominal value of market factors while others (certain hedge fund strategies and CTAs) derive their return not only from primary market factors (stock and bond returns) but also from their ability to take long and short positions whose returns may be captured by factors such as absolute value or by return momentum such as trend following indices.[3]

Exhibit 25.1

Descriptive statistics of hedge fund, CTA, mutual fund and asset benchmarks, 1996–2002

Benchmarks	ARR	StDev	Max	Min	Info.	Sharpe
MFSB	9.92%	8.40%	8.18%	−4.12%	1.18	0.66
GSCI	4.95%	20.40%	16.88%	−12.17%	0.24	0.03
S&P 500	6.87%	17.73%	9.78%	−14.46%	0.39	0.14
Russell 2000	4.17%	21.89%	16.51%	−19.42%	0.19	−0.01
Lehman US Aggregate	7.27%	3.50%	2.70%	−1.75%	2.08	0.82
Lehman High Yield	3.59%	7.86%	7.49%	−7.37%	0.46	−0.11
MSCI World Index	2.40%	15.98%	9.02%	−13.35%	0.15	−0.13
Lehman Global Aggregate	5.28%	5.02%	4.74%	−2.97%	1.05	0.17
US Treasury bill	4.42%	1.45%	0.53%	1.19%		

Hedge funds	ARR	StDev	Max	Min	Info.	Sharpe
HFR Indices						
Equity Market Neutral Index	9.27%	3.54%	3.59%	−1.67%	2.62	1.37
Convertible Arbitrage Index	12.31%	3.18%	3.33%	−3.19%	3.86	2.48
Distressed Securities Index	9.69%	6.07%	5.06%	−8.50%	1.60	0.87
Emerging Markets Total Index	6.81%	17.12%	14.80%	−21.02%	0.40	0.14
Fund of Funds Index	8.08%	6.89%	6.85%	−7.47%	1.17	0.53
Macro Index	9.59%	7.55%	6.82%	−3.77%	1.27	0.68
Equity Hedge Index	14.76%	10.68%	10.88%	−7.65%	1.38	0.97
Fixed Income Arbitrage Index	4.69%	4.62%	3.04%	−6.45%	1.01	0.06
Market Timing Index	12.50%	7.87%	5.96%	−3.28%	1.59	1.03
Merger Arbitrage Index	10.42%	4.12%	2.47%	−5.69%	2.53	1.46
Short Selling Index	5.15%	25.46%	22.84%	−21.21%	0.20	0.03
EACM Indices						
EACM 100	9.69%	4.87%	5.70%	−4.45%	1.99	1.08
Relative Value	7.78%	3.90%	2.30%	−6.07%	1.99	0.86
Long-Short Equity	5.90%	3.10%	2.74%	−2.62%	1.90	0.48
Convertible Hedge	9.50%	5.49%	4.31%	−6.90%	1.73	0.93
Bond Hedge	2.59%	6.07%	2.88%	−7.09%	0.43	−0.30
Relative Value Multi-Strategy	13.00%	7.32%	3.80%	−13.98%	1.78	1.17
Event Driven	10.23%	4.96%	3.37%	−7.48%	2.06	1.17
Risk Arbitrage	8.16%	4.70%	2.96%	−5.98%	1.74	0.80
Bankruptcy/Distressed	9.24%	5.56%	4.72%	−8.17%	1.66	0.87
Event Driven Multi-Strategy	13.28%	5.81%	5.11%	−8.29%	2.29	1.53
Equity Hedge Funds	11.10%	12.91%	14.45%	−9.81%	0.86	0.52
Equity Hedge Domestic Long Bias	7.49%	19.38%	16.51%	−15.11%	0.39	0.16
Equity Hedge Domestic Opportunistic	13.85%	11.87%	15.26%	−5.15%	1.17	0.79
Equity Hedge Global/International	11.21%	11.60%	12.29%	−9.17%	0.97	0.59
Short Sellers	5.87%	23.63%	21.55%	−12.74%	0.25	0.06

(continued)

317

Exhibit 25.1 *continued*

Descriptive statistics of hedge fund, CTA, mutual fund and asset benchmarks, 1996–2002

CTA indices	ARR	StDev	Max	Min	Info.	Sharpe
			CISDM Indices			
US$	8.53%	8.50%	6.56%	−5.12%	1.00	0.48
Equal Weighted	9.39%	9.32%	7.80%	−4.45%	1.01	0.53
Currency Programme	5.01%	5.68%	4.49%	−4.15%	0.88	0.10
Discretionary Adviser Subindex	9.34%	4.89%	4.68%	−1.90%	1.91	1.01
Diversified Adviser Subindex	9.17%	10.33%	10.79%	−6.09%	0.89	0.46
Financial Programme	9.95%	12.31%	9.94%	−7.51%	0.81	0.45
Trend Follower Subindex	9.96%	14.57%	11.49%	−10.02%	0.68	0.38
			Barclay Indices			
CTA Index	6.59%	8.73%	6.45%	−4.77%	0.76	0.25
Currency Index	5.73%	6.80%	6.43%	−3.66%	0.84	0.19
Agricultural Index	0.96%	9.00%	6.47%	−6.52%	0.11	−0.38
Fin./Met. Index	6.33%	8.39%	6.29%	−4.24%	0.75	0.23
Diversified Index	8.24%	12.14%	10.17%	−6.48%	0.68	0.31
Systematic Index	7.53%	10.63%	7.52%	−6.68%	0.71	0.29
Discretionary Index	1.92%	4.91%	4.35%	−2.68%	0.39	−0.51
			EACM Indices			
Global Asset Alloc.	9.03%	8.36%	7.60%	−5.38%	1.08	0.55
Discretionary	7.99%	9.50%	7.21%	−15.87%	0.84	0.38
Systematic	9.46%	12.75%	10.56%	−7.35%	0.74	0.40

Mutual funds	ARR	StDev	Max	Min	Info.	Sharpe
			Lipper Fixed Income Mutual Fund Indices			
A-rated Bond Fund	6.25%	3.87%	3.22%	−2.26%	1.62	0.47
BBB-rated Fund	5.93%	4.05%	3.46%	−2.16%	1.46	0.37
General Bond Fund	6.23%	3.30%	2.98%	−1.92%	1.89	0.55
Global Income Fund	4.99%	4.51%	4.10%	−3.59%	1.11	0.13
Ultra Short Fund	5.18%	0.61%	0.76%	0.01%	8.54	1.26
			Lipper Stock Mutual Fund Indices			
Lipper Cap Appr Fund	3.61%	20.94%	13.02%	−17.18%	0.17	−0.04
Lipper Growth Fund	4.28%	19.08%	9.38%	−16.06%	0.22	−0.01
Lipper Mid-Cap Fund	4.06%	24.29%	17.89%	−20.20%	0.17	−0.01
Lipper Small-Cap Fund	2.99%	24.70%	20.37%	−19.84%	0.12	−0.06

Sources: CISDM, Bloomberg, Lipper, Schneeweis Partners, EACM, HFR, Barclay.

Managed futures, hedge fund, stock and bond indices: simple correlations

Managed futures correlations with commodity, stock, bond and currency indices

Exhibits 25.3 to 25.5 present the correlations among broad-based CTA indices and sub-indices from each of the three CTA index groupings (CISDM, Barclay and EACM) and

Exhibit 25.2

Risk and return for selected indices, 1996–2002

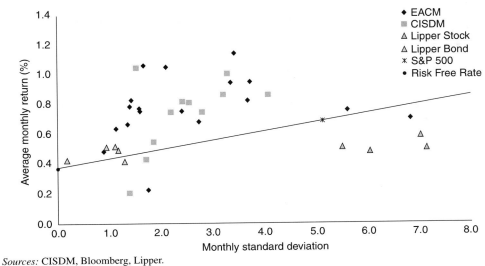

Sources: CISDM, Bloomberg, Lipper.

between those indices and the nominal and absolute values of the cited market factors (for example, MFSB, GSCI, S&P 500, Russell 2000, Lehman US Aggregate, Lehman High Yield, MSCI, Lehman Global). Results show that there are high correlations between overall CTA indices (CISDM CTA and Barclay CTA) and most CTA sub-indices. However, it is important to point out that even within the CTA area, low correlations do exist between certain strategies and markets traded. For instance, there is generally a low correlation between financial and currency CTA sub-indices and currency and agricultural CTA sub-indices. Similarly, the correlation across systematic/trend following CTAs is higher than between systematic/trend following CTA indices and discretionary CTAs.

The correlations between the various CTA indices and the nominal and absolute market factors are consistent with that described in other academic research. Basically, CTA returns have been shown to have a low correlation with traditional stock and bond market factors. Data in Exhibit 25.3 and Exhibit 25.4 reflect those results. Only for Lehman US Aggregate is there a reasonably positive correlation (for example, trend following and systematic indices often greater than 0.40). One reason for this result is that for the period of analysis, bond yields experienced a general downward trend, resulting in positive bond returns as well as positive returns to trend following interest rate futures contracts. Of greater interest is the generally high correlation between systematic CTA returns and absolute values of the cited variables. This result is consistent with other research that has shown that CTAs have the ability to achieve positive returns in up and down markets. Further indication of CTAs tending to profit through trend following systems which are not directly correlated with cash markets is shown in the generally high correlation between CTA index returns and returns to a passive futures-based trend following system (MFSB).

Hedge fund correlations with commodity, stock, bond and currency indices

Exhibit 25.6 and Exhibit 25.7 show the correlation between each of the HFR and EACM

Exhibit 25.3

CISDM CTA correlations

CISDM CTA	Dollar	Equal	Curr	Discret	Divers	Fin	Trend
US$	1.00						
Equal Weighted	0.95	1.00					
Currency Programme Subindex	0.46	0.42	1.00				
Discretionary Adviser Subindex	0.62	0.52	0.23	1.00			
Diversified Advisor Subindex	0.95	0.93	0.31	0.65	1.00		
Financial Programme Subindex	0.93	0.89	0.40	0.45	0.83	1.00	
Trend Followers Subindex	0.94	0.95	0.38	0.47	0.90	0.92	1.00
Nominal factors	Dollar	Equal	Curr	Discret	Divers	Fin	Trend
MFSB	0.78	0.83	0.28	0.44	0.78	0.75	0.80
GSCI	0.13	0.13	−0.02	0.14	0.11	0.16	0.11
S&P 500	−0.16	−0.21	0.15	0.04	−0.21	−0.18	−0.29
Russell 2000	−0.14	−0.18	0.07	0.15	−0.16	−0.21	−0.28
Lehman US Aggregate	0.46	0.41	0.04	0.25	0.44	0.47	0.46
Lehman High Yield	−0.13	−0.17	0.13	0.13	−0.15	−0.19	−0.28
MSCI World Index	−0.17	−0.23	0.10	0.09	−0.20	−0.21	−0.32
Lehman Global Aggregate	0.28	0.28	−0.20	0.08	0.27	0.36	0.29
US Treasury bill	−0.01	−0.01	0.12	0.06	0.00	−0.05	−0.05
Absolute values	Dollar	Equal	Curr	Discret	Divers	Fin	Trend
GSCI	0.08	0.08	−0.13	0.09	0.13	0.09	0.06
S&P 500	0.08	0.14	−0.24	−0.11	0.16	0.16	0.17
Russell 2000	0.21	0.25	−0.25	0.10	0.35	0.20	0.27
Lehman US Aggregate	0.30	0.34	−0.06	0.09	0.29	0.38	0.32
Lehman High Yield	0.23	0.26	−0.15	0.16	0.29	0.26	0.29
MSCI World Index	0.02	0.08	−0.34	−0.12	0.13	0.07	0.13
Lehman Global Aggregate	0.34	0.44	0.03	−0.05	0.32	0.40	0.40

Sources: CISDM, Bloomberg, Schneeweis Partners.

hedge fund indices. Of interest are the differences, if any, in the correlations patterns of the HFR and EACM hedge fund performance indices given in Exhibit 25.6 and Exhibit 25.7 compared to CTA index correlations presented in Exhibits 25.3 to 25.5. First, as in Exhibits 25.3 to 25.5, there exists relatively high correlation between similar hedge fund indices across various reporting firms. In short, the potential benefits of hedge fund investment should be consistent across various hedge fund index providers. Differences between CTAs and hedge funds do, however, exist. First, in contrast to CTA indices, most hedge fund indices are positively correlated with nominal stock and bond returns. Second, a relatively low correlation exists between hedge fund indices and the variable designed to capture trend following strategies (for example, MFSB). Lastly, for hedge funds, there are generally negative correlations between the various hedge fund strategies and the absolute value of the market factors (for example, hedge funds are short volatility). In contrast, systematic CTAs reported a positive correlation between returns and measures of market volatility. Thus, CTAs may offer a means

Exhibit 25.4

EACM CTA correlations

EACM CTA	GAA	Discret	System
Global Asset Allocation	1.00		
Discretionary	0.65	1.00	
Systematic	0.83	0.11	1.00

Nominal factors	GAA	Discret	System
MFSB	0.57	−0.01	0.75
GSCI	0.20	0.15	0.15
S&P 500	0.23	0.53	−0.09
Russell 2000	0.27	0.61	−0.10
Lehman US Aggregate	0.39	0.06	0.46
Lehman High Yield	0.18	0.49	−0.13
MSCI World Index	0.21	0.53	−0.12
Lehman Global Aggregate	0.22	−0.07	0.34
US Treasury bill	0.05	0.12	−0.02

Absolute values	GAA	Discret	System
GSCI	−0.02	−0.13	0.06
S&P 500	−0.05	−0.30	0.16
Russell 2000	0.04	−0.27	0.25
Lehman US Aggregate	0.25	−0.04	0.36
Lehman High Yield	0.09	−0.17	0.25
MSCI World Index	−0.16	−0.37	0.08
Lehman Global Aggregate	0.20	−0.18	0.41

Sources: EACM, Bloomberg, Schneeweis Partners.

to diversify hedge fund returns especially in markets which may show evidence of increasing volatility and, as a result, declining cash market values.[4]

Stock and bond fund correlations with commodity, stock, bond and currency indices

In Exhibit 25.8, the correlation between each of the stock and bond fund performance indices and the nominal and absolute values of the set of explanatory variables is given. Again, of principle interest, are the differences, if any, in the correlation patterns of the CTA and hedge fund performance indices given in Exhibits 25.3 to 25.7 with those given in Exhibit 25.8. The buy-and-hold strategy employed by stock and bond mutual fund managers results in correlation patterns that are very different from CTA indices and some hedge fund indices. First, the correlations among the equity-based mutual fund indices and equity market factors are generally above 0.80. Similar correlations are seen among the government and corporate bond mutual funds and traditional bond market factors such as the Lehman US Aggregate Indices. It is important to point out that these high correlations between equity and bond mutual funds and corresponding equity and bond factors are also shown for hedge funds with equity or bond exposure. As shown in Exhibit 25.6 and Exhibit 25.7, the correlation for equity sensitive hedge funds (hedge equity, event, merger arbitrage) and equity market factors is also often greater

Exhibit 25.5

Barclay CTA correlations

Barclay CTA	CTA	Curr	Agric	Fin	Divers	System	Discret
CTA Index	1.00						
Currency Index	0.68	1.00					
Agricultural Index	0.14	0.06	1.00				
Fin/Met. Index	0.93	0.61	0.07	1.00			
Diversified Index	0.98	0.59	0.14	0.89	1.00		
Systematic Index	0.99	0.66	0.12	0.93	0.98	1.00	
Discretionary Index	0.54	0.39	0.41	0.46	0.52	0.48	1.00
Nominal factors	CTA	Curr	Agric	Fin	Divers	System	Discret
MFSB	0.80	0.50	0.10	0.81	0.80	0.82	0.34
GSCI	0.12	−0.04	0.21	0.06	0.11	0.10	0.35
S&P 500	−0.18	−0.04	−0.02	−0.17	−0.23	−0.20	0.12
Russell 2000	−0.17	−0.09	−0.09	−0.20	−0.19	−0.17	0.05
Lehman US Aggregate	0.42	0.18	−0.11	0.49	0.40	0.44	0.09
Lehman High Yield	−0.16	−0.11	−0.10	−0.16	−0.18	−0.16	−0.05
MSCI World Index	−0.21	−0.07	−0.03	−0.21	−0.25	−0.23	0.10
Lehman Global Aggregate	0.27	0.04	−0.03	0.34	0.26	0.26	0.17
US Treasury bill	−0.02	0.02	0.11	−0.08	−0.01	−0.01	−0.16
Absolute values	CTA	Curr	Agric	Fin	Divers	System	Discret
GSCI	0.08	−0.11	0.15	0.01	0.14	0.08	0.09
S&P 500	0.12	−0.04	0.03	0.20	0.14	0.13	0.12
Russell 2000	0.23	−0.14	0.21	0.21	0.29	0.25	0.17
Lehman US Aggregate	0.30	0.01	0.03	0.37	0.30	0.31	0.20
Lehman High Yield	0.25	0.08	0.15	0.34	0.27	0.26	0.26
MSCI World Index	0.05	−0.12	0.03	0.12	0.09	0.06	0.02
Lehman Global Aggregate	0.40	0.24	−0.11	0.41	0.39	0.39	0.24

Sources: Barclay, Bloomberg, Schneeweis Partners.

than 0.50. Similarly, the correlation for credit sensitive bond-based hedge funds (distressed) and high-yield bond market factors are also often greater than 0.50. Thus, equity sensitive or credit sensitive hedge funds often have similar correlations to market factors as their traditional mutual fund counterpart. Again, in contrast to market neutral based hedge funds and CTAs (but similar to equity and bond sensitive hedge funds), mutual funds often show a negative correlation with the absolute values of the market factors. As a result, a close examination of the strategy employed by the fund is necessary before determining the diversification benefits of a hedge fund relative to a stock and bond portfolio.

Factors determining CTA, hedge and mutual fund returns: regression analysis

Correlation results suggest the factors determining CTA and certain non-equity/bond hedge fund performance differ considerably from the factors that drive stock and bond fund returns.

Exhibit 25.6

EACM Hedge Fund Index correlations

EACM Index	100	Rel Val	L/S Eq	Conv	Bond	Multi	Event	Risk	Bnkrpt	Multi	Equity	DomLng	DomOpp	Gl/Int	Short
EACM 100	1.00														
Relative Value	0.47	1.00													
Long-Short Equity	0.05	0.28	1.00												
Convertible Hedge	0.33	0.69	-0.06	1.00											
Bond Hedge	0.41	0.78	0.18	0.33	1.00										
Relative Value Multi-Strategy	0.40	0.85	0.05	0.48	0.52	1.00									
Event Driven	0.65	0.56	-0.04	0.44	0.39	0.57	1.00								
Risk Arbitrage	0.57	0.44	-0.04	0.38	0.28	0.43	0.91	1.00							
Bankruptcy Distressed	0.58	0.55	0.00	0.41	0.41	0.53	0.91	0.69	1.00						
Event Driven Multi-Strategy	0.65	0.56	-0.09	0.44	0.39	0.59	0.96	0.85	0.80	1.00					
Equity Hedge Funds	0.89	0.26	-0.10	0.24	0.23	0.22	0.57	0.53	0.48	0.56	1.00				
Equity Hedge Funds Domestic Long Bias	0.80	0.16	-0.15	0.21	0.16	0.12	0.57	0.55	0.48	0.55	0.95	1.00			
Equity Hedge Domestic Opportunistic	0.76	0.18	-0.06	0.15	0.17	0.16	0.38	0.37	0.27	0.41	0.88	0.76	1.00		
Equity Hedge Global/International	0.86	0.40	-0.03	0.29	0.33	0.36	0.56	0.49	0.52	0.55	0.85	0.72	0.63	1.00	
Short Sellers	-0.50	-0.21	0.16	-0.26	-0.19	-0.16	-0.62	-0.59	-0.54	-0.60	-0.68	-0.73	-0.46	-0.57	1.00
Nominal factors	100	Rel Val	L/S Eq	Conv	Bond	Multi	Event	Risk	Bnkrpt	Multi	Equity	DomLng	DomOpp	Gl/Int	Short
MFSB	0.00	-0.25	0.11	-0.29	-0.15	-0.24	-0.29	-0.29	-0.26	-0.25	-0.21	-0.24	-0.17	-0.12	0.31
GSCI	0.22	-0.03	-0.02	0.01	0.00	-0.06	0.13	0.17	0.08	0.12	0.22	0.25	0.23	0.10	-0.16
S&P 500	0.49	0.16	-0.16	0.23	0.18	0.09	0.53	0.53	0.44	0.50	0.61	0.67	0.32	0.58	-0.79
Russell 2000	0.70	0.20	-0.17	0.26	0.18	0.15	0.67	0.63	0.55	0.66	0.82	0.88	0.64	0.63	-0.82
Lehman US Aggregate	0.02	-0.19	0.20	-0.10	-0.19	-0.26	-0.16	-0.15	-0.17	-0.13	-0.09	-0.07	-0.10	0.09	0.14
Lehman High Yield	0.47	0.40	-0.03	0.46	0.38	0.21	0.63	0.61	0.56	0.59	0.43	0.47	0.22	0.42	-0.52
MSCI World Index	0.55	0.22	-0.14	0.24	0.21	0.17	0.56	0.57	0.47	0.51	0.66	0.71	0.38	0.63	-0.78
Lehman Global Aggregate	-0.11	-0.34	0.27	-0.17	-0.32	-0.45	-0.25	-0.24	-0.04	-0.27	-0.12	-0.06	-0.12	-0.18	0.11
US Treasury bill	0.22	0.15	0.12	0.09	0.04	0.17	0.19	0.35	0.18	0.24	0.18	0.12	0.24	0.14	-0.02

(continued)

Exhibit 25.6 *continued*

EACM Hedge Fund Index correlations

Absolute values	*100*	*Rel Val*	*L/S Eq*	*Conv*	*Bond*	*Multi*	*Event*	*Risk*	*Bnkpt*	*Multi*	*Equity*	*DomLng*	*DomOpp*	*Gl/Int*	*Short*
GSCI	-0.02	-0.17	-0.27	-0.01	-0.11	-0.14	0.00	0.03	-0.01	-0.02	0.05	0.11	0.02	-0.02	-0.04
S&P 500	-0.21	-0.27	-0.11	-0.04	-0.31	-0.25	0.32	0.36	-0.26	0.27	-0.12	-0.11	-0.11	-0.10	0.06
Russell 2000	-0.09	-0.26	-0.21	-0.18	-0.17	-0.20	-0.37	-0.35	-0.40	-0.28	-0.02	0.03	0.07	-0.09	0.13
Lehman US Aggregate	-0.09	-0.22	0.16	-0.13	-0.12	-0.34	-0.17	-0.10	-0.21	-0.15	-0.12	-0.10	-0.09	-0.14	0.01
Lehman High Yield	-0.19	-0.11	-0.23	-0.03	-0.03	-0.10	-0.35	-0.48	-0.19	-0.32	-0.21	-0.23	-0.19	-0.12	0.08
MSCI World Index	-0.24	-0.20	-0.13	0.01	-0.33	-0.10	-0.32	-0.38	-0.23	-0.29	-0.16	-0.17	-0.11	-0.13	0.13
Lehman Global Aggregate	-0.22	-0.36	0.18	-0.29	-0.28	-0.41	-0.25	-0.19	-0.24	-0.25	-0.26	-0.27	-0.18	0.24	0.19

Sources: EACM, Bloomberg, Schneeweis Partners.

Exhibit 25.7

HFR Hedge Fund Index correlations

HFR Index	*Equity neutral*	*Convertible arbitrage*	*Distress*	*Emerging markets*	*FOF*	*Macro*	*Equity hedge*	*Fixed arbitrage*	*Market timing*	*Merger arbitrage*	*Short selling*
Equity Market Neutral Index	1.00										
Convertible Arbitrage Index	0.20	1.00									
Distressed Securities Index	0.20	0.73	1.00								
Emerging Markets Total Index	0.11	0.49	0.73	1.00							
FOF Index	0.32	0.59	0.78	0.84	1.00						
Macro Index	0.29	0.34	0.50	0.59	0.80	1.00					
Equity Hedge Index	0.31	0.50	0.64	0.71	0.84	0.61	1.00				
Fixed Income Arbitrage Index	0.12	0.31	0.36	0.24	0.34	0.21	0.04	1.00			
Market Timing Index	0.14	0.28	0.34	0.51	0.58	0.51	0.76	-0.08	1.00		
Merger Arbitrage Index	0.36	0.54	0.55	0.48	0.50	0.24	0.55	0.03	0.30	1.00	
Short Selling Index	-0.12	-0.35	-0.53	-0.63	-0.69	-0.47	-0.88	0.04	-0.74	-0.38	1.00

(continued)

Exhibit 25.7 *continued*

HFR Hedge Fund Index correlations

Nominal factors	Equity neutral	Convertible arbitrage	Distress	Emerging markets	FOF	Macro	Equity hedge	Fixed arbitrage	Market timing	Merger arbitrage	Short selling
MFSB	0.10	-0.25	-0.29	-0.22	-0.10	0.32	-0.24	-0.03	-0.12	-0.27	0.29
GSCI	0.12	0.09	0.07	0.13	0.20	0.16	0.24	0.15	0.16	0.18	-0.18
S&P 500	0.13	0.33	0.42	0.60	0.53	0.35	0.68	-0.14	0.68	0.50	-0.68
Russell 2000	0.24	0.45	0.61	0.67	0.70	0.51	0.88	-0.02	0.68	0.59	-0.85
Lehman US Aggregate	0.19	-0.06	-0.12	-0.19	-0.03	0.24	-0.09	-0.07	-0.02	-0.15	0.14
Lehman High Yield	0.07	0.52	0.56	0.50	0.48	0.35	0.49	0.20	0.30	0.52	-0.40
MSCI World Index	0.13	0.34	0.46	0.65	0.58	0.38	0.73	-0.09	0.71	0.51	-0.72
Lehman Global Aggregate	0.11	-0.23	-0.21	-0.26	-0.19	0.04	-0.08	-0.20	-0.07	-0.14	0.07
US Treasury bill	0.33	0.14	0.05	-0.02	0.14	0.02	0.19	0.01	0.14	0.39	0.01

Absolute values	Equity neutral	Convertible arbitrage	Distress	Emerging markets	FOF	Macro	Equity hedge	Fixed arbitrage	Market timing	Merger arbitrage	Short selling
GSCI	-0.17	-0.05	-0.04	0.09	-0.01	0.08	0.05	-0.11	0.16	0.00	-0.12
S&P 500	-0.07	-0.15	-0.37	-0.20	-0.21	-0.05	-0.14	-0.28	0.08	-0.37	0.05
Russell 2000	-0.02	-0.27	-0.27	-0.18	-0.12	0.03	0.01	-0.08	0.11	-0.40	-0.05
Lehman US Aggregate	0.04	-0.18	-0.16	-0.15	-0.10	0.09	-0.08	-0.11	-0.14	-0.14	0.05
Lehman High Yield	-0.34	-0.11	-0.19	-0.12	-0.19	0.04	-0.24	-0.10	-0.02	-0.46	0.10
MSCI World Index	-0.14	-0.11	-0.34	-0.22	-0.24	-0.11	-0.18	-0.28	0.04	-0.39	0.11
Lehman Global Aggregate	0.08	-0.28	-0.33	-0.23	-0.26	-0.03	-0.23	-0.26	-0.32	-0.08	0.25

Sources: HFR, Bloomberg, Schneeweis Partners.

Exhibit 25.8

Lipper Mutual Fund Index

Lipper Index	A rated	BBB rated	Gen bond	Global Inc	Ultra short	Lipper cap appr	Lipper growth	Lipper mid cap	Lipper small cap
A-rated bond fund	1.00								
BBB-rated fund	0.94	1.00							
Gen bond fund	0.91	0.95	1.00						
Global Inc fund	0.67	0.73	0.76	1.00					
Ultra short fund	0.65	0.61	0.63	0.38	1.00				
Lipper cap appr fund	0.00	0.23	0.30	0.26	0.03	1.00			
Lipper growth fund	0.00	0.23	0.30	0.24	0.04	0.97	1.00		
Lipper mid-cap fund	−0.03	0.21	0.26	0.25	0.01	0.98	0.93	1.00	
Lipper small-cap fund	−0.03	0.20	0.25	0.26	0.00	0.93	0.85	0.97	1.00

Nominal factors	A rated	BBB rated	Gen bond	Global Inc	Ultra short	Lipper cap appr	Lipper growth	Lipper mid cap	Lipper small cap
MFSB	0.40	0.27	0.24	0.20	0.34	−0.32	−0.34	−0.32	−0.28
GSCI	0.08	0.12	0.12	0.21	0.08	0.16	0.10	0.20	0.22
S&P 500	0.02	0.24	0.31	0.23	0.07	0.88	0.96	0.80	0.70
Russell 2000	−0.02	0.22	0.26	0.29	0.02	0.90	0.82	0.93	0.97
Lehman US	0.98	0.87	0.84	0.63	0.65	−0.11	−0.10	−0.13	−0.14
Lehman High Yield	0.24	0.51	0.46	0.33	0.16	0.55	0.53	0.53	0.52
MSCI World Index	−0.03	0.20	0.28	0.28	0.01	0.89	0.94	0.83	0.74
Lehman Global	0.64	0.55	0.55	0.77	0.33	−0.10	−0.11	−0.11	−0.09
US Treasury bill	0.00	0.01	0.08	−0.12	0.59	0.12	0.14	0.12	0.08

Absolute values	A rated	BBB rated	Gen bond	Global Inc	Ultra short	Lipper cap appr	Lipper growth	Lipper mid cap	Lipper small cap
GSCI	−0.01	0.02	−0.02	0.03	−0.01	0.11	0.10	0.12	0.09
S&P 500	0.10	0.00	−0.01	−0.05	0.01	−0.10	−0.07	−0.13	−0.17
Russell 2000	0.02	−0.08	−0.05	−0.05	0.04	−0.09	−0.14	−0.04	−0.01
Lehman US	0.57	0.51	0.46	0.38	0.28	−0.07	−0.07	−0.06	−0.06
Lehman High Yield	0.22	0.14	0.15	0.05	0.01	−0.19	−0.20	−0.25	−0.20
MSCI World Index	−0.02	−0.14	−0.14	−0.16	−0.09	−0.18	−0.18	−0.19	−0.19
Lehman Global	0.27	0.17	0.13	0.35	0.05	−0.28	−0.25	−0.24	−0.21

Sources: Lipper, CISDM, Bloomberg, Schneeweis Partners.

Single-factor models, however, may not provide a full description of the explanatory power of multiple factors driving asset return. At the same time, issues in multi-collinearity among factors may result in the signs of the coefficients from the multiple regression analysis not representing individual factor sensitivities to the asset class in question. Exhibit 25.9 gives a correlation matrix for the full set of explanatory variables. These results show few pairwise correlations above 0.50. While the low pairwise correlations indicate that the signs of the explanatory variables in Exhibits 25.10 to 25.12 may reflect the actual sensitivity of the fund indices to the explanatory variables, it is important to remind readers that the importance of the multiple regression is less in the signs of the individual variables than the overall explanatory

Exhibit 25.9

Traditional asset

Index	MFSB	GSCI	S&P 500	RUS 2000	Leh US Agg	Leh High Yield	MSCI	Leh Gl.	US Treas.
MFSB	1.00								
GSCI	–0.01	1.00							
S&P 500	–0.31	0.03	1.00						
Russell 2000	–0.26	0.20	0.69	1.00					
Lehman US Aggregate	0.44	0.07	–0.08	–0.14	1.00				
Lehman High Yield	–0.19	0.03	0.51	0.57	0.08	1.00			
MSCI World Index	–0.32	0.06	0.96	0.73	–0.13	–0.13	1.00		
Lehman Global Aggregate	0.26	0.17	–0.11	–0.11	0.67	0.67	–0.06	1.00	
US Treasury bill	–0.01	0.05	0.15	0.07	–0.02	–0.02	0.13	–0.18	1.00

Nominal index values

Absolute Index	MFSB	GSCI	S&P 500	RUS 2000	Leh US Agg	Leh High Yield	MSCI	Leh Gl.	US Treas.
GSCI	0.12	0.25	0.08	0.06	–0.02	–0.04	0.09	–0.03	0.03
S&P 500	0.16	–0.03	–0.03	–0.18	0.15	–0.27	–0.09	0.19	–0.14
Russell 2000	0.27	0.02	–0.22	–0.06	0.08	–0.24	–0.16	0.15	–0.05
Lehman US Aggregate	0.35	0.22	–0.09	–0.05	0.59	0.12	–0.12	0.49	–0.14
Lehman High Yield	0.30	–0.18	–0.15	–0.17	0.24	–0.11	–0.15	0.20	–0.32
MSCI World Index	0.10	–0.08	–0.17	–0.21	0.03	–0.33	–0.17	0.09	–0.16
Lehman Global Aggregate	0.36	0.10	–0.25	–0.19	0.32	–0.16	–0.25	0.53	–0.20

Absolute index values

	GSCI	S&P 500	RUS 2000	Leh US Agg	Leh High Yield	MSCI	Leh Gl.
GSCI	1.00						
S&P 500	0.07	1.00					
Russell 2000	0.13	0.40	1.00				
Lehman US Aggregate	0.02	0.13	0.14	1.00			
Lehman High Yield	0.05	0.36	0.19	0.19	1.00		
MSCI World Index	0.08	0.87	0.47	0.03	0.38	1.00	
Lehman Global Aggregate	–0.09	0.12	0.13	0.47	0.07	0.05	1.00

Sources: Bloomberg, Schneeweis Partners.

power of the model (for example, *r*-square). Due to potential issues in multi-collinearity, the individual variable's sensitivity to CTA, hedge fund and mutual fund returns may be better reflected by the simple correlation coefficients given in Exhibits 25.6 to 25.9.

Exhibits 25.10 to 25.12 report the regression results. Exhibit 25.10 shows the coefficients using the CISDM CTA indices. Exhibit 25.11 gives the EACM hedge fund regression results and Exhibit 25.12 reports the Lipper stock and bond mutual fund regressions. In each instance, the independent variables are the nominal values (S&P 500, Russell 2000, Lehman

Exhibit 25.10

Regression using CISDM CTA indices

CISDM CTA	Adj r^2	F-Stat	Nominal index coefficients					Absolute index coefficients		
			S&P 500	Russell 2000	Leh US Agg	Leh High Yield	MFSB	Russell 2000	Leh US Agg	Leh High Yield
US$ Weighted	0.60	16.36	0.0356	0.0215	0.4438	−0.0664	0.7526*	0.0139	−0.2000	−0.0287
Equal Weighted	0.66	21.20	0.0324	0.0193	0.1543	−0.1030	0.8798*	0.0191	0.1910	−0.0121
Currency Programme Subindex	0.20	3.59	0.0631	−0.0118	−0.0782	0.0751	0.3593*	−0.1086	−0.3981	−0.1444
Discretionary Adviser Subindex	0.23	4.15	−0.0124	0.0613	0.2134	0.0649	0.2929*	−0.0037	−0.4065	0.0529
Diversified Adviser Subindex	0.61	17.38	0.0098	0.0264	0.5042	−0.0283	0.8672*	0.128*	−0.3537	−0.0017
Financial Programme Subindex	0.57	14.80	0.0901	−0.0069	0.4918	−0.2431	0.9744*	−0.0202	0.5389	0.0348
Trend Follower Subindex	0.65	20.22	0.0324	−0.0013	0.7136	−0.3285	1.2014*	0.0311	−0.0478	0.0516

* Significant at the 95 per cent confidence level.

Source: CISDM, Bloomberg, Schneeweis Partners.

Exhibit 25.11

Regression using EACM hedge fund performance

EACM Index	Adj r²	F-Stat	Nominal index coefficients					Absolute index coefficients		
			S&P 500	Russell 2000	Leh US Agg	Leh High Yield	MFSB	Russell 2000	Leh US Agg	Leh High Yield
EACM 100	0.53	12.86	0.0043	0.1484*	0.2126	0.0760	0.1437*	-0.0049	-0.4691	-0.1130
Relative Value	0.20	3.59	-0.0283	-0.0057	-0.1122	0.2366*	-0.0348	-0.0430	-0.3408	0.0362
Long-Short Equity	0.11	2.22	-0.0215	-0.0137	0.1439	0.0000	0.0273	-0.0438	0.1437	-0.1524
Convertible Hedge	0.21	3.80	-0.0238	-0.0032	0.0020	0.3418*	-0.1321	-0.0205	-0.3479	0.1175
Bond Hedge	0.13	2.55	-0.0036	-0.0278	-0.3985	0.3586*	0.0174	0.0362	-0.1824	0.0965
Relative Value Multi-Strategy	0.12	2.48	-0.0644	0.0219	-0.1961	0.2458	-0.0518	-0.0720	-0.9766	0.0837
Event Driven	0.60	16.88	-0.0061	0.1002*	-0.0127	0.2224*	0.0223	-0.0745	-0.3243	-0.1293
Risk Arbitrage	0.61	17.04	0.0170	0.0716*	-0.0392	0.2040*	0.0212	-0.0411	-0.0799	-0.2763
Bankruptcy/Distressed	0.47	10.34	-0.0233	0.0995*	-0.0439	0.2393*	0.0172	-0.1306	-0.5063	0.0525
Event Driven Multi-Strategy	0.53	12.64	-0.0119	0.1295*	0.0449	0.2238*	0.0286	-0.0518	-0.3867	-0.1630
Equity Hedge Funds	0.68	22.55	0.0692	0.4657*	0.4189	-0.0898	0.0224	0.0831	-0.7385	-0.2405
Equity Hedge Domestic Long Bias	0.78	38.69	0.1573	0.7148*	0.8508*	-0.1504	-0.0493	0.1365	-0.9625	-0.4094
Equity Hedge Domestic Opportunistic	0.44	8.99	-0.1365	0.4659*	0.3635	-0.2431	-0.0758	0.1043	-0.4396	-0.2706
Equity Hedge Global/International	0.41	8.11	0.1870*	0.2166*	0.0423	0.1242	0.1922	0.0085	-0.8135	-0.0415
Short Sellers	0.76	34.34	-0.5530	-0.5743	0.5979	0.0573	0.2182	0.0794	-1.2984	-0.4492

* Significant at the 95 per cent confidence level.

Source: EACM, Bloomberg, Schneeweis Partners.

Exhibit 25.12

Regression using Lipper Mutual Fund Performance Indices

Lipper Index	Adj r^2	F-Stat	Nominal index coefficients					Absolute index coefficients		
			S&P 500	Russell 2000	Leh US Agg	Leh High Yield	MFSB	Russell 2000	Leh US Agg	Leh High Yield
A-rated bond fund	0.98	505.98	0.0016	0.0058	1.0808*	0.0672	0.0108	-0.0076	-0.0465	0.0076
BBB-rated fund	0.96	235.53	0.0108	0.0206*	1.0117*	0.1801*	-0.0108	-0.0150	0.0754	0.0069
Gen bond fund	0.90	97.32	0.0330*	0.0186*	0.8341*	0.0967	0.0026	-0.0041	-0.0952	0.0133
Global Inc fund	0.51	11.62	0.0027	0.0704*	0.8682*	0.0305	0.0150	-0.0228	0.0110	-0.0272
Ultra short fund	0.44	9.20	0.0036	-0.0002	0.1238*	0.0079	0.0123	0.0038	-0.0471	-0.0201
Lipper cap appr fund	0.94	155.63	0.6122*	0.5093*	0.1323	-0.0283	-0.1085	0.1349*	0.0468	-0.1917
Lipper growth fund	0.97	310.08	0.8229*	0.2459*	0.0769	-0.0473	-0.1220	0.1100*	0.2582	-0.2302
Lipper mid-cap fund	0.93	147.56	0.4536*	0.7849*	0.2197	-0.1435	-0.1778	0.2234*	0.1819	-0.5137
Lipper small-cap fund	0.95	181.56	0.0935	1.0607*	0.2182	-0.1619	-0.1354	0.1570*	0.0112	-0.2732

* Significant at the 95 per cent confidence level.

Source: Lipper, Bloomberg, Schneeweis Partners.

US Aggregate, Lehman High Yield and MFSB) and absolute values of the S&P 500, Lehman US Aggregate and Lehman High Yield. For each regression, the r-square, f-statistic and eight slope coefficients are reported. In Exhibit 25.10 the regression results for the CISDM CTA dollar-weighted index are given. For several of the CTA sub-indices, the overall r-square is over 0.60. Thus, the explanatory models provide a substantial explanation for CTA return process. In short, over 50 per cent of the return's total variability is explained by considering the variables in the cited regression. For the various CTA indices, only the MFSB trend following indices are statistically significant.

In Exhibit 25.11, the regression results for the EACM hedge fund indices are given. For certain hedge fund sub-indices (event driven, risk arbitrage), the adjusted r-square is often greater than 0.50 and in certain cases (equity hedge strategies) are close to 0.70. Thus, as for CTAs, market factors explain a large portion of the return of various hedge fund strategies. As important, the signs are generally in line with expectations. For instance, for equity-based indices (event driven, equity hedge, domestic long and global/international) and the Russell 2000 the signs are shown to be statistically significant and have the expected positive signs. Similarly, for credit sensitive hedge fund indices, such as distressed or bankruptcy, which are correlated with high-yield bond indices, the expected signs on the relevant Lehman High Yield debt variables are positive and statistically significant. In contrast, market-neutral strategies, such as long-short equity, convertible arbitrage and relative value, have relatively low r-squares and market neutral equity (for example, long-short equity) shows no correlation with any of the cited variables. This too is as expected, given that a pure hedge play should not be correlated directly with the long return of any of the underlying markets. This suggests that for market-neutral equity, the source of the returns is not captured by the explanatory variables tested, and other variables are needed to fully explain this return.[5]

Exhibit 25.12 repeats this analysis for Lipper stock and bond mutual fund indices. The results are consistent with results reported previously (Sharpe, 1992; Blake et al., 1993; and Elton et al., 1995). The major factor determining the return of a mutual fund is the factor that reflects the primary market in which that fund is trading. For instance, all the major equity-based mutual fund indices have significant positive S&P 500 or Russell 2000 coefficients. Fixed-income mutual funds also report significant coefficients with the Lehman Index.

Implications of results

Considerable research on investment performance in stock, bond, CTA and hedge fund markets concentrates on single-factor models such as beta, standard deviation and drawdown as explanators of performance. In this chapter, a number of factors are used to explain a broad range of managed assets. Results indicate that these factors may help explain the differences in investment return. Adding managed futures and hedge fund products to traditional stock and bond portfolios only makes sense if 1) these products derive return from sources that are distinct from those that drive stock and bond return and 2) the returns from those sources are positive. Results reported herein indicate that certain hedge fund and managed futures strategies do load on different market factors than traditional stock and bond investments. Thus, alternative investments may provide beneficial diversification to traditional stock and bond funds.

Further research is required to develop hedge fund and CTA investment approaches that capture these unique factors more precisely. Unlike equity or bond mutual funds, the lack of a single factor that describes the return process for hedge funds and CTAs means that these investments must be classified according to their style or multi-factor model rather than a single-factor return process. Results presented in this chapter suggest that pure hedge fund style and CTA indices as well as multi-factor models contain important information about returns to actively managed assets in general, and managed futures and hedge funds in particular.

References

Ackermann, C., R. McEnally and D. Ravenscraft (1999), 'The Performance of Hedge Funds: Risk, Return and Incentives', *Journal of Finance*, Vol. 54, No. 3, pp. 833–874.

Agarwal, V., and N. Naik (2000a), 'On Taking The Alternative Route: Risks, Rewards, and Performance Persistence of Hedge Funds', *Journal of Alternative Investments*, pp. 6–23 (Spring).

Agarwal, V., and N. Naik (2000b), 'Multi-Period Performance Persistence Analysis of Hedge Funds', *Journal of Financial and Quantitative Analysis*, Vol. 35, No. 3, pp. 327–342.

Amin, G., and H. Kat (2003), 'Hedge Fund Performance 1990–2000: Do 'Money Machines' Really Add Value', *Journal of Financial and Quantitative Analysis*, forthcoming.

Asness, C., R. Krail and J. Liew (2001), 'Do Hedge Funds Hedge', *Journal of Portfolio Management*, Vol. 28, pp. 20–32 (Fall).

Blake, C., E. Elton and M. Gruber (1993), 'The Performance of Bond Mutual Funds', *Journal of Business*, Vol. 66, No. 3, pp. 371–403.

Brealey, R., and E. Kaplanis (2000), 'Changes in Factor Exposures of Hedge Funds', Working Paper, Bank of England and Institute of Finance and Accounting, London Business School.

Brown, S., and W. Goetzmann (2001), 'Hedge Funds with Style', *Journal of Portfolio Management*, pp. 6–19 (Fall).

Brown, S., W. Goetzmann and G. Ibbotson (1999), 'Offshore Hedge Funds: Survival and Performance 1989–95', *Journal of Business*, Vol. 72, No. 3, pp. 91–117.

Brown, S., W. Goetzmann and J. Park (2001), 'Careers and Survival: Competition and Risk in the Hedge Fund and CTA Industry', *Journal of Finance*, Vol. 56, No. 5, pp. 1869–1886.

Cerrahoglu, B., and D. Pancholi (2003), 'The Benefits of Managed Futures', CISDM Working Paper.

Chan, L., N. Jegadeesh and J. Lakonishok (1996), 'Momentum Strategies', *Journal of Finance*, Vol. 51, No. 5, pp. 1681–1713.

Daglioglu, A., and B. Gupta (2003), 'The Benefits of Hedge Funds', CISDM Working Paper.

Elton, E., M. Gruber and C. Blake (1995), 'Fundamental Economic Variables, Expected Returns, and Bond Fund Performance', *Journal of Finance*, Vol. 50, No. 4, pp. 1229–1256.

Fama, E., and K. French (1993), 'Common Risk Factors in the Returns on Stock and Bonds', *Journal of Financial Economics*, Vol. 33, pp. 3–56.

Fama, E., and K. French (1996), 'Multifactor Explanations of Asset Pricing Anomalies', *Journal of Finance*, Vol. 51, No. 1, pp. 55–84.

Fung, W., and D. Hsieh (1997a), 'Empirical Characteristics of Dynamic Trading Strategies: The Case of Hedge Funds', *Review of Financial Studies*, Vol. 10, pp. 275–302.

Fung, W., and D. Hsieh (1997b), 'Survivorship Bias and Investment Style in the Returns of CTAs', *Journal of Portfolio Management*, Vol. 24, No. 1, pp. 30–41.

Fung, W., and D. Hsieh (1999), 'A Primer on Hedge Funds', *Journal of Empirical Finance*, Vol. 6, pp. 309–331.

Fung, W., and D. Hsieh (2000a), 'Measuring the Market Impact of Hedge Funds', *Journal of Empirical Finance*, Vol. 7, No. 1, pp. 1–36.

Fung, W., and D. Hsieh (2000b), 'Performance Characteristics of Hedge Funds and CTA Funds: Natural Versus Spurious Biases', *Journal of Financial and Quantitative Analysis*, Vol. 35, No. 3, pp. 291–307.

Fung, W., and D. Hsieh (2001), 'The Risk of Hedge Fund Strategies: Theory and Evidence From Trend Followers', *The Review of Financial Studies*, 313–341 (Summer).

Fung, W., and D. Hsieh (2002), 'Hedge-Fund Benchmarks: Information Content and Biases', *Financial Analysts Journal*, Vol. 58, No. 1, pp. 22–34.

Gatev, E., W. Goetzmann and K.G. Rouwenhorst (1999), 'Pairs Trading: Performance of a Relative Value Arbitrage Rule', Working Paper.

Henriksson, R.D., and R.C. Merton (1981), 'On Market Timing and Investment Performance II: Statistical Procedures for Evaluating Forecasting Skills', *Journal of Business*, Vol. 54, No. 4, pp. 513–533.

Kazemi, H., and T. Schneeweis (2003a), 'Market Source of Market Neutral Returns', CISDM Working Paper.

Kazemi, H., and T. Schneeweis (2003b), 'Conditional Performance of Hedge Funds', CISDM Working Paper.

Liang, B. (1999), 'On The Performance of Hedge Funds', *Financial Analysts Journal*, Vol. 55, No. 4, pp. 72–85.

Liang, B. (2000), 'Hedge Funds: The Living and the Dead', *Journal of Financial and Quantitative Analysis*, pp. 309–326 (September).

Liang, B. (2001), 'Hedge Fund Performance: 1990–1999', *Financial Analysts Journal*, Vol. 57, No. 1, pp. 11–18.

McCarthy, D. and R. Spurgin (1998), 'A Review of Hedge Fund Performance Benchmarks', *Journal of Alternative Investments*, pp. 18–28 (Summer).

McCarthy, D., T. Schneeweis and R. Spurgin (1997), 'Informational Content in Historical CTA Performance', *Journal of Futures Markets*, pp. 317–340 (May).

Mitev, T. (1996), 'Classification of Commodity Trading Advisors (CTAs) Using Likelihood Factor Analysis', CISDM Working Paper.

Schneeweis, T., H. Kazemi and G. Martin (2002), 'Understanding Hedge Fund Performance: Research Issues Revisited – Part I', *Journal of Alternative Investments*, pp. 6–22 (Winter).

Schneeweis, T., H. Kazemi and G. Martin (2003), Understanding Hedge Fund Performance: Research Issues Revisited – Part II, *Journal of Alternative Investments*, pp. 8–31 (Spring).

Schneeweis, T., and J. Pescatore, Eds. (1999), *The Handbook of Alternative Investment Strategies: An Investor's Guide*, New York, Institutional Investor.

Schneeweis, T., and R. Spurgin (1998), 'Multifactor Analysis of Hedge Fund, Managed Futures and Mutual Fund Return and Risk Characteristics', *Journal of Alternative Investments*, pp. 1–24 (Fall).

Schneeweis, T., and R. Spurgin (1999), 'Quantitative Analysis of Hedge Fund and Managed Futures Return and Risk Characteristics', *Evaluating and Implementing Hedge Fund Strategies, Second Edition*, Ed. Ronald Lake, London, Euromoney Books, pp. 262–275.

Schneeweis, T., R. Spurgin and D. McCarthy (1996), 'Survivor Bias In Commodity Trading Advisor Performance', *The Journal of Futures Markets*, pp. 1–24 (October).

Sharpe, W. (1992), 'Asset Allocation: Management Style and Performance Measurement', *Journal of Portfolio Management*, pp. 7–19 (Winter).

Spurgin, R. (1998), 'Managed Futures, Hedge Fund, and Mutual Fund Performance: An Equity Class Analysis', *The Journal of Alternative Investments*, pp. 41–55 (Summer).

Spurgin, R., and T. Schneeweis (2003), 'Managed Futures: Volatility or Momentum Capture', CISDM Working Paper.

[1] The use of derived variables which attempt to replicate the factor loading in multi-factor regression models is consistent with research conducted in equity research (Chen and Jordan, 1993).

[2] For background on the MFSB see www.cisdm.org.

[3] Research (Fung and Hsieh, 1998) has shown that the ability of managers to asset allocate (long and short positions) may be reflected by various option-like strategies such as look back options.

[4] As the result of the positive correlation between CTAs and measures of return such as absolute value, CTAs have often been viewed as long volatility. This is a simplistic view. In fact, many CTAs do not directly trade options (a means to trade volatility) but use various trend following programs. The high correlation between CTAs and the MFSB is one indication of such consistent trend following strategies. While correlation results may show that CTAs make money in high ex post volatility markets, that simply reflects trending markets. In fact, research has shown that systematic CTAs primarily make money in high trend/low volatility markets.

[5] Preliminary research on the source of returns to market-neutral equity (H. Kazemi and T. Schneeweis, *Source of Returns to Market Neutral Investment,* CISDM, 2003) shows that returns may be positively correlated with cross-sectional standard deviation (potential price differences in sample set) and negatively correlated with implied volatility (market induces risk premia and thus future directional market moves).

Chapter 26

The due diligence process

Roxanne M. Martino
Harris Alternatives, LLC, Chicago, Illinois

Investing in hedge funds is thought to be extremely risky by the average investor. The press loves to latch on to any morsel of bad news in the hedge fund business and stoke the fires of fear among investors to grab a good headline. All of this often drowns out the message that I have tried to give investors for years: that the proper combination of hedge fund strategies and managers in a fund of funds can be (and has been) an attractive and relatively low-risk way to invest one's money.

How does one achieve this 'proper combination' of strategies and managers? As with any investment, an investor must first set their goals and objectives for this portion of one's portfolio. At Harris Alternatives, our objective over 15 years ago was to manage our own money in a manner that would earn a targeted annual return of 12–15 per cent over the long term with no correlation to the US equity markets' direction and with little volatility of those returns. We set out to find the best and the brightest hedge fund managers to execute the strategies that we identified would accomplish our investment objectives.

Identifying the best and the brightest is the most important, and the hardest, part of a hedge fund investor's job. This is called the due diligence process and it takes up the vast majority of our time as fund of funds managers. What is due diligence? How is it performed? What are some of the common mistakes in the process?

The due diligence process begins with identifying a potential manager. This aspect of the process has changed significantly since I started in this business in 1984. At that time, few people invested in hedge funds and fewer still were investing in more than one. The industry was quite small. There were no conferences other than futures industry conferences; there were no hedge fund industry publications or indexes. The participants in the industry were, in most cases, known to one another. Now, hedge funds number in the thousands and new ones are launched seemingly every day. How do I identify ones worth analysing now? In many cases, our most successful managers have left a larger organisation and are striking out on their own. These managers may already know us, and we know them; this can greatly speed certain aspects of the due diligence process. Other potential managers are referred to us by our existing managers. Of course, some managers contact us; we have found, however, that few of these make it into our portfolios. This highlights one benefit of investing with a fund of funds; a fund of funds manager often has the contacts, industry knowledge and years of experience with managers that can be used to identify talented and worthwhile new entrants. A private investor usually hears of only a few managers in the universe and may not have the time or resources to perform the initial or ongoing due diligence that is required.

Another change that I have seen in the industry is the length of time an investor has to complete the due diligence process. In the past, it took managers years to raise their capital; all the while the managers were honing their investment expertise and building their organisations. A prospective investor could 'wait and watch' while the manager went through the many steps needed to develop a successful investment firm. Today, there is so much capital in the industry that many talented, and some not-so-talented, managers close before they open; that is, before they make one trade in the new organisation, they have raised all the capital they targeted. A prospective investor may not have the opportunity to watch a manager trade; this makes many aspects of the initial due diligence process more difficult, yet more important.

Reference checks

The first step of our due diligence process, and one that a private investor may have a more difficult time doing effectively, is checking references. This goes far beyond calling the 'approved list' that a prospective manager provides us. Other managers that trade in the same area must also be contacted. They should know this prospective manager, and they often have an accurate assessment of his skills and shortcomings. I have found that a manager's peer group is often an excellent judge of his or her skill set; hedge fund managers, while competitive, will often praise a manager they have dealt with, even if it is on the other side of a negotiating table or trading desk. What they say (or do not say) can speak volumes about a manager's ability. Calls should also be made to former colleagues and organisations that the manager has been with: what did he do there? How much responsibility did he actually have? Who controlled his position sizes? Who was his sounding board? I will call people I know within those organisations to try to obtain an accurate picture of the manager's role, ability and risk appetite. I believe it is very important to perform these checks early in the process rather than as the last step; after an investor may have already made up his mind about investing, pertinent information may be ignored. Also, by having these conversations early, you may obtain clues as to what areas require your added attention during the review process. If an investor has spent many days performing due diligence and the reference checks reveal less than stellar information, he may underweight their significance. By calling references early in the due diligence process you will not get 'invested' in the process and be tempted to downplay negative information or clues; they will take on their rightful, important place in your evaluation.

Aligning incentives

What should an investor look for in a hedge fund, or fund of funds manager? The most important requirement is that a prospective manager must have a substantial portion of his liquid net worth invested in his fund. At Harris Alternatives, we 'eat our own cooking' and require the same of our managers. Hedge funds provide a manager with a great deal of freedom to invest your capital along with a financial incentive to take risk, namely a 20 per cent incentive fee. Requiring a side-by-side investment is the best way to mitigate this risk; when a manager has his own money on the line alongside yours, he has a great incentive to manage risk responsibly. Additionally, what possible line of reasoning could a manager present to try to convince me that I should invest my money in his fund, but he shouldn't? He knows the pitfalls and rewards of his strategy better than anyone else – how is his capital placed? Many of our managers are proud to say they make more money on the profits on their invested capital than on their management and incentive fees for their funds. Their goals and their investors' goals are aligned.

Quantitative due diligence

It is important to note that due diligence is heavily qualitative, not just quantitative. It does not take a great amount of skill to invest with a manager who has had excellent returns in the past. That is the key, those returns are 'past'. The difficult part for an investor is to determine if those returns are likely to be replicated in the future; that is the heart of the due diligence process. What are the drivers of performance? Relying too much on past performance is one of the most common pitfalls of any type of investing. You must overlay the qualitative information that you gather about the manager, the organisation, the industry, and the current investing climate to the many quantitative measures that you develop to predict the future prospects for this manager and his strategy. When performing quantitative analysis on a previous performance record, keep in mind such things as the amount of leverage employed over time, the varying levels of capital managed, and any change in strategy or the portfolio management team that generated the record presented. Also, what was the investment environment during the years presented? Be aware of the 'lottery ticket' effect; was there one position that is responsible for generating the majority of the gains? What if you removed this trade or theme from the performance record? Would your assessment change?

Be sure to gather and review all manager-provided information. The memorandum, legal documents and financial statements can make for dry reading but are absolutely essential. The financial statements can reveal a great deal of information that would not come up in a marketing presentation, including capital flows, expenses and important information contained in the footnotes. Also, confirm information given to you verbally with this written information, such as the actual expense ratios in the financials. Be especially wary of managers whose expenses seem out of proportion to the size of their fund and their activity. How have the expense ratios changed over the last few years? Read the memorandum carefully: do you understand the withdrawal provisions, any lock-up period, the ability to suspend redemptions and the option the manager has to hold your capital? Can he distribute securities instead of cash? Examine whether the memorandum details a procedure for a change of control in the fund or for notification of the withdrawal of the manager's capital. Is there a key-man provision present so that you can withdraw your capital if the main investment team is no longer in charge of the capital?

Qualitative due diligence

After you have laid the due diligence foundation through quantitative analysis, reference checks and analysing the source material, the qualitative portion of your review begins in earnest. What should you look for in a hedge fund manager? High integrity, of course, but how can this be measured? Did the manager have regulatory problems in the past? What do his former colleagues say about this aspect of his personality, his integrity and ethics? Ask. Again, remember that the hedge fund structure provides a manager with a great deal of freedom. You will be relying on this manager to do what is right and prudent. If there are any doubts, an investment should not be made. These doubts need not be confined to integrity; there can be doubts about any of the qualities required. I see many managers every year and place them into three broad categories. The first, managers that are talented, have built a quality organisation and are trading a strategy that will meet our investment objectives. The second, managers that immediately fall into the 'no' category: no interest, no capital, no need to follow. Both these categories are very small. Most managers fall into the 'I don't know' category. They are just 'not compelling'. We try to identify the best and the brightest; therefore, 'not compelling' results in a no capital allocation decision also.

The best managers have innate talent, a 'sixth sense' about how to make money and how to control downside risk. You must apply good judgement and common sense to all the qualitative and quantitative information that you have gathered to identify the managers that will be investing your assets. They should have an edge (sometimes they can't even articulate what this is for you) but along with applying our judgement and common sense to our evaluation, we also apply years and years of experience. This helps us identify a manager's edge and helps us recognise that he is different – he is a money-maker. It also assists us in recognising when the edge is no longer present. This is one of the most important components of long-term success in hedge fund investing.

Often, an investor's due diligence process neglects to properly ascertain a manager's portfolio management skills. While this is a basic and required ingredient, it is often extremely difficult to assess. Being a trader or an analyst is different than managing a portfolio; each requires different skills. Good research ideas are not enough; a manager must also understand position sizes, risks to the overall portfolio and entry and exit points. There are many good researchers but few also have excellent portfolio management skills. Both are required in the hedge fund business.

Business risk

Notice that I say 'business'. Many investment people fail to recognise that it is a business. I have seen a number of talented analysts start their own funds and truly believe that they can complete all the 'non-investing' tasks involved in running their own business in the hours between the market's close and its open. This includes, for instance: investor relations, fundraising, trade settlement, personnel management, office space issues, management information systems, regulatory and compliance issues. These are not tasks that you can squeeze into a few hours. These are full-time jobs that require one's full attention. Many potential managers underestimate these tasks as they have never had to worry about them before; many do not even recognise all the bridges they must cross to build and run a business. Hedge funds need appropriate infrastructures to support their business.

Another issue that you must consider in your evaluation is the change in a manager's environment. For example, information flows, once readily available to a manager in his former environment, may no longer be available in his new environment. Was the manager successful because he saw the deal flow – a deal flow he will no longer see when he is on his own? You must assess how a manager's new environment will affect his idea generation; did he rely on the judgement of a colleague as a sounding board or a superior's application of risk limits? Will the manager be decisive when he is on his own? Will he be able to 'pull the trigger'? We meet with managers who explain with great detail their solid investment ideas, yet when asked how big these positions are in their portfolio, they tell us each is less than 1 per cent. Why? Perhaps he was a top analyst at his prior firm but his ideas were presented to a portfolio manager who then put these ideas to work. Many investment people can identify interesting ideas, but few have the guts to act in a timely and meaningful manner to capture substantial profits from these ideas. Few are successful money managers.

A successful hedge fund manager must have clear objectivity and the ability to fight the natural instinct to be stubborn. Many managers risk losing their entire business just to prove an investment thesis is correct; the timing of investing is just as important as the idea itself. We ask managers not just about winning positions but about losing ones also. What has a manager learned from the losers? How did he minimise the loss? If he didn't, what mistakes occurred, how were they resolved, what has the manager changed to ensure that this outcome will not occur again? Also, ask a manager about the terrific investment ideas that he has had that never made money. Listen to him explain what occurred and what lessons he learned.

A hedge fund manager must have unwavering focus and dedication; managing money is not a part-time job. Visit managers frequently in their offices. Glean changes in the environment, in key personnel and in the manager's interests.

Ongoing due diligence

The due diligence process does not end when an investment is made. In fact, that is when the process begins. Due diligence must be ongoing. You must continually monitor and evaluate your current managers as well as potential managers. Changes are frequent and rapid. The majority of our time is spent performing ongoing due diligence. Personnel change, strategies change, markets change and managers' personal situations change. Any of these can have an effect, positive or negative, on a manager's ability to make money. It is an investor's mandate to be aware of these changes and judge their effects, if any, on a manager's ability to make money. Do you need to take action? What course of action is required?

Do your own work; don't rely on others' analysis. 'Cocktail chatter' can be a tool to gather information, but don't substitute this for thorough due diligence. You must be critical of the 'halo effect'; just because a well-known investor has made an allocation to a manager does not mean this manager is talented or appropriate for your portfolio, or even that that investor performed any due diligence at all. Your investment decisions should be based on information that you gathered.

Do not underestimate the time involved in the due diligence process. Effective due diligence takes a great deal of time and energy. Do not short-cut the process. This can be very costly. Due diligence is not only time-consuming, it is also time sensitive; it cannot wait until you have 'a few hours'. When problems occur, you must be willing to address them in a timely manner. An investor must give himself time not only to gather the information, but also time to apply seasoned judgement to this information.

Listen to what the manager has to say and ask questions about his opinions, views and beliefs. Don't just listen to the managers you use, also listen to ones you don't use. Listen to people in the industry. Discern trends, biases, fears and opportunities. Then evaluate this information in light of what you see around you now and what you have seen before. We apply our historical perspective and use it to creatively deduce the future.

Due diligence on funds of funds

Most of these points apply to fund of funds managers as well as hedge fund managers. Some points that an investor should examine with their fund of funds manager include underlying manager turnover. Is this fund adding 20 managers a year and deleting 15? If so, how can they be performing effective, worthwhile due diligence? If they have had major errors or frauds in their portfolio, ask a lot of questions about how this occurred. It shouldn't have.

Ask about the resources available to this fund of funds. Have they developed a useful database? The information flow is overwhelming in the hedge fund business today. Without a database that can make this information useful, portfolio management would be difficult.

Experience is important to all investment managers: how much experience does your fund of funds manager have? Has the performance record that you are examining been generated by the team that you are evaluating? If not, it has no relevance to your evaluation of the judgement that will generate your returns in the future.

Does the fund of funds employ strategy specialists or generalists? While specialists may have a deep understanding of the strategy that they cover, they may also develop tunnel vision and argue extensively for 'their' managers or for 'their' strategy, even when no capital should be allocated to the area. Generalists create a shared body of knowledge and are able to draw on multiple points of view. All investment professionals should support each investment decision.

The due diligence process is an art, not a science. There is no magic checklist that ensures the most talented manager will be selected in a particular strategy. You must perform extensive qualitative and quantitative due diligence steps on an ongoing basis to maintain the strength of your portfolio and its ability to continually meet your investment objectives.

Chapter 27

Understanding continuing trends in hedge funds

Stuart N. Leaf, Paul Isaac and Michael Waldron
Cadogan Management, LLC, New York, New York

Structural issues

Introduction: from the seeds of the past grow the crops of tomorrow

Understanding today's hedge funds and where the future is likely to take them requires a survey of their history and the trends that have brought hedge funds to their current form. By and large, the reality of hedge funds has always been at odds with the public's perception of them, as funds have evolved from 'mysterious' through 'maligned' to merely 'misunderstood'. There will be a brief review of the development of hedge funds from small, largely speculative pools, innocent of today's quantitative portfolio management tools, catering for wealthy individuals and Wall Street professionals, to today's often sophisticated investment vehicles designed for clients ranging from small retail investors to significant institutional investors, including the world's largest pension plans.

The early hedge funds, as personified initially by such pioneers as A.W. Jones and later by such risk arbitrage managers as Leonard Sheriff were strictly the domain of the ultra-high net worth individual. These partnerships, skirting the rules the Securities and Exchange Commission (SEC) had created to protect less affluent and supposedly naive investors, remained secretive and intentionally non-promotional. Due to this high level of silence surrounding the few hedge funds then in existence, and also because of their relative insignificance within the overall landscape of finance and money management, very little interest was shown by the press and consequently by the broader investing and reading public.

It wasn't until the mid to late 1980s that a real resurgence of hedge funds and the emergence of a couple of well-followed and dominant players increased the public's interest. The most documented hedge fund players were Julian Robertson of Tiger and the press favourite, George Soros of Quantum. The image created in the press ranged from that of David (going against the Goliath of the Bank of England and other central banks), Don Quixote tilting at a broad range of windmills and a Barbary Coast pirate pillaging at will! Given the press' desire to sell more papers, the headlines were generally negative. Although the significance of hedge funds' capital relative to the rest of the markets remained limited, perhaps even shrinking in relation to the extraordinary growth of the mutual fund industry, some interesting developments were actually taking place. Certain sophisticated and forward-thinking institutions such as Yale, Stanford and Harvard were beginning to place capital with hedge fund managers. At the same time a number of European private banks (notably the Swiss) were beginning to create products for some of their secretive and ultra-high net worth clients. These two groups were key to the early institutionalisation of hedge fund investing, both in terms of who would invest and how those investments would be evaluated.

The growth of hedge fund investing continued apace during the 1990s, attracting relatively little attention until after the fateful default of Russia on its debt during the summer of 1998. This began a cascade that turned into an avalanche as a major and very leveraged player in the industry, Long-Term Capital Management (LTCM), failed and nearly pushed the entire financial sector over a precipice. This caused an atmosphere in which the term 'hedge fund' became generally vilified and associated with gargantuan levels of greed. Interestingly, however, it is over this period that a broader, although still rather limited range of foundations and endowments in the United States began to take an interest, together with some forward-thinking insurance companies and a limited number of public and private pension funds. In parallel to this was a growing level of investment by European and Japanese institutions, both for their own accounts and for resale to their high net worth clients (see Exhibits 27.1 and 27.2).

Since the new millennium dawned, many endowments, foundations and other institutions (often in conjunction with their consultants) have been systematically reviewing their investment and disbursement policies. This has often resulted in attempts to create less volatile portfolios. The constant increase of global systemic risk has generated considerable interest in hedge funds, particularly as most long-only strategies have suffered from high volatility and historically low returns.

The new interest and investment coming from the institutional sector is looking to fund actuarial or cash flow obligations that have been increasingly difficult to meet, with low (or negative) equity returns and very low bond yields. In the longer run, it is more likely to be driven by the potential of hedge funds to diversify institutional portfolios with a source of return independent of either the fixed-income or equity markets.

Although the increased size and number of hedge funds, combined with the renewed awareness of the risks of traditional equity investing caused by the market down-draft of 2001

Exhibit 27.1

Proliferation of hedge funds: estimated number of global hedge funds, 1988–2004

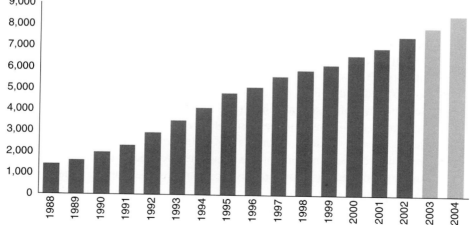

Source: Based on data provided by Van Hedge Fund Advisors International, Inc. Estimates for 2002–04 are projections based on current data and may be revised in the future.

Exhibit 27.2

Estimated global hedge fund assets under management, 1988–2004 (US$ billion)

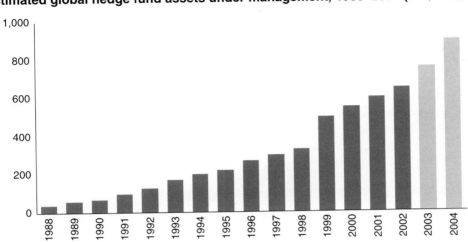

Source: Based on data provided by Van Hedge Fund Advisors International, Inc. Estimates for 2002–04 are projections based on current data and may be revised in the future.

and 2002, have made hedge funds increasingly prominent and press coverage somewhat more regular, they are still widely regarded as exotic variants and not part of mainstream investing. Hedge funds, funds of funds (FOF) and consultants (who have been accelerating up the learning curve in order to provide their clients with the requisite advice) frequently find that, although both the need and acknowledgement of need is present at many institutions, the degree of comfort at the committee and board level to invest in hedge fund vehicles is surprisingly low. An air of mystery and uncertainty remains around hedge funds, making final investment decisions both time-intensive and arduous to consummate.

Paralleling the growing institutional interest in hedge funds over the past few years has been the emergence in Europe, Japan and most recently the United States, of a range of hedge fund products targeted at the 'semi-affluent' investor. Some are mutual fund vehicles, but most have been registered, structured and privately placed funds of funds, targeting the 'retail' investor with minimum initial investments often less than US$100,000. The SEC and other global regulatory authorities have long been concerned about keeping hedge funds out of the portfolios of all but the richest and most sophisticated investors. However, they seem now to be looking at how to allow access to hedged investments within a regulated world. Regulators' concerns have often been based on the lack of statutory and disclosure protections in traditional hedge funds, a concern largely satisfied by the new retail structures. There remains, however, a lingering concern that hedge funds are extraordinarily risky despite many FOF and structured products being, in fact, significantly less risky (using virtually any measurement metric) than their traditional equity counterparts.

The accommodation of retail FOF products to the existing securities laws and their generally low-volatility nature has, thus far, forestalled significant resistance to the emergence of these new products. We are not convinced, however, that this atmosphere will remain. Much will depend on the quality of products offered and the increasing oversight of regulatory authorities going forward. Resistance will also depend on the further development of strategies entailing short selling and fulcrum (incentive) fees within traditional mutual funds. As the use of these techniques becomes more common, and particularly should it grow rapidly, the conceptual opposition to FOF vehicles should continue to decline.

We find it ironic that as the 'veil' of mystery surrounding hedge funds is gradually lifted and the area becomes more accessible to both the institutional and affluent investors, much of the intrinsic value of hedge funds as a group is likely to dissipate. Much of the success of hedge funds over time has been in their being where others weren't or couldn't be. As the term 'alternatives' becomes mainstream, it is hard to see how differential alpha can be sustained at historical levels. The increasing differentiation of hedge fund strategies may leave particular pockets of specialisation less affected than others, especially where illiquidity and interim volatility remain high; but, it is hard to see how the asset class as a whole can escape the effects of increasing acceptance.

Hedge funds: an investment style or a compensation scheme?

Historically, a hedge fund was an investment vehicle that could invest short as well as long and could employ some degree of leverage. Also, in order to create a greater incentive to the hedge fund manager and to better align the manager's interests with those of the clients, a large portion of the total compensation became based on performance-related incentive fees.

Although many hedge fund styles still fit the original definition (such as long-short equities, fixed-income arbitrage, convertible arbitrage, global macro, commodities and futures trading and derivatives trading), others (such as activist equity investing, high-yield, distressed, emerging markets and some pure long-only) often do not have any short component, use no leverage nor employ any exotic investment instruments or techniques. Essentially, they differentiate themselves only through their fee structure! Overall, we believe the term 'hedge fund' will continue to be a catch-all, particularly given how lucrative using that definition can be.

Fees: usurious? And getting worse?

As both cynics and devotees of free markets, we believe that if fees are too high, new market entrants will emerge and, eventually, competition will drive down overall compensation levels. There has already been a tsunami of new entrants into the field. The number of hedge fund managers has increased from hundreds to many thousands over the past two decades and yet not only have fees not declined, they have risen and continue to do so today. Our empirical observations have been that those managers that perform well (whether or not they are nearing capacity limits) have been raising their fees (both their base management and incentive fees). We see no reciprocal discounting by established managers enduring sub-par performance!

Many hedge funds generate most of their alpha by being small, nimble and able to extract value that more sizable investment entities cannot. At some point all funds reach a ceiling of assets under management beyond which their risk-adjusted returns decline. This limit is dependent on a variety of strategy, process and infrastructure elements. Given the high cost of attracting top investment talent, we can understand the need for high base management fees in smaller hedge funds. The range of 1–1.5 per cent might be high (given the potential for incentive fees), but not completely unreasonable, especially if, in theory, it is spread over a general gross level of investment well over 100 per cent of capital. We would argue (and have argued) that a well-capitalised organisation should be able to sustain itself without high base management fees, but this notion is generally brushed aside as being unrealistic! Regardless, we find it dismaying that well-established organisations, with hundreds of millions, even billions of dollars under management, not only charge high base management fees, but look to raise them as well. Why do they do it? They do it because they can!

To us, it seems as though hedge funds are moving toward a 'Hollywood' system where those who thrive become very large and very lucrative (although the glory period may be relatively short) as opposed to an 'industrial' system where more moderate but sustained fee structures and strategies would be the norm. This Hollywood system tends to magnify the hubris of the top performers, supporting the belief that all good luck is actually manifest genius! History is littered with the corpses of self-declared super-investors. We agree with the old saying that 'all Gods are made with clay feet' and are eventually brought tumbling back to earth.

In summary, we see fees sustaining their current high levels for the short to medium term, but anticipate greater downward pressure over time, particularly as total assets under management in the area increase, the percentage of institutional investors grows and the overall alpha generated declines.

The effects of technology on hedge funds

Developing financial technology has had a major impact on the evolution of the hedge fund market. The idea that relatively small investors could compete in active trading in dealer markets would have seemed risible before the age of Bloomberg, Electronic Crossing Networks, conference calls and the use of the internet for all means of research and data retrieval. The ability to access vast libraries of information, simplified versions of which formerly lay at the heart of the intellectual capital of major securities firms has, therefore, been crucial to the proliferation of hedge funds.

The same communications and information technology and its steadily plummeting costs has also allowed hedge funds to operate outside major financial centres and has facilitated hedge fund growth in a variety of ways. By providing alternative venues, it has made hedge funds a popular vehicle with financial professionals anxious to live outside New York City and even outside other major financial centres. These new locations almost always have lower operating and personnel costs and have allowed many smaller funds to survive and even thrive. We see this movement increasing over time, with the side benefit that dispersion of talent is also likely to be a strong draw to new capital from 'local' investors (both high net worth and institutional), comfortable with the manager as a professional and as a community member.

The explosion of heavily IT-dependent markets such as mortgages, options and derivatives has continually created new opportunities for specialised hedge fund strategies. The development of canned screening technologies, programmes that allow for simple yet sophisticated screening of financial data for a broad range of attributes, has enabled even small hedge funds to undertake far-reaching and sophisticated portfolio selection strategies. Massive data libraries have permitted sophisticated correlation analyses among instruments and even synthetic instruments created through sub-hedging strategies. Hedge and trade opportunities exist in geometric proportion to the number of liquid underlying instruments. Technology has permitted the development and dissemination of many new underlying instruments and has created a market of sophisticated spread trading among them.

Inexpensive, reliable communications and IT have encouraged the development of multiple, geographically diversified markets. These, in turn, have fed back into a proliferating web of arbitrage activities among the various markets, including the rise of sophisticated, dynamic multi-factor long-short models with various conditional attributes to their systems.

Our big question, however, is can technology continue to provide managers new ways to generate consistent alpha? As outlined above, to date, technology has created huge opportunities among hedge fund managers, making them privy to information heretofore unobtainable. Value has been created by the managers' abilities to access, appropriately screen and process increasing streams of data and information. However, as the cost of retrieving this data and information decreases, the speed of dissemination increases and the sophistication of systems to sort the information independent of manager input develops, where will the alpha come from? We foresee more and more people having access to user-friendly information at their fingertips. The greater the transparency and liquidity, the fewer the alpha-generating opportunities we will see. Consequently, the time when technology actually begins to become a net alpha 'depleter' might soon be upon us.

Evolution of the prop desk and the trading hedge fund

Securities broker-dealers used to be small, capital constrained businesses until relatively recently. Limited capital combined with limited market liquidity, particularly on the fixed-income side, greatly constrained the ability to trade. The combination of great strides in financial theory, consolidation within the industry to create meaningful balance sheets and rampant technology advances set the scene for firms to increase their specialised trading desks. The institutional compulsion for growth, the decline of agency revenues and the growth of risk management technology at the supervisory level pushed firms into dramatically expanding their proprietary activities during the 1980s and 1990s. These prop desks became a very large contributor to many firms' bottom lines. Two events during the late 1990s have held back the growth of prop desks:

- Nick Leeson single-handedly bringing down the ancient house of Barings; and
- the debacle surrounding LTCM.

The senior management of many global financial institutions realised the potential threat to their survival of the growing trading books in increasingly volatile markets. The 'knock-out optionality' of these businesses was too great a risk and greater limits were imposed. Yet the potential for gain still existed and exists, as does the need to maintain the liquidity of the markets. With the shrinking of the in-house prop desks, many hedge funds have stepped up to the plate and have become 'de facto' outsourced prop desks. Given the difficulty of managing both the risks and the personnel within larger organisations, this is a trend we would anticipate increasing rather than fading (particularly given the fact that the financial institutions can capitalise on hedge funds' growth through their prime brokerage operations).

346

Evolution of the prime brokerage business

Prime brokerage has evolved from a mere support function to a critical element in the establishment and growth of hedge funds. Today, many prime brokers can provide 'turnkey' operations for a new hedge fund, including office space, systems, accounting, legal and documentation support and marketing, most of which can be paid for through soft dollars. This greatly limits the need for many hedge funds to raise seed capital or focus on business issues, freeing them to engage in security selection and portfolio management. We believe this is a mixed blessing, as prime brokers are not a panacea and many hedge funds end up closing because of business rather than portfolio failures.

Initially, prime brokerage, emerging from the operations side of Wall Street firms, was not very glamorous at all. A few larger firms saw an opportunity to turn cost centres into revenue ones and used their scale to adapt the necessary technology they had built in-house for use by outside funds. Beginning in the late 1990s, hedge funds became important clients of larger Street firms and the prime brokerage area a major profit centre. Clients now demand more sophisticated services and competition among the prime brokerage players has dramatically increased.

Initially, many firms were somewhat specialised, with some overlap between the prime brokerage firm's own investment banking and trading activities and those of its clients. Thus, Bear Stearns tended to be prime broker of choice for mortgage-backed, distressed and risk arbitrage funds. Montgomery (now Banc of America) was a specialist in technology shares and had many West Coast clients. Lehman Brothers and some European banks had primarily fixed-income clients. More global firms such as Goldman Sachs and Morgan Stanley had a range of fund strategies and were the primary players in hedge funds trading outside the United States.

Over the past several years, prime brokers have almost become 'venture' backers of hedge funds. They provide investment infrastructure (trading platforms, portfolio accounting, risk tools), business support (office space, IT, other office services) and fundraising through their capital introduction groups. As the quality of these services has increased, firms 'leapfrog' each other with improved technology platforms, greater capital introduction efforts and so on. In addition, the larger firms have looked to 'lock up' the ability to borrow stocks from large institutional investors, making them more competitive for those hedge funds with specific short-selling needs. In the wake of LTCM, it seems the access to leverage is a less competitive issue, as fewer funds seek high borrowing limits. On the other hand, there is competition on the cost and terms of borrowing, as prime brokers rent their balance sheets to hedge funds.

As hedge funds have grown larger (and some have become gargantuan), the balance of power has shifted somewhat in their favour and the larger ones are able to negotiate very favourable terms and use multiple prime brokers. This leads us to wonder if margins will decline somewhat as the prime brokerage industry matures. Regardless, it remains a business that is here to stay and one that is vital in providing many resources to most hedge funds.

Hedge fund indexation

The investible hedge fund index is a fairly recent phenomenon with great conceptual appeal, both from a measurement and investment perspective. Large institutions that must invest across a large number of hedge funds to reach their desired exposure may find an index simple and appealing. Indices may have greater liquidity than actively managed port-folios of hedge funds. They may facilitate broad diversification otherwise beyond the means of investors and increase the efficiency of asset allocation strategies by minimising the deviation of actual performance from theoretical benchmarks.

On the other hand, there have been many structural problems in creating indices. Unlike active equities that are readily traded and continually priced by the market, hedge funds are often very illiquid and may have truly accurate marks perhaps only once a year after their audit. For those creating the index, therefore, the problems are enormous. Many indices want to show long track records and thus invest in larger established funds. This eliminates invest-ment in newer vehicles (even run by experienced managers) and may lead to a need for 'index rebalancing' as older firms cease accepting capital or close altogether. Also, composition of the underlying index is not 'automatic' but rests on considerable subjective judgement, as do some of the pricing issues on specific holdings of the underlying funds. Furthermore, indus-try politics may result in controversy over index composition. Finally, the short average life of hedge funds leads to tremendous issues of 'survivorship bias', making the composition and measurement of any index all the more difficult.

While the idea of the hedge fund index is laudable, it remains to be seen if the difficulties can be resolved and translated into a workable model that, with reasonable consistency, can overcome all the inherent complexities of the discipline.

Regulation

Regulation is a hot topic and deservedly so. Although the concept of the freewheeling risk-be-damned hedge fund is greatly exaggerated, there is certainly the potential within many hedge funds to amplify the risks of a traditional long-only portfolio. Hedge funds are indirect-ly regulated through the restrictions placed on their prime brokers, by the SEC through 'Reg T' and by the regulators controlling banks that provide lines of credit. Nonetheless, hedge funds remain less accountable than most other financial market intermediaries. We believe this is likely to change.

We would expect that hedge funds will be required to register as Registered Investment Advisers and be subject to the audit oversight, ethical standards and limited disclosure required by the SEC.* In our view, many of the more draconian measures (such as requiring full transparency and imposing onerous trading restrictions) are unlikely to be passed as they would dramatically interfere with the ability for hedge funds to trade and thereby negatively impact (possibly in a highly material way) on the liquidity of the overall financial markets, an area that both the SEC and the Federal Reserve are very concerned about.

Sector trends

Long-short equity

Long-short equity, the space in which hedge funds began, remains the dominant strategy in terms of number of hedge funds. Since trading equities has virtually no capital requirements and the skill set seems readily transferable from a number of other careers, the barriers to entry are virtually non-existent. We would expect this to remain a hub of activity for the foreseeable future. Over time, there has been a natural long bias to the area, an understand-able phenomenon given the long-term uptrend of equity markets (particularly during the hedge fund blossoming of the 1980s and 1990s). Although markets are likely to remain tricky and could possibly be in a flat trading range for an extended period of time, we would anticipate the long bias to remain evident. Optimism reigns supreme and short selling is extremely hard to execute!

With more and more capital entering the area, as institutions and individuals alike look for diversifying assets, we see a growing bifurcation within the long-short arena. There are those hedge funds that look to provide steady uncorrelated alpha. As more and more of the liquid names become crowded, the amount of alpha available will decline. We would expect a non-directional portfolio in this area to possibly generate Libor + 400 b.p. returns with low volatility, a product suited primarily to larger institutions with a clearly defined asset allocation model. The higher return, higher volatility side of the market will remain but, by definition, will remain smaller, trafficking in the less liquid and transparent parts of the market. We would anticipate returns still attractive in the area, with a portfolio able to generate 12 per cent + net, but with a growing level of volatility.

Event

This will remain a cyclical sector. For the three years following the onset of the bear market in 2000, the risk arbitrage business became uninteresting, with low interest rates, limited deals and too much capital on the sidelines waiting to enter at a moment's notice. Although we would anticipate a pick-up in corporate activity, we do not expect to see compelling returns until there is a marked up-trend in interest rates.

Corporate restructuring will continue to be prevalent. However, the returns available will again be dependent on capital flows to the area, but because this strategy is largely long-only, will benefit or suffer from equity market moves.

Although none of us possesses a crystal ball, we do not believe that all corporate excesses (particularly leverage-related) have yet been worked out of the system. With or without a mild recovery in the economy, we would expect to see many participants in many industries struggling over the next couple of years. Given the risk profiles at banks, we would also be surprised to see an easy credit environment. Combined, we would surmise there will be an ample supply of distressed paper over the next 24–48 months. Although this area is also highly cyclical and dependent on flows in and out, we would expect the supply of paper to well exceed the demand from skilled practitioners. Although there will be marginal investors entering and exiting, we foresee this will only be noise (admittedly increasing the volatility) and should have limited impact on investment rates of return.

Fixed-income arbitrage

Perhaps the biggest development in this area is the emergence of the credit derivative market, which allows hedging of credit risk through an over-the-counter derivative (often a credit default swap 'CDS' that allows the buyer to 'put' bonds to the seller in case of default). This has created a clearer picture of credit spreads, as CDS prices adjust quite rapidly to reflect the market's opinion about the credit quality of a given issuer. This market allows investors in the credit markets to both hedge and speculate directly on the direction of credit.

While there have been many start-ups in the hedge fund arena, relatively few have been in mortgage-backed securities (MBS) and asset-backed securities (ABS) fixed-income strategies. In part, this is due to high barriers to entry. In order to effectively manage a fixed-income fund, one needs a strong back office to negotiate lending agreements, settle complex trades, and manage liquidity and cost of funds. One also needs a strong technology platform to evaluate various risks, a database describing the terms of complex securities and modelling software to examine the features of these securities under different scenarios. The initial investment is high, and requires significant infrastructure that few can start independently. Also, most lenders prefer large counterparties, and larger, established funds have a cost advantage over smaller start-ups. The few firms that have started tend to have institutional backing of some form.

Finally, as every potential fixed-income security seems to now have an associated derivative, the liquidity in this area has generally increased, as banks, insurance companies and the large government sponsored entities have become significant players. Some hedge funds sprang up as replacements for much of the dealer capital that left the MBS and ABS markets after 1994, and to some extent 1998. However, we sense that the opportunities have not expanded beyond what would be expected with the increasing size of the overall market.

International hedge funds

The greatest trend is continued growth! Outside the United States, the primary centres continue to be the United Kingdom, Hong Kong and Tokyo, although funds are showing up regularly in new and often exotic locations, whether Australia, Denmark, South Africa, Italy or Korea. We believe the diversity and number will continue to increase, absent widespread currency inconvertibility or significant new regulatory restrictions on capital flows.

Talent is located around the globe. The United States has been the greatest advocate and beneficiary of advances in investment theory and practice. However, large markets such as the United Kingdom, Europe overall and Japan have gradually been closing the gap. Many fixed-income funds have always been international (either playing relative value or investing in emerging markets), so this discussion will focus on equity funds.

Developed markets

Europe and Japan have suffered certain structural disadvantages in their equity markets versus the United States. Their markets are narrower and shallower and in many cases significant levels of institutional cross-holdings have further limited the free float. For most prudent hedge funds in both Europe and Japan, this has limited the pool of applicable investments to 200–400 potential mid and large cap companies, rather than the multiple of that available in the United States. Furthermore, the market mentality outside the United States has been geared much more to momentum, growth and GARP investing, with little value culture. This has limited the flexibility for markets to rotate, readjust and equilibrate. In the United States, once a security drops below some 'value threshold', a new crop of buyers emerges willing to accept illiquidity and negative market sentiment in exchange for great fundamentals at the right price. There are also activist investors who are willing to pressure corporate management in order to better realise value. There have been attempts on both fronts in Europe and Japan, but to date they have met with little success, with the value holders continuing to hold cheap securities with little chance of becoming less cheap.

Thus, many European and Japanese hedge funds swim in the same pool and differentiating among them is difficult, as is differentiating between hedge funds and traditional managers investing in the similar securities. Consequently, in order to achieve superior returns, more risk is often taken, mainly in the form of increased leverage or increased concentration.

In the short term, we would not anticipate a real improvement in the fundamentals outlined above, although there is movement in the right direction. In Japan and in Europe, cross-shareholdings are being dismantled. There is a nascent movement towards investor activism and value realisation, although many cultural and practical roadblocks greatly slow the process. Furthermore, the large decrease in total market capitalisation of the major markets decreases overall liquidity. All said, we would expect to see many of the larger European and Japanese hedge funds mired in adequate but unexciting returns. On the other side of the spectrum, we would also anticipate many of the smaller hedge funds, unable to sustain themselves, to go out of business. Nonetheless, we believe there will be opportunities in specific countries and specific sectors for those able to understand the underlying dynamics, although as in most such cases, the level of volatility is likely to be high.

Emerging markets

Apart from more limited liquidity, poorer macro and micro information, often less developed regulatory and legal systems, emerging market equity hedge funds have suffered and will continue to suffer one insurmountable problem: in times of duress, there are virtually no hedges! With Herculean effort, hedges can be found during periods of liquidity, but during the intermittent, yet persistent times of crisis, they often disappear. Governments change the rules, prime brokers call in the shorts, all while demand soars! Hedging an emerging markets portfolio is like buying an insurance policy from a soon-to-be-defunct insurance company. The premium checks get cashed, but when it comes to collecting, there are padlocks on the doors of the company's headquarters! We don't see why this would change going forward.

As such, we view emerging markets 'hedge funds' as members of the 'hedge funds that aren't really hedge funds' group. Money is made by finding the right countries at the right times, moving capital adeptly from opportunity to opportunity and being willing to hold cash when appropriate and engage in the occasional money-making short. There are tremendous inefficiencies in the information flow, tremendous opportunities for gaining an edge and tremendous risks in maintaining an edge! Some funds will generate strong long-term returns, albeit with often breathtaking concomitant levels of volatility. This is an area where we anticipate the future to mirror the past.

Commodity trading advisers (CTAs) and global macro

CTA/macro funds emphasise broad macroeconomic relationships and phenomena, although these sometimes manifest themselves in very particular commodity trades or investments. CTAs have a strong tendency to follow trends, as they typically function with exceedingly high trade leverage, in volatile commodity markets, with short time horizons. Many CTAs are quite small and rely on nimbleness in closing many small losing trades to ride the occasional massive winner.

Macro funds tend to be much larger and often use their size, sophistication and creditworthiness to set themselves up on attractive terms in instruments available to only a limited range of investors. They often trade around their core commitments in much more liquid related instruments accepting basis risk as a matter of course. As large funds may have a number of different trades on at any given time, diversification mitigates the volatility of individual trades and permits accepting high risks on particular portions of the portfolio.

Since these funds often operate as large players in illiquid markets they are often far more opaque to individual investors than funds in liquid securities. This, combined with often very high levels of leverage, both implicit and explicit, creates a strong preference among both individual and institutional investors for known 'brand names' with deep infrastructure and long records. We see no reason why this should change. It is very difficult to anticipate the next great macro trader and, as such, this is definitely a discipline best practised with 20/20 hindsight.

Quantitative strategies

Factor models look at historical relationships among some fairly intuitive measures (such as, price-to-earnings, price-to-book, growth rates and yield) and subsequent performance. These then look to create a portfolio of securities with factors indicating potential future outperformance (longs) and underperformance (shorts). The problem is that many factors are not stable over time and may have significant periods where the factors either do not work (no alpha) or cause underperformance (negative alpha). Many strategies significantly underperformed in 1998, when liquidity came out of the market (and thus more liquid, larger cap stocks outperformed regardless of their factors) and in 1999, when 'GAAP' (growth at any price) investing took over. As these models grow more sophisticated, there is the risk that with a large enough set of factors, one can describe any market. The better managers use human experience to alter the weights of the factors based on their 'read' on the market and based on their own shorter-term testing of the return to a given factor.

Statistical arbitrage, in our opinion, is a replacement for market-making in many cases. While there is evidence that the return on capital for traditional large cap market-makers have been diminished somewhat by decimalisation of trading prices in the United States market (and resulting lower bid/ask spreads) we also believe that there is somewhat less liquidity in certain areas of the market. This is due in part to less block and basket trading being taken on by bulge bracket firms as well as a decline in smaller regional brokerage firms that might have been more willing to make a market in smaller stocks. Thus, the opportunity set for hedge funds operating in mid cap and smaller stocks has increased and many are acting as de facto market makers in some markets. We feel that part of the reason the SEC is looking more carefully at the hedge fund complex is that hedge funds are increasingly important in maintaining liquidity and market stability. In some cases, there have been reports that hedge funds represent up to 60 per cent of the volume in some names.

Some of the biggest developments in the field are coming from the continued application of academic work in the area of 'behavioural finance'. Research is seeking to understand the irrational forms of human behaviour that lead to biases in the market that might be exploited systematically. This research can also give an empirical basis to many of the price patterns that have been statistically observed. Some areas, such as earnings surprise (companies with earnings surprises are more likely to have them because both management and Street analysts are slow to incorporate new developments into their earnings estimates) have been known for some time, and the 'excess' return from naively investing in the strategy has been steadily declining. Other areas, such as the timeframe of different market participants (such as, daily for market-makers, weekly for many managers, quarterly for those who review earnings) are coming under scrutiny.

Statistical arbitrage is a continued race of firms one against the other to find new anomalies and the ability to invest in them without disturbing the market (and thus eliminating the anomaly). Thus, hedge funds in this area need to continue investing in technology, trading platforms and research to ensure continued strong returns. On the risk control side of the portfolio, firms are putting more focus on measures of 'returns to factors' or when various algorithms are working or not. Those firms that have lost money in the past often did so because of an abrupt change in the factors driving aggregate market returns. Given the increased amount of capital allocated to the area and the constant improvement of competing systems, we would anticipate decreasing risk-adjusted returns to this area over time.

Conclusions

Institutions, consultants and individuals are all becoming more sophisticated with regard to portfolio allocation. The globalisation of the world's financial markets and their participants has dramatically increased systematic risk and made true diversification much more difficult to achieve. Investing in hedge funds remains one of the few ways to still generate pure alpha. Yet a dramatic increase in the capital flowing into many of the strategies discussed in this chapter will squeeze both the returns and the alpha that can be generated. The bulk of hedge fund capital will need to settle for lower risk-adjusted returns than have been achieved in the past, but perhaps sufficient to satisfy a clearly defined niche within a well-designed overall financial portfolio. There will remain the outlying fund, operating either under the radar screen or with considerable leverage or concentration that will remain able to generate outsized alpha, but the risks associated with generating that alpha are likely to grow as well.

---

* Editor's note: on 29 September 2003, shortly before this book went to press, the staff of the SEC issued its report entitled 'The Implications of the Growth of Hedge Funds', the culmination of its efforts following the Hedge Fund Roundtable held in May 2003. As of the date of this writing, the Commission itself had not taken any action in response to the report. One of the key recommendations of the staff was that the SEC consider 'requiring hedge fund advisers to register with the SEC as investment advisers, taking into account whether the benefits outweigh the burdens of registration'. In the staff's view, ' … registration of hedge fund advisers would serve as a deterrent to fraud, encourage compliance and the adoption of compliance procedures, provide the SEC with important information … and effectively raise the standards for investment in hedge funds from the "accredited investor" standard to that of "qualified client"'. See http://www.sec.gov/news/studies/hedgefunds0903.pdf for the full text of the report.

Chapter 28

Hedge fund benchmarking and indexation

Jeff Bramel
DB Advisors, LLC, New York, New York

Introduction

This chapter is intended as an overview of the central themes and issues surrounding hedge fund benchmarking and indexation, and is written to be of appeal to a broad cross-section of financial professionals. As such, it favours qualitative description over technical rigour, and many sections are devoted to relatively high-level discussion of the myriad important yet subtle technical aspects of indexation with hedge funds.

Indexation and benchmarking are fundamentally data-intensive, quantitative pursuits with close connections to statistical portfolio analysis. Consequently, many of the underlying issues in this chapter have mathematical and statistical foundations, and most have received (and continue to receive) extensive treatment in academic literature. While such papers are valuable to quantitative financial professionals working in closely related areas, they often fail to serve the broader financial population for two reasons.

1. They are often highly technical in nature, requiring people with an unrelated or tangentially related background to spend considerable time and effort gaining familiarity with the underpinning principles necessary to understand them.
2. They study or model an idealised case that may differ in important respects from the real-world application in ways that are understood by specialists but not by non-specialists.

This chapter addresses these points by avoiding overly technical presentation, and by focusing on considerations likely to be important to the practitioner. By doing so, it aims to provide a general survey of indexation that is of value to the investment professional who has occasional need to understand hedge fund indices, but does not focus on them.

History and evolution of hedge fund indices

The first hedge fund indices were constructed in the early 1990s as simple averages of all the monthly returns available to the constructor. Little if any thought was given to reducing the impact of distortions induced by poor data quality and construction techniques, with the consequence that a host of biases could potentially be present in the resultant numbers. The following are among the more serious problems that existed in one or more early indices.

- No attempt was made to ensure a consistent selection of funds, with the result that the index reflected the performance of a different group of funds every month.

354

- No mechanism was in place to ensure that funds reported their performance by the date necessary for calculation of the index, leading to a bias toward early-reporting funds. In practice, funds with unusually good performance were observed to report their results earlier than those with unusually poor performance, resulting in an upward bias to the reported index number.
- The history of the index was recomputed every time funds were added or deleted, leading to retroactive changes in performance.[1]
- The universe of funds consisted of only those funds still in operation, leading to survivorship bias.
- There was inconsistency in fee treatment.
- Index constituents were not disclosed, impairing research and analysis.

Although hedge fund indexing remains an embryonic endeavour, it is a misconception to believe that it has not yet advanced to the point where indices are capable of providing any useful information. On the contrary, much of what we can say today about the dynamics of the hedge fund industry has emerged from research related to hedge fund indices. Despite the criticisms they attract, hedge fund indices have educated investors about the performance characteristics of various hedge fund strategies, and have for the first time provided meaningful peer-group benchmarks for tracking investment performance. They have also stimulated research into hedge fund performance and provided impetus for the development of new types of hedge fund investment products. Hedge fund indices are also emerging as investment products, with at least five different investable indices or index-tracking funds available today. Whatever shortcomings indices face, it is no longer an open question whether they have begun to benefit the investment community.

Hedge fund indexation problems

There are two primary difficulties that arise when creating hedge fund indices: fund classification and data quality. Both are sources of much criticism of existing indices, and neither is likely to disappear anytime soon. Fund classification encompasses the set of problems that stem from attempting to pigeon-hole into consistent groups fund managers that are almost by definition unique, nimble and prone to adapt their strategies over time in response to market changes. Data quality problems stem from the lack of systematic and timely data gathering about the industry and the consequent inconsistency of quality and quantity of information available for different fund managers, strategies and time periods.

Categorisation

Given that many investors choose hedge funds on the basis of their purported ability to pursue unique investment strategies not available elsewhere, it may seem contradictory to attempt to categorise them in any systematic fashion. Indeed, the development of a hedge fund classification system presents a tremendous challenge and poses consistency problems that a purist would find troublesome. However, despite these problems, the advantages of being able to group hedge funds together in a structurally meaningful way are sufficient enough that almost every hedge fund industry participant relies upon some form of classification scheme.

Ask a financial professional to name a few common hedge fund categories and they will likely be able to respond with phrases like long-short equity, convertible arbitrage, distressed, global macro, and relative value. However, what do these terms really mean? It may be somewhat alarming to realise that despite being commonly employed, none of these categories fits into an entirely consistent framework with the others. Two of them (long-short equity and convertible arbitrage) tell us something about the types of securities being traded. Two (convertible arbitrage and global macro) describe at least in part the trading strategies being used. One (distressed) refers to the type of company whose securities will be traded, but not which securities or how they will be traded; one (global macro) reveals something about the geographical orientation of the fund's investments; and one (long-short equity) explains something about the anticipated market exposure. Finally, one classification (relative value) tells us almost nothing at all, since nearly every type of investment is ultimately a choice about relative value, and all of the other four examples easily fit this description.[2] Thus, these classifications constitute a hodgepodge of overlapping frameworks of asset type, trading strategy, geography and market exposure, any one of which could potentially form the basis for an entire classification scheme. Yet the previous five terms, among others, are so widely utilised (and utilised together) that they have become part of the hedge fund vernacular. What can we say about the de facto classification schemes that are used in practice, and why have more consistent, rigorous and systematic classification schemes not become prevalent?

The attempt to develop a fully systematic classification system from only a single framework, such as asset type, strategy or geography, invariably works well for some categories, but fails to provide enough specificity by itself to segregate the universe of hedge funds into useful sub-categories. Two examples serve to illustrate this point: choosing asset class as a 'pure' framework does not allow differentiation between directional and non-directional strategies, and has difficulty accommodating any hedge fund whose strategy involves relationships across asset classes (such as capital structure arbitrage); likewise, choosing trading strategy does not allow distinction between equity and fixed-income managers. Nor is it entirely satisfactory to impose a systematic multi-tier hierarchical system by multiplying out all the possible combinations of sub-categories within two or more frameworks: we quickly arrive at a very long list of possible permutations and find that many represent few or no hedge funds in practice, while still leaving the problem of how to address hedge funds that span across category boundaries.[3] These problems help explain the lack of success implementing purely systematic frameworks, and lead back to the disappointing reality that most existing hedge fund classification schemes tend to be inconsistent hybrids of different top-level approaches.

The inconsistent use of different, overlapping classification schemes is usually the by-product of an effort to achieve reasonably tight clustering of related hedge funds and little crossover between groups. Put differently, the use of a partially strategy-based and partially asset class-based system has empirically tended to be the best at putting funds into relatively stable 'baskets' that perform similarly to funds of the same type and differently from other fund types, with few ambiguous outliers, across a variety of market conditions. The more tightly a pre-specified categorisation scheme is able to cluster funds together, the more it has succeeded in eliminating extraneous factors and focusing on the core drivers of performance within that category.

There is, however, a limit to the truth of this statement. Note the use of the word pre-specified. Taken to the extreme, one might assume that the very best categorisation framework would be one that looks only at how tightly it can cluster funds based on their performance, disregarding entirely the presence or lack of any structural similarities between these funds. Such categorisation is referred to as statistical clustering, since it relies only on the statistical distribution of fund returns, and not on the stated investment strategies of the funds, and has been applied in the development of at least one hedge fund index.[4] Although this technique may have value in other financial and scientific disciplines, its use is dubious at best with hedge funds (it becomes a classic case of building the results to fit the data). The problem arises because of the relative paucity of consistent data available on hedge funds, a topic discussed in the following section.

Although at present there is no formal standardisation of hedge fund categories, it is worth noting that a study committee has been convened by the Alternative Investment Management Association (AIMA) with the goal of developing an industry standard classification system. At publication time, the committee had not concluded its work, and no results had been announced. If an AIMA sanctioned framework is developed, and if it becomes widely accepted throughout the industry, it is possible that some standardisation across indices will emerge in the future. However, given the continual cycle of innovation for which hedge fund managers are valued, it seems likely that there will always be hedge funds that defy easy classification.

Data quantity and quality

The other major obstacle faced in the creation of a hedge fund index is in obtaining data that is sufficient in quantity, reliable and consistent. Data quantity becomes an issue because, as noted above, most hedge funds provide performance statistics only monthly.[5] The number of data points available within a historically relevant timeframe is therefore limited, handicapping the reliability of analysis done on it.

At present (though years from now this may have changed), most hedge funds provide performance data only once a month. At the current pace of evolution and change in hedge funds and financial markets,[6] it is in many cases difficult to justify that data more than three years old can still have any relevance to today's market dynamics. With perhaps just 36 (or fewer) data points available, it becomes relatively easy to spot 'false positives' in the data clusters (to group unrelated funds together based on similarities that are nothing more than coincidence). However, if one has structural reasons for believing *ex ante* that certain funds should be categorised similarly, and cluster analysis supports this conclusion, then one can have increased confidence that the *ex ante* categorisation scheme is meaningful.[7]

Complicating matters, whatever data is available may not be completely reliable. Data quality problems can be decomposed into two sources: systematic biases that arise from distortions in the way data is reported, captured or catalogued; and non-systematic errors or 'noise' that arises from inaccurate or incomplete information capture (for example, the use of good-faith monthly performance estimates rather than audited final numbers). Broadly speaking, systematic errors are those that cannot be reduced by increasing the sample size, while random errors are those that tend to get cancelled out if enough data points are collected. Systematic biases tend to be of more concern because failure to account for them will lead to systematic distortions of results, whereas random noise can be reduced

357

with larger sample sizes. However, the limited quantity of data available for hedge funds means that random errors are also prone to frequent occurrence if care is not taken to assess the reliability of results.[8]

Many studies have documented the distortions and biases that exist in hedge fund databases: survivorship bias, self-selection bias, instant history bias, early reporting bias and others.[9] It is beyond the scope of this chapter to discuss these deficiencies in depth, other than to note two important observations: (1) the existence of data biases can pose significant challenges to the researcher and investor, and (2) although data biases may render it more difficult to make use of data, they do not mean that the available data should be dismissed (only that users of the data need to be careful to understand the limitations of their information).

It is worth noting that the fundamental difficulties inherent in creating a hedge fund index are closely related to the reasons why a hedge fund index is important in the first place. An index helps present a consolidated picture of the industry, just as it does for equities, fixed-income instruments or any other area of finance. If such a consolidated picture were easily obtainable, there would be little additional value in the indices.

Index weighting schemes

By 'weighting scheme', we refer to the manner in which the index value is computed from the values of its constituents. Hedge fund indices typically use either simple arithmetic averaging or asset-weighted averaging, although other weighting schemes also exist. In simple averaging, all constituents are given an equal weight, so the index value can be computed simply by summing the monthly returns and dividing by the number of constituents. In asset-weighted averaging, the period returns of each fund are weighted by the assets under management of that fund at the beginning of the period, so that a fund with US$200 million under management would be weighted twice as heavily as one with US$100 million under management. A third type of weighting scheme (although 'weighting' is a slight misnomer in this case) is to calculate an index value as a percentile value of the constituents, where the 50th percentile or median is the most common percentile value used.[10] Of course, other variations are possible, whether on one of these themes or others.

The majority of hedge fund indices in existence today still use even-weighted construction (simple averaging), although asset-weighted indices appear to be receiving increased attention. The primary advantage of even weighting versus asset weighting is that it requires no knowledge about the relative sizes of the constituent hedge funds. Since such information can require substantial effort to collect reliably and consistently, it constitutes a major deterrent to the creation of asset-weighted indices. A second reason often cited for the creation of even-weighted indices is that because they minimise asset concentration and maximise diversification, an even-weighted index thereby minimises volatility relative to the average volatility of its constituents.

Two major index providers (CSFB/Tremont and MSCI) publish asset-weighted index families, where the relative weights of the constituents are scaled according to their assets under management. A third index provider, HFR, also provides an asset-weighted composite index. Although more difficult to construct and calculate, asset-weighted indices possess two key advantages: their performance is more representative of the actual dollar returns across their constituent hedge funds, and by properly accounting for the compounding of returns they avoid underperformance bias. The fact that asset-weighted index returns better track actual dollar performance also makes it easier to use them as the basis for index investment products, since they require substantially less rebalancing activity than even-weighted index investment portfolios.

A small number of providers have produced indices using median weighting schemes or other percentile-based construction techniques. Among these is the Zurich Capital Markets index family, which reports the median return of its constituent funds. The PerTrac Online index family reports multiple percentile levels for each index, providing investors with some perspective on the relative performance of top and bottom-tier funds. Like even-weighted averages, median and percentile construction schemes do not require data on assets under management.

Exhibit 28.1

Index weighting scheme comparison

Weighting scheme	Advantages	Disadvantages	Examples
Even-weighted	Simple to compute	Does not compound constituent returns	Bernheim EACM
	Minimises concentration of assets	Exhibits underperformance bias	HFR MAR/CISDM
	All else equal, has lower volatility than asset-weighted schemes	Difficult to track with an investable product due to constant rebalancing	MSCI[*] Hedgefund.net (Tuna) Hennessee InvestorForce (Altvest) Standard & Poor's Van
Asset-weighted	Close approximation of actual dollar investment performance	Complicated to compute	CSFB/Tremont MSCI
	Compounds constituent returns	Requires monthly asset inflow and outflow data	
	Does not exhibit underperformance bias	Risk of domination by small number of very large funds (concentration risk)	
	Easier to track with investable product	All else equal, has higher volatility than even-weighted schemes	
Percentile (including median)	Simple to compute	Not representative of actual economic performance	PerTrac Online (upper and lower percentiles)
	Top-tier and bottom-tier percentile indices possible	Does not model impact of extreme values	Zurich Capital Markets (median)
		Very difficult to track with an investable product	

[*] MSCI offers even-weighted and asset-weighted indices.

Source: Author's own, with information provided by index publishers.

However, one significant drawback is that they do not model the differing magnitudes of constituent returns above and below the median, making them unsuitable as the basis for an index investment product. Exhibit 28.1 compares different index weighting schemes.

Beyond the weighting scheme, the consistency of an index's construction and calculation methodology is also important. If one takes the goal of an index to be the objective representation of the performance of a group of similar instruments, then it stands to reason that an index should have as little subjective or arbitrary component to its construction as possible. The logical extreme of this argument would be an index that is entirely formula-driven, where anyone in possession of the formulas would, without prior knowledge of any of its constituents, be able to construct the index from scratch and calculate its entire performance history throughout time. In reality, all hedge fund indices have at least some degree of subjectivity in their construction. Any hedge fund index that is based on a particular database as its universe is, at minimum, subject to the vagaries of which funds are members of that universe; since there is no standardised reporting requirement for hedge funds, there is no single repository of data that contains information on every fund. Furthermore, because of the complexities arising from uniform treatment of issues as diverse as share classes, currencies, fees, estimates, liquidity, investability, reporting consistency and even errors, in practice it is essentially impossible to construct an index without some subjective element.

Indices handle subjective aspects of their construction by relegating undefined or unanticipated situations to the purview of an Index Committee or equivalent oversight body. The power (and motivations) of such bodies varies greatly. In some indices, the Index Committee may exercise nearly dictatorial power, with the ability to select and remove members of the index at any time, dictate adjustments to reported performance, and make other modifications at any time for any reason. In other cases, they may have power only to act in very limited cases. An equally important consideration is the degree of independence of the committee: are their personal interests connected to the performance, composition, or other aspects of the index? Greatest consistency is usually achieved with an independent oversight board that seldom becomes involved in the index's construction or calculation, although (as with most aspects of indexing) the most appropriate level of subjectivity is naturally connected to the ultimate purposes for which the index is intended.

Indices and investability

Not all hedge funds are open to investment, and as a result, indices may contain constituents into which it is impossible to invest actual money. In practice, some indices restrict their constituents to only those funds still open to new investments, while others make no such restriction.[11] The most notable family of purely investable hedge fund indices is the Standard and Poor's hedge fund index family, which requires an open capacity commitment of its constituents. Recently, HFR, MSCI and CSFB/Tremont have all announced families of investable indices as well.[12] Most other major hedge fund indices include both open and closed hedge funds.

Transparency

Just as different hedge funds offer different levels of transparency, different indices reveal differing amounts of information about how they are constructed and calculated. As with hedge funds in general, the trend has been toward more disclosure, with most newly launched indices making available the names of their constituents and various details about how they are constructed, calculated, and rebalanced. However, a number of hedge fund indices disclose none of this information, making it more difficult to evaluate how appropriate they are for a given purpose. The degree of transparency may be connected to the degree of subjectivity in an index's construction; clearly, an index with few formal rules or policies governing its construction has less available to disclose than a more rigorously defined index.

Transparent disclosure of constituent funds also aids in assessing the suitability of benchmarking a hedge fund's performance with a given index. The classification of hedge funds remains, at present, a subjective and somewhat contentious exercise. Since one person may categorise a fund differently than another, it is often difficult to evaluate the suitability of a particular hedge fund strategy index without direct knowledge of its constituents. It is also difficult to evaluate the consistency of an index's construction and calculation from month to month when no information about its constituents is disclosed. Both of these facts motivate greater transparency and encourage investors to adopt those indices providing it.

Liquidity

Before the advent of index investment products, the only real liquidity question of relevance to an index was whether all its member funds were investable or not. However, as the prevalence of investable hedge fund index products has increased, the liquidity of the constituents has become a more important consideration. Investable indices often have liquidity requirements for member funds, with the possible consequence of systematic selection bias toward certain groups or strategies that tend to feature higher liquidity. For example, many event-driven strategies tend to be relatively illiquid while many managed futures and CTA strategies tend to be highly liquid, leading to a potential over-representation of the latter category in otherwise balanced indices. There is, of course, also the danger that overly stringent liquidity requirements will lead to adverse selection bias, as poorly performing hedge funds desperate to attract new capital modify their investment terms to accommodate index requirements in the hopes of attracting index-related capital.

Why index?

By representing distillations of broader groups of assets or investments, indices can offer benefits to both analysis and investment. As a reference tool, they bring clarity and definition to the hedge fund space by cutting across the bewilderingly broad array of different funds, managers and strategies to distil out the essential elements. As an investment strategy, indexation offers (in theory at least) the possibility of broad asset-class exposure, maximum diversification and potentially lower management fees.

Valid arguments can be made that because of the diversity among even similarly styled hedge funds, an index cannot be a close proxy for any of the individual constituents. While this may be true, it is not necessarily a disadvantage, and comes close to missing the point of creating an index in the first place: it can just as well be argued that it is the very dissimilarities among otherwise 'similar' hedge funds that make such distillations even more vital than with traditional asset classes. An ideal index will retain the common characteristics of the funds it represents while discarding the dissimilar traits or, if you prefer, will retain the systematic elements that drive performance among a particular group of managers, while diversifying away the idiosyncratic risk of individual managers. While clearly the ultimate suitability of an index is dependent on the intended application, it can be readily seen that for many purposes, the informational value of an index is greater when the constituents are less alike.

Consider for a moment the usefulness of an index of assets that all have identical price movement. In such a case, an index tells us nothing, because any one of the underlying assets could be taken as the index with no loss of information. Relaxing this condition just slightly to allow for very minor differences still leaves a collection of assets that are, for many intents and purposes, extremely good proxies of each other, so there is still little value in computing and indexing some sort of composite index. It is only when there are meaningful differences between the members that knowing the average (or median, or other statistical aggregation upon which an index could be based) becomes useful. This is obviously a matter of degree, for what are meaningful differences for one purpose may not be for another.

It is easy to list a broad range of applications of hedge fund indices to research, analysis and benchmarking. The following is by no means an exhaustive enumeration of all such applications:

- performance benchmarking of individual hedge funds;[13]
- determination of hurdle rates;
- comparisons across asset classes;
- comparisons of strategies;
- style and factor analysis;
- decomposition of market risk and idiosyncratic risk;
- portfolio construction and analysis; and
- news, presentations and marketing.

Hedge fund index investing

Until the advent of investable index products, essentially all indexing applications were related to research, analysis or information dissemination applications similar to those listed above. Hedge fund indexation as an investment strategy remains in its infancy. In recent years a number of firms have launched hedge fund index-tracking products with varying degrees of success. In 2001, Zurich Capital Markets and CSFB launched products that tracked the ZCM Institutional Benchmarks and CSFB/Tremont Hedge Fund Index, respectively. These were followed in 2002 by the launch of investable products that tracked the S&P Hedge Fund Index and in 2003 by investable products launched by HFR and MSCI, bringing the total number of investable index product families to at least five. As the hedge fund industry continues to develop, it is likely that the number and diversity of hedge fund index products will continue to increase.

Index investment products come in two forms: those that attempt to provide exact tracking of their benchmark index, and those that do not. Investment products designed to provide exact tracking may rightly be referred to as 'investable indices', while products offering imperfect tracking are more correctly termed 'index-tracking products'. The S&P, MSCI and HFR products are investable indices, while ZCM offerings are designed as index trackers and CSFB offers both types of products.

Products of the latter type typically consist of baskets of hedge funds designed to imitate the performance of the full hedge fund index as closely as possible, but typically provide only 'best-efforts' tracking. In other words, the risk of the product not tracking the index is borne by the investor. The achievable tracking accuracy is dependent on a host of factors including the number and make-up of funds in the index, the proportion of closed (inaccessible) funds, the liquidity of the funds and (since most hedge funds do not accept investments below a minimum threshold size) the amount of capital available to construct the tracking basket. To date there have been relatively few index-tracking products constructed, but anecdotal evidence from those that do exist suggests that relatively tight tracking performance can be achieved, even when a substantial percentage of the funds in the index are not available for investment by the tracking vehicle. Exhibit 28.2 shows predicted and actual tracking error for two investment vehicles tracking the CSFB/Tremont Hedge Fund Index, an asset-weighted index of approximately 400 hedge funds, of which approximately 40 per cent by assets are closed to new investment.

Exact tracking of an index is usually only possible when the index itself is fully investable; even then, because of product management fees and liquidity restrictions on the constituent funds, it may not be possible for the investable product to deliver zero tracking error. If zero tracking error is a requirement, there are usually only two workable approaches. The first is for the index itself to be designed from the outset to mirror the real-world inefficiencies of an investable product. The other alternative is for the investable product to be structured as a derivative security where the issuer agrees to pay the exact performance of the index, effectively issuing an index-linked note backed by the credit of the issuer to deliver on the obligation. In such cases, the issuer usually hedges its own obligations to deliver this

Exhibit 28.2

Hedge fund index tracking error versus fund count

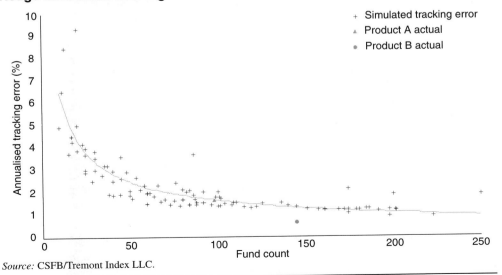

Source: CSFB/Tremont Index LLC.

performance by purchasing an underlying basket of hedge funds that mirrors the actual index as closely as possible, thereby reducing its residual risk to a minimum. Although complex, the derivative product technique has certain potential advantages, such as flexibility and liquidity. In theory a product can be developed with special features of interest to the customer, such as caps and floors on performance, and can be designed to offer enhanced liquidity via secondary market-making by the product issuer.

Investing in hedge fund index products is typically viewed as an alternative to investing in funds of funds (FOFs). Both indices and FOFs offer the investor greater diversification than can be obtained with investments in individual hedge funds, seeking to deliver less volatile return streams.

Three arguments made in favour of hedge fund index investing are that it provides greater diversification than a fund of funds, does so without subjective bias or tilt, and may offer lower fee structures. While a typical fund of hedge funds may have between 10–30 constituent funds, a hedge fund index product may contain considerably more than 100 separate managers. Funds may be selected in a variety of ways: if the index is purely investable, typically all funds in the index are included in the investable product. If not, funds may be selected using a variety of techniques designed to ensure the investable product tracks the index.

Regulatory advantages to indexation may also arise in some countries and jurisdictions. If they are seen as passive, diversified or tracking products by regulators, hedge fund index products may receive different tax or regulatory treatment than products perceived to be active, concentrated or discretionary. In other cases, regulators may have explicitly different rules for indices than for non-indices. Finally, in some cases, derivative products built on indices may offer certain advantages to certain classes of investors.[14]

A survey of hedge fund indices

The number of hedge fund indices is large and expanding. It is possible that at some point in the future a consolidation will occur due to business pressures, but for the moment, few indices have disappeared. Exhibit 28.3 compares several features of many well-known hedge fund indices.

Future trends

What developments are there likely to be in hedge fund indices in the future? One can only speculate, but the following seem plausible.

- *Consolidation.* The number of hedge fund indices has grown rapidly, and over time it is possible that some will gain dominance. The costs of calculating and publishing an index can be substantial, so those that fail to gain dominance may face pressure to merge resources or cease operations.
- *Publication frequency.* As more hedge funds provide intra-month performance updates, it is possible that more indices will move to publish their values more frequently.
- *Category standardisation.* Though efforts are under way by the AIMA and others to develop standardised categories, the diversity of applications of categories still makes some types of classification schemes more suited than others for particular purposes. Category standardisation may therefore take considerable time, if it occurs at all.

Exhibit 28.3

Feature comparison of major hedge fund indices

Index	Number of strategies	Strategies assigned	Constituent weighting	Update frequency	Construction notes	Funds in database	Funds in index	Closed funds	Total assets (US$ billion)	Data start	Funds disclosed?	Investable index products	Website
Bernheim	N/A	Bernheim	Simple average	Monthly	Funds maybe in more than one sub-index.		18		50	1993	No	No	www.hedgefundnews.com
CISDM (Formerly MAR)	9	Self-select	Median	Monthly	Construction methodology is not published.	1,300			120 (database)		No	No	www.marhedge.com
CSFB/Tremont	13	Assigned by Tremont	Asset-weighted	Monthly	Funds must have US$10 million minimum under management, a one-year track record and an audit before being included. Rebalanced quarterly.	2,600	403	Yes	141 (index), 300 (database)	1994	Yes	Yes	www.hedgeindex.com
EDHEC	13	Self-select	Simple average	Monthly	Indices are averages of other published hedge fund indices, rather than individual hedge funds.	N/A	N/A	Yes		2003	Indirectly	No	
Evaluation Associates Capital Markets (EACM)	13	Based on PPM	Simple average	Monthly	Index is rebalanced annually.		100			1990	No	No	www.eacm.com
Hedge Fund Research (HFRI)	16	Based on PPM	Simple average	Monthly	Funds of funds are not included in composite numbers.	1,350	1,350	Yes		1990	No	No	www.hfr.com

Disclaimer: While efforts have been made to provide accurate data, this information has been assembled from a wide variety of sources, including (in some cases) estimates derived from partial or incomplete information when published sources were not available. Furthermore, indices change over time: funds are added, funds are removed, categories change and construction rules may change. Therefore the information in this table should be interpreted with the understanding that it may contain inaccuracies that may be significant.

(*continued*)

Exhibit 28.3 *continued*

Feature comparison of major hedge fund indices

Index	Number of strategies	Strategies assigned	Constituent weighting	Update frequency	Construction notes	Funds in database	Funds in index	Closed funds	Total assets (US$ billion)	Data start	Funds disclosed?	Investable index products	Website
Hedge Fund Research (HFRX)	8	Statistical clustering	Optimised basket	Daily	Funds are qualitatively selected and must pass due diligence assessment. Strategy index constituent weights are chosen 'to maximise correlation with their group'.	1,350		No		2003		Yes	www.hfr.com
Hedgefund.net (Tuna)	33	Self-select	Simple average	Monthly	Index history is revised when new or updated data is received	2,600	2,000	Yes		1979	Yes	No	www.hedgefund.net
Hennessee Group	23	Based on PPM	Simple average	Monthly	No performance or size criteria.	3,000	450	Yes	160 (database)	1987	No	No	www.hennesseegroup.com
InvestorForce (AltVest)	13	Self-select	Simple average	Monthly	No performance criteria for inclusion. Funds may be in more than one strategy.		1,400	Yes		1993	Yes	No	www.investorforce.com
LJH Global Investments	14	Assigned by LJH	Simple average	Monthly	Index is rebalanced either quarterly or semi-annually, depending on the strategy. Funds must have audited financial statements and have gone through some level of LJH due diligence.		800			1989	No		www.ljh.com

Disclaimer: While efforts have been made to provide accurate data, this information has been assembled from a wide variety of sources, including (in some cases) estimates derived from partial or incomplete information when published sources were not available. Furthermore, indices change over time: funds are added, funds are removed, categories change and construction rules may change. Therefore the information in this table should be interpreted with the understanding that it may contain inaccuracies that may be significant.

(continued)

Exhibit 28.3 *continued*

Feature comparison of major hedge fund indices

Index	Number of strategies	Strategies assigned	Constituent weighting	Update frequency	Construction notes	Funds in database	Funds in index	Closed funds	Total assets (US$ billion)	Data start	Funds disclosed?	Investable index products	Website
Magnum	16			Monthly						1994			www.magnum.com
MSCI	164	MSCI	Simple and weighted averages	Monthly	Hierarchical system of categories allowing funds to be re-used among several indices. Funds must have at least US$15 million in assets to be included in index.	1,500	936	Yes	134 (index)	2002	Subscribers only	No	www.msci.com
MSCI/Lyxor Hedge Invest	1	MSCI	Capped median	Weekly	Funds selected by MSCI from among those approved by Lyxor Asset Management. Illiquid strategies are excluded.		60	No		2003		Yes	www.msci.com
PerTrac Online	35	Self-select	Percentile rankings	Monthly	Utilises data from hedge fund.net. Multiple returns corresponding to selected performance percentile rankings are published.	2,400	1,700	Yes		1979	Yes	No	www.pertraconline.com
Standard & Poor's	3	S&P	Simple average	Daily	Funds selected based on ability to guarantee capacity and provide daily reporting.		40	No	26	2002	Yes	Yes	www.spglobal.com

Disclaimer: While efforts have been made to provide accurate data, this information has been assembled from a wide variety of sources, including (in some cases) estimates derived from partial or incomplete information when published sources were not available. Furthermore, indices change over time: funds are added, funds are removed, categories change and construction rules may change. Therefore the information in this table should be interpreted with the understanding that it may contain inaccuracies that may be significant.

(*continued*)

Exhibit 28.3 *continued*

Feature comparison of major hedge fund indices

Index	Number of strategies	Strategies assigned	Constituent weighting	Update frequency	Construction notes	Funds in database	Funds in index	Closed funds	Total assets (US$ billion)	Data start	Funds disclosed?	Investable index products	Website
Van Hedge Fund Advisors	12	Assigned by Van	Simple average	Monthly	No minimum size or track record requirement. Index is never rebalanced. Number of index funds varies monthly.	3,400	about 750	Yes	182 (database)	1988	No	No	www.vanhedge.com
Zurich Capital Markets (ZCM)	5	Statistical clustering	Simple average	Monthly	Reports the median for each strategy, 10 of which are combined into four submedians. They do not provide a composite number	750	55	No	14 (index)	1998	Yes	Yes	www.zindex.com

Disclaimer: While efforts have been made to provide accurate data, this information has been assembled from a wide variety of sources, including (in some cases) estimates derived from partial or incomplete information when published sources were not available. Furthermore, indices change over time: funds are added, funds are removed, categories change and construction rules may change. Therefore the information in this table should be interpreted with the understanding that it may contain inaccuracies that may be significant.

Sources: CSFB/Tremont Index LLC, Strategic Financial Solutions, and Blackstone Group research.

- *Regulation.* The current regulatory environment makes it seem possible that hedge funds may face registration requirements or other regulatory requirements in the future. If this occurs, it could lead to the universal availability of certain types of basic data for all hedge fund managers, allowing indices to converge toward a more consistent fund universe and thereby facilitating more reliable cross-comparison among indices.

- *Indexation as investment strategy.* At present, index products remain too new for much to be said about their long-term popularity or performance. Over time, however, both track records and opinions will accumulate, with consequences for the future of index investments.[15]

- *Transparency.* Just as investors seem to be demanding more transparency of individual hedge funds, so too is it likely they will require more transparency of their indices.

- *Acceptance.* As the popularity of hedge funds increases, hedge fund indices may become increasingly widely quoted metrics of industry performance. While this could benefit the hedge fund industry, there could also be regulatory backlash if widespread awareness of hedge fund indices triggers increased demand for public access to hedge funds.

[1] Imagine the consternation this would cause someone trying to trade derivative products on the index!

[2] This is a somewhat pedantic conclusion, since in practice most classification schemes using the term 'relative value' provide further explanation about what is meant by it, but the present literal interpretation helps make a point that not all categories can be interpreted in the same manner.

[3] An adaptation of the multiplicative multi-framework approach was used by MSCI in the creation of its hedge fund indices, resulting in more than 160 sub-categories with at least one representative hedge fund.

[4] The Zurich Capital Markets Institutional Benchmarks employ this categorisation technique.

[5] However, as the industry matures, more frequent reporting appears to be becoming increasingly common.

[6] For example, the rapid growth of new product families like credit derivatives, the lack of precedent for the current bear market (within the short history of the modern hedge fund community) and the explosive growth in the amount of assets being managed by hedge funds themselves.

[7] This was alluded to in the previous section. By way of analogy: seeing a group of people standing together on a sidewalk does not provide strong evidence that they are friends. However, if we have other (independent) reasons to believe they are friends, and we subsequently see them standing together, it supports the conclusion they are indeed friends.

[8] Statistical confidence intervals are one technique to assess the validity of data-analysis conclusions, but their discussion is beyond the scope of this chapter. Introductory statistics textbooks cover this topic in detail.

[9] See, for example, the extensive collection of academic research work on hedge funds by William Fung and David Hsieh, much of which is available online at http://www.london.edu/hedgefunds/Published_Papers/published_papers.html#Fung

[10] However, as will be discussed, it is not the only percentile in use.

[11] The author is not aware of any hedge fund index that specifically includes *only closed* hedge funds, although such an index might prove a useful research tool.

[12] The HFRX, MSCI/Lyxor Hedge Invest and CSFB/Tremont 60 investable indices. See Exhibit 28.3 for more details on these and other indices.

[13] Some argue that using an index built of hedge funds to benchmark hedge funds is circular, and that a 'real' index consisting of traditional securities is more appropriate. If one accepts this thesis, how does one justify the use of, for example, an equity index to benchmark individual equities?

[14] This is intended as a broad expository overview only, and is not intended to refer to any specific region or endorse any investment strategy or structure.

[15] This chapter does not intend to predict whether such products will ultimately be successful. It only points out that the market is likely to decide within the foreseeable future.

Part IV

Assessing risk and risk control

Chapter 29

Risk control and risk management

Paul Singer
Elliott Associates, LP, New York, New York

Introduction

The risks that are inherent in hedge funds require careful and thoughtful consideration by managers and investors. As the manager of two funds that are designed to compound capital by producing relatively stable returns, I consider the control of risk of primary importance. Gaining some return in excess of the risk-free rate is therefore a secondary objective. Rather than seeking to generate the highest returns, we believe in maximising the probability of longevity and vitality throughout a wide range of market environments.

The important elements in understanding and managing risk, which will be discussed in this chapter, are:

- leverage;
- concentration and position size;
- absolute size;
- the human factor;
- people management;
- counterparty risk;
- sovereign risk;
- liquidity;
- geopolitical risk;
- systemic risk; and
- regulatory risk.

Leverage

The importance of leverage in risk control cannot be overemphasised. It is hard for money managers today to remember life before easily available leverage. In the 1970s and before, at the beginning of the derivatives age, it was much more difficult to obtain leverage for trading than it is today. Now, the amount of leverage available to professional investors is limited only by their creativity. It is available not just in the direct sense of being able to pay for only a small portion of a position (and thus have larger positions per dollar of capital); but also indirectly through options, futures, swaps, contracts for differences and forward contracts. Investors today are not constrained by an amount that they have to put up for many kinds of trades or situations; rather, they have to actively choose the amount that they will invest in a trade.

Life in the leverage lane is simple: it is a magnification process. The less one puts up for any asset, the greater the impact on capital of any fluctuation in the price of the asset. This is as true for US Treasury bills as it is for high technology stocks. There are coarse as well as finely tuned ways of assessing this from a risk management standpoint, but in all cases, the three steps below must be followed.

1. The probabilities and magnitudes of expected fluctuations in the price of the assets to be purchased, as well as their cross-correlation, must be calculated.
2. The extent to which estimates might be wrong, or worse, biased in a particular direction, must be assessed.
3. The magnitude of losses that can result from fluctuations, and the environments in which such losses will result, must be examined.

When these three tasks have been carried out, a leverage can be chosen (that is, the position size in relation to capital) that keeps losses in adverse environments within estimated boundaries.

One of the problems with carrying out this kind of analysis is that many of the relationships being studied have only a relatively limited history. Moreover, it is quite common for an asset to have a particular range of fluctuation for a long period of time which could be years or even decades, and then have bursts of volatility far beyond normal boundaries. Examples abound, but we only have to look at commodities in the early 1970s to see historical boundaries exceeded by a huge amount. For example, aluminium traded in a range of 15–27 cents per pound from 1921–1973. Starting in 1974, the price took off, peaking at 77 cents in 1982.

Financial assets are like life. There are things that we think we know that we really do know. There are other things that we think we know that we turn out not to know. Leverage in an investment portfolio should, in our view, take this into account. In a highly leveraged portfolio, it is not acceptable to be broadly right eight times out of 10, because if you engage in the activity long enough you will make mistakes. Everyone makes errors, but leverage magnifies the problem, so that it has become more and more crucial to be right all the time. With a highly leveraged portfolio, being wrong can amount to almost a capital offence. This places a terrible burden on a money manager.

I try to be realistic, conservative and broad when it comes to choosing leverage. I recognise that protecting our portfolios against ourselves and our foibles as managers and people is as important as protecting them against the vagaries of the world. It does no good to rail against unexpected events in the world. The only thing unexpected should be the exact way that the world surprises us, not the fact of periodic surprises. Sometimes the surprises come out of long calm periods, sometimes as part of a sequence of difficult and confusing events. Yet, when excessive leverage provides pain, I blame the leverage and the manager for taking on the leverage, not the events.

In our portfolios, I tend to choose 25 per cent as the maximum portfolio leverage for all but some quite precisely definable and tame fixed income arbitrage strategies. Twenty-five per cent leverage means that US$1.00 of capital buys up to US$1.25 of long positions in a long or long-short portfolio. There is no magic to 25 per cent. In an adverse environment when most strategies are not working well, any leverage is too much, and vice versa. However, 25 per cent is a figure which should keep us out of trouble during unpredictable adverse periods; it also takes into account that some of the strategies we employ have extremely low risk and low correlation with other strategies, and thus can be leveraged without introducing the risk of large leverage-induced portfolio losses in adverse periods.

An example of a strategy in which we use substantial leverage is bond arbitrage. If we buy a two-year US government bond and sell a strip of Eurodollar futures in the appropriate amounts, we are basically cancelling out the interest rate fluctuation component. What is left is the spread between Eurodollar obligations and US Treasury obligations. This is a form of risk premium spread, and this trade and others like it are sometimes called 'synthetic TED spreads' (TED meaning Treasuries versus Eurodollars). Due to the relatively tight range in which such a spread trades, we might only invest minimum futures margins on the short side and practically nothing on the long side. Since this kind of strategy involves a trading relationship which can be precisely defined, we can decide to use a high degree of leverage.

In contrast, other strategies may warrant the use of leverage, but not to so great a degree. For example, consider a late-stage bankruptcy situation, in which a distressed bond is successfully restructured to become a series of cash flows of quite definable amounts and timing. If we feel that the cash flows are very predictable, we might initiate such a trade at a 12 per cent or 13 per cent cash-on-cash internal rate of return (IRR), and then boost the implied return to close to a 20 per cent IRR by applying a certain amount of leverage, if we believe that overall portfolio risk is not thereby increased by any appreciable degree. Of course, leverage is fungible, and it is foolish to leverage any subset of trades without considering the leverage of the portfolio as a whole, and its increased susceptibility to market fluctuations.

Concentration and position size

Most hedge fund portfolios contain positions and strategies of widely differing size. A hedge fund manager must find a balance between concentration and diversification, and must also choose a maximum position size for any particular position (as well as for positions which are thought to be correlated). Diversification and concentration have their relative strengths and weaknesses, but what is relevant here is what happens when leverage and concentration come together. If a portfolio is leveraged two-to-one, a position which is 20 per cent of one's positions is 40 per cent of capital. From a risk-control standpoint, I have to decide just how much I love my favourite positions. Nobody loves every position equally, and there is a temptation to just build and build the best ones. However, investment life is full of surprises. One example was the great European bond trade of 1993, which became the great bond bust of 1994. As interest rates declined during 1993, a steep yield curve enabled traders to borrow short and lend long at very attractive spreads. The strategy became very popular, given that French bonds, for example, rose 30 per cent in a matter of months. No sooner did expectations of continued profits become widespread than the Federal Reserve unexpectedly raised rates, and the bull market reversed without skipping a beat. The strategy then became much abhorred, as rates in Europe also rose and French bonds declined nearly as much as they had risen, and just as fast.

All other things being equal, a larger maximum position size in relation to capital increases risk. Some people say that concentrating on just a few positions in which you have most confidence and focus is the way to both make money and decrease risk. I agree, but only up to a point. Often a risk manager faces the greatest need to limit position size when the enthusiasm and self-confidence which enable money managers to 'pull the trigger' scream to take a larger position.

I wish I could describe some complicated algorithm that can tell us when a position is big enough. Without any such magic formula, however, what we have to do is this:

- look at each position;
- try to assess the downside case;
- envision what the rest of the portfolio will look like when the downside case occurs;
- assess the quality of our effort and what we or the rest of the world might be missing; and
- choose position size from there.

Effectively, we continuously reassess the notion of position size as it pertains to risk. The same kind of thinking applies to our decision making with respect to diversification. We are involved in a number of different strategies for three reasons:

- we think it lowers the overall risk of the portfolio;
- the value-creation possibilities generated by our research and insights are enhanced when we are able to follow a situation as it metamorphoses from one strategy to another; and
- there are usually a number of different ways to make money that we find attractive.

If every position in the portfolio could be uncorrelated with every other position and also uncorrelated with the markets, we would be happy indeed. However, as the world does not work that way, we approach diversification and seek un-correlation in an incremental fashion. We put money into an area that we think shows promise, move up a learning curve, and then put more money in, while simultaneously trying to assess how the risks of the area relate to other areas of investment. We have had periods in which one or more areas looked absolutely fabulous, but it is part of our discipline to continue to invest in a number of areas, in order to limit pain if we are wrong about any one. At one point several years ago convertible hedging (long convertible bonds and preferreds, and short the underlying common or an option on the underlying common) accounted for 80 per cent or so of our capital, but we came to feel that our risk-limitation goals were better served by engaging in a number of strategies.

Absolute size

We have been facing the issue of absolute size since our formation in 1977, when we had a little over US$1 million of capital. With over US$3.0 billion of investment capital at the time of writing, we are still facing the issue. Old friends remind me that at the US$5 million level, I was telling people that the very labour-intensive convertible hedging we were doing in 1979 simply could not be done with US$10 million, and so on through the years. The fact is size depends on the particular market. Some markets, like worldwide bond and currency markets, can accommodate huge size. On the other hand, certain cute arbitrages cannot accommodate more than a very small amount of money.

The relevance of this to risk control is subtle. I must assess, when evaluating a strategy as well as the absolute size of our funds, whether we can move properly in and out of positions. Large size is an advantage in that it can generate the best call regarding research and

376

merchandise for sale, as well as maximising influence in those businesses which require hands-on negotiating and clout. Large size enables you to:

- pay people better;
- spend more money on the necessary tools of the trade; and
- be a better customer of Wall Street and the City.

However, if you are large, it is important to know how big the exit doors are. Large size makes it harder to move in or out of positions, and can increase the realistically calculated costs of trading (including market impact). It is interesting in this regard that some of the world's greatest traders (like Bruce Kovner, Paul Tudor Jones and Louis Bacon) decided to return significant portions of their investors' capital after 1994, in order to radically downsize.

Being too large in an activity enables the rest of the market to pick you off or 'gun' for you. We once did an option trade that was so compelling that we built much too large a position. We found that as market participants sensed the size of our positions, they 'ganged up' on us. The options that we bought at cheap prices just got cheaper and cheaper, people anticipated our 'rolls' from one option to another, and every trading action that we took seemed to increase our losses. As soon as we unwound the position to stem the losses, prices rebounded to near normal levels. It was quite an expensive lesson for people who were used to trading quietly in the market, rather than being the focal point for attack.

Being too small does not seem relevant to risk, but it is. When you are too small, you can be almost in the dark in terms of information and trading flow. You do not get 'the call', you cannot spend enough money to do the work, and you either have difficulty getting credit lines or can get credit only on adverse terms and conditions. What that amounts to is taking greater risks or being unable to properly evaluate the risks.

The human factor

Risk control from a hedge fund manager's point of view must take into account human foibles. It is a delicate blend of qualities which enables a person to make trading decisions involving large amounts of money in complicated situations, often going against the grain of popular wisdom; or seeing opportunity in the buying and selling decisions of other, equally motivated smart investors. The ability to pull the trigger in favourable markets with a good chance of being right is inherent in every intelligent person. However, a hedge fund manager who wants to survive for a long time needs also to understand how he or she will react in other, perhaps more hostile, environments. When markets turn, or losses mount, people change. Those who thought that they would stay the course lose confidence and become fearful.

In such circumstances, the judgement of the hedge fund managers can be worse than that of the small investor, strange as that seems. Loyalty is more a feature of the little guy, and this can keep him from selling out in adverse periods. He can thus get the long-term rate of return and not be shaken out. His bargain mentality may also make him buy more on the way down, which in many cases is the right thing to do.

In contrast, the hedge fund manager's vivid imagination (which usually works in his favour, of course) can work against him in adverse situations. His profound grasp of the dangers (and terrible repercussions) of portfolio concentration and leverage, or the scary possibilities in a macro situation, can cause him to make stupid decisions. In some cases, bad decisions made in times of adversity are forced, by a realisation of the danger to the business of large losses, or even by an actual margin call.

There are no easy answers about what personal qualities make for survival and longevity, but a successful manager is one who has found a balance between discipline and flexibility, between the courage of his convictions and the need to desert the battlefield in order to live to fight another day.

The year 1998 was a painful year for most hedge fund managers. The years 2001 and 2002 have also provided varying degrees of difficulty for many hedge funds, since common stocks are still the principal asset class owned by hedge funds, and most funds are net long. Notwithstanding the post-bubble market downturn, the ultimate scope of the bear market may not yet be fully visible. The ability of many hedge fund managers to deal with losses and whipsaw while maintaining their equilibrium is yet to be fully tested, but how people react to losses and confusing environments is extremely important to hedge fund investing. Dealing with this is not just a matter of soul-searching and introspection. A hedge fund manager must either:

- run the portfolio in a way that tries to ensure there will not be significant losses (which is what we aim for at Elliott); or
- have a contingency plan ready should the markets turn and become inhospitable.

This plan should not be: 'I will recognise it and take timely defensive manoeuvres'. This is because hedge funds and other professional investors, including big mutual fund groups and broker-dealers, form such a big proportion of the market, and are so plugged into the same information, that it is quite possible that it is their perceptions, not the little guys, which will create major turning points in markets. A model for this was 1987, when one of the world's great investors reportedly created the bottom of the Crash by a monstrous stock futures sale at dozens of Standard & Poor's points under the market, out of either fear or the need for liquidity and protection against further loss.

Hubris is another human factor which has an impact on risk management. The power and wealth created by financial success is something that some people find so intoxicating as to be actually toxic. It is not hard to believe, after a period of success, that one really is a different breed of human, and that one should not be fettered by the same rules that apply to other mortals. This must be guarded against for many reasons, but for the purposes of this chapter suffice it to say that hubris increases risks more than any other factor.

- Hubris decreases the quality and quantity of work.
- Hubris ignores advice.
- Hubris causes people to treat people badly (and for the 'treatees' to decrease their loyalty to the 'treator' and fail to inform him of his errors).

The investment world is so continually fraught with danger that letting down one's guard, or behaving arrogantly, can instantaneously destroy career and capital. Lest we forget, as an illustration, there were smart short sellers in the early 1990s who believed without a doubt that the big US banks couldn't extricate themselves from their financial holes. As we know, interest rates went down, stock prices went up, and in a wonderful (terrible to the shorts) bootstrap operation the banks were saved and the shorts were nailed to the wall.

People management

Financial incentives given to managers also have a bearing on risk management. It is quite typical on Wall Street to allocate to traders particular sums of capital, let the traders manage these sums, and then pay them on the basis of a percentage of the gains. This mode of compensation has profound implications for risk management. In effect, employees who have such a deal have a free option with someone else's money. If they make money, they make a percentage of it as a fee. If they lose money, they do not have to pay a percentage of the losses out of their own pockets. Even if they leave the firm (either by choice or because the losses make them unwelcome), frequently they can start again with a similar deal at another firm. Firms who offer these deals typically choose a year as the period of measurement (to try to prevent gains and losses in different sub-periods from creating bonuses equal to a very high proportion of gains in excess of losses). However, no matter how structured, such deals create very strong incentives to boost position size, and create little incentive to consider the overall risk to the firm of larger positions.

If a hedge fund is paid on a percentage of gains basis, it is hard to resist paying its own portfolio managers on the same basis, regardless of whether the results generated are a group effort or more attributable to the clout and franchise of the firm than to the efforts of the traders and portfolio managers. Nonetheless, this factor of the incentive structure impacting the risk is very important.

A hedge fund manager who is interested in risk management must choose people who can incorporate the culture of the firm into their decision-making, to the extent that risk-minimisation or at least risk-cognisance is part of their own deep-rooted business culture.

It should not be necessary to point out (but it unfortunately is) that the integrity of portfolio managers, traders, and accounting and operational people is essential to risk management. Huge sums of money and huge bonuses and pay ride not only on trading decisions, but also on pricing decisions, as well as on clearing and accounting decisions and procedures. Mistakes and errors of judgement can be extremely costly. A hedge fund manager must make sure that all of the firm's employees, from the highest to the lowest paid, are totally honest and fair. A manager who is very thoughtful about investment and trading risks could easily be vulnerable to huge risks if the firm does not have in place both a culture and procedures that foster accountability and control.

In the Barings episode several years ago, a trader who had made a large amount of money for the firm was reportedly allowed to both trade large positions and clear his own trades. Moreover, it appeared that nobody at the firm was really looking at or supervising his trading and positions from a risk management standpoint. Also, he was geographically removed from the head office. After hundreds of millions of dollars of margin money were sent to meet losses, apparently without anyone adequately questioning what was happening, the breakdown in risk management caused Barings to fail.

It is necessary from a risk management perspective to supervise people properly, to know what they are doing, to have checking systems and money tracking systems to prevent hidden trades, and to have senior employees check prices and markets and marks.

Most hedge funds grow from the seeds that one or two people have sown. The hedge fund manager must create systems, which in many cases have to be home-grown systems, to manage the people who are hired to help the firm grow. Growth creates synergies and opportunities to have a better and more organised result, but control is absolutely necessary to manage risk.

Counterparty and sovereign risk

Running a hedge fund means doing business in complex instruments with a wide variety of firms across the globe. The risk manager must examine carefully the credit of all parties who need to be looked to for performance. Trading brokers only need to clear trades in a pipeline that is just a few days long. At the other end of the risk spectrum, swap counterparties are tied into relationships in which large sums of money change hands in response to market fluctuations occurring over a period which could be many years. In those years, events can transpire which affect firms' financial conditions, so a risk manager must be cautious and thorough in choosing long-term counterparties.

Hedge funds have been in the forefront of investing in developing countries and regions of the globe, and there is no doubt that they have gained fabulous profit opportunities as a result. However, from a risk management standpoint the hedge fund manager must decide which of the regions and countries offer both staying power and a legal, accounting and ethical framework that is developed enough to enable trading to be done with a degree of confidence in the rules and the sustainability of the market. I sense that many such markets are only superficially attractive, and in fact are extraordinarily dangerous, not least because they are often classic insider markets, in which outsiders are the last to be clued in as to what is going on. In many places clearing is manual, insider trading rules are primitive or non-existent, and reported financial information is a joke. Shining skyscrapers, computers, and Led Zeppelin T-shirts should not blind hedge fund managers to these factors. When an emerging market disappears, the disappearance can be total. Included in every risk, of course, is the notion that political changes, taxes or capital controls can instantaneously produce losses and lock-ins that were completely unforeseen at the time the investment was made. America's long, stable history should not blind money managers to the fact that the rest of the world does not necessarily work that way.

This point is valid even for major markets abroad. Hong Kong shut down its market for several days in the 1987 Crash, and the Singapore SIMEX exchange came close to failing. As the world's trading becomes increasingly active, complex and interrelated, more surprises are likely to occur, both local and systemic.

Liquidity

Liquidity is a strange concept. As trading and leverage increase around the world, the liquidity factor becomes more important from a risk point of view. Yet, liquidity is definitely a now-you-see-it-now-you-don't phenomenon. Liquidity can be high, even in new markets. In many cases it is the hedge fund community itself, on the way in, that is supplying all the liquidity. Hedge fund managers must take into account the lessening of liquidity and the widening of bid/ask spreads on the way down. In a real bear market, many assets can have, quite simply, no bid at all. From a bull market perspective, that can seem unbelievable and shocking. Moreover, it is not unusual for liquidity to disappear instantaneously. Some of the other factors I have discussed in this chapter are cumulative in their impact on risk and decision-making, but it is a lack of liquidity which turns a decline in asset prices into a panic. When hedge fund managers lose their confidence that they can get out if they need to, the compulsion to get out increases to the irresistible point in all but the most stolid and resolute managers.

In the case of many foreign markets, it is literally impossible to predict when liquidity will disappear, and with it, the opportunity to trade out when you want to. Even in developed markets, liquidity conditions can change with blinding speed. For example, in the Crash of 1987, just a few weeks after a bull market peak, stocks hit a vacuum in which liquidity practically disappeared. Stocks could only be sold on large price concessions, and if one hesitated for an instant, bids disappeared. The example of the Crash should be sobering to all hedge fund managers except those who think that by some kind of cosmic plan, one is only dealt one such episode in a lifetime.

Geopolitical risk

Before 11 September 2001, it was possible to imagine that history had ended, and that the triumphs of liberal capitalism, advancing globalisation, and galloping productivity, were permanent. Geopolitical problems, even including the small wars which punctuated the last few decades, were not thought to provide important impediments to assuming an unchanging basic framework to investing. All of these assumptions are now questionable. The range of possibilities for the way that some of the global themes could play out is wider than at any time in American history since the Civil War. The war being waged, sporadically but passionately, by Islamic radicals against the West, is fuelled by weapons of ever-advancing efficiency and brutality. The size of the disruptions which can be caused by very small groups of committed individuals is possibly gargantuan. Moreover, any attacks and events could change the investing, trading, and living context in an instant, in major ways. The assumptions on which investment programmes are based could be jostled significantly by the event stream of this war and the accompanying bursts of terrorism. The obvious implication of all this is that risky assets should be priced for a larger margin of safety, but that is not necessarily how the world works. Sometimes risky assets just provide risk.

Systemic risk

Starting a couple of decades ago, a growing portion of human financial cerebral activity has been devoted to constructing complicated, leveraged and illiquid structures which are designed to increase available exposures, create extra agency spread for dealers and brokers, produce complexity so that professional traders can extract more value from the market place, allow concentrations of risk to pile up, or create the appearance of something that does not otherwise exist (like yield). The derivatives boom has proceeded exponentially almost without interruption, but has never been really tested. Every nascent test has been met with frantic easing and other supportive moves by policymakers, and so the pile of the indescribable, the unintelligible and the impenetrable gets higher and higher. It may be true for any particular investor that the availability of complicated structures adds value and enables one to aim at reducing or reshaping risk. However, for the system as a whole, there is little question that the result is an increase in the brittleness of the system. The resilience of the system appears to be enhanced, but the consequences of the tightly woven network of relationships and trades has become increasingly impossible to unwind gently. We cannot be the ones to tell you if and when the vulnerability of the novel structures could feed into a systemic problem, but we think that every hedge fund manager must adopt a humble attitude toward the world of such structures and toward one's perceived ability to protect against systemic risks. It is hard to find out from the outside where the greatest pockets of vulnerability lie, and very few trading firms can go about their business without becoming part of the interwoven network in some important way. Yet, it is worth paying attention to all the aspects of systemic risk, including disaster recovery, assessments of the impact of market shutdowns for extended periods, potential difficulties with clearing firms and currency controls among others.

Regulatory risk

Every market crisis creates waves of populism, recrimination, resentment toward Wall Street, and new laws and regulations. At the time of writing it is not clear what regulators have in store for the hedge fund community.* All practitioners must be flexible and alert enough to be able to adapt their businesses for changes. It is nice to be involved with businesses of such immense potential profitability (for both practitioners and investors) as hedge funds, but totally unconstrained trading and investing is not a basic human right; rather, it is a creature of laws, regulations and practice. The system giveth and the system can taketh away.

Keeping the risk beast caged

Risk is a far more complex consideration than merely the simple but widespread notion of volatility. Keeping the risk beast safely in its cage requires careful, thoughtful management. Given the convoluted and leveraged nature of most hedge funds' portfolios, risk management should be at the very forefront of hedge fund managers' attention. Our style is to try to minimise risk in every way we can, and be glad of what is left by way of a return. We don't love risk for the sake of excitement (some people do). We think of risk as a phenomenon to be watched from afar, like some wonderfully picturesque flaming lava flow from a volcano. It looks inviting and beautiful, but it scorches, if not destroys, those who venture too close.

---

* Editor's note: on 29 September 2003, shortly before this book went to press, the staff of the SEC issued its report entitled 'The Implications of the Growth of Hedge Funds', the culmination of its efforts following the Hedge Fund Roundtable held in May 2003. As of the date of this writing, the Commission itself had not taken any action in response to the report. One of the key recommendations of the staff was that the SEC consider 'requiring hedge fund advisers to register with the SEC as investment advisers, taking into account whether the benefits outweigh the burdens of registration'. In the staff's view, ' … registration of hedge fund advisers would serve as a deterrent to fraud, encourage compliance and the adoption of compliance procedures, provide the SEC with important information … and effectively raise the standards for investment in hedge funds from the "accredited investor" standard to that of "qualified client"'. See http://www.sec.gov/news/studies/hedgefunds0903.pdf for the full text of the report.

Chapter 30

Qualitative aspects of analysing risk and monitoring managers

Guy Hurley
Financial Risk Management, Ltd. London

Introduction

Hedge funds and their returns are a function of a process that can and must be understood by any potential investor. In order to be a comfortable investor, especially in an early stage fund where there is little quantitative information available, it is important to understand:

- the investment philosophy;
- how the philosophy gives rise to an edge, and the nature of that edge;
- how strategy implementation exploits the edge;
- the nature of the associated risks;
- how risk is managed routinely and in crisis; and
- how much returns may be diluted by risk management and implementation costs.

Monitoring these issues regularly is essential in order to check whether the initial thoughts on a fund were correct and to maintain confidence in the investment process going forward.

Hedge funds are not black box money-making machines; hedge funds are the product of the mind-sets of individual hedge fund managers. A hedge fund manager makes dozens of discretionary decisions every day. Even systematic hedge funds are eventually a function of the choices made by the designer and the philosophical premises behind the original underlying system. A quantitative analysis of a fund's return profile will tell an investor how those premises have performed on a month-to-month basis. However, quantitative analysis may not tell you much about the nature of the built-in biases and beliefs a hedge fund manager carries with him and therefore the potential pitfalls embedded in the strategy in the future as the market environment changes.

Hedge fund managers: character analysis

The best way to understand these built-in biases is through a combination of quantitative and qualitative analysis. Qualitative analysis has to start with the hedge fund manager himself. Hedge fund managers, almost by definition, are entrepreneurs and as such are an interesting group. Many of them are 'political émigrés' from large organisations where their ambitions could not be satisfied. Often they are deeply insightful people, whose entrepreneurial streak and desire to innovate could not be contained within the tight parameters of an investment bank. Sometimes they are just weird. However, as entrepreneurs, they tend to share certain characteristics. First, they typically have a need for total control. Second, they feel naturally superior to others. Third, they seek every opportunity to prove it. However, these are characteristics that are not necessarily consistent with trading the markets successfully. Thus, a manager is only as successful as his recent track record.

A successful hedge fund manager is a leader as well as an entrepreneur. Usually leadership skills are nurtured in an organisation as individuals learn how to make sound judgements about situations and people. Experience is the best tutor. Young hedge fund managers often lack leadership experience and end up running funds within their own sets of standards rather than those imposed by others.

Quite often, gifted, entrepreneurial money managers are terrible communicators. The job of the analyst is to understand the investment process however it is presented, or indeed, misrepresented. Just because an individual has a real talent for convertible bond arbitrage does not necessarily mean that he can explain what he actually does. However, the skilled analyst who has met the rest of the convertible bond arbitrage peer universe may eventually be able to infer what the manager's biases are and where the edge is in the underlying portfolio.

The hedge fund manager is more than just a money manager. He is also a human being and prey to all the emotional and behavioural problems that every human being wrestles with in life.[1] This creates a problem for the investor, for eventually the investor has to trust that money manager, in spite of the fact that he is human. This is one of the driving reasons why indexing and passive investing is becoming more popular with certain hedge fund investors: it takes away the whole need for establishing trust in an individual money manager.

Understanding the hedge fund culture

The hedge fund manager defines the culture within his fund. In good funds this is a pervasive culture of risk management, in trade execution, in employee contracts, in establishing credit lines, prime brokers, administrators and in all the multitudinous relationships that make a hedge fund tick. Another distinguishing feature of the successful hedge fund is a culture of thoroughness and attention to detail. Investment processes and risk management are meaningless unless they are an embedded part of the corporate culture. The best way to confirm a fund's culture is to meet the staff one step below the hedge fund manager, such as the risk manager or the head trader, to see whether they buy into the fund culture and atmosphere.

In the heat of the trading day, investment processes may be abandoned. However, it is unlikely that the culture will simply disappear. If a fund has a strong culture of doing the right thing, it becomes easier to establish a level of trust and confidence in the fund.

Understanding the investment philosophy

Broadly speaking, there are only three methods of making money. The first is the 'value' methodology, based upon the idea of buying low and selling high. This is the academically and logically robust idea of buying cheap and selling expensive assets in the expectation the market will recognise the mis-pricing at some stage in the near future. This methodology is based upon the pragmatic and logical notion that valuations will revert to the mean, liquidity is persistent and that rational people invest in the financial markets in a rational way. Over the years, this 'Graham and Dodd' approach has been successful, but there have been periods when the value trap has been sprung. The last significant example of the value trap was in the summer of 2002 and the demise of WorldCom. It is interesting to note how the value trap in credit markets was transmitted around the market. Losses in one part of investors' portfolios forced a reduction of risk appetite across their whole portfolios. These portfolios all shared similar style biases. The ripple effects even led to the selling of the Australian dollar, as value orientated FX investors who owned the Aussie for the interest differential and fundamental economics bailed out because of their losses elsewhere in their portfolios. Value investing as a philosophy was hurt, irrespective of asset class or investment process.

The second way of making money is the opposite of 'value' investing. While value investors might be classified as trend makers, 'momentum' investors are trend followers. These people,[2] are buying high in the expectation that someone will pay a higher price tomorrow. There is no intellectual logic in their methodology; rather they are exploiting the behaviour of the crowd. These managers are predicting the level of future prices, betting on money flows, irrational market behaviour and the divergence of market prices.

The third way of making money is from trading market noise. Strategies pursuing this opportunity set are characterised by high turnover and short holding periods. Some people argue that noise trading is merely value or momentum on a very short-term frequency. However, returns from this group are so idiosyncratic that they deserve to be classified on their own.

It should be possible to classify any hedge fund manager in one of these categories. It does not matter whether the process is statistical arbitrage, macro, equity long-short or whatever. Once the manager is classified, it should be possible to determine what market environment suits the style and what environment is going to create problems for the manager. It is at this point that the manager's biases and core beliefs about the way markets work should emerge. The truly exceptional managers, who have established consistent long-term track records, operate on the basis of two or even all three of these philosophies.

Understanding the edge

At the heart of any hedge fund there must be a repeatable and scalable process that isolates either an arbitrage or a regularly occurring and identifiable characteristic of the market. Furthermore, the manager must demonstrate that he is better at executing the process than his competitors and that he understands the pitfalls of his strategy. In the increasingly competitive hedge fund industry, it is not good enough to be just another convertible bond arbitrageur, or another stock-picker.

This means that there must be an identifiable investment process focused on extracting alpha from the market. The manager must realise that if he says he performs a certain kind of analysis, he will be expected to produce the analysis and explain it. Some manager's revel in this disclosure, for they take pride and pleasure in their craft. Other managers go to great lengths to mask their investment process. The truth is that an appropriate level of process transparency must be a prerequisite for investment. An investor cannot be expected to stick with a manager during the inevitable drawdown period unless he has total understanding of that manager's edge.

The other big risk to a fund manager's edge is intellectual sloth. After a while, it is too easy for a manager to listen to his research team, but only hear the facts that reinforce his existing perspective. Even worse, the decision maker may stop listening to his research team altogether. A good fund manager thinks about organisational design, and makes sure that the decision-making process is intellectually rigorous and robust so that the truth will come out, and force the manager to make decisions in line with the underlying research. In small hedge funds, this is difficult, as the fund manager becomes a mini Napoleon who dominates everything.

Some of the big names in the industry get around this problem by keeping a trading diary. After a while, it becomes hard to contradict what you have written down before and the inconsistencies in thought process become apparent even to the toughest ego. One well-known macro manager has taken this a step further and keeps a diary of how he feels, what he eats, his exercise regime and then maps the results out against his buy and sell orders. In this way he aims to maintain his objectivity.

Integrating the edge, research and the decision-making process is more difficult than it sounds. It can be very painful making decisions that go against previously strongly held views, or buying bonds at 4 per cent yields when you sold them on an up tick at 4.75 per cent last week. Systematic trading is an explicit attempt to avoid these very difficult and emotional decisions.

Reflecting the edge in the portfolio

Once a manager has explained his edge, qualitative analysis is about understanding how that edge is exploited and how all other factor bets are constrained within the portfolio. For example, if an equity long-short fund claims to be the best stock-picker in the world, there are logical implications for the portfolio. The position concentration should be high, with a small number of mid-cap and small-cap holdings. The fund should have little net exposure, but a large gross exposure. By contrast, a manager who claims that he is a great trader will have many large-cap names in his portfolio, a wide range of net exposures but a low gross exposure.

The idea is simple: the portfolio should be built so that the edge is magnified but the noise around that edge is eliminated. The investor is looking for a set of rules and parameters within which the hedge fund will operate. Some of the issues that might be constrained are position sizing, the number of positions, capital allocation, mismatches between longs and shorts and assumptions on correlations between different asset classes.

The delivery of this idea is not simple. The details of the constraints are effectively the rules against which a manager will be monitored and measured on a monthly basis. However, markets fluctuate and managers need to adapt to a changing environment. This raises the issue of the difference between style drift and style evolution. In long-only fund management, style drift is easy to define, but in the alternative space, where constraints are artificial and self-imposed, the separation is more difficult. Historically, the most successful managers have adapted with the world but they have adapted with full disclosure to their clients of all changes they make to their investment process and its constraints.

Understanding risk management

Most hedge funds have an embedded tail risk. That tail risk is often obvious: the risk of a credit default in convertible bond arbitrage or the failure of a takeover like E/Honeywell in merger arbitrage. It is essential that a hedge fund provides adequate transparency to identify what these risks are and the internal rules used to manage these risks. For some funds this is very straightforward at a superficial level, with stop losses at the individual position level and at the portfolio level. The level of complexity can become high as these stop loss levels are examined in detail.

For example, is the stop loss discretionary or is it based upon a basis point loss to the portfolio, in which case how are position sizes determined? Perhaps the stop loss level is decided based upon the average true range of the market but over what look back period? Are stops executed on a 'one-touch' basis or when the market has traded through a price? Is the amount of slippage monitored? As a fund becomes larger, stop losses might not be appropriate. How does a manager unwind a US$1 billion position in the FX markets?

Stop losses on a portfolio basis need close examination as well. Some managers use a decay function on their losses above 8 per cent, so that by 15 per cent, risk is almost eradicated from the portfolio. However, as time goes by and profits return, losses are forgiven and risk rises exponentially. These risk adjustments can lead to enormous implementation costs as markets fluctuate. Other managers trade their profit and loss on a monthly cycle, pyramiding up in good months and pyramiding down in bad months.

Some managers do not use stop losses, but rather look at the Value-at-Risk (VaR) in the portfolio and the incremental VaR to the portfolio from adding and reducing positions. These managers will typically target a VaR and standard deviation over time. While this method of risk management might be appropriate for a macro fund, it is inappropriate for an event-driven fund because the VaR will always underestimate the tail risk.

Good funds think about liquidity constraints and understand that liquidity going into a trade is very different from liquidity exiting a trade. There are plenty of examples of mortgage-backed security funds and emerging market funds finding ample liquidity in the market until they most need it.

Risk management does not stop at market risk and liquidity risk. A crucial risk that needs extensive qualitative analysis is operational risk. The most obvious first point of analysis is the methodology a hedge fund uses for marking its book to market. For commodity trading advisers (CTAs) and equity long-short funds, this is usually straightforward. However, in less liquid over-the-counter strategies like distressed debt and some convertible arbitrage strategies this becomes a real issue. One fund failed after the manager marked the volatility part of its book to model rather than to market because 'there was no market in that maturity'. When the market reappeared, it was several million dollars from the model.

The relationship between the fund and the administrator becomes crucial. Some administrators are rigorous in pursuing an independent valuation policy on all assets. Other administrators are comfortable taking guidance from the hedge funds on asset valuations or taking guidance from investment banks. However, investment banks' traders and salesmen are not immune from smoothing market bids and offers for favoured clients.

Indeed, the whole relationship between the banks and the hedge funds needs to be understood both on an individual detail basis and in the wider context of the fund. For example, in the case of a fixed-income fund, the terms and provisions of the swap agreements need to be related back to the liquidity provisions and any limit on redemptions from the underlying fund. Information needs to be understood in its wider context. This contextual analysis is also needed in understanding the business structure of the fund, the internal controls and the role of non-executive directors in terms of corporate governance. Risk management is all-embracing.

Monitoring a hedge fund

All the understanding of a hedge fund manager's character, culture, investment philosophy, edge, portfolio construction and risk management is stress tested every month. It should be possible to see a fit each month between a manager's process, performance and the market environment.

However, monitoring is about more than understanding return attribution; it should also be contemporaneous and forward-looking. Contemporaneous monitoring is about matching the existing portfolio to the constraints self-imposed by the manager. Any significant break of these rules should be regarded very seriously and might result in a swift exit from the fund.

Forward-looking monitoring means thinking about the seven common tools a portfolio manager can use to modify the exposure profile of his fund in order to fit in with performance objectives, or comply with stop loss limitations, irrespective of the style or asset class. How the manager has adjusted these seven drivers of return (listed below) in the recent past dictates how the portfolio will probably behave in the near future.

1. *Size of individual positions.* The volatility of a portfolio will increase with the size of underlying positions.
2. *Directionality on the portfolio.* The volatility of a portfolio will increase with the level of directionality.
3. *Volatility of individual positions.* The volatility of a portfolio will increase with the volatility of the underlying instruments. Correlation benefits will not help when there is a 'fat tailed' market event.
4. *Time horizon.* The volatility of a portfolio will increase with the length of the holding period.
5. *Diversification.* The volatility of a portfolio falls as genuine diversification increases but be wary of the pitfalls of correlation assumptions.
6. *Leverage.* Generally, but not always, leverage and portfolio volatility are positively correlated.
7. *Optionality.* The volatility of a portfolio normally falls as the level of non-linear pay-offs increase through the use of long option strategies.

However, the best indicator of future performance is the level of humour and humility in the manager. To bring this chapter full circle, eventually an investor has to gauge whether he is still comfortable with the hedge fund manager. Is he still sane and sober, and running his portfolio in the agreed and expected manner? As long as that trust still exists between investor and manager, a happy relationship should ensue. However, once that trust is broken, it is probably better for everyone, irrespective of the lock-in terms, for that investor to move his money elsewhere. The ultimate test is the 'shower test'. If an investor worries about his investment in a hedge fund when he is taking a shower, it is a sure sign that he should not be in that investment. When the shower becomes a worry-free zone, qualitative analysis and monitoring have served their purpose.

---

[1] Some hedge fund investors will deliberately create a provocative atmosphere in a meeting in order to put a manager under stress and hence understand the way he thinks and reacts in difficult environments. The 'stress' interview in the money-raising or money-withdrawing process no longer raises an eyebrow.

[2] CTAs are probably the purest example.

Chapter 31

Assessing risk and risk control: operational issues

Mike Tremmel
Ernst & Young, LLP, San Francisco, California

Introduction

Hedge funds and investment partnerships, together with the products they trade, have greatly proliferated since the mid-1970s. Since then, hedge funds have grown not only in number but also in sophistication. Many have developed different trading divisions, each with its own trading strategy; others have established their own broker-dealers to help facilitate trades and security lending. Over the years, the now estimated US$600 billion plus industry has become more complex in investment techniques, provided absolute returns during uncertain markets and expanded its market beyond wealthy investors and large institutions. Through all this, the hedge fund industry has appeared to monitor itself. However, it is now coming under increased scrutiny by regulators due to its rapid growth. As a result, operating a hedge fund has become increasingly difficult and costly. In this chapter, the following areas of concern for hedge fund operations will be addressed:

- prime brokerage;
- trade authorisation;
- trade capture;
- credit and counterparty risk;
- position and money reconciliation processes with brokers and prime brokers;
- valuation of financial instruments;
- currency exposure; and
- future directions, challenges and opportunities.

In each section, it will become clear that the best way to prevent and resolve operational problems is by establishing and enforcing controls. In today's market place, risk assumes various dimensions and can be difficult to identify and manage without the proper procedures in place. Once implemented, controls reduce a fund's exposure to these various types of risk and allow the fund to concentrate on its investment objectives. A discussion of the various types of controls accompanies each section.

Prime brokerage

The primary activity of a hedge fund is trading. Along with this activity comes a need for custody, clearance, finance and settlement of trades, which is where the prime broker comes in. As defined by the Securities and Exchange Commission (SEC), prime brokerage is a system developed by full-service firms to facilitate the custody, clearance and settlement of securities trades for retail and institutional investors who are active market participants, that is, hedge funds.

Prime brokerage involves three distinct parties.

- *Prime broker.* A registered broker-dealer that clears and finances the hedge fund's trades executed by one or more other registered broker-dealers (executing brokers) as ordered by the hedge fund.
- *Executing broker.* Receives a letter from the prime broker agreeing to clear and carry each trade placed by the hedge fund with the executing broker. The hedge fund then directs delivery of money or securities to be made to or by the prime broker.
- *Hedge fund.* Maintains its funds and securities in an account with the prime broker. Orders placed with an executing broker are affected through an account with the executing broker in the name of the prime broker for the benefit of the hedge fund.

With prime brokerage, trade execution entails an eight-step process, outlined below.

1. *Order placement.* The hedge fund places an order with one of its executing brokers, who in turn buys or sells securities in accordance with the hedge fund's instructions.
2. *Notification.* The hedge fund notifies the prime broker on trade date or, at the latest, the morning of the day after trade date, of the transaction executed through the executing broker.
3. *Recording.* The prime broker records the transaction in the hedge fund's account. At the same time, the prime broker records the transaction in a 'fail-to-receive/deliver' account with the executing broker.
4. *Prime broker confirmation.* The prime broker issues a confirmation to the hedge fund and computes all applicable credit and Regulation T (Reg T) amounts, in keeping with the Federal Reserve Board's regulation governing the amount of credit that brokers and dealers may extend to customers who buy securities.
5. *Executing broker confirmation.* The executing broker confirms the transaction with the prime broker through the Depository Trust Company's (DTC) Institutional Delivery System. DTC is a depository for eligible securities that facilitates clearance between member organisations and banks without the necessity of receiving or delivering actual certificates. The Institutional Delivery System is the common link between brokers and banks that allows for the notification and verification of trade executions.
6. *Affirmation.* The prime broker then begins the affirmation process. Affirmation is the acceptance of settlement responsibility by the prime broker for trades executed by hedge funds with their executing broker. The prime broker has a few business days from trade date to affirm the trade. The affirmation process has three principal steps. First, the prime broker confirms all the information related to the trade (for example, quantity and cost) to that which has been provided by the executing broker through the use of the DTC Institutional Delivery System. Next, the prime broker conducts its credit review to ensure that the trade is within the credit limits established for the hedge fund's account. Finally, the prime broker performs its own due diligence procedures to ensure the creditworthiness of the parties involved. If the prime broker disaffirms the trade then the transaction is reverted back to the executing broker and considered a customer transaction on the books and records of the executing broker subject to Regulation T. If the hedge fund is unwilling to provide the exe-

cuting broker with the required financing for the transaction, then the executing broker will either try to cancel the order, or if it is too late, liquidate the hedge fund's position.

7. *NSCC submission.* If the trade is affirmed, it is then submitted to the National Securities Clearing Corporation (NSCC) for clearance and settlement. The NSCC is an independent organisation established by the New York and American Stock Exchanges and the National Association of Securities Dealers (NASD) as an equally owned subsidiary to provide trade processing, clearance, delivery, and settlement services to its members.

8. *Settlement.* Finally, the prime broker settles with the hedge fund in accordance with regular settlement procedures.

Following this process, the hedge fund needs to reconcile trading activity per the hedge fund's books and records to the prime broker's, which will be discussed later.

In addition to providing custody, clearance and settlement services to hedge funds, prime brokers may also provide the following services:

- multi-currency portfolio accounting and allocation systems, which can provide performance measurement, multi-currency pricing and economic allocations;
- access to research;
- stock borrow capabilities, to facilitate short sale transactions;
- stock loan capabilities, which will allow the hedge fund to earn a rebate on its positions; and
- financing opportunities (repurchase agreements and alternative equity and fixed-income financing arrangements).

Many of these services are relatively new and in some instances still being developed. They are being offered in part to meet the growing needs of hedge funds today, as increasingly complex trading and strategies require additional financing and research, greater reporting capabilities and the like. Many prime brokers have expended major resources, especially in the area of technology, and others continue to do so to develop these services. Prime brokers are developing these services not only to keep up with the needs of hedge funds today, but also to remain competitive. Hedge funds should therefore bear in mind when selecting a prime broker that the extent of services offered will vary from one prime broker to the next.

A hedge fund needs to control the amount of leverage it has with its prime broker and the amount of exposure it has in its positions. Senior management must set leveraging parameters before trading takes place. Each trader should have pre-set limits, depending on the instruments they trade and the capital they have, and management must review traders' portfolio and margin accounts to ensure their compliance with these limits. Regarding exposure, unless real-time systems are in place, the exposure for positions will not be known until the following day. Senior management therefore must review positions and determine if any need to be reduced, closed out entirely or otherwise altered.

Trade authorisation

The individuals trading on behalf of a hedge fund must be careful not to violate its investment parameters. The composition of a hedge fund's portfolio is determined by the fund's investment objectives and its strategy to achieve them, along with its investment limitations, all of which are described in partnership agreements and offering documents.

Limitations may include, for example, a maximum percentage of the fund's capital to be invested in restricted securities. (A restricted security is a security that may be sold privately, but that is required to be registered with the SEC or exempted from such registration before it may be sold in a public distribution. An example is a security issued through a private placement – ie, the direct sale of a block of securities of a new or secondary issue to a single investor or group of investors. The sale or placement is usually made through an investment banker. The securities' public resale is restricted if they are not registered under the Securities Act of 1933, which could make them illiquid and difficult to value.) By imposing such investment limitations, the hedge fund would be able to maintain a higher level of liquidity and reduce valuation issues. Such issues are important to the hedge fund's investors because they affect the fund's performance.

In addition to the fund's traders complying with the partnership agreement, someone independent of the trading function, such as a member of executive management or the hedge fund manager, should review the positions held by the hedge fund on a daily basis to ensure compliance with the investment parameters. Although typically not regulated by the SEC, hedge funds still have a responsibility to their investors to establish control processes and to properly process, record and summarise transactions. Therefore, executive management should establish certain controls over those who trade for the fund, often including limits on:

- size of trades and positions;
- type of securities they may trade in; and
- how much counterparty exposure they may have at any one time.

Counterparty or credit exposure is the risk that a party to a transaction will not fulfil its portion of the obligation, typically as a consequence to a party's insolvency. Most of this risk is eliminated when the hedge fund executes and/or clears its transactions through its prime broker and the prime broker affirms the transaction. However, when the hedge fund enters into an over-the-counter transaction (for example, a swap) outside the prime broker relationship, the hedge fund assumes the counterparty risk. Someone who is independent of the trading function, such as a member of executive management, must review the positions held as well as counterparty exposure on a daily basis and ensure that the control procedures are being adhered to.

What happens when firms fail to follow control procedures on trading operations? In recent years, examples have abounded, as numerous firms have suffered well-publicised breakdowns because of such control failures. Several are described below.

Kidder Peabody

A Kidder bond trader by the name of Joseph Jett allegedly generated US$350 million in phoney trading profits from 1991–94 while masking approximately US$95 million in actual losses. Jett allegedly was able to do this by taking advantage of a flaw in Kidder's accounting system, enabling him to create instant paper profits by trading zero coupon Treasury bonds. Indeed, since Jett was one of its star traders, Kidder had reduced the control processes over his activity.

Barings

A 28-year-old futures trader by the name of Nick Leeson allegedly ran up approximately US$1.3 billion in losses in the Asian futures markets, bringing about the demise of Barings, one of England's oldest securities houses. Leeson's activity went largely undetected because he was able to clear his own trades. Amid an obvious lack of proper segregation of duties and similarly inadequate review of his trading activity and cash requirements, Leeson was in effect controlling his own back office – a total violation of the most basic exchange rules. Leeson, like Jett, was given this power because he was considered to be one of Baring's star traders.

Daiwa Bank

An executive vice president in the bank's New York operations, who both ran the bank's securities custodial operations and traded Treasury bonds (again an improper segregation of duties), had lost approximately US$200,000 in bond trades and spent approximately 11 years trying to recoup those losses by conducting around 30,000 unauthorised trades. He did not succeed, and in fact ran up additional losses of about US$1 billion by allegedly selling bonds from the bank's portfolio without permission and forging records to hide his acts from superiors. He later stated that a lack of risk control at the bank and lax supervision by Japanese and US financial authorities allowed him to continue his wrongdoing for more than a decade.

Sumitomo Corp

A trader by the name of Yasuo Hamanaka had established himself over the previous 10 years as an internationally known powerhouse in the copper market. Backed by Sumitomo's capital, he was actually able to move the copper markets. During 1996, it became apparent that Hamanaka was doubling down on Sumitomo's long copper positions while short sellers were hitting the copper markets hard. Apparently (Sumitomo had not voluntarily shared many details), Hamanaka had built a large inventory of copper, storing it in London Metal Exchange warehouses, while also buying copper futures contracts. Once Hamanaka's buying binge was cut off by Sumitomo officials, the copper markets were destroyed. Sumitomo lost between US$1.8 billion and US$4 billion on the ride down, it has been estimated. As in other cases, it appears Hamanaka was able to build his large positions without sufficient oversight because he was considered a star trader for Sumitomo.

NatWest Group

Losses were concealed by a trader who deliberately mis-priced and overvalued options contracts. The trader input false volatility factors into pricing models for long-dated, out-of-the-money swaptions to falsely increase their value on the books and records of NatWest. In conjunction with the trader's unethical behaviour, the personnel responsible for ensuring that over-the-counter instruments were independently valued for reporting purposes did not execute sufficient procedures for procuring independent quotations. The combination of these factors led to the concealment of losses from management for more than two years. In mid-1997, NatWest management employed an independent investigation team to confirm the net charge against pre-tax earnings, as a result of positions put on by this trader, of approximately US$115 million.

Trade capture

Trade capture is the process of ensuring that all trades entered into by the hedge fund are properly accounted for and recorded. Depending on the size, number of strategies employed and volume of trades, the trade capture process for hedge funds will vary from one fund to another. However, what holds true for all, no matter what their size, is that they use a prime broker to facilitate the custody, clearance and settlement processes of their trading activity.

Although a third party handles these processes, a hedge fund still needs to account for its trading activity in an internal record. Funds may accomplish this with trade blotters, one of which each trader maintains. The trade blotter provides all the relevant information related to the trade including, among other things:

- trade date;
- time stamp;
- security name;
- quantity;
- cost;
- buy/sell; and
- counterparty.

The hedge fund may also consider establishing recorded telephone lines for those who trade for the fund. These serve to settle potential trade disputes between the fund and counterparty.

Hedge funds typically use a portfolio management system to keep track of a fund's positions. On a daily basis, trades should be entered by tax lot from the trade ticket into the portfolio management system. The trade blotter, as well as reports generated by the portfolio management system, should then be used to reconcile daily trading activity between the hedge fund's books and records and those of the prime broker. To increase the effectiveness and efficiency of this process, computerised links should be established with the prime broker. This way, downloads of daily trading activity per the prime broker can be obtained and automated reconciliations can be performed, reducing many of the manual reconciliation processes where transactions may not be accounted for. As noted above, someone independent of the trading function, to ensure proper segregation of duties and reduce the possibility of defalcations, should perform this reconciliation daily.

The reconciliation process ensures that trades entered into by the hedge fund are recorded even if the trader fails to enter a trade on his or her blotter. This issue could be significant if there are subsequent market fluctuations of a position, which the portfolio manager is unaware that the fund is holding, thereby exposing the hedge fund to market risk. Conversely, the hedge fund may have recorded the transaction but the prime broker may not have received settlement instructions. This may impede the settlement process and cause the trade to be unrecognised by the prime broker on settlement date.

The procedures outlined do not fully cover more esoteric instruments such as swaps, structured notes and other non-exchange-traded instruments commonly referred to as derivatives. These instruments are generally entered into directly between the hedge fund and the counterparty and are outside the realm of the prime broker. In addition, many of these instruments are often recorded off-line and therefore are not captured in the hedge fund's portfolio management system.

Some control procedures that a hedge fund may implement to ensure that derivative instruments are properly accounted for and recorded include:

- sending confirmation of these transactions to a responsible individual who is independent of the trading function;
- limiting the number of people who are authorised to trade in derivative instruments; and
- using a 'trader's slate', which may be a manual or computerised listing of trades filled.

Derivative instruments are almost always recorded on this slate. A member of management should review the trader's slate on a daily basis to ensure that all derivative instruments are properly accounted for.

Credit and counterparty risk

With the proliferation of hedge funds, now numbering an estimated 6,000, and the continual emergence of complex derivative instruments, trading puts a significant burden on a hedge fund manager, who must ask:

- who do I transact business with?
- will the counterparty to the transaction be able to fulfil its end of the obligation?

This exposure is known as credit and counterparty risk, and, as discussed earlier, is largely eliminated when a hedge fund executes and/or clears its transactions through its prime broker and the prime broker affirms the transaction. However, what risk does the hedge fund encounter when a transaction is entered into outside of the prime broker? This depends on the nature of the instrument. For OTC derivatives, there are generally two types of risk:

- the probability of the counterparty defaulting and the associated costs of the non-defaulting counterparty finding a new counterparty (that is, replacement cost); and
- the exposure of the net market value of a transaction at the time of the default.

Both of these risks can be reduced through greater use of collateral and continually monitoring and/or reviewing the creditworthiness of counterparties. Some of the instruments which a hedge fund may participate in, and their respective operational risks, are outlined below.

Repurchase agreements

A hedge fund looking to finance securities may enter into a repurchase agreement (repo), which is the sale of a security (usually US government or corporate debt obligations) at a specified price, with a simultaneous agreement to repurchase the security or substantially the same security at a determinable or fixed price on a specified future date. An agreed-upon interest rate is accrued by the seller-repurchaser over the life of the contract. Repos are typically processed through the hedge fund's prime broker.

The risks associated with repos are borne by the hedge fund, even though the transaction is facilitated through the prime broker. Some of the risks a hedge fund faces with a repo include:

- failure on the part of the counterparty to return collateral securities or provide additional cash collateral due to re-pricing;

- insolvency of the counterparty, which may result in a failure to remit principal and interest payments; and
- the existence of multiple transactions entered into by the counterparty, all of which use the same securities as collateral.

Additionally, hedge funds entering into repurchase agreements are exposed to operational risk with respect to refinancing these repurchase agreements. Financing terms associated with repurchase transactions are based upon terms agreed to by the parties involved. Typically, the party that extends the financing to the hedge fund has the ability to change the required amount of collateral. For example, a counterparty initially provides a hedge fund financing at 100 per cent of the market value of the securities being financed; as the original repurchase agreement approaches expiration the hedge fund communicates to the counterparty that they wish to maintain the position and extend the financing; due to market conditions (such as, volatility in the underlying security, concerns over liquidity and concerns over issuer risk) the counterparty may only wish to extend financing at 60 per cent (or any other percentage) of the current market value of the underlying security; the hedge fund is then required to secure cash to pay for the portion of the position no longer financed (40 per cent in this example).

Swaps

A swap is a transaction in which two counterparties agree to exchange streams of payments over time. There are many forms, such as interest rate, currency and equity swaps. Since these transactions are usually entered into by the hedge fund and another counterparty outside of the realm of the prime broker, the hedge fund itself bears the risk of economic loss in the event of non-performance by the counterparty. As a result, the hedge fund must establish proper credit controls.

The operational risks associated with swap transactions primarily focus on counterparty creditworthiness. Below is a partial list of recommended control procedures, which identifies some of the general procedures that should be established when a hedge fund enters into swap transactions.

- Ensuring that those engaged in a transaction have the relevant experience.
- Limiting the size and number of swaps that may be open at any one time. On a daily basis someone independent of the trading function should monitor the open swap positions versus pre-set limits.
- Establishing a credit committee. This committee should set credit limits for each counterparty based upon a review of the financial integrity and current position of a counterparty. This can be accomplished by in-depth financial statement analysis and a review of current financial information. Additionally, the credit committee should be aware of current economic conditions which may have an adverse effect on the counterparty's financial position.
- Confirming all transactions in writing with the counterparty.
- Entering into a master agreement with each counterparty that the hedge fund's credit personnel approve for business. Industry standardised master agreements are used to establish consistent expectations for certain activities and requirements of the included derivative instruments that the parties to the master agreement expect to enter into. Some

of the activities defined in the master agreements include: policies surrounding the type of assets that form acceptable collateral (for example, cash and/or securities); policies defining when each counterparty may request additional collateral (or the return of collateral placed); and policies defining which types of derivative agreements the counterparties may net or set off against one another, if any, in determining the collateral requirements of the counterparties. A list of the master agreements typically used in the industry can be located on the internet at www.bondmarket.com.

- Ensuring that all swaps are properly accounted for. Many swaps are accounted for off-line from the hedge fund's main accounting system. Someone independent of the trading function should review the trader's slate and receive transaction confirmation directly from counterparties and, when available, customer statements of open positions for the existence of swap transactions and reconcile these to the holdings report. This procedure should be performed daily.

- Use generic pricing models to test the counterparty's valuation for reasonableness. Keep in mind, though, that market conditions will always dictate the actual value of these derivative instruments. In addition, the fund should evaluate changes in interest and/or foreign currency rates which may affect the swap. In this way the fund can maintain other positions which serve to effectively hedge its exposure.

Forwards

A forward is an obligation between two parties to buy and sell an underlying financial instrument, foreign currency or commodity at a price specified now, with delivery and settlement at a specified future date. A hedge fund will typically use a forward contract to hedge against adverse changes in interest rates, foreign currencies, prices of commodities and the like. Since these are over-the-counter contracts and their terms are not standardised, they are entered into outside the realm of the prime broker, and therefore the hedge fund bears the risk of economic loss in the case of counterparty non-performance. As with swaps, there are both market and operational risks associated with forwards. The operational risks are primarily focused on counterparty creditworthiness, so the recommended control procedures mirror those outlined for swaps.

The risks associated with forward agreements became apparent when hedge funds and financial institutions around the world were left stranded by counterparties to Russian rouble forward contracts. Generally, the hedge funds were party to contracts that enabled them to sell roubles at an agreed rate. When the Russian economy fell into extreme hardship many counterparties located in Russia (for example, Russian banks or other local financial institutions) walked away from the terms of these contracts. To complicate matters, the Russian government stepped in and froze the execution of Russian rouble contracts. As a result, hedge funds lost millions of dollars in unrealised gains associated with those contracts. (See the 'Currency exposure' section later in this chapter for further discussion of risks associated with positions of foreign currency.)

Forward rate agreement

A forward rate agreement is an agreement between two parties to exchange amounts at a specified future date based on the difference between an agreed-upon interest rate and a reference rate on a notional amount. Hedge funds may enter into these agreements to fix interest costs for a specific future period, or to hedge other transactions.

Since these instruments are over-the-counter, the hedge fund's primary exposures are liquidity and counterparty risk. The fund must therefore evaluate and monitor the credit-worthiness of the counterparty and implement the aforementioned control procedures.

Other credit and counterparty risk concerns

The increase of investment activity in the various emerging markets of the world has led many to focus on new credit and counterparty issues: securities fraud and theft. Occurrences of securities fraud and theft have been documented in certain emerging markets in recent years. Investors in these regions of the world must familiarise themselves with the settlement process, custodial functions and responsibilities, and securities laws that govern trading and investing in these countries. Hedge funds can take further measures to manage credit risk by setting counterparty credit risk limits, reviewing and monitoring concentrations of credit risk and having standards and policies in place for approving credit risk exposures.

Position and money reconciliation processes with brokers and prime brokers

In addition to reconciling its trading activity with the prime broker each day, as discussed, at the end of each month the hedge fund should reconcile ending positions and broker balances (on a trade date and settlement date basis) with those which the prime broker reflects on its monthly statements. Items affecting the cash balances and other areas enumerated above, which may not have been recorded by the fund, include interest, dividends and corporate actions. The prime broker effects the account balances for these items once the fund is entitled to receive or make payments based on its holdings.

Other areas the hedge fund should have an understanding of and review for reasonableness include: the prime broker's calculation of its margin requirements; the buying power available; and what the fund's special memorandum account (SMA) balance is.

Buying power is defined as the equity remaining in a margin account after providing for the margining of existing securities in the account, in accordance with Regulation T and the prime broker's margin requirements. Ensuring that the prime broker's calculation of this balance is reasonable is important to the execution of the hedge fund's strategy, since buying power is the dollar value of securities that the fund can purchase without having to deposit additional funds.

The SMA is an account maintained by the prime broker for the hedge fund in conjunction with the hedge fund's margin account. The SMA creates another form of buying power for the hedge fund in addition to that addressed above. When the value of securities the hedge fund holds increases, the equity in the hedge fund's margin account increases. When the equity in a margin account exceeds the account's minimum requirements, the excess equity is journalised (recorded) by a credit entry to the SMA. While having a balance in the SMA creates buying power for the hedge fund, the balance accumulated in the SMA is only decreased when the hedge fund uses the account's buying power and therefore is not affected by subsequent unrealised losses in positions held. Interest expense for financing positions and short stock rebate calculations should also be reviewed.

Valuation of financial instruments

The valuation of financial instruments relates directly to the performance of the hedge fund and therefore is a critical aspect of its operations. There are prescribed guidelines established for the industry listed in the *American Institute of Certified Public Accountants Audit and Accounting Guide: Audits of Investment Companies* (as outlined below). The valuation policy is typically disclosed in the partnership agreement as well as the offering documents.

Listed securities

Listed securities are those which are traded on a national exchange such as the New York Stock Exchange (NYSE), American Stock Exchange (AMEX) or any established foreign stock exchange. Provided that the security was traded on the valuation date, it is generally valued at the closing market price on that date. If a security is listed on more than one exchange, then the security should be valued at the last quoted sales price on the exchange on which the security is principally traded. If a security was not traded in the principal market on the valuation date, the security should be valued at the last quoted sales price on the previous most active market, if representative.

If a security was not traded on the valuation date, but closing bid and asked prices are available for that date, then the security should be valued within the bid and asked range.

Some funds use the bid price; others use the mean of the bid and asked prices; others still choose a value within the range that they feel is appropriate under the circumstances. All these methods are acceptable if consistently applied and in accordance with the partnership agreement.

When only a bid or asked price is available on the valuation date, or if the spread between the bid and asked price is substantial on that date, the fund should review quotes for several dates and then, based on this information, choose a value it believes is appropriate.

Various services provide prices for listed securities. Many of these services can be accessed with computer links, which help reduce the man hours required to price listed securities.

Over-the-counter (OTC) securities

OTC refers to a market for the securities of companies, which are not listed on a stock exchange. These securities are traded mainly by electronic communications facilitated by organisations such as the Nasdaq, or by telephone between brokers and dealers who act as principals or brokers for hedge funds and who may or may not be members of a securities exchange.

When valuing OTC securities, the hedge fund should not rely completely on the counterparty's valuation. Quotations for OTC securities are available from the financial press, individual broker-dealers and the NASD National Market System (which provides information on the last sales price on Nasdaq).

Like listed securities, OTC securities are generally valued at the closing market price on valuation date. When unlisted securities are not traded on the valuation date, some funds will use the mean of available bid prices; some the mean of the bid and asked prices; and others the mean of price quotations received from a representative selection of broker-dealers. Again, all these methods are acceptable if consistently applied and in accordance with the partnership agreement.

Derivative instruments

Other OTC instruments include interest rate swaps, currency swaps, equity swaps, structured notes and so on, which are often referred to as derivatives. These instruments or contracts generally derive their value from fluctuations in, for instance, interest rates, exchange rates, stock prices, bond prices and indices which are generally valued through the use of models.

There are many generic pricing models available for testing a counterparty's valuation for reasonableness. Since these instruments are often recorded off-line from the hedge fund's main accounting system, when valuing them a fund manager must ensure that all instruments have been included in the valuation process, as well as the resulting profit or loss generated from marking.

Currency exposure

With the growth of international markets and a desire on the part of hedge fund managers to seek out above-average returns for their investors, the investment philosophy for hedge funds has expanded to include trading in international equity and fixed-income markets. Along with the traditional market and credit risk a hedge fund typically experiences when investing, a fund that invests overseas is also exposed to currency risk, foreign settlement issues and the actions of foreign governments.

Currency risk arises in two areas.

- *Broker balances* – to purchase foreign instruments, the fund needs to exchange US dollars for foreign currency and therefore has broker balances denominated in a foreign currency. Accordingly, the fund is exposed to fluctuations in exchange rates.
- *Foreign positions* – the hedge fund is holding positions that are denominated in a foreign currency and is exposed to the appreciation/depreciation in the value of the currency.

The portfolio(s) should be reviewed for these holdings and balances, and appropriate currency hedge positions, such as forward currency contracts, should be maintained to minimise currency exposure.

Foreign settlement issues arise during the trading of foreign securities, which requires an understanding of the trading, delivery and settlement policies of each country in which the hedge fund intends to buy and sell securities. For example, some countries may settle securities within a day or two of trade date, while others may take as long as 30 days. Some countries do not permit the short selling of securities; others do not allow securities to be out on repo.

Many prime brokers are aware of these issues and have either opened satellite offices in these foreign countries to facilitate the clearance of trades at the request of hedge funds, or have positioned themselves with agent banks around the world that do this for them. However, when hedge funds trade in over-the-counter foreign instruments such as forward currency contracts, they assume the responsibility of knowing the market in which they are trading and its regulatory requirements. Therefore, hedge fund managers should ensure that the individuals who are responsible for the settlement of these instruments have the appropriate qualifications and experience.

Foreign governments may impose certain taxes or withholdings (for example, capital gains or dividend withholdings) against the trading activity and accounts of foreign investors.

400

In addition, the assets of a fund maintained in a foreign country are exposed to the actions imposed by the local government. Recent examples include restrictions placed on foreign currency trading and repatriation of funds in various Asian countries and Russia. A fund manager must be familiar with the local tax and regulatory restrictions governing the fund's accounts for all countries in which the fund invests.

Another aspect of trading in international markets is the need for multi-currency portfolio accounting systems. As mentioned earlier, the prime broker may provide this service. However, if the hedge fund has its own portfolio accounting system, before entering into a significant number of foreign currency transactions it must assess the multi-currency capabilities of its system.

Future directions, challenges and opportunities

Regulation and increased disclosure

With hedge funds becoming increasingly available to the broader market, regulation is perhaps inevitable. Studies have been launched by the SEC to examine and gather information to understand the hedge fund industry. Large investors and regulatory bodies such as the SEC are pushing for increased financial statement presentation, transparency and disclosure requirements.* Some examples supporting the issuance or changes of rules, regulations, procedures and practices within the investment industry are given below.

- The *AICPA Audit and Accounting Guide* requires investment companies to present financial highlights either in the notes or as a separate schedule in the financial statements. The objective of financial highlights is to provide the user of the financial statement with information on the total return for each class of shares, the ratio of expenses and net investment income to average net assets of the investment company.
- The Commodity Futures Trading Commission (CFTC) now requires funds of funds to disclose the name and carrying amount of each individual investee fund or material investee pool which equals or exceeds 10 per cent of the fund of fund's net assets. The fund must also disclose management and incentive fee/allocations of the investee funds, the liquidity of the investee funds and the total net income earned from the investee funds. The objective is to provide the user of the financial statements with information on the performance, liquidity and fees of any of the fund's material underlying investee funds or pools.
- The *AICPA Audit and Accounting Guide* requires investment companies to present a condensed schedule of investments, which includes categorising all investments by type (common stock, fixed income, short positions, etc), country or geographical region, and industry. In addition, for each investment constituting more than 5 per cent of the net assets of the fund, it requires disclosure of the name, share or principal amount and type. The CFTC has stated it will not accept any financial statements without the complete presentation of the condensed schedule as outlined in the *AICPA Guide*. The CFTC is moving into a more active role to ensure funds are reporting in accordance with Generally Accepted Accounting Principles (GAAP).
- In January 2003, the FASB issued Interpretation No. 46, 'Consolidation of Variable Interest Entities', which provides new criteria for determining whether or not consolidation accounting is required. The Interpretation may require the fund to consolidate, or provide additional disclosures of financial information for certain of its portfolio investments. This

Interpretation is effective immediately for 'Variable Interest Entities' created after 31 January 2003; otherwise, it is applicable for the first interim or annual reporting period beginning after 15 June 2003 for existing investments determined to be 'Variable Interest Entities'. This Interpretation may require consolidation by the fund of certain investee company assets and liabilities and results of operations. A minority interest may be recorded for the investee company ownership share attributable to other investors. Where consolidation of portfolio companies is not required, additional disclosures may be required of investee company financial information.

Anti-money laundering

In 2001, President Bush signed the USA Patriot Act to assist in intercepting and obstructing terrorism and provide public safety. Section 352 of the USA Patriot Act requires all financial institutions, including investment companies, to establish anti-money laundering (AML) programmes, which include at a minimum developing internal policies, procedures and controls; designating a compliance officer; establishing an ongoing employee training programme; and establishing an independent audit function to test programmes. Concerns of money laundering and tax evasion have become a more important element of the Internal Revenue Service, particularly with respect to offshore hedge funds. Although hedge funds have always adhered to the 'know your investor' requirements through due diligence, in the future hedge funds will be under enhanced scrutiny and it is important that hedge fund managers understand the rules and regulations in each fund's respective jurisdiction, onshore and offshore.

Emerging markets

With the growth that has been taking place in countries classified as emerging markets, hedge funds will continue to experience increased investment opportunities in these markets. As noted above, this raises clearance, settlement and valuation issues, since prices for many of the instruments traded in these markets are not readily available. With this in mind, there is a significant need for individuals who have the appropriate qualifications and experience in these markets and instruments.

Divergence in size

There will continue to be mega hedge funds like Soros and Tiger, employing large numbers of people. However, a significant portion of the hedge fund market is represented by a vast number of smaller firms. Many large institutions have also expanded their activity in the hedge fund arena. However, the one-man hedge fund will continue to thrive, in part due to advances in the services that prime brokers are offering. Many of these services help to alleviate some of the operational issues which hedge funds face.

Proper controls essential

Establishing the various controls needed to reduce the operational risks described in this chapter may seem burdensome. However, proper controls are integral to successful management not only because they help prevent breakdowns but also because, once they are in place, they actually make hedge fund operations less cumbersome. Indeed, they can enhance the success of a fund by allowing it to focus on its main purpose: managing money.

* Editor's note: on 29 September 2003, shortly before this book went to press, the staff of the SEC issued its report entitled 'The Implications of the Growth of Hedge Funds', the culmination of its efforts following the Hedge Fund Roundtable held in May 2003. As of the date of this writing, the Commission itself had not taken any action in response to the report. One of the key recommendations of the staff was that the SEC consider 'requiring hedge fund advisers to register with the SEC as investment advisers, taking into account whether the benefits outweigh the burdens of registration'. In the staff's view, ' … registration of hedge fund advisers would serve as a deterrent to fraud, encourage compliance and the adoption of compliance procedures, provide the SEC with important information … and effectively raise the standards for investment in hedge funds from the "accredited investor" standard to that of "qualified client"'. See http://www.sec.gov/news/studies/hedgefunds0903.pdf for the full text of the report.

Chapter 32

The evolving role of the prime broker

Christopher J. Pesce
Banc of America Securities, LLC,[1] *New York, New York*

Introduction

The growth of the hedge fund industry over the past decade has been phenomenal. Not only has a tremendous amount of capital flowed into the space, there has also been a clear growth in the number of funds and the diversity of strategies they use. Many observers argue that the capital flowing into hedge funds over the past decade will be dwarfed in the next decade, particularly as pension funds look to increase their allocation to the alternative space and traditional money management firms begin establishing hedged products for their traditional customers, which includes the broad base of retail customers. In May 2003, the SEC held round table discussions on this growing industry to better understand the strategies and operating environment of hedge funds. While this chapter will not speculate on what action the SEC may take, it seems safe to say the regulators and legislators are educating themselves in anticipation of the widespread use of hedge fund products by a much broader constituency.*

Suffice it to say that with this massive growth, the role of the prime broker continues to evolve. The hedge fund customer demands more of its prime broker. In response, the role is evolving from that of a service provider to that of a strategic partner.

What a prime broker does

The basic services of a prime broker start with centralised custody and clearing as well as reporting and financing of an account. In simple terms, a money manager has the ability to trade with multiple brokerage houses while maintaining at their prime broker the hedge fund's cash and securities in one centralised master account. Additionally, the prime broker acts as an outsourced back office fulfilling the account reconciliation process. Centralising the hedge fund's balances from other institutions, a fund manager may receive more efficient and favourable financing terms, as well as consolidated portfolio accounting and back office support.

Over the years, though, the prime broker's role in working with hedge fund managers has grown to cover a much wider array of services. Hedge fund managers count on a variety of services that far exceed centralised custody and clearing, including capital introduction, capital accounting, structured products, risk-based margining and synthetic prime brokerage.

In order to be a first-class strategic partner, a financial institution must meet four basic needs of a hedge fund:

- getting started;
- operating the business;

Exhibit 32.1

Equity division: hedge fund strategy

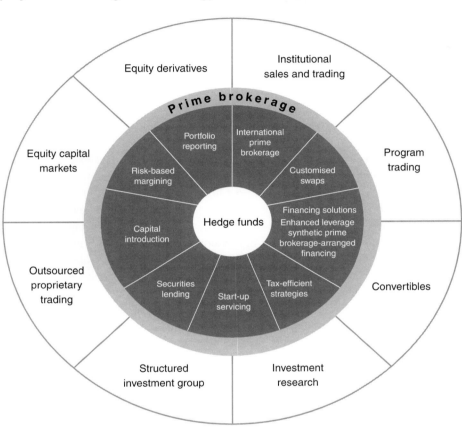

Source: Banc of America Securities LLC.

- capital introduction; and
- generating alpha.

To focus purely on traditional prime brokerage is counter-intuitive to fulfilling these vast needs. In order to be a full-service strategic partner, a firm's entire platform must focus on hedge funds. Exhibit 32.1 is an example of a fully integrated approach to this concept.

The inner ring of the 'wheel' defines traditional stand-alone prime brokerage. The outer ring of the 'wheel' addresses the capital markets aspect of an entire equity division's platform. Due to the myriad of styles, strategies and business-cycle phases of hedge funds, the stand-alone approach to prime brokerage is inadequate. The vast numbers and diverse needs of hedge funds require that prime brokerage and capital markets functions, products and services be delivered in concert. Coupling together and delivering to the hedge fund manager the products, services and functions of stand-alone prime brokerage and capital markets has redefined prime brokerage. Redefined prime brokerage enables the hedge fund manager full access to an entire securities platform rather than a mere slice.

How does a prime broker help a manager start a hedge fund?

Start-up consultation for fund managers

- Developing a business plan.
- Real estate location services.
- Guidance on organisational structure.
- Best practices regarding infrastructure.
- Recommendations on selecting attorneys, accountants, administrators and other key service providers.

Client office space

Start-up and established hedge fund managers rely on their prime broker to assist in identifying the optimal location for their office. Real estate services range from mere referral of real estate brokers to providing completely built-out high-end offices. Hedge fund managers and, most importantly, their investors reap substantial benefits from prime broker-provided office space. Through prime broker-provided office space the hedge fund manager accesses the infrastructure and capabilities of a multi-billion dollar organisation with hundreds of thousands of employees. A few examples of the numerous economies of scale benefits for the hedge fund manager and their investors are:

- architects to help design the office;
- on-site technology, telecommunications, installation and support;
- purchase of computers and other office technology at discounted prices;
- access to security quotation data-feed servers;
- receptionist, conference rooms, kitchen services;
- disaster recovery plans, procedures and capabilities; and
- no long-term lease commitment.

The proficient prime broker provides a true turnkey solution for the hedge fund manager to move seamlessly into a fully functioning working environment. Thus, the hedge fund manager minimises distractions, leverages off of the prime broker's core competencies and, therefore, may focus on their investment strategy. A hedge fund manager in prime broker-provided office space also receives the benefits the prime broker generally delivers to all of its clients. Investors are particularly in favour of start-up funds moving into space supported by a prime broker. This provides investors with the comfort that the fund has its infrastructure supported by a major institution as opposed to the go-it-alone strategy. Not only does this provide comfort due to the level of support it also provides comfort so the manager may focus more time and energy on generating alpha.

Small business/home office consulting

- Domain name registration and e-mail configuration.
- Cost-effective market data feeds, both server and internet based.
- Computer hardware/software configuration, ordering and installation.
- Cost-effective internet connectivity.

Password protected marketing web pages

- Creation of corporate identity (such as logos).
- Design and creation of marketing web pages.
- Streaming audio and video.
- Performance charting.
- Downloadable versions of offering memorandums and subscription documents.

Prime relationship management

Prime relationship managers are senior level relationship liaisons, providing the manager a single point of contact for operations, technology, trading and capital introductions. They are an integral component for a prime broker to establish best practices for itself and its clients. The prime relationship managers constantly interface with hedge fund managers to relay innovation and capabilities, deliver tools and training, and provide access to capital markets services and products. Working with a hedge fund manager from the first day of the prime brokerage relationship will expedite the set-up of technology and training on portfolio reporting and systems that a client will use as well as to act as a sounding board for operational questions. A prime relationship manager queries and receives feedback from a hedge fund manager on the entire capital markets relationship. This valuable feedback ensures that the prime broker is exceeding the hedge fund manager's expectations and is continuously improving its services, products and tools.

Account executives

Essential to quality prime brokerage is streamlined service. The advantage of centralised custody is that the manager does not have to maintain accounts and records with multiple brokerage houses. Absent centralised custody, a money manager must spend an inordinate amount of time with back office work, such as account maintenance and brokerage house reconciliations. Since the prime broker is the custodian for all trading activity, a natural value-added service is the ability for the hedge fund manager to outsource the back office work to a single point of contact. The back office single point of contact is the account executive. The account executive will work with the hedge fund manager to resolve trade breaks, adjust for reorganisations or simple services such as wire transfers. The account executive relieves the hedge fund manager of many time-consuming operational issues and allows him to focus on managing the hedge fund's assets.

How does a prime broker help a hedge fund operate?

Trading

In addition to assigning a traditional trader on a brokerage house's desk, prime brokers may provide trading solutions for their clients. On-line trading is an easy to use, cost-effective standard offered as an alternative to calling a sell-side trade desk. Another concept offered by prime brokers is a buy-side trading desk. The use of a buy-side desk is a cost-effective way for the hedge fund manager to outsource the trading function. An outsourced trader can execute anywhere on the Street either by following a hedge fund manager's direction or working on their behalf to get the best execution.

Portfolio reporting

Hedge fund managers rely on prime brokers for more than just operational support. It is imperative that a prime broker provides state of the art technology in servicing their hedge fund clients. Innovative reports and reports delivery systems are essential to a hedge fund manager and the daily operation of their fund. Working with a prime broker eliminates the need for the manager to go out and purchase a portfolio reporting system, a major responsibility of a prime broker is to provide numerous portfolio accounting reports on a daily and monthly basis. With the proliferation of the internet, most hedge funds are able to log onto a secure website and view their portfolio reports. Some of the basic reports may include the items below:

- *Valuation analysis.* A report that provides summarised portfolio information such as realised and unrealised gains and/or losses for the day, month, quarter and year for the entire portfolio.
- *Daily profit and loss.* A listing of gains and losses for each security in the portfolio including price and percentage change.
- *Client position summary.* A portfolio holding report listing positions, unit cost, total cost, market price, market value as well as unrealised gains and losses for the day.
- *Working appraisal.* Similar to the client position summary, however it shows the positions by tax lot giving the client the cost basis of their positions.
- *Daily transaction journal.* A recap of the previous day's activity including, for example, trade, funds in and out, and dividend expenses.

In addition to these basic daily and monthly reports, a prime broker may also provide useful monthly and annual accounting reports such as various tax layering and 'wash sale' reports for the fund. Most hedge fund accountants and bookkeepers will log directly onto a client's site and pull this preliminary information for monthly bookkeeping, capital accounting and general year-end tax work such as estimated K1s.

Most portfolio reporting systems also offer detailed (unaudited) performance charting, earnings estimates and advanced portfolio statistics such as weighted average beta, average monthly returns, and standard deviation of returns and Sharpe ratios.

Risk and transparency reporting

It is becoming more and more important that hedge fund managers address risk control for their fund as well as provide some level of transparency for their investors. Risk reporting helps a manager monitor risk on both the security and portfolio level. Risk analysis takes options and other derivatives into account. Some of the various types of risk reporting are outlined below:

- *Value-at-Risk.* Analysis that measures the portfolio's expected gain or loss for a specified holding period.
- *Equivalent shares.* Converts derivatives to their underlying share equivalent for optimal hedging and risk exposure. This type of report also calculates the beta-adjusted value on both a security and portfolio level.
- *Derivative risk statistics.* Provides the greek's for a portfolio, namely the delta, gamma, lambda, theta and rho. It allows the portfolio manager to monitor a hedged position on a daily basis.

- *Transparency reports.* Certain investors require a higher degree of transparency in order to invest in a hedge fund. Transparency reports may include sector and country broken out by long and short exposure.

Capital accounting

Prime brokers may also provide solutions for hedge fund managers that wish to perform their capital accounting in-house instead of outsourcing. Whether by an in-house team of bookkeepers or accountants or a firm's proprietary software, capital accounting provides the following:

- maintaining financial records;
- preparing financial statements;
- calculation of fees or reallocations; and
- partner level economic allocations.

A quality portfolio system will also give the user the ability to download reports into Excel, a must for any hedge fund wishing to create their own spreadsheet models.

Securities lending

The primary function of a securities lending group is to facilitate a hedge fund's short selling by borrowing the stock from their own 'box' as well as going to another institution and posting cash as collateral against the borrowed stock. Some securities lending organisations will maintain a matched book, where the securities lending group is also a net lender to 'the Street' of hard-to-borrow securities. For the hedge fund manager and the prime broker, this is critically important as it protects against a buy-in of the borrowed security. Each prime broker works in sync with their securities lending group to provide short sale approvals for the hedge fund manager. A recent innovation is the ability for the manager to electronically make and receive online approvals for short sale transactions.

Business administration

Prime brokers may facilitate the outsourcing of the hedge fund manager's human resource needs. By partnering with a human resources firm the prime broker may assist a hedge fund manager's access to services such as payroll, health insurance and 401k benefits and administration. They may also provide assistance in compliance documentation as well as recruiting needs as the fund grows.

How do prime brokers help hedge funds find capital?

Capital introduction

Capital introduction is quickly becoming the driver in the prime brokerage relationship with the hedge fund manager. Prime brokers are responding to this growing need. Capital introduction benefits the hedge fund manager by eliminating the amount of time and resources spent on increasing the assets of the hedge fund. The matrix in Exhibit 32.2 illustrates how a prime broker may help hedge fund managers access capital.

Exhibit 32.2

Capital introduction services

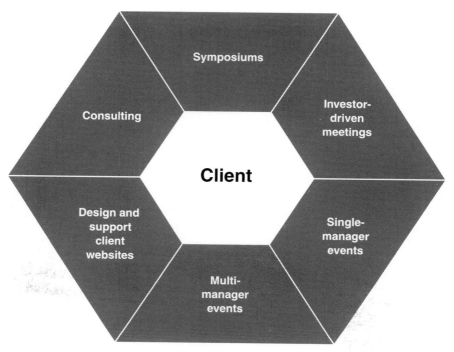

Source: Banc of America Securities LLC.

The goal of a capital introduction group is to match the right type of investor with the right type of client. This can be done with targeted events such as one-on-one meetings or single-manager events that are attended by a number of pre-screened investors. There also is the symposia format that may have multiple managers speaking at an all-day conference where the audience is made up of qualified investors. A capital introduction group will also assist in helping hedge fund managers follow up with various meetings and requests for information. Invariably, it is performance that ultimately drives the attainment of new capital but the capital introduction efforts of a prime broker are an essential component of a hedge fund manager's marketing effort.

How do prime brokers help hedge funds generate alpha?

It is estimated that 50 per cent of all trading activity done on the Street is from hedge fund managers. With this explosive growth of the hedge fund industry, as well as a greater variety of investment styles, it is important for a prime broker to stay ahead of the curve in offering new products and services to the hedge fund manager. Some of the newest products offered by full service prime brokers include:

- equity derivatives;
- equity capital markets;

- outsourced proprietary trading;
- structured investments;
- investment research;
- convertible trading; and
- program trading.

Conclusion

As the growth of the hedge fund industry accelerates the demand for prime brokerage services, the need for hedge funds to develop a strategic alliance with a capable financial institution will grow as well. Services and products of the largest banks will need to be coordinated and packaged for both the hedge fund and their investors.

Those institutions with the greatest level of resources including balance sheet, credit rating, lower cost of capital, greatest access to investor capital and core prime brokerage and investment products, will be the providers of choice to the hedge fund community and their investors. Very similar to the global custody business there will be tremendous consolidation in the prime brokerage business. The market will simply not support the role of boutique providers that cannot provide for all of the needs of hedge fund managers and their investors. Simply put, it will be the universal bank model and not the investment bank model that will offer the breadth and the depth of product to become the most complete strategic partner.

* Editor's note: on 29 September 2003, shortly before this book went to press, the staff of the SEC issued its report entitled 'The Implications of the Growth of Hedge Funds', the culmination of its efforts following the Hedge Fund Roundtable held in May 2003. As of the date of this writing, the Commission itself had not taken any action in response to the report. One of the key recommendations of the staff was that the SEC consider 'requiring hedge fund advisers to register with the SEC as investment advisers, taking into account whether the benefits outweigh the burdens of registration'. In the staff's view, ' ... registration of hedge fund advisers would serve as a deterrent to fraud, encourage compliance and the adoption of compliance procedures, provide the SEC with important information ... and effectively raise the standards for investment in hedge funds from the "accredited investor" standard to that of "qualified client"'. See http://www.sec.gov/news/studies/hedgefunds0903.pdf for the full text of the report.

---

[1] Chris Pesce was assisted by Jonathan J. Bloom, Managing Director, Banc of America Securities LLC (who is the Head of Synthetic Prime Brokerage and Swap Sales) and Gary J. Kniffen, Vice President, Banc of America Securities LLC, Northeastern US Prime Brokerage Sales.

Chapter 33

Hedge fund transparency

James R. Hedges IV
LJH Global Investments, Naples, Florida

Introduction

Since hedge funds traditionally have been offered privately in the United States as limited partnerships they are not allowed to advertise and are exempt from disclosure requirements facing traditional, registered investment funds.* As a result, there are no incentives for managers to be forthcoming with their performance data and portfolio holdings. By further setting up as offshore funds, many hedge funds are able to avoid further scrutiny or tax requirements imposed in the United States.

Considered for a long time to represent niche or frontier investing, not only did hedge funds garner a small portion of investors' wealth, they also attracted little public attention. In the early years of the hedge fund industry, managers often provided only quarterly performance results and audited annual statements without investors clamouring for more disclosure. However, the US$39 billion weakling in 1990 has grown into a US$600 billion gorilla in the early 2000s, a growth rate only matched by the explosion in the number of arcane investment strategies that hedge funds engage in. The unfortunate 'blow-up' of Long-Term Capital Management (LTCM) in 1998 managed to do two things: first, it demonstrated to both investors and regulators the impact that hedge funds can now exert on investors' wealth and on the financial system; and second, it exposed how little even seasoned investment professionals knew about what hedge fund managers were up to. On the verge of becoming a mainstream investment, hedge funds are now attracting much greater attention as both investors and regulators are demanding more transparency and accountability.

In public debates or pronouncements, the key word is transparency, not disclosure. Whether intended or not, it signifies a stronger requirement. A fund cannot provide transparency without disclosure. However, it can disclose all its positions and yet what a manager is up to may not be transparent, at least to most investment professionals. Disclosure by hedge fund managers has varied from a monthly or quarterly release of performance results without a single fact about their investments to complete daily details on individual investment positions. Why would hedge funds be singled out for increased scrutiny? A contrast between hedge fund and mutual fund investing puts matters into perspective.

Hedge fund versus mutual fund investing

Although mutual funds are required by the Securities and Exchange Commission (SEC) to offer total transparency in annual and semi-annual reports, few 401K statements, if any, include a listing of all fund holdings. Most investors are quite content to receive periodic performance reports and would probably not welcome thick reports detailing all their funds' holdings simply for the sake of transparency. In order to understand why mutual fund investors are not clamouring for information, it is useful to think like a police detective confronted with a crime. Who has the motive and the opportunity?

Mutual fund managers perform in a tightly regulated environment. For the most part they are allowed to invest only in vanilla instruments such as stocks and bonds, with strict guidelines for below-investment-grade securities. There are strong restrictions on the use of derivatives, and leverage is highly limited. They often buy and hold. Shorting is allowed, but used by only a small community of funds. Incentive fees are prohibited. Mutual fund managers typically are paid a fee equal to a fixed percentage of assets under management no matter how well they perform, although some have a 'fulcrum' fee. With very little performance-based upside to their compensation structure, there is nothing to gain by taking extra risks and trying innovative strategies. Also, the SEC and the state regulatory bodies can conduct extensive examinations of all books and records and compliance procedures of any registered investment adviser. Consultants conduct quantitative and qualitative due diligence and monitor the funds. Finally, the principals of these funds are required in many cases to get ethics training.

The nature of the instruments traded, the vanilla strategies executed and the scrutiny of regulators ensure that mutual fund managers have little scope and no incentives to behave opportunistically in ways that may jeopardise investors' wealth. With consultants and regulators monitoring these funds, investors may enjoy a free ride on this monitoring process.

In contrast to mutual funds, hedge fund managers face no restrictions on the types of instruments that they can trade. They are paid an incentive fee that is a function of performance (for example, 20 per cent of profits). There is the possibility that the quest for a high pay-off may cause some managers to lose caution and take unfortunate actions. The potential combination of illiquid instruments, derivatives (futures and options) and leverage uniquely present in many hedge fund operations, the low barriers to entry in the business and the very flexibility of their business models leave the door open for an unscrupulous manager to behave opportunistically to the detriment of investors if no one is looking. With no comprehensive regulatory oversight in place, no free ride on the due diligence and monitoring is available unless investors are participating through a fund of hedge funds. Therefore, investors may feel with some justification that hedge fund managers have both the motive and the opportunity. Consequently, they need to know what managers are up to through increased disclosure in order to protect their interests.

Furthermore, with US$600 billion of investors' wealth hanging in the balance, monitoring of hedge funds has become a matter of regulatory concern. Well-publicised 'blow-ups' such as LTCM, Lipper, Maricopa and Manhattan, offer a clear illustration that hedge funds have risks that most investors have not traditionally faced with mutual funds.

Advantages and disadvantages of transparency

The advantages of greater transparency are rather practical, particularly from the standpoint of a hedge fund investor. More transparency means more information available to both present and prospective investors. It means an improved ability to monitor performance and assess risks, therefore enabling fully informed investment decision making. At the very least, transparency enables investors to become more aware before they commit themselves to an investment. Alternatively, it also enables them to be more comfortable about their personal wealth invested in a fund by reducing the levels and the likelihood of fraud, misrepresentation and price manipulation.

Transparency can also allow investors to minimise exposures to certain investments made by the hedge fund manager. For example, if an investor notices that his manager has a huge position in a particular security, that investor can choose to hedge that risk by either taking an opposite position or entering into a simple derivatives contract such as an option.

From a fund manager's viewpoint, increased transparency has its advantages as well. The process of disclosing data to fund investors can be an important communication tool for the manager at the same time it benefits investors. Managers can use disclosure as a means to educate and maintain dialogue with their investors, thereby keeping up relationships with investors who are the long-term foundation of the hedge fund.

The overriding disadvantage of transparency facing a hedge fund manager concerns disclosure of fund holdings. The greatest fear of fund managers is that their transactions and positions become known by other traders, putting them at a competitive disadvantage. This can easily happen to a manager that has entered into a sizeable, but relatively illiquid position. For example, if a large hedge fund invested a substantial amount in a given security that was thinly traded, and other investors and brokers in this security knew of the position size, traders could take advantage of the manager. In addition, most hedge funds seek out stocks that are not covered by mainstream analysts. They hope to find a 'diamond in the rough' and build a large position in the stock. When a manager is building such a position, it is certainly not to his/her advantage to have total transparency. These situations have arisen before and in some cases have proven to be disastrous to hedge fund managers.

Another fear of hedge fund managers is that competitors will replicate their proprietary trading models if full transparency is provided. Many quantitative or model-driven managers develop robust systems (sometimes referred to as 'black boxes') that are responsible for daily trading activity. The typical system contains an algorithm or neural net that generates signals on whether to buy or sell a given security or commodity. Traders often develop these systems after conducting intensive research on historical price trends, volatility and other technical relationships. If competitors have access to the trades that a manager makes, they may be able to reverse engineer the models being used, putting a manager again at a significant competitive disadvantage.

Finally, managers are also reluctant to disclose positions when they have a significant short position in a particular security. Companies do not look kindly on investors who short their shares. If the company that is being shorted finds out, it may become difficult for the hedge fund manager to communicate with the company. Consequently, if a manager cannot obtain information, then the trade becomes much riskier.

Transparency is not a free good

There is no disagreement regarding the need for transparency. The real debate centres on the level of detail regarding portfolio composition that the funds should disclose to their investors, and whether this disclosure makes managers' actions and strategies more readily understood. Disclosure of information is only as good as the ability of investors to process it in both timely and cost-effective manners.

Providing the position details on all the interest-only and principal-only tranches, floaters and inverse floaters, and the like, in a specific mortgage fund, for example, may tell investors very little about the level of risk of the fund unless they have the analytical skills and the quantitative tools to make sense out of these complex instruments. As a matter of fact, such disclosure may perversely provide investors with a false sense of security. The required analytical skills and quantitative tools needed to analyse risk in certain strategies and instruments used by many hedge funds are costly to acquire and may not be worth the cost given the size of one's individual investments in a hedge fund. For those investors with limited expertise and cost concerns, the disclosure of key portfolio characteristics suitably aggregated may be more revealing and therefore more useful in making timely assessments of a fund risk–return profile.

Analytical ability and cost considerations have led to the delivery to hedge fund investors of various forms of transparency and to the emergence of third party financial information processing services. The bottom line is that where there are costs involved in preparing and releasing information and where certain types of disclosure may reveal proprietary information, transparency must be managed.

Separate accounts are an increasingly popular vehicle, in part because they allow full disclosure to an investor. Unlike an investor in a partnership, he/she owns the portfolio and therefore may obtain complete transparency of each position in the account directly from the prime brokers. Separate accounts offer additional benefits: portfolio directives such as loss limits or exposure restrictions can be customised. Unwanted asset classes can be easily eliminated. Leverage, credit quality and valuation errors or fraud can be easily monitored as well as deviations from investment guidelines or style drift. Stop loss rules for both individual holdings in the account and for the overall account itself can also be customised. Indeed, since the investor has direct ownership, he/she can terminate a manager at any time and assume control of the assets. Risk analytics may further be obtained directly from the prime broker at no additional charge to the investor. The extra level of transparency and control offered by separate accounts must be balanced by the following: all costs incurred to manage the separate account (for instance, accounting, auditing and trading) are borne by the single investor rather than being proportionately borne by multiple investors. In addition, hedge fund managers typically require a minimum of US$15–20 million or more to initiate a separate account. Since many hedge fund managers are unwilling to accept managed accounts, an investor insisting on this investment vehicle may have to settle for second-best managers. Due to the large required minimums, managed accounts have been the favourite investment vehicle of large investment houses, institutional investors and a few large funds of hedge funds. However, as some recent blow-ups show, even sophisticated investors with cutting edge analytics and with the benefit of full transparency offered by separate accounts may not always be able to avoid problems.

A small but increasing number of hedge funds are willing to provide full transparency to their investors subject to non-disclosure or other conditions. However, investors anticipating the receipt of such disclosure must first grapple with the following issues: should they purchase off-the-shelf information processing/risk management systems if available or should they build their own proprietary systems? Such decisions must take into consideration, for instance, the complexity and variety of individual hedge fund positions, the proprietary view of risk, the level and types of risk analytics required, reporting flexibility and development costs vs. licensing fees. Should the project be outsourced or carried out in-house? Additional issues regarding, for instance, security, turnaround time, hardware, software and product support cost also need to be addressed.

Few investors are in a position to go this route alone. Existing platforms such as RiskMetrics and Measurisk have emerged in recent years to offer a turnkey solution to investors who require full transparency. These third party financial service companies stand between a hedge fund manager willing to provide position details and investors willing to pay. These companies receive full detailed positions monthly, weekly or daily, depending on the manager, which they then process using proprietary risk analytics before making summary reports available to paying investors. To encourage managers to provide full position reports, a more condensed risk report is generally also provided to the managers.

The workhorse of these systems is the concept of Value-at-Risk (VaR), a measure of market sensitivity. This measure provides an estimate of the loss that could occur with a given probability over a certain horizon. This new standard of risk measure has proved very popular with consultants, investment boards and many other members of the investment community including academics. Statistically derived, it appears 'objective'. It is also intuitively appealing and very convenient for aggregating portfolios. Although a discussion of the merits of VaR is beyond the scope of this chapter, it suffices to note that this technique of analysis does not come without serious limitations. For example, VaR only reflects 'normal' market behaviour; it gives no information on the direction of exposure; and it provides no information on the potential magnitude of losses in the tail of the distribution of returns.

Although the usefulness of these VaR based systems is limited, their marketing appeal is undeniable, a fact that has not escaped the attention of many funds of hedge funds. However, because of the high subscription cost of these risk systems and the reluctance of many managers to provide position details, full transparency through third party risk platforms has been the route chosen by only a limited number of funds of hedge funds. The same cost considerations also make such a direct approach unappealing to a high net worth investor.

A weakness of the previous approaches to disclosure is that they still do not achieve the goal of transparency, that is, they still do little in revealing a manager's strategies and intentions. Consider, for example, a distressed securities portfolio. A routine VaR analysis of the senior notes held in the portfolio is likely to prove meaningless. Admittedly, full disclosure of securities and their prices may help investors determine how a manager or fund administrator is pricing the portfolio, and that prices are consistent with prime brokers' valuations. However, it will not shed any light on a manager's strategy and intentions. For example, the manager may hold defaulted corporate debt that is hard to price or has a very wide bid/ask spread, because he is anticipating a positive announcement in the short run that will increase their value with the intention of selling them shortly afterward. Others may be held for longer periods, waiting for the firm to come out of bankruptcy proceedings and receiving shares of equity before selling. Many other complex considerations may be involved. Unless a manager directly communicates his views and horizon for each security held, transparency is unlikely to be achieved even with the best analytical tools.

An alternative approach that seems to have been garnering more industry support is for fund managers to disclose portfolio summary statistics instead of detailed security positions. These statistics can be used by an investor in tandem with other reports to monitor overall portfolio exposure and risk. The information provided should be sufficient to clearly determine concentration levels, long and short exposure levels, leverage usage and levels of liquidity. Such an approach (a) is cost-effective, (b) is within the analytical reach of many investors and (c) allows for a timely assessment of a portfolio. It also provides quantitative and qualitative information without exposing proprietary trading information about the fund.

416

The good news is that a large number of managers are already providing such statistics on a monthly basis. Positions aggregated by, for instance, geography, sector, industry or credit ratings are routinely provided by managers, as is disclosure of their top five or 10 long and short positions. Transparency can be enhanced further if hedge fund managers provide substantive comments: (a) on the strategy level, especially if they are willing to elaborate on their intentions regarding sector or industry exposures, and (b) on the position level, by discussing the rationale behind their top holdings. Such analyses will not only contribute to the education of investors but will also allay fears and suspicions by giving investors an understanding of what their hedge fund managers are up to.

Hedge funds have been improving their disclosure not because of the pressure of impending regulation, but in response to the quiet workings of a competitive capital market. While regulators have debated standards of disclosure for hedge funds, competitive pressures have provided an incentive to disclose information voluntarily. Fund managers not willing to provide adequate disclosure are facing increasing penalties in the form of difficulties in their ability to retain existing investors and to attract additional investments, especially from institutional investors but also more high net worth individuals as well. Increasingly, many funds of hedge funds and institutional investors are requiring managers to agree to meet minimum transparency standards before they will invest with them.

Recent developments

Transparency also has been driven by the movement toward 'structured' products with either more regulatory oversight or greater built-in transparency. These products might prove to be a bridge from current hedge fund products that provide transparency on a not so consistent basis, to a platform of new, hybrid alternative products built to meet the increasing demands for 'safer', more transparent and regulated products. It is convenient to distinguish between structured products and registered hedge funds.

The two main types of structured products are: (a) principal protected notes and (b) private placement variable life insurance vehicles. Principal protected notes come in a variety of forms, but in the traditional structure a portion of investors' money is invested in zero coupon bonds and the remaining portion is invested in a fund of hedge funds. The bond portion guarantees repayment of the principal at maturity while the fund of funds portion is aimed at upside potential either directly or through warrants. There is a required liquidation of the fund of funds assets and immediate reinvestment into the risk-free asset should net asset value fall below a pre-set limit. Depending on the structure of the notes, exposure to the risky hedge fund portion could also be managed dynamically, leveraging and de-leveraging depending on performance. More recent structures have involved insurers or banks paying for participation in the fund upside with the insurance product being structured as a two-tranche senior/junior deal.

Private placement variable life insurance products (also referred to as 'insurance wraps') are portfolios of hedge funds 'wrapped' inside an insurance policy. Note that many hedge funds are limited partnerships. As such they are pass-through entities, meaning that all investment income is taxable on a current basis. Furthermore, investors may be subject to a current income tax liability even though the fund may not make any cash distribution of earnings. Insurance wraps can circumvent these problems by taking advantage of a section of the Internal Revenue Code which allows investments to accumulate tax-free provided that they are within a life insurance policy. Insurance wraps offer many additional benefits that do not concern us here. An important feature of insurance wraps is that policy investments must be held in segregated accounts. They require a structure that will qualify for 'look through' treatment under the diversification rules of Treasury Reg. 1.817(h) and avoid 'investor control'. That is, the policyholder under an insurance wrap may not pick and choose the underlying funds on an ongoing basis, but rather must rely on an independent adviser.

In order to: (a) satisfy providers of these principal guarantees and (b) effectively manage and monitor these structures and/or ensure that the insurance policy can meet its policy obligations such as death benefit payout, surrenders and loans, hedge funds participating in these structured products are generally held to higher standards of transparency with respect to pricing, risk management and reporting. Attractive liquidity terms are also required. The possibility of being 'stopped out' and having to liquidate does not permit investment in funds with long lock-up and redemption periods and other inflexible terms.

Finally, registered hedge funds are single or multi-manager products that comply with the terms of the Investment Company Act of 1940. Such funds can be made available to a wider range of investors by offering lower minimums. They may also become more marketable to pension funds and other institutional investors as they are not subject to the restrictions of the Employee Retirement Income Security Act that limits the amount of money that unregistered funds can attract from retirement plans to 25 per cent of total assets. However, with these benefits comes greater oversight not only from regulators but also independent directors, who face pressure to play a strong role in corporate governance and compliance. Such fiduciary responsibility is likely to translate into more stringent requirements for transparency and ongoing monitoring.

As registered funds and structured products grow in popularity and managers vie for these sources of capital, competitive pressures are expected to produce more voluntary compliance and disclosure.

---

* Editor's note: on 29 September 2003, shortly before this book went to press, the staff of the SEC issued its report entitled 'The Implications of the Growth of Hedge Funds', the culmination of its efforts following the Hedge Fund Roundtable held in May 2003. As of the date of this writing, the Commission itself had not taken any action in response to the report. One of the key recommendations of the staff was that the SEC consider 'requiring hedge fund advisers to register with the SEC as investment advisers, taking into account whether the benefits outweigh the burdens of registration'. In the staff's view, ' ... registration of hedge fund advisers would serve as a deterrent to fraud, encourage compliance and the adoption of compliance procedures, provide the SEC with important information ... and effectively raise the standards for investment in hedge funds from the "accredited investor" standard to that of "qualified client"'. See http://www.sec.gov/news/studies/hedgefunds0903.pdf for the full text of the report.

Part V

Hedge funds and public policy

Chapter 34

What bankers don't know

Henry Kaufman
Henry Kaufman & Company, Inc., New York, New York

Tears in the fabric of the global financial system appeared during the late summer of 1998. Stock markets in the United States and abroad tottered, declining 15 per cent or more from mid-year peaks. Private investors, banks, and other financial institutions suffered huge losses when Russia defaulted on rouble bonds, and the outstanding obligations of a long list of emerging market governments and corporations plunged in value. One big US hedge fund – Long-Term Capital Management – essentially went broke and had to be taken over by its creditors, with the Federal Reserve nervously hosting the proceedings.

Grave consequences loomed. A substantial slowing in economic activity became likely. More credit problems began to come to light and with it a greater preference for liquidity by lenders and investors. A debt liquidation ensued in the developing world and selectively in some parts of the industrialised world. A global recession became increasingly difficult to avoid.

Whatever the ultimate outcome, such disturbing events reflected a lack of leadership and of vigilance at a variety of levels and in a large number of countries. A number of self-proclaimed sophisticated people risked a great deal of money without demanding to know what they were getting into. It proves that neither investors, nor lenders, nor official regulatory agencies, know the extent of the amount of leverage that was being deployed by major participants in the global markets and no one knows who will be repaid and who won't.

Once again ignorance proved to be most conspicuous with regard to those risk exposures that are off-balance sheet, utilising financial derivatives. Whether in the form of futures, forwards, swaps, options, or securities pieced together from a combination of several of them, financial derivatives have been used not just to manage risk or to reduce risk, but to take sizeable speculative positions in the market place. Many derivatives create leverage by allowing users to magnify their purchases or sales of securities, much like they do when they borrow cash or securities to finance their activities.

The misnamed 'hedge funds' have been particularly aggressive in making use of derivatives to make leveraged bets on market movements rather than to hedge risks. If they are right, their profits are multiplied. But when markets move against them, their losses swell. In the case of Long-Term Capital Management, the losses swelled to near fatal magnitudes.

Why did banks, securities firms, and other major lenders fail to appreciate how dangerous it can be to lend to highly leveraged institutions such as hedge funds, especially through financial derivatives? I would give four reasons.

First was heightened competition among financial institutions. The nature of entrepreneurial finance is to stretch risk taking to enhance returns. The stock market had put lofty valuations on the shares of the largest financial institutions, implicitly sanctioning their activities in riskier lines of business. Competition was driving down profit margins in safer, more analysable areas. Lending to outfits like hedge funds was more than merely a source of prestige. It promised higher returns than attainable elsewhere. Getting involved in transactions in financial derivatives with these counterparties was an integral part of the relationship with the client – or so the rationale went. The competitive pressures were so intense that the bankers did not insist on doing proper due diligence. Their ignorance of how the money was being bet was sometimes breathtaking.

Second was complexity. Even those who would ordinarily be considered sophisticated bankers can sometimes get in over their heads when contending with the bewildering array of novel products created by specialists in financial derivatives. And it is often the most complex that are of interest to the highly leveraged portfolio managers. No one gave much thought as to how these instruments would behave at times of stress.

Third was misplaced infatuation with mathematics and quantification. The credo of many leveraged funds is to proclaim how ingenious their computer models are and bedazzle lenders. Never mind that the statistical properties of these models are far from robust, since they are estimated on the basis of past data that may or may not hold up under greatly changed financial circumstances. Lots of money has been lost on the assumption that a model that correctly predicts the past can predict the future.

Fourth was the illusion of boundless liquidity. When markets are rallying and the good times seem endless, portfolio managers and their bankers alike believe that they can buy or sell any security instantly without a significant impact on price. So portfolio managers pursue strategies that require a high volume of transactions, each yielding a small profit, while lenders view the collateral they hold as easily evaluated and readily marked to market. Those assumptions are nonsense during times of stress, such as were experienced in several sectors of the financial markets in 1998. And without liquidity and instant marketability, the poor computer models that drive many of the investing decisions of highly leveraged funds can't cope.

Up to now, the regulatory attitude toward hedge funds and highly leveraged portfolio management in general has been studied indifference, if not outright admiration. But that was before those renowned operators lost their Midas touch. And it was before the share prices of lending banks plummeted by a third or more in the space of a few weeks. And it was before the safety and soundness of the financial system was thought to be at risk from the unwinding of just one hedge fund's losing bets.

To conclude that putting in place tough restraints on hedge funds will cure the excesses in the financial markets is rather simplistic. The need is to put in place supervision and regulations that will limit excesses in all major financial markets and institutions.

Chapter 35

Hedge funds and dynamic hedging[1]

George Soros
Soros Fund Management, New York, New York

I welcome this opportunity to testify before your distinguished committee. I believe that the committee is right to be concerned about the stability of financial markets because financial markets have the potential to become unstable and require constant and diligent supervision to prevent serious dislocations. Recent price volatility, particularly in the market for interest rate instruments, suggests that it is appropriate to take a close look at the way markets operate.

A different view of markets

I must state at the outset that I am in fundamental disagreement with the prevailing wisdom. The generally accepted theory is that financial markets tend towards equilibrium and, on the whole, discount the future correctly. I operate using a different theory, according to which financial markets cannot possibly discount the future correctly because they do not merely discount the future; they help to shape it. In certain circumstances, financial markets can affect the so-called fundamentals which they are supposed to reflect. When that happens, markets enter into a state of dynamic disequilibrium and behave quite differently from what would be considered normal by the theory of efficient markets. Such boom/bust sequences do not arise very often, but when they do, they can be very disruptive, exactly because they affect the fundamentals of the economy.

The time is not sufficient to elaborate on my theory. I have done so in my book *The Alchemy of Finance*. The only theoretical point I want to make here is that a boom/bust sequence can develop only if the market is dominated by trend following behaviour. By trend following behaviour, I mean people buying in response to a rise in prices and selling in response to a fall in prices in a self-reinforcing manner. Lopsided trend following behaviour is necessary to produce a violent market crash, but not sufficient to bring one about.

The key question you need to ask, then, is what generates trend following behaviour? Hedge funds may be a factor and you are justified in taking a look at them, although, as far as my hedge funds are concerned, you are looking in the wrong place. There are at least two other factors which I consider much more relevant and deserving of closer scrutiny. One is the role of institutional investors in general and of mutual funds in particular. The second is the role of derivative instruments.

Institutional investors

The trouble with institutional investors is that their performance is usually measured relative to their peer group and not by an absolute yardstick. This makes them trend followers by definition. In the case of mutual funds, this tendency is reinforced by the fact that they are open-ended. When money is pouring in, they tend to maintain less-than-normal cash balances because they anticipate further inflows. When money is pouring out, they need to raise cash to take care of redemptions. There is nothing new about this, but mutual funds have grown tremendously, even more than hedge funds, and they have many new and inexperienced shareholders who have never invested in the stock market before.

Derivatives

The trouble with derivative instruments is that those who issue them usually protect themselves against losses by engaging in so-called delta, or dynamic, hedging. Dynamic hedging means, in effect, that if the market moves against the issuer, the issuer is forced to move in the same direction as the market, and thereby amplify the initial price disturbance. As long as price changes are continuous, no great harm is done, except perhaps to create higher volatility, which in turn increases the demand for derivative instruments. But if there is an overwhelming amount of dynamic hedging done in the same direction, price movements may become discontinuous. This raises the spectre of financial dislocation. Those who need to engage in dynamic hedging, but cannot execute their orders, may suffer catastrophic losses. This is what happened in the stock market crash of 1987. The main culprit was the excessive use of portfolio insurance. Portfolio insurance was nothing but a method of dynamic hedging. The authorities have since introduced regulations, so-called 'circuit breakers', which render portfolio insurance impractical, but other instruments which rely on dynamic hedging have mushroomed. They play a much bigger role in the interest rate market than in the stock market, and it is the interest rate market which has been most turbulent in recent weeks.

Dynamic hedging has the effect of transferring risk from customers to the market-makers and when market-makers all want to delta hedge in the same direction at the same time, there are no takers on the other side and the market breaks down.

The explosive growth in derivative instruments holds other dangers. There are so many of them, and some of them are so esoteric, that the risks involved may not be properly understood even by the most sophisticated of investors. Some of these instruments appear to be specifically designed to enable institutional investors to take gambles which they would otherwise not be permitted to take. For example, some bond funds have invested in synthetic bond issues which carry a 10- or 20-fold multiple of the normal risk within defined limits. And some other instruments offer exceptional returns because they carry the seeds of a total wipeout. It was instruments of this sort which forced the liquidation of a US$600 million fund specialising in so-called 'toxic waste', or the residue of collateralised mortgage obligations that generated a selling climax in the US bond market on 4 April 1994.

The issuers of many of these derivative instruments are commercial and investment banks. In the case of a meltdown, the regulatory authorities may find themselves obliged to step in to preserve the integrity of the system. It is in that light that the authorities have both a right and an obligation to supervise and regulate derivative instruments.

Generally, hedge funds do not act as issuers or writers of derivative instruments. They are more likely to be customers. Therefore, they constitute less of a risk to the system than the dynamic hedgers at the derivatives desks of financial intermediaries. Please do not confuse dynamic hedging with hedge funds. They have nothing in common except the word 'hedge'.

What are hedge funds?

I am not here to offer a blanket defence for hedge funds. Nowadays, the term is applied so indiscriminately that it covers a wide range of activities. The only thing they have in common is that the managers are compensated on the basis of performance and not as a fixed percentage of assets under management.

Our type of hedge fund invests in a wide range of securities and diversifies its risks by hedging, leveraging and operating in many different markets. It acts more like a sophisticated private investor than an institution handling other people's money. Since it is rewarded on absolute performance, it provides a healthy antidote to the trend following behaviour of institutional investors.

But the fee structure of hedge funds is not perfect. Usually there is an asymmetry between the upside and the downside. The managers take a share of the profits, but not of the losses; the losses are usually carried forward. As a manger slips into minus territory, he has a financial inducement to increase the risk to get back into positive fee territory, rather than to retrench as he ought to. This feature was the undoing of the hedge fund industry in the late 1960s, just as I entered the business.

The Quantum Group of Funds

I am proud to say that the Quantum Group of Funds, with which I am associated, is exempt from this weakness because the managers have a substantial ownership interest in the funds they manage. That is a key point. Our ownership is a direct and powerful incentive to practise sound money management. At Soros Fund Management, we have an operating history stretching over 25 years during which there was not a single occasion when we could not meet a margin call. We use options and more exotic derivatives sparingly. Our activities are trend bucking rather than trend following. We try to catch new trends early and in later stages we try to catch trend reversals. Therefore, we tend to stabilise rather than destabilise the market. We are not doing this as a public service. It is our style of making money.

So I must reject any assertion or implication that our activities are harmful or destabilising. That leaves, however, one other area of concern: we do use borrowed money and we could cause trouble if we failed to meet a margin call. In our case, the risk is remote, but I cannot speak for all hedge funds.

It has been our experience at Soros Fund Management that banks and securities firms exercise great care in establishing and monitoring our activities. As we mark our portfolios to market daily, and communicate with banks regularly, they can monitor their credit exposure. I believe that it is a sound and profitable business for them and that our activities are a far sight simpler to monitor than most of their activities.

Supervision and regulation

Nevertheless, this is an area that the regulatory authorities need to supervise and, if necessary, to regulate. If regulations are to be introduced, they ought to apply to all market participants equally. It would be wrong to single out hedge funds.

And if it comes to regulations, beware of the unintended consequences! For instance, it may seem advisable to introduce margin regulations on currency or bond transactions, but that may drive market participants to the use of options or other derivatives which may be even more destabilising. One of the driving forces behind the development of derivatives was a desire to escape regulation.

I should like to draw a distinction between supervision and regulation. I am for maximum supervision and minimum regulation. I should also like to draw a distinction between information gathering and disclosure. I think the authorities need a lot more information than the general public. In fact, information we are legally obliged to disclose has, on occasion, caused unwarranted price movements.

Let me conclude by saying that this is a propitious moment to assess the new risks created by new instruments and other new developments. Financial markets have recently suffered a serious enough correction that an inquiry is unlikely to precipitate the kind of dislocation which it ought to prevent.

I should like to emphasise that I see no imminent danger of a market crash or meltdown. We have just punctured a bit of a bubble that had developed in asset prices. As a result, market conditions are much healthier now than they were at the end of last year. I do not think that investors should be unduly fearful at this time.

This concludes my general remarks. I have answered your questions in writing and shall endeavour to answer any specific questions you may have now. Thank you Mr. Chairman, and the members of the committee, for providing me this opportunity to share my perspective with you.

Questions

Q: Top bank assets under management in bank trading accounts have grown over 500 per cent over the past four years. In fact, they are considerably larger than the assets of hedge funds. In what ways do hedge funds compete with bank trading accounts?

A: We are basically customers of banks, not competitors. But they do have proprietary trading accounts. They are more or less doing the same thing we are doing, and I think it is an area of legitimate concern, and an area for close supervision, I would say.

Q: Many instruments that companies, hedge funds and investment banks deal in are designed to limit risks of one kind or another. But does systemic risk increase or decrease? Would we be better off with somewhat smaller markets and somewhat less refined products? Or have we built up a quasi-gambling system?

A: The instruments of hedging transfer the risk from the individual to the system. As more of these instruments are used – because manufacturers and traders don't want to take a currency risk – more risk is passed on to the system. So there is a danger that at certain points you may have a discontinuous move. In currencies, you don't call it a crash, but an overshoot, a large move in the value of a currency. Since the risk has been passed on from the individual to the system, it behoves the people who are in charge of the system to provide stability. When everybody is out for themselves, they can destroy the system. This is the point I'm really trying to bring home. There is this danger.

Q: What do you do about it? Governments don't have near the resources of the private sector actors.

A: I think the people in charge of the monetary system need to coordinate economic policies so that currency fluctuations are not too great; so that you don't have fundamental imbalances.

Q: Do hedge funds move markets?

A: I am sure that they don't because Soros Fund Management represents about 15 per cent of the hedge fund industry. And we are probably more active in currencies than the average hedge fund. I'm sure that our average daily trading does not exceed US$500 million. Now, that US$500 million is a very large amount of money in absolute terms, but in terms of the US$1 trillion or more that trades daily, it is something like four-tenths of 1 per cent of the total volume. I think that puts it in perspective.

Q: You say that the banks can monitor their loans to hedge funds fairly easily, that they have good information, mark to market daily, and so on. And your investors are sophisticated, willing to take market risks and, presumably, could afford to lose their investment if that is what happens. So what's the public policy issue here?

A: We are subject to the same rules and regulations that apply to everyone as far as disclosure is concerned. So, for instance, our portfolio is available to the public the same way as any other large institutional portfolio. We have reporting obligations. If we own more than a certain percentage of a company, we have to report. So far as markets are concerned, we are actually regulated in exactly the same way as any other institution. Where we are not regulated is in our relationship with our shareholders. In other words, there is no Securities and Exchange Commission protecting the shareholders against the misdeeds of the management. But since I am a large shareholder in the funds that I manage, I think that the shareholders have a protection that is more reliable than any regulation could possibly be – namely, I am putting my own money where I am putting their money. There is no need for shareholder protection in the case of this kind of partnership.

Q: You said in your testimony that you fully support more information sharing and more supervision.

A: I think that the authorities ought to be in a position to assess, let's say, the role of hedge funds in the recent market decline. They ought to be able to put their hands on some kind of information. And we certainly are ready to cooperate with them. I think it would probably be detrimental, however, if we were forced to disclose our positions more or less in real time. That would make it very difficult for us, and I think it would probably cause unwarranted trend following by other investors, although they ought to know better. So I don't think that more disclosure would be good. But if the authorities feel they don't have enough information, we are certainly at their disposal to provide them with it.

Q: You warned us to beware of unintended consequences in designing regulations. Could you give us an example of where this principle could work to our disadvantage?

A: One of the obvious things one would think of is to introduce margin regulations for bond and currency transactions. There are no such margin regulations at the present time. There is a margin requirement for stock transactions. You have to put up 50 per cent in cash. You don't have anything like it in fixed interest – in bonds. And yet bonds can also vary in price. So maybe there should be a margin requirement on bonds, perhaps of 5 per cent or 10 per cent. But if you establish too onerous a margin, then instead of buying bonds, investors will buy options on bonds, because that is a way to avoid putting up a margin.

Q: Are not derivatives materially changing in terms of their impact on the global and on the domestic market?
A: They are. A lot of new and more esoteric instruments have been brought into existence. There has been a remarkable shift of the terrain as far as derivatives are concerned. It is an appropriate area for investigation. If, for example, you look at recently developed instruments that separate interest from principal, they are very interesting instruments. But I am not quite sure that they are really necessary.

Q: What do you believe to be the regulatory implications of the growth of finance offshore?
A: I think that any kind of regulation now needs to be international. The main regulation that has been imposed is the Bank for International Settlements' capital requirements, an international agreement. I think the issue that now needs to be addressed is capital requirements with regard to derivative instruments, and I think this needs to be addressed in an international forum.

---

[1]   An edited version of testimony given to the US House of Representatives Committee on Banking, Finance and Urban Affairs on 13 April 1994.

Chapter 36

Hedge funds and financial markets: implications for policy

Barry Eichengreen
University of California, Berkeley, California

Donald J. Mathieson
International Monetary Fund, Washington, DC

Introduction

During the 1990s, episodes of instability in international financial markets heightened the attention of government officials and others to the role played by institutional investors, and hedge funds in particular. This was the case in 1992, following the crisis affecting the Exchange Rate Mechanism (ERM) of the European Monetary System. It was the case in 1994, a period of turbulence in international bond markets. It was again the case in 1997 in the wake of the financial upheavals in Asia. In each case, it was suggested that hedge funds precipitated major movements in asset prices, either through the sheer volume of their own transactions or via the tendency of other market participants to follow their lead.

Yet for all this attention, little concrete information was available about the extent of hedge funds' activities. No consensus existed on their implications for financial stability and on how policy should be adapted. The goal of this chapter is therefore to provide a basis for understanding these issues better.[1]

Hedge fund operations

Better understanding starts with clearer definition. Hedge funds can be defined as eclectic investment pools, organised as private partnerships and often resident offshore for tax and regulatory purposes, whose managers are paid on a fee-for-performance basis. Their prospectuses and legal status place few restrictions on their portfolios and transactions. Consequently, their principal partners and managers are free to flexibly use a variety of investment techniques, including short positions, transactions in derivative securities and leverage, to raise returns and cushion risk.

The questions posed in this chapter include the following. In what kind of activities do hedge funds engage? How large are their assets? Under what circumstances might their investment and trading activities significantly influence market outcomes? To what supervision and regulation are they subject? How should exchange rate and debt management policies, financial market regulation, and monetary and fiscal policies more generally be adapted to the presence of these large investors in international markets?

It is important to emphasise the fragmentary nature of information on this subject. Hedge funds are a rapidly growing part of the financial sector, but they are not subject to the same reporting and disclosure requirements as banks and mutual funds. In the United States, the fact that hedge funds operate through private placements and restrict share ownership to high net worth individuals and institutions frees them from many of the disclosure and regulation requirements of the Securities and Exchange Commission (SEC).* Offshore funds are subject to even less regulation. This makes it difficult to construct a comprehensive enumeration of hedge funds, much less to assemble information on their activities.

Hedge funds and market moves

In the popular view, hedge funds are often among the first investors to take positions against unsustainable currency pegs and other misaligned asset prices. According to one variant of the argument, through their aggressive use of leverage hedge funds are able to take large positions that precipitate major market moves, for example, by selling a currency short in such quantities that the issuing central bank finds its reserves depleted and is forced to abandon its exchange rate peg. In another variant of the argument, hedge funds may be small relative to international markets, but because fund managers have reputations as acute prognosticators, news of their positions can prompt other investors to follow their lead, and the combined transactions of the leaders and followers can precipitate major market moves. In this view, hedge funds play an important role in the herd behaviour that amplifies volatility in international markets.[2]

There is scant empirical evidence with which to attempt to verify these hypotheses. The fragmentary data that exist on the hedge fund industry suggest that hedge fund capital, and in particular the capital of 'macro' hedge funds that take large directional positions in currency markets, is small relative to the resources at the command of other institutional investors. At the same time, hedge fund capital is substantial relative to smaller emerging markets, although macro funds concentrate a substantial share of their resources in particular emerging markets only under exceptional circumstances.

The limited econometric evidence that is available on herding, reported in a later section, provides some indication that hedge funds herd together, but it does not suggest that other investors regularly follow hedge funds' lead. Nor does the case study evidence all point in one direction. It is possible to point to market moves where news of hedge funds' trades and positions provided the signal for other investors to follow, the 1992 ERM crisis being the most frequently cited example. However, it is equally possible to cite episodes where other investors were first to take a position against a currency peg, and where hedge funds, instead of leading, in fact followed the market. Similarly, it is possible to point to instances where hedge funds took a position against a currency and lost instead of making money. Nor are hedge funds' activities limited to shorting currencies and other assets. In a number of important instances, hedge funds have taken long positions in depreciating currencies, for example buying them in the wake of a crisis in anticipation of their subsequent recovery.

Thus, isolating the role of hedge funds in a particular crisis, such as that in Asia in 1997, requires a detailed analysis of the episode in question. Below we provide such an analysis.

Policy implications and options

Regulation of collective investment vehicles can be justified on three grounds: consumer protection, systemic risk and market integrity. Few regulators see a need for stricter regulation on the first two of these three grounds. Large investors, in the regulators' view, can generally fend for themselves and the systemic risk issues raised by hedge funds, although of concern, are viewed as largely under control by existing regulatory measures.

This leaves market integrity. The concern here is that hedge funds can dominate or manipulate markets. In the case of the foreign exchange market, the concern that individual traders should not dominate or manipulate the market reflects the authorities' desire for autonomy for the conduct of macroeconomic policy and insulation from market pressures. It reflects the fear that large traders can precipitate a crisis that arbitrarily shifts an economy from a 'good' to a 'bad' equilibrium.

Limited measures to strengthen supervision, regulation and market transparency might be considered to deal with this concern. It would be possible, for instance, to strengthen and replicate in other markets the large trade and position reporting mechanisms in place in countries like the United States as a way of rendering hedge fund operations more transparent. It would be possible to limit the ability of hedge funds and other investors to take positions in financial markets by requiring banks and brokers to raise margin and collateral requirements. Similarly, it would be possible to limit the ability of hedge funds to take short positions in currency markets by restricting the ability of financial institutions to lend domestic assets to non-residents.

However, the analysis that follows does not suggest a strong case for supervisory and regulatory measures such as these targeted specifically at hedge funds. Hedge funds, after all, are only one part of the constellation of institutional investors active in international financial markets. The analysis suggests that the most important action policymakers can take to protect their economies against uncomfortable market movements is to avoid offering one-way bets in the form of inconsistent policies and indefensible currency pegs. They need to adopt policies that keep their economies away from the 'zone of vulnerability' where multiple equilibria and self-fulfilling speculative attacks can arise. They need to strengthen the ability of clearance, settlement and payments systems to withstand asset-price volatility. In addition, they need to provide better information about government policy and private sector financial conditions in order to weaken the tendency for incompletely informed investors to 'follow the herd' and thereby magnify the repercussions of the positions taken by large institutional investors, including but not limited to hedge funds.

The hedge fund industry

Hedge funds are private investment pools. In the United States, they typically offer their shares in private placements and limit the number of investors to make use of exemptions to regulations under the Securities Act of 1933, the Securities Exchange Act of 1934 and the Investment Company Act of 1940. They are managed on a fee-for-performance basis; typically, management is rewarded by a 1 per cent management fee and 20 per cent of profits, although management and investment fees vary. Most funds require shareholders to provide advance notification if they wish to withdraw funds: notice can vary from 30 days for funds with more liquid investments to three years for other funds.

Diversity within the hedge fund industry

Two problems arise as soon as one attempts to build on these regularities. First, practices vary enormously. Market participants distinguish two main classes of funds: firstly, macro hedge funds taking large directional (unhedged) positions in national markets based on 'top-down' analysis of macroeconomic and financial conditions; and secondly, relative value funds that take bets on the relative prices of closely related securities (Treasury bills and bonds, for example) and are less exposed to macroeconomic fluctuations. Relative value funds tend to be more highly levered than macro funds because the amount of capital needed to establish a position is relatively small on the instruments they hold.

As soon as one looks more closely at these sub-categories, one detects further diversity. Some macro hedge funds take positions mainly in mature markets; others take positions mainly in emerging markets. A number of the largest macro funds do both and spread their holdings across equities, bonds and currencies (both short and long positions), and hold commodities and other less liquid assets such as real estate in both developed and emerging markets. However, the majority of macro funds hold a more limited range of assets. In all but the most exceptional circumstances, only a fraction of their portfolios is allocated to emerging markets; this reflects the risk of a concentrated stake and the costs of establishing and liquidating large positions in smaller markets. Only dedicated emerging market funds, which are a small minority of the hedge fund universe, allocate a substantial share of their portfolios to positions in emerging markets.

Similarly, within the relative value category one finds hedge funds specialising in fixed-income arbitrage, merger arbitrage and distressed securities arbitrage (that these activities are referred to as arbitrage should not be taken to imply that they are free of risk). Most funds engaging in these activities limit their holdings to the mature markets, if not the United States, because their institutional knowledge does not carry over to other countries.

The fuzzy line between hedge funds and other institutional investors

A second problem with defining and describing hedge funds is that other investors engage in many of the same practices. Individual investors and their institutional investor counterparts buy stocks on margin. Commercial banks use leverage in the sense that a fractional-reserve banking system is a group of levered financial institutions whose total assets and liabilities are several times their capital. The proprietary trading desks of commercial and investment banks take positions, buy and sell derivatives, and alter their portfolios in the same manner as hedge funds. Insurance companies and university endowments are among the most important investors in hedge funds. For all these reasons, any line between hedge funds and other institutional investors is increasingly arbitrary.

Quantitative dimensions

No reliable estimates exist of the number of hedge funds and the value of hedge fund capital. Commercial services that report on hedge funds rely on fund managers for information. This may bias upward average returns, since the worst performing managers are least likely to provide information. Newer, smaller funds may be picked up only with a lag. Estimates of hedge fund capital may suffer from double counting insofar as some commercial services combine data for funds of funds (hedge funds that invest in other hedge funds) with other categories.

Above all, there is the problem of who to include. Should one include individuals or family groups taking highly levered positions? Should one include limited partnerships or limited liability companies that invest primarily in assets other than public securities and financial derivatives, or that do not use leverage or short selling? Should one include managed futures funds, which limit their activities to futures markets? Differences in how the various commercial services answer these questions help to account for their widely varying estimates of the total number of hedge funds and hedge fund capital under management.

According to Managed Account Reports, LLC (MAR), the number of funds came to more than 1,100 in 1997 (the year of the Asian financial crisis, which is the focus of this article), of which approximately one-quarter were funds of funds. The corresponding estimates of capital were just under US$110 billion including funds of funds, and US$90 billion excluding them. Of this US$90 billion total, US$30 billion was in the hands of macro funds and US$31 billion in the hands of global funds.[3]

While there are good reasons to think that these data, based on a relatively narrow definition of the hedge fund universe, provide a lower bound on the size of the industry at that time, there is no question about the implication, namely that hedge fund capital pales in comparison with capital of other institutional investors. In the mature markets, the assets of institutional investors exceed US$20 trillion. Moreover, these other institutional investors engage in many of the same practices as hedge funds. This creates doubt that hedge funds can dominate, or corner, particular markets under most circumstances.

Use of leverage and derivatives

Some long-established macro funds regard fees on complex derivatives as prohibitive and make little use of them. They see it as possible to take positions in anticipation of large market moves more cost effectively by using 'plain vanilla' forwards and futures. Some newer macro funds do, however, pursue more specialised trading strategies, using at least some complex derivative securities. Relative value funds are also inclined to use derivatives insofar as their core activity is trolling for mis-priced securities, which may themselves be hidden within complex derivatives that combine several underlying assets.

Hedge funds obtain leverage by buying securities on margin, putting up collateral, and/or using collateralised borrowing in repo markets.[4] Hence, their use of leverage is correlated with the mix of assets in their portfolios, those arbitraging US Treasury securities typically being more highly levered than those taking long positions in emerging equity markets.[5] In practice, neither hedge funds nor those who provide them with credit think in terms of leverage; rather they continuously 'stress test' their portfolios, attempting to predict the drawdown that will come with a two or three standard deviation market move.

This makes it difficult to generalise about hedge funds' use of leverage. In 1997, Van Hedge Fund Advisors estimated that 70 per cent of hedge funds used leverage but that only 16 per cent borrowed more than one dollar for every one dollar of capital.[6] Macro funds used leverage more aggressively: 83 per cent of the macro funds surveyed by Van Hedge Fund Advisors acknowledge using leverage, and more than 30 per cent borrowed more than a dollar for every dollar of capital. Some funds of course levered their capital many more times than this. Market participants suggest that macro funds lever their capital four to seven times on average.

A look ahead

Most market participants see the growth of the hedge fund industry as a normal corollary of financial development. Individual and institutional investors wish to diversify their portfolios with a variety of investments having returns that are not highly correlated. This suggests that hedge-fund-style investment vehicles are likely to grow more important in the future.

Indeed, the existence of a growing client base willing to pay performance fees is inducing entry by independent investment managers, while investment banks and securities houses for their part are setting up hedge fund look-alikes to take advantage of their brand name. As these branded leveraged funds grow in number and size, the line of demarcation between hedge funds and other institutional investors becomes increasingly difficult to draw.

Some commentators suggest that entry and maturation will mean that the supernormal profits that some hedge fund investors have come to expect will be severely reduced due to competition. Hedge funds that offer extraordinary profits will have to assume extraordinary risks. The counter-argument is that because hedge funds are freer than, say, mutual funds to go short as well as long, they may be able to continue offering more attractive risk–return packages.

Hedge funds and market dynamics

This section describes the core principles of the investment strategies of the macro hedge funds that are most active in currency markets. Building on this analysis, it considers the possibility that hedge funds play a distinctive role in the herd behaviour that may sometimes characterise those markets. It analyses some institution-based arguments for why hedge funds are less likely than other institutional investors to engage in positive-feedback trading that amplifies market volatility.

Investment strategies

The diversity of investment strategies that is a defining characteristic of the hedge fund industry applies even within the sub-category of macro hedge funds that engage in 'top-down' country analysis and are most likely to take large positions in currency markets. That said, it is possible to point to several common characteristics of the strategies utilised by managers of these funds.

First, managers of macro funds seek to identify countries where macroeconomic fundamentals are far out of line, so that changes in asset prices (and the associated profits) will be large when they finally occur. Investors are aware that macro funds assume considerable risk, in return for which they expect considerable returns. Managers therefore have an incentive to identify cases where they anticipate large changes in asset prices.

Second, managers are especially attracted to investments where the risk of large capital losses is effectively nil – for example, to an exchange rate that may be devalued but under no circumstances will be revalued. This explains their focus on countries with currency pegs.

Third, hedge funds are most likely to take large positions when the cost of funding is low. Cheap funding allows them to take and hold a position even when they are uncertain about the timing of events. For example, they may expect a country to devalue with significant probability but be uncertain about the date. When funding is cheap, they can take and hold a position against that currency without worrying excessively about the cost.

Fourth, hedge fund managers are attracted to liquid markets, where they can do large trades at low cost. Having to pay a hundred basis points when putting on a position and another hundred basis points when taking it off can wipe out an otherwise attractive profit opportunity and neutralise the advantages of cheap funding. In emerging markets in particular, limited liquidity and the limited size of accepted deals can constrain the ability of hedge funds and other investors to build up positions. The bank that is the counterparty to such transactions would normally limit the size because of the difficulty of offloading them. Breaking the transaction into smaller components with different counterparties is possible but involves additional cost, takes additional time and creates additional price uncertainty in execution. Moreover, where the government has capital controls in place or restricts the ability of domestic banks to do business with offshore counterparties, hedge funds may find it more difficult to put on positions than commercial and investment banks that operate both offshore and onshore. Finally, managers are wary of being identified as on the other side of government or central bank transactions for fear of economic retaliation or political retribution. Anonymity is particularly difficult to maintain in smaller, less liquid markets.

Herding and market dynamics

One popular generalisation is that hedge funds are nimble and quick off the mark. Their managers have a reputation for astuteness. The rumour that hedge funds are taking a position may thus encourage other investors to follow. Hedge funds' transactions, especially when they are large, will not escape the notice of other investors. Thus, hedge funds can serve as the lead steer when the financial herd begins to move. The recent theoretical literature in which foreign exchange markets are characterised by multiple equilibria suggests that such 'lead steers' can be important. In these models they can precipitate a crisis in two ways. First, they can themselves undertake a volume of sales sufficient to drive interest rates to levels that the authorities regard as unacceptably high, leading them to abandon a currency peg that they would otherwise be prepared to maintain. Second, they can serve as the leaders who other smaller traders follow. In this case it will be unnecessary for large traders to actually take large positions, they only need to signal their intention of doing so. This mechanism is consistent with models of herding in foreign exchange markets.

That said, there is also reason to be sceptical that hedge funds are always the leaders in market moves. Hedge funds have low overheads; a small staff can mean that they have limited capacity to monitor conditions simultaneously in many markets. Many are consumers rather than producers of information (relying on the publications of, among others, the IMF). Insofar as other institutional investors have better access to information and more extensive research capability, hedge funds may in turn follow their lead.

Systematic evidence on these relationships is scanty. One relevant study is Wei and Kim (1997), who analysed the correlation between the positions taken by large foreign exchange traders (including commercial banks and other financial entities) and subsequent exchange rate changes, and found no evidence of an association. They concluded that this casts doubt on the assumption that large participants like hedge funds have better information about future exchange rate movements or are otherwise better able to predict market moves.

Another relevant study is Kodres and Pritsker (1997), who analysed data reported to the Commodity Futures Trading Commission by broker-dealers, commercial banks, foreign banks, hedge funds, insurance companies, mutual funds, pension funds, and savings and loans who took large positions in futures markets.[7] The authors found that herding within their various groups of institutional investors is statistically significant for some but not all futures contracts, but that it explains no more than 13 per cent, and in most cases less than 5 per cent, of total position changes among large participants. Hedge funds are found to herd among themselves in the S&P 500 index contract and the three-month Eurodollar contract. Smaller funds were detected as herding with larger ones in the Japanese yen contract and the S&P 500 index contract.

However, given that hedge funds are small relative to other investors, it is more important to determine whether those other investors follow the hedge funds' lead. We therefore extended this analysis to test whether there was a significant tendency for other categories of investors to take the same positions as hedge funds in the current or immediately subsequent period. Here the evidence is mixed or actually negative. There is in fact a negative correlation between the positions of hedge funds and the positions of other traders in the same period, and there is little correlation between the positions of hedge funds in the immediate past period and the current positions of other traders. There is little evidence here, in other words, that hedge funds play a singular role in herding in financial markets.

Feedback trading

While hedge funds have the flexibility to take short positions, they can also be the first to take long positions in currencies that have depreciated in the wake of a speculative attack, providing much-needed liquidity to illiquid markets and helping the currency to establish a bottom. The expectation on the part of their clients that hedge funds will make above-normal returns will, other things being equal, discourage managers from buying the same assets being purchased by other investors or shorting the same assets being unloaded by other investors, as the prices of those assets will already reflect moves by others.

Thus, while managers of macro funds search for fundamentally overvalued currencies against which to go short, they also search for currencies that have recently depreciated and are trading for prices lower than warranted by fundamentals, with the goal of buying them on the rebound. In this sense they can function as 'stabilising speculators'.

There is some evidence consistent with this view. Kodres and Pritsker (1997) find that hedge funds, and large hedge funds in particular, tend to negative feedback trade, that is, their current position changes depend negatively on past price changes. They buy when prices fall and sell when prices rise, which, other things being equal, should stabilise the markets.

There are two reasons to think that hedge funds may be less inclined than other investors toward 'positive feedback' trading strategies that amplify market moves. First, hedge funds, unlike most mutual funds, are not bound by their prospectuses to invest inflows of funds in the same manner as existing capital. A mutual fund that enjoys high returns may attract new investors and be bound by its prospectus to buy more of the recently appreciated asset; hedge funds have more flexibility.

Second, other institutional investors may be forced to liquidate declining positions and thus sell into a falling market. Other institutional investors may be forced to cut their losses by their internal controls. A mutual fund that makes losses may suffer withdrawals. A mutual fund manager who allows losses to mount in anticipation of a subsequent reversal may find himself a former mutual fund manager before that reversal takes place, which creates an understandable reluctance to let the position ride. Hedge funds may be better able to ride out these fluctuations because their investors are often locked in for substantial periods and because some have credit lines on which they can draw when asked to put up additional margin or collateral. On the other hand, pension fund managers and insurance company directors operating under relatively inflexible mandates regarding portfolio composition may be compelled to purchase assets whose prices have fallen in order to restore the overall balance of asset allocation.

Supervision and regulation

Regulations affecting collective investment vehicles such as hedge funds fall under three headings: those motivated by issues of investor protection, those related to issues of market integrity, and those related to issues of systemic risk.

The first category of regulation focuses on ensuring that small investors receive adequate information about the risks of their investments. However, since participation in hedge funds tends to be limited to high-wealth individuals and institutions, hedge funds are generally exempt from regulations promulgated on these grounds. Regulations covering issues of market integrity are designed to ensure a level playing field for all market participants. Typically, these regulations (insider trading restrictions, position limits, order execution priorities, restrictions on the ability to 'corner' or 'squeeze' a market, and so on) apply to all participants, including hedge funds. Most transaction and large position reporting requirements serve to both protect the integrity of markets, by assuring all participants that those with undue influence in particular markets will be observed (and reprimanded) by the authorities, and monitor systemic risk. Systemic risk is also limited by prudential regulations on large institutions, typically banks, brokers and other financial intermediaries that are designed to ensure they are adequately monitoring and managing their exposure to counterparties and not extending credit imprudently. Hedge funds are included among the relevant counterparties, and regulators, when interviewed in 1997, seemed generally satisfied that they pose no special problems of systemic risk. However, they expressed concern that the difficulty of obtaining information on hedge funds complicates the efforts of the counterparties to assess the creditworthiness of potential hedge fund customers and that not all banks have the expertise needed to evaluate the credit risk associated with some hedge funds' complicated derivatives holdings. The collapse of the mega-hedge fund Long-Term Capital Management in August 1998 confirmed that these problems of transparency can be serious and that relying on credit providers and counterparties to monitor the risk taken on by hedge funds might not suffice. This episode, together with the efforts of hedge funds to broaden their customer base, has breathed new life into the debate over the need for further regulation.

Hedge funds and recent crises

This section reviews what is known about hedge funds' activities in episodes of market turbulence during the 1990s, with particular attention to emerging markets in 1997.

The 1992 ERM crisis

The 1992 ERM crisis is the episode where hedge funds are most frequently cited as having played an important role. The prologue was the flow of capital into high-yielding ERM currencies between 1987 and 1991 in what was known as the 'convergence play'. This was a trend in which hedge funds participated. The key ingredients were cheap funding (in Deutschmarks, among other currencies), attractive yields in countries such as Italy, and the belief that exchange rates, having been credibly pegged, were unlikely to move against investors sufficiently to offset the interest differential.

However, starting in 1992, problems of competitiveness cast into doubt the assumptions underlying the convergence play. Italy's multilateral relative unit labour costs rose strongly, by some 20 per cent, in the 16 quarters leading up to the crisis. Worries that the lira was overvalued were heightened by the country's deteriorating current account and weakening profitability of businesses. Sterling appreciated strongly in the period preceding the United Kingdom's 1990 entry into the ERM, creating comparable worries of overvaluation, and the current account deficit widened in 1992. Finland and Sweden suffered massive external shocks because of the collapse of their trade with Russia. On top of this, Denmark's rejection of the Maastricht Treaty in its June 1992 referendum cast into doubt the priority European countries attached to their currency pegs.

All this meant that countries for which the convergence trade had been a source of funding for their current account deficits found it more difficult to obtain external finance, and that in turn implied that the exchange rate stability upon which the convergence trade was predicated might prove an illusion. Seen from this perspective, the decline of the US dollar (which fell by 17 per cent against the Deutschmark between mid-March and early September 1992, further eroding European competitiveness) and the 75 basis point increase in the Bundesbank's official discount rate on 16 July (which increased the cost of funding) were only the final nails in the coffin.

Hedge funds were early to recognise the significance of these trends and to position themselves accordingly.[8] They participated (although they were far from the only players) in the build-up of long positions in the heyday of the convergence play. They participated (although they were again far from the only players) when investors unwound these long positions, and they were among the first to begin shorting European currencies. They entered into over-the-counter forward sale contracts of European currencies with banks in anticipation of being able to buy back those currencies at lower prices after their realignment. The banks covered their positions by selling an equivalent amount of the currency on the spot market and entering into currency swaps of the same maturity as the forward contracts to cover the foreign exchange maturity mismatch.[9]

How large were these transactions? The short answer is that no one knows. One well-known macro fund that reportedly accounted for about 15 per cent of hedge fund capital was able to use collateral and margining to fund a US$10 billion short position in sterling. However, other macro funds did not make equally aggressive use of leverage to short sterling.[10] Hedge funds as a group are also reported to have made profits taking short positions in the forward foreign exchange market in Italian lire.[11]

Thus, if hedge funds played a role in precipitating the crisis, they did so by acting as market leaders that other institutional investors followed. Their actions in 1992 'to position themselves favourably for possible exchange rate realignments in the ERM apparently served as a signal for other institutional funds managers to re-examine their own . . . positions,' in the words of the 1993 Capital Markets Report. 'Thus, although hedge funds have less than US$10 billion [sic] in capital, their potential influence on forex markets [was] larger.'[12] However, mutual funds, pension funds, insurance companies and non-financial corporations provided the 'real financial muscle'; pension funds, insurance companies and mutual funds in Canada, Germany, Japan, the United Kingdom and the United States alone had more than US$11 trillion under management.

Bond market turbulence in 1994

Hedge funds, proprietary traders at banks and securities houses, and institutional investors were again viewed as playing a significant role in the bond market turbulence of 1994. Hedge fund capital had increased significantly (doubling by some estimates) in the second half of

1993 as high-income investors searched for yield in the prevailing low interest rate environment. While they were far from the only investors to take such positions, hedge funds led the march back into European bonds (especially high-yielding bonds) once calm returned to foreign exchange markets in the second half of the year.[13] The widening of ERM margins from 2.25–15 per cent in August 1993 encouraged the belief that European interest rates would fall on the grounds that authorities wishing to stimulate economic activity now had more room to cut interest rates. Given that recovery was slower to get under way in Europe than in the United States, it was expected that European central banks would be quicker to capitalise on the opportunity. Similarly the depressed state of the Japanese economy implied lower interest rates there than in the United States. Managers funded their European bond positions in yen, capitalising on the low level of interest rates in Japan. With interest differentials seen as increasingly favouring dollar-denominated fixed-income assets, they went long on the dollar and shorted the yen and the Deutschmark.

In the event, expectations of falling European interest rates were disappointed by two 25 basis point increases in US rates, in February and March 1994 (reflecting the strength of the US economy), the stabilisation of Japanese rates (reflecting the buoyancy of equity markets in Japan) and a decision by the Bundesbank Council on 17 February not to lower official rates. Bond yields rose sharply throughout the mature markets from 50 basis points to more than 150 basis points between 3 February and 30 March 1994, as hedge funds and other investors scrambled to close out their long positions.

However, hedge funds as a group did not make large profits on these market movements. On the contrary: having placed large bets that interest rates would decline, they suffered heavy losses when this did not occur. Indeed, although they had double-digit rates of return in 1993, most categories of hedge funds lost money in 1994.

The 1994–95 Mexican crisis

Hedge funds played a limited role in the next episode of financial market turbulence, the Mexican crisis of 1994–95. Studies concluded that domestic residents and not international investors played the leading role in the crisis.[14] In a world of globalised financial markets, the studies concluded, foreign investors managing internationally diversified portfolios may find it difficult to keep abreast of conditions in a myriad of countries. The smaller the emerging market, the less the incentive for large investors to do so. Consequently, domestic residents with a comparative advantage in accessing and processing the relevant information may be first to take a position against a currency peg. In addition, the deregulation of domestic financial markets and international financial transactions, which long inhibited position-taking by domestic residents, makes it easier for them to do so.[15]

The structural characteristics of developing countries' financial markets may have prevented hedge funds and other international investors from playing a large role in the 1994–95 currency crises.[16] In Mexico, as in other emerging markets, hedge funds and proprietary traders were prevented from borrowing the domestic currency from domestic banks against a small margin in order to sell it forward, reflecting moral persuasion by the authorities and restrictions on capital account convertibility. Even where they might have been able to borrow the domestic currency, they worried about the ability of their domestic counterparties to deliver on the forward contract due to prospective capital controls and possible bankruptcies of the counterparties.

Interim summary

Several regularities emerge from this review of earlier episodes. First, while hedge funds sometimes take sizeable positions, so do banks, corporates and institutional investors, all of whom manage assets many times larger than those of the hedge funds. Second, while there is some evidence, especially for 1992, that hedge funds can be early to take positions against shaky currency pegs, in most cases that evidence is only anecdotal. Third, although hedge funds made substantial profits betting on changes in macroeconomic variables in 1992, they did not make money on all their forward foreign exchange market positions in that year, and they made substantial losses from such bets in 1994. Their forecasts are not infallible, nor does emulating their positions guarantee profits. Fourth, hedge funds worry about the liquidity and the risk of their positions, not just about the return, and are less inclined to take large positions in small, relatively illiquid markets.

The 1997 crisis in emerging markets

The process leading up to this crisis extends back some years. The story begins with the markets' enthusiasm for the fixed-income debt of emerging economies, in particular of high-growth East Asia, starting with Malaysia and then extending to Indonesia, Thailand and other countries. Hedge funds were initially long in these markets.[17] Their positions were paralleled by those of other institutional investors, including commercial and investment banks who built up the largest books in the carry trade.

International investors were encouraged to establish and maintain these positions in, but not limited to, fixed-income markets by low interest rates in the major financial centres. They funded themselves in the markets of industrialised countries and invested in East Asia. The ample credit of which they made use reflected the low level of interest rates in Japan and the United States.[18] Using low-cost funding to buy high-yielding East Asian fixed-income securities was attractive so long as East Asian exchange rates did not move. In the case of Thailand, in 18 of the 20 quarters through the second quarter of 1997 this carry trade was profitable, the pegged exchange rate ruling out large exchange rate surprises. (See Exhibits 36.1 and 36.2; for details see Exhibit 36.3.) Hedge funds participated in this build-up, although they were not dominant players in the carry trade, in which commercial banks, investment banks, pension funds, mutual funds and other institutional investors all participated.

Notwithstanding the stability of the Thai baht, a growing number of investors began to worry that the period of financial stability might be drawing to a close. The first episode of pressure on the currency was in July 1996, following the collapse of the Bangkok Bank of Commerce and the central bank's injection of liquidity to support the financial system. The second episode was in early 1997, following the release in January of disappointing fiscal and export performance data. Hanbo's collapse in January 1997 may also have been important for changing investors' perceptions of Asian economic and financial prospects. International investors who were important players in the carry trade began closing out their positions. At this stage, the liquidation of long positions in Thai securities by domestic corporates and banks, proprietary trading desks of commercial and investment banks, treasuries and foreign exchange desks of the major money centre banks, mutual funds, hedge funds and retail investors was probably more important in weakening the baht than short sales.[19]

Exhibit 36.1

US dollar carry trades in the Thai baht, 1992–97

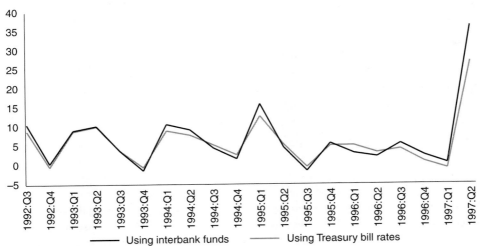

Sources: Bloomberg; International Monetary Fund, *International Financial Statistics*; and IMF staff estimates.

Exhibit 36.2

Japanese yen carry trades in the Thai baht, 1992–97

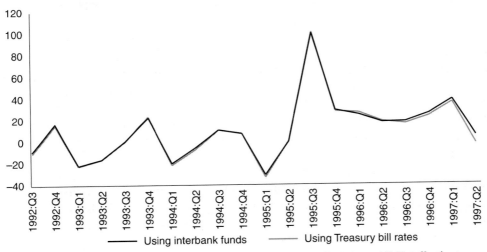

Sources: Bloomberg; International Monetary Fund, *International Financial Statistics*; and IMF staff estimates.

The carry trade was then further disturbed by changes in global financial conditions. There were increases in interest rates in the United Kingdom and Germany in the spring of 1997. Japanese long rates ticked up from 2–2.5 per cent when the outlook for the Japanese economy appeared to brighten after March, and short rates firmed with talk that the Bank of Japan might raise rates by the end of the year. Perhaps most important was the appreciation of the United States dollar against the yen, which undermined the competitiveness of Asian

Exhibit 36.3

The Asian carry trade

International commercial and investment banks were heavily involved in dollar and yen carry trades in Asia beginning in 1992. One technique was to borrow on the interbank market in dollars and yen, to convert the proceeds into local currency, and to on-lend on the local currency short-term interbank market. At the end of the loan period, principal and interest were converted back into dollars or yen, closing out the interbank loan.[a] An alternative was for banks and other institutional investors to borrow in the dollar or yen short-term debt market (through, for example, a Treasury term repo agreement), to convert the proceeds into local currency and to hold a time deposit. A final technique was to utilise the money markets; international investors issued money market securities in mature markets and invested the proceeds in local currency-denominated money market instruments (promissory notes, bankers' acceptances, and other short-term corporate or government paper).[b] And, of course, hybrids of these three techniques were also used.

Data for the Thai baht confirm that all three techniques were profitable for an extended period. Returns computed using the interbank market (subtracting from the interest rate differential the realised change in the exchange rate over the holding period) suggest that in 18 of the 20 quarters up to mid-1997 the carry trade generated a higher spread than investing in the mature markets (Exhibit 36.1). The returns on the yen carry trade were profitable in 13 of these 20 quarters, showing greater variability due to volatility in the yen exchange rate (Exhibit 36.2). Carry trades using term repos and Thai time deposits tell a similar story.

The effects of speculative pressure in the period leading up to the crisis, as well as the authorities' response, are evident in the limited time series available on the local money market instruments series for Thailand (see table below). Although returns on dollar carry trades were substantial in the second quarter of 1997 because the squeeze applied at the time of the speculative attack raised yields while not allowing the baht–dollar exchange rate to move, returns to both carry trades turned sharply negative with the depreciation of the baht in the third quarter.

Yields on US dollar and Japanese yen carry trades in the Thai baht (using money markets)[c]

	Index returns in yen[d]	Japanese yen Libor (3-month)	Profit from yen carry trade	Index returns in US dollar[d]	US dollar Libor (3-month)	Profit from US dollar carry trade
1996: Q3	15.66	0.52	15.09	8.88	5.63	3.13
1996: Q4	23.42	0.49	22.85	6.03	5.56	0.45
1997: Q1	36.24	0.58	35.52	3.97	5.77	−1.73
1997: Q2	−1.33	0.66	−1.98	34.47	5.79	27.54
1997: Q3	−64.90	0.56	−65.15	−71.32	5.77	−73.47

[a] In practice, both the borrowing and lending legs were frequently rolled over into the next period without unwinding them, as long as doing so continued to be profitable.

[b] Domestics got in on the game as well: some local entities issued short-term debt on international markets and on-lent domestically at higher spreads.

[c] All returns are annualised.

[d] Computed by converting Thai money market index returns into US dollars and yen.

Sources: International Monetary Fund, *International Financial Statistics*; Bloomberg; Peregrine Securities; and IMF staff estimates.

economies in whose basket pegs the dollar had the heaviest weight. For all these reasons it became less attractive to borrow in the United States, Europe and Japan to hold positions in, among other countries, Thailand.

However, the main factors to which international investors pointed as the rationale for these portfolio shifts were problems with Thai fundamentals. Those who anticipated a devaluation had an incentive to sell the baht forward. While they saw devaluation coming, however, they were uncertain about its timing. However, the probability of currency appreciation was negligible; portfolio managers perceived the existence of a one-way bet, which encouraged them to maintain their positions.

Hedge funds' forward sales of baht are impossible to estimate precisely. Of the Bank of Thailand's US$28 billion forward book at the end of July 1997, approximately US$7 billion is thought by market participants to represent transactions taken directly with hedge funds. Hedge funds may have also sold the baht forward through offshore counterparties, onshore foreign banks and onshore domestic banks, which then offloaded their positions to the central bank. There is no way of breaking out the magnitude of these transactions.

Although hedge funds apparently sold some long-dated forward contracts on the baht in February 1997, the bulk of hedge funds' forward sales to the Bank of Thailand appears to have occurred only in May at the tail-end of the process. If herd behaviour contributed to the crisis, then the hedge funds were at the rear, not the front of the herd, which appears to have been led by domestic corporates, domestic banks and international commercial and investment banks. Hedge funds also appear to have closed out their positions soon after the initial depreciation of the baht.

After 2 July 1997, corporates with unhedged foreign currency exposure rushed for foreign exchange cover, fuelling the currency's depreciation. These domestic entities entering the period with unhedged foreign currency liabilities appear to have played a larger role than hedge funds in the baht's continued decline.

In the view of market participants, the baht is the only Asian currency for which the hedge funds collectively took significant short positions. The hedge funds appear to have been surprised by the extent of the contagion, managers not having seen comparable problems with fundamentals in other countries. Many of them were therefore taken off guard by the sharp movement of other Asian currencies. Van Hedge Fund Advisors estimates that offshore hedge funds lost 7 per cent of their value in August 1997, due largely to the decline of emerging stock markets. According to market participants, the main entities taking short positions in Indonesia, Malaysia and the Philippines were money centre commercial banks and investment banks and domestic investors, who were better able to short due to their superior access to inter-broker markets and domestic credit.

Besides the Thai baht, the one other significant build-up of hedge fund positions was on the Indonesian rupiah. Most of these were in fact long positions taken after the initial depreciation, reflecting the view that the rupiah had overshot and the expectation that it would soon recover. Domestic banks and corporates not only had incurred large amounts of external debt but had sold options against the rupiah's depreciation, using the premiums as a source of income. International banks may have had reasonably complete knowledge of domestic banks' and firms' off-balance sheet exposure, having been the counterparties to the latter's sales of options. They were aware that if the rupiah began to depreciate these entities would rush to hedge their exposures. These anticipations precipitated foreign investor flows out of the currency, led by the international commercial and investment banks but accompanied by little if any activity on the part of the hedge funds. Indonesian banks and corporates changed sides following the widening of the band, as they attempted to hedge their external debts and options positions. The hedge funds are reported to have come in later, on the view that the rupiah had overshot, going long.

It appears that only a few hedge funds took modest positions on the Malaysian ringgit. None appears to have 'ridden' the ringgit for any substantial range of its fall from 2.5–3.5 ringgit per US dollar. Reflecting their holdings of Malaysian equities, many hedge funds incurred losses from the ringgit's depreciation. The initial pressure on the currency appears to have emanated from institutional investors closing out long equity positions, reflecting their concern that the stock market was overvalued, rather than a build-up of speculative short positions reflecting concerns about the sustainability of the external debt and the state of the domestic banking system.

There are no indications that hedge funds took significant positions against the Philippine peso. The limited 'on-balance sheet' channels available for shorting the currency suggest that it was primarily domestic banks and international commercial and investment banks with onshore operations that took positions in expectation of depreciation.[20]

While international investors, including but not limited to hedge funds, claim to have felt for some time that fundamentals warranted taking short positions against the Korean won, there were few avenues for doing so, either on or off-balance sheet. There are few signs of a build-up in such positions in the period leading up to the currency's sharp decline. As the crisis built up, outflows were still inhibited by the costs to foreign investors of liquidating long equity positions. In this case, the predominant source of pressure on the currency appears to have come from domestic entities.

An appraisal

This appraisal covers two areas: the implications of the crisis, and policy options in light of the activities of hedge funds.

Implications of the crisis

There are suggestive parallels between the 1997 crisis and the ERM crisis of 1992. In 1992 international investors were attracted into European securities by high European interest rates, ample cheap funding and the mirage of pegged exchange rates, just as the combination of high interest rates, cheap funding and the mirage of pegged exchange rates more recently attracted money into Asia. In 1992, it was called the 'convergence play' rather than the 'carry trade', but the phenomenon was fundamentally the same. In 1992, the process was disrupted by the build-up of problems with competitiveness, and the reversal of opinion was catalysed by a depreciating US dollar, which reinforced the declining competitiveness of the European economies, and by rising interest rates, which made funding more expensive. In 1997, carry trades were wound down in response to the perception that Thailand in particular was suffering from mounting competitiveness problems. This time the reversal of opinion was catalysed by an appreciating US dollar, which made Asian economies less competitive, and a small but significant rise in European and Japanese interest rates.

A difference between 1992 and 1997 is the role of the hedge funds. For 1992 there is wide agreement that hedge funds were early to recognise the possibility that exchange rate pegs might not be sustained and that the positions they took to avail themselves of this possibility provided the signal for other investors to follow. For 1997 it is much less clear that hedge funds were earlier than other investors to take short positions against Asian currencies and that their trades were a signal for other investors to follow, rather than vice versa. Hedge funds had large short positions on the Thai baht, but not on Asian currencies in general, and even in Thailand they were not obviously earlier than other international investors in building up those positions. Compared with international banks, hedge funds have less staff on the ground; the smaller an economy, the less likely hedge funds are to devote their limited analytical resources to investment opportunities in its market, and the more likely they are to follow rather than lead other investors. The fact that hedge funds appear to have followed rather than led other investors in Mexico in 1994–95 is consistent with this view.

Two fundamental differences distinguish the recent Asian crisis from those in both Europe and Mexico. First, because in the Mexican crisis the authorities used controls and moral suasion to limit the ability of offshore counterparties to borrow domestic currency and securities from onshore banks, those investors with the best access to the domestic broker market, such as investment banks and domestic banks and corporates, were in a position to act as market leaders. Second, and closely related, investment banks have dramatically expanded their operations in emerging markets. Both facts point to the likelihood that other institutional investors, and not merely hedge funds, were major participants in 1997.

Finally, the 1997 crisis, like the bond market turbulence of 1994, reminds us that hedge funds' market bets are not always right; they lose as well as make money. In 1994, they bet on a decline in interest rates in industrialised countries and suffered losses when interest rates unexpectedly rose. In 1997, they anticipated the depreciation of the Thai baht and made profits on short positions in forward currency contracts but appear to have been taken off guard by the virulence of the contagion incurring, on balance, substantial losses from their positions in other Asian financial markets.

Policy options

As noted earlier, regulation of collective investment vehicles can be justified on three grounds: investor protection, systemic risk management, and market integrity. Few regulators, particularly in the United States and the United Kingdom, the leading markets where hedge funds operate, see a need for additional regulation on grounds of investor protection or systemic risk. They are of the view that wealthy investors can largely fend for themselves. To be sure, regulators are concerned that banks under their supervision are adequately monitoring the credit risk associated with their exposure to particular hedge funds. They recognise that the dearth of public information on hedge funds may make it difficult for potential counterparties to assess the creditworthiness of a hedge fund customer. While major banks typically obtain and analyse detailed financial statements from hedge funds before extending them credit, regulators also recognise that not all banks may have the sophistication to fully understand the market and counterparty risks associated with the hedge fund industry and that a small but significant risk to systemic stability may remain. However, they regard these as problems best dealt with by existing supervision of banks and other counterparties rather than by new regulations.

This leaves market integrity. The concern here is that hedge funds, with at least US$80 billion of capital, and macro hedge funds, with at least US$25 billion of capital, can dominate or manipulate markets. In the case of the foreign exchange market, the concern that individual traders should not dominate or manipulate the market reflects the authorities' desire for autonomy for the conduct of macroeconomic policy and insulation from market pressures. However, those markets are also inhabited by a large number of other participants. Even accounting for leverage, the positions that can be taken by hedge funds pale in comparison with the position-taking capacity of mutual funds, pension funds, insurance companies and the proprietary trading desks of investment and commercial banks. Whether they manage hedge funds, compete with hedge funds, serve as counterparties to hedge funds, provide credit to hedge funds, or keep an eye on hedge funds from official quarters, many observers are sceptical that hedge funds are large enough to dominate markets.

Overall, the case for supervisory and regulatory initiatives directed specifically at hedge funds is not strong. However, if policymakers wish to proceed, options exist for rendering hedge fund operations more transparent and of further assuring officials that hedge funds are not dominating or manipulating markets.[21] These include extending large trader and position reporting systems, and limiting the ability of individual traders to take large short positions against the domestic currency by restricting the ability of financial institutions to loan that currency.

Large trade and position reporting

Other countries could emulate the large trade and position reporting requirements in effect in countries such as the United States. As noted, this would increase transparency and reassure officials that individual traders, including hedge funds, are not dominating particular markets. Implementing large position or transaction reporting is more difficult in an over-the-counter environment than when an asset is traded on an exchange. Transaction reporting is particularly difficult when transactions occur on the interbank market rather than in a centralised location. However, experience in the United States suggests that periodic large-position reporting is feasible even in this kind of decentralised environment. However, to be totally effective, such requirements would have to apply in all jurisdictions in which foreign exchange transactions could be booked. Otherwise, were reporting requirements be regarded as onerous (because, for example, of fears of repercussions when large trades became known to the authorities) the foreign exchange transaction could move offshore.

A partial response would be to make domestically owned bank and non-bank subsidiaries abroad subject to the reporting requirement, as is the case in the United States for entities with foreign exchange positions in excess of US$50 billion. It would be more difficult, of course, to require international banks and multinational corporations that operate in a country but are chartered or incorporated abroad to report on all large currency transactions undertaken outside its borders. It is perhaps revealing that this is not attempted by the US reporting system for foreign currency positions.

A watertight reporting system would therefore have to be applied in all jurisdictions. How much leakage would otherwise occur depends on how onerous traders regarded the reporting requirement.

More comprehensive reporting requirements

Even in the United States, only large trades and positions are subject to reporting requirements. In particular, the US$50 billion minimum threshold for weekly and monthly reporting of foreign exchange positions in the United States would not catch most foreign exchange transactions of hedge funds and other investors. If more comprehensive reporting requirements are viewed as desirable, lower thresholds would have to be considered.[22]

Requiring hedge funds in particular to report comprehensive data on all their transactions and positions would pose special difficulties. In the United States it would be necessary to lift the 'trader' exemption from the Securities Exchange Act, which frees hedge funds and others dealing solely for their own account from having to file detailed financial reports with the SEC. The problem of where to draw the line is more general: if small investor partnerships are required to report all their investments, should the same also be asked of family groups and individual investors?

Moreover, enforcing more comprehensive reporting requirements for hedge funds would be difficult because hedge funds are so mobile. While large trades and positions would presumably be reported to the regulators of the national markets on which they were taken, more comprehensive reporting on balance sheets and financial dealings would have to be administered by the territory of incorporation (if the fund has corporate form) or, more likely, the place of residence of the majority of trustees (if, as is more typically the case, the fund is unincorporated). If such reporting requirements were regarded as onerous, coordination among the Group of 10 countries, for example, would not suffice, since hedge funds are free to locate in Bermuda or the Cayman Islands.

Limiting position taking

Policymakers might contemplate a variety of measures to limit the ability of hedge funds and other international investors to take positions in domestic financial markets. By taxing short-term capital inflows (as countries like Chile have done), it would be possible to discourage hedge funds and other international investors from putting on long positions in domestic markets that might then be closed out suddenly. Hedge fund managers emphasise the importance they attach to being able to put on and take off positions with a minimum of transaction costs, an emphasis that suggests that this class of investors might be particularly sensitive to such measures.

In addition, a growing literature (for example, Cowan and De Gregorio, 1998) suggests that these last measures can have the further advantage of limiting the magnitude of capital inflows during periods when funds are flowing to emerging markets, damping down asset-price booms and preventing distortions in the structure of relative prices, and of limiting countries' vulnerability to disruptions of their external accounts if and when capital flows suddenly reverse direction.

Similarly, by requiring banks and brokers to raise margin and collateral requirements, it would be possible to limit the use of leverage by hedge funds and other investors. These last initiatives would have to be coordinated internationally, of course, since hedge funds can obtain credit in a variety of national markets. They would have to be coordinated across assets to prevent hedge funds and other investors from shifting assets subject to increased margin requirements to other assets, including derivatives, not so covered. In addition, there is the possibility that higher margin requirements would induce hedge funds and others to shift from purchasing securities on margin to obtaining leverage through the use of bank credit lines: see the discussion of the practice in the section on use of leverage.

Finally, by limiting the ability of financial institutions to provide the domestic credit needed to short the currency and to loan the securities needed to short equity and fixed-income markets, it might be possible to limit the ability of hedge funds and other investors to

447

take short positions. By slowing the development of active and liquid bond markets, it might be possible to discourage trading in those assets by hedge funds and other investors that prefer to transact in markets where positions can be easily taken and easily liquidated.

However, strong limits on position taking could prevent hedge funds and other international investors from acting as contrarians. While hedge funds may be among the first institutional investors to short a currency when there is evidence of inconsistent macroeconomic fundamentals and shaky currency pegs, they may also be among the first buyers to jump back into the market after a crisis in which a depreciating currency overshoots and the foreign exchange market dries up. As already noted, and elaborated in the section on feedback trading, there are reasons to think that hedge funds' structure and incentives incline them less than other investors toward positive-feedback trading strategies that amplify asset-price volatility. It is not clear, therefore, that discouraging position taking by hedge funds would reduce that volatility.

In addition, attempts to impose position limits or margin requirements will provide incentives for financial market participants to arrange transactions in unregulated or offshore jurisdictions, neutralising efforts to constrain their activities.

Finally, in terms of economic growth, the costs of policies of financial repression (for that is what is being discussed) are high. Slowing the development of active and liquid bond markets by imposing position limits, margin requirements, and other permanent restrictions on trading may discourage position taking by hedge funds and others, but this does not make the policy desirable. Repressed markets may be stable, but this does not mean that they are efficient or conducive to growth. Indeed, the evidence that financial liberalisation leads to financial deepening and accelerating growth is incontrovertible.[23] If measures are adopted to discourage position taking by hedge funds and other investors, it is critically important that these measures do not encourage a relapse into costly policies of financial repression.

Improving information to discourage herding

That said, because some hedge fund managers have well-publicised reputations for astuteness, the news that they have taken positions in particular assets or markets may encourage other less well-informed investors to follow their lead (in an example of the information cascades phenomenon described earlier). In other words, hedge funds may play an important role in the herd behaviour that sometimes characterises financial markets and that can force difficult adjustments on policymakers and shift the market from a better to a worse equilibrium.[24]

Herding of this sort (that is, herding based on information cascades) takes place when information is asymmetric and incomplete, rendering market participants uncertain about a government's policies or intentions and causing them to infer those policies or intentions from the actions of other traders. The solution is to provide better information to the markets on government policies and the condition of domestic financial institutions in order to encourage investors to trade on fundamentals rather than to run with the herd.

This means releasing information about current government policies and about contingencies that might affect future government policies, as well as using interest rates and other financial variables under the government's control to clearly signal policy priorities. It means not presenting hedge funds and other private investors, whose combined resources constitute a market vastly larger than the assets of central banks and governments, with an incentive to take large positions against a currency by offering them the irresistible combination of inconsistent policies and unsustainable currency pegs.

448

References

Bank for International Settlements (1995), *Central Bank Survey of Foreign Exchange Market Activity in April 1995: Preliminary Global Findings*, Basle (24 October).

Caldwell, T. (1995), 'Introduction: The Model for Superior Performance', *Hedge Funds: Investment and Portfolio Strategies for the Institutional Investor*, Eds. J. Lederman and R. A. Klein, New York, McGraw-Hill, pp. 1–17.

Cowan, K., and J. De Gregorio (1998), 'Exchange Rate Policies and Capital Account Management: Chile in the 1990s', *Managing Capital Flows and Exchange Rates: Perspectives from the Pacific Basin*, Ed. R. Glick, Cambridge, Cambridge University Press.

Dale, T. (1995), 'The Foreign Exchange Market in London', *Bank of England Quarterly Bulletin*, pp. 361–68 (November).

Devenow, A.A., and I. Welch (1996), 'Rational Herding in Financial Economics', *European Economic Review*, Vol. 40, pp. 603–615 (April).

Flood, R.P., and P.M. Garber (1984a), 'Collapsing Exchange-Rate Regimes: Some Linear Examples'. *Journal of International Economics*, Vol. 17, pp. 1–13 (August).

Flood, R.P., and P.M. Garber (1984b), 'Gold Monetization and Gold Discipline', *Journal of Political Economy*, Vol. 92, pp. 90–107 (February).

Flood, R., and N. Marion (1997), 'Perspectives on the Recent Currency Crisis Literature', (unpublished), International Monetary Fund, Washington, DC; and Dartmouth College, Hanover, NH.

Frankel, J.A., and S.L. Schmukler (1996), 'Country Fund Discounts and the Mexican Crisis of December 1994: Did Local Residents Turn Pessimistic Before International Investors?', *Open Economies Review*, Vol. 7, Suppl. 1, pp. 511–534.

Frankel, J.A., and S.L. Schmukler (1997), 'Country Funds and Asymmetric Information'. (unpublished), University of California, Berkeley, CA; and World Bank, Washington, DC.

Fung, W., and D.H. Hsieh (1997), 'Empirical Characteristics of Dynamic Trading Strategies: The Case of Hedge Funds', *Review of Financial Studies*, Vol. 10, pp. 275–302 (Summer).

International Monetary Fund (1993a), *International Capital Markets: Part I. Exchange Rate Management and International Capital Flows*, World Economic and Financial Surveys, Washington, DC.

International Monetary Fund (1993b), *International Capital Markets: Part II. Systemic Issues in International Finance*, World Economic and Financial Surveys, Washington, DC.

International Monetary Fund (1994), *International Capital Markets: Developments, Prospects, and Policy Issues*, World Economic and Financial Surveys, Washington, DC.

International Monetary Fund (1995), *International Capital Markets: Developments, Prospects, and Key Policy Issues*, World Economic and Financial Surveys, Washington, DC.

International Organization of Securities Commissions (1997), *International Regulation of Derivative Markets, Products and Financial Intermediaries.*

449

Kodres, L.E., and M. Pritsker (1997), 'Directionally-Similar Position Taking and Herding by Large Futures Market Participants', (unpublished), International Monetary Fund and Board of Governors of the Federal Reserve System, Washington, DC.

Krugman, P. (1979), 'A Model of Balance of Payments Crises', *Journal of Money, Credit and Banking*, Vol. 11, pp. 311–325.

Kuper, S. (1997), 'Hedge Funds: Gentler Face for 'Evil Geniuses'', *Financial Times* (19 September).

Martinson, J. (1997), 'Niederhoffer: Speculator Sticks with Thailand Despite Loss', *Financial Times* (17 September).

Morris, S., and H.S. Shin (1995), 'Informational Events that Trigger Currency Attacks', Working Paper 95–24, Federal Reserve Bank of Philadelphia, Philadelphia, PA.

Obstfeld, M. (1984), 'The Logic of Currency Crises', *Cahiers Economiques et Monétaires*, Vol. 43, pp. 189–213.

Obstfeld, M. (1986), 'Rational and Self-fulfilling Balance-of-Payments Crises', *American Economic Review*, Vol. 76, pp. 72–81 (March).

Obstfeld, M. (1996), 'Models of Currency Crises with Self-Fulfilling Features', *European Economic Review*, Vol. 40, Nos. 3–5, pp. 1037–47 (April).

Ul Haq, M., I. Kaul, and I. Grunberg (Eds.) (1996), *The Tobin Tax: Coping with Financial Volatility*, New York, Oxford University Press.

United States Congress, House of Representatives (1994), 'Statement and Testimony of George Soros', *Risks that Hedge Funds Pose to the Banking System*, Committee on Banking, Finance and Urban Affairs, 103 Congress, 2nd Session (13 April).

Wei, Shang-jin, and J. Kim (1997), 'The Big Players in the Foreign Exchange Market: Do they Trade on Information or Noise?' *NBER Working Paper 6256*, National Bureau of Economic Research, Cambridge, MA.

World Bank (1997), *Private Capital Flows to Developing Countries: The Road to Financial Integration*, New York, Oxford University Press.

---

* Editor's note: on 29 September 2003, shortly before this book went to press, the staff of the SEC issued its report entitled 'The Implications of the Growth of Hedge Funds', the culmination of its efforts following the Hedge Fund Roundtable held in May 2003. As of the date of this writing, the Commission itself had not taken any action in response to the report. One of the key recommendations of the staff was that the SEC consider 'requiring hedge fund advisers to register with the SEC as investment advisers, taking into account whether the benefits outweigh the burdens of registration'. In the staff's view, ' … registration of hedge fund advisers would serve as a deterrent to fraud, encourage compliance and the adoption of compliance procedures, provide the SEC with important information … and effectively raise the standards for investment in hedge funds from the "accredited investor" standard to that of "qualified client"'. See http://www.sec.gov/news/studies/hedgefunds0903.pdf for the full text of the report.

---

[1] This was not the first time that the IMF considered the role of hedge funds in international financial dynamics. The 1993 International Capital Markets Report analysed their role in the 1992 ERM crisis. The 1994 Report had a chapter entitled 'Bond Market Turbulence and the Role of Hedge Funds'. The 1995 Report analysed their activities in a chapter entitled 'Increasing Importance of International Investors'. See International Monetary Fund (1993a, 1993b, 1994, 1995).

2 Formally, herding is a situation in which traders emulate the actions of other traders. The phenomenon is not necessarily predicated on irrationality. Models of rational herding are typically built on one of three effects. The first is payoff externalities, in which the payoffs to an agent adopting an action increase in the number of other agents adopting the same action. Second are principal-agent models in which managers, in order to preserve or gain reputation when markets are imperfectly informed, prefer to 'hide in the herd' in order not to be easily evaluated, or to 'ride the herd' to prove their quality. Third are models of information cascades, in which agents infer information from the actions of others and optimally act alike. The notion that other investors regard hedge fund managers as relatively well informed and therefore follow their lead is most obviously interpreted in terms of this third effect. For a survey, see Devenow and Welch (1996).

3 Macro funds engage in 'top-down' analysis, looking at national macroeconomic and financial variables such as the current account, the inflation rate and the real exchange rate, whereas global funds engage in 'bottom-up' analysis, investing globally but picking stocks on the basis of individual companies' prospects.

4 Haircuts (the share of the portfolio that cannot be traded but must be held as collateral) vary with the riskiness of the underlying securities, from 50 per cent on equities to 3–10 per cent on foreign exchange transactions to 1 per cent or 2 per cent on US Treasury bonds. At the beginning of the 1990s, when hedge funds were less familiar to the banking community, they were subject to more substantial haircuts. Haircuts declined as hedge funds acquired a track record and became more of a known entity. Better-known hedge funds can buy structured derivative products without putting up capital initially but make a succession of premium payments when the market in those securities trades up or down to trigger levels. In addition, some hedge funds negotiate secured credit lines with their banks (at least one large relative value fund has a large unsecured credit line). However, credit lines being expensive, managers use them mainly to finance calls for additional margin when the market moves against them.

5 This distinction grows less clear with the rise of margin optimisation, or cross-margining, where closely offsetting positions can be netted to reduce required margin.

6 Communication from Van Hedge Fund Advisors, 5 December 1997. Borrowed funds are typically used to take both long and short positions. Thus, figures such as those in the text pertain to the sum of long and short positions.

7 These reports are made under the provisions of the Large Trader Reporting System, described later. Kodres and Pritsker's results need to be treated with caution insofar as investors (including hedge funds) in currency markets tend to transact in forward and spot rather than futures markets.

8 See International Monetary Fund (1993a).

9 Because those transactions were generally undertaken with other banks, the initial forward sale typically set in motion a chain of subsequent transactions until the initial position was distributed among a number of investment banks and other investors willing to hold it. The circle was closed when the hedge fund purchased the currencies previously sold short in the spot market at the time the forward contract expired.

10 In Congressional testimony, George Soros, who managed this fund, estimated that it accounted for about 15 per cent of the hedge fund industry at the time but that it was more active in currencies than the typical hedge fund. United States Congress (1994, p. 44).

11 On the other hand, they were reported to have lost money on currencies that were devalued later, such as the Spanish peseta. Again, see International Monetary Fund (1993a).

12 International Monetary Fund (1993a, p. 11).

13 For a discussion of this topic see International Monetary Fund (1994).

14 Frankel and Schmukler (1996). See also International Monetary Fund (1995).

15 As Frankel and Schmukler (1996) note, the fact that the Mexican Bolsa, on which transactions by Mexican residents dominate, responded more quickly than closed-ended mutual funds, through which foreigners invest in the Mexican market, is consistent with this view.

16 International Monetary Fund (1995, p. 7).

17 From 1991 to 1992 in the case of Malaysia and in 1993 in the case of Thailand and Indonesia. At least one prominent macro fund went short in Asian equities (including but not limited to Japanese banks), but it was the exception, not the rule.

18 Revealingly, the genesis of the Asian carry trade, starting with Malaysia in 1991–92, coincided with the Federal Reserve's policy of keeping interest rates low so as to promote the recovery of the US economy from the recession in the early 1990s.

19 Too sharp a distinction should not be drawn between investors who closed out their long positions and those who shorted the baht; both actions were logical responses to the perceived rise in currency risk. Nor should those who shorted the baht in the forward foreign exchange market be regarded as more actively speculating against Thai

financial markets: some of those who shorted the currency in the forward market did so in order to hedge the currency risk to which they were exposed as a result of their desire to maintain long positions in equity and fixed-income markets.

[20] On-balance sheet channels refer to the use of domestic currency credit that, when converted into foreign currency, creates a short position on the local currency. The use of forwards or swaps to go short on a currency is often referred to as 'off-balance sheet,' as this is where such transactions are typically recorded.

[21] While national monetary authorities have been known to complain that they lack information on who is on the other side of the foreign exchange market, it is important to emphasise that there is nothing peculiar in this respect about either hedge funds or currency markets. To be sure, the foreign exchange market is an over-the-counter market. It is decentralised: individual banks quote their own bid and offer prices, which are then disseminated by financial services like Reuters. However, in most major equity, fixed-income and commodity markets, just as in foreign exchange markets, most transactions are undertaken by traders whose identity is unknown to other traders. While the identity of the buyer or seller may be known to the dealer or broker who is the counterparty to the individual transaction, the dealer does not share that information. On the New York Stock Exchange, all that specialists report in real time is the amount and price of each sale so as to facilitate the printing of the trade on the tape (on the commodity futures exchanges, buyers and sellers themselves are not required to report transactions as they occur; rather, the prices at which shouted transactions are concluded are overheard by pit observers, who relay the information to exchange officials who control the tape). All that other buyers and sellers therefore know is the change in prices and amounts as they scroll across their screens. This can be seen as the defining feature of an efficient, competitive market, in which anonymous buyers and sellers react to the price signals sent by other anonymous buyers and sellers

[22] The reportable position of greater than US$50 billion in the United States implies that between 30 and 40 entities are captured for weekly reporting. In the Bank for International Settlements (1995) survey of foreign exchange turnover, the Federal Reserve Bank of New York reported on 147 foreign exchange dealers. Since most of the participants in the position reporting scheme are commercial banks (for instance, 29 out of 36 in Wei and Kim's 1997 study using these data were commercial banks), setting a reporting threshold such that about 20 per cent of the active institutions are required to report may be sufficient to be able to monitor market developments. Alternatively, instead of aiming for a given proportion of market participants, the threshold can be set by comparing it to daily turnover. For example, daily turnover in the five currencies covered by the United States large position reporting requirements amounted to US$166 billion in April 1995 (the last time a turnover survey was officially conducted). Assuming positions (a stock variable) are roughly proportional to turnover (a flow variable), the equivalent reporting threshold for the Thai baht, where the daily turnover was estimated to be US$5 billion in May 1996, would be about US$1.5 billion; for the Indonesian rupiah, the threshold would be about US$1 billion; and for the Czech koruna, about US$150 million. The problem with setting a threshold using information from the highly liquid, competitive foreign exchange market of New York is that it may not be representative of the market structure in emerging market currencies. For example, the largest 20 dealers in the New York market accounted for 70 per cent of the turnover in April 1995. In an emerging market country, it is more likely that five or six banks account for the same share of turnover. More important than the higher market concentrations is the loose connection between turnover and positions. For instance, turnover can be quite high and yet intermediaries may be unwilling to hold (or be prohibited from holding) outstanding positions of any substantial size. Alternatively, large positions may be in place but turnover may be extremely low. Further complicating the establishment of thresholds are the large fluctuations in activity levels in emerging market currencies. A given position may appear 'large' during a period in which the market is liquid, but a much smaller position may be able to move the market in a period in which market liquidity has dried up. Thus, if the authorities set the reporting level low to accommodate the latter situation it may capture too many participants, driving the market to other locations. However, if the threshold is high enough to reduce the reporting burden, it may fail to warn the authorities of upcoming volatility when markets become illiquid.

[23] A recent compendium of research on this question can be found in World Bank (1997). To be sure, precipitous liberalisation associated with inadequate supervision and regulation of domestic financial institutions can create problems and provide justification for going slow, but this has little to do with hedge funds.

[24] This possibility arises in a situation of multiple equilibria. Morris and Shin (1995) show that it is possible to have multiple equilibria when investors have less than perfect information about the economic environment.

Chapter 37

Short selling, hedge funds and public policy considerations[1]

James S. Chanos
Kynikos Associates, New York, New York

Introduction

Despite the mystique surrounding short selling, the concept behind the practice is very simple. Short sellers manage a portfolio of securities they consider to be overvalued. Their portfolios are designed to profit if the securities they have sold short fall in value. Typically a good short seller selects portfolio securities by conducting a rigorous financial analysis and focusing on securities issued by companies that appear to have:

- materially overstated earnings;
- an unsustainable or operationally flawed business plan; and/or
- engaged in outright fraud.

Given how difficult the practice of short selling is, it helps enormously to have many years of experience in the equity markets.

In almost any market environment, professional short sellers are a small percentage of those actively engaged in the markets. The bull market of the 1990s drove a number of previously short-only funds into alternative strategies or out of the market altogether. In the less robust market environment following 2000, however, a number of new participants have emerged and, with them, heightened public, corporate and regulatory scrutiny of the practice of short selling has ensued, as it does during almost every prolonged market downturn. Nevertheless, I firmly believe, based on experience and empirical analysis, that short selling is beneficial to the markets not only in the technical aspects of providing liquidity or a hedge against long positions, but also as an important bulwark against hyperbole, irrational exuberance and corporate fraud. As Bernard Baruch said nearly 90 years ago: 'To enjoy the advantages of a free market, one must have both buyers and sellers, both bulls and bears. A market without bears would be like a nation without a free press. There would be no one to criticise and restrain the false optimism that always leads to disaster.'[2]

Who sells short?

There are three main categories of market participants who sell short, and they do so for differing reasons.

The first category is exchange specialists, market-makers and block traders who will sell short for technical reasons in order to maintain customer liquidity and price stability.

The second category of short sellers are those who are engaging in market-neutral arbitrage and are seeking to take advantage of temporary or minute price discrepancies in markets or in similar securities.

While the above activities are common market techniques, they are not what the public generally has in mind when any discussion of short selling arises. The last category of short sellers is the investor expressing his or her view that a specific stock or market index is over-valued and will decrease in price over time. It is this activity that is often associated with hedge funds and is also the frequent target of corporate criticism.

Regulatory requirements and economic costs of short selling

First and foremost, it is important to note that short selling, like any market activity, is subject to the full body of anti-fraud and anti-manipulation provisions of the securities laws. There is no loophole or grey area of which I am aware in the federal securities laws that makes it illegal to manipulate the price of a stock upward but simultaneously permits the manipulation of the price of a stock downwards. In fact, and contrary to the allegations of some, short selling is one of the most heavily regulated market strategies around.

First, open short interest is disclosed monthly by both the New York Stock Exchange and the Nasdaq stock market for every listed company. Any investor can take a look and see how much short interest exists for any particular company. So the charge that short selling is a wholly opaque practice is spurious.

Second, alone among market transactions, short selling is subject to the 'uptick rule' on both the New York Stock Exchange and the Nasdaq stock market. Every short sale transaction must be disclosed as such. The uptick rule requires that a short sale could, in fact, only be made at (zero plus tick) or above (plus tick) the last transaction price. Thus, it is mechanically impossible for short sellers to drive down the price of the stock. It is an open question whether the harm done to price efficiency in the market place is warranted by the supposed protection offered to investors against so-called 'bear raids'. An inquiry into the transaction-by-transaction functioning of the uptick rule may in fact disclose that significant numbers of sell orders get trapped behind the gate, thus making it more difficult for investors of all sizes and sophistication levels to sell their securities when they wish.

Third, Regulation T, administered by the Federal Reserve Board, requires that short accounts post at least 50 per cent of the value of all shorted shares as a margin requirement. Of course, margin calls can arise if the price of the shorted stock increases, thus triggering additional collateral deposits in order to meet the requirements of Regulation T.

Collateral requirements on securities loans used by shorts to deliver shorted securities pose a further control on short selling. Short sale proceeds are used to collateralise borrowed securities and they are not available to leverage the portfolio and enable additional short sales. This represents a further control on short selling.

Lastly, many institutional investors such as pension funds, mutual funds and endowments have been prohibited or are severely restricted in shorting stock by the prudent investor rules under which managers operate such funds.

To this regulatory burden, there are also significant economic costs and market risks. Short-sellers typically must hold their short positions for extended periods (often months) until the market realises how badly overvalued a particular stock is and the price declines. Holding the short positions is expensive and risky for the short seller. A joint Harvard Business School-University of Michigan Business School working paper in 1999 summarised these factors:

> The proceeds from a short sale are not available to the short seller. Instead, the proceeds are escrowed as collateral for the owner of the borrowed shares. Typically, the short-seller receives interest on the proceeds, but the rate received ('the rebate') is below market rate. The difference is compensation to the lender of the stock. Thus, short-sellers cannot directly use the proceeds from short sales to hedge their short positions. . . . The tax treatment of short positions contributes to the high cost of short selling. All profits from a short sale are taxed at the short-term capital gains rate, no matter how long the short position is open. Finally, the short-seller is required to reimburse the stock lender for any dividends or other distributions paid to the shareholders of the shorted stock while the short position is open. . . . The standard stock-lending practice is that the loan must be repaid on demand. This practice exposes the short-sellers to the risk of being 'squeezed'.[3]

The fact that there is a significant regulatory and economic burden to short selling is not to say that it cannot be a profitable transaction. Nevertheless, I would hope that this brief overview of the regulatory and economic forces in play, when anyone chooses to short stock, puts to rest the carping of critics who allege that this is a lightly regulated or wholly unregulated endeavour that one would enter into cavalierly.

Short sellers as financial detectives[4]

The public benefit of the 'long' side of the market is well understood by almost everyone today: companies raise capital to fund investment, research and job creation; retail and institutional investors seek out equity investments in order to share in the creation of wealth that flows from well-managed, honest companies.

The public benefit from the short side of the market is less well understood, but no less valuable. As Edward Chancellor, the noted expert on the history of finance, wrote in 2001: 'we need more, not less, shorting activity if, in the future, we are to avoid wasteful bubbles, such as the recent technology, media and telecoms boom'.[5]

Many of the major corporate frauds and bankruptcies of the past quarter century were first exposed by short sellers doing fundamental research: Enron, Tyco, Sunbeam, Boston Chicken, Baldwin United, MicroStrategies, Conseco, ZZZZBest and Crazy Eddie are but a few examples of this phenomenon.

The short sellers provide a kind of independent research that is the market place's best antidote to the myriad conflicts of interest so amply revealed in the recent global settlement with 10 leading Wall Street investment banking firms. Short sellers ask the tough questions and dig out the discrepancies in the financial statements and other regulatory filings made by publicly traded companies.

Paul Asquith and Lisa Meulbroek, in a Harvard Business School working paper, found a strong correlation between short interest and subsequent negative corporate returns:

> Using data on monthly short interest positions for all New York Stock Exchange and American Stock Exchange stocks from 1976–1993, we detect a strong negative relation

between short interest and subsequent returns, both during the time the stocks are heavily shorted and over the following two years. This relationship persists over the entire 18 year period, and the abnormal returns are even more negative for firms which are heavily shorted for more than one month.[6]

For an investor seeking warning signs in the market, corporate conflicts with short sellers may be just the canary in the mineshaft that is needed. As *The New York Times* reported early in 2003:

> If you own shares in a company that declares war on short sellers, there is only one thing to do: sell your stake. That's the message in a new study by Owen A. Lamont, associate professor of finance at the University of Chicago's graduate school of business. . . . The study, which covers 1977 to 2002, shows not only that the stocks of companies who try to thwart short sellers are generally overpriced, but also that short sellers are often dead right.[7]

In fact, Owen Lamont's study confirms anecdotal evidence collected by the National Association of Securities Dealers in 1986 as part of former SEC Commissioner Irving Pollack's report to the NASD entitled 'Short Sale Regulation of Nasdaq Securities':

> The Pollack Report chose 11 securities for analysis, based upon media articles, complaints from issuers, and indications of unusual trading patterns. . . . The Pollack Report found that, with respect to two of the securities studied, rumours of extensive short selling were unfounded – large short positions did not exist. With respect to the nine other securities, six of the issuers suffered significant operational losses and five of the issuers were the subject of adverse regulatory action.[8]

In testimony presented to Congress in 1989, the SEC's Associate Director of Enforcement, John Sturc, was even more pointed in dissecting the underlying reasons that issuers and others complain about short sellers. John Sturc outlined five reasons that the SEC 'frequently finds that the complaints of downward manipulation that we receive from issuers or their affiliates do not lead to sustainable evidence of violations of the antifraud provisions of the federal securities laws . . .', including:

> . . . negative statements which persons holding short positions are alleged to have disseminated to the marketplace may be true or may represent expressions of investment opinion by professional securities analysts . . . *many of the complaints we receive about alleged illegal short selling come from companies and corporate officers who are themselves under investigation by the Commission or others for possible violations of the securities or other laws* [emphasis added].[9]

Short sellers also help stabilise falling markets by buying shares to close out their short positions. This results in market support and can reduce volatility and market declines caused by a lack of buyers.

An example of research-based short selling: Enron[10]

It may be useful to understand some of the mechanics of research-based or informationally motivated short selling. My own early negative view of the Enron Corporation is one example of why and how a short seller develops his investment view.

My involvement with Enron began normally enough. In October 2000, a friend asked me if I had seen an interesting article in *The Texas Wall Street Journal*, which is a regional edition, about accounting practices at large energy trading firms. The article, written by Jonathan Weil, pointed out that many of these firms, including Enron, employed the so-called 'gain-on-sale' accounting method for their long-term energy trades. Basically, gain-on-sale accounting allows a company to estimate the future profitability of a trade made today and book a profit today based on the present value of those estimated future profits.

Our interest in Enron and other energy trading companies was piqued because our experience with companies that have used this accounting method has been that management's temptation to be overly aggressive in making assumptions about the future was too great for them to ignore. In effect, 'earnings' could be created out of thin air if management was willing to push the envelope by using highly favourable assumptions. However, if these future assumptions did not come to pass, previously booked earnings would have to be adjusted downward. If this happened, as it often did, companies wholly reliant on gain-on-sale accounting would simply do new and bigger deals (with a larger immediate earnings impact) to offset those downward revisions. Once a company got on such an accounting treadmill, it was hard for it to get off.

The first Enron document my firm analysed was its 1999 Form 10-K filing, which it had filed with the SEC. What immediately struck us was that despite using the gain-on-sale model, Enron's return on capital, a widely used measure of profitability, was a paltry 7 per cent before taxes. That is, for every dollar in outside capital that Enron employed, it earned about seven cents. This is important for two reasons; first, we viewed Enron as a trading company that was akin to an energy hedge fund. For this type of firm, a 7 per cent return on capital seemed abysmally low, particularly given its market dominance and accounting methods. Second, it was our view that Enron's cost of capital was likely in excess of 7 per cent and probably closer to 9 per cent, which meant from an economic point of view, that Enron was not really earning any money at all, despite reporting 'profits' to its shareholders. This mismatch of Enron's cost of capital and its return on investment became the cornerstone for our bearish view on Enron and we began shorting Enron common stock in November 2000 for our clients.

We were also troubled by Enron's cryptic disclosure regarding various related-party transactions described in its 1999 Form 10-K, as well as the quarterly Form 10-Qs it filed with the SEC in 2000 for its March, June and September quarters. We read the footnotes in Enron's financial statements about these transactions over and over again and we could not decipher what impact they had on Enron's overall financial condition. It did seem strange to us, however, that Enron had organised these entities for the apparent purpose of trading with their parent company, and that they were run by an Enron executive. Another disturbing factor in our review of Enron's situation was what we perceived to be the large amount of insider selling of Enron stock by Enron's senior executives. While not damning by itself, such selling in conjunction with our other financial concerns added to our conviction.

Finally, we were puzzled by Enron's and its supporters' boasts in late 2000 regarding the company's initiative in the telecommunications field, particularly in the trading of broadband capacity. Enron bragged about a huge, untapped market in such capacity and told analysts that the present value of Enron's opportunity in that market could be US$20 to

US$30 per share of Enron stock. These statements were troubling to us, because our portfolio already contained a number of short ideas in the telecommunications and broadband area based on the snowballing glut of capacity that was developing in that industry. By late 2000, the stocks of companies in this industry had fallen precipitously, yet Enron and its executives seemed oblivious to this fact. In addition, despite the obvious bear market in pricing for telecommunications capacity and services, Enron still saw huge upside in the valuation of its own assets in this very same market, an ominous portent.

Beginning in January 2001, we spoke with a number of analysts at various Wall Street firms to discuss Enron and its valuation. We were struck by how many of them conceded that there was no way to analyse Enron, but that investing in Enron was instead a 'trust me' story. One analyst, while admitting that Enron was a black box regarding profits, said that, as long as Enron delivered, who was he to argue.

In the spring of 2001, we heard reports, later confirmed by Enron, that a number of senior executives were departing from the company. Further, the insider selling of Enron stock continued unabated. Finally, our analysis of Enron's 2000 Form 10-K and March 2001 Form 10-Q filings continued to show low returns on capital as well as a number of one-time gains that boosted Enron's earnings. These filings also reflected Enron's continuing participation in various 'related-party transactions' that we found difficult to understand despite the more detailed disclosure Enron had provided. These observations strengthened our conviction that the market was still overpricing Enron's stock.

In the summer of 2001, energy and power prices, specifically natural gas and electricity, began to drop. Rumours surfaced routinely on Wall Street that Enron had been caught 'long' in the power market and that it was being forced to move aggressively to reduce its exposure in a declining market. It is an axiom in securities trading that no matter how well 'hedged' a firm claims to be, trading operations always seem to do better in bull markets and to struggle in bear markets. We believe that the power market had entered a bear phase at just the wrong moment for Enron.

Also in the summer of 2001, stories began circulating in the market place about Enron's affiliated partnerships and how Enron's stock price itself was important to Enron's financial well-being. In effect, traders were saying that Enron's dropping stock price could create a cash flow squeeze at the company because of certain provisions and agreements that it had entered into with affiliated partnerships. These stories gained some credibility as Enron disclosed more information about these partnerships in its June 2001 Form 10-Q, which it filed in August of 2001.

To us, however, the most important story in August of 2001 was the abrupt resignation of Enron's CEO, Jeff Skilling, for 'personal reasons'. In our experience, there is no louder alarm bell in a controversial company than the unexplained, sudden departure of a chief executive officer no matter what 'official' reason is given. Since we viewed Jeff Skilling as the architect of the present Enron, his abrupt departure was the most ominous development yet. Kynikos Associates increased its portfolio's short position in Enron shares following this disclosure.

The effort we devoted to looking behind the numbers at Enron, and the actions we ultimately took based upon our research and analysis, show how we deliver value to our investors and, ultimately, to the market as a whole. Short sellers are the professional sceptics who look past the hype to gauge the true value of a stock. Let me now turn to the question of whether, in light of the important work they do, short sellers should be subject to greater, or perhaps less, regulation.

Is there a need for regulatory change?

It is important to separate the questions regarding additional regulation of hedge funds, on the one hand, and the possibility of additional regulation of short selling, on the other. Unfortunately, the two are often linked, even though there is little evidence that there is a relationship between the two that warrants changes in public policy.[11]

Short selling

As outlined above, short selling is already a heavily regulated strategy with significant legal and economic constraints. Strong capital markets in the United States require a robust short side; restrictions on short selling impede the market's efficiency and decrease the amount of independent research necessary to mitigate against irrational exuberance and outright fraud. Short selling represents only a very small fraction of market activity. It is very costly and full of risk for the short seller to execute and maintain a position, waiting for the rest of the market to realise the stock is overvalued.

There are already tight regulatory requirements and economic costs that restrict short selling. Imposing further barriers and restrictions upon short sellers may shrink an already small number of professional short investors and further limit their incentive and ability to serve as the counterbalance to hype and irrational optimism that frequently drive stock valuations to unsustainable heights, resulting in the misallocation of capital in our markets.

Any manipulation of stock prices, whether upward or downward, should be prosecuted to the full extent of the law, and I firmly believe that the enforcement agencies (federal, state and SRO) must have the tools necessary to accomplish that objective. However, I believe that the record (as evidenced by the NASD's Pollock Report in 1985, the SEC's testimony in 1989 and Owen Lamont's study in 2002) demonstrates that the allegations about illegal short manipulation activity are frequently spurious. One can even go back to the Senate investigation that led to the enactment of the Securities Act of 1933. It started out as an investigation of alleged bear raids and short manipulation in the 1929 market crash, but found instead issuer and investment banker hype, conflicts of interest and inadequate disclosure. The investigation vindicated short selling as an important market activity and led instead to the enactment of the federal securities laws, regulating issuers and investment bankers.

In a more modern context, the SEC testified before Congress in 1989 (again addressing allegations of short selling and market manipulation) that it 'frequently' found the negative statements of short sellers to be true; and, that it also found that 'many of the companies from whom we receive complaints about alleged illegal short selling are themselves under investigation for possible violations of the securities or other laws at the time they make the complaints'.[12]

Obviously, we will willingly comply with any new law or regulation that is enacted. However, it is my hope that a careful examination of any allegations of regulatory gaps will reveal that the facts do not support the case for new regulatory action.

In fact, the SEC itself contemplated relaxing restrictions on short selling at a number of points in the 1990s, most recently issuing a concept release in 1999 on the topic. I believe that the facts underlying those releases are much the same today as they were then. Thus, I would hope that there would be as much consideration to removing antiquated and inefficient regulations as there is to imposing new regulations.

459

Hedge funds

Chairman Donaldson in his 10 April 2003 testimony on hedge funds to the Senate Committee on Banking, Finance and Urban Affairs identified a number of the important issues to be considered in reviewing and considering changes to private investment fund regulation. Retailisation of hedge funds was one of the problems he identified.[13] From a business perspective, I know that I am not comfortable soliciting funds from individuals who simply meet the minimum criteria of the Regulation D/accredited investor/3(c)(1) exemption of either US$200,000 in annual income or US$1 million in net worth. As a business practice, I do not find that I can make a presumption that an individual or business entity that meets those criteria is sufficiently knowledgeable about the risks associated with Kynikos' investment strategy to make an informed decision. Short selling is an inherently risky proposition. Profits are limited to a maximum of 100 per cent of the proceeds on the date of sale; losses, however, can be infinite, depending on how high the stock price moves after the sale. Private investment companies like Kynikos also set different rules for withdrawal of funds than do most mutual funds or other traditional money managers. I do not want someone who is not able to tolerate these risks to invest with me. It is simply not good business. Therefore, the prerequisites for investing in our funds are much more stringent than they are for these other managed investment vehicles.

When Regulation D was adopted over 20 years ago, its definitions for accredited investors of US$200,000 of annual income or US$1 million in net worth were considerably higher standards than they are today. In general, the investment strategies of private investment funds involve substantial risk and illiquidity. They are not appropriate for the average investor.

I do not know, as a matter of public policy, what the right level of income or net worth is to make a presumption about market sophistication. I am aware that when Congress enacted an expansion of the 3(c)(7) exemptions in 1997, that it used the criteria of US$5 million in investible assets (a more selective barrier) as the presumptive basis for market sophistication. Given the increase in the number of hedge funds over the past decade, perhaps it is appropriate to re-examine the Rule 506 accredited investor/3(c)(1) standard.

In addition to the NASD's recent move to improve broker-dealer suitability standards for sales of hedge funds, additional steps can be taken to keep investors limited to those who can understand and bear the risks associated with private investment funds. One such step would be setting a higher minimum investor qualification standard than the current accredited investor definition. This could include both a higher net worth and a limit to an investment in a fund to a percentage of that net worth (some states, such as California and North Carolina, historically have used a cap on privately placed investments at 10 per cent of the investor's net worth as a rough benchmark or limit, while others have used a 20 per cent limit).

This change would not necessarily require an amendment to Regulation D's definition of 'accredited investor'. Other regulatory provisions could be amended, for example, the pending rulemaking under Section 18 of the Securities Act of 1933 to pre-empt state filing requirements for sales to qualified purchasers, would define 'qualified purchasers' by reference to the Regulation D definition of 'accredited investors': Rel. No. 33–8041, 66 Fed. Reg. 66839 (December 2001). Why not set a somewhat higher investor qualification standard for private placements that seek to rely on pre-emption to avoid all state filings?

In addition to the retailisation issue, Chairman Donaldson in his 10 April testimony also noted conflicts of interest, valuation, performance reporting, fraud, misappropriation of assets, and relations with prime brokers and other service providers. Each of these is a significant issue that all managers of a private investment fund should be required to address as a condition to operating in a relatively unregulated format.

One simple means to address these issues would be to impose some basic prudential restrictions on hedge funds that wish to rely upon the regulatory exemptions from investment adviser registration, 17 C.F.R. §§ 275.203(b)(3)-1 & 275.222–2 (which treat a private investment fund as a single client of the manager for purposes of determining whether the manager has 15 or more clients and is thus subject to registration and regulation under the Investment Advisers Act). The rule could be amended to require a look through to count the investors in the fund if the fund does not meet certain basic investor qualification and investor protection requirements such as:

- minimum investor qualifications above current accredited investor levels (addresses retailisation issue);
- custody of private investment fund assets in a broker-dealer or bank and compliance with SEC interpretations on constructive custody (addresses misappropriation of assets, fraud and transparency issues);
- annual audit and delivery of financial statements to investors (addresses fraud and transparency issues);
- quarterly unaudited financial reports to investors (addresses transparency issue);
- clear disclosure of financial arrangements with interested parties such as investment manager, custodian, prime broker, portfolio brokers, placement agents and other service providers, both in terms of description and with some periodic historic quantification of amounts paid to each category and benefits received (addresses conflict of interest, transparency and fraud issues);
- clear disclosure of investment allocation policies (addresses conflict of interest, transparency and fraud issues); and
- clear, objective and transparent valuation standards, that are clearly disclosed, not stale, and subject to audit, for use in calculating current unit values for investor reports, admissions and withdrawals and calculations of performance and volatility information (addresses valuation, transparency and fraud issues).

Simple, basic standards on each of the above points could be added to Advisers Act Rule 275. 203(b)(3)-1(a)(2)(i) as a condition to reliance on the 'single client' treatment of a private investment fund. Those investment managers who operate investment funds that meet these standards would be allowed to treat the fund as a single client and thus continue to avoid registration under the Advisers Act. It may be appropriate to exempt family partnerships, family trusts, and gift and estate situations and 'knowledgeable employee' funds from these requirements (to mirror exemptions contained in current Investment Company Act §§ 2(a)(51)(A)(ii) and (iii); 17 C.F.R. §§ 270.3c-5, 270.3c-6 on the grounds that these types of closely held arrangements do not involve marketing to unrelated investors). Investment managers that operate private investment funds that do not meet these standards would be required to look through the investment fund and treat each of its investors as a client, thus subjecting the investment manager to registration, SEC examination and regulation under the Investment Advisers Act.

While we are not advocates of increases in the general regulation of private investment funds or short selling, we are concerned that the misdeeds of a few could result in a backlash against the industry. Requiring private investment funds to follow a few basic requirements on investor qualifications and investor protection along the lines set forth above as a condition to continuing to operate in a relatively unregulated fund environment could protect both investors and the private investment fund industry from the actions of a few bad actors.

[1] Adapted from a prepared statement for the US Securities and Exchange Commission roundtable on hedge funds panel discussion: Hedge Fund Strategies and Market Participation. 15 May 2003.

[2] Bernard Baruch, testimony before the Committee on Rules, House of Representatives, January 1917.

[3] Dechow, P., A. Hutton, L. Meulbroek, R. Sloan (1999), *Short Sellers, Fundamental Analysis and Stock Returns,* Working Paper, Harvard Business School, University of Michigan Business School, May, pp. 3–4.

[4] See Alex Berenson (2003), 'The Number: How the Drive for Quarterly Earnings Corrupted Wall Street and Corporate America', Chapter 9, *Detectives and Archeologists*, New York, Random House.

[5] Edward Chancellor (2001), 'A Short History of the Bear', Guest Analysis, www.theprudentbear.com, 29 October, p. 6.

[6] Asquith, P. and L. Meulbroek (1996), *An Empirical Investigation of Short Interest,* Working Paper (Harvard University, Boston, MA).

[7] 'If Short Sellers Take Heat, Maybe It's Time to Bail Out', Gretchen Morgenson, *The New York Times*, 26 January 2003.

[8] I. Pollack (1986), *Short Sale Regulation of NASDAQ Securities*; see Prepared Statement of Richard G. Ketchum, Director, Division of Market Regulation and John H. Sturc, Associate Director, Division of Enforcement, Securities and Exchange Commission, Before the House Committee on Government Affairs, Subcommittee on Commerce, Consumer, and Monetary Affairs, 6 December 1989.

[9] Prepared Statement of Richard G. Ketchum, Director, Division of Market Regulation and John H. Sturc, Associate Director, Division of Enforcement, Securities and Exchange Commission, Before the House Committee on Government Affairs, Subcommittee on Commerce, Consumer, and Monetary Affairs, 6 December 1989, pp. 434–435.

[10] This section of testimony is drawn largely from testimony that I presented before the Committee on Energy and Commerce, United States House of Representatives, *Lessons Learned From Enron's Collapse: Auditing the Accounting Industry,* 6 February 2002.

[11] See, for example, Edward Chancellor (2001), 'A Short History of the Bear', Guest Analysis, www.theprudentbear.com, 29 October.

[12] Oral Testimony of John H. Sturc, Associate Director, Division of Enforcement, Securities and Exchange Commission before the Committee on Government Operations, Subcommittee on Commerce, Consumer, and Monetary Affairs, United States House of Representatives, 6 December 1989.

[13] Testimony of William J. Donaldson, Chairman, Securities and Exchange Commission; Senate Banking Committee; 10 April 2003.

Part VI

Legal and regulatory issues

Chapter 38

Structuring hedge funds: an overview of business, legal and regulatory considerations for managers

Philip H. Harris, Andrew S. Kenoe, Sarah Davidoff and Michael A. Lawson[1]
Skadden, Arps, Slate, Meagher & Flom, LLP, New York, New York

Introduction

The structuring of a hedge fund is an interdisciplinary legal and regulatory exercise, with regard to both (a) the numerous legal speciality practice areas involved (for example, tax, the Employee Retirement Income Security Act (ERISA), securities and commodities laws, investment company and investment advisers acts, and US and non-US local laws) and (b) the combination of legal considerations and economic, political, geographical and marketing components. Consequently, in creating a hedge fund, most investment managers find themselves confronted by a myriad of seemingly disparate legal and regulatory considerations that can result in significant economic and reputation costs if not properly addressed. The goal in structuring a hedge fund is to manoeuvre through this regulatory and legal obstacle course to achieve a structure that affords the investment manager efficiency and flexibility in marketing, trading, management and administration. Ultimately, the structural success of a hedge fund (ie, the degree of economic efficiency and administrative ease with which it operates) largely depends on the analytical rigour applied to these elements. The more rigorous the analysis and the more precisely these goals are delineated, the more focused the legal or regulatory responses to them can be, subject to varying compromises among incompatible regimes. A well-structured hedge fund, in the final analysis, is one that has the simplest (but not simplistic) structure in relation to the nature of its investors and trading strategies while simultaneously providing the maximum economic efficiency and investment and operational flexibility.

Finally, as the industry develops and regulatory and media interest increases, the structure needs to be able to adapt to regulatory changes as well. This article is based on current law, but readers should be aware that substantial changes are occurring at a rapid pace in both the United States and the European Union.

Threshold questions

The initial structuring requires investment managers and their advisers to answer certain threshold questions.

- What is the fundamental nature of the product being offered?

- What is the investment objective of the proposed fund and any future funds (and in what types of instruments will the fund invest)?
- What trading strategies will be employed (and over what term will the fund hold such instruments)?
- Who are the fund's investors, where are they located and what is their legal status?

Ancillary queries concern the organisational form of the product (trust, partnership or corporate vehicle); the tax treatment of the jurisdiction form; and the jurisdiction of its organisation, as certain forms, tax treatments and jurisdictions are more amenable to certain types of products and investor needs. The product's targeted market must be identified (eg, taxable US, tax-exempt US or non-US individuals and institutions) in unison with the means used to sell the fund (third party placement agents or the issuer directly). The narrower the focus on these issues, the more precise the structuring process will be.

After these threshold matters have been analysed, the process of assembling a fund's various components can begin. Of course, the typical response to the questions posed above is often that there is no certainty regarding any of these issues and that the structure needs to be flexible enough to be sold anywhere to any type of person, and be able to invest in almost anything.

Types of organisation

The nature of the product and the investor base to which it will be marketed will determine to a great extent the product's organisational structure. This section sets forth the most typical structures for US-based hedge funds, offshore hedge funds and complexes of hedge funds that combine both US and offshore jurisdictions and investor types.

Domestic funds

Hedge funds marketed primarily to US taxable investors have historically been domiciled in the United States.[2] In order to (i) avoid an additional level of income tax, (ii) capitalise upon the US federal, state and local tax savings currently afforded to capital gains and (iii) allow certain fund losses to be available to reduce its investors' own tax liabilities, these funds are organised as income tax pass-through entities, either as limited partnerships, Delaware statutory trusts or limited liability companies (LLCs). Hedge funds today commonly seek various types of investors. This simple structure, therefore, is no longer common because managers seek to satisfy the needs of a diverse investor base.

Limited partnerships

Limited partnerships historically were the most frequently encountered organisational form of domestic hedge fund, combining pass-through tax treatment for investors with the advantage of a market-recognised product. Delaware is a favoured jurisdiction amongst investors due to its highly developed, well-delineated limited partnership law and the familiarity of its courts with investment partnerships. However, limited liability companies, described below, are now the most frequent form of single-vehicle hedge funds for a variety of reasons.

The investment manager (or an affiliate) usually functions as the general partner, the entity to which investors grant exclusive management (including investment advisory) authority for the fund. The fund often delegates advisory authority to an investment adviser, who makes the actual trading decisions, although the general partner entity may also perform this role, thereby eliminating the need for a separate investment adviser.[3] If the investment manager cannot or does not wish to serve as a general partner for regulatory, liability or other reasons, the fund may be structured so that an administrative entity serves as the general partner with the regulated entity serving as the investment adviser.[4]

Under Delaware law, a general partner of a Delaware limited partnership has unlimited liability;[5] for this reason, the general partner itself is virtually always organised as a limited liability entity, typically a limited liability company, thus shielding its owner (ie, the investment manager and the principals) from personal liability. In organising the general partner entity, certain special considerations should be addressed. For example, the value of the investment manager's interest in the fund is, at the outset, substantially less than it is likely to be once the fund is fully established. Since these interests will have their lowest value during the fund's preliminary stages, it may be advantageous, for individual estate and gift tax purposes, to gift or sell interests in the general partner (or investment adviser) to beneficiaries or family members before the fund is developed and has assets. Similarly, the investment manager should decide at this stage if it desires a deferral mechanism for deferring current income, as such income deferrals generally must be made prior to the beginning of the taxable year in which such income will be earned.[6]

A hedge fund organised as a limited partnership typically issues non-voting limited partnership interests to its investors (unless the manager is a bank or an affiliate of a bank, which triggers special structuring, voting and regulatory capital issues).[7] Although hedge funds generally issue only one class of interests, interests in a Delaware limited partnership may be issued in multiple classes or series or with preferred interests for leverage or other purposes. Each class may either (i) share on a *pari passu* basis in the same portfolio but on differing economic or governance terms[8] or (ii) have its own designated portfolio. In addition, each series may be designated to have separate and distinct assets and liabilities, so that there is no cross-liability among the series under Delaware law. For example, this structure is useful if an investment manager would like to offer various investment strategies. The manager may offer all strategies within one vehicle rather than incurring the administrative and other costs of establishing and maintaining several vehicles. Notwithstanding the clarity of state law, to date the separateness of the series structure has not been litigated in a bankruptcy scenario.[9] Similar economics can be achieved in Delaware statutory trusts.

Part of the attraction of the limited partnership as a hedge fund structure is that a holder of a limited partnership interest is statutorily liable to the partnership[10] only for the amount of its investment.[11] Because of their 'limited' status, limited partners may participate in management only on a restricted basis; for example, they may sit on an advisory board or vote for the removal of the general partner or the investment adviser. If they take too active a role in the fund's management, however, they could be deemed to be themselves a general partner, thereby losing their limited partner status and subjecting themselves to unlimited liability.

The organisational documents for a Delaware limited partnership include:

- a certificate of limited partnership, which must be filed with the Secretary of State in the state of Delaware in order for the fund to be legally organised;
- a limited partnership agreement, which defines the economic and governance provisions of the fund; and
- an advisory agreement between the investment adviser and the fund, to the extent applicable to the structure.

Limited liability companies

Limited liability companies (LLCs) are now the primary structures for investment vehicles for US taxable investors. Currently, all of the states have adopted LLC statutes. Again, Delaware is a common choice for organising a hedge fund. One of the chief benefits to this form is that it eliminates the need for a general partner (ie, the creation of an entity with unlimited liability). This makes the LLC an especially attractive structure for hedge funds sponsored by investment managers that either cannot serve as general partners or do not want to undertake the administrative, economic or legal burden of organising and maintaining an entity to function as general partner.[12] The manager (ie, the general partner equivalent) is statutorily shielded from liability to the same extent as a corporate officer or director and can be an entity itself.

A hedge fund organised as a LLC affords the same flexibility in terms of management as a limited partnership. It may be managed by a manager who may, but is not required, to hold a membership interest in the fund. Alternatively, management may be vested in the membership (ie, the investors) at large, or in a combination of a manager/managing member and the membership. As with a limited partnership, investment advisory authority may be delegated to an investment adviser. Structurally, this means that a managing member that is an investment manager may either engage a fund manager with no direct economic stake to undertake the general management of the fund, or perform such duties itself. Interests in LLCs may be issued in series in the same manner and with the same benefits as interests in limited partnerships issued in series as described above.

The organisational documents for a LLC include:

- a certificate of formation, upon the filing of which with the Secretary of State in the state of organisation the fund is legally organised; and
- a limited liability company agreement, which defines the economic and governance provisions of the fund.

Neither a Delaware limited partnership nor a LLC is required to publicly disclose or file the names of its holders or any of its governance documents.

Privately offered registered investment companies

Another alternative that is suitable for certain pension investors' specialised needs (including as a shield against unrelated business taxable income (UBTI) or a means through which an investor may invest in a portfolio of securities without regard to certain limitations imposed under ERISA) involves the creation of an investment company that is registered under the Investment Company Act. An investment company is subject to full Securities and Exchange Commission (SEC) regulation as an investment company and is privately placed (so as to avoid regulation as a public offering under the Securities Act of 1933) to at least 100 security holders, virtually all of whom may hold nominal amounts of a debt or equity instrument. See 'Securities Act of 1933 – Private placement'. Such a vehicle can obtain pass-through income tax treatment as a regulated investment company (provided it satisfies the asset diversification and other income tax-related requirements) or can elect to be taxed as a partnership (assuming that it can be structured so as to avoid becoming a 'publicly traded partnership taxable as a corporation' for US federal income tax purposes and UBTI is not a concern). However, the adviser must register with the SEC and there are substantive leverage limits, meaningful restrictions on affiliated transactions and a significant regulatory overlay involved that make the utility of this structure very limited, except for investors in hedge funds and third party funds of funds that are primarily institutional. The SEC and the National Association of Security Dealers (NASD) are also currently examining the propriety of offering these funds to retail investors.

Offshore funds

Hedge funds sponsored by US investment managers that are marketed primarily to US investors exempt from US federal income tax[13] and/or US and non-US persons and institutions, are generally domiciled in a tax haven jurisdiction to avoid taxation at the fund level and shield investors from certain IRS filing requirements.[14] Legal structures that can be used in organising offshore funds include:

- corporations issuing both debt and equity;
- unit trusts;
- undertakings for collective investments in transferable securities (UCITS);
- limited partnerships, including partnerships that are taxable as corporations for US federal income tax purposes;[15]
- LLCs;
- series or umbrella funds; and
- multi-class funds.

The legal systems of certain jurisdictions may not provide for all of these forms. The Cayman Islands, for example, does not provide for UCITS funds, but does offer a variety of corporate, trust and partnership forms. Our current preference in nearly all scenarios is the Cayman Islands unit trust. Due to the flexibility it provides to adjust the structure at minimal expense to accommodate virtually any investor base and economic structure, the Cayman Islands unit trust structure has all the benefits of other structures with less complexity, and allows a manager to build or add on to the fund without restructuring or creating new entities.

Marketing considerations can affect the choice of structure if certain forms are better known and more widely accepted by investors in the targeted jurisdiction. For example, partnerships are typically less known to non-US investors and more difficult to market internationally than corporate or trust vehicles. Moreover, certain investors may have particular regulatory considerations; for example, some Asian-based investors can book a structured note (ie, a note whose economics are limited to the fund's performance) as debt (which, for US purposes, would clearly be viewed as equity), which makes a corporate vehicle issuing 'notes' a viable vehicle for such investors.[16] Similarly, certain European investors frequently require a 'convenience listing' for their interests; Luxembourg and Ireland have traditionally provided such listings, although some funds list their shares on the Cayman Islands Stock Exchange.[17]

The particular structure chosen for an offshore fund must achieve the desired tax results both for the fund and its investors. Therefore, the question of structure is partially a jurisdictional question, as only certain jurisdictions offer certain organisational forms, partially a governance question and partially a cost/benefit analysis. International tax treaty issues also can affect the analysis. Often a balance must be struck between the competing concerns of various investor groups, management and the specific trading strategies to be employed. Ultimately, a particular structure may, in some cases, have favourable regulatory or marketing implications to particular investors in certain jurisdictions, and be neutral or (in the worst case) negative to other investors and/or management. These competing concerns lead to more complex structures that address the needs of particular investors while still maintaining a common pooling of investments.

Complex structures

Frequently, the organisation of fund complexes, including mirror funds (ie, two or more funds that each follow similar or identical investment strategies but are domiciled in different jurisdictions) or master/feeder structures, may be the only practical approach to gain access to multiple markets with different regulatory and marketing concerns, and satisfy the different needs of different investor profiles.

In master/feeder arrangements, all investment activity occurs at the master fund level. Feeder funds, targeted for different types of non-US and US investors, invest all of their investable assets in the master fund. This arrangement permits economies and efficiencies in portfolio management to be achieved at the master fund level, while permitting diversity in the form of the product offered to investors at the feeder fund level. Master funds are structured as limited partnerships or as other pass-through entities domiciled in an offshore jurisdiction such as a series of a Cayman Islands' unit trust that has elected to be treated as a partnership for US tax purposes,[18] with the various feeders as any combination of limited partnerships and various corporate entities, trusts or other vehicles. In the case of limited partnerships, a corporate entity affiliated with the investment manager usually serves as its general partner. Structurally and operationally, such master funds are similar to domestic partnerships (although, as noted, they are usually not domestic). A variation of the master/feeder structure is a multi-class arrangement, which uses separate classes of shares to represent interests in a single investment portfolio. Depending upon various factors, these classes may have separate liabilities and assets. These arrangements provide many of the same benefits as a master/feeder arrangement. Feeders can assess varying load charges; incur leverage; be denominated in different currencies from the master; or enter into derivatives transactions, altering the management of the pool as a whole at the master level. Tax allocation, tax withholding rules and other criteria all need to be balanced in these structures. Certain types of investments, such as real estate and physical commodities, create special complexities and can mandate locating a master fund onshore or offshore or force separation into mirror funds.

In contrast to the master/feeder structure (in which several investment vehicles share pro rata in one portfolio), in a 'series fund' structure[19] multiple investment portfolios are created within one legal vehicle. Interests in each portfolio represent separate series of shares or units, which series, in turn, can be further subdivided into separate classes. Investors can select the portfolios in which they invest, each of which can have different objectives, fee structures, leverage or other variants (including separate distribution channels). Mirror structures can also be used.

While funds of funds have become popular in the private equity markets relatively recently, funds consisting of multiple underlying hedge funds have existed for a number of years. Index funds and sector-based pools are also using this format. The attraction of such a structure is that a portfolio can be built to meet the diversification and risk needs of a particular investor base. For example, an investment manager can assemble a portfolio of hedge fund investments using diversification principles to achieve varying levels of market correlation, volatility and risk; or the portfolio can provide the marketing advantage of mixing varying trading strategies or market sectors. Special considerations relating to funds of funds include liquidity concerns, multiple levels of fees and operational concerns (such as audit timing, information reporting, valuation methodology and the mechanics of purchasing and redeeming interests).

Swap structures and structured notes are sometimes used to (i) provide investors access to an offshore fund in which, for regulatory reasons, they would be unable to invest directly and (ii) provide a leverage mechanism. For example, an equity swap between a financial institution (or similar entity) and an investor can provide for payments between the parties that are linked to the performance of a particular fund. This device can be used to enable an investor to participate in a fund's investment experience, even if the investor is located in a jurisdiction in which the fund cannot be offered, or to leverage an investment.[20]

Similarly, an investor can buy a structured note from either a third party or the fund on which the payout is linked to the fund's investment performance. This can be used to overcome regulatory limitations, applicable to either the fund or the investor, prohibiting a direct investment in the fund by the investor.

Annuity and insurance products

In general, these products are tax-deferred insurance policies with premiums paid and invested in various underlying products (including one or more hedge funds). Recently, a number of products have been structured for US taxable investors that, when combined with estate and gift tax planning, can maximise the tax-deferred returns or, in some cases, avoid tax entirely on appreciation over an extended period of time. These products are quite complex and involve numerous regulatory issues, including issues under the Investment Company Act, the Commodity Exchange Act and US state insurance regulations as well as non-US considerations. For US tax purposes there are certain diversification and control tests, and the products are not without risks. In addition, there are meaningful requirements concerning sale by licensed insurance brokers, status tests for the insurance companies and look-through rules under the securities laws that need to be considered. These products can provide advantages to many investors, but in marketing them, care must be taken to assure that each investor understands the risks involved. Investment managers often work with the participating insurance company to structure these products. Ultimately, when properly structured through certain restrictions on liquidity, such products can provide the investment manager with a stable asset base and provide benefits to the investors.

US REGULATORY FRAMEWORK

Securities Act of 1933 (Securities Act) and Regulation D thereunder; blue sky

Private placement

As a general premise, all securities sold in the United States (including interests in a hedge fund) must be registered with the SEC, unless an exemption from the registration requirements of the Securities Act is available. Because such registration would subject the fund to regulation under the Investment Company Act and substantive disclosure, regulation and reporting obligations that would generally be undesirable, and if it is an offshore fund impossible, interests in a hedge fund (other than certain funds of funds) are virtually always sold in the United States pursuant to an exemption from the Securities Act's registration requirements, either the private placement exemption under Section 4(2) or the safe harbour thereunder contained in Regulation D. Generally, to fall within the parameters of either exemption, those involved in the marketing of the fund must observe the following.

- No general solicitation through newspapers, the Internet, etc.
- Sales only to 'accredited investors'[21] as defined under Regulation D.
- A 'reasonable belief' that investors are accredited.[22]
- Records must be kept of all solicitations made in the United States.
- No interviews or cooperation with the US press or with press likely to be located in or directed to the United States during the offering period. Separately, this could result in the manager being deemed to hold itself out publicly as an adviser, and thus it could be required to register as an investment adviser with the SEC and could create a public offering of the hedge fund's interests.[23]

It is important to abide by the foregoing, because an unregistered public offering would give rescission rights to each of the fund's investors at the original purchase price, which would effectively give such investors a put right (typically for five years under newly adopted US law) exercisable at any time, including when the fund's performance is down. As a general matter, all press contacts need to be closely monitored and evaluated on an ongoing basis for their effect on sales and regulatory status.

Non-US sales are subject to local laws, which in most countries also prohibit public offerings. Therefore all public pronouncements need to be reviewed by local counsel.

Internet offerings

The SEC has stated that a website that makes available online offering documents for hedge funds, if operated within certain parameters, does not constitute a public offering within the United States. To fall within these parameters, the SEC requires the website be accessible only to pre-qualified persons through a password-protected mechanism of some sort. In order to become qualified, a person would be required to demonstrate status as an 'accredited investor'.[24] Once admitted as a subscriber, the investor would be given a password, which would enable the investor to have access to the website. Similarly, if the website is to provide offering materials of (i) 3(c)(7) funds, the subscription questionnaire should elicit responses which would allow the provider to form a reasonable belief that the subscriber is a 'qualified purchaser' and (ii) offshore funds, additional disclosure should be made that the information provided does not constitute a public offering in the United States of the securities of those funds represented on the website. The regulatory protections currently in place satisfy regulatory concerns regarding the nature of the investors and their status. If proper legends are present, there are no restrictions on offshore sales, even if potential investors can otherwise gain access to the site from the United States. This is a rapidly evolving area of the law in many jurisdictions (eg, the United Kingdom and Switzerland have also issued similar rules for sales within their jurisdictions).

Related 'blue sky' considerations

Prior to 11 October 1996, private offerings of hedge funds (both US and offshore) to US persons were required to comply with the various state blue sky laws. Although exemptions were available for institutional investors in most states, filings were occasionally necessary. The National Securities Markets Improvement Act of 1996 (NSMIA) pre-empts blue sky requirements (other than fees, sales reports and the ability to require filing a copy of any document filed with the SEC) if the offering is exempted from registration with the SEC by compliance with Regulation D (including filing Form D) or is made to qualified purchasers as defined under the Investment Company Act (see 'Investment Company Act').

In order to ensure such pre-emption, a fund must file a Form D with the SEC within 15 days after its initial sale. Many hedge funds engage in de facto continuous offerings of the same security and consideration must be given to filing federally as well as a notice filing in states where sales occur. Certain investment managers and/or placement agents are reluctant to file a Form D, as the form requires disclosure of the total amount raised and any applicable selling commissions. For such clients, an initial sale can be made for their own respective accounts in advance of third party sales, thereby complying with the rule while obviating the need to disclose the fund's size or any applicable selling commissions.

Securities Exchange Act of 1934 (the Exchange Act)

Section 12(g)

Entities formed under the laws of the United States issuing securities (including interests in hedge funds) in the United States with total assets of US\$10 million or more and a class of equity securities held of record by 500 or more persons (whether or not such persons reside in the United States) are required to register such class of securities pursuant to Section 12(g) of the Exchange Act in the absence of an exemption therefrom. There are special rules to determine the number of record holders. Registration under Section 12(g) would subject a fund to the periodic reporting requirements of the Exchange Act. However, the structure of the disclosure is designed for operating companies, and creates compliance difficulties for hedge funds. The SEC has indicated that it is prepared to utilise the exemptive provisions of Section 12(h) and grant partial exemptive relief to a hedge fund limiting the amount of disclosure required to something that is probably similar to that required of a registered investment company.[25]

Rule 12g3-2 contains two exemptions from the Section 12(g) registration and reporting requirements, both of which are available only to offshore funds (ie, foreign private issuers) but only one of which is viable for a hedge fund.

Under Rule 12g3-2(a), securities of any class of equity issued by an offshore fund would be exempt from Section 12(g) if there are fewer than 300 holders of record of the class resident in the United States. This exemption is self-executing and requires no action by the fund. The exemption is available as long as the number of US holders of record is less than 300, regardless of the number of holders residing outside the United States or the amount of assets of the fund. The exemption becomes unavailable at the end of any fiscal year in which interests are held of record by 300 or more persons resident in the United States.

Therefore, a US organised hedge fund may have up to 499 holders of record of any equity class of its interests[26] (whether US or non-US) and an offshore fund may have up to 299 US holders of record and an unlimited number of non-US holders of record before having to register such interests under the Exchange Act.[27]

Disclosure issues

Under Section 10 of the Exchange Act and pursuant to Rule 10b-5, with respect to an offering in the United States, a material misstatement, a misleading statement or the omission of a material fact in a fund's offering materials can (if certain other requirements are established) render the fund liable to those investors who purchased interests in reliance upon such misstatement or omission and subsequently suffered a pecuniary loss in their investment. This means it is incumbent upon an investment manager to conduct thorough due diligence on trading descriptions, models, performance data and similar information that may be set forth in a fund's offering materials in order to avoid liability for a material misstatement or omission that could give rise to 10b-5 liability and ultimately grant rescission rights to investors. Non-US offerings are subject to local laws which, other than those of the European Union, are generally not as well developed as in the United States. Generally, it is prudent to adhere to US or EU disclosure standards in these jurisdictions, which provides a fair measure of protection to the investment manager and the fund.

Broker-dealer issues

Under the Exchange Act any sales agent who sells in or from the United States is required to be registered as a broker-dealer (or be an associated person of a registered broker-dealer) both federally and, depending on the nature of the investors, with the states through the Central Registration Depository. An exemption is available in certain circumstances for sales made by the investment manager (the so-called 'Issuer Self-Exemption' under Rule 3(a)4-1 of the Exchange Act). In order to qualify under this 'safe harbour' exemption, no person can be directly or indirectly compensated for selling a fund's interests unless all its requirements are met, including, among other things, that persons selling are not disqualified for regulatory reasons, have currently or within one year been associated with a registered broker-dealer and that the persons have a substantial ongoing role with the investment manager other than selling interests in the fund.

Failure to be registered if it is otherwise statutorily required can result in substantial sanctions to the fund and the investment manager (in particular if the investment manager or an affiliate is a NASD member), as well as give rescission rights to investors at their original purchase price both from a US federal and a state perspective. Many people erroneously believe that they can be a finder, or pay a finder a cash fee and that such persons are not required to be registered as broker-dealers. 'Finder' is a very narrow concept that does not include the normal range of selling activities (such as delivery of offering materials and discussions regarding the fund) that the typical selling agent utilises. Care must be taken by the investment manager that paid agents are properly registered so that any failure to comply by the agents does not cause liability to the investment manager or give rise to rescission rights.

Investment Company Act of 1940 (the Investment Company Act)
Exemptions from registration

Section 3(c)(1) of the Investment Company Act has historically excluded from substantially all of its regulatory framework those funds whose interests are beneficially owned by no more than 100 persons (a 3(c)(1) fund). Section 3(c)(7) was added to the Investment Company Act in the late 1990s, authorising a new type of unregistered fund (a 3(c)(7) fund) that, for Investment Company Act purposes, may have an unlimited number of investors so long as each is either a 'qualified purchaser' (as defined below) or a knowledgeable employee. The Exchange Act and certain tax considerations, however, provide other numerical limits.

3(c)(1) funds

Section 3(c)(1) of the Investment Company Act excludes from the definition of an investment company subject to regulation under the Investment Company Act investment funds whose securities (other than short-term paper) are beneficially owned by no more than 100 persons and which are not making a public offering. Section 3(c)(1) further imposes certain look-through rules that must be used to determine the number of beneficial owners. For any beneficial owner that is a registered investment company, a 3(c)(1) fund, a 3(c)(7) fund or an offshore fund that is a 3(c)(1) or 3(c)(7) fund or that would have to register if it were organised under US law, there is an automatic look-through to the investing fund's security holders[28] if the investing fund owns more than 10 per cent of the voting securities of the 3(c)(1) fund.[29]

3(c)(7) funds

Section 3(c)(7) became effective on 9 April 1997. An investment fund that qualifies as a 3(c)(7) fund may have an unlimited number of investors without having to register under the Investment Company Act and without regard to the 10 per cent voting look-through that applies to 3(c)(1) funds so long as the investor was not formed for the purpose of making the investment (which is also a separate requirement for 3(c)(1) funds). In order to qualify as a 3(c)(7) fund, an investment fund must have the following characteristics:

- each investor must be a qualified purchaser;[30] and
- the fund is not making and does not propose to make a public offering of its securities.

Investors in a 3(c)(7) fund must be 'qualified purchasers' at the time they make their respective investments.[31]

Investment Advisers Act of 1940 (the Advisers Act)

Investment advisers registered with the SEC may not charge performance fees (generally measured based upon the amount of both realised and unrealised gains and losses), unless the client (as defined under the rules of the Advisers Act, including all investors in a 3(c)(1) fund) is (i) not a US person, (ii) a qualified purchaser or (iii) a qualified client.[32]

An investment manager that is required to register (or is registered) with the SEC also has to comply with all the other requirements of the Advisers Act, including detailed record-keeping, proxy voting and custody rules. In general, if an investment manager has fewer than 15 clients in any year, less than US$30 million under management, does not hold itself out publicly as an adviser and does not advise a US registered investment company, it is not permitted to register with the SEC. However, some managers with at least US$30 million under management decide to register with the SEC for marketing purposes or due to certain ERISA requirements. The manager may have state filing obligations if it has an office or investors in a particular state. Both registered and unregistered advisers are subject, however, to the anti-fraud provisions of the Advisers Act.

Commodity Exchange Act of 1974 (CEA)

Generally, if a fund invests in futures or options on the US contract markets, or if the investment manager is located in the United States with US investors in the fund and it trades in offshore markets, then the fund must have a registered commodity pool operator (CPO), the investment manager must be registered as a CPO or a commodity trading adviser (CTA) with the CFTC and the fund must file its offering documents with the CFTC. A CPO or CTA must also join the National Futures Association (NFA), a self-regulatory organisation.

The following sets forth certain of the more common exemptions from registration under the CEA.

- *No futures trading* – no filings.
- *Rule 4.12(b) exemption* – less than 10 per cent of assets in futures, prefiling ('instant filing' for funds of funds) with CFTC is required; disclosure of conflicts; waiving performance; periodic updates and other NFA member information is mandatory.
- *Rule 4.7 exemption* – only a notice of exemption is filed; no filing of documents, no review by CFTC; no mandated disclosure so long as all investors are qualified eligible clients (QECs). QECs must meet high net worth and investment tests of US$2 million, be qualified purchasers or other alternative tests unless they are not US persons as defined by the CFTC.

The CFTC has outstanding proposed rules that would eliminate the CPO registration requirements for 3(c)(7) funds and 3(c)(1) funds in certain circumstances.

Anti-money laundering

On 18 September 2002, the Financial Crimes Enforcement Network (FinCen) proposed a new rule that clarifies that hedge funds must comply with the anti-money laundering (AML) requirements of the Bank Secrecy Act (BSA). The BSA requires every financial institution to establish an AML programme, and the proposed rule effectively includes hedge funds in the definition of a financial institution. The proposed rule also sets forth guidelines that hedge funds are to follow in establishing AML programmes. We note that the rule may not be adopted in the form in which it was proposed.

On 26 October 2002, FinCen and the Treasury Department issued an interim final rule that defers application of the BSA until the final rules are issued. At the time of this writing, the rules are to be finalised shortly. In the meantime, managers should consider their readiness to implement the guidelines set forth below and the possible reputation risks involved in having a problem investor before being required by FinCen to implement a programme. Many hedge fund complexes have already implemented AML programmes.

Generally, the proposed rule requires that each hedge fund adopt an AML programme reasonably designed to prevent the fund from being used to launder money or finance terrorist activities. Each programme must be approved in writing by the fund's board of directors, trustees, general partner or, in the absence of the foregoing, senior management. The proposed rule provides that such programmes are to be in place within 90 days following the publication of the final rule. Please note that the proposed rule would require hedge funds to file a notice with FinCen to identify themselves and to provide basic information about their business.

Under the proposed rule, the BSA does *not* apply to hedge funds that (i) only give their investors the right to redeem any portion of ownership interests beginning two years following the date the interests were purchased; (ii) have total assets of less than US$1 million as of the most recently completed calendar quarter; (iii) are organised outside of the United States, sell ownership interests only to non-US persons and are sponsored by non-US persons; (iv) are owned by one family; (v) are employees' securities companies; or (vi) are employee benefit plans not considered pools by Rule 4.5(a)(4) under the Commodity Exchange Act.

The following guidelines are set forth in the proposed rule to be followed by hedge funds in establishing an AML programme.

- Policies, procedures and internal controls are to be established and implemented in such a way that they are reasonably designed to prevent the fund from being used to launder money or finance terrorist activities and to comply with the requirements of the BSA. As proposed, the only BSA requirement applicable to unregistered investment companies is the obligation to report the receipt of cash and certain non-cash instruments totalling more than US$10,000 in one transaction or two or more related transactions. Hedge funds would not be subject to the BSA requirements regarding investor verification and filing suspicious activity reports (SARs). However, funds would be strongly encouraged to voluntarily file SARs with FinCen. In addition, hedge funds are not currently subject to the BSA know-your-customer (KYC) requirements. However, it is anticipated that FinCen will issue KYC guidelines for hedge funds at a future date.
- The programme is to provide for independent testing for compliance and that such testing be conducted by company personnel or by a qualified outside party.
- A person or persons responsible for implementing and monitoring the operations and internal controls of the programme are to be designated.
- Ongoing training is to be provided to the appropriate persons.

Hedge funds should also be aware of the economic sanctions administered by the US Treasury Department's Office of Foreign Assets Control (OFAC) which prohibit US persons (ie, US citizens, US residents, companies organised in a US jurisdiction and persons in the United States) from engaging in certain transactions with persons, entities or governments of certain countries.

OFAC has stated that 'all investments and transactions in the United States' or *involving US persons anywhere in the world* fall under US jurisdiction and must comply with OFAC's regulations. All investments and contributions should be scrutinised to ensure they do not represent obligations of, or ownership interests in, entities owned or controlled by sanctioned targets. We recommend that managers screen their investments and investor contributions against OFAC lists of specially designated nationals and blocked persons. This is an ongoing obligation. Several companies have developed software programmes that can assist managers with OFAC screening.

In addition, many other jurisdictions are in the process of changing or creating AML, embargo and trade sanctions, or similar laws, regulations, requirements (whether or not with force of law) or regulatory policies. Many financial intermediaries are in the process of changing or creating responsive disclosure and compliance policies, and hedge funds could be requested or required to obtain certain assurances from their investors; disclose information pertaining to them to governmental, regulatory or other authorities, or to financial intermediaries; or engage in due diligence or take other related actions in the future.

Privacy regulations

The 1999 Gramm–Leach–Bliley Financial Modernization Act obligated certain federal agencies (including the FTC, the SEC and the CFTC) to adopt regulations that require financial institutions to comply with restrictions on the use of non-public personal information obtained from individuals and to provide such individuals with notice of their privacy policies and practices. As a result, hedge funds are now required to furnish notices to new investors before they make an investment and annually to existing investors. The notice should contain a description of the fund's policy regarding disclosure of non-public personal information and, to the extent required by the applicable regulations, a provision allowing the investor or client to opt out of disclosure of non-public personal information by the fund or adviser. In addition, hedge funds are required to formulate and follow policies that maintain the security of customer information.

Basic economics

Compensation

Generally, an investment manager's compensation consists of (i) a base advisory fee in an amount equal to a percentage interest of the fund's total assets (currently, advisory fees range from anywhere between 1–3 per cent) and (ii) a performance allocation or fee,[33] as the case may be, in an amount equal to a percentage (currently, generally ranging between 5–30 per cent) of the net increase in an investor's investment. In the hedge fund arena, performance-based compensation is almost always measured on a 'high water mark' basis, so that any losses suffered by an investor during a prior period are made up before any such compensation becomes due for a current period. In order to effectuate this, each investor in a pass-through structure (such as a partnership or a LLC) is given a memorandum account, a so-called 'loss carryforward account', which will track losses over previous periods of performance. Performance-based compensation becomes due only if the balance in such account is zero and returns are positive. Depending on the accounting principles applied, corporate structures either have loss carryforward directly reflected in the fund's net asset value (NAV) (in the case of series 'roll-ups' or equalisation factors) or provide for a similar sort of memorandum account (in the case of structures following partnership accounting principles).[34]

Accounting

Funds structured as partnerships and LLCs follow standard partnership accounting practices. Such funds establish a capital account for each investor, into which the investor's share of net profit and net loss is allocated and from which the investor's share of any performance allocation is reallocated to the entity entitled to it (ie, the general partner, special limited partner[35] or the managing member).

For those funds organised as corporations or trusts, or that otherwise offer investors interests represented by shares, notes or units, and have not elected status as a partnership for US tax purposes, partnership accounting principles can be grafted onto the basic corporate governance terms. In such instances, each investor may be given its own series of interests (shares, notes or units as the case may be), which series functions as the equivalent of a capital account. For each such series a loss carryforward account is established to which such series' share of net loss is effectively allocated. A NAV for the fund is determined by aggregating the NAVs of the various series. In the alternative, a separate series may be issued upon each closing of interests over a specified period of time (usually a year); at the end of such period, all interests for which there is a no loss carryforward are 'rolled up' into one series, with investors thereafter having the same series.[36]

Organisational expenses

Organisational expenses are typically borne by the fund. Placement fees may be borne by the adviser or may be borne by the fund directly. Although US GAAP no longer permits organisational expenses to be amortised over a five-year period, accountants will generally permit such amortisation for US hedge funds, if the amount being amortised is determined to be immaterial or, if material, provided disclosure is made that US GAAP is not being followed with regard to this aspect of the fund's financial statements.

ERISA-employee benefit plans

If 25 per cent or more of any class of a fund's equity is held by employee benefit plans (including non-US plans) and any portion of any class of equity is from pension plans subject to ERISA, the fund's assets may be subject to ERISA under the look-through provisions of the so-called 'plan asset rules'.

The look-through provisions impose ERISA's fiduciary responsibility restrictions on persons with discretionary authority over the fund and prohibit certain transactions with or in securities of persons who are 'parties in interest' to ERISA plans that hold equity in the fund (which includes persons who are related to or who provide services to such ERISA plans).[37]

Exceptions

In general, the look-through provisions of the plan asset rules will not apply in the following situations:

- *mutual funds* – if the fund is registered under the Investment Company Act;
- *publicly offered securities* – if the equity in the fund that is held by an ERISA plan is part of a class of securities that is widely held, freely transferable and registered under the Exchange Act;
- *venture capital operating companies* – if at least 50 per cent of the fund's long-term assets are invested in operating companies with respect to which it has certain management rights; and
- *the 25 per cent rule* – if less than 25 per cent of each class of equity interest in the fund is held by benefit plan investors (including plans not subject to ERISA and non-US pension plans).

Even if the look-through provisions of the plan asset rules were to apply, a number of exemptions may be available to exempt parties to such transactions from the imposition of the applicable ERISA penalties with respect to certain of the transactions of the fund (assuming the conditions set forth in such exemptions are met). Sample exemptions include the following: (i) QPAM – if the investment manager or other fiduciary exercising discretion over the fund is a qualified professional asset manager (QPAM),[38] the transactions executed under the QPAM's authority would generally be exempt from penalty; or (ii) group trusts/insurance company pooled separate accounts – group trusts maintained by a bank or insurance company pooled separate accounts composed exclusively of ERISA plans, in which no one plan owns more than 10 per cent of the beneficial interests of the trust or account, may engage in certain prohibited transactions without incurring the penalties on prohibited transactions.[39]

Tax considerations

As noted earlier, tax considerations weigh heavily among the principal factors that determine which structure will produce the most flexibility and economic benefit to the investors and the investment manager. At the same time, however, tax considerations are not typically the driving force of the structure; rather they should be thought of, at least in some instances, as limitations to be recognised and dealt with and, in others, as potential opportunities.

Overall, in the structuring of a hedge fund, the major tax considerations can be simply stated: the fund should be structured so that (i) investments in the fund's chosen asset classes can be managed effectively without generating, to the extent practicable, income or gain that is taxable *at the fund level*, and (ii) the fund's distributions of cash or other property to its investors are not themselves subject to additional income or withholding taxes. Beyond those major considerations, the fund manager and structurer will also need to consider the ability to preserve (or create), where possible, certain favoured types of income (eg, long-term capital gains instead of ordinary income), and, in some cases, the ability to defer recognition of income to the investment manager.

Domestic funds

As noted above, where a domestic vehicle will serve as the fund, unless a regulated investment company (ie, a company registered under the Investment Company Act that meets the various tax standards regarding its income and diversification of its assets) will be used, the fund will be established as an entity that will need to be able to be characterised as a partnership for US federal and state tax purposes (eg, a limited partnership, a LLC, or a business trust).[40] Care needs to be exercised in making sure that the fund is not at risk of being treated as a publicly traded partnership taxable as a corporation.[41]

For US federal and most state income tax purposes, an entity classified as a partnership is not generally subject to income tax on its net income and is similarly not generally subject to US federal or state withholding tax on amounts paid to it by US payers. The owners of the entity, however, are required each year to include in their own income tax returns their respective shares of the fund's taxable income for such year, regardless of whether any amounts have actually been distributed. Conversely, distributions of earnings by such an entity to its owners are generally not subject to withholding nor result in additional taxable income to the owners. Accordingly, for funds that expect to have only US persons as investors, a domestic partnership entity[42] makes for a very simple, familiar and relatively non-intrusive tax choice. However, if the fund expects to employ any material degree of leverage and hopes to accept tax-exempt organisations (eg, pension funds, endowments, charitable remainder trusts) as investors, the partnership form will not be attractive because the fund's use of leverage will be attributed to the tax-exempt and render all or a portion of the tax-exempt's share of the fund's income subject to income tax as UBTI.

Similarly, if a fund's investment purpose includes engaging in activities that could be considered to be engaging in the conduct of a trade or business within the United States (eg, conducting a financing business), US investors will be largely indifferent, provided that such business does not cause the fund to be treated as 'predominantly engaged' in the business of writing insurance.[43] Non-US investors, however, could be substantially adversely affected, particularly those that did not invest in the fund in connection with their pre-existing conduct of a trade or business in the United States.[44] Well-advised funds that may engage in activities that are not firmly within the traditional 'trading in stocks or securities' safe harbour of Section 864(b) are very careful about the way in which they acquire potentially troublesome assets (eg, interests in bank loans) so that they can defend themselves against a potential IRS assertion that they may be beyond the bounds of Section 864(b).

Non-US investors in a domestic partnership fund will be subject to US federal income and withholding tax at a 30 per cent rate (or a lower rate if the income is protected by an applicable treaty) on their share of the fund's US source dividend income and US source interest income that does not qualify as 'portfolio interest' or is not otherwise exempt from US income tax (eg, municipal interest, discount on commercial paper with original maturity of no more than 183 days, interest on bank deposits). The determination of whether the interest qualifies as portfolio interest is made as if the non-US investor were the direct payee of the interest.[45] In general, capital gains recognised by the fund will not be taxable to non-US investors in the fund. (Naturally, there are exceptions, including any gains that are attributable to 'US real property interests', which are taxed pursuant to FIRPTA as if they were effectively connected income.)

Non-US funds

Many non-US investors prefer not to become direct partners in a US partnership or LLC so as to avoid the unnecessary tax costs discussed above. Similarly, US tax-exempt organisations will generally avoid investment in the equity of leveraged US partnership entities. Both types of investors usually prefer a fund that is organised as a corporation or that elects to be treated as a corporation for US tax purposes in a non-US jurisdiction. Obviously, the chosen jurisdiction of incorporation is usually one that will impose little or no tax on the fund's income and not subject the fund's distributions to withholding or other tax. (Although there are others, the typical jurisdictions used are found not too far from the United States; eg, Bermuda, the Cayman Islands, the British Virgin Islands.)

As all of an offshore fund's US source income must either satisfy one exemption from US federal income tax or another (or be subject to US federal income tax) offshore funds are ideal only for investment strategies that generate only immaterial amounts of income potentially subject to US federal income tax. Fortunately, most types of interest income and capital gains on stocks and securities recognised by a fund that is an investor or trader (as opposed to, for example, a dealer or a lender) will be exempt from such tax, and, as such, offshore funds can provide for a great deal of international appeal and flexibility. US persons (other than tax-exempt organisations) who invest in an offshore fund, however, find themselves subject to a withering array of anti-income tax deferral regimes, some of which actually produce results that are more disadvantageous than would be the case if the investor purchased the assets directly or invested in a domestic partnership fund that held the same assets.

PFICs

A fund established as a non-US corporation will, as a general rule, be a passive foreign investment company (a PFIC).[46] A US shareholder that owns stock in a PFIC, either direct-ly or indirectly through certain attribution rules, may be subject to an interest charge with respect to certain dividend distributions made by the PFIC in respect of such US shareholder's stock and on any gain recognised by such US shareholder upon the direct or indirect disposition of its stock in the PFIC. In addition, in the case of individual US investors, any gain recognised upon disposition of the fund's shares will be treated as ordinary income only, not capital gain, and if an individual dies holding shares in a PFIC, those shares will not receive the benefit of the usual fair market value step-up-at-death rule. The interest charge and these other adverse consequences are avoided if the fund allows the US shareholder to make an election (a QEF election), to treat the PFIC as a qualified electing fund (a QEF). In such event, the fund is treated (at least as to income and gain) much like a pass-through vehicle, and the US share-holder is taxed currently on its pro rata share of the QEF's ordinary earnings and net capital gains. The shareholder's ability to make the QEF election depends on the fund's willingness to provide all of the information (essentially, the fund's annual ordinary earnings and net cap-ital gains, as calculated for US federal income tax purposes) necessary for investors who make the election to report their share of income each year.[47]

CFCs

A fund may also either itself constitute, or invest, directly or indirectly, in stock of, a con-trolled foreign corporation (CFC). In general, a foreign corporation will constitute a CFC if more than 50 per cent of its outstanding stock (measured by vote or value) is owned either directly or indirectly through certain attribution rules by US shareholders each owning 10 per cent or more of such foreign corporation's total voting power. In general, any US per-son that owns directly or by application of certain attribution rules 10 per cent or more of the total voting power of a CFC's outstanding voting stock (a US 10 per cent shareholder) is currently required to include as ordinary income its pro rata share of certain items of income (eg, dividends, interest and most capital gains) earned by the CFC (subpart F income) whether or not such income is actually distributed to such shareholder. Thus, investors that are US 10 per cent shareholders may be currently required to include as ordi-nary income their distributive shares of a fund's pro rata share of subpart F income earned by the CFC, even if all or a substantial portion of the fund's income is capital gain. Generally, for any taxable year of a US 10 per cent shareholder in which the CFC also con-stitutes a PFIC, the CFC tax rules take precedence over the PFIC tax rules. However, the PFIC tax rules continue to apply with respect to CFC shareholders that are US persons but are not US 10 per cent shareholders.

Combination structures

When the fund has been structured as a master-feeder fund and/or the investment structure of the fund is as a fund of funds, the PFIC and CFC rules can have somewhat complicated effects. For example, in a master-feeder structure, if the 'master' fund were structured as a corporation for US federal income tax purposes (which may be preferable for US tax-exempt investors), US taxable domestic investors will have to face the QEF regime instead of the generally more preferable pure flow-through treatment that a partnership structure would afford.[48]

In general, fund of funds structures face more difficulties with the anti-deferral regimes. For example, only the first owner that is a US shareholder (actual or deemed) in the chain of ownership of PFIC stock may make a QEF election with respect to such stock.[49] Thus, a fund structured as a fund of funds (and all of its US investors) will be unable to make a QEF election with respect to PFIC stock that it holds indirectly through any unaffiliated US pass-through entity (eg, a partnership, LLC or trust) and that US investment fund that holds the PFIC stock may be unwilling to make a QEF election with respect to such stock. Thus, the fund of funds will have to monitor its investments in underlying investments, but will have no control over whether they make QEF elections with respect to PFIC stock that they hold.

As an alternative to making a QEF election, a fund that invests in a PFIC could make an election (a PFIC mark to market election) to mark to market each year marketable (generally, publicly traded on an established securities exchange) PFIC stock that it holds directly or indirectly through a foreign partnership, foreign trust or foreign estate. Mark to market, in this context, means recognising as ordinary income or loss each year an amount equal to the difference between the fund's adjusted tax basis in such PFIC stock and its fair market value. Losses will be allowed only to the extent of net mark to market gain previously included by the fund pursuant to the election for prior years. The PFIC mark to market election applies to the taxable year for which such election is made and to all subsequent taxable years, unless the PFIC stock ceases to be publicly traded or the IRS consents to revocation of the election. By making the PFIC mark to market election, a fund could ameliorate the adverse tax consequences arising from ownership of PFIC stock, but in any particular year may be required to take into account income in excess of the distributions it receives from the PFIC and proceeds from the dispositions of PFIC stock.[50] As a practical matter, the effect is to potentially change capital to ordinary income but should not result in an acceleration of income as compared to an investment in a flow-through fund.

Investment manager issues

Investment managers should also be aware that their own tax situation can be improved with careful structuring. Although the details and the items that are most important to any given manager will vary depending on the manager's own situation, managers should always consider, for example, whether it will be possible to provide themselves the potential to affect the character and timing of income taxes on some or all of their carried interest (or other compensation). For investment managers in funds with only tax-exempt or non-US investors, deferral should generally be available, at least to managers that are individuals (or partnerships with only individual partners).[51] In addition, for non-corporate investment managers that conduct their business in locations that impose taxes on the income of unincorporated business (eg, New York City), it may be desirable to split the non-incentive-based compensation from the incentive-based compensation and pay the latter to a separate entity that can more clearly be defended as not being engaged in a business or as otherwise not subject to such tax. For individual managers, their advisers should always consider, at the outset of structuring and organising a new fund, whether any part of the manager's interest in the fund should be transferred (outright or in trust) to achieve charitable or estate planning goals of the manager. Transferring interests in a fund at a time when its value is speculative may save substantial income or estate tax costs while conferring significant potential economic benefits to the transferee.

Documentation

In general, documentation for a hedge fund will consist of organisational documents, offering materials (usually a brochure and/or private placement memorandum (a PPM) and flip charts for personal meetings) and any subscription documents (which generally consist of a subscription agreement). There may also be ancillary materials, such as forms of legal opinions or schedules.

The PPM is the primary marketing piece and also the primary legal disclosure document. Great care must be taken to ensure that the PPM is accurate and complete from a legal perspective since it generally provides protection from liability for all disclosed matters. Therefore, good risk disclosure and accurate descriptions of the investment strategies are crucial. In addition, since the PPM is a primary selling document, it needs to be comprehensible from a marketing perspective.[52] The subscription documents are purely legal, and, as such, manifest and elicit the information necessary to determine regulatory status and any applicable exemptions. As the legal and regulatory regimes of differing jurisdictions are inconsistent, subscription documents tend to be lengthy and burdensome to investors.

Conclusion

The foregoing is meant to provide an overview of some of the primary issues involved in organising a hedge fund. The regulatory regimes around the world and in the United States that govern hedge funds or from which they seek exemptions are inconsistent, have conflicting policies and are not necessarily harmonised for this type of product. Therefore, an investment manager needs good counsel, accountants and service providers with significant experience in order to organise and properly operate its hedge fund.

---

[1] This chapter expresses the views of the authors only, and is not intended to provide legal or tax advice to any person, nor does it create an attorney–client relationship. No person should rely on this chapter in lieu of seeking legal counsel.

[2] While US taxable investors may invest in offshore funds, they generally will require an offshore fund that is taxed as a corporation for US federal income tax purposes to provide for certain accounting procedures to enable them to make an election to treat the fund as a qualified electing fund (QEF election). Providing this information can sometimes prove difficult for an offshore fund with corporate tax status. See the section 'General tax considerations'.

[3] As noted below, in some cases it may be preferable for tax reasons to bifurcate these two roles. See 'Investment manager issues'.

[4] Note, however, that if the investment manager is serving only as the investment adviser and not as the general partner, it will have to receive its performance-based compensation pursuant to an advisory agreement (which may have disadvantageous tax consequences for an investment manager that is an individual or group of individuals) or through some other cash flow mechanism. In the alternative, the general partner or an affiliated entity admitted to the partnership as a limited partner (ie, the special limited partner) may receive the performance-based compensation as an allocation. See the section 'Basic economics'.

[5] This is true not only under Delaware law, but also under both the limited partnership statute of every other US jurisdiction and the Revised Uniform Limited Partnership Act.

[6] Deferral will not be available for all investment advisers. See the section 'Investment manager issues'. Additionally, deferral of fee income on offshore hedge funds has come under increased scrutiny by the Internal Revenue Service and the US Congress.

[7] Under new accounting rule FAS 46 the assets of a fund may be consolidated on the balance sheet of the manager.

[8] For example, if certain investors (including the investment manager and its affiliates) are to be subject to different fees or have different voting rights, a separate class of interests may be issued to each such investor group.

[9] This would permit a single partnership effectively to be comprised of a series of separate funds, which, in turn, may have different groups of investors sharing in each such designated portfolio (as described above). Note, however, that this has other regulatory effects under the Investment Company Act and Employee Retirement Income Security Act (ERISA). See the section 'Investment Company Act of 1940'.

[10] A subscription agreement will customarily require an investor to indemnify the fund, the general partner, the investment adviser and the other investors for any liability attaching to any negligence or misrepresentation on its part that results in a loss to the fund. Since the subscription agreement is not statutorily mandated, but rather governed by general principles of contract law, the exposure under this indemnification can be made unlimited.

[11] Under Delaware law and that of most other US jurisdictions, this may include (within a specified timeframe and under certain specific circumstances) amounts previously distributed.

[12] Although the investment manager may encounter similar burdens as a managing member (see herein), depending on the specific circumstances of the investment manager, these will generally be less than those related to serving as a general partner of a limited partnership.

[13] US tax-exempt investors are generally concerned about UBTI (see the section 'Tax considerations'). If, however, these concerns are not present, such investors can invest directly in the US-based partnership or LLC.

[14] Historically, popular offshore jurisdictions have included he Netherlands Antilles, Luxembourg, the Channel Islands, Ireland, Bermuda, the Bahamas, the Cayman Islands, the British Virgin Islands and Jersey. Increased regulatory burdens have made jurisdictions such as Luxembourg and Bermuda less desirable, while increased flexibility, competent administrative and legal assistance and the development of indigenous stock exchanges have made certain other tax havens (such as the Cayman Islands) increasingly attractive choices. These jurisdictions compete for this business so there is a levelling effect. Also, international anti-money laundering requirements, discussed below, have set a standard for all jurisdictions.

[15] See endnote 40 below.

[16] Further, Japanese investors, for example, typically may purchase interests in a secondary offering although some interests, such as partnerships, are not considered securities. Thus, a partnership that functions like a corporation, may be desirable. Historically, interests to be sold into the Japanese markets, were 'seasoned', that is, held for two days by another investor (usually an affiliate of the placement agent, if there is one, or an unaffiliated entity) or the investment manager.

[17] Certain regulated entities requiring such 'convenience listings', however, only recognise certain exchanges (primarily Luxembourg or Ireland).

[18] For US regulatory purposes, all of the investors from the feeders would generally be attributed to the master if it were located in the United States. As a result, absent special circumstances, in a global offering the master fund is normally located offshore.

[19] These are frequently organised as unit trusts (but can also be corporations, LLCs or limited partnerships) that consist of one or more classes of interest, each with its own designated pool of assets and (depending on the jurisdiction in which the vehicle is organised) with no cross-liability.

[20] Similarly, a total return swap can be implemented at the fund level to lever the fund itself. These and other swaps or derivative transactions can have tax effects, however, and should be carefully evaluated.

[21] An 'accredited investor' for these purposes includes a) an individual which either has a net worth of US$1 million (including the individual's residence), or in the last two years has had either an annual income of US$200,000 or a combined annual income (with spouse) of US$300,000, b) a bank or other financial institution, c) a tax-exempt or other entity with assets in excess of US$5 million or d) any entity in which all such entities beneficial owners are 'accredited investors'.

[22] The belief that an investor is an 'accredited investor' may be predicated upon representations made in the subscription documents.

485

[23] If the fund is organised as a complex with various onshore/offshore vehicles, it would be possible to hold a press conference in the United States, to suspend sales of the US fund for a certain period of time (ie, a 'cooling off' period), but continue to sell the offshore funds to non-US persons outside the United States.

[24] See endnote 21.

[25] Registration under Section 12(g) does not authorise a public offering of securities. Such an offering requires either registration under the Securities Act or the availability of an exemption therefrom. Exemptions from Section 12(g) are not exemptions from Securities Act registration.

[26] Note that the statute clearly states that a US-organised entity may have up to 500 holders of interests of one class of equity. Therefore, if a fund were to issue various classes of interests that were different enough in their terms so as to constitute a different class of equity interest, such as voting or senior securities (or a combination thereof), then each such class could itself have up to 499 holders of record. In the master/feeder context, where the feeders are organised for specific, demonstrable business purposes and not designed to evade Exchange Act limitations, each feeder should generally count as one record holder. This determination can only be made in each case based on the particular facts and circumstances.

[27] See the section 'Investment Company Act' for a discussion of the number of potential investors with regard to registration under the Investment Company Act.

[28] Moreover, the SEC will integrate a 3(c)(1) fund's beneficial holders with those of another 3(c)(1) fund managed by the same manager if the two funds are effectively the same (ie, if a reasonable investor would consider an investment in one to be the equivalent of an investment in the other). However, a 3(c)(1) fund is not integrated with a 3(c)(7) fund nor is any 3(c)(7) fund integrated with any other 3(c)(7) fund for purposes of determining beneficial ownership of the 3(c)(1) fund. Sponsors of private investment funds may therefore create parallel funds – one with 100 or fewer investors, as many as all of whom may be non-qualified purchasers, and one or more other funds, each with an unlimited number of qualified purchasers. Also, a 3(c)(1) fund may invest in a 3(c)(7) fund as long as the 3(c)(1) fund is a qualified purchaser and is not organised for the purpose of investing in the 3(c)(7) fund.

[29] The look-through rule limits the ability to create funds of funds in the 3(c)(1) fund arena, since such funds may not own more than 10 per cent of the voting securities of another 3(c)(1) fund without becoming subject to a 'look-through' (which could cause the underlying 3(c)(1) fund to violate its 100 investor limit).

[30] Qualified purchasers include:

(i)   any natural person that owns not less than US$5 million in 'investments' (as defined by the SEC);

(ii)   any company directly or indirectly owned entirely by two or more closely related natural persons, their estates or foundations, charities, or trusts formed by or for their benefit that owns not less than US$5 million in 'investments' (ie, a family company); this provision essentially permits family entities that have at least US$5 million in investments to be qualified purchasers even if no single family member meets the US$5 million threshold;

(iii) any person, acting for its own account or the accounts of other qualified purchasers (which would include qualifying 3(c)(1) funds), that in the aggregate owns and invests on a discretionary basis not less than US$25 million in 'investments';

(iv)   any other trust not formed for the specific purpose of acquiring the fund's securities and as to which both the person with investment discretion with respect to the trust and each of the contributors is a qualified purchaser under (i), (ii) or (iii) above;

(v)   any person who received securities of a 3(c)(7) fund as a gift or bequest, or due to an involuntary event (such as death, divorce or legal separation) from a qualified purchaser; and

(vi)   any entity in which all beneficial owners of all securities issued are qualified purchasers.

[31] Prior capital commitments (common in the private equity fund context) that are called by the fund are not new investments by the investor. However, in the fully funded hedge fund context, qualified purchaser status needs to be verified any time an investor makes a new investment.

[32] A qualified client includes:

• a natural person or an entity who has a net worth (with respect to natural persons, together with assets held jointly with a spouse) of more than US$1.5 million; or

• a natural person or an entity who has at least US$750,000 under the management of the manager.

[33] In the domestic context, whether the compensation is structured as a fee paid by the fund or an allocation from one capital account to another may be determined, in part, upon the nature of the investment manager. If it is an individual or a pass-through vehicle, there is a tax advantage to be achieved by properly structuring the performance compensation as an allocation, an advantage that does not exist for corporate entities.

[34] It is also possible for an investment manager to only charge the pool as a whole for increases in value and have a single class of interests. However, this mechanism gives a free ride to anyone who invested when the fund's value was down and is unfair to investors who invest mid-period when the fund's value is up, and, therefore, is not common.

[35] In those instances in which the investment manager is not serving as the general partner or managing member.

[36] A variation of the 'roll-up' is 'equalisation', a method designed to formulaically 'equalise' into one class interests that have been subject to varying performance.

[37] It should be noted that in the fund of funds structure, so long as no single entity or group of related entities owns 50 per cent or more of the target fund and the target fund does not own 10 per cent or more of the equity of any portfolio company, it is unlikely that a target fund would be a 'party in interest' to an ERISA plan that holds an equity interest in the investing fund.

[38] QPAM is defined as (a) a bank, (b) an insurance company, (c) a savings and loan association or (c) an adviser registered under the Advisers Act that meets certain capital requirements and has at least a certain amount of client assets under management.

[39] Generally, such exemptions do not exempt self-dealing transactions in which the fund manager may otherwise engage in connection with the operation of the fund (eg, buying or selling securities or other assets with affiliates of the manager).

[40] Since the final promulgation of Regulation Sections 301.7701-2,-3 and -4 (the so-called 'check-the-box' regulations), entity classification is, in many instances, within the taxpayer's control without regard to legal or economic characteristics.

[41] In most, but not all, instances, 3(c)(1) funds will automatically qualify for a private placement safe harbour initially. Other funds that would not be regulated investment companies if they were organised as domestic corporations may find that they are confident that 90 per cent of their gross income will always qualify as income specified in Section 7704(d), in which case they would qualify for another exemption from being at risk of being taxed as a corporation. Funds that cannot rely on either of those exemptions need to structure their transferability and liquidity arrangements with care in order to minimise this risk. Moreover, funds that meet with unexpected success or growth and migrate to 3(c)(7) as their basis for continuing exemption risk losing the private placement safe harbour at a time when it may be more difficult to address transferability and liquidity arrangements.

[42] For the sake of simplicity, in this section of the chapter we shall use the term 'partnership' to mean any entity that is characterised as a partnership for relevant tax purposes. (As noted above, these entities include, trusts, partnerships, LLCs and even corporations organised in certain jurisdictions such as the Cayman Islands and Bermuda. Domestically formed corporations are not eligible to be treated as partnerships for US federal income tax purposes.)

[43] In the unlikely event such a thing were to occur, the fund would be treated as a corporation for US federal income tax purposes: Section 7701(a)(3).

[44] The adverse effects include (i) quarterly withholding with respect to the non-US investor's share of the fund's income effectively connected with the fund's US trade or business(es) (effectively connected income), without regard to amounts distributed, and (ii) in the case of corporate investors, being subject to the branch profits tax of Section 884.

[45] In determining whether the interest income in question is being earned by a 10 per cent shareholder (within the meaning of Section 871(h)(3)) of the obligor, the non-US investor is not attributed voting stock owned (actually or constructively) by their US partners in the fund. See Section 318(a)(5)(C).

[46] A foreign corporation will constitute a PFIC in any taxable year in which at least 75 per cent of its gross income is derived from passive sources (eg, dividends, interest) or at least 50 per cent of its assets, generally as measured by fair market value, produce or are held for the production of passive income.

[47] Taxable US investors in domestic partnerships that invest in non-US corporations or other funds treated as corporations for federal income tax purposes may also be subject to these PFIC rules.

[48] On occasion, the master fund will be a US partnership or LLC with various offshore feeder entities. In those situations, the US taxable investors may invest directly in the master fund (or a US partnership feeder if different fees will or may apply to different feeders) and will face the 'normal' tax considerations discussed above with respect to domestic partnership funds. The offshore feeder entities will, of course, face the panoply of tax considerations that non-US investors encounter when they invest in a domestic partnership (eg, potential interest

and dividend withholding as well as potential Section 1446 withholding if the partnership is determined to have effectively connected income).

[49] Note that if a domestic fund invests directly in the stock of a PFIC and the PFIC furnishes the required information, the domestic fund (rather than its investors) is the only person who can make a QEF election with respect to its stock in the PFIC. If the fund is an offshore entity, its US investors (to the extent that they are not tax-exempt organisations) would have to make the QEF election for themselves. In many instances, however, a fund (and especially an underlying fund in a fund of funds structure) will not agree to provide the necessary information, and the US investors will be forced to live with the potentially adverse consequences of owning an interest in a PFIC.

[50] It is unclear in the fund of funds context whether a fund will be able to make a PFIC mark to market election with respect to PFIC stock that it holds indirectly through an underlying investment treated as a domestic partnership for US federal income tax purposes.

[51] Income deferral by offshore hedge funds has very recently come under increased scrutiny by the Internal Revenue Service. In addition, a pending Senate bill would affect the ability of offshore corporate hedge funds to defer fee income.

[52] A common question regarding documentation is whether prior performance results can be used in marketing. This area is quite complex and the SEC has conflicting positions. In general, if a person or entity is exclusively responsible for a track record, this record can be used to market other products that use substantially the same strategies and parameters. The touchstone is that the record and its use not be false or misleading. Results normally have to be provided net of fees and expenses although gross returns can be used in certain circumstances. Clear explanations of the record and differences or special facts relating to the track record need to be provided with the performance information. The use of a track record is a difficult topic and must be analysed separately in each case. The ability to use prior performance is a very important marketing issue, as it is often difficult to raise initial capital without a track record.

Chapter 39

Investing in hedge funds: an overview of business, legal and regulatory considerations for investors

Eric Sippel
Eastbourne Capital Management, LLC, San Rafael, California

Christopher Rupright
Shartis, Friese & Ginsburg, LLP, San Francisco, California

Introduction

Hedge funds[1] have attracted a wide range of investors seeking excess risk-adjusted returns. Understanding a manager's historical performance record and investment style is obviously important to investors. In addition, though, it is important for investors to understand the documents and terms governing their investment. Ideally, for both the investor and the manager, the terms of the hedge fund will strike a balance between the manager's desire for the flexibility necessary to achieve stated objectives and the needs of the investors in that fund.

Before implementing an investment in a hedge fund, a prospective investor should review (and ask a lawyer to review) the governing documents of that fund. These documents typically include a private placement memorandum and a 'charter' document (which should be thought of as the contract between the hedge fund and its investors).[2] If there is a conflict or inconsistency between the private placement memorandum and the charter document, the terms of the charter document typically control, although the investors may then have a claim of misrepresentation against the hedge fund sponsor.

As part of the process of preparing the governing documents, the hedge fund manager establishes the terms of the hedge fund. The hedge fund manager is influenced by the nature of the likely potential investors in that fund (that is, institutional or high net worth individuals, onshore or offshore) and the fund's investment strategy.

Since a hedge fund is not registered with any government agency, the legal restrictions on the terms of a hedge fund are relatively minimal.* In contrast, US federal law imposes significant restrictions on the terms and activities of a mutual fund that is registered with the US Securities and Exchange Commission.[3]

Primary factors influencing a hedge fund's terms

Types of investors

Different types of investors will have different needs and perspectives regarding their investment in a hedge fund. They may also have different levels of experience, knowledge and sophistication regarding investing in general, and hedge funds in particular. The amount that they invest will also determine the negotiating strength those investors may have with the hedge fund to change terms that are not attractive to them. The terms of a hedge fund may be significantly influenced by these differences in prospective investors.

High net worth individuals

Traditionally, most investors in hedge funds have been high net worth individuals with a minimum net worth of at least US$1 million.[4] Most hedge funds have a significant minimum investment requirement, ranging from US$250,000 to over US$1 million; as a result, most high net worth individuals who invest in a hedge fund have a net worth significantly in excess of US$1 million. Although not a legal requirement, many investors and hedge fund managers suggest that an investor should not invest more than a small percentage of his or her net worth in a particular fund.

Fund of funds/family offices

Hedge funds have also traditionally attracted assets from funds of funds and family offices. A fund of funds is an investment fund that invests primarily in other investment funds. A fund of funds generally attracts assets from high net worth individuals, although more recently offshore funds of funds have been established to attract assets from foreign institutions.

Institutional investors

Although some institutional investors (that is, foundations, endowments, pension plans, insurance companies and banks) have invested in some large and well-established hedge funds for many years, they have recently begun investing in smaller hedge funds. Other institutional investors that have not traditionally invested in hedge funds are also beginning to do so.

Investment activity

There is a range of investment activities in which a hedge fund may engage. A hedge fund is typically managed differently from the long-only/buy and hold/significant diversification strategies (the 'traditional strategies') typically implemented by more conventional investment managers (such as those advising mutual funds and institutional separate accounts). To reflect these alternative investment strategies, the governing documents of most hedge funds provide the hedge fund manager with significant flexibility to invest the fund's portfolio in a manner that the manager believes is in the fund's best interests without significant restrictions and to change the strategies without investor consent.[5] Although such flexibility may introduce an element of uncertainty in many cases, investors often invest with a hedge fund manager to take advantage of the manager's ability to modify the hedge fund's strategy in response to changing market conditions. Sophisticated investors also carefully scrutinise statistics of past performance to understand the risk–reward characteristics of a manager's past performance. It is incumbent upon investors to inquire about these issues.

490

Some hedge funds are managed more aggressively than traditional strategies. This aggressiveness may be implemented through leverage, significant short selling, concentration (of the number and size of positions) and purchase or short sale of illiquid securities (for example, thinly traded bonds or stocks or venture capital investments). Leverage can be implemented through margin trading and the use of options, futures and other derivative instruments. When discussing leverage with a hedge fund manager, a potential investor should be careful to identify how that manager defines leverage. In some cases managers focus on gross exposure and in other cases they focus on net exposure. For example, some hedge fund managers believe that if they are 100 per cent invested on the long side and 100 per cent invested on the short side that they are not employing leverage; other managers believe that this is use of 100 per cent leverage.

Other hedge funds are managed more conservatively than traditional strategies. For example, market-neutral strategies have been utilised by hedge funds for many years. Recognising the conservative nature of such strategies, Congress amended the Internal Revenue Code in 1997 to allow mutual funds to engage in significant short sale activity. To date, however, only a limited number of mutual funds have been established offering market-neutral strategies.[6] Hedging strategies can provide more conservative portfolio management, which may be implemented through short sales, diversification and the use of options, futures and other derivative instruments.

Other hedge funds may combine aggressive and conservative techniques to attempt to achieve a desired level of risk-adjusted returns.

Significant hedge fund terms

Fees

Fees charged by hedge fund managers typically exceed those charged by investment advisers implementing traditional styles. In addition to fees based on a percentage of assets (usually 1–2 per cent), hedge fund managers also receive performance fees or allocations (typically 20 per cent) that are based on the profitability of the fund.[7] Except for a few notable exceptions, hedge fund managers usually have significantly fewer assets under management than traditional money managers. They believe that this smaller size enables them to manage the fund's portfolio more effectively and actively. Hedge fund managers believe (and prospective investors must determine) that the enhanced risk–reward characteristics of the alternative investment strategies that they offer, combined with the significantly smaller asset base, justify the significant fees that they receive.

Of course, fees are influenced by supply and demand characteristics, including, among other things, the type of investor that a hedge fund may attract. An institutional investor who invests significant amounts with a hedge fund manager is more likely to have greater leverage[8] to negotiate a fee discount than a large number of dispersed high net worth individuals who in the aggregate may invest that amount.[9]

Some hedge funds include a hurdle or benchmark rate in their performance fee calculation as an attempt to make the fee structure more attractive to investors. These rates are sometimes fixed (generally ranging between 5 per cent and 10 per cent) or variable and based on an index (for example, the three-month Treasury bill rate or the return of the S&P 500 index or the Russell 2000 index). There are three ways to calculate a hurdle rate: the deductible formula, the catch-up formula and the cliff formula.

The deductible formula provides that the performance fee is equal to the designated percentage of the net profits in excess of the hurdle. The catch-up formula provides that the performance fee is equal to the designated percentage of the net profits only to the extent that the investor receives a return equal to the hurdle rate. The cliff formula provides that the performance fee is equal to the designated percentage of the net profits as long as the gross return to the investor (before the calculation of the performance fee) is at least equal to the hurdle rate. For example, assume that an investor's capital account balance on the first day of a period is US$100,000, the designated performance fee percentage is 20 per cent, the hurdle rate is 10 per cent for that period and the return for that period is US$11,000. The performance fee using the deductible formula is: 20 per cent (US$11,000 – US$10,000) = US$200. The performance fee using the catch-up formula is: US$1,000 (that is, the lesser of US$11,000 – US$10,000 and 20 per cent of US$11,000). The performance fee using the cliff formula is: 20 per cent (US$11,000) = US$2,200.

Withdrawals

Withdrawal provisions of hedge funds are significantly more restrictive than those of mutual funds, which allow daily redemptions. In addition to the economic advantages, portfolio managers are often attracted to managing hedge funds because they do not have to manage the portfolio with the uncertainty created by the potential for unlimited daily withdrawals. This allows hedge fund managers greater freedom to construct the portfolio without worrying about unexpected short-term redemptions.

Generally, hedge fund managers do not want 'fast money'. They would like investors to view their hedge fund as a long-term investment. Most domestic hedge funds (and many offshore hedge funds) have a one-year lock-up to signal this desire to prospective investors; that is, investors may not withdraw any assets from the fund until after the first anniversary of their admission to the fund (or in some cases, at the end of the first calendar year following the date of their admission to the fund). Some hedge funds, though, impose a longer lock-up.

Withdrawals from a hedge fund are only permitted periodically. Quarterly withdrawals are common, although many funds only permit annual or semi-annual withdrawals and other funds permit withdrawals monthly. Furthermore, 30–90 days' prior written notice is commonly required.

These provisions are designed to give the portfolio manager sufficient time to liquidate positions in an orderly fashion to fund the redemption. For example, smaller capitalisation securities are often liquidated over several weeks to avoid a negative impact on the price of those securities, thereby benefiting all investors.

Hedge funds often restrict withdrawal as of any permitted withdrawal date to less than 25 per cent of the assets of the fund. This is designed to avoid a massive liquidation of the fund's portfolio, which could have a significantly negative impact on the prices of the securities in the fund's portfolio, thereby hurting not only those investors who are withdrawing but also those who are remaining in the fund.

Funds that have a significant percentage of their assets in illiquid positions generally have more restrictive withdrawal provisions. Often illiquidity is a matter of degree. Some securities are thinly traded (for example, US micro-cap stocks are relatively illiquid, but more liquid, than many securities of all capitalisations in emerging markets). Other positions may be illiquid because of the significant size of the position. Venture capital investments are illiquid until these securities become publicly registered (if ever) or the issuer becomes a public company and Rule 144 under the Securities Act of 1933 is available.

The degree and percentage of anticipated illiquidity in a hedge fund's portfolio will affect the restrictiveness of the withdrawal provisions of that fund. For example, some crossover funds that have a significant portion of assets in venture capital investments may have long lock-up periods (two to five years is common), restrict the percentage of an investment that can be withdrawn in any one year, allow withdrawals only once in a year and provide lengthy notice periods. Other crossover funds are organised more like venture capital funds – that is, the investors invest at the commencement of the fund, periodically receive distributions and receive the remainder of their investment when the fund is finally liquidated, with no withdrawals permitted in the interim.

Many hedge funds include key man provisions that allow a special right of withdrawal without regard to any of the withdrawal restrictions if the portfolio manager of the fund is no longer managing the fund (for example, if the portfolio manager resigns, dies or becomes disabled). Usually these key man provisions allow for a common date for all investors to withdraw from the fund with sufficient notice to provide for an orderly liquidation that would minimise the impact on the portfolio.

Monitoring and reporting: transparency

The extent and frequency that investors can monitor their investment in a hedge fund depends on the hedge fund manager's desire for confidentiality and the nature of the investors. At a minimum, the financial statements of hedge funds are generally audited annually. Most hedge fund managers provide a monthly or quarterly letter to investors describing their market outlook and some performance statistics. Funds with significant institutional investor participation tend to provide more extensive reporting during the year. A prospective investor in a hedge fund should review prior communications with that fund's investors as part of their due diligence process.

Although there are many reasons why a hedge fund may blow up, the four most common reasons have been the following:

- the fund employed too much leverage;
- the hedge fund manager misappropriated assets of the fund;
- certain positions were valued improperly; and
- the fund was concentrated in illiquid positions that could not be sold to meet redemptions (sometimes a hedge fund manager will then inaccurately report performance results to hide negative results that may be a consequence of some of these strategies).

Hedge fund managers are generally reluctant to reveal their positions to investors. They are usually concerned with investors copying or countering their trades, which could negatively impact the portfolio. Hedge fund managers are also reluctant to reveal their short positions either because they are concerned about short squeezes or because they do not want management of the companies they have shorted to become aware of the short position.

Despite this desire for confidentiality, many sophisticated hedge fund investors (usually sophisticated funds of funds and consultants) desire additional transparency to monitor the portfolio. Since they are paying significant fees and are often responsible for their own clients' or investors' money, they want to be sure that the hedge fund manager delivers the portfolio management services and risk–reward characteristics that are expected. These fund of funds managers and consultants believe that they add value for their clients by monitoring the manager's portfolio exposures and performance using a variety of statistical measures. In addition, hedge fund investors should monitor their funds to continually assess 'blow-up' risk. Hedge fund managers should also consider whether they are more likely to retain assets of their investors if they provide greater information. First, greater information can allow an investor to monitor blow-up risk. Second, greater information reduces the potential for surprise; if an investor in a fund is aware of the significant positions held by that fund and those positions decline in value during a period, the investor should not be surprised if the fund's performance is poor during that period.

Hedge fund managers can provide information to investors without disclosing actual securities positions. Some investors require funds in which they have invested to provide the complete portfolio to a third party risk evaluation firm. That third party firm enters into a confidentiality agreement with the fund under which it agrees that it will not provide the identity of the positions to its client and will not provide any information regarding that fund to any person other than its client. That third party firm would then provide various statistical risk measures to its client to enable that client to monitor its hedge fund investments. Instead of positions, some hedge fund managers provide their investors with information regarding the use of leverage and liquidity of positions and the percentage of the fund's assets invested long and short and by sectors, country and capitalisation.

Valuation

Investors should be aware that most hedge fund documents provide the hedge fund manager with the flexibility to value investments in their exclusive discretion, consistent with the manager's fiduciary duties to the fund. Valuation is relatively easy with liquid positions for which there is an established and deep market. The hedge fund manager generally adopts the valuation of the prime broker, custodian or other reporting service used by the manager.

Illiquid and more esoteric investments (such as derivative instruments) may be more difficult to value. Investors (and managers) must be mindful of potential conflicts of interest that may arise from this. A more aggressive valuation of a position will benefit existing investors when a new investment is made in the fund at the expense of new investors. A more conservative value will have the opposite effect. Investors withdrawing from the fund will benefit from overstatement of the value of the portfolio; remaining investors will be harmed.

The hedge fund manager will also benefit from a more aggressive valuation of an investment. Asset-based fees will be higher because the asset base is greater. Performance fees will be higher because unrealised profits will be greater. Of course, the performance record will also show better results.

Several of the well-publicised collapses of hedge funds in recent years involved aggressively high valuations of a portfolio with significantly illiquid assets that later proved inaccurate. The hedge fund manager realised greater fees and the investors who withdrew prior to disclosure of the overvaluation received a disproportionate share of the fund's assets on withdrawal. Further, earlier withdrawals were often funded by liquidating the more liquid positions in a portfolio, which significantly increased the proportion of illiquid positions in the portfolio and the concomitant risk relating to valuation. The investors in the fund at the time that the overvaluation was disclosed were left holding the bag.

Investors should understand the extent and nature of the illiquid positions in a hedge fund portfolio and how they are priced. Many hedge fund managers price illiquid positions conservatively. It is difficult, however, for an investor to determine if a hedge fund manager values illiquid positions aggressively or conservatively, unless they have independent contact with the manager's counterparties, administrators and auditors.

Hedge fund managers that aggressively price illiquid positions endanger the credibility of the hedge fund industry. Potential investors may be reluctant to invest in hedge funds if they are prone to overvaluation problems. Although the accounting firms that conduct the annual audits of the financial statements review the valuation of illiquid securities, they do so only on an annual basis several months after the end of a year. The unfair effects of overvaluation may have already occurred during the year. In addition, an auditing firm may not have the ability to accurately value illiquid investments and may rely heavily on the hedge fund manager. Unfortunately, the hedge fund industry has yet to adopt a standard that could protect against valuation problems relating to illiquid securities.

Conclusion

Before investing in a hedge fund, prospective investors must understand the terms that will govern their investment. The key point for investors to understand is that the manager generally seeks to define terms that will give him flexibility in pursuing alternative investment strategies. The ability to pursue flexible strategies is often what makes hedge funds successful in coping with or profiting from changes in investment conditions. This flexibility manifests itself in broad authority over investment management strategy, restrictions on withdrawals, valuation provisions and the degree to which a manager may keep the fund's positions confidential. Performance fees allow a manager to have a relatively small amount of assets under management and to be rewarded based on the profitability of the fund. In the long run, both the manager and the investor share the objective of achieving excess returns on some risk-adjusted basis. Ideally, a well-thought out document will facilitate this objective by balancing the needs of the manager with those of the investor.

The terms of a fund are designed to enhance the hedge fund manager's ability to achieve excess returns on a risk-adjusted basis. The terms are not, however, as flexible as some types of investors may desire. For example, a professional investor who has many potential hedge funds in which it can invest and needs to balance asset allocation continually will be more concerned with liquidity provisions than a high net worth individual. A hedge fund manager must balance investors' desires with the need to create terms that will provide the hedge fund with the best opportunity to create excess returns for all investors.

---

* Editor's note: on 29 September 2003, shortly before this book went to press, the staff of the SEC issued its report entitled 'The Implications of the Growth of Hedge Funds', the culmination of its efforts following the Hedge Fund Roundtable held in May 2003. As of the date of this writing, the Commission itself had not taken any action in response to the report. One of the key recommendations of the staff was that the SEC consider 'requiring hedge fund advisers to register with the SEC as investment advisers, taking into account whether the benefits outweigh the burdens of registration'. In the staff's view, ' ... registration of hedge fund advisers would serve as a deterrent to fraud, encourage compliance and the adoption of compliance procedures, provide the SEC with important information ... and effectively raise the standards for investment in hedge funds from the "accredited investor" standard to that of "qualified client"'. See http://www.sec.gov/news/studies/hedgefunds0903.pdf for the full text of the report.

[1] The label 'hedge fund' is a misnomer; it is possible that a fund may not hedge at all. The market defines a hedge fund as any private investment fund that primarily buys and sells publicly traded securities. An investment fund is private if it is not registered with the US Securities and Exchange Commission or any foreign regulatory agency. Some offshore hedge funds are, however, listed on foreign stock exchanges.

[2] The charter document for a limited partnership is the limited partnership agreement; the charter documents for an offshore corporation or limited duration company are generally the memorandum and articles of association.

[3] For example, the Investment Company Act of 1940 imposes significant restrictions on leverage (including short selling), concentration and the percentage of illiquid positions in the portfolio.

[4] Rule 205–3 under the Investment Advisers Act of 1940 requires an advisory client who is charged a performance fee to have a net worth in excess of US$1.5 million. Many states have adopted this federal performance fee rule. Many hedge fund managers are registered as investment advisers with the SEC or a state securities administrator.

[5] Many institutional investors establish separate accounts or separate investment funds with hedge fund managers, rather than investing directly in their main fund, so that some contractual restrictions can be imposed on the hedge fund manager. Generally, those separate accounts or funds are significant enough in size to the hedge fund manager to accept the additional burdens of managing a separate account or fund (which may include, among others, tax disadvantages to receiving fees from a separate account and operational issues).

[6] Mutual funds are significantly limited in the degree of leverage that may be employed. In contrast, many market-neutral hedge funds employ significant leverage.

[7] Most US-based hedge fund managers charge this fee on an investor-by-investor basis, rather than charging the fee at the fund level.

[8] This leverage may be derived from the absolute size and potential longevity of the investment and the hedge fund manager's recognition that the institutional investor has a greater range and number of investing options.

[9] There may also be significant differences in the marketing and client relations costs incurred by a hedge fund manager in respect to institutional and high net worth investors that may justify fee differences .

Chapter 40

Marketing alternative investment funds: law and regulation in Europe

Eric C. Bettelheim[1]
Mishcon de Reya, Solicitors, London

This chapter examines the legal and regulatory framework applicable to marketing alternative investment funds under key EU Directives, as well as under applicable laws and regulations in the United Kingdom, Germany and France, and in Switzerland, the leading western European jurisdiction outside the EU. In addition, the chapter sets out key elements in the US legal and regulatory framework. Each case focuses on the manner in which overseas and domestic hedge and alternative investment funds can be marketed to sophisticated investors by using private placement or other applicable exemptions.

EU Directives

The UCITS Directive

The principal EU Directive relating to investment funds is the UCITS (Undertakings for Collective Investments in Transferable Securities) Directive. This Directive was designed to establish a common framework for mutual recognition of investment funds among EU member states. Its original scope, however, was restricted to funds investing primarily in transferable securities and to money market funds. Although UCITS funds may use derivatives for hedging (termed efficient portfolio management), the Directive is not designed to accommodate funds which use alternative investments – investments other than transferable securities – for significant portions of their portfolios.

Where a fund promoter establishes a fund in an EU jurisdiction which does qualify as a UCITS fund, other EU member states are required to accord reciprocity and to permit the fund to be marketed to the public in the same manner as domestically established funds. Although formal filings are required in order to benefit from such reciprocal recognition,[2] the process is streamlined and the burden on a fund promoter wishing to promote its fund to the public in a number of EU jurisdictions is radically reduced.

Since the reciprocity mechanism is available only to funds established in EU jurisdictions with investment restrictions in line with those set out in the Directive, the UCITS Directive is of very limited practical significance for promoters of alternative investment funds. For example, a fund established in Luxembourg under Part I of that country's investment funds law, applicable to funds complying with the investment restrictions of the Directive, can be listed on the Luxembourg Stock Exchange and, after the reciprocity filings referred to above, may be marketed to the public in one or more other EU jurisdictions. In contrast, a fund established under Part II of Luxembourg's investment funds law, applicable to funds which do not comply with the UCITS Directive, can still be listed on the Luxembourg Stock Exchange, but neither the fact of its establishment in Luxembourg nor its Luxembourg listing will enable the fund promoter to market it in other EU jurisdictions, except under applicable domestic private placement exemptions.

The scope of the UCITS Directive has recently been widened somewhat, by EC Directive 2001/108/EC, to permit investment by UCITS funds in financial instruments, other than transferable securities, which are sufficiently liquid. In addition, the European Commission is, before 13 February 2005, to forward the European Parliament a report on the application of the UCITS Directive. The report will focus on how to deepen and broaden the single market for UCITS, in particular with regard to cross-border marketing, the functioning of the Investment Services Directive (ISD) passport (see below) for management companies, the scope of the Directive as it applies to different types of products (institutional funds, real estate funds, master feeder funds and hedge funds) and an evaluation of the organisation of funds. Until that time, the distribution of hedge and alternative investment funds is largely confined to compliance with each EU member state's domestic legislation and regulation.

The ISD

The aim of the ISD is to provide a means for those carrying on investment business in one EU member state to be 'passported' to allow them to do business in other EU member states without authorisation or licensing in each such state. The ISD provides a single European passport, under which an investment business that is authorised in the EU member state in which it has its head or registered office (its home state) may offer services into, or establish branches in, other EU member states (or host states). Home states are responsible for prudential (capital) supervision, while host states are responsible for enforcing uniform rules on conduct of business, applicable to all firms doing business in them.

This aspect of regulation has become more important in recent years in relation to the marketing of investment funds. Before the ISD came into force, on 1 January 1996, many EU jurisdictions did not require authorisation of entities selling investments on a private placement basis and without a place of business in the jurisdiction. However, at the same time as they passed legislation implementing the ISD, a number of jurisdictions amended their applicable laws and/or regulations to require authorisation of all businesses offering investment services into the jurisdiction. The United Kingdom, with its overseas person exemption (discussed below), is a notable exception.

The United Kingdom

The Financial Services Act 1986 has been replaced by the Financial Services and Markets Act 2000 (FSMA). Like the FSA, the FSMA sets the boundary between legal and illegal financial services activities within the United Kingdom. FSMA provides a comprehensive framework for a single regulator for the financial services industry, the Financial Services Authority (FSA). FSMA operates by preventing anyone from carrying on or purporting to carry on, any regulated activity by way of business in the United Kingdom, unless they are authorised to do so, or exempt from doing so. Businesses present in the United Kingdom are prevented from engaging in the financial promotion of funds, unless the firm is authorised, the communication is approved by an authorised firm or an exemption applies. Any contract made in breach of either of these provisions is unenforceable and amounts to a criminal offence. FSMA extends to foreign firms selling into the United Kingdom as well as those operating in the United Kingdom.

Exempt persons under FSMA

FSMA provides that certain exempt persons can conduct all or some regulated activities without needing authorisation, for example the Bank of England. Lawyers and accountants, in carrying out their professions, are also exempt through their membership of professional bodies. Appointed representatives contracted to conduct regulated activities (normally as selling agents) for authorised firms may be exempt provided that the authorised firms which appoint them undertake responsibility for their conduct and compliance with FSMA and FSA regulations. An individual's exempt status only removes the requirement to be authorised as far as it applies to the general prohibition. The restriction on financial promotion of funds still applies. The promotion itself must be approved by an authorised firm unless covered by a specific exemption.

Regulated activities under FSMA

Since FSMA now covers deposit taking and insurance, the concept of 'regulated activities' is wider than under the preceding legislation. A regulated activity is now considered to be any activity which:

- is an activity of a specified kind;
- is carried on by way of business; and
- relates to an investment of a specified kind.[3]

Firms are caught by this provision if they have a registered office in the United Kingdom or carry on any of their activities from the United Kingdom. Therefore, any regulated activity carried on in or connected to the United Kingdom requires authorisation. Firms that do not have a permanent place of business in the United Kingdom may receive an exemption to promote regulated activities or products to UK-based customers.

Collective investment schemes

In the United Kingdom, collective investment schemes (CISs) are the vehicles by which investors can pool their funds to invest in a variety of investments, typically to spread the risk. This covers virtually all forms of investment funds. Traditionally in the United Kingdom there were two types of CIS vehicles: investment trusts and unit trusts. While both still exist, they largely have been superseded, particularly in the hedge and alternative investment fund sector, by open-ended investment companies (OEICs) and more recently by limited partnerships. This is largely the case because of the limitations of trust structures as well as their history as funds offered to the general public.

Investment trusts

Investment trusts provide an undifferentiated pro-rata interest in the trust funds which are typically invested in listed securities. Often listed on the stock exchange, interests in an investment trust typically trade at a significant discount to their net asset value and can be illiquid. They are not subject to corporation tax as other holding companies are.

Unit trusts

Units in a unit trust are marketed continuously to investors by the fund manager who is required to maintain a two-way (bid and offer) market for the units. Such schemes are restricted in what they can invest in. Their open-ended nature means that units may be bought and sold at any time at or near the underlying net asset value of the trust, but typically at a spread which favours the manager.

Open-ended investment companies

OEICs were introduced under the European Communities Act 1972. Later they were authorised for distribution in the United Kingdom. Like unit trusts they pool the resources of investors to provide a fund for investment by professional fund managers. Structurally OEICs are limited liability companies and hence are simpler to establish and manage than trust structures. Shares in OEICs have a single price for purchase and sale based on net asset value.

Limited partnerships

Limited partnerships, which have long been used in the United States, are governed in the United Kingdom under the Limited Partnership Act 1907 (the Act). They consist of one or more general or managing partners who are liable for the obligations of the partnership, and one or more limited partners who are only liable for the debts of the partnership to the extent that they have agreed to contribute to its capital or withdrawn capital from it. A limited partner cannot take part in the management of the firm and has no implied authority to bind the firm. The Act imposes strict rules of registration on a limited liability partnership, which, if not complied with, may jeopardise the partnership's limited liability status. Overseas partnerships, often Delaware LLCs, are also increasingly popular among promoters of hedge and alternative investment funds in the United Kingdom.

All CIS schemes marketed to or from the United Kingdom must be authorised if they are to be marketed to the general public. Furthermore, managers, trustees, depositaries and selling agents of such schemes must be authorised by the FSA. If the marketing is restricted to other authorised persons, professional investors and experienced investors, authorisation is not required. Such funds are 'unauthorised collective investment schemes' and make up a large proportion of current offers of hedge and alternative investment funds.

Promotion of CISs

There are a variety of restrictions on the promotion of CISs unless:

- the firm is authorised;
- the promotional material is approved by an authorised firm;
- an exemption applies;
- the scheme itself is authorised, exempt or recognised;

- the promotion is 'otherwise than to the general public'; and/or
- the promotion falls within a Treasury exception created by a statutory instrument.

Previously labelled 'investment advertising', the new definition of 'financial promotion' is much wider in scope. It now covers cold calling and solicited calls by authorised persons. Authorised persons involved in financial promotion are now subject to detailed rules laid down by the FSA.

The definition of financial promotion is to 'communicate [or cause to be communicated] an invitation or inducement to engage in investment activity'.[4] With regard to the financial promotion of CISs the FSMA 2000 (Promotion of CIS) (Exemptions) Order 2001 sets out the UK rules in detail. Fundamentally, it prohibits all communication originating outside the United Kingdom if it is capable of having an effect in the United Kingdom. However, there is an exception for unsolicited non-personal (letter, mail or brochure) communications, which are only exempt if they are made from outside the United Kingdom and relate to an overseas scheme. In this area of activity, FSMA has implemented the most stringent restrictions that the United Kingdom has seen to date.

The previous statute did provide for a number of exemptions to the financial promotion of CIS schemes which have been carried forward under FSMA. These exceptions include arrangements:

- operated otherwise than as a business;
- treated as other types of investment, for example deposits, contracts of insurance, depositary receipts and clearing services;
- sharing the use or enjoyment of property (time sharing), occupational pension schemes or employee share schemes;
- with a primary commercial purpose (including franchises);
- parallel investment management schemes; and
- that set up UK bodies corporate (other than OEICs) such as investment companies.

If a firm is authorised, recognised or exempt, an exception for the financial promotion of CISs to the general public will be available. Authorised firms may generally promote to the public five categories of schemes: two domestic and three overseas. These are:

- unit trusts;
- investment trusts;
- recognised schemes that comply with the UCITS Directive;
- recognised schemes authorised in designated countries; and
- individually recognised schemes.

Overseas CISs may be promoted by authorised firms to the public in the United Kingdom if they are recognised by the FSMA in one of three ways. Firstly, they are recognised where the CIS consists of a passported UCITS and the operator has given the FSA not less than two months' notice of wishing to market the scheme in the United Kingdom. Secondly, they are recognised where the CIS consists of a class of scheme specified from an overseas country or territory designated by statutory instrument. This allows the Treasury to passport schemes from Jersey, Guernsey, the Isle of Man and Bermuda, which again require two months' notice to be recognised. Finally, the individual CIS schemes that do not fall within the previous two categories, but nevertheless match the criteria of those imposed upon UK authorised schemes may be recognised.

A new approach

In May 2003, the FSA, recognising changing consumer needs and market developments, announced proposals for reforming the regulation of CISs. The reform proposes to broaden investor choice and give the industry more operational flexibility, whilst simultaneously safeguarding investors' interests. The key proposals are, briefly, as follows.

- A new category of non-retail schemes will be introduced. The schemes will be restricted to investment by institutional and expert investors, and therefore subject to less stringent product regulation than retail schemes.
- The current distinct categories of retail schemes will be rationalised into two broad categories – UCITS and non-UCITS. The former will retain the Directive-imposed requirements on the spread and quality of the assets in the fund, whilst the latter will afford investors a much wider range of illiquid assets, such as property, in which to put their savings.
- The quality of the information sent out by providers is also set to improve. Short form reports will replace long form reports and accounts in a bid to attract and cater for the non-professional investors.
- The FSA will lift its ban on onshore authorised funds charging performance fees. The charging rules for unit trusts will be aligned with those for OEICs and performance fees will be allowed for both products, bringing the United Kingdom in line with the majority of the EU.

The consultation period ended in October 2003 and the FSA plans to make final rules in 2004, at which point they will be available for use by existing UK schemes. The rules will apply to all UK schemes from February 2007.

The United States

The offer and sale of fund interests in the United States requires consideration of several regulatory regimes: the federal regimes of the Securities and Exchange Commission (SEC) and the Commodity Futures Trading Commission (CFTC), as well as the securities (blue sky) laws of the 50 states.

Under US federal law, fund interests are generally securities under the Securities Act 1933 and may only be offered or sold in the United States in compliance with or pursuant to an exemption from that Act and the SEC's rules made under it. Funds that have a primary purpose of investing in securities, but do not have an applicable exemption, are required to register with the SEC as investment companies under the Investment Company Act 1940. Their advisers may be required to register with the SEC as investment advisers under the Investment Advisers Act 1940 or similar state laws. The organisers and advisers of funds using futures or options on futures are generally required to register with the CFTC as commodity pool operations (CPOs) or as commodity trading advisers (CTAs).

Any sale of fund interests or other securities in, from or into the United States may be regulated under US securities laws. For securities to be sold to the general public in the

United States by means of inter-state commerce (broadly speaking, any mailing, telephoning (including internet) or travelling across state lines or into the United States from abroad) the securities must be registered with the SEC. In order to do so, a Securities Act registration statement, including a prospectus, must be filed with the SEC. Issuers of registered securities typically become subject to continuing reporting requirements under the Securities Exchange Act 1934.

An exemption from the registration requirements under the Securities Act applies to transactions by an issuer of securities not involving any public offer. Thus funds may be sold by private placement. The most common private placement exemption used is that available under Regulation D made by the SEC under the Securities Act. Rule 506 of Regulation D provides that an offer is private if the offeror does not engage in general solicitation and all purchasers are accredited investors, and/or no more than 35 purchasers are unaccredited investors. Among the categories of accredited investors are the following:

- authorised banks;
- registered broker-dealers;
- registered investment companies;
- licensed insurance companies;
- pension plans for which investment decisions are made by a plan fiduciary which is a bank, insurance company or registered investment adviser, or any pension plan with assets of more than US$5 million;
- trusts with assets of more than US$5 million for which investment decisions are directed by a sophisticated person with sufficient knowledge to evaluate relevant investment risks and which were not formed for the purpose of acquiring the fund interests offered;
- individuals whose net worth, individually or jointly with a spouse, exceeds US$1 million; and
- individuals whose income has exceeded US$200,000, or US$300,000 jointly with a spouse, in each of the most recent years and who have a reasonable expectation of reaching the same income level in the current year.

In addition to compliance with federal securities laws, the public offer of fund interests may require separate registration under blue sky laws in the states in which they are offered for sale. Although in many states the SEC filings may be used to achieve registration in a routine fashion, in certain states regulators require that additional information is filed before offers or after sales, and in many states filing fees are payable. Any offer or sale of securities pursuant to the exemption provided under Rule 506 of Regulation D is automatically exempt from registration under state laws. This, however, does not preclude individual states from imposing filing requirements or fees on persons who rely on this exemption.

The Investment Company Act requires the registration of all entities primarily engaged in the business of investing or trading in securities. Funds that trade securities clearly fall within this definition. The most useful exemptions enabling a fund to avoid regulation under the Investment Company Act are those applicable to funds of which the outstanding securities are owned by investors, all of whom are qualified purchasers (as further explained below), or which are beneficially owned by fewer than 100 persons and which do not publicly offer their securities. Under an SEC staff interpretation, an offshore fund need not count non-US investors for the purposes of this exemption. Thus, so long as an offshore fund has investors that are all qualified purchasers or has fewer than 100 US investors and does not make a public offer in the United States, it is not required to register under the Investment Company Act. In certain circumstances, the Investment Company Act, as interpreted by the SEC, requires looking through an investing entity to its beneficial owners (particularly where it is a fund or other entity formed for the purpose of making investments) for the purpose of counting the number of investors. However, the SEC has granted no action relief where the investing entity has invested less than 40 per cent of its assets in a fund. Where multiple funds have control and similar investment characteristics, they may be amalgamated for the purpose of counting the number of investors.

Qualified purchasers include the following:

- individuals who own, individually or jointly with a spouse, securities and other investments worth at least US$5 million;
- companies owned directly or indirectly by two or more individuals who are related as sibling or spouse, or who are descendants or spouses of such persons;
- persons, acting for their own account or for the account of other qualified purchasers, who in aggregate own or invest on a discretionary basis not less than US$25 million in investments; and
- trusts outside the second category above not formed for the specific purpose of acquiring the fund interests offered when the trustee (or other person authorised to make investment decisions) and each settler or other person who has contributed assets to the trust is a qualified purchaser under one of the other categories set out above.

Under the Investment Advisers Act any person giving advice with respect to the value of, or advisability of investing in, securities may be required to register with the SEC as an investment adviser. The Act provides an exemption from the registration requirement for investment advisers that had fewer than 15 US clients during the preceding 12 months and that do not hold themselves out to the public as investment advisers, or act as investment advisers to any registered investment companies. If an adviser exceeds the 15-person limit it is required to register with the SEC, if it has more than US$25 million in assets under management. If the adviser does not meet this threshold it is generally prohibited from registering as an adviser with the SEC, but it may be required to register as an adviser with the appropriate state(s). The SEC's position for the purpose of calculating the 15-person limit is that a typical fund, in which the funds of all investors are invested in the same investments, is treated as a single client.*

If a fund engages in commodity or financial futures or options transactions, registration as a CPO or CTA may be required under the Commodity Futures Modernisation Act of 2000. Any person or organisation that operates or solicits monies for a fund trading in CFTC-regulated futures or options is required to register with the CFTC as a CPO. There are certain exemptions from the registration requirement to register as a CPO:

- CPOs with total funds under management of less than US$200,000 and with no single fund having more than 15 participants;
- CPOs that limit their use of futures and options contracts to 10 per cent of the fair market value of their funds' assets; and
- investment companies registered with the SEC which enter into futures and options transactions for bona fide hedging purposes, provided that such a company commits no more than 5 per cent of its total net assets to initial margin and option premiums; that it is not

marketed as a futures fund; and that prospective participants are informed of the purpose of, and restrictions on, the company's use of derivatives.

CPOs with funds that are limited to qualified eligible participants are required to register as CPOs with the CFTC, but are subject to a reduced compliance burden. Qualified eligible participants include:

- investment professionals, including registered futures brokers and securities broker-dealers, and CPOs and CTAs with at least US$5 million under management; and
- any corporation, unincorporated entity or individual that owns or controls a portfolio of at least US$2 million in securities, or that has deposited at least US$200,000-worth of margin and option premiums for trading in commodity futures and options (or a combination of the two), provided that individuals meet net worth criteria and that other entities meet total asset size criteria broadly similar to those applicable to accredited investors (discussed above).

Any person or organisation that is engaged in business that includes advising US citizens or residents concerning trading in CFTC-regulated contracts, or that trades such contracts on a discretionary basis, is required to register with the CFTC as a CTA. CTAs that have advised fewer than 15 people in the preceding 12 months are exempt from registration if they do not publicly hold themselves out as CTAs. The CFTC's position for the purpose of calculating the 15-person limit is that, if a CTA advises a fund, it thereby advises each investor that participates in the fund. CFTC regulations exempt a CPO, including one that is exempt from CPO registration, from the obligation to register as a CTA if advice is given only in relation to funds for which the CPO is registered or exempt. Although they are required to register with the CFTC, reduced compliance burdens apply to CTAs with clients that are all qualified eligible clients – a category broadly similar to qualified eligible participants (discussed above).

France

Under Regulation 98–04 of the French Commission des Opérations de Bourse (COB) there are significant difficulties in marketing funds to French investors. Even private placements of fund shares can only be carried out in accordance with very stringent guidelines. The most restrictive is that fund interests must not be offered or sold through any financial intermediary or selling agent, regardless of whether such selling agent is domiciled and/or licensed in France. Further, no prospectus, or other descriptive or advertising material in any form, may be mailed to investors. The COB further abolished the earlier exemption which allowed for the distribution of funds to a limited number of French investors. This was known as the 'pre-existing private placement exemption'.

Now foreign funds and French funds require COB approval for them to be marketed to French investors. In order to obtain approval foreign hedge funds are required to fall within the UCITS or non-UCITS classification and need to comply with the French legislation that applies to foreign hedge funds. One of the requirements is that foreign funds must have 90 per cent of their investments in securities listed on a regulated stock market. Such funds need to be seen to use derivatives for hedging purposes and not for speculation. Hence, futures, swaps and options cannot exceed 10 per cent of the assets of the fund.

505

COB approval is, however, only required in relation to proactive marketing of the foreign fund. Such marketing occurs where the potential investor is solicited by the fund. This approach can be oral or written. However, where an investor has not been solicited and responds to an unsolicited request by the fund, which is based in France, the COB rules do not apply.

Germany

The position in Germany is now governed by the German Foreign Investment Fund Law (GFIFL). Under this regime, both UCITS and non-UCITS funds need to be registered in Germany. However, the regime places strict measures on the marketing of non-UCITS funds, which in reality means that such funds cannot be marketed in the German market.

One significant exemption is that unregistered funds may be marketed to investors who have an established relationship with the financial advisers with whom the transaction is made. Furthermore, there are no provisions in respect of the type and numbers of investors that may be approached in this way. The result is that a domestic bank or securities firm is essential to the promotion of overseas hedge and alternative investment funds in Germany.

In addition, where the investment in the hedge fund is incidental to a larger transaction the German regulators can authorise a 'no action' letter. As a result investment in hedge funds in Germany may be undertaken via vehicles which make the hedge fund investment incidental to a larger transaction.

Switzerland

Investment funds in Switzerland are governed by the Mutual Funds Act, which came into force in 1995. Unlike previous Swiss legislation, it did not clearly set out a distinction between exempted private offers and public offers, which require authorisation by the Federal Banking Commission (FBC). Until the Act was passed, Swiss securities law practitioners had generally accepted that solicitation of up to 20 investors could be carried on, as this did not constitute public solicitation and was therefore permissible with respect to funds, which were not registered with the FBC.

An ordinance, which took effect on 1 November 1997, amended the scope of the Mutual Funds Act and restored the private placement exemption with respect to institutional investors – banks, insurance companies, pension funds and treasury departments of large corporate investors. Under the ordinance, up to 20 Swiss institutional investors can be targeted, provided that there is no public solicitation, without triggering the registration requirement.

The FBC will not generally grant public offer authorisation to foreign investment funds unless they are subject to supervision in their home jurisdiction under a regulatory system comparable to that provided under Swiss law. Among jurisdictions which the FBC has concluded are comparable are the United States, all EU member states, and Guernsey and Jersey. Low-tax jurisdictions, such as the British Virgin Islands or the Cayman Islands, have not yet been approved. In early 1997, two derivatives funds established in Ireland became the first derivatives funds organised by an entity other than a bank or a Swiss corporation to be approved by the FBC.

It is also important to bear in mind that the offer and sale of fund shares falls within the scope of the newly enacted Swiss Stock Exchange Act, which requires that any entity offering securities to Swiss residents must be authorised by the FBC. In the case of the Man funds referred to above, the promoter's Swiss affiliate was given approval to distribute the funds. A number of Swiss financial institutions have recently established vehicles designed to provide Swiss investors with access to hedge funds established in jurisdictions for which, for the reasons set out above, public offer authorisation is precluded. Typically, these Swiss vehicles are structured as closed-end holding companies, which invest in a series of hedge funds through an intermediate company. Such Swiss closed-end vehicles do not constitute mutual funds under Swiss law. These vehicles are required to observe certain restrictions – for example, redemptions are limited to 10 per cent of the shares, and shareholders' approval is required for any share capital increase or decrease.

Conclusion

The restrictions on the marketing of hedge and alternative investment funds continue to vary widely throughout Europe, and in both the EU and the United States such products are essentially limited to private placements to sophisticated and high net worth investors. Retail products for the general public are being developed both in the United Kingdom and the United States but are unlikely to be permitted in the EU until the review of the UCITS Directive has been completed. Nevertheless, the hedge fund industry is growing rapidly on both continents and continues to move towards the mainstream of investment products.

* Editor's note: on 29 September 2003, shortly before this book went to press, the staff of the SEC issued its report entitled 'The Implications of the Growth of Hedge Funds', the culmination of its efforts following the Hedge Fund Roundtable held in May 2003. As of the date of this writing, the Commission itself had not taken any action in response to the report. One of the key recommendations of the staff was that the SEC consider 'requiring hedge fund advisers to register with the SEC as investment advisers, taking into account whether the benefits outweigh the burdens of registration'. In the staff's view, ' ... registration of hedge fund advisers would serve as a deterrent to fraud, encourage compliance and the adoption of compliance procedures, provide the SEC with important information ... and effectively raise the standards for investment in hedge funds from the "accredited investor" standard to that of "qualified client"'. See http://www.sec.gov/news/studies/hedgefunds0903.pdf for the full text of the report.

---

[1] The author gratefully acknowledges the assistance of Ben Dhesi and Laura Tyler of Mishcon de Reya in the preparation of this chapter.

[2] The information required by each member state in such filing differs in detail; however, broadly, each member state requires the filing of the home jurisdiction's certificate of compliance with the UCITS Directive, the fund prospectus and constitutional documents and its latest annual and semi-annual reports, together with certain basic information relating to the fund, its managers and promoters, and a description of the intended method of marketing.

[3] Section 22 FSMA.

[4] Section 21(1) FSMA.

Chapter 41

Marketing alternative investments: law and regulation in the United States[1]

Nicholas S. Hodge
Kirkpatrick & Lockhart LLP, Boston, Massachusetts

Introduction

Until recently, alternative investment products such as hedge funds were invariably structured so as to qualify for exemptions from registration under the Investment Company Act of 1940 (the 1940 Act) and the Securities Act of 1933 (the 1933 Act). Most still do, and these exemptions substantially dictate how these products can be marketed in the United States. More recently, certain alternative investment products have been registered as closed-end funds or as mutual funds under the 1940 Act, and the shares of some of these funds have been registered under the 1933 Act. Registration under these statutes can dramatically enhance distribution options. This chapter will briefly review US law and regulation as it relates to the marketing of various types of alternative investment products.

1933 Act limitations on marketing

Within the United States, hedge funds and other alternative investment products are typically structured as limited partnerships or limited liability companies. The fund sponsor sells interests in the fund in order to raise the money that is invested in portfolio securities or commodities in accordance with the fund's investment strategy. The limited partnership or limited liability company interests that the sponsor sells are themselves securities. To sell these interests, the sponsor must comply with US federal and state law applicable to the offer and sale of securities. Most sponsors choose to offer the interests pursuant to an exemption from registration under the 1933 Act. While there are numerous exemptions available under the 1933 Act, hedge fund sponsors rely exclusively on the exemption in Section 4(2) of the 1933 Act. Section 4(2) exempts from the registration requirements of the 1933 Act 'transactions by an issuer not involving any public offering'. An offering that is not public is generally called a private offering, and the Section 4(2) exemption is referred to as the private placement exemption.

The choice of exemption under the 1933 Act is dictated by the requirements for an exception under the 1940 Act. The 1940 Act regulates entities that are in the business of investing in the securities of other companies. A fund that invests in securities, such as a typical hedge fund, must either register as an investment company under the 1940 Act or seek an exception from the definition of 'investment company'. Funds organised in the United States typically rely on the Section 3(c)(1) or Section 3(c)(7) exception under the 1940 Act.

A fund that meets all of the requirements of either of these sections will be deemed not to be an investment company for purposes of the 1940 Act and will therefore not be required to register under the 1940 Act. A requirement of each of these sections is that the fund not be making and not currently propose to make a public offering of securities. The fund must therefore make private offerings of its securities under Section 4(2) of the 1933 Act.

An offshore fund may make offers and sales of its securities in the United States or to US persons outside the United States, but only in accordance with the Section 3(c)(1) or Section 3(c)(7) exception under the 1940 Act. Thus, to the extent that an offshore fund sells its interests in the United States or to US persons, it must do so in accordance with all of the requirements of the private placement exemption.

Section 4(2) itself provides no guidance as to what constitutes a public or private offering. In 1982, the Securities and Exchange Commission (SEC), which is the federal agency charged with enforcing US securities laws, adopted a rule intended to facilitate private offerings of securities. Rule 506 of Regulation D provides a relatively objective set of criteria for qualifying for the private placement exemption. A fund that offers and sells securities in accordance with all of the requirements of Rule 506 is deemed to have made a valid private offering under Section 4(2). Rule 506 is not the exclusive means of qualifying for the private placement exemption; however, a fund that does not rely on Rule 506 cannot be as certain that it has met the requirements for the exemption, since the judicial and administrative interpretations of Section 4(2) are vague and inconsistent.

A failure by a fund to meet all of the requirements for the private placement exemption can give rise to a right of rescission on the part of the investor, meaning that the investor can demand a return of its purchase price plus interest. An investor is of course most likely to exercise such a right if the fund has lost its money. If the fund no longer has sufficient assets to meet rescission claims, the fund sponsors may be exposed to personal liability. Moreover, if investors challenge the availability of the private placement exemption in an attempt to establish a right of rescission, the burden of proving the availability of the exemption is on the fund that is claiming the exemption. Ambiguities in the law tend to work against the party having the burden of proof. Therefore, a fund sponsor that is relying on the private placement exemption is well-advised to conduct its offering in a manner that conforms as nearly as possible to settled interpretations. It is also important to note that a failure to meet all of the requirements of the private placement exemption, such as making a single offer in a manner that is inconsistent with the exemption, may contaminate the entire offering, giving all investors in that offering a right of rescission.

Two requirements of Rule 506 bear particularly on marketing: the requirements that sales be made to 'accredited investors' (as defined in Regulation D) and the prohibition against making offers by any means of general solicitation or general advertising. As discussed below, these requirements substantially limit the fund's marketing options.

Accredited investors

The US Supreme Court has held that the essence of a private offering is that those to whom the offers and sales of the securities are made must be sufficiently sophisticated in business and financial affairs to be able to watch out for their own interests. This sophistication standard is highly subjective, and prior to the adoption of Regulation D issuers of securities were frequently uncertain as to whether a prospective investor was sufficiently sophisticated.

When the SEC adopted Regulation D, it provided relatively objective standards of sophistication by recognising certain financial criteria as proxies for investor sophistication. It did this by defining eight categories of so-called 'accredited investors' that the SEC considers sophisticated. Accredited investors include an individual with a net worth (or joint net worth with a spouse) in excess of US$1 million, and an individual with income in excess of US$200,000 in each of the last two years and who reasonably expects to have the same level of income in the current year (or joint income with a spouse in excess of US$300,000 in each of those years). Entities are generally accredited if they have assets in excess of US$5 million and were not formed for the purpose of making the investment.

Sales can be made under Rule 506 to an unlimited number of accredited investors. While Rule 506 permits a fund to sell securities to up to 35 non-accredited investors in any given offering, most hedge funds choose not to sell to non-accredited investors at all. If a sale is made to even a single non-accredited investor, the fund becomes subject to an onerous disclosure requirement under Rule 502 of Regulation D that otherwise would not apply. While all fund sponsors must disclose all material facts when offering and selling fund interests, it is preferable from the sponsor's standpoint not to be subject to the specific and extensive disclosure requirements of Rule 502.

Prohibition against general solicitation

A fund that is relying on the private placement exemption is severely limited in its marketing activities by the prohibition against general solicitation and general advertising. With limited exceptions, a fund cannot advertise its offering on the internet or radio, in newspapers, or by any other general means. It cannot offer its securities at a seminar or meeting where attendees have been invited by any general solicitation or advertising. Similarly, a fund sponsor cannot answer questions from a reporter about its offering if it expects that the reporter will write a story about the offering that will be published in a newspaper or on the internet.

The SEC has made clear that a fund conducting a private offering may offer its securities to prospective investors with whom it (or a broker-dealer acting on its behalf) has a pre-existing relationship and for whom it believes the offering would be suitable. The SEC has also made clear that the pre-existing relationship standard is not the only means of complying with the prohibition against general solicitation and advertising, although it has not been particularly clear in describing other acceptable methods. Whether or not a general solicitation has occurred must be evaluated on a case-by-case basis, taking into account the facts of each situation. However, as noted above, a fund sponsor who strays too far from settled law in this area may find it difficult to meet the burden of proving the availability of the private placement exemption.

The development of the internet has created particular hazards for fund sponsors, since the internet makes it possible to communicate with large numbers of people in indiscriminate fashion. The SEC has, for example, already deemed the posting of a notice of an offering on a fund's website to constitute a general solicitation if access to the website is unrestricted. However, the internet also presents fund sponsors with opportunities. The SEC has recognised that the ability to transmit information rapidly by electronic means can be affirmatively helpful to existing and potential investors, as long as it is effected in a manner that is consistent with the prohibition against general solicitation and general advertising. Thus, the SEC has permitted the following practices.

- A fund sponsor may deliver the private placement memorandum and other offering documents electronically to a specific prospective investor if the making of an offer to that investor does not otherwise constitute a general solicitation.
- The SEC has issued interpretations that enable a hedge fund sponsor to post a notice of its offering on a password-protected internet site maintained by a third party. The third party, which charges the hedge fund a fee for this service, uses an investor suitability questionnaire to determine whether a prospective investor is an accredited investor that can be allowed access to the website. This determination is made without reference to any particular offering of securities. If the prospective investor is deemed suitable, it is provided with a password to access the website, where the prospective investor can review hedge fund offerings that have been listed. The SEC has conditioned its acceptance of this procedure on a requirement that the investor wait at least 30 days before purchasing any issue of securities offered at the site.

The staff of the SEC has recommended that the prohibition against general solicitation be eased or eliminated for offerings by funds relying on the Section 3(c)(7) exception. The staff noted that there is little policy justification in prohibiting general solicitation in such offerings, since all of the investors will meet a high suitability requirement. At this time, we do not know whether or when the SEC will adopt this recommendation.

1940 Act limitations on marketing

A fund that relies on the Section 3(c)(1) or the Section 3(c)(7) exception under the 1940 Act is not only limited to offering its interests in private offerings. Each of these exceptions imposes additional requirements that limit a fund's ability to market its interests. The Section 3(c)(1) exception limits the number of beneficial owners in the fund to 100. The sponsor of such a fund will usually impose a high minimum investment amount (typically US$1 million) so that the fund will have sufficient assets under management even with just 100 investors. The Section 3(c)(7) exception requires that all investors in the fund be so-called 'qualified purchasers' at the time of sale, a relatively high standard that includes individuals with at least US$5 million in investments (as defined) and companies with at least US$25 million in investments.

Advisers Act limitations on marketing

Hedge fund managers must either register as investment advisers under the Investment Advisers Act of 1940 (the Advisers Act) or analogous state statutes, or qualify for exemptions from registration under those laws. Many hedge fund managers prefer to operate pursuant to exemptions from investment adviser registration. The federal exemption from registration and some state exemptions from registration are premised on the adviser's not holding itself out to the public as an investment adviser. An adviser would be considered to be holding itself out as an investment adviser if, for example, it advertised its business in a newspaper or over the internet. The SEC has adopted a rule that makes clear that merely to offer securities of a hedge fund in a valid private offering would not constitute holding out by the investment adviser. If the adviser were to violate the prohibition against general solicitation or otherwise fail to meet the requirements of the private placement exemption in connection with the offering of a hedge fund, the adviser would likely also lose the benefit of its exemption from registration under the Advisers Act and may lose its exemption from state investment adviser registration.

The Advisers Act and certain state investment adviser statutes generally prohibit a registered adviser from taking a performance-based fee, which is to say a fee based on the capital gains or capital appreciation of the assets under management. A performance-based fee (usually a performance allocation) is a feature of nearly all hedge funds, however, so hedge fund advisers that are subject to this prohibition must qualify for an exemption from it. Rule 205–3 under the Advisers Act provides such an exemption if each customer of the adviser (or each investor in the case of a fund) is a so-called 'qualified client'. A qualified client is an individual or company with a net worth of at least US$1.5 million or with at least US$750,000 under management with the adviser. If the client is itself a company relying on the Section 3(c)(1) exception from the 1940 Act, it is necessary to look through that client and ascertain that all of its investors are qualified clients.

Registered advisers are also prohibited from compensating finders who direct customers or investors to the adviser unless certain requirements are met. One of these requirements is that the prospective customer or investor be informed that the finder is being compensated for making the referral.

1934 Act limitations on marketing

The Securities Exchange Act of 1934 (the 1934 Act) generally requires that persons who are in the business of selling securities on behalf of others be registered as broker-dealers. While the SEC has recognised a limited exception to this requirement for so-called 'finders' who are not in the business of acting as brokers, many individuals and companies that purport to be operating within that exception do not meet its requirements. As a general matter, a hedge fund that wishes to pay a third party to market the interests in the fund must engage a registered broker-dealer to do so.

New products

If a fund and its manager rely on the exemptions described above, they will be subject to multiple overlapping restrictions on marketing. Some fund sponsors have developed new products that do not rely on one or more of these exemptions to enhance their ability to market the interests in their funds. Two of these new products are described below.

Registered funds of hedge funds

A registered fund of hedge funds is registered under the 1940 Act as a closed-end investment company. It invests in hedge funds that are excepted from the definition of investment company under the 1940 Act.

The shares in the fund may be registered for sale under the 1933 Act, in which case sales can be made without regard to the prohibition against general solicitation and general advertising. Even if the shares are registered for sale under the 1933 Act, however, as a condition to declaring effective the registration statements of such funds, the SEC has frequently required that the shares be sold only to accredited investors. This requirement does not derive from the private placement exemption because the offering is registered under the 1933 Act. The SEC is apparently imposing the accredited investor standard in an attempt to assure that funds of hedge funds will be marketed only to investors that are capable of understanding their relatively complex structures. The SEC has also sometimes imposed a minimum offering amount (usually US$25,000), presumably for the same reason.

Because the fund is registered under the 1940 Act, sales are not limited to qualified purchasers, nor is there a limit on the number of investors in the fund. However, since the adviser to any fund registered under the 1940 Act must be registered under the Advisers Act, sales can be made only to qualified clients if the adviser to the fund of hedge funds receives performance-based compensation. Sales must also be limited to qualified clients if the fund of hedge funds invests in hedge funds that rely on the Section 3(c)(1) exemption from the 1940 Act and that are managed by registered investment advisers. Sales of funds of hedge funds need not be limited to qualified clients if there is no performance-based compensation at the fund of hedge funds level, and if the fund of hedge funds invests only in hedge funds that rely on the Section 3(c)(7) exception from the 1940 Act or only in funds that are managed by unregistered investment advisers.

Long-short mutual funds

A significant change in the Internal Revenue Code in 1997 paved the way for a new breed of mutual fund that can invest both long and short. Prior to this change, if an investment company derived 30 per cent or more of its gross income from securities held for less than three months, it would not qualify for pass-through tax treatment under Subchapter M of the Internal Revenue Code. Failure to qualify for pass-through tax treatment would mean that the investment company would be taxed as a corporation, which would be a very undesirable result. Securities sold short were always considered to be held for less than three months, because they were sold immediately. Few investment companies even attempted to operate within the confines of this so-called 'short-short' rule.

Congress amended the Internal Revenue Code in 1997 to eliminate the short-short rule. This has led to the creation of numerous mutual funds that can offer many strategies of the sort used by hedge funds in the context of a 1940 Act registered fund. Such funds sell their shares publicly to an unlimited number of investors in minimum amounts as low as US$500. Sales are not limited to qualified clients if there is no performance-based fee to the adviser, or if the performance-based fee is a fulcrum fee (a fee that is based on the net asset value of the fund that increases or decreases proportionately with the performance of the fund relative to an appropriate index).

Even with the elimination of the short-short rule, registered investment companies do not enjoy the same latitude to engage in short selling and certain other investment strategies as hedge funds. Section 18 of the 1940 Act limits the ability of registered investment companies to issue so-called 'senior securities'. The SEC has interpreted the term senior securities to include not only senior classes of stock, but all type of indebtedness with a term of over 60 days and various other instruments that could expose the fund to leveraged losses. These include short selling, entering into reverse repurchase agreements and entering into forward contracts.

Because each of these activities has the potential to create a senior security, a fund entering into them must comply with the requirements of Section 18 or take steps to cover the transaction in ways approved by the SEC to limit the potential for loss by the fund. If the transaction is covered in an approved fashion, the SEC takes the position that no senior security has been created, and therefore compliance with Section 18 is unnecessary.

Compliance with Section 18 is a possibility in the case of a borrowing by a registered investment company, as long as all of the requirements of that section are met. Section 18 forbids an open-ended investment company (which continuously offers and redeems its securities) from borrowing, except from a bank, and then only subject to 300 per cent asset coverage. The asset coverage requirement will be met if, after the borrowing, the fund has assets equal to at least 300 per cent of its indebtedness. In other words, a fund with US$100 in assets could borrow US$50 from a bank, since, following the borrowing, the fund would have a total of US$150 in assets (including the borrowed funds) and US$50 in debt. As a practical matter, however, such funds do not typically borrow from banks because the cost of credit is too high.

Compliance with Section 18 becomes more difficult, and in many cases impossible, in the case of the various other leveraged transactions that the SEC considers to be senior securities. Unless the proposed transaction is entered into with a bank, for example, an open-end fund simply cannot comply with Section 18.

Therefore, to enter into transactions of this sort, funds routinely cover potential losses in one of the manners approved by the SEC. This renders compliance with Section 18 unnecessary. Coverage can be achieved either by being long in the instrument underlying the transaction or by segregating certain assets. In the case of a short sale, for example, the fund can sell short against the box or can segregate assets in required amounts. If the fund chooses to segregate assets, the SEC requires that the fund segregate assets on its records or on its custodian's records equal to the current market value of the securities shorted, marked to market daily. The fund can deduct from the amount required to be segregated any collateral deposited with the broker in connection with a short sale, but not the proceeds of the short sale itself, which are being held by the broker. The amount deposited as collateral will vary, but will ultimately be dictated by Federal Reserve Board Regulation T, New York Stock Exchange requirements, Nasdaq requirements and house margin requirements. The segregated assets may be any liquid securities or cash. The segregated assets are not available to the fund for investment, to make redemptions or to pay expenses.

Through the use of new products such as these, hedge fund strategies are being made available to larger numbers of investors. They are also being made available to investors who may not have been able to invest directly in hedge funds, either because they were not able to invest the high minimum investment amount typically required of hedge fund investors or because they were not accredited. The SEC and the National Association of Securities Dealers, Inc, are monitoring these developments and have expressed concern about whether sales are being made to unsuitable investors. If their investor protection concerns can be satisfied, these trends can be expected to continue.

---

[1] This chapter is for informational purposes only and does not contain or convey legal advice. The information herein should not be used or relied upon in regard to any particular facts or circumstances without first consulting with a lawyer. Christina Lim and Irene Brennan assisted in the preparation of this chapter, and Mark Goshko provided helpful comments on it.

Chapter 42

The evolution and outlook for regulation of hedge funds in the United States[1]

Nicholas S. Hodge
Kirkpatrick & Lockhart LLP,[2] *Boston, Massachusetts*

Introduction

It has been a hallmark of hedge funds since their inception that they have operated relatively free from US federal and state securities regulation. As a result, hedge funds have had far greater flexibility in the management of their assets than their more heavily regulated counterparts that are registered under the Investment Company Act of 1940 (the 1940 Act). Creative hedge fund managers have exploited this flexibility to engage in the many investment strategies that are described in various chapters of this book.

However, hedge funds have never been entirely free from regulation under federal and state law, and the current trend is toward greater regulation on a number of fronts. This is a brief review of the background of hedge fund regulation in the United States and likely future developments.

Current regulatory environment

Hedge funds typically qualify for exemptions from registration under the 1940 Act and the Securities Act of 1933. The advisers to hedge funds frequently qualify for the Section 203(b)(3) exemption from registration under the Investment Advisers Act of 1940 (the Advisers Act). These exemptions are available without regard to the dollar amount under management. As a result, enormous amounts of money have been managed in hedge funds without much regulatory oversight.

Due to these exemptions, hedge funds are relatively free to pursue creative trading strategies. The restrictions on borrowing, for example, that apply to registered investment companies under Section 18 of the 1940 Act are wholly inapplicable to hedge funds. To be exempt from registration under various federal securities laws is not tantamount to being entirely exempt from regulation, however. Hedge funds and their advisers are currently subject to many regulatory requirements. These requirements do not generally restrict the manager in devising and implementing the fund's trading strategies, nor do they usually entail oversight by regulatory authorities, but they may considerably enhance investor protection by imposing other limitations on the fund, its adviser and any broker-dealer acting on their behalf. These requirements include, significantly, the anti-fraud requirements of federal and state securities law, such as Section 10(b) and Rule 10b-5 under the Securities Exchange Act of 1934, which prohibit fraud in connection with the purchase or sale of a security.

Consequently, an investor who purchases an interest in a hedge fund in reliance upon a material misstatement or omission in the offering material may be entitled to a return of its original investment.

Further, the advisers to hedge funds are subject to the anti-fraud provisions of the Advisers Act even if they are exempt from registration under that Act. The anti-fraud provisions forbid all investment advisers from engaging in any course of business that is fraudulent, deceptive or manipulative. In addition, in 1963 the US Supreme Court interpreted the anti-fraud provisions of the Advisers Act to impose a fiduciary duty on all advisers. A fiduciary duty requires the adviser to act in the utmost good faith with respect to the investor and not to advance its own interests at the expense of those of the investor to whom the duty is owed. A fiduciary duty is the highest obligation known under the law, and it requires the adviser to adhere to a code of conduct that far exceeds the standards of general good faith business dealings. It is the same duty as that owed by a trustee to the beneficiaries of a trust. This duty would, for example, typically forbid an adviser from taking an investment opportunity that was of limited availability for its own account if the investment opportunity would be suitable for a hedge fund under its management and the fund had sufficient assets to make the investment itself.

The following are some of the other regulatory requirements to which hedge funds and their advisers may currently be subject.

- Institutional investment managers that exercise discretion with respect to equity securities having an aggregate fair market value of at least US$100 million are required to file Form 13F with the Securities and Exchange Commission (SEC), disclosing the names of the issuers of the securities and the market value of each holding. The manager is not required to disclose short positions or holdings of debt securities. The manager may request that the SEC treat the filing as confidential.
- Every broker-dealer is currently required by the USA Patriot Act to have an anti-money laundering compliance policy to detect and cause the reporting of suspicious activity. The Department of the Treasury and the Financial Crimes Enforcement Network have proposed rules that would expand anti-money laundering regulation to investment advisers. The advisers affected would be those that are registered with the SEC and those that operate pursuant to the Section 203(b)(3) exemption if they have US$30 million or more under management.
- As fiduciaries, advisers to hedge funds are generally required to obtain best execution when purchasing or selling securities on behalf of the fund. An adviser may pay a brokerage commission that is higher than the minimum commission available in exchange for research and execution services provided by the broker-dealer if the amount of the extra commission is reasonable in relation to the value of the services provided. In the absence of appropriate disclosure or the consent of the investors in the fund, however, the adviser may not for any other reason generally pay a brokerage commission that is higher than the minimum commission available.
- Hedge funds are subject to privacy regulations promulgated by the Federal Trade Commission, which require the funds to adopt policies regarding the disclosure of non-public personal information about natural persons that are investors in the funds.
- The manager of a hedge fund that trades in commodity futures contracts and commodity option contracts may be required to register as a commodity pool operator (CPO) or commodity trading adviser (CTA) under the Commodity Exchange Act, which is enforced by the Commodity Futures Trading Commission (CFTC).

- The Employee Retirement Income Security Act of 1974 (ERISA) regulates persons who manage or control the assets of an employee benefit plan. If the assets of a hedge fund are considered 'plan assets' under ERISA, the manager of the fund is generally a fiduciary for ERISA purposes and must also comply with specific prohibited transaction rules.
- Broker-dealers, which both market interests in hedge funds and trade securities on behalf of hedge funds, are heavily regulated under the Securities Exchange Act of 1934 and under the rules of the National Association of Securities Dealers, Inc (the NASD). Among other things, NASD rules limit the extent to which NASD members may distribute so-called new issues (public offerings of equity securities) to certain categories of restricted persons, including the managers of hedge funds.

The development of the hedge fund industry and hedge fund regulation

While there has been recurrent regulatory concern about hedge funds, three general themes emerge:

- whether the investors who invest in hedge funds are adequately protected by the securities laws;
- whether the banks and other counterparties who lend money to hedge funds and otherwise do business with them are adequately protected; and
- whether hedge funds pose risks to the financial markets in general.

What follows is an examination of how these concerns developed as the hedge fund industry grew and expanded.

From the time of their initial development in the late 1940s, hedge funds have relied extensively on the private investment company exception provided in Section 3(c)(1) of the 1940 Act, which is available to a fund that conducts no public offering of securities and has no more than 100 beneficial owners. The exception appeared in the original 1940 Act and reflected Congress's view that private investment companies were not within the purview of the 1940 Act. The 100 beneficial owner limit was intended to represent the largest investor base that would be likely to be composed of people with personal, family or similar ties. No filing need be made with the SEC to obtain the benefit of the Section 3(c)(1) exception, and the SEC is therefore generally unaware of the creation of a Section 3(c)(1) fund.

The hedge fund industry grew considerably in the 1980s. Prior to 1992, the SEC and Congress still had taken little note of hedge funds. In January 1992, the SEC, the Department of the Treasury and the Board of Governors of the Federal Reserve System issued a Joint Report on the Government Securities Market. The Joint Report addressed abuses that had been occurring in the government securities market and included a discussion of the impact of hedge funds. The Joint Report indicated that the regulatory issues relevant to these funds 'involve not so much the protection of the investors who invest in them but the potential of these funds, due to their size, active market presence and use of leverage to cause market disruptions'. The Joint Report lamented that regulators 'have little, if any, authority to gain access to information about hedge fund activities'.

In response to that Joint Report, on 18 March 1992, Congressman Edward Markey, then Chairman of the House Subcommittee on Telecommunications and Finance, wrote to Richard

Breeden, then Chairman of the SEC, about hedge funds. Congressman Edward Markey expressed concern about 'the potential for highly speculative investment entities (about which the SEC has little or no information) to engage in activities which could potentially result in disruptions in our nation's financial markets'. Chairman Richard Breeden responded to Congressman Edward Markey's letter on 12 June 1992, indicating in part that:

> There does not appear, at the present time, to be any need for legislation specifically addressing hedge funds . . . . Since 1987, the Commission has apparently received no investor complaints and has instituted no enforcement actions against hedge funds. To the extent that additional information about the trading of hedge funds is necessary to understand any systemic effect of their trading, the large trader reporting system for equity securities and the proposed large position reporting system for government securities should be adequate.

By 1996 the attitude of Congress toward hedge funds was sufficiently positive that Congress created an entirely new exception under the 1940 Act on which hedge funds could rely. The new exception, set forth in Section 3(c)(7) of the 1940 Act, is available to a fund if all of its investors are 'qualified purchasers', as defined in the 1940 Act, and if the fund is not making and does not intend to make a public offering of securities. The term 'qualified purchaser' generally encompasses individuals who have at least US$5 million in investments (as defined) or entities with at least US$25 million in investments or US$25 million under management. The creation of this exception made possible the development of larger hedge funds, the investors in which are generally very sophisticated.

The tendency of some hedge funds to leverage their portfolios aggressively came under particular scrutiny in 1998 on the occasion of the near collapse of Long-Term Capital Management (LTCM). Founded in 1994, LTCM was an enormous debt arbitrage fund whose managers were well known and highly respected in the financial community. By August of 1998 the fund had over US$125 billion in assets with less than US$5 billion in equity, implying a balance sheet leverage ratio of more than 25-to-1. The financial markets' reaction to Russia's devaluation of the rouble in August 1998 resulted in huge losses for LTCM. By September it was clear that LTCM would not be able to meet its obligations, resulting in tremendous financial exposure to LTCM's trading counterparties and creditors. These counterparties met under the auspices of the Federal Reserve Bank of New York to seek an alternative to the default of LTCM, since such a default could have had devastating consequences for the counterparties themselves and for the financial markets in general. The counterparties invested US$3.6 billion in new equity in the fund, and a default was averted. The near-disaster prompted The President's Working Group on Financial Markets to conduct a study and to issue a report in April 1999. In that report the Working Group recognised that the principal issue was excessive leverage, not hedge funds per se. The Working Group specifically acknowledged that other financial institutions 'are often larger and more highly leveraged than most hedge funds'. The Working Group urged that public companies publicly disclose their material financial exposures to significantly leveraged institutions, including hedge funds, and recommended that financial institutions enhance their practices for counterparty risk management. The Working Group also expressed concern about the 'opaqueness' of hedge funds and urged that more information about hedge funds be made public.

Climate change: new perceptions of hedge funds

The bull market that had begun in the early 1980s came to a famously abrupt end in 2000 with the rapid decline in the technology and internet sectors. Both individuals and institutions that held significant long positions suffered heavy losses. Investors who have pursued long-only strategies since 2000 have generally been unable to preserve their capital, much less to recoup their losses. This has given rise to much greater interest in the long-short strategies frequently adopted by hedge funds. Until that time, hedge funds had been widely regarded as high risk investment vehicles; since 2000 hedge funds have come to be understood in many quarters as more conservative than traditional investment vehicles. The managers of pension plans, endowments and other institutions have come to believe that long-short strategies should be an essential part of their portfolios. Consequently, the hedge fund industry has grown vigorously since 2000. The growth is reflected both in dollars under management (currently estimated to be US$600 billion) and in the types of investment vehicles available. The first fund of hedge funds to be registered under the 1940 Act was sponsored in 2001, and an increasing number of registered investment companies pursue long-short strategies. The increase in hedge fund activity has also lured new participants into the industry, including major financial services firms.

With the tremendous growth in the hedge fund industry in recent years has come, perhaps inevitably, an increase in the incidence of fraud. Most of this fraud has been in the form of simple misappropriation of fund assets by the managers of small start-up funds. The SEC brought only four enforcement actions against hedge funds in 2000, five in 2001 and 12 in 2002. Some of this increase is likely attributable simply to the enhanced level of hedge fund activity. On the other hand, it is possible that dishonest elements are being attracted to this industry because of the relative absence of regulatory oversight.

Regulatory concern has also recently been focused on short selling by hedge funds, which has brought substantial gains to hedge funds during the bear market. The SEC and senior management of some public companies have accused certain funds of issuing false research reports regarding companies after taking short positions in their stock.

The late 1990s also saw the development of hedge fund products by mutual fund companies. The SEC has raised numerous concerns about the operation of hedge funds and mutual funds by the same managers. The principal concerns relate to the allocation of investment opportunities that are of limited availability. If a fund manager stands to gain 20 per cent of the profits of a hedge fund but receives only a fee based on assets under management from the mutual fund, the manager has a strong personal interest in allocating the investment opportunity to the hedge fund.

The dramatic increase in hedge fund activity corresponded with an equally dramatic decline in other securities activity, as initial public offerings dried up and the bear market set in. Broker-dealers sought new opportunities for themselves, and some found them in the hedge fund industry. This gave rise to concerns on the part of the SEC and the NASD that some broker-dealers were marketing hedge funds to investors for whom they were unsuitable. In a Notice to Members on this subject, the NASD reminded the broker-dealer community that 'certain hedge funds are for the first time being offered to a broader investor segment' and therefore it is essential that members perform appropriate due diligence and individual suitability assessments and ensure that their promotional efforts are fair and balanced.

The SEC in 2003 conducted a series of examinations of broker-dealers to determine whether the firms were taking excessive credit risks relative to hedge funds.

Yet another recent trend has been the so-called retailisation of hedge funds (or, as Rick Lake of Lake Partners would say, the democratisation of hedge funds).[3] For 50 years, hedge fund strategies have been available only to a small number of very wealthy investors, typically in minimum investments of US$1 million. As the benefits of certain hedge fund strategies have become more apparent to the market place in general in recent years, individual investors who do not have high net worth are seeking to reap these benefits themselves. Long-short strategies, for example, are now available to the average investor in the context of long-short mutual funds and closed-end registered investment companies that invest in hedge funds. The minimum investment for some of these funds is as low as US$500. The SEC and the NASD have questioned whether average investors are capable of understanding these investment products and whether broker-dealers are marketing these investments solely to investors for whom they are suitable.

The increase in hedge fund activity has also given rise to pressures for reform from certain segments of the mutual fund industry, which claims that it has not been provided a level regulatory playing field to compete against hedge fund managers. Some mutual fund industry representatives assert that if hedge funds continue to enjoy a more favourable regulatory environment, the best portfolio managers will inevitably leave mutual funds to manage hedge funds, where they will serve only the wealthy elite. The reforms advocated include disclosures of hedge fund holdings, a requirement that hedge fund managers adopt codes of ethics and a requirement that hedge fund managers be limited to the same type of performance-based fee that is available to mutual funds. As noted above, institutional money managers are in fact currently required to disclose the equity securities under their management to the SEC on Form 13F, but these disclosures are not made on a fund-by-fund basis, and they omit short positions and holdings of debt securities. Consequently some critics believe the Form 13F filings do not provide sufficient insight into specific hedge fund trading practices. Mutual funds may charge a performance-based fee, a so-called 'fulcrum fee' which increases or decreases in relation to a specified benchmark. Because the managers of mutual funds must be registered investment advisers, however, a mutual fund cannot otherwise charge a performance-based fee unless all of the investors meet a specific suitability requirement. Hedge fund managers that operate pursuant to exemptions from registration under the Advisers Act and applicable state law need not require fund investors to meet this suitability requirement.

It is noteworthy that most of the hedge fund abuses identified to date (misappropriation of fund assets, market manipulation by short sellers, abuses in the allocation of investment opportunities and marketing to unsuitable investors) are not unique to the hedge fund industry and are already prohibited by law or by NASD rules.

Future regulatory developments

These developments (increased fraud, conflicts of interests from mutual fund firm sponsorship of hedge funds and sales by broker-dealers to unsuitable investors) have resulted in regulatory and political pressures for an examination of hedge fund practices. The SEC commenced such an examination in June 2002 by sending questionnaires to numerous hedge funds and by conducting interviews of hedge fund managers. The SEC held a two-day roundtable discussion about hedge fund regulation in May 2003, at which industry leaders, academics and lawyers offered their perspectives to the SEC and its staff. The SEC staff acknowledged the importance and positive influence of hedge funds in the financial market place. At the same time, the SEC staff sought to understand better the actual and potential abuses in the industry with an eye to adopting intelligent regulatory reforms. While counterparty risk and financial market risk were addressed, the principal focus of the roundtable was on investor protection. Is the disclosure that is being provided to hedge fund investors adequate? Are hedge funds being marketed to investors for whom they are unsuitable? Are hedge funds valuing their assets accurately? Are hedge fund managers adequately addressing conflicts of interest in allocating investment opportunities to hedge funds and other accounts? As SEC Chairman William Donaldson concluded the roundtable, he asked the staff to recommend legislative and rule changes. The staff submitted its report on 29 September 2003. In the report the staff made recommendations to the SEC about possible hedge fund regulatory reforms. At this time, we do not know whether or when the SEC will adopt the recommendations made by the staff. Among other things, the staff recommended the following to the SEC.

- Require hedge fund managers to register under the Advisers Act. This would enable the SEC to conduct periodic audits of hedge fund managers and more effectively oversee their operations, without impeding the functioning of the hedge funds they manage. Registration under the Advisers Act would subject hedge fund managers to record-keeping and custody requirements. It would also in effect require each investor in a hedge fund to be a 'qualified client', as defined in Rule 205-3 under the Advisers Act (a person or company with a net worth in excess of US$1.5 million or with at least US$750,000 under management with the adviser).
- Adopt a requirement that hedge fund advisers file with the SEC and deliver to investors a disclosure statement specifically designed to meet the needs of hedge fund investors. The disclosure statement would address conflicts of interest, risk factors and lock-up periods and would be required to be updated periodically.
- Require registered investment companies that invest their assets in hedge funds to disclose in their fee tables the estimated fees of the underlying funds.
- Permit general solicitation by funds that rely on the Section 3(c)(7) exception from the 1940 Act.
- Consider taking steps to enable the wider use of absolute return strategies in the context of registered investment companies.

Meanwhile, in August 2003 the CFTC adopted new rules that expand exclusions from the definition of CPO under CFTC Rule 4.5 and create new exemptions from CPO registration for operators of certain private funds. One of these new exemptions is now available without regard to the amount of options and futures trading activity conducted by the fund if the investors meet certain qualification standards. The CFTC simultaneously adopted rules that expand exemptions from registration available to CTAs. One of the new rules changed the interpretation of Section 4m of the Commodity Exchange Act, which exempted from the CTA registration requirements any CTA that, during the preceding 12 months, had not furnished commodity interest trading advice to more than 15 persons and that did not hold itself out to the public as a CTA. In the past the CFTC required the CTA to look through every entity it advises, such as a hedge fund, and count each investor toward the 15-person limit. The new rule eliminated the look-through requirement.

While it is impossible to predict accurately the future of hedge fund regulation, it is unlikely that Congress and the SEC will subject hedge funds to regulation that is unnecessarily burdensome. Congress and the SEC are well aware that excessive regulation within the United States would simply drive the hedge fund industry offshore, where the industry would be even more difficult for US authorities to regulate.

---

[1] This chapter is for informational purposes only and does not contain or convey legal advice. The information herein should not be used or relied upon in regard to any particular facts or circumstances without first consulting with a lawyer.

[2] Christina Lim and Irene Brennan assisted in the preparation of this chapter and Mark Goshko, Cary Meer, Marc Mehrespand and Maya Ruettger-Cruciana provided helpful comments.

[3] 'Democratisation of Hedge Funds' is a registered service mark of Lake Partners, Inc.

Appendices

Appendix 1

AIMA's illustrative questionnaire for due diligence of hedge fund managers[1]

Alternative Investment Management Association

The purpose of this document is to serve as a guide to investors in their relations with hedge fund managers. This due diligence questionnaire is an unavoidable process that investors must follow in order to choose a manager. Most hedge fund strategies are more of an investment nature rather than one of trading activity. Each strategy has its own peculiarities. The most important aspect is to understand clearly what you plan to invest in. You will also have to:

- identify the markets covered;
- understand what takes place in the portfolio;
- understand the instruments used and how they are used;
- understand how the strategy is operated;
- identify the sources of return;
- understand how ideas are generated;
- check the risk control mechanism; and
- know the people you invest with professionally and, sometimes, personally.

Not all of the following questions are applicable to all managers but we recommend that you ask as many questions as possible before making a decision.

DISCLAIMER

Whilst AIMA has used all reasonable efforts to produce a questionnaire of general application in connection with a due diligence appraisal of hedge fund managers, in any particular case an investor is likely to have its own individual requirements and each hedge fund manager its own characteristics. As a result, prior to any individual investor sending out the questionnaire, it is strongly recommended that the questions are reviewed and, where necessary, amended to suit its own requirements and its state of knowledge of the hedge fund manager's operations.

In addition, responses to the questionnaire should not be relied upon without review and, where considered appropriate, further investigation. In order to obtain the best possible information on any specific hedge fund manager additional questions should be raised to clarify any point of uncertainty, and where practicable verbal examination should be undertaken. In particular, AIMA recommends that in respect of special areas of concern, such as fund performance or risk profile, independent third party data should, if possible, be obtained in order to verify these facts.

Accordingly, none of AIMA, its officers, employees or agents make any representation or warranty, express or implied, as to the adequacy, completeness or correctness of the questionnaire. No liability whatsoever is accepted by AIMA, its officers, employees or agents for any loss howsoever arising from any use of this questionnaire or its contents or otherwise arising in connection therewith.

Other AIMA questionnaires available for selection of:
Fund of Funds Managers
Fund of Funds Custody and Administration
Fund Administration (excl. Fund of Funds) for Managers
Fund Administration (excl. Fund of Funds) for Investors
Managed Futures Managers
Prime Brokers

AIMA's illustrative questionnaire for due diligence of HEDGE FUND MANAGERS

CONTENTS

Manager information

Fund information

Data overview

Strategy

Risk

Investment research

Investor service/reporting

Administration

Published by
The Alternative Investment Management Association Ltd (AIMA)
Lower Ground Floor, 10 Stanhope Gate, London W1K 1AL
Tel +44 (0)20 7659 9920   Fax +44 (0)20 7659 9921
www.aima.org

MANAGER INFORMATION

CONTACT INFORMATION

Company name:	
Address:	
Telephone:	
Fax:	
E-mail:	
Name of contacts:	
Title of contacts:	
Telephone of contacts:	
E-mail of contacts:	

COMPANY

Please give a brief history of the firm:	
Legal entity:	
Domicile:	
Branch offices or other locations, if any: • What functions are performed at these branches and locations?	
Which regulatory authority is the company registered with? • Type (class):	
• Date of registration:	
• Are all the employees registered with the same authority?	
List any affiliations, directorships and memberships of the company and/or its principals:	

COMPLIANCE

Who is responsible for compliance in the firm?	
Please describe any current or potential conflict of interest:	
Does the firm or adviser have any relationship which may affect its trading flexibility, eg, associated broker-dealer?	
Please list your accountant and attorney of the company:	
Is there any material, criminal, civil or administrative proceedings pending or threatened against the firm or any of its principals, or have there ever been any such matters?	
• If yes, please provide full details:	
What are the firm's employee own account dealing procedures?	
Do any of the firm's principals have other business involvement?	
• If yes, describe and quantify how much of their professional time is dedicated to each?	

MANAGER ORGANISATION

How large is the firm in terms of full time individuals?	
Describe the firm's ownership structure, name of its owners, their percentage ownership, and their role within the firm.	

Percentage ownership of principals?	
Short background of principals (education, career background etc)	
• Please, attach information if necessary	
How many investment professionals (portfolio managers, analysts, etc) in the firm?	
What are the average years of professional experience in the firm, both years as a professional as well as years in the firm?	
Please enclose an organisation chart depicting the names of senior managers in charge of the following areas:	
• Trading:	
• Reporting, performance analysis:	
• Research and development:	
• IT/Programming:	
• Administration:	
• Marketing and business development:	
• Others (please specify):	
What has been the turnover rate among the firm's personnel?	
Where do the primary trading, research, and portfolio management activities take place?	
Where are the accounts maintained?	
Are outside representatives or consultants used for any activities? If so, give details.	
MANAGER REFERENCES	
Please provide at least two references for the firm and for each of the principals involved in the management of the fund?	
1 • Name:	
• Profession:	
• Company:	
• Title:	
• Telephone:	
• Fax:	
• E-mail:	
• Current and past relationship with the firm or its principal:	
2 • Name:	
• Profession:	
• Company:	
• Title:	
• Telephone:	
• Fax:	
• E-mail:	
• Current and past relationship with the firm or its principal:	
FUND PROMOTERS	
What external promoters, if any, have been appointed by the management company for its products?	
Duration of your professional relationship?	

FUND INFORMATION

FUND DETAILS

Contact details:	
• Name:	
• Address:	
• Tel:	
• Fax:	
• E-mail:	
• Internet:	
• Fund structure:	
• Legal entity:	
• Domicile:	
Date of inception:	
Is the fund listed on any exchange(s)?	

FEES

Management fee:	
Administration fee:	
Incentive fee:	
Hurdle rate/High water mark:	
Sales fee:	
Redemption fee:	
Any other fees:	
What costs, if any, are recharged to the fund?	
Are your fees calculated and charged in terms of equalisation structure by:	
• issuing a different series of shares every time shareholders subscribe?	
• the Equalisation Share method?	
• the Equalisation and Depreciation Deposit method?	
• the Equalisation-Adjustment method?	
• Others:	
Do you ever share fees with a third party?	
Have any investors been granted rebates?	
Disclose any soft dollar agreement.	

LIQUIDITY

Minimum initial investment:	
Minimum subsequent investment:	
Subscription frequency (when):	
Redemption frequency (when):	
Redemption notice period:	
Redemption cash proceeds time period:	
Do you have any lock-up period or any other liquidity constraints?	
Do you allow for transfer of shares between nominees?	

ADMINISTRATOR

Details:	
• Name:	
• Address:	
• Telephone:	
• Fax:	
• E-mail:	
• Name of contact:	
• Telephone of contact:	
• E-mail of contact:	
Duration of your professional relationship?	

AUDITOR

Details:	
• Name:	
• Address:	
• Telephone:	
• Fax:	
• E-mail:	
Duration of your professional relationship?	

CUSTODIAN

Details:	
• Name:	
• Address:	
• Telephone:	
• Fax:	
• E-mail:	
Duration of your professional relationship?	

LEGAL ADVISER

Details:	
• Name:	
• Address:	
• Telephone:	
• Fax:	
• E-mail:	
Duration of your professional relationship?	

BANKS AND PRIME BROKER

Please list the banks used by the fund:	
Please list the prime brokers used by the fund, as well as the duration of your professional relationship:	

DIRECTORS OF FUND

Please list the number of directors, their names and the degree of relationship with manager and service providers?	
Duration of your professional relationship?	

DATA OVERVIEW

FUND ASSETS

Please list the size of assets by investment vehicle:	
Please list the size of the fund's net assets:	
List the total assets under management, and their respective changes over the last year:	
What percentage of assets is represented by the largest investor?	

CAPACITY MANAGEMENT

What is the maximum capacity of your fund?	
What is the projected timeframe to reach capacity?	
Will new money be accepted after capacity is reached?	
How will front/back-office operations be affected in the event of significant increase in assets under management, and what measures will be taken?	

WITHDRAWALS

What were the largest withdrawals in your fund since inception?	
• Date:	
• % of equity:	
• Reasons:	

MANAGEMENT TEAM'S CO-INVESTMENT

What is the total amount invested by the principals/ management in the fund and other investment vehicles managed pari passu with the fund?	
Has the management reduced its personal investment?	
• Date:	
• Amount:	
• Reasons:	
Disclose conditions of subscription/redemptions of team and owners' assets.	

FUND PERFORMANCE

Historical performance since inception:	
• Monthly NAVs since inception (in table format):	
• Monthly RoR since inception:	
Please explain any major factors affecting performance and drawdowns (ie, a manager change, a change in strategy, etc):	
Is the fund performance audited?	

DRAWDOWNS

List the 5 maximum drawdowns, in percent of equity for each fund, the recovery period, and explain why they have happened:	
Over the past 12 months, how many daily drawdowns greater than 5% have occurred, and what was the length of recovery?	

MANAGER TRACK RECORD	
Number of portfolios/accounts managed by the firm:	
Number of funds managed/advised by the firm:	
• Names of these funds:	
Total assets managed/advised by the firm:	
Oldest continuously active account:	
Largest current account:	
Length of track record:	
Has the track record been audited?	
What is your level of portfolio turnover?	
Average annual commission costs as a percentage of total assets:	
• Brokerage to equity ratio	
• Administrator fee to equity ratio	
• Custodian fee to equity ratio	
• Auditors' fee to equity ratio	

STRATEGY	
Characterise your investment style in terms of:	
• Strategy:	
• Hedging:	
• Market exposure:	
• Portfolio concentration in terms of amount of instruments and exposure bias (min/max/avg. number of instruments, min/max/avg. long or short bias):	
• Geographical market focus:	
List the instrument types you use by percentage:	
Describe your strategy (in as much detail as possible):	
What is your trading philosophy?	
• Do you believe that there are persistent structural inefficiencies in the area you invest in? Please explain:	
• How do you think these market inefficiencies will change over time?	
What makes your strategy unique?	
What makes your strategy different from your peers?	
Describe your strategy for today's market:	
What are the strengths/weaknesses of your investment strategy?	
• Why do you feel you will generate absolute returns?	
In which markets do you believe your strategy performs best/worst? (Give examples of time periods):	
• Volatility:	
• Trends:	
• Liquidity:	
• Correlation:	

533

What is your average holding period for:	
• All investments	
• Profitable investments	
• Losing investments	
Does the strategy have a long or short bias?	
What investment criteria must new positions meet?	
How do you invest new capital into the market?	
How do you deal with redemptions?	
Have the strategy or trading processes changed over time due to capital flows?	
Have you encountered position limit problems? If yes, please explain.	
Describe your cash management policy?	
Do you outsource this function? If so, please give name of provider and method used.	

RISK

LEVERAGE

Discuss your leverage exposure policy and its management over different market cycles:	
What are your portfolio financing constraints/limits? Discuss sensitivity (cost) to Libor levels:	

HEDGING

How is the portfolio hedged?	
How do you determine size and limits for each position/basket?	
How often do you re-hedge?	
Are short positions profit centres?	

DIVERSIFICATION

Discuss the depth of diversification:	
How do you calculate the correlation between each investment in the portfolio?	
What are the main sources of marginal risk in your strategy?	
How has performance been distributed across positions and time?	

RISK MANAGEMENT

Discuss position and stop loss limits and their management:	
How often are these limits applied? When were their peaks observed?	
How do you adjust your risk capital allocation when there is a significant increase in equity due to trading profits?	
Do you have a risk manager?	
Do you use an external risk monitor? If so, who, and why that particular one?	
Please describe the operational risk management policy:	

How do you measure minimum liquidity of positions:	
What system/software is used in your middle office?	
EXTERNAL CONTROLS	
Are any third parties involved in verifying adherence to risk limits, eg, the fund's administrator?	

INVESTMENT RESEARCH

What outside sources are used?	
What proportion of research is generated internally?	
Describe the typical flow of an investment idea from inception to a trading position:	
Describe your back testing of investment ideas?	
Have you published or commissioned any research/ academic papers?	

INVESTOR SERVICE/REPORTING

Can the prospectus/offering memorandum be transmitted to us electronically?	
Who calculates the NAV?	
What is the frequency of calculation.	
Do you make any adjustments to the NAV valuation received from your source? If yes, please explain what kind in terms of:	
• Liquidity	
• Time zone	
• Size	
• Holding period	
• Other	
• Percentage of adjustments to total NAV	
• What instruments subject to adjustments	
Can fund performance (NAV, RoR) be transmitted to us electronically on a regular basis, and at what periodicity?	
List all reports and correspondence usually sent to clients, and please explain the frequency and the detail the manager reports performance to investors.	
Can you provide copies of historical reports?	
• Please provide examples:	
Are investors informed when minor/major changes are made to the trading, money management, or risk control methods?	
What databases, publications, or other available sources does the manager regularly report performance figures to? If none, explain why?	
What portfolio data can you provide (electronically) in terms of:	
• Position:	
• Concentration:	
• Exposure:	
• Performance attributes:	
• Hedge:	
Can all trades be reported on a daily basis to the client?	

ADMINISTRATION	
Please indicate any material facts about your fund that are not mentioned in the offering memorandum (domicile, legal issues, political situation, tax etc.)	
How do you manage trade data and keep track of open positions? • Please specify the systems in use:	
How is performance of each account calculated, and how often?	
What type of information is maintained internally on each account?	
Is there an electronic feed to brokers and administrators, and how is it used?	
Can you link to any third party risk management systems (like Measurisk)?	
Does your management program automate trade allocations to investor accounts?	
If not, how are trade allocations to investor accounts executed?	
Has this method been audited by a regulatory body?	
How are trading errors dealt with?	
What contingency plans do you have in terms of: • Computer system fault? • Incapacitated investment decision makers? • Technical failure at prime broker's location? • Presence of in-house computer technician? • Back-up systems?	

Please attach the most recent disclosure document, information memorandum, and marketing literature.

In the event of amendments to the aforementioned documents, notably the memorandum, please ensure that we will receive those directly from you within reasonable time, as well as copies of proxy's and notification of the Annual General Meeting (the latter only for information purposes).

Please state the name and title of the officer at your firm who has prepared and reviewed this questionnaire.

Name:	
Date:	
Position:	

---

[1] © Alternative Investment Management Association (AIMA), January 2002.

Appendix 2

Regulatory and investor protection issues arising from the participation by retail investors in (funds-of-) hedge funds[1]

Report of the Technical Committee of the International Organization of Securities Commissions, February 2003

Introduction

During its 17 and 18 February 2003 meeting the IOSCO Technical Committee approved for public release the report entitled *Regulatory and Investor Protection Issues Arising from the Participation by Retail Investors in (Funds-of-) Hedge Funds.* Work on this project was initiated in May 2002 when the Technical Committee mandated its Standing Committee on Investment Management (SC5) to look into the regulatory issues arising from participation by retail investors in hedge funds.[2] This IOSCO Technical Committee report identifies specific regulatory issues created by hedge funds and details approaches for addressing the impact these issues have on retail investors.[3]

The backdrop for this paper begins with the many studies and reports undertaken on the subject of hedge funds and the risks posed by uncontrolled leverage, especially in light of the collapse of Long-Term Capital Management in 1998. Most of that work, however, concentrated on the possible systemic effects of hedge funds that possessed a certain level of assets and that were leveraged to an extent that would affect adversely regulated markets. In order to differentiate these funds from the majority of hedge funds that were neither large nor highly leveraged, these funds were described as Highly Leveraged Institutions (HLIs). Direct and indirect retail participation in HLIs was relatively small and it was felt that the large sophisticated or institutional investors in those funds were capable of protecting their own interests. It now appears that hedge funds and similar vehicles, especially funds-of-hedge-funds, are increasingly targeting and attracting retail investment.

In late 2001, SC5 updated a brief questionnaire on the extent of retail participation in hedge funds in the jurisdictions represented on SC5. The results of the questionnaire suggested that there was growing retail participation in highly leveraged instruments, including those offered by hedge funds, if not directly, then through fund-of-hedge-funds type vehicles. It was observed that, in many jurisdictions, while direct retail participation in a hedge fund is prohibited unless the fund complies with all of the normal regulatory restrictions on collective investment schemes ('CISs'), in some jurisdictions, CISs are permitted to invest in funds which in turn invest in hedge funds.

The increased participation of retail investors in hedge funds and fund-of-hedge-funds raises various regulatory issues especially related to investor protection issues. Although the terms 'retail participation,' 'retail investors,' and 'retail investment' vary by jurisdiction, it is well-accepted in regulatory circles that these terms refer to investors other than those normally referred to as 'professional,' 'qualified' or 'sophisticated' investors.[4]

A project in this area was therefore considered useful for the following reasons:

- There may be particular risks that need to be disclosed to retail investors about their investment in these vehicles;
- Existing regulation (or exemptions from regulation) may be based on premises that need to be tested or may no longer be correct, e.g., that retail investment is not permitted;
- The existing regulation of the extent to which CISs may invest in derivatives or use certain trading techniques, such as short selling, may need reassessment; and
- Significant investment by CISs in highly leveraged instruments raises questions about the CISs' internal controls and processes for managing the risks posed by those investments.

This paper is exclusively concerned with retail investor protection issues and does not treat questions relating to such matters as systemic risk and exposure to hedge funds by banks and investment firms. Furthermore, parts of this paper focus primarily on hedge funds as they determine the underlying issues for funds-of-hedge-funds.

Regulatory issues raised by the existence of hedge funds

Several issues can be identified:

- What are hedge funds and can they be sufficiently identified in legal terms to enable specific regulation?
- Are hedge funds by their very nature riskier for retail investors than 'normal' funds, and, if so, is this a bad thing?
- If direct investment in hedge funds is not open for retail investors, should it be open indirectly in the form of funds-of-hedge-funds?
- Should hedge funds, including funds-of-hedge-funds, be subject to the same rules as more traditional CISs?
- Should special authorisation and supervision requirements be imposed on hedge funds with retail investor participation with regard to organisational aspects, taking into account the investment strategy, the expertise required for management, management information, technology and the appropriate internal controls?
- Are there additional disclosure requirements that need to be placed on hedge funds in order to make their risk profiles and strategies comprehensible to retail investors?
- Do regulators have sufficient expertise in-house in order effectively to authorise and supervise complex hedge funds?

Scope of the types of CISs involved

Before entering into a discussion of the regulatory aspects of retail investment in hedge funds, it is necessary to attempt, at least broadly, to arrive at an adequate description of such funds. As a premise it is assumed that a hedge fund will always be a vehicle for collective investment. A hedge fund is not the normal-type CIS that is open-ended and invests primarily in listed securities, whilst being conservative in its use of derivatives. 'Funds-of-hedge-funds' refer to CISs that invest primarily in a number of underlying hedge funds, which may or may not be affiliated to the manager of the fund-of-funds.

In the 1999 IOSCO Technical Committee report on *Hedge Funds and Other Highly Leveraged Institutions*, HLIs were, for the purposes of that report, described as, ' . . . institutions which are significant traders for their own account in financial instruments and which display some combination of the following characteristics:

- they take on significant leverage;
- they are subject to little or no direct prudential regulation; and
- they are subject to limited disclosure requirements as they are seldom public companies'.[5]

This description does not appear to be useful for the purposes of this paper. Firstly, the scope of the previous IOSCO work focused only on that small subset of funds that potentially posed market stability issues. Secondly, not only hedge funds, but other CISs (or their management companies) also trade in financial instruments for their own account. Thirdly, most hedge funds do not use significant leverage.

An approach for identifying hedge funds is to look at the kinds of characteristics of and strategies employed by institutions that would consider themselves to be hedge funds. Hedge funds have at least some of the following characteristics:

- borrowing and leverage restrictions, which are typically included in CIS regulation, are not applied, and many (but not all) hedge funds use high levels of leverage;
- significant performance fees (often in the form of a percentage of profits) are paid to the manager in addition to an annual management fee;
- investors are typically permitted to redeem their interests periodically, e.g., quarterly, semi-annually or annually;
- often significant 'own' funds are invested by manager;
- derivatives are used, often for speculative purposes, and there is an ability to short sell securities;
- more diverse risks or complex underlying products are involved.

The distinguishing characteristics of hedge funds are not limited to this and the (near) future could result in this list needing to be adapted to take account of market dynamics.

The investment strategies tend to be quite different from those followed by 'traditional' asset managers. Furthermore, these strategies do not fit within neat definitional categories because each fund usually follows its own proprietary strategies. In a recent discussion paper, the Financial Services Authority of the United Kingdom – after having mentioned the foregoing – lists the following three most common broad fund types:[6]

- Event driven funds investing in securities to take advantage of price movements generated by corporate events. This group includes merger arbitrage funds and distressed asset funds.
- Global macro funds that take long and short positions in major financial markets based on views influenced by economic trends and events.
- Market neutral funds where the manager attempts to minimise (or significantly reduce) market risk. This category includes long-short equity funds, convertible bond arbitrage funds, and fixed income arbitrage.

On the basis of the foregoing descriptions, it will be possible to identify a CIS as being a hedge fund in the broad sense of the term. This is a fairly pragmatic approach that is, for instance, followed by the Securities and Futures Commission (SFC) of Hong Kong. Section 8.7 of the SFC Code on Unit Trusts and Mutual Funds states: 'The following criteria apply to collective investment schemes that are commonly known as hedge funds (or alternative investment funds or absolute return funds). Hedge funds are generally regarded as non-traditional funds that possess different characteristics and utilise different investment strategies from traditional funds. In considering an application for authorisation, the Commission will, among other things, consider the following: (i) the choice of class of assets; and (ii) the use of alternative investment strategies such as long-short exposures, leverage and/or hedging and arbitrage techniques'.[7]

Given the broad range of investment instruments and economic and financial objectives employed by hedge funds, such a pragmatic approach assists the identification of such funds for regulatory purposes. Nevertheless, it will, at the end of the day, most likely be next to impossible to arrive at a definition of 'hedge funds' that is a) accepted internationally and b) sufficiently precise for 'universal' implementation in laws and statutes regulating CISs.

Existing regulatory regimes for hedge funds

In 1999, SC5 conducted a survey among its members with regard to the regulatory environment for hedge funds in the various jurisdictions. This survey was updated in late 2001.

The following observations can be made on the basis of the survey:

- Most jurisdictions consider hedge funds to be CISs. In a few jurisdictions, hedge funds do not fall under the concept of collective investment due to their legal structure.
- There appear to be three types of regulatory starting points. Hedge funds:

  1. are prohibited outright;
  2. fall within the scope of the general regulatory framework for CISs; nevertheless, hedge funds often profit from exclusions or exemptions from the applicability of the general framework when they are, for example, open only to professional/qualified investors;
  3. are not considered to be a CIS and are therefore not prohibited from being offered.

- There is no common definition for hedge funds.
- Compared to the 1999 survey, hedge funds seem to be more available in different jurisdictions (either directly or, which is the predominant case, indirectly via funds-of-funds) for retail investors. The changes do not appear to be specifically aimed at hedge funds, but result from relaxation of regulation in the field of funds-of-funds, investment restrictions, the use of derivatives and short-selling techniques.
- In those jurisdictions that allow (funds-of-) hedge funds, very few 'pure' hedge funds exist that fall under the supervisory framework for CISs and that attract investment from the general investor public. Investment in 'pure' hedge funds is mostly restricted to sophisticated or professional investors. The funds-of-hedge-funds, however, are not necessarily restricted to such investors.
- Statistics are few and far between. Some jurisdictions have data, but because of the lack of a common definition, it was not possible to make a reliable estimate of the size of the

(retail or non-retail) investment in hedge funds. Nevertheless, as stated before, there is a noticeable growth, particularly in funds-of-hedge-funds.

An approach to the investor protection issues

A number of observations can be made regarding the investor protection regulatory implications of allowing hedge funds to be sold into the retail market:

1. As mentioned above, it is not really possible to define hedge funds. This means that it will be extremely difficult to arrive at a legally sound description for the purposes of laws and statutes.[8]

2. The primary concern for CIS regulators is that investors can adequately assess the proposition, including whether an investment in a hedge fund is suitable for their investment needs. The hedge fund must disclose adequate information about its strategy (including the risks involved) and the terms and conditions involved in investing in the fund. In addition, the investors' interests need to be reasonably protected, for instance by risk diversification requirements.

3. Whether investment vehicles may, or may not, have a useful role in the capital markets, is up to the markets to decide.

4. The major issues with regard to hedge funds seem to be two-fold. In the first place there is the issue of systemic risks and exposure to hedge funds by banks and investment firms: this is outside the scope of this paper and has been adequately addressed by other fora. In the second place, there is the notion that hedge funds are inherently risky, and should therefore not be open to non-qualified retail investors. Given the diversity in the kinds of hedge funds, it would probably be unwise generally to conclude that hedge funds as a group are riskier than certain 'normal' funds that are specialised (e.g., funds investing in the IT-sector or in private equity). Indeed, the use of hedging techniques may in fact produce a more predictable return.

5. Most regulators are more concerned with funds-of-hedge-funds than hedge funds themselves as the former are the primary vehicles for attracting retail investment in this sector.

It is for individual national governments and regulators to determine whether or not hedge funds are suitable for sale to the retail market. However, where a jurisdiction does permit hedge funds (or funds-of-hedge-funds) to be marketed to the retail public, there are a number of issues that the regulator may wish to consider, which are described in more detail below.

In the light of the observations made above, it is useful to explore whether the principles embodied in the regulation of CIS are relevant for the regulation of hedge funds (including funds-of-hedge-funds). It is argued here that this is the case and that, if jurisdictions are willing to permit retail investment in (funds-of-) hedge funds, it is not necessary, from a viewpoint of investor protection, to develop new approaches that significantly divert from those principles in order to accommodate hedge funds. The main objective of CIS-regulation, after all, is not to prevent the incurring of losses on investments, but to create a framework within which products are offered that are suitable for retail investors. This can be achieved by, among other things, ensuring that the risks involved are disclosed in such a fashion that they are understandable for retail investors.

The 1995 IOSCO *Principles for the Regulation of Collective Investment Schemes* provides a sufficient framework for the regulation of (funds-of-) hedge funds. Two of those principles may, however, not fit especially well. The first is principle 7 on Asset Valuation and Pricing, especially the statement that a CIS must redeem its units at the request of any investor, given the situation that hedge funds often do not have a pure open end status. The second is principle 8 on Investment and Borrowing Limitations, which are directed at traditional funds. Even though a broad interpretation of this principle could be applied for hedge funds, such funds may use unusual or innovative leverage or limited investment strategies, which may conflict with this principle. Therefore, subject to additional disclosure being provided, in order to carry out their investment objective hedge funds may need to be exempted from regulation that is more appropriate to traditional CIS, particularly regulation of investment restrictions and practices.

Another IOSCO document prepared by IOSCO's Working Party 5 (the predecessor of SC5), *Disclosure of Risk, a discussion paper*, September 1996, is also relevant. Certainly in 1996 the document was drafted with a 'mindset' for traditional funds. It is, nevertheless, also applicable to hedge funds. See especially paras 2.2 and 2.4 of this document. Para 2.2 states: 'In order to make an informed decision, an investor who is contemplating investment in a CIS needs to understand both the potential rewards and the associated risks.' Para 2.4 states: 'Risk disclosure by a CIS should assist investors in understanding the relationship between risk and return, so that investors evaluating CIS performance do not focus solely on return, but also on the risk assumed to produce the return. Risk disclosure should help investors assess whether a CIS's potential return is an adequate reward for the risks taken.'

A number of disclosure issues can be identified that are either unique to hedge funds or magnified in the case of hedge funds:

- **Fund strategy and disclosure of risks** – Hedge funds employ a diverse range of strategies, many of which are unfamiliar to retail investors. It is therefore important that the strategy of the fund is explained in a way that is comprehensible to retail investors and that the risks inherent in the strategy are clearly stated. Unwillingness to provide full disclosure seems to be a characteristic of many hedge funds, the reason often given that such disclosure would enable competitors to gain insight into their 'unique' strategy.[9] It can be questioned whether this is a valid argument. In disclosure documents of normal CISs, a description of the investment policy, aims and risks will be given, but that is not to say that the manager will give insight into why particular choices will be made to buy or sell certain stocks. This follows from the fiduciary relationship between the investor and the manager: the investor mandates the manager to make decisions within certain (often broad) parameters.
- **Target performance/prospective financial information** – It is much harder for investors to judge whether a hedge fund is performing well or not than for traditional funds (where ready comparisons can usually be made against widely available indices). Therefore, in order for investors to gauge the performance of the fund it is necessary for them to have more of an indication of the performance that the hedge fund manager is targeting (whether this be an absolute level of performance or relative to a given benchmark).
- **Fees and charges** – Hedge funds generally charge a performance fee as well as a management fee. In order that this is readily comprehensible to investors, the basis of this fee needs to be set out clearly.

- **Past performance** – Given the emphasis in hedge fund strategies on the skills of the manager rather than general market movements, it is particularly important that timely information on performance of the fund is available as it is less likely that returns will be correlated with general market movements.
- **Lock up periods/liquidity** – Many hedge funds place restrictions on when investors can withdraw their money and/or have a notice period in advance of payment of withdrawal. These should be stated clearly so that investors are aware that they will not have instant access to their money. All funds-of-funds and single strategy hedge funds which invest in illiquid assets should also disclose this clearly to investors.
- **Valuation** – Some hedge fund strategies involve investing in illiquid, hard to value securities. Where the fund invests in illiquid securities, it is important that the basis for valuing the portfolio is clearly made and that the risks of investing in illiquid underlying investments are properly explained.
- **Related parties/outsourcing/service providers** – Hedge funds commonly outsource part of their operations to related parties. It is important that this, and any related consequences for fees, is fully disclosed. Where significant reliance is being placed on service providers such as prime brokers to perform services such as valuation and reconciliation, this should be disclosed. It is important that the custodians and accountants to the fund have appropriate expertise in the strategies that it follows.
- **Issues specific to funds-of-funds:**
- *Information on underlying funds and how they are selected* – If investors are to have any idea about the risk profile of a fund-of-funds, they will need information about the nature and risks of the underlying funds (as well as the criteria used by the fund-of-funds manager in selecting the underlying funds).
- *Due diligence on underlying funds* – One of the critical functions performed by the manager of a fund-of-funds is the performance of due diligence on underlying funds. However, the investor generally has no recourse in the event of a problem with the underlying fund. It is therefore important that the investor receives a clear explanation of the due diligence process and liability of the manager if anything goes wrong with the underlying funds.
- *Diversification* – The number of underlying funds the fund-of-funds invests in and the concentration in individual underlying funds is an important component of the risk of the fund-of-funds. Ideally, the fund should disclose the maximum percentage of its capital that it will invest in any one fund and the minimum number of funds that it will hold. This could be usefully supplemented by recent data showing the composition of the fund at a given point in time.
- *'Double' fees* – It is customary for management and performance fees to be payable both at the fund-of-fund level and from the fund-of-funds to the underlying funds. Investors should be made aware that investing through a fund-of-funds structure means that, in effect, two sets of fees are payable on the investment. This could be helpfully illustrated by an example showing the total amount of fees payable from the investors' money.
- *Investment activity at fund-of-funds level* – Normally, funds-of-funds invest on a long-only basis in underlying funds without taking positions themselves. If the fund-of-funds plans to 'overlay' the investments in underlying funds by making investments itself, this should be clearly disclosed to investors.

543

The foregoing means that a regulator applying the traditional approach vis-à-vis hedge funds has two basic choices:

- authorisation of a hedge fund if the regulator is, among other things, satisfied that the investment policies and risks are adequately disclosed in the prospectus (and is therefore willing if necessary to exempt the hedge fund from traditional CIS regulation that would restrict how the hedge fund meets its investment objectives or strategies) and that the fund is otherwise suitable for retail investors, or
- non-authorisation of the fund or restricting the offering of the fund to professional or qualified investors if the manager is unwilling to provide the level of disclosure required for retail investor participation.

This approach would also seem to be applicable to funds-of-hedge-funds. With indirect investment by a CIS in offshore or unauthorised CISs, regulators may be concerned that the investors will indirectly hold investments that would otherwise not be permitted in the regulator's own jurisdiction. The methods regulators employ to address these concerns (varying from additional disclosure requirements to prohibitions on master/feeders) can also be applied when a CIS invests in offshore or unauthorised hedge funds. For the regulation of funds-of-hedge-funds it is furthermore of utmost importance that the manager applies, and is tested on, a sufficient degree of due diligence when selecting hedge funds into which the manager may wish to invest. This includes the necessity of being sure that the hedge fund is valued correctly and in a timely fashion. Without a stringent due diligence process by the manager of the fund-of-hedge-fund, the interests of the investors could be affected adversely.

Depending on the legal framework for the regulation of CISs in the jurisdiction, the potential responses of the regulator include:

- prohibiting direct or indirect retail investment, as the view is taken that the underlying product is too risky or complex or otherwise unsuitable for retail investors;
- allowing limited indirect investment through a professional fund manager;
- imposing additional competency and experience requirements on the manager;
- additional attention to the due diligence applied by the manager of funds-of-hedge-funds when selecting hedge funds;
- permitting direct investment but limiting it to more sophisticated investors, by imposing a minimum subscription level;
- requiring additional disclosure about the risks associated with the investment and the strategies followed by the fund;
- requiring investors to sign an acknowledgment of the risk/complexity warning;
- placing greater emphasis on the proficiency of sellers of the hedge fund to understand the product before recommending it to their clients;
- placing greater emphasis on the manager's internal control processes, including valuation procedures.

Of course, the regulator will be challenged by the supervision of hedge funds as they often employ styles, techniques and technology that are 'state-of-the-art'. This means that it may be difficult for a regulator to judge whether or not the investment policy and risks are adequately disclosed and to judge, during on-site inspections, whether the manager is operating in conformity with its stated policies. The regulator must have sufficient comfort in this respect. That could be achieved through staff training and/or through the use of specific statements of independent parties (such as the external auditor). Finally, it is believed that the March 2002 IOSCO Technical Committee report on *Investment Management: Areas of regulatory concern and risk assessment methods* provides a framework that can easily be applied when assessing the regulatory risks of retail investment in hedge funds.

Summary and recommendations

In this paper a number of approaches have been identified that can be used by regulators when they choose to allow forms of retail investment in (funds-of-) hedge funds. Systemic risks of exposures to hedge funds by banks and investment firms, which have been considered at length by both the IOSCO Technical Committee and the Financial Stability Forum in recent years, are outside of the remit of this paper and have not been considered.

Definition

Before being able to set rules, it is necessary to determine the types of CISs involved by making clear what hedge funds are. It is however very difficult to arrive at an adequate definition of hedge funds. It is easier to find a broad consensus with a negative description and the use of some identifying characteristics and investment strategies, which are detailed above.

An approach to investor protection regulatory issues

The possibilities for retail investment in hedge funds have significantly grown over the past years. Some jurisdictions allow forms of direct retail investment and many jurisdictions allow indirect retail investment.

Where a jurisdiction does permit the marketing and selling of hedge funds to retail investors, the key regulatory concerns that arise are:

1. That the retail investor may not adequately understand the risks involved in or the complexity of the product; and
2. That the manager may not have the competence or the processes and controls required to adequately manage the fund and explain this clearly to his investors.

These two concerns lead to the following guidelines:

Disclosure: The investor should be able to know what the risks of the fund are

Investors in hedge funds often face a complex combination of risks: market risk, operational risk, credit and counterparty risk etc. In order to understand those risks hedge funds have to disclose their strategies in detail. That means that a complete list should be given with the strategies a fund follows and a description per strategy of the risks involved and the handling of those risks by the fund. It is however not necessary for the funds to reveal their current individual investments, for that would make their market position rather difficult. However hedge funds marketed and sold directly to retail investors should be subject to the same disclosure requirements as other CIS (with annual and semi-annual disclosure of holdings being the minimum requirements). In addition, this paper identifies a number of areas which present particular disclosure issues in relation to hedge funds. IOSCO members may wish to consider whether their disclosure requirements are adequate in these areas.

Competent management

The management and internal control process of hedge funds may require additional attention of the regulator. The complexity of the risks, the investment strategies, the management of the administrative organization and the valuation of the assets can demand special skills. The regulator should consider the adequacy of those skills, while accepting that it is impossible to second-guess the commercial judgments being made by the manager and for which the manager is responsible.

This is also important for funds-of-hedge-funds. The manager should be able to make a considered choice between the many funds he could invest the fund's money in. That means that he must at least understand the strategies of the funds and that he should apply adequate due diligence. But he also should be able to explain to his investors how the fund selection takes place, what the procedures for monitoring the funds are, what criteria are used for switching the investments between funds and how the valuation takes place. In addition, managers of hedge funds should be held to the same general standards in managing their hedge funds as they would be in managing any other publicly offered CIS.

Regulation of hedge funds poses challenges for regulators. Regulators should not seek to lead or anticipate the market. The primary responsibility for managing and controlling the risks lies with the CIS operator. The regulator's responsibility is to set, oversee and enforce appropriate regulatory requirements, in the interests of protecting the investor.

Concluding remarks

Further research work on such investor protection issues as identification of hedge funds, their authorisation and methods of valuation may be useful. However, it should be noted that the members of SC 5 do not consider retail investment in (funds-of-) hedge funds to be high. Even though such funds manage to attract considerable attention from regulators and the financial press, the amount of retail investment involved is still quite modest in a relative sense. Furthermore, existing regulatory and supervisory structures applicable to CISs generally have proven to be sufficiently flexible to address investor protection issues raised by (funds-of-) hedge funds.

This is not to say that hedge funds do not give rise to a number of other regulatory issues that are important, such as:

- short selling;
- fee structures;
- whether the use of derivatives by hedge funds could lead to a more relaxed regulation of use of derivatives by traditional funds;

- the use of benchmarks as a source of information for investors to compare the results of the CISs they invest in; and
- the methods of distribution and the quality of the advisors.

These issues are, however, not limited to hedge funds as a phenomenon, and may warrant broader consideration than just in the hedge funds context.

---

[1] Reproduced here with the kind permission of the Technical Committee of the International Organization of Securities Commissions.

[2] As discussed below, it is very difficult to come up with a satisfactory definition of the term 'hedge funds'. Nonetheless, over time, the term has referred consistently to an investment vehicle that pools the monetary contributions of multiple investors and employs a variety of investment strategies. For the purposes of this paper, only the term 'hedge funds' has been used, although similar considerations apply to other funds which are not regulated.

[3] As of the last quarter of 2001, it was estimated that there were between 4,000–5,000 hedge funds that managed US$400–500 billion in capital. See The Financial Stability Forum (FSF), *Recommendations and Concerns Raised by Highly Leveraged Institutions: An Assessment*, March 2002, at 1–2 (http://www.fsforum.org/Reports/HLIreviewMar02.pdf). The amount of this pool that is contributed by retail investors is not clear.

[4] Some jurisdictions define a retail investor by reference to their income or net worth. For example, in the US, retail investors are those who do not meet the 'accredited investor' standard of either (1) income of US$200,000 for the last 2 years and a reasonable expectation of making at least this in the current or coming year or (2) net worth of US$1 million.

[5] IOSCO Technical Committee, *Hedge Funds and Other Highly Leveraged Institutions*, November 1999, page 4.

[6] UK Financial Services Authority, Discussion Paper 16: *Hedge Funds and the FSA*, August 2002.

[7] The Swiss Federal Banking Commission also applies a pragmatic approach through a licensing procedure for 'funds with special risk.' This qualification is not based on economic factors such as volatility, but on the legally binding investment policy as laid down in the prospectus. The Central Bank of Ireland has recently introduced a regime for the authorisation of 'funds of unregulated funds' which invest more than 10% of their assets in entities such as hedge funds and alternative investment funds.

[8] The term 'hedge fund' is often used as a reference to a particular investment strategy (or strategies). That strategy can be carried on in as many different structures as there are structures – it can be done in closed ended funds (companies), open ended funds, trusts or even through fund links in life insurance policies. So the 'structure' does not necessarily form any part of their definition.

[9] Opaqueness on the part of hedge funds transfers, of course, upwards into the quality of the information that is provided by the funds-of-hedge-funds that invest in them.